Lecture Notes in Business Information Processing

373

More information about this series at http://www.springer.com/series/7911

Witold Abramowicz · Rafael Corchuelo (Eds.)

Business Information Systems Workshops

BIS 2019 International Workshops
Seville, Spain, June 26–28, 2019
Revised Papers

 Springer

Editors
Witold Abramowicz ⓘ
Poznań University of Economics
and Business
Poznan, Poland

Rafael Corchuelo ⓘ
University of Seville
Seville, Spain

ISSN 1865-1348   ISSN 1865-1356   (electronic)
Lecture Notes in Business Information Processing
ISBN 978-3-030-36690-2   ISBN 978-3-030-36691-9   (eBook)
https://doi.org/10.1007/978-3-030-36691-9

This Springer imprint is published by the registered company Springer Nature Switzerland AG
The registered company address is: Gewerbestrasse 11, 6330 Cham, Switzerland

Preface

In 2019 we had a great opportunity to organize the 22nd edition of the International Conference on Business Information Systems (BIS 2019), that has grown to be a well-renowned event for scientific and business communities. This year the main topic of the conference was "Data Science for Business Information Systems." The conference was jointly organized by the University of Seville, Spain, and the Poznań University of Economics and Business, Poland, and was held in Seville, Spain.

During each edition of the BIS conference series we make the effort to provide an opportunity for discussion about up-to-date topics from the area of information systems research. However, there are many topics that deserve particular attention. Thus, a number of workshops and accompanying events are co-located with the BIS conference series. The workshops give researchers the possibility to share preliminary ideas and initial experimental results, and to discuss research hypotheses from a specific area of interest.

Nine workshops and one accompanying event took place during BIS 2019. We were pleased to host well-known workshops such as AKTB (11th edition), BITA (10th edition), iCRM (4th edition), and iDEATE (4th edition), as well as relatively new initiatives such as ISAMD, DigEx, BSCT, SciBOWater, and QOD. Each workshop focused on a different topic: knowledge-based business information systems (AKTB), challenges and current state of business and IT alignment (BITA), integrated social CRM (iCRM), Big Data and business analytics ecosystems (iDEATE), Blockchain (BSCT), digital customer experience (DigEx), maritime systems (ISAMD), water management (SciBOWater), and data quality (QOD).

Additionally, BIS 2019 hosted a Doctoral Consortium. It was organized in a workshop format, thus the best papers from this event are included in this book. Moreover, all authors had the possibility to discuss their ideas on PhD thesis and research work with a designated mentor.

The workshop authors had the chance to present their results and ideas in front of a well-focused audience; thus the discussion gave the authors new perspectives and directions for further research. Based on the feedback received, authors had the opportunity to update their workshop articles for the current publication. This volume contains **57** articles that are extended versions of papers accepted for BIS workshops. In total, there were 139 submissions for all mentioned events. Based on the reviews, the respective workshop chairs accepted **57** in total, yielding an acceptance rate of **41%**.

We would like to express our thanks to everyone who made BIS 2019 workshops successful. First of all, our workshops chairs, members of the workshop Program

Committees, authors of submitted papers, and finally all workshops participants. We cordially invite you to visit the BIS website at https://bisconf.org/ and to join us at future BIS conferences.

June 2019

Witold Abramowicz
Rafael Corchuelo

Contents

AKTB Workshop

AKTB 2019 Workshop Chairs' Message

AKTB 2019 was the 11th Workshop on Applications of Knowledge-Based Technologies in Business, organized in conjunction with the BIS conference series. It continued the successful series of AKTB workshops in Poznan, Berlin, Vilnius, Larnaca, Leipzig, etc. AKTB 2019 invited researchers, practitioners, and policy makers to share knowledge of efficient computational intelligence methods for implementing business information systems in finance, healthcare, e-business, and other application domains. We requested original papers which could provide advanced services based on innovative data science approaches for the information systems users, and propose efficient solutions for smart business and process modeling. Authors from 15 countries submitted 22 articles to the AKTB 2019 workshop. Each paper was evaluated by two or three independent reviewers of the Program Committee (PC). The highest ranked ten articles, representing the research trend from nine different countries, were accepted for presentation during the conference and the second stage of reviewing before including them into the post-conference proceedings. The PC of AKTB 2019 invited one additional paper disclosing the evaluation of the interdependent effect for Likert scale items. The 21 outstanding researchers who represent prestigious scientific institutions from 8 countries joined the PC as paper reviewers. They evaluated the quality of the articles by taking into account the criteria of its relevance to the workshop topics, originality, novelty, and quality of presentation. We appreciate the level of work and expertise of the PC members, whose reviews provided deep analysis of the submitted research works and highlighted valuable insights for the authors. High standards followed by reviewers ensured a high quality workshop event, excellent presentations, intensive scientific discussions, and added value to the post-conference workshop proceedings. We would like to express our gratitude for the joint input of many people who made AKTB 2019 a success: to all authors of submitted papers, members of the PC, the Kaunas Faculty of Vilnius University, Department of Information Systems of the Poznan University of Economics, ETSI Informática, the University of Seville, and to the outstanding efforts of the Organizing Committee of the 22nd International Conference BIS 2019.

Virgilijus Sakalauskas
Dalia Kriksciuniene

Organization

Chairs

Virgilijus Sakalauskas   Vilnius University, Lithuania
Dalia Kriksciuniene   Vilnius University, Lithuania

Program Committee

María Dolores Afonso Suárez	University of Las Palmas de Gran Canaria, Spain
Lia Bassa	Foundation for Information Society, Spain
Dumitru Dan Burdescu	University of Craiova, Romania
Ferenc Kiss	Budapest University of Technology and Economics, Hungary
Dalia Kriksciuniene	Vilnius University, Lithuania
Dariusz Krol	Wrocław University of Science and Technology, Poland
Roman Lewandowski	University of Social Sciences, Poland
Audrius Lopata	Vilnius University, Lithuania
Dale Luksaite	Kauno Kolegija University of Applied Sciences, Lithuania
Saulius Masteika	Vilnius University, Lithuania
Laima Papreckiene	Kaunas University of Technology, Lithuania
Justyna Patalas-Maliszewska	University of Zielona Góra, Poland, and University of Vienna, Austria
Tomas Pitner	Masaryk University, Czech Republic
Giedrius Romeika	Vilnius University, Lithuania
José Raúl Romero	University of Cordoba, Spain
Vytautas Rudzionis	Vilnius University, Lithuania
Virgilijus Sakalauskas	Vilnius University, Lithuania
Darijus Strasunskas	HEMIT, Norway
Ilona Veitaite	Vilnius University, Lithuania
Sebastián Ventura	University of Cordoba, Spain
Danuta Zakrzewska	Institute of Information Technology Technical University of Lodz, Poland

A Practical Grafting Model Based Explainable AI for Predicting Corporate Financial Distress

Tsung-Nan Chou[✉]

Chaoyang University of Technology, Taichung 41349, Taiwan
tnchou@cyut.edu.tw

Abstract. Machine learning and deep learning are all part of artificial intelligence and have a great impact on marketing and consumers around the world. However, the deep learning algorithms developed from the neural network are normally regarded as a black box because their network structure and weights are unable to be interpreted by a human user. In general, customers in the banking industry have the rights to know why their applications have been rejected by the decisions made by black box algorithms. In this paper, a practical grafting method was proposed to combine the global and the local models into a hybrid model for explainable AI. Two decision tree-based models were used as the global models because their highly explainable ability could work as a skeleton or blueprint for the hybrid model. Another two models including the deep neural network and the k-nearest neighbor model were employed as the local models to improve accuracy and interpretability respectively. A financial distress prediction system was implemented to evaluate the performance of the hybrid model and the effectiveness of the proposed grafting method. The experiment results suggested the hybrid model based on the terminal node grafting might increase the accuracy and interpretability depending on the chosen local models.

Keywords: Decision tree grafting · Explainable AI · Deep neural network

1 Introduction

The machine learning and artificial intelligence (AI) technology have been successfully applied to many financial services to solve various decision-making problems. However, the pervasive deep learning techniques developed from the neural network is considered as a black box and cannot be explained by humans because their network architecture and weights are difficult to be interpreted. Consequently, their processed results are unable to confirm whether the decision-making and analysis are reasonable. In addition, in the case of a consumer loan application, if the financial institution rejects an applicant's loan, the borrower has the rights to ask for the reason why the loan is not approved. In such a situation, the credit decision generated by the automated decision system using the deep learning algorithm needs to explain how the judgment process work. In order to avoid possible irreparable harm from the automated decision-making systems, the General Data Protection Regulation (GDPR) approved by the European

© Springer Nature Switzerland AG 2019
W. Abramowicz and R. Corchuelo (Eds.): BIS 2019 Workshops, LNBIP 373, pp. 5–15, 2019.
https://doi.org/10.1007/978-3-030-36691-9_1

Union in 2016 and enforced in 2018 stipulates that rejected applicants have the rights to know the details of the process leading to their rejection [1]. Therefore, for the most common applications of machine learning in finance, legal consultation, and medical diagnosis, the user must be informed with the reasons for decision or judgment. Otherwise, even the decision is correct, or the prediction model is highly accurate, the result is still doubtful.

Unlike the difficulty of understanding why artificial intelligence has failed, humans can understand and discover their decision and judgment errors and then correct them to avoid making the same mistakes. Therefore, many researchers have tried to develop different methods to make the black boxes of artificial intelligence understandable without affecting their efficiency and performance. As a result, the research area such as the explainable AI (XAI), which is concerned with how to make humans understand the reasons for judgment under artificial intelligence, is getting more attention. However, while using XAI models for prediction, these models need to deal with the tradeoff between model interpretability and accuracy [2]. Generally, an effective XAI model could be used to explain the decision rules generated, but the performance of the model might be affected. Since the artificial intelligence is originally designed to solve a large amount of data analysis problems that humans are difficult to handle, whether the AI models can be understood is closely related to the complexity of the algorithms they used. In general, the more complex a model is, the more difficult to interpret its decision-making and reasoning processes. How to make artificial intelligence interpretable without affecting its performance for an automated decision-making system will be a challenge for researchers. In deep learning techniques, the generative adversarial network (GAN) could be used to train two neural networks against each other to maximize learning outcomes and explore the internal workings of neural networks to provide interpretability [3]. However, the training of GAN is time-consuming and might be unstable. In contrast, the decision tree generates a set of decision rules that are easy for the human to interpret, and the algorithm could be one of the solutions that help the banking industry to be compliant with the GDPR requirements. Although the concepts of explainability and interpretability are different for XAI applications, both are used interchangeably in this paper because the applied decision trees are interpretable models that also provide understandability to know how the results are achieved. The following sections introduce the methods and strategies used in this study briefly.

2   Research Methods and Experiment Design

Some machine learning algorithms such as decision trees, Bayesian inference or Sparse linear models (SLIM) [4] intrinsically provide human interpretability that is easy to understand. Alternatively, many research approaches attempt to realize how the machine learning model work by examining their global or local interpretability, and some others use model-specific or model-agnostic to distinguish the way in which interpretability can be generated. In general, model-agnostic approaches such as partial dependence plot (PDP), Shapley value and local interpretable model-agnostic explanations (LIME) provide interpretability that is compatible with any classification, regression, or reinforcement learning models [5]. The PDP model [6] generally changes the value of a certain characteristic variable one by one while controlling other variables, and interprets the relationship between the characteristic variable and the target variable by a line graph. Comparatively, Lundberg and Lee [7] proposed the Shapely explanations method, using the Shapley value designed by Lloyd Shapley [8] to explain the importance of feature variables. In general, the deep learning models use the training sample to learn the relationship between the input and output variables. If the sample data increases, the mapping of relationship becomes more complicated and makes the constructed model difficult to understand. The LIME algorithm uses a small number of regional samples to construct a simple local model, and the importance of the variable with respect to a testing sample is calculated by the local model rather than the global model previously trained. In brief, this algorithm uses the local model as a proxy model to interpret the original black-box global model [9]. Since the LIME algorithm is model-agnostic, the global model can be any machine learning or deep learning algorithm, while the local model can apply a simple linear regression or a decision tree to fit the target values predicted by the original global model.

This paper proposed a practical grafting method with intent to overcome the tradeoff between accuracy and interpretability in machine learning based on the integration of the global model and the local model. In the first place, each of five common machine-learning models was applied as a global model to evaluate its individual performance. Especially, the decision tree (DT) and fuzzy decision tree (FDT) were used as the global modes due to their explainable ability. Both models worked as a skeleton or blueprint to concatenate the local models. To balance the tradeoff between accuracy and interpretability, the deep neural network (DNN) and k-nearest neighbor methods (KNN) were chosen as local models, where the former intended to increase the accuracy and the latter attempted to increase the interpretability. Finally, the terminal node grafting method that integrated the global and the local models based on three fusion strategies were implemented to examine the performance of the hybrid model. The methods and strategies used in this study were briefly described as following.

2.1 Interpretable Global and Local Models

According to the leading auditing and consulting company PwC's subjective ranking for the explainability of machine learning techniques [10], the decision tree acquired the highest score among all compared models, while the neural network attained the lowest score. Therefore, both the decision tree (DT) and the fuzzy decision tree (FDT) were chosen as the global models due to their highly explainable ability. In contrast to the DT model, the FDT model was employed as a counterpart to examine whether the fuzzy membership and inference mechanism could improve the model performance. The k-means algorithm was also used to generate optimized fuzzy membership partitions for the input variables [11, 12]. Moreover, the random forest (RF) model was another compared model since it randomly chose variables and samples to build several decision trees and combined the outcomes of multiple decision trees into a single average result. Apart from the tree-based models, the KNN and DNN models were applied not only as an independent model to compare their performance, but also as a local model in conjunction with the DT or the FDT global model to construct a hybrid system. The number of hidden layers and the corresponding processing units within the sequential DNN model [13] were examined with different experimental configurations. Furthermore, the dropout layers with a cut-off value of 0.1 were used to control the overfitting problem. The activation functions such as Sigmoid, Tanh and ReLU were assessed in different hidden layers and another SoftMax function was employed in the last fully connected layer.

2.2 The Decision Tree Grafting

By analogy with grafting in plants, heterogeneous models could concatenate on the terminal or internal nodes of a decision tree that worked as the root system. For the grafting performed on internal trunks or branches of a decision tree, the structure of the original tree was altered and the new hybrid tree became more complex. However, if the grafting performed on the terminal nodes, the structure of the original tree remained unchanged. The terminal node grafting might at least not affect the interpretability of the original decision tree and night also improve the model accuracy depending on what kind of local model applied. Some research work [14] have demonstrated that the combination of both pruning and grafting might effectively provide the best general predictive accuracy. Although most of the grafting approaches added the new branches with another decision tree to increase accuracy, we proposed a practical grafting method by using the DNN and the KNN models as the local models rather than using the tree-based model. Both the terminal node grafting and the internal node grafting were developed to improve the accuracy and interpretability of the hybrid model.

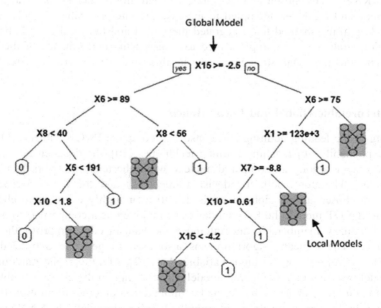

Fig. 1. The terminal node grafting

As shown in Fig. 1, for any decision path ended with a terminal node, the subset of training data partitioned by this path was collected to train another specified local model if it performed poor accuracy. The model interpretability remained unchanged if using the inexplicable DNN model as a local model, while using the KNN model might increase the model interpretability. The other grafting method was the internal node grafting illustrated in Fig. 2. The internal nodes (or decision nodes) of a decision tree performing lower accuracy were removed and replaced with a local model such as the DNN or the KNN model. The branches of a decision tree resembled the clustering function to partition the training data into smaller subsets for training the local models.

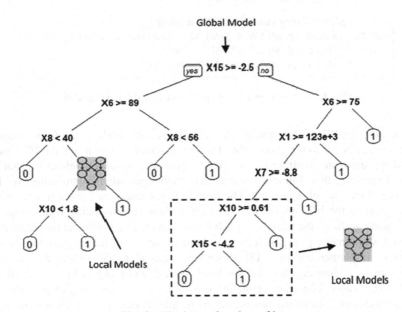

Fig. 2. The internal node grafting

2.3 The Model Integration Approaches

The strength of the FDT model, with respect to other machine learning models, was its inductive learning and linguistic rule construction that inherited from the decision tree and fuzzy inference. Some applications such as medical diagnosis benefited greatly from its interpretative power based on the readable rules. As the global model was the root system and implemented as the skeleton or blueprint of a decision-making framework, the model required to provide the explainable ability to help people understand and trust its outcomes. Therefore, both the DT model and the FDT model were selected as global models because of their interpretable decision rules and the ability to handle inexact and uncertain information. The tree structures of both models were converted to a set of if-then decision rules with a slight difference at multiple antecedent statements. In contrast to the DT model, the FDT model applied the k-means algorithm to partition all input variables into three fuzzy subsets denoted as

MF1, MF2, and MF3. The decision rules generated by the DT and the FDT models comprised 6 and 10 rules, respectively. As the excerpted rules illustrated in Fig. 3, the fuzzy rules derived from the FDT model were controlled by the maximum of four input variables in the non-crisp antecedents to reduce the complexity of the global model.

Examples of decision rule (The DT model):
If X15 < -2.47 & X6 >= 75.135 & X1 < 1231.5 Then Y=1
If X15 < -2.47 & X6 >= 75.135 & X1 >= 1231.5 & X7 >= -6.43 Then Y=0
If X15 >= -2.47 & X6 < 88.875 Then Y=1

Examples of fuzzy rule (The FDT model):
If X15 =MF3 & X8=MF1 & X13=MF2 & X12=MF1   Then Y=1
If X15 =MF3 & X8=MF2 & X7=MF3   Then Y=0
If X15 =MF3 & X8=MF3 & X12=MF2   Then Y=1

Fig. 3. The excerpted rules of the DT and the FDT models

Generally, the DT model searched for a single suitable if-then rule from its trained rule set and applied it to the prediction of a testing sample. In contrast, the FDT model required to aggregate multiple fuzzy rules to evaluate the overall effect on that prediction. Therefore, this difference raised two challenges for implementing the FDT model as a global model in grafting. The first challenge concerned about how to use the multiple rules of the FDT model to train each of their corresponding local models. In terminal node grafting, the training data that complied with a single decision rule of the DT model was directly partitioned as an individual subset for training the local model. In contrast, implementing the FDT model as a global model required to combine several subsets of training data for the local models according to the aggregation of multiple fuzzy rules. The other challenge was how to integrate the global model with the local model to achieve the best synthesis results. If the FDT model was used as a global model, each of its activated fuzzy rules imposed a different weighting effect on the prediction of the testing sample.

Accordingly, three fusion methods were developed to quantify the effect of fuzzy rules on their concatenated local models and calculate the synthetic outcome for the testing data. The first fusion method was a weighted sum approach. The evaluation of a testing sample was calculated by the weighted sum of the outputs from its corresponding local models, where the weights were the relative importance derived from the activated fuzzy rule associated with the local model. In addition, the second fusion method evaluated the testing sample based on the average output of the local models triggered by their corresponding activated fuzzy rules from the global model. Moreover, because each of the activated fuzzy rules represented a weighted vote to its associated local model, the evaluation of a testing sample in the third fusion method was decided by the activated fuzzy rule that acquired the relative majority. In this paper, the FDT model implemented with the KNN model based on three fusion methods were denoted as the FDT-KNN (1) to FDT-KNN (3) models. Comparatively, the FDT model integrated with the DNN model were denoted as the FDT-DNN (1) to FDT-DNN (3) models.

3 Experiment Results

To evaluate the integrated performance of the global and the local modes based on different grafting and fusion methods, a financial distress prediction system was implemented with various experimental configurations. The dataset for experiments comprised the financial and corporate information of 32 distress and another 32 healthy companies declared by the authoritative Taiwan Economic Journal (TEJ) in accordance with various criteria and definitions during the period of 2008 and 2015. Furthermore, the dataset consisted of 15 independent variables were subdivided into 80% for the training dataset and another 20% for the testing dataset. The DT, FDT and KNN models were all regarded as interpretable models regardless of whether they were used as the global or local model. Totally, five experiments were established to evaluate the performance of the model grafting strategies based on four metrics including accuracy, kappa, sensitivity, and specificity. Considering the tradeoff between the accuracy and interpretability for training tree-based global models, the complexity parameter (CP) controlling the number of splits in a decision tree by examining the misclassification error for each branch was evaluated with 0.01 and 0.001, and both were denoted as the DT1 and DT2 models in the first experiment. Moreover, the minimum number of samples in a terminal node and the maximum depth and height of a tree were also controlled to construct a concise global model. As shown in Table 1, the experiment result reported that the DT2 model demonstrated better training accuracy of 0.89, only 5% difference from the simpler DT1 model. However, the DT2 model created a larger rule set of 12 if compared to the smaller DT1 model generating 6 rules only. Although the accuracy of DT1 model was slightly lower than the DT2 model, the DT1 model was selected as the global model to concatenate local models because it was easier to interpret, and the local models might recover the minor decrease of accuracy during grafting experiments.

Table 1. The DT model trained with different CP Parameters.

Trained model	Accuracy	Kappa	Sensitivity	Specificity
DT1 (CP = 0.01)	0.84	0.67	0.86	0.81
DT2 (CP = 0.001)	0.89	0.78	0.91	0.87

The second experiment intended to compare the performance of the five common models described in Sect. 2 prior to working as either a local model or global model. As indicated in Table 2, the FDT model was inferior to the other four models although all models achieved the accuracy over 0.70. The accuracy of the FDT model was 0.73, a 6% deteriorated from the original DT model being reported. The reason why the DT model performed better than the FDT model was that the latter was pruned to preserve a similar tree structure as its counterpart DT model for further comparison of predictive accuracy after grafting, and the crisp inputs needed to be transformed into fuzzy inputs for a fuzzy inference rule. As the random forest was an ensemble approach that combined multiple decision trees into a single predictive model to reduce variance and bias, the experiment result unquestionably suggested the RF model was the best model and achieved an accuracy of 0.85, which outperformed all other common models.

Table 2. The performance comparison of five machine-learning models

Model	Accuracy	Kappa	Sensitivity	Specificity
DT	0.79	0.58	0.88	0.71
FDT	0.73	0.48	0.94	0.56
RF	0.85	0.70	0.94	0.77
KNN	0.80	0.60	0.94	0.67
DNN	0.81	0.63	0.90	0.74

The model grafting created a hybrid model that combined the global model with the local model to increase the overall interpretability and accuracy. Both the DT and the FDT models could be employed as a global mode because they provided better interpretability for the human to understand. On the other hand, the KNN model used as a local model with an attempt to increase more interpretability, while the DNN model was applied to improve predictive accuracy. The performance of the terminal node grafting based on using the DT model as a global model was reported in Table 3. As opposed to the single DT model obtained the accuracy of 0.79, the DT-based grafting result indicated a moderate improvement, and the accuracy was increased to 0.87 for concatenated with the DNN model and 0.82 for the KNN model respectively. Although the DT-DNN model achieved higher accuracy, however, the DT-KNN model gained more interpretability by slightly losing the accuracy of 5%.

Table 3. The grafting performance of the DT-DNN and DT-KNN models

Model	Accuracy	Kappa	Sensitivity	Specificity
DT-DNN	0.87	0.73	0.88	0.85
DT-KNN	0.82	0.65	0.96	0.70

Since the FDT model required to concatenate several local models together due to the multiple fuzzy rules been activated simultaneously, three fusion methods were applied to merge the outcomes of the FDT model with its corresponding local models. By referring to Table 4, the accuracy of the FDT-DNN (3) model using the third fusion method performed the lowest accuracy of 0.73, the same as the result of using the FDT model alone. On the other hand, the FDT-DNN (1) model using the first fusion method improved the accuracy to 0.88 and it was considered as the best model if compared to the other two fusion methods.

Table 4. The grafting performance of the FDT-DNN models

Model	Accuracy	Kappa	Sensitivity	Specificity
FDT-DNN (1)	0.88	0.75	0.92	0.84
FDT-DNN (2)	0.82	0.65	0.9	0.75
FDT-DNN (3)	0.73	0.46	0.75	0.72

In the final experiment, the KNN model was employed as a local model in conjunction with the FDT model to evaluate three fusion methods. As reported in Table 5, the FDT-KNN (1) model outperformed the other models and achieved an accuracy of 0.84. However, this result was slightly lower than that of the FDT-DNN (1) model using the same fusion method and suggested that the KNN model might not be able to improve the predictive accuracy substantially. Although the DNN model aided the hybrid model to improve the predictive accuracy, the KNN model implicated more explanations could be obtained to learn how the results were achieved.

Table 5. The grafting performance of the FDT-KNN models

Model	Accuracy	Kappa	Sensitivity	Specificity
FDT-KNN (1)	0.84	0.68	0.98	0.72
FDT-KNN (2)	0.81	0.63	0.94	0.71
FDT-KNN (3)	0.76	0.51	0.69	0.82

As a highlight, while using only a single model in the experiment, the RF model achieved the highest predictive accuracy among five testing models. However, the interpretability of the RF model was limited since the model applied an ensemble of a number of decision trees. Moreover, by using a hybrid model that integrated a global model with several local models, the predictive results varied and depended on which fusion method was used in model grafting. As the experiment results suggested, the first fusion method surpassed the other two fusion methods, and the combination of the FDT and DNN models might outperform the single RF model in predictive accuracy. Conversely, by using the FDT model in conjunction with the KNN model, the predictive accuracy was slightly worse than the RF model. If considering the DT model instead of the FDT model to concatenate with the local models, the combination of the DT and the DNN model also performed better than the single RF model. Consequently, both the DT and FDT model grafted with the DNN model might be the favorable hybrid solutions to increase predictive accuracy, even by losing a bit of interpretability if compared with the KNN model.

4 Conclusion

To create a fully interpretable framework required combining an explainable global model with flexibly selected local models to prevent from losing accuracy or interpretability. In this paper, a practical grafting approach was proposed to integrate the global model and the local model together with the intent to improve the overall interpretability and accuracy of the resulting hybrid model. Both the DT and the FDT models were chosen as the global models due to their highly explainable ability. On the other hand, the inexplicable DNN model and the explainable KNN model were applied as local models to improve the accuracy and interpretability respectively. By employing a signal model in the experiment, the result indicated the RF model was the best model with the predictive accuracy of 0.85. However, if we implemented a hybrid model based on three fusion methods in the terminal node grafting, the FDT-DNN (1) model was considered as the most competent model under all experiments and achieved the highest accuracy of 0.88. In addition, the experiment result also suggested that both the DT and the FDT models were capable of providing the explainable ability and could be combined with the DNN model to improve model performance by using the proposed grafting technique. Although the KNN model might deliver additional interpretability to the hybrid model, the predictive accuracy was slightly decreased. This research work can be further extended to implement the internal node grafting and compare its performance with that of terminal node grafting described in this study.

References

1. Goodman, B., Flaxman, S.: European union regulations on algorithmic decision-making and a "right to explanation". AI Mag. **38**, 50–57 (2017)
2. Adadi, A., Berrada, M.: Peeking inside the black-box: a survey on explainable artificial intelligence (XAI). IEEE Access **6**, 52138–52160 (2018)
3. Karras, T., Aila, T., Laine, S., Lehtinen, J.: Progressive growing of GANs for improved quality, stability, and variation. arXiv:1710.10196v3 [cs.ne] (2018)
4. Ustun, B., Rudin, C.: Supersparse linear integer models for optimized medical scoring systems. Mach. Learn. **102**(3), 349–391 (2016)
5. Došilović, F.K., Brčić, M., Hlupić, N.: Explainable artificial intelligence: a survey. In: 2018 41st International Convention on Information and Communication Technology, Electronics and Microelectronics (MIPRO), pp. 0210–0215 (2018)
6. Berk, R., Bleich, J.: Statistical procedures for forecasting criminal behavior: a comparative assessment. Criminol. Public Policy **12**(3), 513–544 (2013)
7. Lundberg, S.M., Lee, S.I.: A unified approach to interpreting model predictions. In: Advances in Neural Information Processing Systems (NIPS 2017), vol. 30, pp. 4765–4774 (2017)
8. Roth, A.E. (ed.): The Shapley Value, Essays in Honor of Lloyd S. Shapley. Cambridge University Press, Cambridge (1988)
9. Ribeiro, M.T., Singh, S., Guestrin, C.: Why should I trust you? Explaining the predictions of any classifier. In: Proceedings of the 22nd ACM SIGKDD International Conference on Knowledge Discovery and Data Mining, pp. 1135–1144 (2016)
10. Rao, A., Golbin, I.: What it means to open AI's black box. Next in Tech, PwC Blogs. http://usblogs.pwc.com/emerging-technology/to-open-ai-black-box (2018), last accessed 2019/04/14
11. Levashenko, V., Zaitseva, E.: Fuzzy decision trees in medical decision making support system. In: Proceedings of 2012 Federated Conference on Computer Science and Information Systems, pp. 213–219 (2012)

12. Guillaume, S., Charnomordic, B.: Learning interpretable fuzzy inference systems with Fispro. Int. J. Inform. Sci. **181**(20), 4409–4427 (2011)
13. Liu, W., Wang, Z., Liu, X., Zeng, N., Liu, Y., Fuad, E.A.: A survey of deep neural network architectures and their applications. Neurocomputing **234**, 11–26 (2017)
14. Webb, G.I.: Decision tree grafting from the all tests-but-one partition. In: Proceedings of the 16th International Joint Conference on Artificial Intelligence (IJCAI), vol. 2, pp. 702–707 (1999)

Data Analytics in the Electronic Games

Tomáš Porvazník, František Babič[(✉)], and Ľudmila Pusztová

Department of Cybernetics and Artificial Intelligence,
Faculty of Electrical Engineering and Informatics,
Technical University of Košice, 040 01 Košice, Slovak Republic
tomas.porvaznik@tuke.sk, frantisek.babic@tuke.sk,
ludmila.puzstova.2@tuke.sk

Abstract. This paper aims at the use of data analytics methods in mobile games. The main goal was to predict future purchases of players in the selected mobile game. The result presents the information about whether the player is going to buy any of the offered bonus packages or not. This information is crucial for marketing and possible ways of monetization. From the perspective of data analytics, the goal is the creation of a classification model in line with the CRISP-DM methodology. We used the following algorithms in the modeling phase: Random forest, Naive Bayes, Linear regression, XGBoost, and Gradient Boosting. All generated models were evaluated by contingency tables, which presented models accuracy as the ration between successfully predicted values to all predicted samples. The results are plausible and have the potential to be deployed into practice as a baseline model or support for personalized marketing activities.

Keywords: Mobile games · Data analytics · Monetization

1 Introduction

Everybody knows what mobile games are. We play them in our free time, on the bus, some of us even at work. Mobile games sector is a highly competitive, and the development of a successful game is a challenging and complex issue. A few years ago, you came to the shop and bought a physical copy of the game. Nowadays, the process is even more straightforward with the availability of online mobile stores. But the players prefer another model for mobile games; it is called a fremium. The 2018 report by Nielsen gaming research company SuperData has revealed that so-called freemium games – games that are free to play but typically enable microtransactions for users to purchase upgrades and gizmos – are dominating the entertainment market, generating a massive $88 billion in the past year. This fact motivated us to start a collaboration with one of the game development companies creating free-to-play games. During the analytical process, we communicated intensively with the experts; not only during the data understanding but also in the evaluation phase.

The paper is organized as follows: an introduction with motivation, related work, methodology, and used methods. The description of the performed analytical project is in line with the CRISP-DM methodology. The conclusion summarizes the results.

W. Abramowicz and R. Corchuelo (Eds.): BIS 2019 Workshops, LNBIP 373, pp. 16–25, 2019.
https://doi.org/10.1007/978-3-030-36691-9_2

1.1 Electronic Games

Field of electronic games is growing every day. Generally speaking, it is a game played on some electronic device, whether it is a console, mobile phone or computer. Some of the most popular mobile games count their daily active users in millions. The Q4 and Full Year 2018 Store Intelligence Data Digest report[1] pointed out that worldwide app revenue grew 22.7% in 2018 to $71.3 billion and new app installs topped 105.3 billion, increasing 11.1 percent over 2017. In the mobile games world, the hyper-casual titles dominated the download charts for 2018, led by releases from Voodoo (Helix Jump) and Lion Studios (Love Balls).

If the mobile game uses the freemium model, the idea is that they make a lot of money. But, they have to have a good monetization strategy. The recommended way how to do this effectively is to follow the ARM model invented by Lewis in 1898 [1]. ARM stands for Acquisition, Retention, and Monetization. You may say that mobile games did not even exist back then. That is because this model is not focused on mobile games but business in general. Gain new customers, make them stay and in the end, monetize them. In each step, you have to define relevant key performance indicators [2].

The first step in the model is an acquisition. Use every available source and gain as many players as possible. Viral sources are better than those nonviral because nonviral sources cost studio money. Once your game went viral, you are all good. K-factor is a metric representing several users who come from virality (social media shares). The second kind of acquisition, nonviral, is based on ads and marketing. There are few indicators if your ad campaign is successful. One of them is Cost per Install. This key performance indicator measures how much you need to spend on ads to gain one user.

The second step in the ARM model is retention. Longer, the user will stay the higher profit you will have from him. If the user is coming back to the game regularly, there is a bigger chance of monetizing him. For example, you can you two approaches to motivate him: reward him for coming back or punish him for not doing so. The punishment method is outdated. The modern game studios are using rewarding even for failure in the game. It is all mind games. In this step, there are also a few essential key performance indicators like daily active users, monthly active users, and an average total in-app time. Let's say you have gain users and they are coming back every so often.

The next step will be to monetize the users. In-app purchases and ads are the only ways of profiting in the freemium model. This step aims to convert as many players to paying ones as possible. Not every player is willing to spend money in the game. The fact is that paying users to represent only a fraction of all players, mostly less than 5%. Those paying users are commonly separated into three categories. First, there are minnows. The players, who spend a little bit of money, maximum of 5$ in their lifetime (total time spend in the game). Next, the dolphins, those spend up to 20$. And the smallest group but with the highest earnings is called whales. Those players spend more than 20$, sometimes even more than 100$. The game must be designed in such a way that it will encourage users to pay. To monitor monetization there are several key

[1] https://sensortower.com/blog/top-apps-games-publishers-2018.

performance indicators like Average revenue per daily active users, to see the fluctuations of purchases during the day, or Average revenue per paying user, to see how much money are users spending.

2 Methodology

Data analytics, data mining, or knowledge discovery in databases represents a process in which we want to find knowledge was yet unknown, is relevant and can be needed asset to the company [3]. This process is iterative, meaning, you can go forward and backward between the steps of the process.

In our case, we decided to use the CRISP-DM methodology [4, 5]. It is a widely accepted approach on how to organize and implement analytical projects through six main phases, such as Business understanding, Data understanding, Data preparation, Modeling, Evaluation, and Deployment.

Business understanding deals with a specification of business goal followed with the transformation to the specific analytical task. Based on this specification, we can select appropriate mining methods and necessary resources.

Data understanding stars with a collection of necessary data for the specified task and ends with a detailed description including some statistical characteristics.

Data preparation is usually the most complex and the most time-consuming phase. Generally, take 60–70% percent of the overall time. It contains data aggregation, cleaning, reduction, or transformation. The result covers prepared data for modeling.

Modeling deals with an application of suitable data mining algorithms on the pre-processed data. Also, it is necessary to specify the correct metrics for results evaluation, e.g., accuracy, ROC, precision, recall, etc.

The evaluation phase is oriented towards the evaluation of generated models and obtained results based on specified goals in business understanding.

The deployment contains the exploration of created models in real cases, their adoption, maintenance, and collection of acquired experiences and knowledge.

2.1 Data Analytics in Mobile Games

We shortly present some existing works or studies with similar topics. A first case study from 2010 [6] focused on a situation when a user leaves the game. The authors applied neural networks to the data characterizing the player's initial behavior. They used data about 6 430 players and created a few models like Random Forest, Naïve Bayes, Linear regression, XGBoost, Gradient Boosting, and Stacked Ensemble. The most successful one was the linear regression model with 77.3% accuracy. The result represented a piece of valuable information for the game developers to modify and improve the relevant part of the virtual environment.

In 2012 game studio, which created one of the most popular FPS (First Person Shooter) game decided to use clustering technique on players of their game [6]. They targeted the attributes like score, level, total gameplay time, accuracy when shooting, and many more. Then they've used algorithms like k-Means and SIVM (Simplex Volume Maximization). The results covered seven clusters representing the style of gameplay. The interesting fact was that two of these clusters did not correspond to the known characters. The main finding was the identification of the two primary playing techniques like the combat-oriented and support-oriented style. This knowledge helped developers adjust the abilities of the characters in the game, and improve the gameplay.

The German data analysts aimed to predict the purchases in the mobile game following the freemium model [7]. They divided the task into two goals: (1) the classification task to predict whether the player is going to purchase something at all; (2) a regression task to estimate the number of purchases by individual players. They used data about 100 000 in-game purchases in the popular puzzle game. The first step was to extract a sample of the users and focus on three factors: logins, played rounds, and purchases. The paying players represented only 2% of the total players. Based on it, the authors used oversampling to balance the ratio between payers and non-payers. They applied algorithms like Random Forest and Support-Vector Machine with and without balancing. They predicted purchases in one, three, and seven days. The findings were not shocking. They found out that the attribute which affects the outcome the most is the fact if there were any purchases by the player before. If the player did buy something in the past, he would most likely do it again. Next step was the regression task. The estimation of the number of purchases is essential for the Lifetime value KPI. They started with the average purchases in one day on one player. On the sample of 10 000 players, the average was 0.057. When extended to three days, the value was 0.050, and in seven days, 0.037. Since the target value should be the whole number, they decided to use a decision tree algorithm with Poisson distribution (PRT). The combination of two created models led to the nearly flawless prediction of players purchases.

2.2   Used Methods

In this section, we shortly introduce the methods applied in the modeling phase to the pre-processed data.

Decision trees are one of the best-known tools used for classification and prediction. In principle, decision trees can be defined as a structure for predicting a target attribute using decision rules. It is a classifier with a tree structure. Random forest is a classifier that, as its name suggests, consists of multiple decision trees [8]. It consists of two phases. In the first phase, the algorithm builds a data behavior model based on the data training set. In the second phase, the assembled model is used to predict the values of the identified cases. The process consists of several iterations, while in each of them, the algorithm tries to create a stronger one with the help of weaker classifiers. It uses a different subset of the training data attributes and assigns the resulting classes based on the single classifier voting principle. The error rate of the algorithm depends on the correlation of the individual trees being built, as well as, of course, the strength of the built classifiers.

Bayesian classifiers are based on the probability principle with which a new record belongs to a particular target attribute class. They calculate the conditional probabilities of individual attribute values for all target classes based on the Bayes' theorem [9, 10]:

$$P(H|X) = (P(H|X) * P(H))/(P(X))$$

The conditional probability means that we assume that the attributes affecting object assignment to the class are independent of each other. This assumption is often referred to as the Naive Bayesian classification [11].

Linear regression is the simplest form of regression. Two-dimensional linear regression models the target attribute Y as a linear function of another known X attribute according to the line equation [12]:

$$Y = \alpha + \beta * X$$

Regression coefficients α and β are calculated using the least squares method, which minimizes the error between the approximation line and the real values. We used the generalized linear regression model.

Gradient boosting is a machine learning technique for regression and classification problems, which produces a prediction model in the form of an ensemble of weak prediction models, typically decision trees (Wikipedia). This approach was first time introduced by Leo Breiman [13]. When strengthening, each new tree is applied to the modified version of the original dataset. After its evaluation, the algorithm will increase the weights of those examples that are difficult to classify and reduce for those that have easy classification. The second tree is created from these modified data, and this approach improves the prediction of the first tree. The new model contains both classification trees, classification error is determined, and a third tree is created predicting the deviations. This process repeats based on the specified number of iterations. The final classification is based on the weighted sum of predictions from the built trees.

XGBoost is a very popular open source implementation of the decision tree strengthening algorithm. This machine learning library has been winning many data analytics competitions. It tries to predict the target variable accurately by combining estimates of simpler and weaker models. Subsequently, the algorithm maps the input data for each tree to one of its sheets, which contains the intermediate score. XGBoost minimizes the function that combines convex loss function (the difference between predicted and actual values) and the punishment function for the complexity of the algorithm. The process of such learning is iterative. New trees are added to predict the errors of previous ones and then in combination, represent the final prediction.

K-Nearest Neighbor (k-NN) is a simple algorithm that stores all available records and classifies new ones based on a similarity measure. A record is classified by a majority vote of its k neighbors measured by a distance function [14].

3   Analytical Project

The whole analytical project was organized within the CRISP-DM methodology.

3.1   Business Understanding

Our business goal was to understand the player's behavior in the virtual environment to make targeted marketing in-game more efficient. From an analytical point of view, we solved the classification task which will predict if the player is going to purchase something (do the microtransaction), and if so, which specific package. For this purpose, we used the development environment of the Python programming language called Rodeo.

We had available data with two types of microtransactions in the investigated mobile game: (1) an in-game currency - you are forced to spend it, and if you run out of it, you need to buy it; (2) the offer for special packages occurring every once in a while. In this situation, the game usually offers a few of them, everyone targeted at different players depending on their gameplay.

We performed the experiments in the development environment of the Python programming language called Rodeo. The Pandas open source library provides high-performance, easy-to-use data structures, and data analysis tools. We used this library for transformations. Seaborn is a Python data visualization library based on mat-plotlib. It provides a high-level interface for drawing attractive and informative statistical graphics. We used it for exploratory data analysis. H2O is open-source software for big-data analysis; we used it for application of the selected machine learning algorithms to the pre-processed data.

3.2   Data Understanding

The data contained information about players and their purchases from the selected period within 65 attributes. The target value was the result of the offer if the player bought the related package or not. Also, the data contained information about what type was purchased, total spend money, time of registration, time of purchase, information about the device, or current game status.

We visualized all distribution within suitable graphs like histograms or boxplots. Next, we provided a correlation analysis to investigate the possible relations between numerical attributes. In the case of nominal variables, we used relevant statistical tests.

3.3   Data Preparation

We started with a reduction of the unwanted and not needed redundant data. After that, we split the date attributes to day, month, and year. We created a new attribute representing the time between registration into game and time of purchase. Next, we replaced the missing values as one of the most critical steps of this phase. In case of categorical attributes and if the missing value had a meaning (like NaN value means no purchase was done), we replaced them with the 'Empty' value. In the case of the numerical attributes, we replaced the missing values with the algorithm of k-Nearest Neighbor, meaning it was calculated based on similarity to other objects.

Also, we investigated the distribution of the target attribute that was heavily unbalanced. As we mentioned before, paying players to represent only a fraction of total players. In our case, it was about 7%. That was the reason why we chose to go with the oversampling technique. The oversampling will take classes with fewer objects and artificially copy some of the objects to match the number of the majority class. This operation helped use to balance the target classes almost to 400 thousand records.

3.4 Modeling and Evaluation

The Random forest represents a bagging-based algorithm, and with the default parameters, we obtained 73% accuracy of the classification model. We tried several iterations with different settings, and the accuracy gradually increased to the highest value of 89%. The set of parameters for the best model was following: automatic balancing; the number of built trees limited to 25 with depth 42; the sample_rate parameter determining the rate at which the lines are sampled setting to 0.8; 10-fold cross-validation with cross-validation prediction. The automatic balancing means an additional modification of input data by algorithm itself. It is an optional parameter selecting appropriate balancing method based on the distribution, the number of target attribute's values, and the classes of other attributes in the training set.

In the case of the Naive Bayes algorithm, we started with 58% value related to the default parameters. Similar as in the first case, we tried several iterations to improve this value. The best model with 65% accuracy was: 10-fold cross-validation and automatic balancing; the Laplace equalization setting to 2, and the minimum probability for low data observations as 70.

The most successful iteration with the XGBoost resulted in 78.9% accuracy; the baseline was 72%. The best parameters combination was: 10-fold cross-validation and automatic balancing, multinomial as distribution type, the number of trees 65, the learning speed 0.6. Gradient boosting brought quite similar results, the best accuracy 80.27%, with a difference in the number of trees (50), the tree depth (30), and the learning speed (0.9).

We applied linear regression model with different distributions; except for Gaussian, also Poisson, binomial, and gamma. Each of them serves a different purpose and depends on the distribution type and choice of function. The best accurate model was 87.27% with the following partial predictions: 1st class 95%, 2nd class 87.4%, 3rd 90.4%, and 4th 90.2%. We set up these parameters: 10-fold cross-validation and automatic balancing, multi-nominal, and normalization of numeric attributes.

Finally, we applied an automatic machine learning method to the data provided by the H2o library. The AutoML algorithm uses 10-fold cross-validation and trains several algorithms. We selected the Stacked ensemble, Random forest, Extremely-randomized forest and Gradient Boosting Machines The resulted model is described by following metrics like Root Mean Square Error (RMSE), Mean squared error (MSE), Mean Absolute Error (MAE), Root Mean Squared Logarithmic Error (RMSLE) [15], see Table 1.

Table 1. The results of AutoML

Model	RMSE	MSE	MAE	RMSLE
Stacked ensemble	0.084	0.007	0.042	0.032
DRF	0.086	0.007	0.037	0.031
XRT	0.204	0.042	0.140	0.074
GLM	0.621	0.385	0.489	0.137

The model with the lowest error was the Stacked ensemble model, the combination of two models: Random Forest and Gradient Boosting. This approach improved the accuracy to 91%. It is a process called stacking, and the chosen models have to use the same principles. Therefore it must be based on decision trees.

For clustering, we needed only numeric attributes. Therefore we transformed the categorical attributes within the dummy coding. 'Dummy' is a duplicate variable representing one level of the categorical variable. The presence was represented by 1, and absence by 0. After this transformation, we applied the k-NN algorithm to the data. We expected four clusters similar to the four target classes. Figure 1 visualizes the result.

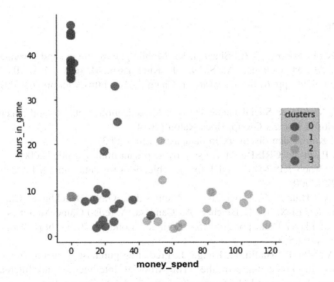

Fig. 1. The clustering results. (Color figure online)

The blue cluster represents players who did not buy anything but stayed in the game for a long time. The green one covers players who remained in the game for a shorter time but spent a lot of money. Red cluster is somewhere between those two, and the orange one represents a specific group played the game more than nine hours and spent almost no money.

4 Conclusion

This paper aims to use data analytics in mobile games. A better understanding of the player's in-game behavior represents a significant step forward in the marketing activities and also in the overall improvement of the relevant virtual environment. We applied suitable machine learning or exploratory data analysis methods in line with the CRISP-DM methodology to solve the classification task as useful as possible. We tried five various algorithms with different parameters. The best accuracy 91% was obtained by the combination of the Random Forest algorithm and gradient boosting. Obtained results are plausible and have potential to be deployed into practice. Being aware of what package a player will buy when he first enters a game opens new opportunities for companies to provide better user experience in parallel with optimizing the marketing and monetization processes.

Acknowledgements. The work was partially supported by the Slovak Grant Agency of the Ministry of Education and Academy of Science of the Slovak Republic under grant no. 1/0493/16, The Slovak Research and Development Agency under grant no. APVV-16-0213 and the Cultural and Educational Grant Agency of the Ministry of Education, Science, Research and Sport of the Slovak Republic under grant no. 005TUKE-4/2017.

References

1. Alomari, K.M., Soomro, T.R., Shaalan, K.: Mobile gaming trends and revenue models. In: Fujita, H., Ali, M., Selamat, A., Sasaki, J., Kurematsu, M. (eds.) IEA/AIE 2016. LNCS (LNAI), vol. 9799, pp. 671–683. Springer, Cham (2016). https://doi.org/10.1007/978-3-319-42007-3_58
2. Fields, T.: Mobile & Social Game Design: Monetization Methods and Mechanics. CRC Press, Taylor & Francis Group, Boca Raton (2014)
3. Paralic, J.: Knowledge discovery in databases, Elfa (2003)
4. Chapman, P., et al.: CRISP-DM 1.0 step-by-step data mining guide (2000)
5. Shearer, C.: The CRISP-DM model: the new blueprint for data mining. J. Data Ware-Hous. **5**(4), 13–22 (2000)
6. Drachen, A., Thurau, C., Togelius, J., Yannakakis, G.N., Bauckhage, Ch.: Game data mining. In: Seif El-Nasr, M., Drachen, A., Canossa, A. (eds.) Game Analytics: Maximizing the Value of Player Data, pp. 205–253. Springer, London (2013). https://doi.org/10.1007/978-1-4471-4769-5_12
7. Drachen, A., Sifa, R., Hadiji, F., Runge, J.: Predicting purchase decisions in mobile free-to-play games. In: Proceedings of the 11th Artificial Intelligence and Interactive Digital Entertainment International Conference, pp. 79–86. AAAI Press (2015)
8. Breiman, L.: Random Forests. Mach. Learn. **45**, 5–32 (2001)
9. Russell, S., Norvig, P.: Artificial Intelligence: A Modern Approach. Prentice Hall, Upper Saddle River (2003)
10. Devroye, L., Gyorfi, L., Lugosi, G.: A Probabilistic Theory of Pattern Recognition. Springer-Verlag, New York (1996). https://doi.org/10.1007/978-1-4612-0711-5

11. Friedman, N., Geiger, D., Goldszmidt, M.: Bayesian network classifiers. Mach. Learn. **29**, 131–163 (1997)
12. Kenney, J.F., Keeping, E.S.: Linear regression and correlation. In: Mathematics of Statistics, vol. 1, pp. 252–285. Van Nostrand, Princeton (1962)
13. Breiman, L.: Arcing the edge. Statistics Department, University of California, Berkeley (1997)
14. Altman, N.S.: An introduction to kernel and nearest-neighbor nonparametric regression. Am. Stat. **46**(3), 175–185 (1992)
15. Shcherbakov, M.V., et al.: A Survey of Forecast Error Measures. World Appl. Sci. J. **24**, 171–176 (2013). (Information Technologies in Modern Industry, Education & Society)

Evaluating the Interdependent Effect for Likert Scale Items

Dalia Kriksciuniene[1], Virgilijus Sakalauskas[1(✉)],
and Roman Lewandowski[2]

[1] Institute of Applied Informatics, Vilnius University,
Universiteto str.3, Vilnius, Lithuania
{dalia.kriksciuniene,
virgilijus.sakalauskas}@knf.vu.lt
[2] Management Faculty, University of Social Sciences, Lodz, Poland
r.lewandowski@ameryka.com.pl

Abstract. Likert scale items are used for surveys exploring attitudes by collecting responses to particular questions or groups of related statements. The common practice is asking respondents to express their level of agreement by applying the seven or five-point scale from 'strongly disagree' to 'strongly agree'. Although the Likert scale methodology serves as a powerful tool for asking attitudinal questions and getting measurable answers from the respondents, the surveys fail to identify level of importance of the individual questions used for characterizing the explored phenomena. Moreover, the Likert scale methodology does not enable to distinguish which of the questions are the causes, and which of them are the effects of the explored problem. The objective of the research is to propose an original method for evaluating the cause-effect relationship and strength of interdependences among Likert scale items. The classical DEMATEL technique is modified for analysis of the interdependence among factors in order to overcome the subjective origin of expert evaluations, generally applied for its implementation. The Spearman Rank Order Correlations of Likert scale items were explored as a consistent replacement of subjective group direct-influence matrix. The modified influential relation map built for Likert scale items revealed improvement scopes by defining causal relationships and significance of the questions of the survey, and added value for long-term strategic decision making. The viability of the proposed model is illustrated by a case study of service quality survey data collected at the rehabilitation hospital in Poland.

Keywords: Likert scale survey · DEMATEL · Cause-effect relation · Influential relation map · Healthcare quality

1 Introduction

In order to investigate problems requiring description of attitudes from different perspectives, we need to explore factors influencing process changes. The examples of such problems are in broad variety of domains, such as the quality of healthcare, customer satisfaction, or the service level of the society. The prevalent instrument

© Springer Nature Switzerland AG 2019
W. Abramowicz and R. Corchuelo (Eds.): BIS 2019 Workshops, LNBIP 373, pp. 26–38, 2019.
https://doi.org/10.1007/978-3-030-36691-9_3

applied for this purpose is a survey performed as Likert scale questionnaire, developed by Likert [12]. It is designed to measure attitudes by rating the degree to which the respondents agree or disagree with a provided statement. The Likert scale questionnaire enables to investigate the survey results not only in a qualitative manner but also perform a quantitative analysis.

Likert scale item typically have five level rating scale: strongly disagree, disagree, neutral, agree, strongly agree. The other number of levels and different ordered categories from lowest to highest is also acceptable [1, 7, 18]. We could find a number of articles discussing the various aspects of creating [18], interpreting [22], making in-depth analysis [2, 11] or disclosing the findings in different areas [5, 10, 14]. Besides its numerous advantages, the Likert scale questionnaire methodology provides quite limited and controversial analytical possibilities [19].

Our research objective is to propose an original method for evaluation the Likert scale items and explore the interdependences and cause-effect relationships among survey questions. This will support the decision makers to improve the Likert scale surveys and to enhance analysis and interpretation of the researched problems.

The explored problem is highly compatible to the classical DEMATEL (Decision Making Trial and Evaluation Laboratory) method, which was firstly developed by Geneva Research Centre of the Battelle Memorial Institute [3, 4]. The DEMATEL approach enables to visualise the structure of complicated causal-effect relationships among factors of a system. By using this method, we can confirm the interdependence of the system attributes and clarify critical factors of complex system. The DEMATEL finds wide application in various fields, such as group decision-making [13], sustainable production and consumption [16], managing performance improvement [15, 21], competency modelling [9], importance–performance analysis [6].

The DEMATEL method starts from building direct-influence matrix composed of expert decisions about the interdependence and strength of all explored factors. This requirement is hardly realised in case of Likert scale items. Generally, we have sets of survey questions describing the problem are, however their individual importance and interdependence is unclear even for specialists. In order to remove the necessity of expert opinion, we proposed modification of the DEMATEL method by replacing the subjective direct-influence matrix with Spearman Rank Order Correlations matrix obtained from the survey database of Likert scale factors.

The article is organized as follows. The characteristic of the proposed method is described in Sect. 2. A case study and application of our technique is demonstrated in Sect. 3, where the Polish rehabilitation hospital service quality survey data is explored. The paper is summarized by the main findings and conclusion of the research.

2 Research Method

We investigate the behavior of some process described by a Likert scale questionnaire. Assume we have n questions-factors $Q_1, Q_2, \ldots, Q_n$ reflecting some characteristics of the investigated process and having any quantity of ordered response levels. The sample of m respondents who took a survey form the survey data set SD(m, n) suitable for analysis.

The proposed method consists of 6 major steps:

1. *Grouping of question-factors.* In general, a big number of question-factors lead to difficulty of distinct identification of their interrelationships. Therefore, we group the factors to bigger groups according to the topics they explore $G_1, G_2, \ldots, G_k$, $k < n$. We advise to use no more than 10 groups, and for more relevant grouping purposes we can invite the concrete domain authorities.

2. *Setting the group $G_1, G_2, \ldots, G_k$ interrelation directed graph.* This graph should express vision of the domain experts about the direction of influences between group $G_1, G_2, \ldots, G_k$ members. Unlike in classical DEMATEL method, we do not require to predict integer value of the influence strength.

3. *Create the adjacency matrix from the directed graph.* The adjacency matrix is a square matrix with elements 0 or 1, indicating whether pairs of nodes of the directed graph are adjacent or not. The adjacency matrix is created for n questions-factors $Q_1, Q_2, \ldots, Q_n$ considering the presence of factor influence according group $G_1, G_2, \ldots, G_k$ interrelation as it was marked in the directed map. We construct the adjacency matrix $AM(n, n)$ with zeros on its diagonal.

4. *Calculate the Spearman Rank Correlations from survey data set SD(m, n).* Spearman's Rank correlation coefficient is used to summarise the strength and direction (negative or positive) of a relationship between two variables. It takes value from the interval $(-1, 1)$. After calculation Spearman Rank correlation for survey data set $SD(m, n)$ we get the correlation matrix $SRC(n, n)$ reflecting the strength and direction of the initial question-factor set.

5. *Get the questions-factors direct influence matrix Z(n, n),* which indicate the direct influence that one factor has on another. To do this we multiply the absolute values of matrix $SRC(n, n)$ entries by the corresponding elements of $AM(n, n)$. As it was stated in the DEMATEL method description, all factors relation values have to be positive, all principal diagonal elements equal to zero.

6. *Applying the classical DEMATEL for deriving direct influence matrix Z(n, n).* In the classical DEMATEL algorithm, the direct influence matrix is formed from aggregated subjective expert decisions about factors' influence strength on each other, while in our case we use the modified Spearman's Rank correlation matrix. This lets us to avoid subjectivity and necessity to organise expert pool.

Next, we describe the DEMATEL algorithm to convert the interrelations between factors into structural model of the system and divide them into groups according to their cause-effect profiles [17].

The $Z = \{z_{ij}\}_{i,j=1}^{n}$ denotes the direct influence matrix, and s is the normalizing constant:

$$s = \max\Big(\max_{1 \le i \le n} \sum_{j=1}^{n} z_{ij}, \max_{1 \le j \le n} \sum_{i=1}^{n} z_{ij}\Big) \tag{1}$$

We aim to construct the *total – influence matrix T(n, n)*. The total influence matrix T expresses the aggregated direct and indirect effects of our factors:

$$T = \frac{Z}{s} + \left(\frac{Z}{s}\right)^2 + \left(\frac{Z}{s}\right)^3 + \ldots + \left(\frac{Z}{s}\right)^l \overset{l \to \infty}{\longrightarrow} \frac{Z}{s} \cdot \left(I - \frac{Z}{s}\right)^{-1} = \left(I - \frac{Z}{s}\right)^{-1} - I \quad (2)$$

where I denote the identity matrix.

The total-influence matrix enables to evaluate the direct and indirect effects which one factor has on the others. By summing the rows of total-influence matrix T, we get a vector $R = \{R_i\}_{i=1}^n$ which indicates the strength of direct and indirect effects dispatching from factor Q_i to other factors. The sum of total-influence matrix T columns $C = \{C_j\}_{j=1}^n$ signifies the direct and indirect effects value that factor Q_j is receiving from others factors.

The vector $R + C' = \{R_i + C_i'\}_{i=1}^n$, where C' denotes a transposed matrix, gives an index aggregating total received and given effects by the factor Q_i. In the literature [17] this vector is called "*Prominence*" as it illustrates the degree of the central role that the factor plays in the system.

Alike, the difference vector $R - C' = \{R_i - C_i'\}_{i=1}^n$ indicates the net effect that factor Q_i contributes to the system. We will call it "*Relation*": if this difference is positive, factor Q_i is net causer, if it is a negative - net receiver. In case of positive difference, all corresponding factors make a **cause group**, which has the total net influence on the other factors. The *Relation* factors with the negative difference form an **effect group** which is influenced by the other factors.

Finally, DEMATEL let us create the **influential relation map** (IRM) by mapping the dataset of pairs $(R + C', R - C')$ and visualize it by using the four-quadrant graphical chart (see Fig. 1).

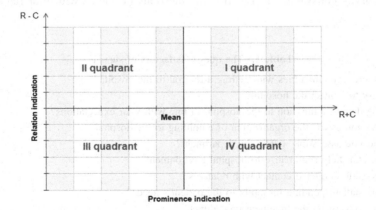

Fig. 1. Four quadrant influence relation map

The factors from quadrant I have high prominence and relation and can be identified as core factors or intertwined givers. The factors falling in quadrant II are seen as driving factors or autonomous givers as they have low prominence but high relation. The III quadrant factors are characterized by low prominence and relation and are relatively disconnected from the system. These are called independent factors or autonomous receivers. The factors in the quadrant IV are called impact factors or intertwined receivers, which are influenced by other factors and cannot be directly improved. They have high prominence but low relation.

The IRM provides decision makers with new advanced valuable insights about the character of individual Likert scale items, reveal complex cause-effect relationship among questions-factors and can support for their improvement within the survey to get a more precise characteristics of the explored process.

3   Experimental Research of the Method

The data used for our experimental research was taken from a children rehabilitation hospital in Poland. The hospital administration cares about the performance aspects which can be identified as quality of treatment, personnel helpfulness, infrastructure and admission conditions. Therefore, the patients or their parents are asked to respond to the survey about satisfaction of provided medical rehabilitation services. The questions of the surveys aim to ask about various aspects of the performance so that the respondents could express their attitudes. The main purpose of such questionnaire from the managerial perspective is to find the positive and negative influencing factors of the rehabilitation processes, assess the impact of specific actions and decisions, and to find strategies for the treatment quality improvement ways.

The data base of survey answers was collected as the Likert scale data. In order to get the comprehensive portrait of the situation of the hospital it is necessary to evaluate the interrelation and define cause-effect nature of factors among the Likert scale items. The following research illustrates the possible solution of this problem.

The survey consists of 20 Likert-scale questions (Table 1) with four rating-scale levels.

Table 1. The questions-factors of survey

1. Were there any difficulties with getting a referral to the hospital?
2. Is it easy to contact the hospital?
3. Was the date of admission to the hospital in line with your expectations?
4. How do you assess the organization of admitting to the hospital?
5. How do you assess the staff in the department?
6. Did the staff help acclimatize to hospital environment?
7. Has the staff facilitated contact with relatives?
8. Was the staff responding promptly to the patient's needs?
9. How do you assess the treatment procedures?
10. Did the staff inform in a clear and exhaustive way about the performed procedures?
11. Did the staff perform all the treatments with due diligence?
12.Did the staff provide comprehensive information about the disease and treatment?
13. Did recommended treatment program meet your expectations?
14. Is the treatment effective?
15. Were the tips for further treatment comprehensive?

(continued)

Table 1. (*continued*)

16. Was the quality of the equipment appropriate to your requirements?

17. Were the meals delicious?

18. Were the meals aesthetically served?

19. How do you assess the therapists - educator?

20. Were leisure activities organized by the hospital?

The responses to Likert scale items make collection of Likert scale data file of 228 records i.e. 228 hospital patients provided responses to this survey. The fragment of the data file is presented in Table 2.

Table 2. Fragment of the survey data file (first 11 responses of total N#228)

	1	2	3	4	5	6	7	8	9	10	11	12	13	14	15	16	17	18	19	20
1	4	4	4	4	4	4	3	3	4	4	4	4	4	4	4	4	4	3	3	3
2	4	4	4	4	4	3	4	4	4	4	4	4	4	3	4	4	4	3	3	3
3	4	4	4	4	4	3	4	4	4	4	4	4	3	2	4	4	4	3	3	3
4	4	4	4	3	3	3	2	3	4	4	4	3	4	4	4	4	4	4	4	3
5	4	1	4	4	4	3	4	4	4	4	4	4	3	3	4	4	4	4	4	3
6	4	4	4	3	4	2	4	3	4	4	4	4	3	4	3	4	4	3	4	3
7	4	4	2	2	2	4	3	2	2	3	2	2	3	2	2	4	4	1	2	2
8	4	4	4	4	4	3	4	4	4	4	4	4	4	4	3	4	4	4	4	4
9	4	4	4	4	4	3	4	4	4	4	4	4	4	4	3	4	4	3	4	4
10	4	4	4	4	4	3	4	4	4	3	3	4	3	1	4	4	4	4	3	3
11	4	4	4	4	4	3	4	4	4	4	4	4	4	4	4	4	4	4	3	3

Each survey question can be interpreted as a quality evaluation factor and processed according to the method described in the previous section. In order to have a more explicit interpretation of the method we illustrate it by following the research steps defined in the previous section.

1. **Grouping of question-factors.** According to the research framework, we group the question-factors to meaningful groups. For this task, we have involved hospital authorities, who have selected 4 factors: Process of admission to hospital; Personnel helpfulness; Quality of treatment; Infrastructure and food. The allocation of questions to the corresponding factors are in Table 3.

Table 3. Questions related to grouping factors

Grouping factors	Questions no.
Process of admission to hospital	1–4
Personnel helpfulness	5–11
Quality of treatment	12–15
Infrastructure and food	16–20

2. **Setting the grouping factors interrelation directed graph.** This step also was supported by expert opinion of hospital authorities. They stated that all factors have a direct influence on *Quality of treatment* item, but it influences only *Infrastructure and food*, which shows a direct impact on all other factors. The *Personal helpfulness* influence *Process of admission to hospital*. This relation is shown in Fig. 2 as a directed graph.

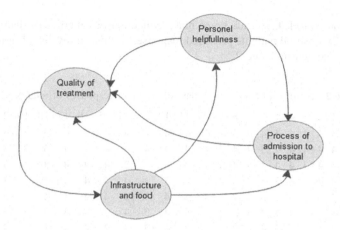

Fig. 2. Grouping factors interrelation directed graph

3. **Create the adjacency matrix from the directed graph.** The adjacency matrix *AM (20, 20)* is created for 20 questions-factors considering their influence directions from Fig. 2. As an example, questions 12–15 representing the *Quality of treatment* will have 1's values in columns of adjacency matrix corresponding the *Infrastructure and food* group questions: 16–20; The *Personal helpfulness* questions (5–11), will have 1's in columns corresponding the *Quality of treatment* and *Process of admission to hospital* group questions: 1–4 and 12–15. The adjacency matrix is presented in Table 4.

Table 4. Adjacency matrix *AM(20, 20)*

	1	2	3	4	5	6	7	8	9	10	11	12	13	14	15	16	17	18	19	20
1	0	1	1	1	0	0	0	0	0	0	0	0	1	1	1	1	0	0	0	0	0
2	1	0	1	1	0	0	0	0	0	0	0	0	1	1	1	1	0	0	0	0	0
3	1	1	0	1	0	0	0	0	0	0	0	0	1	1	1	1	0	0	0	0	0
4	1	1	1	0	0	0	0	0	0	0	0	0	1	1	1	1	0	0	0	0	0
5	1	1	1	1	0	0	0	0	0	0	0	0	1	1	1	1	0	0	0	0	0
6	1	1	1	1	1	0	1	1	1	1	1	1	1	1	1	1	0	0	0	0	0
7	1	1	1	1	1	1	0	1	1	1	1	1	1	1	1	1	0	0	0	0	0

(*continued*)

Table 4. (*continued*)

	1	2	3	4	5	6	7	8	9	10	11	12	13	14	15	16	17	18	19	20
8	1	1	1	1	1	1	1	0	1	1	1	1	1	1	1	1	0	0	0	0
9	1	1	1	1	1	1	1	1	0	1	1	1	1	1	1	1	0	0	0	0
10	1	1	1	1	1	1	1	1	1	0	1	1	1	1	1	1	0	0	0	0
11	1	1	1	1	1	1	1	1	1	1	0	1	1	1	1	1	0	0	0	0
12	0	0	0	0	0	0	0	0	0	0	1	0	1	1	1	1	1	1	1	1
13	0	0	0	0	0	0	0	0	0	0	1	1	0	1	1	1	1	1	1	1
14	0	0	0	0	0	0	0	0	0	0	1	1	1	0	1	1	1	1	1	1
15	0	0	0	0	0	0	0	0	0	0	1	1	1	1	0	1	1	1	1	1
16	1	1	1	1	1	1	1	1	1	1	1	1	1	1	1	0	1	1	1	1
17	1	1	1	1	1	1	1	1	1	1	1	1	1	1	1	1	0	1	1	1
18	1	1	1	1	1	1	1	1	1	1	1	1	1	1	1	1	1	0	1	1
19	1	1	1	1	1	1	1	1	1	1	1	1	1	1	1	1	1	1	0	1
20	1	1	1	1	1	1	1	1	1	1	1	1	1	1	1	1	1	1	1	0

4. *Calculate the Spearman Rank Correlations from survey data set.* This calculation was done by using the STATISTICA software. The square matrix *SRC(20, 20)* of Spearman Rank correlation is depicted in Table 5.

Table 5. Spearman Rank correlation *SRC(20, 20)*

Var	1	2	3	4	5	6	7	8	9	10	11	12	13	14	15	16	17	18	19	20
1	1,00	0,29	0,11	0,06	0,06	0,00	0,02	-0,03	-0,07	0,13	-0,07	0,11	0,03	0,03	0,16	0,05	0,10	0,13	0,02	0,00
2	0,29	1,00	0,18	0,14	0,03	-0,01	0,01	0,08	-0,04	0,15	0,00	0,25	0,18	0,05	0,09	0,05	0,23	0,14	0,19	0,05
3	0,11	0,18	1,00	0,40	0,14	-0,05	0,31	0,28	0,03	0,22	0,21	0,19	0,27	0,12	0,22	0,16	0,28	0,29	0,23	0,22
4	0,06	0,14	0,40	1,00	0,35	-0,16	0,45	0,35	0,12	0,29	0,33	0,37	0,31	0,10	0,35	0,30	0,20	0,26	0,24	0,25
5	0,06	0,03	0,14	0,35	1,00	0,06	0,33	0,50	0,15	0,24	0,24	0,27	0,20	0,16	0,08	0,26	0,37	0,28	0,13	0,26
6	0,00	-0,01	-0,05	-0,16	0,06	1,00	-0,08	-0,06	0,09	-0,11	-0,20	-0,25	-0,06	0,00	-0,11	-0,09	-0,04	-0,09	0,03	-0,07
7	0,02	0,01	0,31	0,45	0,33	-0,08	1,00	0,27	0,10	0,19	0,18	0,33	0,26	0,08	0,26	0,30	0,19	0,27	0,24	0,23
8	-0,03	0,08	0,28	0,35	0,50	-0,06	0,27	1,00	0,15	0,30	0,34	0,33	0,28	0,04	0,22	0,35	0,40	0,43	0,23	0,34
9	-0,07	-0,04	0,03	0,12	0,15	0,09	0,10	0,15	1,00	0,29	0,22	0,11	0,13	0,02	0,10	0,19	0,03	0,08	0,24	0,17
10	0,13	0,15	0,22	0,29	0,24	-0,11	0,19	0,30	0,29	1,00	0,47	0,47	0,24	0,19	0,33	0,25	0,13	0,33	0,21	0,19
11	-0,07	0,00	0,21	0,33	0,24	-0,20	0,18	0,34	0,22	0,47	1,00	0,30	0,38	0,12	0,24	0,42	0,10	0,26	0,12	0,23
12	0,11	0,25	0,19	0,37	0,27	-0,25	0,33	0,33	0,11	0,47	0,30	1,00	0,33	0,14	0,41	0,33	0,18	0,26	0,26	0,16
13	0,03	0,18	0,27	0,31	0,20	-0,06	0,26	0,28	0,13	0,24	0,38	0,33	1,00	0,18	0,25	0,38	0,19	0,21	0,13	0,35
14	0,03	0,05	0,12	0,10	0,16	0,00	0,08	0,04	0,02	0,19	0,12	0,14	0,18	1,00	0,03	-0,02	0,10	0,09	0,07	0,07
15	0,16	0,09	0,22	0,35	0,08	-0,11	0,26	0,22	0,10	0,33	0,24	0,41	0,25	0,03	1,00	0,20	0,10	0,16	0,18	0,28
16	0,05	0,05	0,16	0,30	0,26	-0,09	0,30	0,35	0,19	0,25	0,42	0,33	0,38	-0,02	0,20	1,00	0,21	0,28	0,11	0,27
17	0,10	0,23	0,28	0,20	0,37	-0,04	0,19	0,40	0,03	0,13	0,10	0,18	0,19	0,10	0,10	0,21	1,00	0,58	0,08	0,32
18	0,13	0,14	0,29	0,26	0,28	-0,09	0,27	0,43	0,08	0,33	0,26	0,26	0,21	0,09	0,16	0,28	0,58	1,00	0,18	0,32
19	0,02	0,19	0,23	0,24	0,13	0,03	0,24	0,23	0,24	0,21	0,12	0,26	0,13	0,07	0,18	0,11	0,08	0,18	1,00	0,13
20	0,00	0,05	0,22	0,25	0,26	-0,07	0,23	0,34	0,17	0,19	0,23	0,16	0,35	0,07	0,28	0,27	0,32	0,32	0,13	1,00

5. *Get the questions-factors direct influence matrix Z(20, 20).* In this step we multiply the absolute values of matrix *SRC(20, 20)* entries by the corresponding elements of *AM(20, 20)*. The result matrix shows direct influence survey question-factors values to each other.

6. **Apply the classical DEMATEL for direct influence matrix Z(20, 20).** After designing direct influence matrix for investigated factors we apply the classical DEMATEL algorithm to get the **influential relation map** (IRM), which will provide analysis of the cause-effect relationship among question-factors and calculate the strength of interrelation among Likert scale item.

After applying Eqs. (1) and (2) we estimate the total-influence matrix $T(20, 20)$ and the vectors R, C, $R + C$ and $R - C$. The results are presented in Table 6.

Table 6. DEMATEL algorithm results

Question no.	R	C′	R + C′	R − C′
1	0,246	0,411	0,657	−0,166
2	0,374	0,564	0,938	−0,190
3	0,483	1,135	1,617	−0,652
4	0,572	1,398	1,969	−0,826
5	0,417	0,995	1,412	−0,578
6	0,453	0,304	0,757	0,150
7	0,994	0,719	1,713	0,274
8	1,133	0,996	2,128	0,137
9	0,600	0,547	1,148	0,053
10	1,250	0,863	2,113	0,387
11	1,176	0,890	2,067	0,286
12	0,902	1,934	2,836	−1,032
13	0,906	1,708	2,613	−0,802
14	0,310	0,666	0,976	−0,356
15	0,728	1,519	2,247	−0,792
16	1,676	0,805	2,481	0,872
17	1,540	0,715	2,255	0,825
18	1,840	0,832	2,672	1,008
19	1,147	0,512	1,660	0,635
20	1,570	0,803	2,373	0,767

From Table 6, we explore dispatching (R) and receiving (C) effects from other factors, and the *Prominence* $(R + C')$ and *Relation* vectors $(R - C')$. The groups were defined as the **cause** factor group, which has a net influence on the other factors (the question with positive $R + C'$) and **effect** group, which is influenced by the other factors (the question with negative $R - C'$).

More detailed question-factor interrelation can be visualized by mapping the dataset of pairs $(R + C', R - C')$ as four-quadrant graphical chart - the **Influential Relation Map** (see Fig. 3).

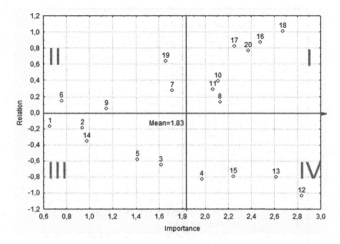

Fig. 3. Four quadrant influence relation map

From quadrant I (Fig. 3) the cause factor group consists of questions 18, 16, 20, 17, 10, 11, 8 which have the significant influence strength on other factors as compared to the influence mean (1.83) of all factors. Therefore, in order to achieve a good healthcare quality and patients' satisfaction of treatment, the primary attention should be paid to a group of *Infrastructure and food* (questions 16, 17, 18 and 20) and some aspects of *Personnel helpfulness* (questions 8, 10, 11). These 'influencers' mostly affect the *Quality of treatment* group (12, 13, 15 from IV quadrant), which have the biggest impact on all system behaviour. These findings are also consistent with the research about the quality of infrastructure [8] and interpersonal contacts with staff which significantly affect patients' satisfaction [20].

The question-factors from quadrant II (6, 7, 9, 19) show low prominence but high relation and can be seen as driving factors or autonomous givers. We can interpret them in two ways, considering both perspectives of managerial and the respondents. It can be stated that the questions have low importance on the final evaluation of health treatment or we can make an insight that the formulation of the questions was not understood by respondents, therefore their answers could not be clearly linked to their attitude on performance aspects.

The III quadrant joins all question-factors (1, 2, 3, 5, 14) with low prominence and relation and relatively disconnected from the system. They are autonomous receivers, independent factors and do not impact whole system behaviour. So we can exclude the questions related to group *Process of admission to hospital* from the survey and do not notice any marked difference in the evaluation level of hospital healthcare quality and patient satisfaction of treatment.

To verify the conclusion of irrelevant role of III quadrant question-factors to whole system progress, we applied the Reliability and Item Analysis, which is generally applied to evaluate the quality of particular survey items and determine the overall reliability of Likert scale survey.

| Question No | Cronbach alpha value if deleted specific question. The maximum possible values is marked in bold | | | | |
	Step 1 with all Questions	Step 2 Drop 6 Question	Step 3 Drop 14 Question	Step 4 Drop 1 Question	Step 5 Drop 2 Question
1	0,815599	0,826741	**0,831292**		
2	0,814767	0,825990	0,830724	**0,831901**	
3	0,805995	0,817424	0,821861	0,822278	0,823468
4	0,802063	0,813048	0,817205	0,817114	0,817764
5	0,804048	0,816606	0,821571	0,821326	0,821222
6	**0,827178**				
7	0,808080	0,819665	0,823855	0,823808	0,823925
8	0,794876	0,807369	0,811214	0,810543	0,810278
9	0,815395	0,826775	0,831096	0,831155	0,831704
10	0,802340	0,813927	0,819193	0,819064	0,819967
11	0,808603	0,819270	0,823755	0,823445	0,823847
12	0,802386	0,813410	0,817893	0,818078	0,819467
13	0,807181	0,818438	0,823114	0,823081	0,823931
14	0,819804	**0,831241**			
15	0,809276	0,820450	0,824561	0,825184	0,825814
16	0,808148	0,819367	0,822649	0,822356	0,822722
17	0,804023	0,816403	0,821706	0,821873	0,823949
18	0,799634	0,811849	0,816293	0,816380	0,817289
19	0,813992	0,825045	0,829314	0,829637	0,830659
20	0,807655	0,819702	0,824127	0,823924	0,824066

Fig. 4. Reliability and Item Analysis

For this purpose, we applied STATISTICA software, its Reliability and Item analysis tool. The reliability of survey is evaluated by estimating Cronbach alpha coefficient, which take values from lowest 0 to maximum reliability equal to 1. Cronbach alpha measures internal consistency of the Likert scale and can help to improve the survey. Reliability and Item analysis tool not only lets us to measure Cronbach alpha coefficient for the entire survey, but it also supports the decision which Likert scale item should be deleted to improve reliability and increasing Cronbach alpha.

By applying this tool to our Likert scale survey we found the questions which reduce the reliability of this questionnaire: in (Fig. 4) the initial survey Cronbach alpha was 0,827178 and we gained improvement to 0,831901 value by dropping out the questions 6, 14, 1, 2. The conclusion is well supported by results presented in Fig. 3, as the same items belong to III quadrant or have very low importance value (Item 6). These findings show the advantages of proposed method over a simple Reliability and Item analysis, as the four quadrant influence relation map provide more deep insights about the system status, and the causal analysis leading to higher quality decisions.

This case study confirmed the advantages of proposed method for evaluating the Likert scale items interdependent effect. The possibility to visualise the structure of complicated causal-effect relationships among factors of a system play core role for long-term strategic decision making and indicating improvement scopes of survey.

4 Conclusions and Main Results

The Likert scale have demonstrated sufficient advantages for measuring attitudes, and is widely applied for performance evaluation in various domain areas. Measurement of qualitative factors can require a group of questions which could express the characteristics of the attitudes explored. However, the analytical capabilities of the approach are limited to basic statistical characteristics.

The article introduces the method of evaluating the interdependence strength among the Likert scale items. We proposed to apply modified DEMATEL method to measure the cause-effect relationship and estimate the impact magnitude for rating scale survey data it's possible. We propose to solve the disadvantage of the classical DEMATEL technique and to replace its subjective expert judgement matrix with the modified Spearman Rank Order Correlations matrix estimated for Likert scale items.

The case study based on data collected at children rehabilitation hospital in Poland, provided relevant illustration of the proposed method and enabled us to evaluate the relationships among Likert scale items, set cause-effect factors and estimate conditional influence rate of each survey question.

The application of our technique provides an instrument for the researchers to measure the reliability of the survey, improve individual questions and create influential relation map of the Likert scale items which serve for long-term strategic decision making and indicating improvement scopes.

Acknowledgement. This work was performed within the framework of the COST action "European Network for cost containment and improved quality of health care" http://www.cost. eu/COST_Actions/ca/CA15222, and was also supported by funding from National Science Centre, Poland (grant number: 2015/17/B/HS4/02747).

References

1. Brown, S.: Likert Scale Examples for Surveys (2010). www.extension.iastate.edu/documents/anr/likertscaleexamplesforsurveys.pdf
2. Wu, C.-H.: An empirical study on the transformation of Likert-scale data to numerical scores. Appl. Math. Sci. **1**(58), 2851–2862 (2007)
3. Gabus, A., Fontela, E.: Perceptions of the world problematique: communication procedure. In: Communicating with Those Bearing Collective Responsibility (DEMATEL Report no. 1), BATTELLE Institute, Geneva Research Centre, Geneva, Switzerland (1972)
4. Gabus, A., Fontela, E.: World problems, an invitation to further thought within the framework of DEMATEL. BATTELLE Institute, Geneva, Switzerland (1972)
5. Harpe, E.S., Pharm, D.: How to analyze Likert and other rating scale data. Curr. Pharm. Teach. Learn. **7**(6), 836–850 (2015)
6. Hu, H.Y., Lee, Y.C., Yen, T.M., Tsai, C.H.: Using BPNN and DEMATEL to modify importance–performance analysis model—a study of the computer industry. Expert Syst. Appl. **36**(6), 9969–9979 (2009)
7. Joshi, A., Kale, S., Chandel, S., Pal, D.K.: Likert scale: explored and explained. Br. J. Appl. Sci. Technol. **7**(4), 396–403 (2015)

8. Kabengele, M.E., Chastonay, P.: Satisfaction of patients: a right to health indicator? Health Policy 100(2–3), 144–150 (2011). https://doi.org/10.1016/j.healthpol.2010.11.001
9. Kashi, K., Jiri, F.: Utilizing DEMATEL method in competency modeling. Forum Scientiae Oeconomia 2(1), 95–106 (2014)
10. Kriksciuniene, D., Sakalauskas, V.: AHP model for quality evaluation of healthcare system. In: Damaševičius, R., Mikašytė, V. (eds.) ICIST 2017. CCIS, vol. 756, pp. 129–141. Springer, Cham (2017). https://doi.org/10.1007/978-3-319-67642-5_11
11. Kriksciuniene, D., Sakalauskas, V., Lewandowski, R.: Process mining of periodic rating scale survey data using analytic hierarchy process. In: Abramowicz, W., Paschke, A. (eds.) BIS 2018. LNBIP, vol. 339, pp. 86–95. Springer, Cham (2019). https://doi.org/10.1007/978-3-030-04849-5_8
12. Likert, R.: A technique for the measurement of attitudes. Arch. Psychol. 22(140), 55 (1932)
13. Lin, Ch.J., Wu, W.: A causal analytical method for group decision making under fuzzy environment. Expert Syst. Appl. 34(1), 205–213 (2008)
14. Murray, J.: Likert data: what to use, parametric or non-parametric? Int. J. Bus. Soc. Sci. 4(11), 258–264 (2013)
15. Seleem, S.N., Attia, E.-A., El-Assal, A.: Managing performance improvement initiatives using DEMATEL method with application case study. Prod. Plann. Control 27(7–8), 637–649 (2016). https://doi.org/10.1080/09537287.2016.1165301
16. Shao, J., Taisch, M., Ortega Mier, M., d'Avolio, E.: Application of the DEMATEL method to identify relations among barriers between green products and consumers. In: 17th European Roundtable on Sustainable Consumption and Production - ERSCP 2014, Portoroz, Slovenia, 14–16 October 2014, pp. 1029–1040 (2014)
17. Si, S.-L., You, X.-Y., Liu, H.-C., Zhang, P.: DEMATEL technique: a systematic review of the state-of-the-art literature on methodologies and applications. Math. Probl. Eng. 2018(1), 1–33 (2018)
18. Subedi, B.P.: Using Likert type data in social science research: confusion, issues and challenges. Int. J. Contemp. Appl. Sci. 3(2), 36–49 (2016)
19. Sullivan, G.M., Artino Jr., R.A.: Analyzing and interpreting data from Likert-type scales. J. Grad. Med. Educ. 5(4), 541–542 (2013). https://doi.org/10.4300/JGME-5-4-18
20. Tasso, K., et al.: Assessing patient satisfaction and quality of care through observation and interview. Hosp. Top. 80(3), 4–10 (2002). https://doi.org/10.1080/00185860209597996
21. Tsai, W.H., Chou, W.C.: Selecting management systems for sustainable development in SMEs: a novel hybrid model based on DEMATEL, ANP, and ZOGP. Expert Syst. Appl. 36(2), 1444–1458 (2009)
22. Warmbrod, J.R.: Reporting and interpreting scores derived from Likert-type scales. J. Agric. Educ. 55(5), 30–47 (2014)

Knowledge-Based UML Use Case Model Transformation Algorithm

Ilona Veitaite[1(✉)] and Audrius Lopata[2]

[1] Kaunas Faculty, Institute Social Sciences and Applied Informatics,
Vilnius University, Muitines g. 8, 44280 Kaunas, Lithuania
`ilona.veitaite@knf.vu.lt`
[2] Faculty of Informatics, Kaunas University of Technology, Studentų g. 50,
51368 Kaunas, Lithuania
`audrius.lopata@ktu.lt`

Abstract. Transforming and generating models is a meaningful process in Model Driven Engineering (MDE). Theoretical and practical researches for MDE have remarkably progressed recently in managing with the increase of complexity within information systems (IS) during their development and support processes by growing the level of abstraction using different kinds of models as information storage – as knowledge storage of problem domain. As models expand in use for developing systems, the possible transformation among models grows in importance. The main scope of the article is to present transformation algorithm of Unified Modelling Language Use Case model generation from Enterprise Model (EM). The transformation algorithm is presented in details and depicted by steps. The presented generation process steps are illustrated by particular UML Use Case example following the transformation algorithm step by step.

Keywords: Problem domain · Enterprise modelling · Knowledge-based · UML · IS engineering · MDA · MDE · Transformation algorithm

1 Introduction

The Model Driven Architecture (MDA) approach delivers a clear separation of the business logic from the execution logic that is less stable. It places the models at the center of the development of the information systems and software [1, 2, 4]. The Object Management Group (OMG) has proposed a modelling language called UML (Unified Modelling Language) for describing all kinds of object-oriented software artifacts in late 1980s [3, 6, 12]. UML models are gaining increasing attention from researchers and practitioners in the recent years. UML has been instrumental in this transition from code-oriented to model-oriented software development techniques. A key role is now performed by the concept of meta-model [9, 13].

In this article particular Enterprise Meta-Model (EMM) is used. EMM is formally determined Enterprise Model composition, which contained of a formalized Enterprise Model (EM) alongside with the general principles of control theory. EM is the main

W. Abramowicz and R. Corchuelo (Eds.): BIS 2019 Workshops, LNBIP 373, pp. 39–48, 2019.
https://doi.org/10.1007/978-3-030-36691-9_4

source of the requisite knowledge of the specific problem domain for IS engineering and IS reengineering processes [5, 7, 15].

2 Enterprise Meta-model

Enterprise modelling has become an inseparable part of IS development process. Core of enterprise modelling theoretical basis is the theoretical enterprise model, which main goal is to identify the necessary components and elements for IS engineering. And Enterprise Meta-Model manages Enterprise Model composition (Fig. 1). Enterprise Model stores knowledge that is necessary for IS development process and will be used within all stages of IS development life cycle [7, 11].

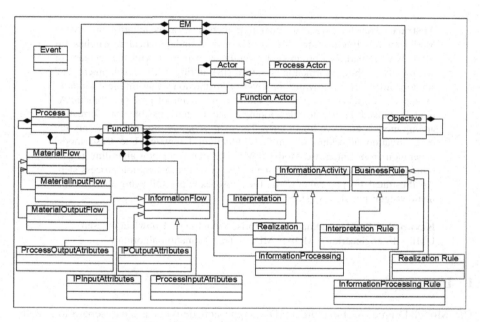

Fig. 1. Class diagram of Enterprise Meta–model [5, 7]

Design methods of information systems indicate the combination of systems engineering processes, i.e. how, in what order and what UML model to use in the IS development process stages and how to implement the process. It is important for software developers to be able to compare and select the most suitable models for a particular problem domain. Each of these models can be used individually, but more important is the fact that each model is the projection of the same system, which is developed [7, 10].

3   Transformation Algorithm of UML Use Case Model

UML Use Case models are usually referred to as dynamic models used to describe a series of actions that some system or systems should or can implement in contribution with one or more external users of the system. Each use case should grant some observable and valuable result to the actors or other participants of the system. UML Use Case model elements [12, 14].

Table 1. UML Use Case model elements [14, 17].

Enterprise Model element	UML Use Case model element	Description
Actor	Actor	An actor is behavioural classifier which defines a role played by an external entity
	Subject	A subject is a classifier which represents business, software system, physical system or device under analysis, design, or consideration, having some behaviour, and to which a set of use cases applies
Function, Process	Use Case	A use case is a type of behavioural classifier that describes a unit of functionality performed by actors or subjects to which the use case applies in collaboration with one or more actors
Business Rule	Extend	Extend is a directed relationship that specifies how and when the behaviour defined in usually supplementary (optional) extending use case can be inserted into the behaviour defined in the extended use case
	Include	Use case include is a directed relationship between two use cases which is used to show that behaviour of the included use case is inserted into the behaviour of the including use case
	Association	Each use case represents a unit of useful functionality that subjects provide to actors. An association between an actor and a use case indicates that the actor and the use case somehow interact or communicate with each other

As all problem domain knowledge that is necessary for IS development process is stored in Enterprise Model and it is already verified and validated, it can be used in UML models generation process. Elements from Enterprise Model is the input and objects generated to UML Use Case model elements is output, they are presented in the table (Table 1).

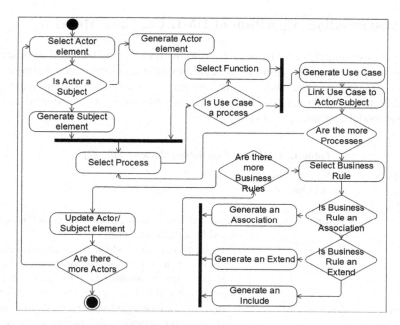

Fig. 2. UML Use Case model transformation algorithm [16]

Figure 2 presents UML Use Case generation from Enterprise Model transformation algorithm. Initial element in this generation process is Actor/Subject, after actor/subject element is generated, Use Case element is selected and generates, then Include, Extend and Association relationships elements are selected and generated. Transformation algorithm is illustrated by following steps:

- Step 1: The initial element Actor from Enterprise Model for UML Use Case model generation is selected.
- Step 2: If Actor element is initial element of UML Use Case model, then Actor element is generated, else Subject element is generated.
- Step 3: Process element from Enterprise model, which is related with the initial Actor element is selected.
- Step 4: If Process element is Use Case element related to Actor/Subject, then Use Case element is generated, else Function element is selected.
- Step 5: Function element is generated as Use Case element.
- Step 6: Business Rule element as link of Actor/Subject element from Enterprise Model which is related with the Process/Function element is selected.
- Step 7: If Business Rule element is UML Use Case model's simple Association element and serves as link between Actor/Subject and Process/Function elements then Association is generated from Enterprise model, else if it is Extend element, then Extend element is generated from Enterprise model, else Include element is generated from Enterprise model.
- Step 8: There is checking if there are more Business Rules in Enterprise Model related to UML Use Case model. In case, there are, algorithm goes back to step 3.

- Step 9: UML Use Case elements Actor/Subject and Process/Function are linked according to Business Rules.
- Step 10: UML Information flow element Actor/Subject is updated.
- Step 11: There is checking if there are more Actors/Subject elements in Enterprise Model related to UML Use Case model. In case, there are, algorithm goes back to step 1.
- Step 12: Else all UML Use Case model elements and links are generated from Enterprise Model.

Generation of UML Use Case model is illustrated with the example of Check-out from parking subsystem example [14]. Verified and validated problem domain information, in this case of Check-out from parking example, is stored in Enterprise model. Example shows, how Client checks out from parking, by giving payment for the service; how Operator of parking manages check-out process; how Payment service provider receives the payment; how Administrator manages all users.

Detailed stages of Parking check-out example processes stored in Enterprise Model are described:

- Stage 1: Client wants to check-out from the parking.
- Stage 2: Client checks-out from the parking, by getting necessary help information. Operator manages check-out process by providing necessary information to the client.
- Stage 3: Client pays the payment for the parking time. Operator supervises payment process.
- Stage 4: Payment for the parking is performed. Payment service provider gets the payment.
- Stage 5: System administrator manages all users: clients and operators.

Transformation algorithm of UML Use Case model generation Parking check-out example from Enterprise Model process is illustrated by following steps:

- Step 1: The initial element Actor from Enterprise Model for UML Use Case model generation is selected.
- Step 2: If Actor element is initial element of UML Use Case model, then Actor element is generated, else Subject element is generated.

First two steps of transformation algorithm is presented in Table 2.

Table 2. Step 1 and step 2 in UML Use Case model generation process

Transformation algorithm part	Enterprise Model element	Generated UML Use Case model element

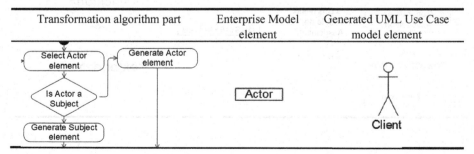

- Step 3: Process element from Enterprise model, which is related with the initial Actor element is selected.
- Step 4: If Process element is Use Case element related to Actor/Subject, then Use Case element is generated, else Function element is selected.
- Step 5: Function element is generated as Use Case element.

Other three steps of transformation algorithm is presented in Table 3.

Table 3. Step 3, 4, 5 in UML Use Case model generation process

Transformation algorithm part	Enterprise Model element	Generated UML Use Case model element

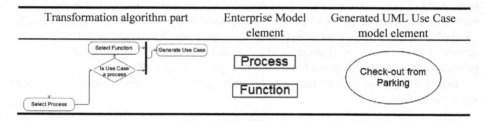

- Step 6: Business Rule element as link of Actor/Subject element from Enterprise Model which is related with the Process/Function element is selected.
- Step 7: If Business Rule element is UML Use Case model's simple Association element and serves as link between Actor/Subject and Process/Function elements then Association is generated from Enterprise model, else if it is Extend element, then Extend element is generated from Enterprise model, else Include element is generated from Enterprise model.

Other two steps of transformation algorithm is presented in Table 4.

Table 4. Step 6 and 7 in UML Use Case model generation process

Transformation algorithm part	Enterprise Model element	Generated UML Use Case model element

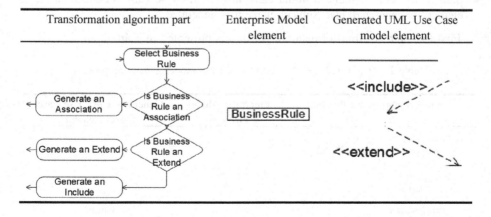

- Step 8: There is checking if there are more Business Rules in Enterprise Model related to UML Use Case model. In case, there are, algorithm goes back to step 3.
- Step 9: UML Use Case elements Actor/Subject and Process/Function are linked according to Business Rules.
- Step 10: UML Information flow element Actor/Subject is updated.

Other three steps of transformation algorithm is presented in Table 5.

Table 5. Step 8, 9 and 10 in UML Use Case model generation process

Transformation algorithm part	Enterprise Model element	Generated UML Use Case model element

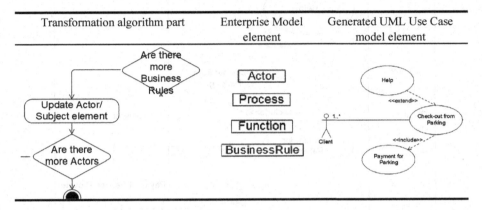

After 10 steps of the transformation algorithm generating of Parking Check-out data from Enterprise Model three stages from client side – Client wants to check-out from the parking, Client checks-out from the parking, by getting necessary help information and Client pays the payment for the parking time – is shown in the Fig. 3.

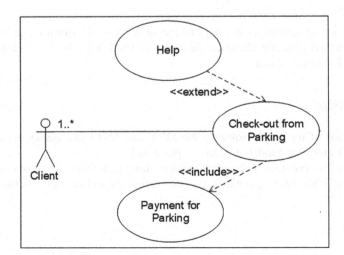

Fig. 3. UML Use Case Model example: Parking check-out: Client part

When all the steps of transformation algorithm, representing all stages, are implemented, the whole Parking check-out process as UML Use Case model with four actors, four use cases, all the relationships between elements, such as association, extend and include is presented in Fig. 4.

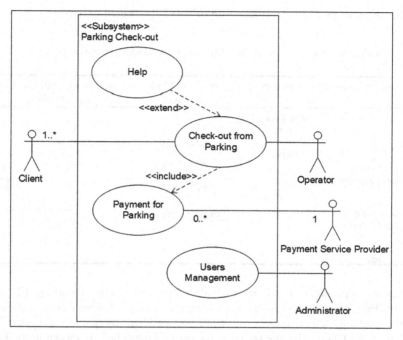

Fig. 4. UML Use Case Model example: Parking check-out

After the implementing all the steps of transformation algorithm it can be certainly stated that chosen example illustrates accuracy of the UML Use Case elements generated from Enterprise model.

4 Conclusions

In the first part of the article some of the MDE and MDA challenges are discussed. Further, the Enterprise Model structure is presented.

According to previous researches, in the next part there is presented detailed explanation of UML Use Case model transformation algorithm, which is illustrated by steps.

Final part describes particular problem domain example – Parking check-out, which data is stored in knowledge-based Enterprise Model and there are described all the stages of the example. Therefore, there are presented transformation algorithm steps for the UML Use Case model generation from the Enterprise Model and example's client side is illustrated with graphical schemes.

The illustrated Parking check-out example reveals that all verified data stored in Enterprise Model is enough for UML models generating process and it is possible to declare, that each and every element of UML models can be generated from the Enterprise Model using transformation algorithms and this can perform knowledge-based information system development cycle design stage.

References

1. Alouini, W., Guedhami, O., Hammoudi, S., Gammoudi, M., Lopes, D.: Semi-automatic generation of transformation rules in model driven engineering: the challenge and first steps. Int. J. Softw. Eng. Appl. 5(1), 73–88 (2011)
2. Bézivin, J.: From object composition to model transformation with the MDA. In: The Proceedings of TOOLS'USA, TOOLS-39, Santa Barbara. IEEE, August 2001
3. Bézivin, J., Ploquin, N.: Tooling the MDA framework: a new software maintenance and evolution scheme proposal. J. Object-Oriented Program. (2001)
4. Bondé, L., Dumoulin, C., Dekeyser, J.L.: Metamodels and MDA transformations for embedded systems. In: Boulet, P. (ed.) Advances in Design and Specification Languages for SoCs, pp. 89–105. Springer, Boston (2005). https://doi.org/10.1007/0-387-26151-6_8
5. Butleris, R., Lopata, A., Ambraziunas, M., Veitaitė, I., Masteika, S.: SysML and UML models usage in knowledge based MDA process. Elektronika ir elektrotechnika 21(2), 50–57 (2015)
6. Czarnecki, K., Helsen, S.: Classification of model transformation approaches. In: OOPSLA 2003 Workshop on Generative Techniques in the Context of Model-Driven Architecture (2003)
7. Gudas, S.: Informacijos sistemų inžinerijos teorijos pagrindai. Vilniaus universiteto leidykla (2012). ISBN 978-609-459-075-7
8. Gudas, S., Lopata, A.: Meta-model based development of use case model for business function. Inf. Technol. Control 36(3) (2007). ISSN 1392 – 124X 2007
9. Kriouile, A., Addamssiri, N., Gadi, T.: An MDA method for automatic transformation of models from CIM to PIM. Am. J. Softw. Eng. Appl. 4(1), 1–14 (2015)
10. Lopata, A., Veitaite, I.: UML diagrams generation process by using knowledge-based subsystem. In: Abramowicz, W. (ed.) BIS 2013. LNBIP, vol. 160, pp. 53–60. Springer, Heidelberg (2013). https://doi.org/10.1007/978-3-642-41687-3_7
11. Lopata, A., Ambraziūnas, M., Gudas, S., Butleris, R.: The main principles of knowledge-based information systems engineering. Electron. Electr. Eng. 11(1(25)), 99–102 (2012). ISSN 2029-5731
12. Object Management Group: OMG website. https://www.omg.org/about/omg-standards-introduction.htm. Accessed 25 Apr 2018
13. Parviainen, P., Takalo, J., Teppola, S., Tihinen, M.: Model-Driven Development. Processes and Practices. VTT Working Papers 114 (2009)
14. UML diagrams website. https://www.uml-diagrams.org/. Accessed 24 Apr 2018

15. Valatavičius, A., Gudas, S.: Toward the deep, knowledge-based interoperability of applications. Inf. Sci. **79** (2017)
16. Veitaite, I., Lopata, A.: Transformation algorithms of knowledge based UML dynamic models generation. In: Abramowicz, W. (ed.) BIS 2017. LNBIP, vol. 303, pp. 59–68. Springer, Cham (2017). https://doi.org/10.1007/978-3-319-69023-0_6
17. Veitaitė, I., Lopata, A.: Knowledge-based UML models generation from enterprise model technique. In: Damaševičius, R., Mikašytė, V. (eds.) ICIST 2017. CCIS, vol. 756, pp. 314–325. Springer, Cham (2017). https://doi.org/10.1007/978-3-319-67642-5_26

Design of a Social-Based Recommendation Mechanism for Peer-to-Peer Insurance

Jyh-Hwa Liou[1], Ting-Kai Hwang[2(✉)], Sai-Nan Wu[3],
and Yung-Ming Li[3]

[1] Center for General Education, Hsin Sheng College of Medical Care
and Management, Taoyuan City, Taiwan
alioujh@gmail.com
[2] Department of Journalism, Ming Chuan University, Taipei, Taiwan
tkhwang@mail.mcu.edu.tw
[3] Institute of Information Management, National Chiao Tung University,
Hsinchu, Taiwan
yml@mail.nctu.edu.tw

Abstract. Peer-to-peer insurance platforms are prospering due to the development of financial technology, but it is difficult to find suitable co-insurers group without risk considering at current online platforms. To improve the advantage of peer-to-peer insurance, in this research, we design a social-based co-insurers recommendation mechanism through analyzing users' inclination, posts, background, similarity, and relationship to put peers-risk-sharing idea into realistic action.

Keywords: Peer-to-peer insurance · Co-insurance · Group formation · Social-based recommendation

1 Introduction

In the insurance industry, moral risk has always been a difficult problem to solve. "Moral risk" refers to the selfish act taken to maximize the utility of the contractor when the contracting party does not fully assume the risk consequences. Peer-to-peer (Here after P2P) insurance provides insurers with the possibility of low premiums that can be used to deal with moral risk. The P2P concept could spread to the insurance market, enabling for digital insurances [1]. With the popularity of social network, people join groups by launching family members, friends, or people with common interests. It is likely that individuals who seek for insurance with the groups they join instead of turning to insurance companies. Moenninghoff et al. argued that such alliances reduce information asymmetry and moral hazard [6].

For the company, group members who join in the same group need to consider the benefits of other members; the fraud rate will be lower than the general insurance. At the same time, by relying on peer group members to sell/market insurance and assist each other's risk management and loss prevention needs, P2P groups appear to eschew traditional brokers and agents, chipping more off the cost of products [2]. For users, P2P insurance model make the user's risk sharing come true, and it brings back high

© Springer Nature Switzerland AG 2019
W. Abramowicz and R. Corchuelo (Eds.): BIS 2019 Workshops, LNBIP 373, pp. 49–60, 2019.
https://doi.org/10.1007/978-3-030-36691-9_5

returns with less pay compared to ordinary insurance. The aims of P2P insurance are to save money through reduced overhead costs, increased transparency, reduced inefficiencies, and especially to reduce the inherent conflict between insurance carriers and their policyholders at the time of a claim [3, 4]. Insuring in self-selecting groups can improve the quality of the risk by redefining the traditional insurance structure, and P2P models can offer unique benefits.

The P2P insurance platform is now rapidly operated in different countries. It lets insurers to join the risk-sharing pool, but it is hard for them to figure out who is suitable to be their co-insurers due to lack of an efficient searching engine. Therefore, most people do not know how to utilize the existing platform. People who want to participate in P2P insurance group have no idea about finding appropriate group members. There is no good way to find a trusted partner. Hence, how to assist insurers to find their co-insurer is an important issue in P2P insurance platform.

Recently, social-based recommender systems have become a popular research and are extending individual recommender systems. In social network scenario, the notion of decision trust can be applied. An agent (i.e. the truster) is willing to rely on another one for decision making in the situation with the feeling of similarity, closeness or security [9]. Social-based recommendation takes advantage of the influence of social relationships in decision making with the available social data through social networking systems. Trust relationships in particular can be exploited in such systems for rating prediction and recommendation, which has been shown to have the potential for improving the quality of the recommender and alleviating the issue of data sparsity, cold start, and adversarial attacks [5].

The objective of this study is to design a group formation mechanism to put peers-risk-sharing idea into realistic action. We propose a social-based co-insurers recommendation mechanism that can help insurers by providing a list of potential co-insurers based on their social activity and social relationship. On the other hand, we help insurers aggregating similar risk-taking group to reduce the uncertainly cost and enhance their efficiency to form their insurance group through the close connection in the insurance community. Using this mechanism, the members in the P2P insurance group can get insurance protection with lower fee, and P2P insurance firms can cut down their cost and the risk of insurance fraud.

2   The System Framework

The purpose of the research is to develop a social-based group formation mechanism and offer insurers a reliable suggestion to find co-insurers. The behavior of a group is drastically different from an individual acting alone. While in a group, improving satisfaction of the interests for each member is an emphasis. To achieve high group satisfaction, certain criteria should be considered while members accept or agree on a selection.

The processes of the proposed mechanism will start to detect who are near the group leader and compute their degree of social influence and individual preference. Each user has three criteria of willingness to join a group or not: (1) individual preference, (2) social influence and (3) social relationship. Each criterion has its own weight for the user in a particular circumstance. Measuring the willingness-to-join of every person near the group leader, this mechanism takes top-k people with higher willingness as candidate group members to form several candidate groups. By computing the cohesion of each candidate groups, this mechanism selects a group with highest cohesion to provide the group member list to the group leader and invite all the group members to join the group for P2P insurance.

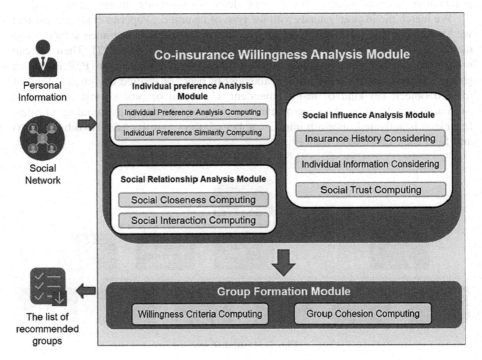

Fig. 1. The system architecture

The system architecture is shown as Fig. 1, and described as follows:

(1) First of all, we set the user who use this mechanism to form a group for P2P insurance as the group leader (or center), then set the group leader's insurance inclination as the theme of the group. After that, we compute the similarity of co-insurer's preference with the group.

(2) Second, after determining the target insurance objects, the purposed mechanism based on the insurers' social relationship and social influence between insurers would find out the latent relationship in the social network. Furthermore, it eliminates the perceived risk and enhances the connection.

(3) Thirdly, based on the score of three main calculations, we compute the weights and find out the willingness of the co-insurer to join the group leader's group.

(4) Lastly, we calculate the cohesion of the groups and sort them to generate the recommended list of group members.

2.1   Individual Preference Analysis Module

When a user uses our recommendation mechanism, the user will be set as the leader of the co-insurance group, and then the recommendation mechanism will form several the most suitable co-insurance group for the leader according to the leader's insurance needs and social network relationship. So, when the recommendation mechanism provides potential co-insurers for the leader, the first step is considering whether the potential co-insurers' needs and the group (leader)'s insurance theme are matched.

We match the insurer's needs with the type of insurance. Paperno et al. suggest that we should construct a hierarchical tree to further match the insurance subjects and user's interest or needs by referencing certain classification index [7]. Then we can understand the insurance scenario. So, we follow their classification: P2P insurance groups can be created on the basis of likeness of peers or insured objects: (1) kind of insured object, (2) kind of insured incident, (3) social or professional affinity and (4) home/work location. Any person can create a team and define its initial set of rules. Insurance is activated once a minimal number of peers join the team (two by default) and fund their distributed wallets.

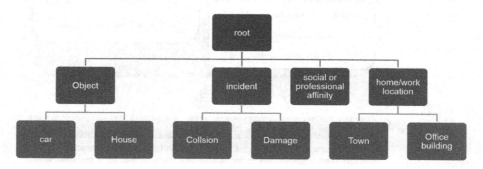

Fig. 2. Insurance tree

According to the pattern above, we built the InsurTree as a three-layers tree structure. The first layer is root layer. The second layer includes insurance objects that classify different insurance needs. The third layer, leaf nodes, lists details of the insurance objects in insurance policy. By doing so, we can use InsurTree to help our mechanism identify users' insurance object. We draw a part of InsurTree in Fig. 2.

In order to discover the potential co-insurer who would probably have the same interest to the insurance objects, the similarity between each potential co-insurer and the group leader would be calculated as a filtration basis.

First, we take the group leader m into the InsurTree and create a new vector for the group leader m. It utilizes the index of nodes to represent the categories m belongs and denote the vector as $\vec{M}$ which the value of each dimension is 1 if the category matches the node or 0 if the category does not match the node. We take the data of the potential co-insurer n likes and posted to match the InsurTree to identify and classify them. Then a vector denoted as $\vec{N}$ represents all the categories related with the data. The value of each dimension in $\vec{N}$ is the number of appearance of the category and sub-categories in pages and tag data. The dimensions of the two vectors are the same to compute the similarity correctly.

2.2 Social Relationship Analysis Module

Social Interaction Computing

The interaction between two users, denoted as u_1 and u_2 on social media, is measured by (1) the number of the two users be tagged together in comments and posts, including statuses, check-ins and photos and we denote it as $Tag(u_1, u_2)$, (2) the number of comments written by the two users under a same post which is created by them and we denote it as $Comment(u_1, u_2)$, and (3) the number of likes given by the two users in comments and posts, including statuses, check-ins and photos which they own and we denote it as $Like(u_1, u_2)$. The interaction between two users, u_1 and u_2, is measured by Eq. 1.

$$Interaction(i, j) = Tag(i, j) + Comment(i, j) + Like(i, j) \qquad (1)$$

The $Interaction(u_1, u_2)$ value should be normalized to be a value ranged from 0 to 1 before go to the next step.

Social Closeness Computing

In order to compute the degree of closeness between the group leader and others, the interaction between users who are in the social network of the group leader is required on social media. We denote $Paths(i, j)$ as a set containing all the social paths, which are the routes to connect the group leader i with the nearby person j. Each social path has a set of links, which connects two users in the particular social path. The two sets are shown as Eq. 2, where n is the number of elements of the set.

$$Paths(i, j) = \{Path_1(i, j), Path_2(i, j), \ldots, Path_n(i, j)\} \qquad (2)$$

The influence of $Interaction(u_1, u_2)$ value of two users who are not direct friends with the group leader should be reduced due to its social degree far from the group leader. We denote $Degree(i, Path_n(i, j))$ as the social degree from the group leader i to the particular link $Link_n(i, j)$.

The social closeness between the group leader i and the coinsurer j can be measured by Eq. 3, which value is equal to a particular social path with maximal value. The $Max()$ function is to find the maximal value of its parameter.

$$SocialCloseness(i, j) = Max\left(\sum \frac{Interaction(i, j)}{Degree(i, Link_n(i, j))}\right), \forall Path_n(i, j)$$
$$\in Paths(i, j) \qquad (3)$$

Finally, $SRA_{score}(u_i, u_c)$ represents the relationship score between insurer i and co-insurer j, including their interaction and closeness in social network as shown in Eq. 4.

After computing all users' relationship, we would have a sorted list of candidates. Then, we would pass this list to the next module.

$$SRA_{score}(i, j) = Interaction(i, j) + SocialCloseness(i, j) \tag{4}$$

2.3 Social Influence Analysis Module

Insurance History Considering

In this part, we consider the co-insurer's insurance history in our system. Similar to the record of loans, a good history of lending is a strong proof of credit. In this system, more co-insurance experience the users have, more trust they are worthy of, if the user and leader were in the same co-insurance group. It is more significant than common co-insurance record. $Count(i)$ represents the number of successful insurance transaction records for the co-insurer i on this system. $Count_{con}(i, j)$ represents the number of successful co-insurance group records for the co-insurer i with the group leader j on this system, p as a constant which is greater than 1.

$$History(i, j) = Count(i) + p^{Count_{con}(i,j)} \tag{5}$$

Individual Information Considering

In this part, we would start to collect related information from the platforms. There are different kinds of preference that insurer would consider before insuring, including the premium level, period of claim, and co-insurers' similarity considering: gender, hometown, identity, etc. Each consideration has different extents representing acceptance in different situations. As people group with others that has same background, they might have the similar financial planning. For exploring the similar background, we used the information regarding age, gender, occupation status, hometown, income level and marital status. If an insurer shares the same consideration of background, we would assign a value to the characteristic item described as below.

$$Con_{age\_range}(i, j) = \begin{cases} 1, & if\ age\_range(i) = age_{range(j)} \\ 0, & otherwise \end{cases} \tag{6}$$

$$Con_{gender}(i, j) = \begin{cases} 1, & if\ gender(i) = gender(j) \\ 0, & otherwise \end{cases} \tag{7}$$

$$Con_{educationlevel}(i, j) = \begin{cases} 1, & if\ education\_level(i) = education\_level(j) \\ 0, & otherwise \end{cases} \tag{8}$$

$$Con_{incomelevel}(i, j) = \begin{cases} 1, & if\ income\_level(i) = income\_level(j) \\ 0, & otherwise \end{cases} \tag{9}$$

Then, we used $Consideration(i, j)$ to represent the consideration similarity degree between insurer i and co-insurer j in Eq. 10.

$$Consideration(i, j) =$$
$$Con_{age_{range}}(i, j) + Con_{gender}(i, j) + Con_{educationlevel}(i, j) + Con_{incomelevel}(i, j) \tag{10}$$

Social Trust Computing

The social closeness would be measured as Eq. 3 and social trust between insurer i and co-insurer j is computed as Eq. 11.

$$SocialTrust(i, j) = \left(\frac{1}{\min(length(i, j))} \right) * q^a \tag{11}$$

We set $Length(i, j)$ as the length of i with j, q as a constant which is greater than 1, and a as the number of the straight friend of co-insurer with group leader.

The final SIA_{score} is computed as Eq. 12. Then we applied max-min normalization to normalize the value of score to be between 0 to 1 after computing all the values in the candidate co-insurers.

$$SIA_{score}(i, j) = SocialTrust(i, j) + Consideration(i, j) + History(i, j) \tag{12}$$

2.4 Group Formation Module

Willingness Criteria Computing

Each user has his/her own weights of criteria which affect the willingness to participate in a group or not. The measurement of willingness to join a group is various due to different circumstances. In this section, we compute the personal weights of three criteria which influence the willingness of a user to join a group in a specific situation.

According to the analytic hierarchy process (AHP), which is well-known to organize and analyze complex decision-making problems with multi-criteria [8]. First we construct matrix M_{PRI} to determine pairwise weight ratios, shown in Eq. 13. Each element A_{ij} represents the relative weight of criterion i in terms of criterion j.

$$M_{PRI} = \begin{bmatrix} 1 & A_{PR} & A_{PI} \\ 1/A_{PR} & 1 & A_{RI} \\ 1/A_{PI} & 1/A_{RI} & 1 \end{bmatrix} \tag{13}$$

where A_{PR} represents the relative weight between social influence and personal preference relevance. A_{PI} represents the relative weight between personal preference relevance and context relevance. A_{RI} represents the relative weight between social influence and context relevance. Next, to compute criteria weight for matrix M_{PRI}, Eq. 14 is used:

$$W_i = \frac{1}{3} \sum_{j=1}^{3} \frac{a_{ij}}{\sum_{i=1}^{3} a_{ij}} \tag{14}$$

where W_i is the relative value of criteria i ($\alpha = w_1$, $\beta = w_2$, $\gamma = w_3$). Notice that if group members are unable to express their weight preferences for each criteria, then the default weight distribution will be equally allocated between the three.

Using the weight values of three criteria, this mechanism can have the ability to measure the willingness-to-join that the person j who is near the group leader i will want to join the group to purchase target product p together in a specific circumstance.

Group Cohesion Computing

We denote N_{gs} as twice as leader's preference of group size and choose top-k people with higher willingness-to-join to the group. The number of people chosen is k at most, where k is equal to N_{re} multiplies with a certain integer. Because we need to consider the great diversity of the group members combination and its value of group cohesion and the higher ratio of willingness simultaneously, but we also need to limit the search range of people near the group leader. Therefore, a group leader can make about $C_{N_{gs}}^k$ combinations for different groups. We denote $G(i, N_{gs})$ as a set containing all the candidate groups as following Eq. 15 and send it to the next approach, group cohesion computing, to compute which is the best group that the group leader i wants.

$$G(i, N_{gs}) = \{G_1(i, N_{gs}), G_2(i, N_{gs}), \ldots, G_n(i, N_{gs})\} \quad (15)$$

This group cohesion computing approach will run after receiving the $G(i, N_{re})$ set from the candidate group forming approach. The $G(i, N_{re})$ may have a great diversity of combinations.

We measure the cohesion of these groups by three steps: (1) the density of network, (2) the social closeness between group members and (3) the average score of willingness-to-join and social closeness in the network.

The density of network can be measured by Eq. 16, where T is the number of ties and N_{nd} is the number of nodes in the network.

$$Density(G_n(i, N_{gs})) = \frac{2 * T}{N_{nd} * (N_{nd} - 1)} \quad (16)$$

Measuring the density of each candidate group, this mechanism filters the top groups with highest density to do the next step. Because it is possible that there are several groups with equal highest density, we need to do advanced filtering.

The second step is to compute the social closeness between group members as the strength of each tie. The approach here only considers about social closeness because we have computed the preference and context before the candidate group forming. Thus we ensure that all the group members are near the group leader with certain degree of preference to the target product. What we care about now is the strength of social relationship between group members.

The third step is to compare which network is the best one to recommend to the group leader. We use the strength of ties to measure the group cohesion in this step. The type of ties are not all the same, because the ties from nearby people to the group leader i are measured by willingness-to-join and the other ties between nearby people are measured by social closeness. Due to the different types of ties, we need to calculate separately. We denote T_{jw} as a set of all the ties measured by willingness-to-join and denote T_{sc} as a set of all the ties measured by social closeness. The representations of the two sets are Eqs. 17 and 18, where n and m is the total number of ties of the specific type.

$$T_{jw} = \left\{ T_{jw}^1, T_{jw}^2, \ldots, T_{jw}^n \right\} \tag{17}$$

$$T_{sc} = \left\{ T_{sc}^1, T_{sc}^2, \ldots, T_{sc}^m \right\} \tag{18}$$

Next, to compute the average values of T_{jw} and T_{sc} using the Eqs. 19 and 20 are as following.

$$Average\left(T_{jw}\right) = \frac{\sum_{i=1}^{n} T_{jw}^i}{n} \tag{19}$$

$$Average(T_{sc}) = \frac{\sum_{i=1}^{m} T_{sc}^i}{m} \tag{20}$$

The average of strength of ties can represent the average cohesion of the network. After get the average values of T_{jw} and T_{sc}, we aggregate these two average values to compute the cohesion of the whole network by using the Eq. 21. We decide to multiply these two average values because multiplying can make the higher value higher. It is useful to show the difference distinctly between each network.

$$Cohesion(G_\alpha(i, N_{re})) = Average\left(T_{jw}\right) * Average(T_{sc}), \forall G_\alpha(i, N_{re}) \in G(i, N_{re}) \tag{21}$$

3 Experiments and Results

In this section, we will describe the experiments of the propose model. First, we choose Facebook as our experimental social media platform, because it is one of the most popular social networks. And we used PHP, Html5, CSS3, JavaScript to develop a web system and collected social data from Facebook. Finally, we used analytical software IBM SPSS and Microsoft Office Excel to evaluate and draw experiment results.

3.1 Data Collection

We constructed the InsurTree, collected user preference and their individual criteria weight. After we get authorization of users, we collected their social network information in the past 6 months. Finally, we collected 113 participants aged from 17 to 50 years old using the web-based service. There were 67 males and 46 females among the participants. Each participant has 379 friends in average, and we collected 2736 posts, 69768 reactions and 42120 comments.

3.2   Measurement Computing

Suitability Computation

In order to evaluate the accuracy of the ranking score calculated by the proposed mechanism, the computation of each sub-module was used as the benchmarks to compare with the ranking score computed by PRI module and personalized weight module. If certain customer's weight could not be acquired, the system category relative weight value was used as replacement. Each computation of the ranking score is as follows.

1. Random model: Computing the willingness score by random among the *IP_score*, *SIA_score*, and *SRA_score* multiplied with relative weight derived from personalized weight.
2. II model: Computing the ranking score by *IP_score* and *SIA_score* only with relative weight derived from personalized weight.
3. IR model: Computing the ranking score by *SIA_score* and *SRA_score* only with relative weight derived from personalized weight.
4. PR model: Computing the ranking score by *IP_score* and *SRA_score* only with relative weight derived from personalized weight.
5. PRI model: Computing ranking score by aggregation of *IP_score*, *SRA_score* and *SIA_score* respectively multiplied with the personalized weight.

3.3   Evaluation

We measure the three different criteria weighting from users' feedbacks. We ask users to evaluate the accuracy of weight by review recommendation results via picking up items (donors or campaigns) which are suitable for him/her. We measure the accuracy by the equation described below, where $\emptyset_{recommended}$ represents the set of our mechanism produced the first recommendation group members and $\emptyset_{recommended \cap join}$ represents the set of recommended insurers who are selected by the group leader and are willing to join in the co-insurance group.

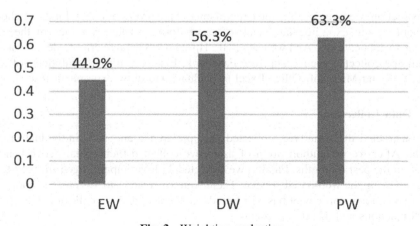

Fig. 3. Weighting evaluation

$$Accuracy = \frac{\left|\emptyset_{recommended \cap join}\right|}{\left|\emptyset_{recommended}\right|} \tag{22}$$

We show the result of weighting evaluation in Fig. 3. It is known that the personal weight has better performance than other two weights, because they have different motivations for each other (intrinsic or extrinsic motivation or both important). Not surprisingly, the accuracy of equality weight is similar with the default weight, because those weights are quite close.

4 Conclusions

This research proposes a recommendation mechanism for P2P insurance group formation. The criteria of recommending a co-insurer to join a group is evaluated according to three factors: individual preference, social influence and social relationship. The willingness of a co-insurer to join a group is measured by the values of the three factors multiplied with corresponding personal weights of criteria. The weight of each criteria is computed by using AHP.

In order to select the appropriate members in a insurance group, we introduce the group formation method. In the group formation module, we identify the set of users with high willingness score and form candidate groups by combination. After combination, we compute the density of each group to execute the first filtering, and then calculate the group cohesion measured by the willingness to join the group and their values of social closeness to execute the second filtering to generate the best group member list for the group leader who will to format the co-insurance group.

The evaluation results show that the proposed contextual group formation mechanism has higher scores on the evaluation of weight, elimination rate, misplace rate, likeness and satisfaction. In the measurement of multi-criteria, we found that individual preference is the most fundamental criterion in the group formation, which affects much on the likeness and satisfaction of recommendation.

References

1. Arumugam, M., Cusick, K: General insurance 2020: insurance for the individual. In: Sydney: Institute of Actuaries of Australia (2008)
2. Banham, R.: Will peer-to-peer insurance startups disrupt the industry? http://www.iamagazine.com/magazine/read/2016/08/01/will-peer-to-peer-insurance-startups-disrupt-the-industry. Accessed 21 Mar 2019
3. Insights, C.B.: Insurance tech startups raise $1.7 B across 173 deals in 2016. Insurance Tech Insights. https://www.cbinsights.com/blog/2016-insurance-tech-funding. Accessed 21 Mar 2019
4. CB Insights: There's an inherent conflict of interest at the heart of the insurance business model. Insurance Tech Insights. https://www.cbinsights.com/blog/insurance-business-model-tech-challenges. Accessed 21 Mar 2019

5. Gao, P., Miao, H., Baras, J.S., Golbeck, J.: Star: semiring trust inference for trust-aware social recommenders. In: Proceedings of the 10th ACM Conference on Recommender Systems, pp. 301–308. ACM (2016)
6. Moenninghoff, S.C., Wieandt, A.: The future of peer-to-peer finance. Schmalenbachs Zeitschrift für betriebswirtschaftliche Forschung 65(5), 466–487 (2013)
7. Paperno, A., Kravchuk, V., Porubaev, E.: Teambrella: a peer to peer insurance system. https://teambrella.com/WhitePaper.pdf. Accessed 21 Mar 2019
8. Saaty, T.L.: How to make a decision: the analytic hierarchy process. Eur. J. Oper. Res. 48(1), 9–26 (1990)
9. Victor, P.: Trust Networks for Recommender Systems. Doctoral Dissertation. Ghent University (2010)

Mining Personal Service Processes

Towards a Conceptualization for the Time Perspective

Birger Lantow$^{(\boxtimes)}$, Tom Baudis, and Fabienne Lambusch

University of Rostock, Albert-Einstein-Str. 22, 18059 Rostock, Germany
{birger.lantow,win.office,
fabienne.lambusch}@uni-rostock.de

Abstract. The process of digital transformation opens more and more domains to data driven analysis. This also accounts for Process Mining of service processes. This work investigates the use of Process Mining in the domain of Personal Services with a special focus on the Time Perspective and the early stages of the mining process. Based on a literature analysis as well as expert and focus group interviews with practitioners in family care, it is shown that a shift in used approaches and concepts of Process Mining is required in order to meet the requirements of the domain. Furthermore, a conceptualization for describing the Time Perspective in Process Mining is suggested.

Keywords: Process Mining · Personal Services · Conceptual model · Time Perspective · Process Management · Applied time

1 Introduction

Digitalization is one of the dominant topics of our time. Information and communication technologies have become an integral part of everyday life and lead to changes in many areas of work. Two fundamental aspects of Digitalization are the transformation of analogously stored information into digital data and the execution of more and more processes by machines or intelligent IT-systems [1].

The central task for the future will be to develop concepts for digital change that support not only industries with highly structured processes, but also economic sectors with knowledge-intensive and weakly structured processes [2] and especially for work with a high degree of uncertainty like in *Personal Services* [3]. Due to the special characteristics and the increasing importance of *Personal Services*, innovative ideas and sustainable advancements are needed for the digital change in this sector. A major challenge is to determine how services that are primarily characterized by the interactive work of individuals [4] can be meaningfully supported by IT-systems. Addressing this, concepts such as *Adaptive Case Management* (cf. [7]) have been developed to support weakly structured, knowledge-intensive work.

From the perspective of *Process Mining*, this development has some implications. First, there is a new data lake connected with new domains that produce process related data by using information systems. This goes hand in hand with a demand to make these data available for analysis. Second, existing *Process Mining* approaches might

W. Abramowicz and R. Corchuelo (Eds.): BIS 2019 Workshops, LNBIP 373, pp. 61–72, 2019.
https://doi.org/10.1007/978-3-030-36691-9_6

not fit to new demands and data. Furthermore, new questions to be answered by *Process Mining* might arise. Before developing new mining algorithms, first data and demands should be analyzed. Thus, the focus lies on the first steps of a *Process Mining* project. In order to address real world problems by performing research in this field, possibilities and concepts of *Process Mining* need to be structured in a framework that is accessible to practitioners and aligned with their needs.

This work presents results of an ongoing project on *Process Management* for family care that connects research at Rostock University with several local companies. *Process Mining* potentially plays a role in all phases of *Process Management* [5]. Thus, it has become a major topic of this project. Although being restricted to a specific domain of *Personal Services*, there is a big potential of generalization by analyzing local problems and solutions.

In the following we concentrate on the results with regard to the *Time Perspective* for mining *Personal Service* Processes. Section 2 discusses shortly the theoretical background of *Process Mining*, *Personal Services*, and conceptualizations of time. Based on this discussion, a literature review in Sect. 3 shows that there is little research on the area so far. Filling this gap, a conceptualization of time is presented, that is aligned with the practitioners' needs. Section 4 at last summarizes and discusses limitations as well as future work on the topic.

2   Theoretical Foundations

This section defines the relevant terms and the focus of this work. Section 2.1 addresses the foundations of *Process Mining*. This is followed by a discussion of *Personal Services* (Sect. 2.2) and existing conceptualizations of time (Sect. 2.3).

2.1   Process Mining

The "*Process Mining* Manifesto" by the IEEE *Process Mining* Task Force [5] provides a good overview of the topic. *Process Mining* is seen as a discipline between data mining on the one hand and process modelling and analysis on the other hand. The main purpose is the extraction of process knowledge from event logs. According to the *Process Mining* Task Force, there are four perspectives addressed.

At first, the *Control Flow Perspective* focusses on the sequence or order of activities within a process. The goal is to find a good characterization of all possible pathways and to present the result for example in a process modeling language such as BPMN, event-driven process chain (EPC) or Petri nets [6]. The second perspective is the *Organizational Perspective*. It focuses on information about resources within the event log, which actors are involved at all and how they relate to each other. Mining goals are for example finding a corporate structure by identifying employees according to their roles or presenting them in the form of a social network. The *Case Perspective* is the third perspective. Here, the focus lies on the characteristics of individual processes, called cases. Besides using the control flow, a characterization of cases can be based on involved actors and roles as well as certain process instance data values. The last perspective is the *Time Perspective*. The focus is on the timing and frequency of events. The availability of time stamps for events is a prerequisite for analyzing this perspective. For example, it is possible to discover bottlenecks or service level compliance can be measured. The use of resources can be monitored and predictions about remaining processing times of ongoing case instances can be made [5].

Although, we concentrate on the *Time Perspective*, dependencies to elements of the other perspectives will have to be considered. As already discussed, time refers for example to resources (*Organizational Perspective*), ongoing cases (*Case Perspective*) or service levels of a process which are connected to certain events in the control flow (*Control Flow Perspective*).

In [5], the IEEE *Process Mining* Task Force also describes general stages in a *Process Mining* project. At the beginning in "Stage 0" (plan and verify), a plan for the project and a goal must be defined. "Stage 1" (extract) describes the extraction of event data, models, objects and questions from the relevant IT systems and stakeholders such as the management and domain experts as well. This stage results in an identification and understanding of available historical data (event logs), handmade process models, objectives of *Process Management* in form of KPI (Key Performance Indicators), and/or a set of questions to be answered by *Process Mining*. In "Stage 2", a control flow model is created and connected to the event log. Thus, analysis can be performed and first questions from "Stage 1" can be answered. Furthermore, data may be filtered and parameters of the analysis be varied. At "Stage 3" the control flow model can be enhanced based on the analysis and extended to reflect the other perspectives, additional questions can be answered. The last "Stage 4" provides an integration of historical and current operational data.

The focus of our work lies on the first two stages. Our interviews with domain experts and focus group research have shown, that there is a general interest in the possibilities of *Process Mining*, especially when practitioners realize the potential of harvesting the digital traces of their work (event logs). However, having knowledge-intensive processes (see Sect. 2.2) it is hard to create control flow models [7]. Additionally, objectives and questions have a broader focus than "traditional" business *Process Management* and optimization approaches. This requires a deeper look on potential objectives and questions of *Process Mining* in that domain in order to support the early stages. We assume that there should be a feed-back from identified objectives and questions to the data that is actually collected in event logs, in addition to the stage model by the *Process Mining* Task force. Thus, the data model is adapted to *Process Mining* requirements. This requires a focus on the early stages as well.

2.2 Personal Services

Services in general are especially distinguished from tangible goods. According to a literature review by Zeithaml et al. [8], the four consistently cited characteristics of services are intangibility, inseparability of production and consumption, heterogeneity (potential for high variability in the provision), and perishability (inability to be inventoried). The authors of this article furthermore call intangibility the fundamental difference from goods, as services are rather performances that cannot be sensed in the same way as goods.

Although services are different from goods and characterized by intangibility, they can still be directed at goods or include tangible actions. A classification approach for services proposed by Lovelock [9] distinguishes between two dimensions of services. The first dimension represents the direct recipient of the service, which describes whether the service is directed at people or things. The second dimension represents the nature of the service act that distinguishes between tangible and intangible actions. For services relating to people, the different proportions of tangible and intangible elements refer to whether the service rather affects the body or the mind of a person. Services directed at people's bodies are characterized in particular by the fact that the person must be physically present when the service is provided (e.g. health care). Production and consumption take place simultaneously. In the case of services with mostly intangible actions, the service is aimed at affecting the person's mind rather than the body and thus, can influence the attitudes or behavior of a person. Instead of the physical, the mental presence is required to provide the service (e.g. psychotherapy). The actual core of the service is therefore information-based and can, for example, also be made accessible in a digital form in some cases. Then, the time of production by the provider does not necessarily have to correspond to the time of consumption by the customer.

Regardless of the proportion of tangible or intangible actions, both classes of services described above have in common that the direct recipients of the services are persons instead of things. Already Halmos [10] denoted those services as personal which are concerned with the change of the body or the personality of a client. Bieber and Geiger point out that a great challenge of *Personal Services* lies in the fact that the recipient of the service is at the same time in the role of a co-producer [3]. They state that *Personal Services* are characterized particularly by the close, indissoluble connection between persons who have to interact with each other. This interaction as a key element in *Personal Services* reduces the predictability and increases the uncertainty in the corresponding work processes. Since service activities that seem similar (e.g. working in a call center) can still differ in their degree of knowledge intensity depending on the specific field of activity, services can also be classified as knowledge-intensive or simple [3]. We refer here in particular to knowledge-intensive *Personal Services*.

While standard process models exist in other service domains such as the Technical Customer Service (e.g. [11]), in the domain of *Personal Services* such a reference model seemingly does not exist. However, Fließ et al. [12] describe a straightforward service model. At its core, the model consists of the three phases *pre-service, service,* and *post-service. Pre-service* describes the preparation of a service, while *service* describes the actual provision of services in interaction with the customer, and *post-service refers* to the follow-up. We extend this model with two additional phases, which are described in the following. From the point of view of information processing, the registration of a client as the starting point for the relation between customer and service provider is also important; this is where the first information about the client becomes available. Therefore, the phase of *client intake* is added. Moreover, *Personal Services* are often integrated into a longer-term meta-process, which then also has longer-term objectives. One example would be the restoration of mobility in the context of physiotherapy. This means that phases of direct, short-term service provision may be intertwined with overarching coordination tasks to achieve objectives.

Therefore, we add the phase of *coordination*. The extended version of the service phases is shown in Fig. 1.

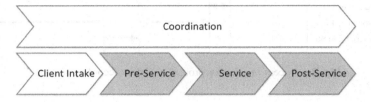

Fig. 1. Extended service phases

The grey elements in the figure show the core phases proposed by Fließ et al. [12], which are passed during each service operation. The two added phases, in contrast, are not necessarily executed during each service operation. Since the nature of *Personal Services* is the interaction between people, human interaction and relationships play a strong role for service performance and thus should be considered when analyzing services processes. Assuming a long-term meta-process which is especially important in therapy and coaching settings, there are also long term relationships that should be considered in *Process Management*.

2.3 Conceptualizations of Time

Research on conceptual models of time mainly focuses on temporal logic. Domain independent models have been developed to describe absolute or relative time, events or time intervals and their relationships as well as periodicity. Examples for this research stream can be found for example in the survey by Gaidukovs and Kirikova [13] or the W3C Time Ontology[1] introduced in [14].

Time elements that are defined based on these concepts become a meaningful information only if they are applied and thus related to a certain domain. This enables the use of time elements for information models in that domain. We calls this *Applied Time* in contrast to *Abstract Time*. Considering business process analysis and optimization, there is a generally accepted set of applied time intervals. For example, von Muehlen and Shapiro define in [15]: Turnaround Time, Wait Time, Change-over Time, Processing Time, and Suspend Time (see Fig. 2). Furthermore, deviations of these time intervals from desired/planned values can be described. Examples are Earliness, Lateness, or Tardiness [16]. The common ground of these and additional applied time concepts is the focus on process execution progress. Thus, objectives and *Process Mining* questions can be based on this set of concepts when process execution progress is in focus. With regard to resources that are used in a process, resource utilization and thus availability, idle, and processing times are commonly considered.

---

[1] https://www.w3.org/TR/owl-time/.

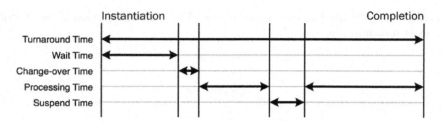

Fig. 2. Process metrics for process analytics according to [15]

Considering the discussion in Sect. 2.2, neither the fact that human beings are resources in *Personal Services* nor the special nature of long term relationships are considered using these common applied time concepts. Section 3 discusses additional applied time concepts addressing these and other aspects relevant for practitioners.

3   Mining Personal Service Processes and the Time Perspective

After defining and discussing important terms in the previous section, the current status of research and new ideas addressing the already shown shortcomings of the generally accepted approaches are shown in the following. Section 3.1 shows the current state of research based on a systematic literature review. This is followed by a presentation of empirical investigations in Sect. 3.2. At last, Sect. 3.3 discusses the developed conceptual model for the *Time Perspective* in *Process Mining*.

3.1   Related Work

As already stated in the introduction, this study is part of a project introducing *Process Management* and *Process Mining* in family care companies. Considering "Stage 0" and "Stage 1" of a *Process Mining* project, process KPI and questions to be answered by *Process Mining* have to be defined. In order to support this task, a systematic literature analysis has been performed. The portals of Scopus, Springer, AISeL, and IEEE have been used to look for literature addressing *Process Mining* in the Social Sector. Using several search terms, 266 publications in total have been found and screened for relevance. Only two [17, 18] turned out to address the topic. However, their focus was on the integration of sensor events in *Process Mining* but not on specific challenges of *Process Mining* in the Social Sector.

A follow-up search on Scopus for publications addressing time in conjunction with *Process Mining* lead to 30 documents. Most of them discussed how event time information can be used to derive control flow models. Only five considered the *Time Perspective* as part of the process analysis. Process execution progress as discussed in Sect. 2.3 was in the focus of three of them [19–21]. Kohawaia [22] described the mining of personal processes with activities like relaxing, grooming etc. Thus, humans as resources in processes and their specific characteristics were considered. Still, the purpose of the approach was a transfer of *Process Mining* technologies to personal time management and not its application to *Business Process Management*. Fernandez-Llatas et al. [23] discussed the importance of process related data in time analysis. Concretely, the conditions of patients were considered. However, the main focus was on the technical implementation of the approach. Consequently, the step from "Stage 1" to "Stage 2" was addressed (cf. Sect. 2.1).

A very general set of questions resulting from "Stage 1" as suggested in [5] can be found in [6]. Out of 14 formulated questions, 3 addressed time:

- What are the throughput [turnaround, the author] times of my cases?
- What are the service times for my tasks?
- How much time was spent between any two tasks in my process?

All of them focus on process execution progress. This is in line with the examples given for *Time Perspective* analysis described by the Process Mining Task Force in [5].

3.2 Empirical Results

We collected first empirical data on possible objectives and questions for *Process Mining* in the domain of family care by guided expert interviews [24]. The interview guide contained two main phases. In the first phase, the participants have been asked to name interesting information for analysis with regard to each of the four *Process Mining* perspectives. In the second phase, the participants rated the importance each item of the general question set from [6]. One interview was conducted with the managing director of a family care company (A), a second interview with a case worker from that company (B). It was revealed that the participants had a different focus on the analysis of their processes compared to the focus set by the classical process analysis and optimization regardless of the perspective. With respect to the *Time Perspective* they suggested the analysis of times with regard to the relationship between customer and service provider as discussed in Sect. 2.2 (participant A: getting acquainted, developing trust,...) or the temporal context of the process (participant B: weekday, weekend, vacation time, summer, winter,...) in the first interview phase. In the second interview phase, most items of the general question set for *Process Mining* were rated at least important for analysis. However, on further inquiry to the rating, the participants realized that they were unsure about the underlying concepts. After then explaining for example turnaround times, it revealed that turnaround times might not be an appropriate KPI because they are barely connected to the quality of service in this domain. Furthermore, if the focus is on a long term relationship there are not necessarily turnaround times that can be measured.

In order to provide the practitioners the room to develop a common understanding of the possibilities of *Process Mining* and of analyzable objectives that are important for the domain, a focus group interview [24, 25] has been conducted. The interview involved five participants from three social care companies, including a managing director of each company. A first conceptual model of relevant concepts of the *Process*

Mining perspectives has been developed and agreed on during the focus group interview. The result for the *Time Perspective* is sketched in Fig. 3.

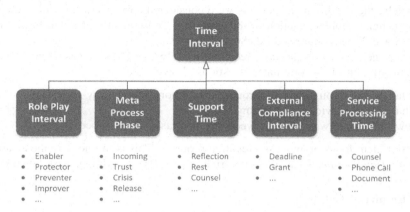

Fig. 3. Conceptualization of time from focus group interview

Five classes of time intervals have been identified in the focus group interview. Examples of concrete applied time intervals are given for the classes. Starting from left to right, "Role Play Interval" refers to roles that the employees of the social care companies have to play in the interaction with their clients und the time intervals that the respective roles are held. "Meta Process Phase" refers to the phases that can be identified in the long-term relationship between service provider and client (cf. Sect. 2.2). "Support Time" refers to activities that support the actual service performance but are not part of the service process. An "External Compliance Interval" reflects regulatory time intervals from government and intervals of monetary funds availability. A "Service Processing Time" is a time interval of actual service performance. Although these times largely depend on the client's needs in family care, they need to be monitored because they are budgeted by governmental funding.

The resulting conceptualization is very specific to the domain of family care. For example, the development of trust or the handling of personal crises are parts of the meta-process in addition to the process described in Sect. 2.2. However it shows, that several time concepts are relevant to *Personal Service* process analysis and a view just on process execution progress and activities is too limited.

3.3   Conceptualization of Time for Mining Personal Service Processes

In order to provide guidance for the first stages of *Process Mining* in the domain of *Personal Services*, the found concepts have been generalized and amended. Tis has been done based on related work (cf. Sects. 2 and 3.1) and further focus group interviews. The result is shown in Fig. 4.

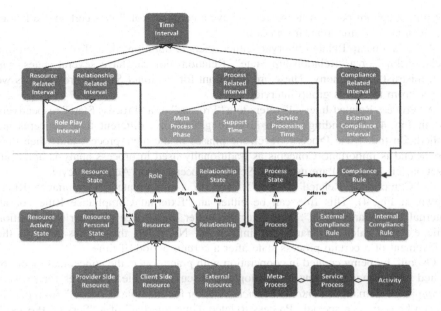

Fig. 4. Conceptualization of time for mining personal services (Color figure online)

The applied time concepts (blue/gray in Fig. 4) are defined by linking them to concepts of other *Process Mining* perspectives. There are four main relevant classes: "Resource Related Intervals", "Relationship Related Intervals", "Process Related Intervals", and "Compliance Related" intervals. These classes are not necessarily disjoint. A further specialization of the classes is possible based on the specializations and association of the referenced concepts of the other perspectives. For reasons of clarity and limited space this is not shown in Fig. 4. In order to demonstrate the applicability and reusability of the model, the concepts of the first focus group interview (gray in Fig. 4) have been aligned with the defined classes.

A "Resource Related Interval" refers to a Resource or a resource-related concept (green in Fig. 4). This addresses the *Organizational Perspective* of *Process Mining*. Considering *Personal Services*, the resources are human beings in general. Due to the importance of the client in service processes (cf. Sect. 2.2), not only provider side resources (employees) should be considered, but also the client side. The focus group interviews showed that also external stakeholders, for example by third party service providers, can influence the service outcome. A "Resource State" can be used to define a "Resource Related Interval". There are specializations for provider, client, or external resources possible. Furthermore a distinction is made between, "Resource Activity State" which refers to activity and rest times of resources (cf. Sect. 2.3) and "Resource Personal State". The latter refers to the personal condition and was suggested in focus group interviews. When humans are performing together, this always has a component of personal "Relationship". People in relationships play official and unofficial "Roles".

The time a certain person ("Resource") plays a certain "Role" in a certain "Relationship" can also be important for analysis.

A "Relationship Related Interval" either refers to durations of a "Role" played in a "Relationship" or a "Relationship State". Relationships can have several states, e.g. trust, mistrust, or harmony. These are important for *Personal Service* provision as we learned from the focus group interviews.

A "Process Related Interval" refers to a "Process" or a "Process State" respectively (red in Fig. 4). Depending on the level of granularity, different time concepts are applied. On the "Meta Process" level, the phases of the meta-process and when they start or end is important. Concepts as traditionally used in process analysis and optimization (cf. Sect. 2.3) are used for "Service Process" and "Activity" level.

A "Compliance Related Interval" refers to a time-related "Compliance Rule" (brown in Fig. 4). This rule can be either an "External Compliance Rule" or an "Internal Compliance Rule". The latter are under the service provider's disposition while external rules can hardly be influenced. Normally, these rules refer to the achievement of a certain process state after a certain period of time.

Overall, by being created in cooperation with practitioners the conceptual model of applied time provides means to develop and discuss possible objectives for *Process Mining* in the domain of *Personal Services*. Taking for example "Counsel" from Fig. 3, this can be seen as a special "Process Related Time Interval" of a "Service Process", being a "Support Time" when counseling colleagues. In this case, it would also be a "Resource Related Time Interval" connected to a "Resource Activity State" in the specialization of for example a "Support Activity State". If it is counseling clients, it wouldn't be a "Support Time" but a "Service Processing Time" and so on. This illustrates the potential of avoiding ambiguities by the conceptual model. Based on a clear definition, measurement or analysis procedures can be defined as well a required data.

4 Summary and Outlook

The literature analysis performed in Sect. 3.1 showed that there is little research available for mining *Personal Services*. Furthermore, the overall investigations show that there are special requirements to *Process Mining* in the area. The developed conceptual of applied time provides a first step for filling this gap. It provides support for the first *Process Mining* stages. Being developed in a specific sub-domain of *Personal Services*, a further evaluation of the conceptual model in different contexts should be one of the next steps. Since the model provides an abstraction from concrete concepts of family care, transferability to other contexts is generally given. However, its utility has to be proven. Considering the increasing focus of *Company Health Management (CHM)* on the personal well-being of employees, an application in *CHM* might also be possible. The focus on the peculiarities of humans as resources may help to identify or develop appropriate data sources and mining approaches for *Personal Services* as well as *CHM*.

The conceptual model of applied time will also be applied to the analysis of already existing event data within the ongoing project with Social Care companies.

Furthermore, additions in the existing information model and thus the collected event data are planned. Thus, a further validation based on data from practice will be possible.

A future formalization of the model using Semantic Web standards and their integration support would foster the integration of heterogeneous data sources for *Process Mining* and the alignment with existing domain concepts.

References

1. Motahari-Nezhad, H.R., Swenson, K.D.: Adaptive case management: overview and research challenges. In: Conference on Business Informatics, pp. 264–269, Wien (2013)
2. Kurz, M., Herrmann, C.: Adaptive case management – anwendung des business process management 2.0-konzepts auf schwach strukturierte Geschäftsprozesse. In: Sinz, E.J., Bartmann, D., Bodendorf, F., Ferstl, O.K. (eds.) Dienstorientierte IT-Systeme für hochflexible Geschäftsprozesse, pp. 241–265. University of Bamberg Press, Bamberg (2011)
3. Bieber, D., Geiger, M.: Personenbezogene dienstleistungen in komplexen dienstleis-tungssystemen – eine erste annäherung. In: Bieber, D., Geiger, M. (eds.) Personenbezogene Dienstleistungen im Kontext komplexer Wertschöpfung, pp. 9–49. Springer, Wiesbaden (2014). https://doi.org/10.1007/978-3-531-19580-3_1
4. Bauer, R.: Personenbezogene Soziale Dienstleistungen: Begriff, Qualität und Zukunft. VS Verlag für Sozialwissenschaften, Wiesbaden (2001). https://doi.org/10.1007/978-3-322-91616-7
5. van der Aalst, W., et al.: Process mining manifesto. In: Daniel, F., Barkaoui, K., Dustdar, S. (eds.) BPM 2011. LNBIP, vol. 99, pp. 169–194. Springer, Heidelberg (2012). https://doi.org/10.1007/978-3-642-28108-2_19
6. van der Aalst, W., et al.: The process mining toolkit: ProM. Process Mining Group, Eindhoven University of Technology (2013). http://www.promtools.org/
7. Lantow, B.: Adaptive case management - a review of method support. In: Buchmann, R.A., Karagiannis, D., Kirikova, M. (eds.) PoEM 2018. LNBIP, vol. 335, pp. 157–171. Springer, Cham (2018). https://doi.org/10.1007/978-3-030-02302-7_10
8. Zeithaml, V.A., Parasuraman, A., Berry, L.L.: Problems and strategies in services marketing. J. Mark. **49**(2), 33–46 (1985)
9. Lovelock, C.H.: Classifying services to gain strategic marketing insights. J. Mark. **47**(3), 9–20 (1983)
10. Halmos, P.: The personal service society. Br. J. Sociol. **18**, 13–28 (1967). https://doi.org/10.2307/588586
11. Däuble, G., Özcan, D., Niemöller, C., Fellmann, M., Nüttgens, M., Thomas, O.: Information needs of the mobile technical customer service -a case study in the field of machinery and plant engineering. In: Proceedings of the 48th Annual Hawaii International Conference on System Sciences (HICSS), Manoa, pp. 1018–1027 (2015)
12. Fließ, S., Dyck, S., Schmelter, M., Volkers, M.J.D.: Kundenaktivitäten in dienstleis-tungsprozessen – die sicht der konsumenten. In: Fließ, S., Haase, M., Jacob, F., Ehret, M. (eds.) Kundenintegration und Leistungslehre, pp. 181–204. Springer, Wiesbaden (2015). https://doi.org/10.1007/978-3-658-07448-7_11
13. Gaidukovs, A., Kirikova, M.: The time dimension in information logistics. In ILOG@ BIR, pp. 35–43 (2013)

14. Hobbs, J.R., Pan, F.: An ontology of time for the semantic web. ACM Trans. Asian Lang. Inf. Process. **3**(1), 66–85 (2004)
15. zur Muehlen, M., Shapiro, R.: Business process analytics. In: vom Brocke, J., Rosemann, M. (eds.) Handbook on Business Process Management 2. IHIS, pp. 243–263. Springer, Heidelberg (2015). https://doi.org/10.1007/978-3-642-45103-4_10
16. Brucker, P.: Scheduling Algorithms, 5th edn. Springer, Berlin (2007). https://doi.org/10.1007/978-3-540-69516-5
17. Vitali, M., Pernici, B.: PiE - processes in events: interconnections in ambient assisted living. In: Ciuciu, I., et al. (eds.) OTM 2015. LNCS, vol. 9416, pp. 157–166. Springer, Cham (2015). https://doi.org/10.1007/978-3-319-26138-6_19
18. Vitali, M., Pernici, B., Interconnecting processes through IoT in a health-care scenario. In: IEEE 2nd International Smart Cities Conference: Improving the Citizens Quality of Life, ISC2 2016 - Proceedings (2016)
19. Garcia, A.O., Dominguez, L.C., Martinez, A.V.: Analysis of hospital processes from the time perspective using process mining. IEEE Lat. Am. Trans. **16**(6), 1741–1748 (2018)
20. Zhou, H., Lin, C., Deng, Y.P., Wan, Z.C.: Determine execution time and selection probabilities in process mining via petri nets. Adv. Mater. Res. **760**, 1951–1958 (2013)
21. Van der Aalst, W.M.P., Schonenberg, M.H., Song, M.: Time prediction based on process mining. Inf. Syst. **36**(2), 450–475 (2011)
22. Khowaja, A.R.: Process mining techniques: an application to time management. In: Proceedings of SPIE - The International Society for Optical Engineering (2018)
23. Fernandez-Llatas, C., Sacchi, L., Benedi, J.M., Dagliati, A., Traver, V., Bellazzi, R.: Temporal abstractions to enrich activity-based process mining corpus with clinical time series. In: 2014 IEEE-EMBS International Conference on Biomedical and Health Informatics, BHI 2014, pp. 785–788 (2014)
24. Döring, N., Bortz, J.: Forschungsmethoden und evaluation. Springer, Wiesbaden (2016). https://doi.org/10.1007/978-3-642-41089-5
25. Edmunds, H., American Marketing Association: The focus group research handbook. NTC Business Books, Chicago (1999)

Company Investment Recommendation Based on Data Mining Techniques

Svetla Boytcheva[1,2]([⊠]) [iD] and Andrey Tagarev[1]

[1] Sirma AI trading as Ontotext, Sofia, Bulgaria
svetla.boytcheva@gmail.com,
{svetla.boytcheva,andrey.tagarev}@ontotext.com
[2] Institute of Information and Communication Technologies,
Bulgarian Academy of Sciences, Sofia, Bulgaria

Abstract. There are about seventy thousand companies listed on various stock markets worldwide and there is public information on about three hundred thousand companies on Wikipedia but that is only a small fraction of all companies. Among the millions others are hiding the future technological innovators, market disruptors and best possible investments. So, if an investors has an example of the kind of company they are interested in, how can they successfully find other such investment options without sifting through millions of options?

We propose non-personalized recommendation approach for alternatives of company investments. This method is based on data mining techniques for investment behaviour modelling. The investment opportunities are discovered using the idea of transfer learning of indirectly associated company investments. This allows companies to diversify their investment portfolio. Experiments are run over a dataset of 7.5 million companies, of which the model focuses on startups and investments in the last 3 years. This allows us to investigate most recent investment trends. The recommendation model identifies top-N investment opportunities. The evaluation of the proposed investment strategies show high accuracy of the recommendation system.

Keywords: Knowledge-based models · Data mining · Investment recommendation system

1 Motivation

There are millions of companies worldwide and thousands of new ones are being created on any given day. The pace of innovation means that in many cases, the most interesting companies that utilize novel approaches and technologies are going to be among the ones created recently and those are also the companies

This research is partially supported by projects that received funding from the European Union Horizon 2020 Research and Innovation Programme – euBusinessGraph (Grant Agreement no. 732003) and InnoRate (Grant Agreement no. 821518).

© Springer Nature Switzerland AG 2019
W. Abramowicz and R. Corchuelo (Eds.): BIS 2019 Workshops, LNBIP 373, pp. 73–84, 2019.
https://doi.org/10.1007/978-3-030-36691-9_7

that are most in need of capital and expert support. There are many important incubators and groups of angel investors who focus on following these fledgling companies and identifying the most promising ones but due to the sheer volume of potential candidates, in each of these cases the investors are only looking at companies at a very specific stage of development, in a limited geographical location and focused on a specific technology or problem. This means that the number of investment option being considered by any such investor is limited by these factors but that is not a benefit, just a natural limitation on the number of companies that human experts can analyze and consider. In reality any given opportunity is most likely being tackled by multiple companies, probably utilizing different tools or based in different locations. This means that a better way to identify potentially interesting investment opportunities than personal knowledge of a company would be vastly beneficial.

Beyond the sheer number of companies that need to be considered, a further challenge is the very sparse information available for the smaller companies that present the best investment opportunities. Generally speaking, the amount of information available on a company lags behind its importance and waiting for complete detailed information to become available before even considering a company as a candidate will exclude many of the best investment opportunities. This means that any automated approach to the problem not only needs to drastically narrow down the number of potential candidates but must be robust enough to work with only incomplete information about a company.

In this paper we will present an approach to identify promising investment alternatives. Our approach will focus on working with startups and newly created companies with only sparsely available data and the selection methods will be based on statistical analysis of historical investment behavior. The complexity of the problem is high enough, that complete automation of the recommendations isn't a viable option. In our experiments, we focused on the pre-selection step i.e. given a company, we aim to return a list that contains some interesting investment alternatives. This means that a human expert will still go through each candidate in the list to select the relevant ones, but the task is reduced from working with millions of candidates to mere dozens.

2   Related Work

Prediction, forecasting and recommendation systems are widely used in the area of business and finance. Zibriczky [22] presents domain-based review of recommendation systems in Finance, where he investigates applications in online-banking and multi-domain solutions, loans, stocks, real estate, insurance polices and riders, assets allocation and portfolio management, investment opportunities and business plans. Variety of methods are used for recommendation systems like collaborative filtering [13], content–based filtering [11], knowledge–based recommendation [14], case–based recommendation [9], hybrid methods [18], association rules mining [10], fuzzy methods [6], artificial neural networks [12], and support vector machines (SVM) [8]. Investigation of the Venture capital's (VC) investment behaviour is quite challenging task, due to its sparsity, thus application of classical recommendation methods for venture capital investments are limited. Yingsaeree et al. [19] define computation finance taxonomy that shows which method is more appropriate for which domain application and which research task. Usually VCs invest in quite few companies from not so diverse industries. Stone et al. [15] propose Top-N recommendation system for venture finance using supervised learning approaches, textual description, fixed set of industry classes, and industry hierarchy. This method alongside with other methods is integrated in NVANA platform that aims to assist in the appraisal of early-stage venture [16]. Zhao et al. [21] present five portfolio-based risk-aware recommendation algorithms for predicting new investments, by using CrunchBase dataset. The authors in [20] propose utility-based recommendation algorithm based, on the idea of transfer learning. This approach allows to cope with the problem of personalized recommendation system usage for VCs that lack a history of investment portfolio by profiling investors and using equity funds information. The majority of the proposed solutions are personalized, but we aim to develop method that is non-personalized, data-driven and unsupervised. Thus we will use data mining techniques to identify patterns of investment opportunities.

3 Datasets

Our experimentation is based on a large custom fused dataset available in an RDF triple store. We will now examine the constituent parts of the dataset, the shape of the unifying model and the database used to store it.

3.1 The Data

Our experiments are carried on a custom dataset created at Sirma AI that was created by the data fusion of five large commercial datasets. These datasets contain information on companies, investors and historical information on financial transactions between these entities. As part of the data fusion process, instances of the same entity or event present in multiple datasets were identified and merged in the final dataset. After the data fusion process, the finalized custom dataset we are working with contains 7.5 million companies and investors and 1.5 million investment events.

Table 1 lists the feature counts and their coverage over the dataset. The only two features that we can always rely on are company name (not actually used for suggestions) and RDF rank which is a measure of a company's importance in the overall graph. Investor count and funding amount are also calculated for every company but in cases where the company has received no investment yet, both numbers are zero. This is still useful information, of course, but it makes the 100% coverage number not quite correct. The rest of the features deal with investment, industry, size and foundation year which get progressively less common for newer companies but they are still present in a useful number of cases. Finally, the company description is potentially the most valuable single feature but its coverage for new companies is even worse than the 34% coverage

Table 1. Company feature coverage in the dataset

Feature	Coverage
Name	100%
Rank	100%
Investor count	100%
Funding amount	100%
Country	91.3%
Region	68.8%
City	61.7%
Industry	46.3%
Foundation year	44.7%
Description	34.0%
Employee count	9.9%

figure suggests and using it in a useful manner requires some serious Natural Language Processing which will not be discussed in this paper.

3.2   The Knowledge Graph

The fully-fused dataset is in the form of a Linked Data graph represented as RDF triples. All triples in the dataset conform to the unified data model that defines the shape and types of data available in the graph.

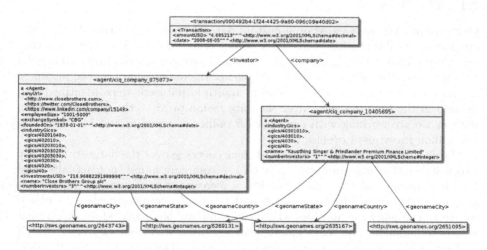

Fig. 1. Part of the Knowledge Graph model

Figure 1 shows a relevant portion of the total Knowledge Graph model, specifically the connection between a company and an investor through an investment event. As we can see, there are a variety of features available for the different entities in the model, notably the features we discussed in Sect. 3.1.

This connection between company and investor through an investment event is going to form the basis for training our algorithms. The idea is, in essence, to examine the different portfolios of investments chosen by a particular investor and search for certain patterns within them, thus concluding what makes a certain company a good fit for a given investment portfolio.

It is also worth bearing in mind that the various steps of the algorithms described are going to affect some changes on the contents of the knowledge graph itself in the form of certain features. Firstly, we will mark all potential candidates, excluding companies that were founded before January 1st 2014 or that have gone bankrupt. Secondly, we are going to cluster all potential candidates into a number of classes depending on their features. These steps are not reflected in Fig. 1 but they do not change the relevant part of the model in any major way. They are, however, crucial in order to translate the candidate selection rules generated by the algorithms into SPARQL queries that select the actual candidates from among all available companies.

3.3 The Database

The Knowledge Graph is stored in GraphDB[1] – a highly-efficient, robust and scalable RDF database. It allows the incorporation of clustering results through reasoning based on forward-chaining of entailment rules and the retrieval of candidates through the use of graph pattern matching rules translated into the powerful SPARQL language.

4 Methods

We propose an unsupervised data-driven method for non-personalized recommendations for company investments. The learning method is based on three main steps (Fig. 2) - investigation of the investment behavior, identification of investment type and generation of investment strategy.

The main idea behind the investment opportunities is to investigate direct and indirect associations in company investments. Direct association, also called frequent patterns, represent different sets of companies that appear together in the investment portfolios of multiple companies. In contrast, indirectly associated companies (Fig. 3) are seldom found in the investment portfolio of the same company, but they co-occur with common a set of companies (called the mediator set) in a large number of investment portfolios.

---

[1] GraphDB web page. https://www.ontotext.com/products/graphdb/ Accessed 12 Jun 2019.

4.1   Indirect Association Rules Mining

Companies in our dataset S will be called *items* $V = \{v_1, v_2, ..., v_n\}$. For the collection S we extract the set of all different companies' investment portfolios $P = \{p_1, p_2, ..., p_N\}$, where $p_i \subseteq V$. This set S corresponds to transactions and for each of them is associated unique transaction identifier (*tid*).

Given a set S of tids, the support of an itemset I is the number of tids in S that contain I. We denote it as $supp(I)$. We define a threshold called *minsup* (minimum support). Frequent itemset (FI) F is one with at least minimum support count, i.e. $supp(F) \geq minsup$. The task of frequent pattern mining (FPM) of S is to find all possible frequent itemsets in S.

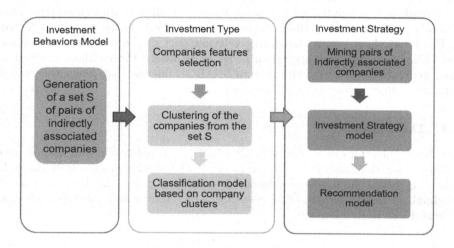

Fig. 2. Investment strategy model

The following definition for indirect association rules was proposed by Tan and Vipin [17]:

Definition 1 *(Indirect associated pair). An itempair $\{A; B\}$ is indirectly associated via a mediator set $C = \{C_1, ..., C_n\}$ if the following conditions hold :*

1. $sup(A; B) < minsup$ *(Itempair Support Condition)*
2. There exists a non-empty set C such that $\forall C_i \in C$:

(a) $sup(A; C_i) \geq ts$; $sup(B; C_i) \geq ts$ *(Mediator Support Condition)*.
(b) $d(A; C_i) \geq conf$; $d(B; C_i) \geq conf$ where $d(p; Q)$ is a measure of the dependence between p and Q *(Dependence Condition)*.

Condition (1) is needed because an indirect association is significant only if both items seldom occur in the same company's investment portfolio, i.e. they are negatively correlated. Condition (2a) is needed to guarantee statistical significance of the mediator set C. Condition (2b) is needed to guarantee that only items highly dependent on both A and B are used to form the mediator set C. Items in C form close neighborhood.

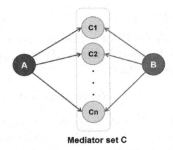

Fig. 3. Indirect association of companies A and B via mediator set $C = \{C_1, ..., C_n\}$

4.2 Investment Behaviours Model

This task starts with preprocessing of the transactions data by converting raw data into item sets by applying hashing – replacing each item (company) with a unique ID and removing duplicates. Each item set is stored in ascending order by id in order to hasten the data mining process. In the initial step we create a model of investments behaviour based on data mining methods for indirect association rules mining (IARM), FPM and Association Rules (ARs). The experiments use Java implementations of the algorithms IndirectRules [17], FPMax [5], and FPGrowthARL [7] from SPMF² (Open–Source Data Mining Library). A set $A = \{(I_1, J_1), ..., (I_m, J_m)\}$ of pairs of indirectly associated companies and set $U = \{X | \exists(X, Y) \in A \vee \exists(Y, X) \in A\}$ of startups involved in some pair in A are generated in result.

4.3 Investment Type Identification

This module starts with company features selection $\Phi = \{f_1, ..., f_t\}$. The set of startups U is clustered by density based clustering method [4] into clusters $K = \{K_1, ..., K_M\}$. The JRip classification algorithm [3] is applied to the clusters in order to generate classification rules. JRip was selected because this algorithm results in a small number of ordered rules with high accuracy. The algorithm runs through 4 stages: Growing a rule, Pruning, Optimization and Selection. It has a high time complexity and is considered relatively slow. In our case the execution time is not significant because it is applied just once during the model creation. The precision and number of rules generated are most important as they will be applied multiple times over big dataset and the overall decision and recommendation process relies on them.

In addition the generated classification rules are applied to the entire datasets S of companies.

---

² Open–Source Data Mining Library SPMF. http://www.philippe-fournier-viger. com/spmf/index.php Accessed 12 Jun 2019.

4.4   Investment Strategy

An indirectly associated pair (IAP) of companies are symmetric, thus $\forall (I, J) \in A, \exists (J, I) \in A$. Then for each ordered pair $(I, J) \in A, \exists$ a vector with company's features and the corresponding clusters:

$$(f_1(I), ..., f_t(I), cluster(I), cluster(J)) \tag{1}$$

Inductive logic method CN2 [1,2] is applied to learn patterns of investment strategies. For each cluster $K_i \in K$ are selected all companies $I \in U$ such that $cluster(I) = K_i$. Their corresponding vectors are marked as positive, and all remaining vectors are marked as negative. The target value is the cluster of the second company J in the IAP (I, J). The CN2 rule induction algorithm, applied over these vectors, generates ordered classification rules in the form:

$$rule_{il} : if \, (condition) \, then \, cluster = K_j. \tag{2}$$

where $condition$ is a conjunction of attribute-value pairs of company's features. The main objective of this step is to produce generalized rules, based on the common features of IAPs. Thus for a company X from cluster K_i the most appropriate cluster K_j can be recommended and investment opportunities can be selected from it. The generated CN2 classifier is applied for each company $X \in K_i$ and a rule $rule_{il}$: applicable to the features of X is identified. Some additional equivalence relations are added for part of the features - $same\_as$. A new vector is generated for each IAP (X, Y):

$$(rule_{il}, f_1(Y), ..., f_t(Y), same\_f_i(X, Y), ..., same\_f_k(X, Y)) \tag{3}$$

CN2 is applied again with the rule as a target value and ordered classification rules in the form are generated:

$$R_{ab} : if \, (condition) \, then \, rule = rule_{pq}. \tag{4}$$

where $condition$ is a conjunction of attribute-value pairs of company's Y features. The later rules R_{ab} for restriction of the investment opportunity companies features by

4.5   Investment Recommendation

For a given company X classification rules are applied in order to associate the corresponding cluster K_i Fig. 4. Then we apply transfer rule $rule_{ij}$ to identify the most appropriate investment strategy. The investment strategy ranks the possible alternative investments clusters. The associated cluster K_j with highest rank is selected. Additional restrictions for the required features of companies from K_j are applied from the rule R_{ab} that corresponds to $rule_{ij}$. Based on these restrictions the possible investment opportunities $\{Y_1, Y_2, ...\}$ from K_j are filtered and ranked. From the investment alternatives for company X, the top-N companies $\{Y_1, Y_2, ..., Y_N\}$ are presented by the recommendation system to the user Fig. 5.

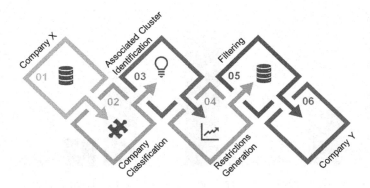

Fig. 4. For given company X recommendation process for investment opportunities

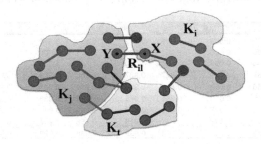

Fig. 5. Investment opportunity

5   Experiments and Results

From the original dataset of 7.5 million of companies the subset of investors who invested recently in startups (last 3 years) was selected. This produced a training dataset containing 112,062 tids and 322,445 companies which was used for experiments. For creating the investment behavior model 2,078,271 indirect association rules were generated using $minsup = 0.000025$ (about 3 investments per startup), $minconf = 0.5$ and $minlift = 1.0$ and 135,717 direct associations (frequent itemsets). There were 1,203 companies in total involved in some indirect association.

Example 1: Some indirect associations that are generated in this step, where a and b are indirectly associated items, i.e. investment alternatives:

```
(a=27 b=37|mediator=26) #sup(a,mediator)=3 #sup(b,mediator)=3
#conf(a,mediator)=1.0 #conf(b,mediator)=0.75

(a=155843 b=155844|mediator=155837 155839 155840 155850)
#sup(a,mediator)=3 #sup(b,mediator)=3
#conf(a,mediator)=1.0 #conf(b,mediator)=1.0
```

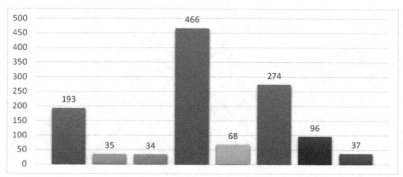

Fig. 6. Startups from the training set grouped in 8 clusters

	TP Rate	FP Rate	Precision	Recall	F-Measure	MCC	ROC Area	PRC Area	Class
	0.772	0.008	0.949	0.772	0.851	0.832	0.938	0.839	cluster1
	1.000	0.000	1	1.000	1	1.000	1	1	cluster2
	1.000	0.000	1	1.000	1	1.000	1	1	cluster3
	0.987	0.049	0.927	0.987	0.956	0.929	0.975	0.927	cluster4
	0.956	0.008	0.878	0.956	0.915	0.911	0.983	0.891	cluster5
	0.945	0.013	0.956	0.945	0.95	0.936	0.987	0.963	cluster6
	0.979	0.007	0.922	0.979	0.949	0.945	0.994	0.954	cluster7
	0.919	0.000	1	0.919	0.958	0.957	0.988	0.946	cluster8
Weighted Avg.	0.939	0.024	0.94	0.939	0.938	0.920	0.976	0.926	

Fig. 7. JRip classification rules accuracy for 8 clusters

Applying density based clustering these companies are grouped into 8 clusters (Fig. 6). The largest cluster (cluster4) contains US-based companies from technological industries that predominate in startups datasets and have common investment model. Despite this imbalance, the classification method JRip generated 39 rules with high accuracy (Fig. 7). In all generated rules the industry feature values were used as a condition. There were 5 rules that used the rank feature value as additional criterion and a few rules used some of the other features like funding, number of the investors and foundation year. The CN2 algorithm generated 215 rules for associated cluster identification and 99 rules for investment opportunity recommendation for 201 features. Weighted Relative Accuracy (WRAcc) was used as evaluation measure of rules search. Beam width was set to 20, and the learning mode to exclusive, the maximal length for rules was set to 15, and statistical significance – 1.0. Evaluation results for 10–fold cross validation with training set size 66% show high precision – 0.959, recall – 0.958 and F1–measure – 0.958.

In Example 1 the company $a = 27$ is classified in $cluster6$, and the company $b = 37$ is in $cluster1$. The features vectors (rank, investors, funding, foundationYear, location, numberEmployees, industry, cluster) for IAP of companies with IDs 27 and 37 are:

```
27:(0.00032,2,0.09,?,3175395,?,45103010;451030;45;4510,cluster6)
37:(0.00042,3,0.0,?,3175395,1-10,202010;20;20201070;2020,cluster1)
```

where "?" denotes missing value. We can see that both companies have comparable ranks, number of investors, same country location, but operate in different industry sectors.

For example for the company "Even Financial, Inc." the top 5 investment alternative recommendations generated were startup companies with the same location, comparable rank, similar number of employees and investors and funding, but from different industries – software, electronics, finance, technologies, merchandise. This shows that the experimental results support the main objective of the investment recommendation system to diversify the investment portfolio.

6   Conclusion and Further Work

We set ourselves the task of attempting to identify potential investment alternatives based on the historical data of investment events contained in our Knowledge Graph with over 7.5 million companies and 1.5 million financial transactions. We explored a variety of statistical approaches to the problem and evaluated their performance, finally identifying the most promising combination of algorithms for the task. Some initial feedback from financial experts is that there are some useful leads in the investment candidates suggested by the final algorithm although this is very much a pre-selection step and serious analysis by a human expert is required.

The immediate next step would be to define a more rigorous metric for evaluation and engage some domain experts to carry out. This would allow us to identify the specific strengths and weaknesses of the selected approach and provide a numerical evaluation of the performance so it can be used as a baseline in further iterations.

From a feature engineering perspective, the most useful next step would be to tackle the company descriptions with the use of a modern NLP approach that would perform meaningful text processing. This would most likely take the form of a neural network approach that can identify semantic similarities between company descriptions and reduce the similarity to a number that can be input into the existing algorithms.

References

1. Clark, P., Boswell, R.: Rule induction with CN2: some recent improvements. In: Kodratoff, Y. (ed.) EWSL 1991. LNCS, vol. 482, pp. 151–163. Springer, Heidelberg (1991). https://doi.org/10.1007/BFb0017011
2. Clark, P., Niblett, T.: The CN2 induction algorithm. Mach. Learn. **3**(4), 261–283 (1989)
3. Cohen, W.W.: Fast effective rule induction. In: Machine Learning Proceedings 1995, pp. 115–123. Elsevier (1995)

4. Ester, M., Kriegel, H.P., Sander, J., Xu, X., et al.: A density-based algorithm for discovering clusters in large spatial databases with noise. Kdd **96**(34), 226–231 (1996)
5. Grahne, G., Zhu, J.: High performance mining of maximal frequent itemsets. In: 6th International Workshop on High Performance Data Mining, vol. 16, p. 34 (2003)
6. Guo, H., Sun, B., Karimi, H.R., Ge, Y., Jin, W.: Fuzzy investment portfolioselection models based on interval analysis approach. Math. Probl. Eng. **2012**, 15 (2012)
7. Han, J., Pei, J., Yin, Y., Mao, R.: Mining frequent patterns without candidate generation: a frequent-pattern tree approach. Data Min. Knowl. Discov. **8**(1), 53–87 (2004)
8. Huang, W., Nakamori, Y., Wang, S.Y.: Forecasting stock market movement direction with support vector machine. Comput. Oper. Res. **32**(10), 2513–2522 (2005)
9. Musto, C., Semeraro, G., Lops, P., De Gemmis, M., Lekkas, G.: Personalized finance advisory through case-based recommender systems and diversification strategies. Decis. Support Syst. **77**, 100–111 (2015)
10. Paranjape-Voditel, P., Deshpande, U.: A stock market portfolio recommender system based on association rule mining. Appl. Soft Comput. **13**(2), 1055–1063 (2013)
11. Pazzani, M.J., Billsus, D.: Content-based recommendation systems. In: Brusilovsky, P., Kobsa, A., Nejdl, W. (eds.) The Adaptive Web. LNCS, vol. 4321, pp. 325–341. Springer, Heidelberg (2007). https://doi.org/10.1007/978-3-540-72079-9_10
12. Quah, T.S.: Improving returns on stock investment through neural network selection. In: Artificial Neural Networks in Finance and Manufacturing, pp. 152–164. IGI Global (2006)
13. Sayyed, F., Argiddi, R., Apte, S.: Generating recommendations for stock market using collaborative filtering. Int. J. Comput. Eng. Sci **3**, 46–49 (2013)
14. Shiue, W., Li, S.T., Chen, K.J.: A frame knowledge system for managing financial decision knowledge. Expert Syst. Appl. **35**(3), 1068–1079 (2008)
15. Stone, T., Zhang, W., Zhao, X.: An empirical study of top-n recommendation for venture finance. In: Proceedings of the 22nd ACM international conference on Conference on Information & Knowledge Management, pp. 1865–1868. ACM (2013)
16. Stone, T.R.: Computational analytics for venture finance. Ph.D. thesis, UCL (University College London) (2014)
17. Tan, P.-N., Kumar, V., Srivastava, J.: Indirect association: mining higher order dependencies in data. In: Zighed, D.A., Komorowski, J., Żytkow, J. (eds.) PKDD 2000. LNCS (LNAI), vol. 1910, pp. 632–637. Springer, Heidelberg (2000). https://doi.org/10.1007/3-540-45372-5_77
18. Tseng, C.C.: Portfolio management using hybrid recommendation system. In: 2004 IEEE International Conference on e-Technology, e-Commerce and e-Service, EEE 2004, pp. 202–206. IEEE (2004)
19. Yingsaeree, C., Nuti, G., Treleaven, P.: Computational finance. Computer **43**(12), 36–43 (2010)
20. Zhang, L., Zhang, H., Hao, S.: An equity fund recommendation system by combing transfer learning and the utility function of the prospect theory. J. Financ. Data Sci. **4**(4), 223–233 (2018)
21. Zhao, X., Zhang, W., Wang, J.: Risk-hedged venture capital investment recommendation. In: Proceedings of the 9th ACM Conference on Recommender Systems, pp. 75–82. ACM (2015)
22. Zibriczky, D.: Recommender systems meet finance: a literature review. In: CEUR-WS: Proceedings of the 2nd International Workshop on Personalization and Recommender Systems in Financial Services - FINREC 2016, vol. 1606, pp. 3–10 (2016)

BITA Workshop

BITA 2019 Workshop Chairs' Message

A contemporary challenge for enterprises is to keep up with the pace of changing business demands imposed on them in different ways. Today, there is an obvious demand for continuous improvement and alignment in enterprises but unfortunately many organizations do not have proper instruments (methods, tools, patterns, best practices, etc.) to achieve this. Enterprise modeling, enterprise architecture, and business process management are three areas belonging to traditions where the mission is to improve business practice and business and IT alignment (BITA). BITA has many times manifested through the transition of taking an enterprise from one state (AS-IS) into another improved state (TO-BE), i.e. a transformation of the enterprise and it's supporting IT into something that is regarded as better. A challenge with BITA is to move beyond a narrow focus on one tradition or technology. There is a need to be aware of and able to deal with a number of dimensions of the enterprise architecture and their relations in order to create alignment. Examples of such dimensions are: organizational structures, strategies, business models, work practices, processes, and IS/IT structures. Among the concepts that deserve special attention in this context is enterprise architecture management (EAM). An effective EAM aligns IT investments with overall business priorities, determines who makes the IT decisions and assigns accountability for the outcomes. IT governance is also a dimension that traditionally has had a strong impact on BITA. There are ordinarily three governance mechanisms that an enterprise needs to have in place: (1) decision-making structures, (2) alignment process, and (3) formal communications.

This workshop aimed to bring together people interested in BITA. We had invited researchers and practitioners from both industry and academia submit original results of their completed or ongoing projects. We encouraged a broad understanding of possible approaches and solutions for BITA, including EAM and IT governance subjects. Specific focus was on practices of business and IT alignment, i.e. we encouraged submission of case study and experience papers. The workshop received 11 submissions. The Program Committee selected seven submissions for presentation at the workshop. We thank all members of the Program Committee, authors, and local organizers for their efforts and support.

Ulf Seigerroth
Kurt Sandkuhl
Julia Kaidalova

Organization

Chairs

Ulf Seigerroth	Jönköping University, Sweden
Kurt Sandkuhl	Rostock University, Germany
Julia Kaidalova	Jönköping University, Sweden

Program Committee

Marite Kirikova	Riga Technical University, Latvia
Michael Fellmann	University of Rostock, Institute for Computer Science, Germany
Andreas L Opdahl	University of Bergen, Norway
Janis Stirna	Stockholm University, Sweden
Christina Keller	Jönköping University, Sweden
Vladimir Tarasov	Jönkoping University, Sweden
Alexander Smirnov	SPIIRAS, Russia
Nikolay Shilov	SPIIRAS, Russia
Björn Johansson	Lund University, Sweden
Jānis Grabis	Riga Technical University, Latvia
Stijn Hoppenbrouwers	HAN University of Applied Sciences, The Netherlands
Birger Lantow	University of Rostock, Germany
Henderik Proper	Public Research Centre Henri Tudor, Luxemburg

An Exploration of Enterprise Architecture Research in Hospitals

Johannes Wichmann[1,2(✉)] and Matthias Wißotzki[1]

[1] Wismar University of Applied Sciences, Philipp-Mueller-Street 14,
23966 Wismar, Germany
johannes.wichmann@hs-wismar.de
[2] University of Rostock, Albert-Einstein-Street 22, 18059 Rostock, Germany

Abstract. In the age of digitalization, enterprises, such as hospitals, have to be able to quickly react on new treatment patterns. The enterprise architecture management as a holistic view concept concerning an enterprises' IT infrastructure addresses such challenges, as the aim of the procedure is to foster the business-it-alignment. Considering, that analyzing IT infrastructures and respectively the maturity of them in hospitals is very complex for managers and stakeholders, an overview about the conducted research within this area is necessary. Therefore, this research provides a systematic literature review to represent an integral sight about relevant publications regarding the enterprise architecture management in hospitals.

Keywords: Systematic literature review and SLR · Enterprise architecture management and EAM · Hospitals

1 Introduction

In the age of digitalization, enterprises e.g. hospitals meet new challenges with different changes in services, patient treatments and organizational processes. To handle these challenges and to develop smart and fast services for patients, an appropriate architecture framework for the enterprise is necessary [1, 2]. Given that a hospital consists of a number of different components, e.g. business rules, processes, goals and actors, any of them contain a related sub-model while all of them result in the enterprise architecture of an organization [3]. The fact that integral approaches in terms of information technologies often lacks attention [4–7] and therefore the enterprise architecture maturity in hospitals is low [8–10], the aim of this paper is to provide an overview about process, business and reference models in terms of enterprise architectures within the hospital context during the last 18 years. To realize this goal, a systematic literature review (SLR) was conducted. Following the systematic literature review method by Kitchenham et al. [11], three main steps with corresponding sub-steps were necessary to accomplish a SLR. The first iteration was defined as the *review planning* and requires the definition of research questions (RQs), literature resources and a time frame for the examination (Sect. 2). Subsequently within the second step called *conduction of the review* (Sect. 3), the relevant articles were selected and data for answering the research questions was collected. The final stage of the systematic

© Springer Nature Switzerland AG 2019
W. Abramowicz and R. Corchuelo (Eds.): BIS 2019 Workshops, LNBIP 373, pp. 89–100, 2019.
https://doi.org/10.1007/978-3-030-36691-9_8

literature analysis (SLA) contains the *review report* (Sect. 4) including the papers' conclusion as well as the outlook about the current state of enterprise architecture related research activities in hospitals. Finally, Sect. 5 represents the conclusion and outlook and discusses the limitations within the current research, presented by the RQ5 in Sect. 4, to encourage further research regarding the gaps in enterprise architecture management in hospitals and approaches to tackle them.

2   Review Planning

In order to ensure that this paper will be transparent, conclusive and provides a comprehensive summary, contents like research activity including research teams and coherences, research approaches and identified concepts were relevant as the foundation for determining the research questions. The review was performed between April 2018 until February/March 2019.

2.1   Research Questions

The first part of the SLA process required the definition of research questions (RQ):

1. How much Enterprise Architecture activity in Hospitals has there been since 2000?
2. What are the addressed research topics?
3. Who is leading the Enterprise Architecture research in Hospitals?
4. What are the research approaches used?
5. What are the limitations of the current research?

The research papers selected as relevant will be examined and answered by the aforementioned RQs (Sect. 4).

2.2   Source Selection

Following the determination of research questions, the source selection process has to be defined. In order to gain a holistic view about the enterprise architecture management, the most important databases for computer and medical science, information systems as well as peer-reviewed literature in the academic community were needed. Those are AISeL, IEEE, Scopus, and SpringerLink. To gain a large validity while examining the publications, it was necessary that they were freely available. Concretely, the publications published at the databases, the Rostock University, the Wismar University of Applied Sciences as well as a guest account of the Helmut Schmidt University Hamburg had access to, were examined. Following this, the envisaged databases had to provide the possibility to execute user-defined search-strings. The application ensured that the specification of search results dedicated the aim of this research, as relevant publications hat to be determined.

2.3   Time Frame Selection

To ascertain, that the selected research publications represent the current state and that they are contemporary, an appropriate time frame was necessary. Given that, the determination of the envisaged period proves itself to be problematic as different other publications with similar research perceptions use different time frames. Malik et al. [12] conducted their research of data mining and predictive analytics application for the delivery of healthcare services between 2001 and 2015. Erdogan and Tarhan [13] chose the period from 2005 until 2017 to ascertain research publications referring process mining in healthcare. Wißotzki [14] investigated capability research within the enterprise architecture management context from 2000 to 2014. Since this research handled the investigation of enterprise architecture management in healthcare, respectively hospitals, a time frame from 2000 until 2018 was determined appropriate considering the periods selected by the researchers with similar research aims.

3   Conduction of the Review

After identifying the questions, sources and time frame, this section summarizes the selection of publications, determines their relevance, depicts the data extraction and tasks derived from the data synthesis. This chapter provides the explanation for publications in terms of relevance and their dedication for answering the aforementioned RQs.

3.1   Article Selection

As it is the aim of this paper to gain a holistic view of publications in the research area, search strings were necessary to refine the results. To ensure that, purposeful sampling strategies following Palinkas et al. [40] were used. First, a Criterion-e emphasis was chosen to determine the relevant paper by using the terms *clinic, sanatorium* combined with *enterprise architecture, business architecture, business reference model, process model, BPMN, IT architecture, digital transformation, reference architecture* and *architecture framework*. To avoid medical publications, a full text analysis for the terms *IT, information systems, information technology, IT system, computer technology* and *technology system* was conducted. Afterwards, a similarity approach considering the homogeneity by Palinkas et al. [40] was used. In order to reduce variation, sub-groups were implemented according the publications' focus and will be presented in RQ2 and later discussed in RQ5. A paper was selected as relevant if the research was conducted in a hospital context with a focus regarding enterprise architecture or at least some kind of process management and improvement dedicated to enhance the hospitals' work performance. The conscious broader approach followed the researcher's underpinning, that process improvements are an important part of EAM, especially in the early stage of EAM implementation [41] and therefore relevant for this research considering the assumption of low EA maturity in hospitals mentioned in Sect. 1. Ultimately, after eliminating non-relevant publications, **405 articles** were selected as pertinent. **220/405**

publications were issued in **173 conference proceedings** and **185/405 articles** in **110 journals**. 1258 researcher in 57 countries investigate in this context.

3.2 Data Collection

Within the data collection, the publications classified as relevant were completely read, analyzed and the data was extracted und documented by the following restrictions: *publication year, author(s), title, keyword(s), research approach, research methodology, research question, journal/conference name, relevance: hospital, IT, process management, frameworks*. The aspects were used as columns in a literature database to secure the collected data and as the foundation to describe the following review report.

4 Review Report

In relation to the aforementioned research questions (Sect. 2), this section will represent the review process and answer the RQs.

RQ1: *How much Enterprise Architecture activity in Hospitals has there been since 2000?*

As presented in Fig. 1 (dotted line), the enterprise architecture research in hospital became more and more popular since 2000.

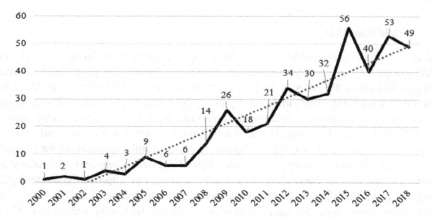

Fig. 1. Trend and number of relevant publications per year

Concerning the topic of this research, an increasing interest in enterprise architecture research can be noticed in 2008 and 2009 with a surge from 14 to 26 publications. Simultaneously, enhanced numbers of process research papers [15, 16] as well as simulation [17, 18] and mining publications [19] regarding this context emerged. The ongoing development of BPMN based on Version 1.1 published in 2008 [20] and the general increasing of computer performances [21] might be explanations for this phenomenon. Between 2015 and 2018, the majority of publications arose (47%). Thomas et al. [22] mentioned that new technologies, such as micro-services, are a suitable solution for data analysis in hospitals and therefore could be the reason for the increased amount of publications. The most relevant database for the research process was Scopus, with 220 publications overall, including 149 journal articles (JA), 3 book chapters and 68 conference proceedings (CP). AISeL was very important for CPs (100, 8 JA), same as IEEE (60 CPs). In addition to that, the IEEE Access, Engineering and Transactions series were useful as well, with 11 JA. Concerning SpringerLink as the last investigated database and after eliminating redundancy, 5 JA were considered. In addition to that, Fig. 2 exemplifies the most relevant conferences for this research.

- Americas Conference on Information Systems
- European Conference on Information Systems
- Hawaii International Conference on System Sciences
- International Conference on Information Systems
- Pacific Asia Conference on Information Systems
- Bled eConference
- Winter Simulation Conference
- International Conference on Health Informatics
- IEEE International Conference on Healthcare Informatics

Fig. 2. Relevant conferences with ≥ 4 publications

As represented via Fig. 2 the AMCIS is the most relevant conference for the approach (27/220), followed by the ECIS (20/220), HICSS (13/220), ICIS (10/220) and PACIS (10/220). The most intensive research activities have been ascertained between 2015 and 2018 with ≥ 40 articles per year and 47% of all relevant publications. The increase of published literature from 32 articles in 2014 to 56 publications in 2015 is conspicuous. Furthermore, the explicit architecture management focus in publishing developed from 3 in 2014 to 8 in 2015. The same holds true for journals, who became more relevant for the community, as only 14 articles were intended in 2014, whereas 27 were issued in 2015. By comparing the search string output between conference proceedings and journal articles with architecture management interest, it is apparent that 49 investigations were conducted via conference proceedings while 20 were issued in journals. Considering 2018, it might be possible, that the number of 49 articles could rise, given the fact that only the conferences and journals could be considered, who already submitted their publications. Therefore, this research will be a foundation for further investigations regarding literature in enterprise architecture management for hospitals. Concerning the journals, the Lecture Notes in Computer Science (12/185) is the most relevant journal for this investigation, followed by the Lecture Notes in Business Information Processing (10/185), Procedia Computer Science (9/185), the Journal of Biomedical Informatics (8/185) and Studies in Health Technology and Informatics (7/185). In opposite to the five most relevant conferences (36%), one of the top five journals conducted every fourth publication. Anyhow, the portion of publications in relation to a specific conference or journal could be considered heterogeneous. For further investigations, conferences like the Bled eConference, the IEEE conferences as well as, on the behalf of journals the Communications of the Association of Information Systems or the IEEE journals could be implicit relevant for enterprise architectures in hospitals.

RQ2: *What are the addressed research topics?*

Considering, that many different disciplines are important for the development of enterprise architectures, the following section will describe the top ten with an amount ≥ 6 publications by categorizing them. Furthermore, the fundamental interests will be exposed.

-1- *Process Management* (132 publications) includes *Clinical Pathways* and *Lean Management* and handles process publications through various hospital departments. As processes are a key element concerning architecture management, respectively the business layer [23], this category is very important for the research. -2- *Architecture Management* (69) contains all publications regarding framework implementation (e.g. Archimate, TOGAF etc.) with different characteristics (e.g. Design Thinking, service-oriented architecture). -3- *Platform Development & Management* (40) depicts different implementations of systems and devices and their outcome on hospitals. -4- *Process Mining* (38) contains *Data Management* and aims to divine different scenarios in hospitals, e.g. duration of staying, surgeries for specific treatments etc. -5- *Decision Management* (35) represents articles who contain topics like forecasting of inpatients, predicting durations of surgeries and optimal allocation of CT scan capacity. -6- *Conformance Management* (16) deals with awareness in relation to clinical guidelines, health IT policy, medication compliance, appointment rule designs and organizational constrains. -7- *Simulation Management* (16) deals with simulation based planning and scheduling of hospital processes while -8- *Quality Management* (9) describes hangovers in service systems as well as data quality in hospitals. -9- *Knowledge Management* (8) implements the knowledge to improve patient centered care, surgical workflows and performances of hospital professionals. -10- *Petri Net Models* (6) investigate process repair methods.

Concerning the publications with explicit enterprise architecture management reference, 69 paper were ascertained. Thereby it is conspicuous, that the subjects' importance is rising. Between 2000 and 2008, 12 publications were published, while 24 were released within the last 4 years. As a variety of the research paper affect different disciplines, e.g. process management in order to improve the hospital information infrastructure, this might be an indication to conduct further investigations.

RQ3: *Who is leading the Enterprise Architecture research in Hospitals?*

In order to gain a holistic view about the authors and institutes active in this research area, them and their relevant institutions have been documented as well. For further investigations, it will be helpful to be aware of the engaged scientists in the enterprise architecture research in hospitals. Moreover, research connections between institutions will be demonstrated to clarify task forces within this area. Figure 3 exemplifies every research-involved country with five proportions concerning their amount of researcher.

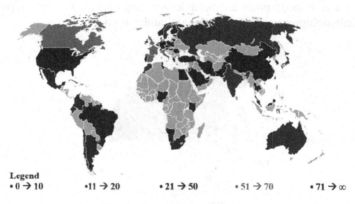

Legend
• 0 → 10   •11 → 20   • 21 → 50   • 51 → 70   • 71 → ∞

Fig. 3. Researcher per Country

Altogether 57 countries were involved in the research process, with the USA contributing the most, as every sixth scientist belongs to the United States of America (221/1258). In addition, Germany (140/1258) and China (73/1258) belong to the top category of 71+ researcher within this area, followed by Italy (69/1258), Spain (62/1258), France (60/1258), the Netherlands (54/1258), the United Kingdom (54/1258) and Canada (53/1258) as part of the second category with 50 to 70 scientists. Regarding the relevant institutions, a cooperation between the College of Biomedical Engineering and Instrument Science as part of the Zhejiang University in Hangzhou China on one side and the Department of Mathematics and Computer Science, respectively the Data Science Center and Analytics for Information Systems on the other, exist. In conclusion, the alliance published 24 relevant articles. Whereas Huilong Duan is the most active researcher in China (9/24), Will M. P. van der Aalst (7/24) and Ronny S. Mans (5/24) are the brisk counterparts in the Netherlands. Besides the Chinese-Netherland-Connection, the Chair of Business Informatics, Esp. Systems Engineering as part of the Faculty of Business and Economics of the Dresden University of Technology is active within this research area as well. Under guidance of the holder of the chair, Werner Esswein, the team contributed 9 relevant paper. Furthermore, the Royal Melbourne Institute of Technology in Australia (7/405), the Shandong University of Science and Technology (5/405) and the Polytechnic Institute of Leiria (4/405) are worth considering as important institutions concerning this research.

RQ4: *What are the research approaches used?*

In order to the SLAs demand of completeness, the research approaches and methods of the relevant publications have to be ascertained. Considering IS research, Wilde et al. [24] and Oesterle et al. [25] determined two generally research approaches, the design science research on one hand and behavioristic research methods on the other. Proto-typing, simulation, reference modeling, conceptual-deductive, argumentative-deductive analysis and action research are the main elements in design science research. Grounded theory, quantitative-empirical analysis, qualitative-empirical analysis, case studies, experiments and ethnographies are behavioristic approaches. Figure 4 represents the research methodologies used for the relevant publications.

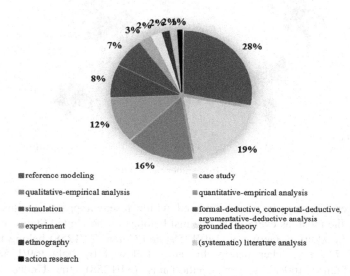

Fig. 4. Research approaches

RQ5: *What are the limitations of the current research?*

As mentioned and illustrated in RQ2, different research disciplines were determined relevant concerning this research. In order to research approaches within a discipline and with similar aims, the emerging of resembling limitations was conspicuous. To ensure, that validity is given in regard to the limitations, those of the top five categories of RQ2 will be presented and were:

-1- Process Management with constraints concerning the business IT alignment and the willingness to implement new systems, respectively insufficient change management [26]. Furthermore, deficient documentations of supply chains [27] or working activities [28] aggravated the modeling and improving of processes. In unison, the *-2- Architecture Management* clarified similar problems with unclear EA architect roles [8], inappropriate enterprise frameworks [1], communication problems, management understanding, commitment and weak EA governance [8, 29] as well as low EA maturity [8]. Regarding the *-3- Platform Development & Management* the

unwillingness in terms of change is present as well [30]. Besides that, the platform developments were often limited to an initial test, which requires a longtime study for further evaluation [31] or only designed for specific departments or process sections of a hospital, without a holistic approach [17]. In relation to *-4- Process Mining* different tools, like ProM [32] or pMineR [33] were used and given that case studies were conducted, further research is necessary to validate the findings [13, 32–34]. To foster the *-5- Decision Management*, a better documentation of hospital activities and pathways is necessary for this discipline as well [35]. In addition to that, the findings connect to the ones of *-3- Platform Development & Management*, as the scope of the prototypes were narrow [36] and often addressed a specific treatment case [37, 38]. By considering the purposive sampling method regarding the limitations of the homogeneous groups, the mentioned paper were selected as representatives of their respective groups, as they are determined as most relevant by the user-defined search-string. Following the EA maturity model levels of Jahani et al. [41] and Kaisler et al. [42] the maturity of the representatives is presented by Fig. 5.

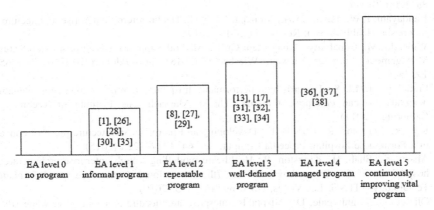

Fig. 5. EA maturity ranking of representative publications

5   Conclusion and Outlook

As hospitals face new challenges in terms of information technology and architectures, the aim of this research was to represent a holistic view about enterprise architecture management within this area. Therefore, a relevant time frame, databases, conferences, journals, the research community as well as methodologies and limitations were presented. By considering the findings represented in Fig. 5, the gaps in enterprise architecture management in hospitals become clear. Given the user-defined search-string, none of the determined researches provides an enterprise architecture level 5 with a continuously improving vital program. Respectively, further research regarding enterprise architecture management could focus on this or else existing approaches (like [36] to [38]) could be developed continuously to assure a holistic enterprise architecture over all functions and processes within a hospital.

Nonetheless, this research was limited by quantitative and qualitative factors. The former could be eliminated by an extension of the selected time frame or additional library literature infrastructures to evoke supplementary publications. Concerning qualitative aspects, the SLA procedure might be converted differently, as the design of the search string and the assessment of relevant articles is handled in a diverse manner by every researcher. For further research, different restrictions have to be considered, as they influence the enterprise architecture implementation process [1, 39]. Therefore, researcher should concretely determine their field of investigation to assure, that specific restrictions, e.g. by countries, are heeded. Additional systematic literature reviews could encounter this limitation.

References

1. Haghighathoseini, A., Bobarshad, H., Saghafi, F., et al.: Hospital enterprise Architecture Framework (Study of Iranian University Hospital Organization). Int. J. Med. Inform. **114**, 88–100 (2018)
2. Handayani, P.W., Pinem, A.A., Munajat, Q., et al.: Health referral enterprise architecture in Indonesia. Health Inform. Res. **25**(1), 3–11 (2019)
3. Wißotzki, M.: Capability Management Guide. Method Support for Enterprise Architectures Management. Springer Vieweg, Wiesbaden (2018). https://doi.org/10.1007/978-3-658-19233-4
4. Frandinho, J.M.D.S.: Towards high performance hospital enterprise architectures: elevating hospitals to lean enterprise thinking. Thesis, Massachusetts Institute of Technology, Cambridge (2011)
5. Rijo, R., Martinho, R., Ermida, D.: Developing an Enterprise Architecture proof of concept in a Portuguese hospital. Procedia Comput. Sci. **64**, 1217–1225 (2015)
6. Ahsan, K., Shah, H., Kingston, P.: Healthcare modelling trough enterprise architecture: a hospital case. In: Proceedings of the 7th International Conference on Information Technology – ITNG, Las Vegas, USA, pp. 460–465 (2010)
7. Oliviera, J., Nightingale, D.: Adaptable enterprise architecture and long term value added partnerships in healthcare. In: Proceedings of the 15th European Conference on Information Systems – ECIS, St. Gallen, Switzerland (2007)
8. Olsen, D.H.: Enterprise Architecture management challenges in the Norwegian health sector. Procedia Comput. Sci. **121**, 637–646 (2017)
9. Ajer, A.K.S., Hustad, E., Vassilakopoulou, P.: Enterprise architects' logics across organizational levels: a case study in the norwegian hospital sector. In: MCIS 2018 Proceedings, p. 6 (2018)
10. Schooley, B., Hikmet, N.: Design of an enterprise architecture for electronic patient care record (ePCR) information exchange in EMS. In: Proceedings of the 19th Americas Conference on Information Systems – AMCIS, Chicago, USA (2013)
11. Kitchenham, B.: Procedures for performing systematic reviews. Keele University, Keele (2004)
12. Malik, M.M., Abdallah, S., Ala'raj, M.: Data mining and predictive analytics applications for the delivery of healthcare services: a systematic literature review. Ann. Oper. Res. **270**(1–2), 287–312 (2018)
13. Erdogan, T.G., Tarhan, A.: Systematic mapping of process mining studies in healthcare. IEEE Access **6**, 24543–24567 (2018)

14. Wißotzki, M.: An exploration on capability research. In: Proceedings of the 19th IEEE International Enterprise Distributed Object Computing Conference – EDOC, Adelaide, Australia, pp. 179–184 (2015)
15. Rojo, M.G., Rolon, E., Calahorra, L., et al.: Implementation of the Business Process Modeling Notation (BPMN) in the modelling of anatomic pathology processes. Diagn. Pathol. 3(1), 22 (2008)
16. Gemmel, P., Vandaele, D., Tambeur, W.: Hospital Process Orientation (HPO); the development of a measurement tool. Total Qual. Manag. Bus. Excellence 19(12), 1207–1217 (2008)
17. Fitzgerald, J.A., Dadich, A.: Using visual analytics to improve hospital scheduling and patient flow. J. Theor. Appl. Electr. Commer. Res. 4(2), 20–30 (2009)
18. Denz, C., Baumgart, A., Zoeller, A., et al.: Perspectives of OR management: from process analysis to simulation-based planning and scheduling. Anasthesiologie und Intensivmedizin 49(2), 85–93 (2008)
19. Mans, R.S., Schonenberg, H., Song, M., et al.: Process mining in healthcare – a case study. In: Proceedings of the International Conference on Health Informatics, Funchal, Portugal, vol. 1, pp. 28–31 (2008)
20. Object Management Group: About the Business Process Modeling Notation Specification Version 1.1. https://www.omg.org/spec/BPMN/1.1. Accessed 19 Apr 2019
21. Xiu, L.: Time Moore – exploiting Moore's law from the perspective of time. IEEE Solid-State Circuits Mag. 11(1), 39–55 (2019)
22. Thomas, M.A., Abraham, D.S., Liu, D.: Federated machine learning for translational research. In: Proceedings of the 23th Americas Conference on Information Systems – AMCIS, New Orleans, USA (2018)
23. Cabrera, A., Abad, M., Jaramillo, D., Gómez, J., Verdum, J.C.: Definition and implementation of the enterprise business layer through a business reference model, using the architecture development method ADM-TOGAF. In: Mejia, J., Muñoz, M., Rocha, Á., Calvo-Manzano, J. (eds.) Trends and Applications in Software Engineering. AISC, vol. 405, pp. 111–121. Springer, Cham (2016). https://doi.org/10.1007/978-3-319-26285-7_10
24. Wilde, T., Hess, T.: Forschungsmethoden der Wirtschaftsinformatik. Wirtschaftsinformatik 49(4), 280–287 (2007)
25. Oesterle, H., Becker, J., Frank, U., et al.: Memorandum on design-oriented information systems research. Eur. J. Inf. Syst. 20(1), 7–10 (2011)
26. Cordeiro, A.L.A.O., Fernandes, J.D., et al: Structural capital in the nursing management in hospitals. Texto contexto – enferem 27(2), 1–10 (2018)
27. Chanpuypetch, W., Kritchanchai, D.: A design thinking framework and design patterns for hospital pharmacy management. Int. J. Healthcare Manag. 30(1), 1–9 (2019)
28. Ceglowski, A., Churilov, L.: Towards process-of-care aware emergency department information systems. Int. J. Healthcare Syst. Inform. 3(4), 1–16 (2008)
29. Azevedo, C.L.B., Almeida, J.P.A., Van Sinderen, M., et al.: Towards capturing strategic planning in EA. In: 19th IEEE International Enterprise Distributed Object Computing Workshop – EDOCW, Adeliade, Australia, pp. 159–168 (2015)
30. Nan, S., Van Gorp, P., Lu, X., et al.: A meta-model for computer executable dynamic clinical safety checklists. BMC Med. Inform. Decis. Mak. 17(1), 170 (2017)
31. Mettler, T.: Contextualizing a professional social network for health care. Experiences from a action design research study. Inf. Syst. J. 28(4), 684–707 (2018)
32. Ganesha, K., Dhanush, S., Swapnil Raj, S.M.: An approach to fuzzy process mining to reduce patient waiting time in a hospital. In: Proceedings of the 4th International Conference on Innovations in Information, Embedded and Communication Systems – ICIIECS, Coimbatorie, India, pp. 1–6 (2017)

33. Gatta, R., Montesi, M., Marchetti, A., et al.: Generating and comparing knowledge graphs of medical processes using pMiner. In: Proceedings of the Knowledge Capture Conference, Austin, USA, p. 36 (2017)
34. Kukreja, G., Batra, S.: Analogize process mining techniques in healthcare: spesis case study. In: Proceedings of the 4th International Conference on Signal Processing, Computing and Control – IPSCC, Solan, India, pp. 482–487 (2017)
35. Tsuru, S., Wako, F., Omiri, M., et al.: Problem solving for volatilizing situation in nursing: developing thinking process supporting system using NursingNAVI® contents. In: Studies in Health Technology and Informatics, vol. 210, pp. 541–545 (2015)
36. Lærum, H., Bremer, S., Bergan, S., et al.: A taste of individualized medicine: physicians' reactions to automated genetic interpretations. J. Am. Med. Inform. Assoc. 21(e1), e143–e146 (2013)
37. Tofangchi, S., Hanelt, A., Böhrnsen, F.: Distributed cognitive expert systems in cancer data analytics: a decision support system for oral and macillofacial surgery. In: Proceedings of the 38th International Conference on Information Systems – ICIS, Seoul, South Korea, pp. 1–21 (2017)
38. Riekert, M., Premm, M., Klein, A., et al.: Predicting the duration of surgeries to improve process efficiency in hospitals. In: Proceedings of the 25th European Conference on Information Systems – ECIS, Guimarães, Portugal, pp. 2842–2851 (2017)
39. Chen, Y.P., Hsieh, S.H., Cheng, P.H., et al.: An agile enterprise regulation architecture for health information security management. Telemed. J. e-health: Official J. Am. Telemed. Assoc. 16(7), 807–817 (2010)
40. Palinkas, L.A., Horwitz, S.M., Green, C.A., et al.: Purposeful sampling for qualitative data collection and analysis in mixed method implementation research. Adm. Policy Ment. Health Ment. Health Serv. Res. 42(5), 533–544 (2016)
41. Jahani, B., Javadein, S.R.S., Jafari, H.A.: Measurement of enterprise architecture readiness within organizations. Bus. Strategy Ser. 11(3), 177–191 (2010)
42. Kaisler, S.H., Armour, F., Valivullah, M.: Enterprise architecting: critical problems. In: Proceedings of 38th Hawaii International Conference on System Sciences – HICSS, Big Island, USA, pp. 1–10 (2005)

In Search for a Viable Smart Product Model

João Barata$^{(\boxtimes)}$ and Paulo Rupino da Cunha

CISUC, Department of Informatics Engineering, University of Coimbra,
Pólo II, Pinhal de Marrocos, 3030-290 Coimbra, Portugal
{barata,rupino}@dei.uc.pt

Abstract. Smart products integrate physical and digital materialities, taking advantage of sensors, mobile technologies, and advanced data processing capabilities. This type of systems is a top priority for managers, offering the capacity to sense, communicate, adapt, and anticipate the needs of business stakeholders. We use the lens of the Viable System Model (VSM) theory to align business strategies and smart products. The proposed model was tested in a real case of information systems development for safety in construction. The findings emerge from a design science research that is part of a larger project to introduce smart technologies in the construction industry. A viable product model (VPM) represents the necessary and sufficient conditions for the smart product cohesion and endurance in different environments, aligned to the business needs. For theory, we present a product-level adoption of VSM and propose guidelines for business-smart product alignment. For practice, the results can assist managers in creating new smart products that adhere to their strategy and capable of dealing with unexpected events.

Keywords: Viable Product Model · Viable System Model · Industry 4.0 · Smart product · Construction

1 Introduction

Products are increasingly digitalized, reconfiguring the socio-technical relationships with users, adding new capabilities to physical objects, and changing their traditional lifecycles. It has been recognized that "*the most important feature of digital innovation is successful generation of new IT-enabled products, processes, and services. Despite its salience, exploration of digital innovation outcomes has received very little attention in the literature*" [1]. Products, or, more precisely, the new smart and digital-physical products [2], concern different C-level executives of the organization, matching the relevance of IT for process improvement initiatives. We agree with [3] that "*IS scholars need to question and complement their received models of aligning IT to business strategy (…), must imagine new digital strategy frameworks that identify new sources of value creation such as generativity, heterogeneity, digital product platforms, and meaning-making capability [...developing] new strategic frameworks that are aimed at deliberately harnessing the unique capabilities of digital technology that are embedded into products*".

Over three decades ago seminal studies identified the competitive importance of aligning business and IT investments [4], focusing strategic developments "*as the*

© Springer Nature Switzerland AG 2019
W. Abramowicz and R. Corchuelo (Eds.): BIS 2019 Workshops, LNBIP 373, pp. 101–112, 2019.
https://doi.org/10.1007/978-3-030-36691-9_9

interplay between a dynamic environment and bureaucratic momentum" [5] where the technologies are at the core of organizational transformation. More recently, "alignment" is seen as a dynamic process that requires continuous adjustments between business functions and applications [6]. Several studies suggest the positive impact of alignment in company performance, namely in the aspects of (1) IT-business communications; (2) value analytics; (3) approaches to collaborative governance; (4) nature of the partnership; (5) scope of IT initiatives; and (6) development of IT skills [7]. However, there is a lack of studies that address the emergent smart products and their alignment to organizational strategies.

Business/IT alignment (BITA) is essential for business viability, so it is warranted to examine it using the lens of influential theories such as the Viable System Model (VSM), originally proposed by the British theorist and professor Stafford Beer [8]. VSM has been widely discussed during the last decades and asserts the necessary and sufficient conditions for the viability of an organization [8–10]. The necessity to align business and IT at the product level [11] and the opportunity to explore a sound theory for *viable systems* in this context motivated two research goals for this paper:

1. Understand how the Viable System Model theory has been addressed in business/IT alignment literature for product level of analysis;
2. Design a Viable System Model for smart products, aligning industry 4.0 strategies and information technologies.

The rest of the paper is organized as follows. Section 2 explains our design science research approach, aiming to integrate smart technologies in construction safety. Subsequently, we review relevant literature on VSM and smart products. Section 4 presents the design and development of the Viable Product Model (VPM). In Sect. 5, we discuss the findings and suggest specific guidelines to align business and product-level IT adoption. Finally, we highlight the main contribution to the field of BITA, the study limitations, and the avenues for future research.

2   Research Approach

The design-science research (DSR) paradigm [12] has its foundations in the work of [13]. DSR enables the creation and evaluation of artifacts to solve specific organizational problems, which can "*be in the form of a construct, a model, a method, or an instantiation*" [12], integrating informational, technological, and social aspects. Although the maturity of the use of industry 4.0 technologies (e.g. Internet of Things (IoT), mobile, cloud) is high in sectors such as automotive, their use in more traditional industries needs further research.

The research presented in this paper is part of a larger DSR project that aims to create smart products for occupational health and safety (OHS) in construction [14]. The project has involved two companies of a Portuguese construction group (C1: consulting, training, safety inspections; and C2: construction equipment supplier) that were interested in adopting industry 4.0 technologies in their businesses. After developing several prototypes for safety with IoT and a comprehensive system to improve OHS in construction, it became clear that the alignment of smart products for

OHS required a viable model of the business and of the technological portfolio. It was necessary to represent the fundamental building blocks of smart products and their relation to the environment in the construction site, ensuring the conditions to become viable. The Viable System Model [8] seemed to be an interesting solution to test.

According to [15], after the (1) identification of the problem and motivation and (2) definition the objectives for a solution, DSR evolves through (3) design and development, (4) demonstration, (5) evaluation, and (6) communication. Our design and development proceeded with a structured literature review to identify the use of VSM for product modeling and, particularly, for the design of smart products. Afterward, we adopted VSM to the product level of analysis in BITA and demonstrate its use with a smart product for construction safety. The evaluation of the research enabled us to propose guidelines to model viable products, aligning technological innovations with the business strategy (industry 4.0 in our case). The communication step of DSR is in the form of a scientific publication and sharing our results with the participating companies.

3   Literature Review

We have selected Google Scholar for our review of the core literature. It was selected because it offers wide coverage of highly-cited documents and citations in three essential fields to the topic of business IT alignment, namely, (1) Business, Economics & Management, (2) Engineering & Computer Science, and (3) Social Sciences [16].

Surprisingly, a search in Google Scholar with the keyword combination "business IT alignment" AND "viable system model" (April 6, 2019; excluding patents and citations) only returned 43 results. Among these contributions we can find the keynote speech by Prof. Jose Perez Rios at PoEM 2013, presenting how VSM can be used for information systems development *"constructing models with sufficient variety (the capacity to deal with complexity) to respond to current problems"* [17]. We attended that inspirational keynote that was our starting point to reflect about the potential of VSM for product development efforts. Yet, none of the studies found in our initial search adopted VSM to ensure smart product development is aligned with company strategy.

In a second review round we used the keywords "viable system model" AND ("Iot" OR "internet of things"), since we were particularly interested in the smart product design supported by IoT. This search has yielded 117 results, suggesting that the efforts to adopt VSM in the IoT context are more popular. Nevertheless, we could not find any study for our purpose and extended the review with additional keywords, namely, "viable system model" + "smart product". We obtained 3 results, with only two of them using VSM [18, 19]. The work of [19] presents a research in progress for a VSM meta-model for manufacturing control with smart objects, while [18] reviews key literature to identify challenges in the design of systems that react to unpredicted events. We still could not find empirical studies for the product-level of alignment that merges physical and digital elements in new product development.

The third review round identified studies addressing product viability (not restricted to smart products) and VSM used the keyword combination "viable product model" in

Google Scholar. This search returned 15 studies, however, none adopted VSM for the purpose of product viability. The second round of search terms using "viable system model" + "product level" (18 studies) and "viable system model" + "product model" with 25 results. Other keywords used in our research were "viable system model" + "smart product service system" (0 results) and "viable system model" + "product service system" with 22 results. Among these, we highlight [20] where VSM is used to analyze the integration of products and services in defense contracts. The authors argue that servitization requires a shift from a product-centric view to a relational-process view of solutions and evaluates variety in this type of contracts. This work – although not addressing the design of product-service systems and its alignment to organizational strategies – has strengthened our belief that VSM can provide a valuable lens for product-service system contexts. The next subsection discusses the fundamentals of VSM.

3.1 Viable System Model

The work of Stafford Beer was hugely influenced by W. Ross Ashby (1903–1972), author of the law of requisite variety – a measure of the number of states a system can take up, stating that it could succeed *"only if it disposed of as much variety as the environment in which it existed"* [21]. Ashby created an electromechanics device named homeostat that simulated the ability of organisms to keep the blood temperature constant independently of the environmental conditions [22]. This device was an inspiration to the efforts of S. Beer to create adaptive organizations, including the automatic factory controlled by computers [8, 21]. In fact, *"VSM is primarily a tool to observe institutions and to support connectivity in the quest for desirable transformation"* [10].

Our study resorts to key VSM definitions summarized by [10]. First, a viable system is *"able to maintain a separate existence"*, possessing the capacity to respond to known and unexpected events (e.g. catastrophes). Second, an organization *"is a 'closed' network of people in interaction producing a whole"* with rules and mechanisms for decision making, identified by human relations. Third, the organization structure *"emerges from stable forms of communication, or mechanisms, which permit the parts* [e.g. people roles or departments] *of an organisation to operate together as a whole* [...and] *suggests the relevance of understanding both the contribution of technology and other resources to organisational processes and the influence of structure in the design of communication and information systems"*.

There are two key mechanisms for viability, namely, *cohesion* and *adaptation* [8, 10, 21]. The first mechanism allows people to produce collective meaning, aligning individual (autonomous) interests with the entire organization. This mechanism involves functions of implementation, cohesion, negotiation, coordination between different units (e.g. lateral communication) and monitoring. The second mechanism is an adaptation, because organizations must evolve according to the (internal/external) environmental changes that occur over time, requiring appropriate policies and intelligence functions. Both mechanisms are essential for recursive organizations (all its units have a structure that enables knowledge meaning creation, regulation and implementation [10]) where all its sub-systems are also viable systems [23]. The VSM model is represented in Fig. 1.

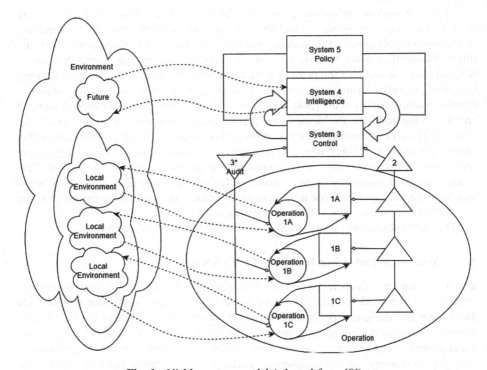

Fig. 1. Viable system model (adapted from [8]).

The VSM includes at least five main levels or systems that are inspired by biology [10]. System 1 includes the primary activities that support the business (e.g., different subsidiaries of an organization as presented by [21]). According to [9], these autonomous units *"conduct and optimize the daily business-in the 'here and now'"*. System 2, like the nervous system, allows communication and interconnections between System 1 elements and with System 3 (executive management), related to the controls and resources that allows managers to react to changes in Systems 1–2. System 4 is responsible for monitoring and understanding adaptation needs (e.g., research and development, orientation toward the long-term), collecting and showing information from the outside world, and lower levels of VSM. Finally, System 5 directs the whole organization, defining policies, norms, values, and balancing the different parts of the firm [8–10].

According to [8], the performance of System 1 activities can be measured according to its actuality (what the activity is accomplishing now with existing resources), capability (what it should be achieving now with the same resources) and potentiality (*ought to be*, developing resources and removing constraints – a main responsibility of System 4). Moreover, recursion is a key aspect in VSM because *"any viable system contains, and is contained in, a viable system*" [8], allowing to consider multiple levels of abstraction in the model creation. Each System 1 element can be seen as a viable system.

There are multiple relationships to consider [8, 9]. The vertical channel (relation between System 1 and System 3) includes the negotiation of objectives and exceptional intervention if cohesion is at risk. Relationship 1-2-3 attempts to reduce complexity and filters information from System 1, while 3* allows auditing the company system. Relationship 3-4 includes the process of strategic development and stability, balancing long-term *vs* short term needs, and the internal and external environment analysis. Finally, relationship Systems (3-4)-5 aims to moderate interactions between Systems 3 and 4, solving conflicts. Problems in these systems and their relations pose risks to the viability of the organization, which is composed of a structure with multiple layers that recursively interact. In this context, a *"product is thus not a separate object; objects are recursively constructed objects in language. The perceiver and the perceived arise together in the discourse of value creation"* [24]. More recently [24] adopted the VSM and requisite variety to propose a framework describing the systemic relations of value co-creation for product innovation and development.

The next subsection explores VSM for the product level of alignment.

3.2   Towards a Viable Product Model with VSM

The VSM lens has been recently used to address business/IT alignment issues, for example, in the work of [25] and [26] for IT governance. VSM can be used for diagnosing and designing organizations, as illustrated in the five case studies of [27], namely, *"transformation of a company"*, *"redesign of a meta-system"* for the top management, *"enhancing cohesion"* of different divisions of the organization, *"developing strategy"*, and *"examining corporate ethos"* to change auditing approaches.

Some examples adopt VSM for enterprise architecture management [28, 29], but most of the studies adopting the VSM address the organizational context and its self-regulation capacity, namely, corporations, public organizations, or nations [9]. Interestingly, a decisive influence in the VSM theory comes from a specific machine with the capacity to 'sense' the environment – Ashby's homeostat. Therefore, VSM should be a potential theory for the design of smart 'viable' products that can sense the environment and adapt to different conditions that are relevant to the business strategy.

We found two contributions particularly relevant for our purpose, one of them presented by [30], who adopted VSM for a product level of analysis in the shop floor. This study exemplifies the use of intelligent product model for a production and control system using RFID in industrial applications. The second study applied VSM to the analysis of a smart network for electricity production. The authors of [31] have studied how the *"smart capability functions at a strategic, business process and technical level"*, contributing for a product-oriented view of VSM theory. Both refer to the production/manufacturing stages, opening an opportunity to expand research in this area addressing the case of smart products. Our research focuses on the structure and mechanisms (e.g., cohesion, adaptation) for BITA at the smart product level of analysis.

4   A Viable Smart Product Model for OHS in Construction

The design and development involved two researchers and a master's student of informatics, responsible for the coding in the prototype development phase of DSR. The initial phase was conducted in close collaboration with the practitioners designated by the construction group, namely, two OHS assessors, the top managers of the construction equipment company and of the consulting company, and two construction technicians designated to assist in field testing. The first artifact used for occupational health and safety in construction using smart technologies aimed at presenting a global picture of the infrastructure, equipment, and main purposes of the stakeholders (Fig. 2).

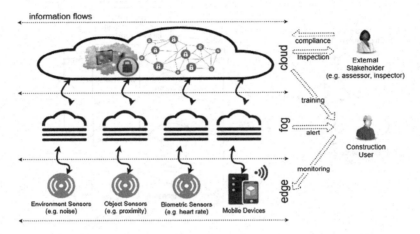

Fig. 2. Integrated smart OHS [14].

There are three key elements in the cyber-physical IoT infrastructure (bottom-left).

- The *personal mobile device*: worker monitoring and alert system based on a smart wristband – biometric information, RFID, and GPS;
- The *environment sensors kit* (unpractical to include in the worker wearables), including light, temperature and humidity, noise, and air quality (requires GPS);
- The *objects sensors*, including RFID antennas (collision detection or fall protection), PPE - personal protection equipment (e.g., helmet), and site access.

The system is used for alerting the user, gathering biometric data, and identification, for example, for collision detection systems using RFID. Moreover, it concentrates the environmental parameters in a portable, low-cost toolkit, making it affordable to use in different areas of the site. Finally, it ensures wearable use (identifies PPE) – if the wearable is not in use, the worker may not enter the site or use specific equipment. The arrows represent the value obtained from data analysis (training, alerts, and inspections), and the purpose of data collected via IoT (monitoring and compliance). On the bottom-right, the external stakeholders that need to access OHS data are represented, and, on the top, we can see the cloud infrastructure. The smart OHS system needed to ensure that it provided cohesion and adaptation to the environmental conditions: a viable product model. The model for the product level of analysis is presented in Fig. 3.

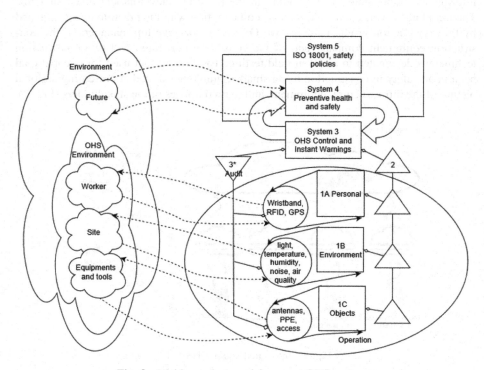

Fig. 3. Viable product model – smart OHS system.

The design of a viable smart product must consider the five interrelated systems included in the VSM theory [8], enabling cohesion and adaptation mechanisms. System 1 includes the key operation units of the smart OHS that will be implemented via IoT, namely, (1A) *personal mobile device*: worker monitoring and alert system based on a smart wristband, (1B) *environment sensors kit* requiring feedback (System 2) from the personal mobile device 1A; and (1C) *objects sensors* that will require feedback from 1A and 1B. System 2 represents the feedback system made possible by the IoT sensors that interact with the local environment - aligned with the strategy for smart OHS. System 3 implements the immediate actions (e.g. avoid unauthorized access to the site or alert of imminent fall or collision with equipment), while providing audit from health and safety assessors and consultants. System 4 includes the algorithms to generate alerts or safety warnings, for example, warn the user to rest according to the weather conditions (collected via weather sensors) and biometric signals. Finally, System 5 is materialized by the health and safety regulations, ensuring alignment between the operation (1, 2), the environment and the metasystem (3-4-5).

We identify different levels of recursion [8, 10] in VPM because each autonomous product (1A, 1B, 1C) is also a viable product according to the VSM, interacting within the operation system and with the structural recursion levels above. This DSR enabled the formulation of the following design principles for viable smart product models:

- *Adopt a top-down approach starting the model with System 5 and then System 4 elements.* Smart products must be a result of overall company policies and future development expectations. Therefore, System 5 must clarify the policies (in our case, occupational health and safety and industry 4.0) and then System 4 envisions candidate technologies and the potential adaptation to future events.
- *Update System 3 (control) as System 4 and System 1 evolve.* It is necessary to balance resources needed to develop System 1 parts of the smart product and the adaptation requirements identified in System 4.
- *Follow an outside-in approach to design System 1.* Contrarily to the usual application of VSM for diagnosing the business, parts (or all) of System 1 components may not yet exist when planning smart products that adhere to the environment. Therefore, it is important to detail the complete setting for the smart product operation.
- *Promote synergies with System 2*, which provides cohesion between all the components of the smart product, lateral communication, and vertical communication with System 3 (which, in turn, allows auditing (3*) via sensors existing in System 1 level).
- *Present the VSM theory using the human body analogy.* We confirmed in this case the findings of [32], that VSM does not provide a common language for managers, requiring a previous presentation of the concepts.
- *Adopt a cyclic approach to the design of the viable product model.* A single iteration (System 5&4-4&3-1&3-2) provides an initial version of the model, but it is necessary to understand the implications of System 1 for the higher levels. For example, specific technologies may not be applicable (e.g., too expensive), requiring manual control procedures at level 3 (e.g., human audits). Designers should navigate through the five levels of the VPM for consistency and reevaluate the capabilities of the system.

5 Discussion

Smart products must be aligned with the business strategy, in cohesion with other organizational systems and ensuring adaptation to environmental changes. As stated by [33] "*if the technologies driving Industry 4.0 develop in silos and the OHS initiatives of manufacturers are fragmentary, hazards will multiply and some of the gains made in accident prevention will be lost*". According to the company managers in our project consortium, a comprehensive model for wearable technologies in construction needs to support (1) training, (2) monitoring critical parameters, (3) user alerts (e.g., collision, fall), and (4) voluntary regulatory compliance (OHS standards audit and evidence). A VPM approach surfaces the different purposes of technology, its interactions with the local environment, and recursion with managerial functions.

Few studies have used VSM theory as an inspiration for product developments that are aligned to the business. Most of the research focuses on diagnosing [32] or transforming already existing organizations [27]. Our study shows that VPM can be used for the development of smart products integrated with the business strategy.

We presented the final model to the companies participating in our research to understand the communication capabilities of this artifact. They found the relation between the environment and System 1 important to understand the needs of regulations, and System 3 to identify what type of data they could get from the viable smart product. Regarding Systems 5, 4, and 2, they found that information more relevant to the implementors of the solution. We found that System 2 was transparent to them (more important to integrate the smart product IoT system by technical staff), System 5 was a representation of their own vision and regulations (more important to third party), and System 4 was, in this case, mostly developed by the research team, who identified the future opportunities and needs for adaptation. This case revealed that the interest of each systems in VSM can vary according to each stakeholder. Additional research is necessary to understand how the VSM representation can improve its communication capabilities according to multiple viewpoints of smart products development.

6 Conclusions

We presented a Viable Product Model artifact based on VSM theory to the design of smart products. The results are attained from (1) a DSR project aiming to introduce smart technologies for safety in construction, and (2) a structured literature review focusing on VSM for BITA at the product-level of analysis, contrasting to the usual adoption of VSM for business units and departments. Digitalization is changing products in all sectors of the economy, requiring new models to capture the alignment between business needs and pervasive IT. The multiplication of IoT systems creates challenges to align synergies within these systems and the (internal and external) social realms of the organization. One central conclusion in our work is that VSM theory can be adopted to model viable smart products in the emerging fourth industrial revolution.

Some limitations must be stated. The first stems from the literature review, namely, the restriction of the source database and the selected keywords. We decided to use Google Scholar, which is the most comprehensive search engine [16], but other databases can be used. Secondly, to our knowledge this is the first attempt to adopt VSM for smart product developments, focusing on the product-level of alignment in a single organization. A more in-depth evaluation of the pros and cons of the VPM is necessary, and other cases may follow to improve the approach. More field work is necessary since current results are mainly supported in the literature review and the preliminary findings of one case. Thirdly, although the model results were positive for the company managers, there are risks of the Hawthorn effect in social studies, suggesting that the observed participants' behavior could be "*related only to the special social situation and social treatment they received*" [34]. Finally, we did not yet explore the full potential of VSM for detailing the relations between specific sensors and actuators in System 1, the integration in System 2, and the detailed information flows with the environment and other Systems (3-4-5). The model that we present in this paper can be improved, including, for example, sensor specifications and detailed data models.

Future research opportunities are promising. First, looking to the possibility to adopt VSM to other types of interactive products. Another possibility is to align the VPM with VSM for the same organization, for example, aligning viability of the product with other levels (recursions) of viable systems such as departments. We also found an opportunity to explore VSM in the entrepreneurship context, namely, its potential to model minimum viable products that are popular in start-ups. Finally, it is possible to develop different VPM representations (viewpoints) to improve its utility to BITA with enhanced communication capabilities according to the needs of each stakeholder.

We plan to test the proposed model in our information systems course, to evaluate the potential of the tool for training smart product specification aligned with the company strategies. Additionally, the next step of our DSR will adopt VPM to a smart tower crane. One of the companies belonging to the construction group rents tower cranes and wants to use IoT to improve safety (e.g. prevent collision with the building during hoisting processes; alert the user in critical weather conditions), maintenance (monitor the equipment use and alert the supplier for maintenance procedures), and other smart capabilities to improve their tower crane rental business.

References

1. Kohli, R., Melville, N.P.: Digital innovation: a review and synthesis. Inf. Syst. J. **29**, 200–223 (2019)
2. Hendler, S.: Digital-physical product development: a qualitative analysis. Eur. J. Innov. Manag. **22**, 315–334 (2018)
3. Yoo, Y., Henfridsson, O., Lyytinen, K.: The new organizing logic of digital innovation: an agenda for information systems research. Inf. Syst. Res. **21**, 724–735 (2010)
4. Luftman, J., Brier, T.: Achieving and sustaining business-IT alignment. Calif. Manag. Rev. **42**, 109–122 (1999)
5. Mintzberg, H.: Patterns in strategy formation. Manag. Sci. **24**, 934–948 (1978)
6. Zhang, M., Chen, H., Li, X., Lyytinen, K.: Evolvement of business-IT alignment: a conceptual model and intervening changes from resource allocation. IEEE Access **6**, 9160–9172 (2018)
7. Luftman, J., Lyytinen, K., Zvi, T.: Ben: enhancing the measurement of information technology (IT) business alignment and its influence on company performance. J. Inf. Technol. **32**, 26–46 (2017)
8. Beer, S.: The Heart of Enterprise. Wiley, Hoboken (1979)
9. Schwaninger, M., Scheef, C.: A test of the viable system model: theoretical claim vs empirical evidence. Cybern. Syst. **47**, 544–569 (2016)
10. Espejo, R.: The viable system model. Syst. Pract. Action Res. **3**, 219–221 (1990)
11. Porter, M.E., Heppelmann, J.E.: How smart, connected products are transforming companies. Harv. Bus. Rev. **93**, 96–114 (2015)
12. Hevner, A.R., March, S.T., Park, J.: Design science in information systems research. MIS Q. **28**, 75–105 (2004)
13. Simon, H.: The Sciences of the Artificial, 3rd edn. MIT Press, Cambridge (1996)

14. Barata, J., da Cunha, P.R.: Safety is the new black: the increasing role of wearables in occupational health and safety in construction. In: Abramowicz, W., Corchuelo, R. (eds.) BIS 2019. LNBIP, vol. 353, pp. 526–537. Springer, Cham (2019). https://doi.org/10.1007/978-3-030-20485-3_41
15. Peffers, K., Tuunanen, T., Rothenberger, M.A., Chatterjee, S.: A design science research methodology for information systems research. J. Manag. Inf. Syst. 24, 45–78 (2007)
16. Martín-martín, A., Orduna-malea, E., López-cózar, E.D., Martín-martín, A.: Google Scholar, Web of Science, and Scopus: a systematic comparison of citations in 252 subject categories. J. Informetr. 12, 1160–1177 (2019)
17. Grabis, J., Kirikova, M., Zdravkovic, J., Stirna, J.: The practice of enterprise modeling. In: 6th IFIPWG 8.1 Working Conference, PoEM (2013)
18. Zimmermann, E., Bril, H., Haouzi, E.L., Thomas, P., Thomas, A., Noyel, M.: A hybrid manufacturing control based on smart lots in a disrupted industrial context. In: 20th IFAC World Congress, pp. 9585–9589 (2017)
19. Cardin, O., et al.: Coupling predictive scheduling and reactive control in manufacturing hybrid control architectures: state of the art and future challenges. J. Intell. Manuf. 28, 1503–1517 (2017)
20. Batista, L., Davis-Poynter, S., Ng, I., Maull, R.: Servitization through outcome-based contract – a systems perspective from the defence industry. Int. J. Prod. Econ. 192, 133–143 (2017)
21. Pickering, A.: The science of the unknowable: Stafford Beer's cybernetic informatics. Kybernetes 33, 499–521 (2004)
22. Ashby, W.R.: Design for a Brain: The Origin of Adaptive Behaviour. Wiley, New York (1952)
23. Espejo, R.: Aspects of identity, cohesion, citizenship and performance in recursive organisations. Kybernetes 28, 640–658 (2002)
24. Espejo, R., Dominici, G.: Cybernetics of value cocreation for product development. Syst. Res. Behav. Sci. 34, 24–40 (2017)
25. Huygh, T., De Haes, S.: Using the viable system model to study IT governance dynamics: evidence from a single case study. In: Proceedings of the 51st HICSS, p. 9 (2018)
26. Coertze, J., Von Solms, R.: Towards a cybernetics-based communication framework for IT governance. In: Proceedings of the 48th HICSS, pp. 4595–4606 (2015)
27. Schwaninger, M.: Design for viable organizations. Kybernetes 35, 955–966 (2006)
28. Buckl, S., Matthes, F., Schweda, C.M.: Towards a method framework for enterprise architecture management–a literature analysis from a viable system perspective. In: CAiSE 2010 Workshop. Business/IT Alignment and Interoperability, pp. 46–60 (2010)
29. Kandjani, H., Tavana, M., Bernus, P., Nielsen, S.: Co-evolution Path Model (CePM): sustaining enterprises as complex systems on the edge of chaos. Cybern. Syst. 45, 547–567 (2014)
30. Herrera, C., Thomas, A., Belmokhtar, S., Pannequin, R.: A viable system model for product-driven systems. In: Proceedings of the IESM, pp. 1–10 (2011)
31. Shaw, D.R., Snowdon, B., Holland, C.P., Kawalek, P., Warboys, B.: The viable systems model applied to a smart network: the case of the UK electricity market. J. Inf. Technol. 19, 270–280 (2004)
32. Hildbr, S., Bodhanya, S.: Guidance on applying the viable system model. Kybernetes 44, 186–201 (2015)
33. Badri, A., Boudreau-trudel, B., Saâdeddine, A.: Occupational health and safety in the industry 4.0 era: a cause for major concern? Saf. Sci. 109, 403–411 (2018)
34. French, J.: Experiments in field settings. In: Festinger, L., Katz, D. (eds.) Research Methods in Behavioral Sciences, p. 101. Dryden Press (1953)

Strategic IT Alignment and Business Performance in SMEs: An Empirical Investigation

Fotis Kitsios and Maria Kamariotou[(✉)]

Department of Applied Informatics, University of Macedonia,
Thessaloniki, Greece
kitsios@uom.gr, mkamariotou@uom.edu.gr

Abstract. New competitive challenges have forced Small-Medium Enterprises (SMEs) to re-examine their internal environment in order to improve competitive advantage. IT investments can improve firm performance in a way that it would be in "alignment" with business strategy. The purpose of this paper is to analyze the contemporary impact of IT and business strategy on Information Systems (IS) planning success, incorporating all these constructs into a model that is tested using Regression Analysis. Data were collected from IS executives in Greek SMEs.

Keywords: Strategic Information Systems Planning · Alignment · Success · Performance · IT strategy

1 Introduction

As businesses are obliged to deal with the environmental uncertainty and complexity, IT executives have to develop Information Systems (IS) that support business strategy, and accommodate decision making in order to increase competitive advantage [20, 23, 29]. As new competitive challenges and requirements have been raised due to the growth of international business, firms are forced to re-examine their internal business environment in order to increase their performance and achieve a competitive advantage. However, IS could be a source of sustainable competitive advantage only if the IS strategy will be aligned with business strategy. Thus, many companies have spent their resources in order to increase their competitive advantage by looking at their IT strategy [24–26, 39]. This is a crucial challenge for businesses and especially for Small-Medium Enterprises (SMEs).

As the current financial crisis has negatively affected plenty of activities of SMEs, they have already acted in a new complex financial environment where uncertainty increases and the market characteristics completely change. Except for difficulties in their financial aspect, their relative lack of technological, managerial and human capabilities may limit their ability to bowl over the financial crisis [3, 9, 27]. Moreover, the lack of strategic planning negatively influences this difficulty. Formal processes in SMEs that are related with strategic management and information handling help managers to focus on strategies, structures and processes that aim to enhance firm

© Springer Nature Switzerland AG 2019
W. Abramowicz and R. Corchuelo (Eds.): BIS 2019 Workshops, LNBIP 373, pp. 113–123, 2019.
https://doi.org/10.1007/978-3-030-36691-9_10

performance. Thus, IT investment has been a crucial issue for CIOs because IT influences business performance and help executives to align business strategy and organizational performance. In complex environments, businesses could develop formal processes using standardized rules and procedures which enhance the minimization of environmental uncertainty and manage economic consistency [22, 28, 29].

Traditionally, the concept of alignment is conceptualized as the extent of fit between IT and business strategy. Several studies found that there is a positive relationship between alignment and performance [24, 29, 30]. With regard to the relationship between alignment and performance researchers argue that SMEs can use different paths in order to achieve a great extent of alignment according to their capabilities and market position. Thus, a more extensive planning would be more effective because it would support planners understand the impact of the environment and better respond to it. If IS executives invest too many efforts, many conflicts among team members can be raised as well as the process could be delayed. On the other hand, if CIOs avoid investing too much time into the process, IS plans could be inefficient so IS goals could not be achieved. Consequently, the assessment of the process is significant because IT managers can reduce these unsatisfactory results [31]. Unfortunately, IS strategy has been studied as a homogenous topic and limited studies delving into comparing the state of relevance across planning or alignment. Previous researchers have examined the relationship between the strategic planning of IS and the success as well as the obstacles that managers face in large companies [13–15].

Despite the fact that studies on strategic alignment in SMEs investigate some of the same topics as research conducted with larger firms, SMEs' uniqueness warrant investigation on their own. Nevertheless, SMEs represent a distinct grouping of firms where firm size and resource constraints have a noticeable influence on alignment factors and outcomes [18, 30]. Management literature has shown that advances in IT are leading to increasing levels of adoption and use of IT in SMEs and are pushing technology further and further into SMEs processes and operations. Because many competitors and suppliers now use IT in their operations, executives (and researchers) need to be aware of how the alignment of business and IT strategies impacts firms [30, 32]. Therefore, the purpose of this paper is to analyze the contemporary impact of IT and business strategy on Information Systems (IS) planning success, incorporating all these constructs into a model that is tested using Regression Analysis.

The structure of this paper is as following: after a brief introduction to this field, the next section includes the theoretical background regarding the alignment between business and IT strategy and the impact on planning success. Section 3 describes the methodology, while Sect. 4 shows the results of the survey. Finally, Sect. 5 discusses the results and concludes the paper.

2 Theoretical Background

In complex environments, SMEs tend to formalize processes using certain rules and procedures which support the limitation of environmental uncertainty. Formalization supports the development of aspects which encourage communication among the individuals and sharing of new information. Also, they transform the generation of new ideas through the inflicted structures into real plans, enhancing the growth of innovation. As the environment is getting more and more complex, the need for innovation is increasing if businesses are to be helped to be competitive so as to survive [3, 9, 21].

The concept of Strategic Information Systems Planning (SISP) has been associated with the ability to formulate business strategy using IS, techniques and methodologies which were used to support organizations in identifying potential opportunities to develop IS with greater competitiveness [37]. SISP has been considered as an integrated process which contains specific phases. These phases represent the components of the planning process such as the identification of the key planning issues, the analysis of internal and external environment, the analysis of strategy alternatives, the formulation and the implementation of strategic planning.

The first phase of the process named Strategic Awareness includes activities such as the identification of key planning issues and objectives, the development of the planning team and the encouragement of top management to participate in the process. In the second phase CIOs conduct a situation analysis in order to collect data regarding current business systems, current organizational systems, current information systems, external environment and external IT environment. The third phase of the process named Strategy Conception refers to the identification of important IT objectives, opportunities for improvement and high-level IT strategies. In Strategy Formulation IS executives identify new business processes, new IT architectures, specific new projects and priorities for new projects. In the last phase, IT managers define change management approaches and action plans and they evaluate them [1, 2, 5–8, 11–15, 18].

The findings of studies which examine the relationship of SISP phases and success conclude that IS executives focused their efforts on the Strategic Conception phase. Although planners focus on this phase, they cannot identify the suitable alternative strategies. As a consequence, their efforts do not positively influence SISP success. So, they cannot achieve their objectives. The most common problems which have been raised during the SISP process are the lack of participation and the failure to apply strategic IS plans. Executives cannot be committed to the plan, consequently the members of the team have difficulties to implement the IS strategy. Moreover, results show that executives only focus on the implementation of IS strategy because they consider this process difficult and they ignore its formulation [4–8, 10, 11, 14–17, 23].

Results from existing studies indicate that many CIOs put too many efforts to SISP process while others too little. If IS executives invest too many efforts, many conflicts among team members can be raised as well as the process could be delayed. On the other hand, if they avoid investing too much time into the process, IS plans could be inefficient so IS goals could not be achieved. Consequently, the assessment of the process is significant because IS executives can reduce these unsatisfactory results [5, 8, 14].

Many researchers mentioned that CIOs concentrate more on Strategy Conception and Strategy Implementation and they do not invest time on Strategic Awareness and Situation Analysis. These findings confirm that the implemented plans are ineffective and unsuccessful and they do not meet the objectives [1, 5, 8, 14, 15]. Furthermore, when IS executives concentrate their efforts on the implementation of the process, they may reduce SISP horizons, but the strategic goals cannot be achieved. IT managers do not understand the strategic objectives and how they can increase business value because they invest time on the horizon of the project and on minimizing its cost due to limited IT budget [1].

The results indicate that executives should pay attention to implementing Situational Analysis with greater meticulousness, so that they can apply Strategy Conception and Strategy Implementation Planning with greater agility rather than now. Planners should focus on the analysis of current business systems, organizational systems, IS, as well as the business environment and external IT environment. If planners understand those elements, they can improve the result of the planning process excluding the increased time and cost which the process is needed. When executives analyze the environment, they can determine important IT objectives and opportunities for improvement, they can evaluate them in order to define high-level IT strategies in their business' strategy conception [13].

Based on the analysis of the existing literature, the following hypotheses are defined (Table 1):

Table 1. Hypotheses.

Hypotheses	References
H1: Strategic awareness positively affects SISP success	[2, 5, 13–15, 18]
H2: Situation analysis positively affects SISP success	[2, 5, 13–15, 18]
H3: Strategy conception positively affects SISP success	[2, 5, 13–15, 18]
H4: Strategy formulation positively affects SISP success	[2, 5, 13–15, 18]
H5: Strategy implementation positively affects SISP success	[2, 5, 13–15, 18]

Relevant literature argued that SISP success is "the degree to which the objectives of SISP are achieved" [17]. Traditionally, the concept of success has been viewed in four dimensions, namely alignment, analysis, cooperation and capabilities. The first one refers to the understanding of executives to use IS in order to support business strategy and to identify opportunities in order to support the strategic direction of the firm. Furthermore this dimension includes variables such as the alignment between IT strategy with the strategic plan of the organization, the education of top management regarding the importance of IT and the adaption of technology to strategic change. The second dimension is merely preoccupied with the generation of new ideas to reengineer business processes through IT. An important issue is the understanding of information needs through subunits, the understanding of the dispersion of data, applications, and other technologies throughout the firm in order to develop a "blueprint" which will improve organizational processes. In this way CIOs can understand how the organization actually operates and evaluate internal business needs and the capability of IS to meet those needs. The third dimension refers to the ability of managers to develop clear guidelines of managerial responsibility for plan implementation, to identify potential sources of resistance to IS plans, to support open lines of communication with other departments in order to achieve a general level of agreement regarding the risks/tradeoffs among system projects and avoid the overlapping development of major systems. Finally, the last dimension includes a list of capabilities such as the ability to identify key problem areas, the ability to anticipate surprises and crises, the flexibility to adapt to unanticipated changes and the ability to gain cooperation among user groups for IS plans [5–8, 14, 15, 17, 18].

3 Methodology

A field survey was developed for IS executives. The instrument used five-point Likert-scales to operationalize two constructs: SISP phases and success. The SISP process constructs measured the extent to which the organization conducted the five planning phases and their tasks. The success constructs measured using four dimensions named alignment, analysis, cooperation and capabilities. The questionnaire was based on previous surveys that examine the relationship between SISP phases and success [2, 13–15].

Four IS executives were asked to participate in a pilot test. Each one completed the survey and commented on the contents, length, and overall appearance of the instrument. Then, a sample of IS executives in Greek SMEs was selected from the icap list. This methodology was followed by previous researchers who examined the same hypotheses and studied the relationship between SISP phases and success [14, 15]. SMEs which provided contact details were selected as the appropriate sample of the survey. The survey was sent to 1246 IS executives and a total of 294 returned the survey. Data analysis was implemented using Regression Analysis.

4 Results

Respondents in this study were employed in a variety of industries, well educated, and experienced. 16% of them worked in agriculture and food, 11.3% in business services, 10.6% in retail and the rest in other industries. 35.2% had some postgraduate studies and 44.7% had a degree. They also had 16–25 years of IS experience. The internal consistency, calculated via Cronbach's alpha, ranged from 0.738 to 0.932, exceeding the minimally required 0.70 level [14]. Table 2 presents the basic characteristics of dependent and independent variables as explained in the previous sections. As can be seen in Table 2, respondents score on average (success) 3.61 on a scale of 1–5 with a standard deviation of 0.88. A standard Pearson correlation analysis was conducted and tested on two-tailed significance. Table 2 shows similar significant results of the two-tailed zero-order and partial correlation analyses.

The normal P-P and scatter plots (Fig. 1) showed that data is normally distributed (i.e., all residuals cluster around the 'line'), complies with the assumptions of homogeneity of variance (i.e., homo-scedasticity) and linearity. Residual errors are in fact evenly distributed and not related to the value of the predicted value, suggesting that the relationship is, in fact, linear and the variance of y for each value of x is the same, this confirming the homoscedasticity assumption [38]. Univariate outliers were checked for using z-scores and all values were within acceptable range. In succession, multivariate outliers were checked using Mahalanobis and Cook's distances. No

Table 2. Descriptive statistics.

	N	Mean	Std. Dev.	Zero-order correlation	Partial correlations
Independent variables					
Strategic awareness	294	3.84	0.82	0.733	0.032
Situation analysis	294	3.91	0.71	0.730*	0.170*
Strategy conception	294	3.87	0.78	0.763***	0.240***
Strategy formulation	294	3.74	0.80	0.773***	0.229***
Strategy implementation planning	294	3.61	0.88	0.788***	0.369***
Dependent variable					
Success	294	3.71	0.67		

influential outliers were detected. Multicollinearity was checked using variance inflation factors (VIF). Table 3 presents the results of the regression analysis.

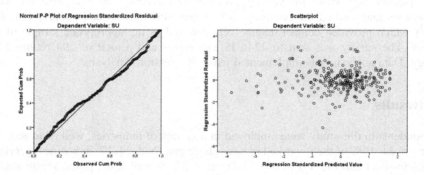

Fig. 1. Normal P-P plot of regression standardized residual and residual scatter plot

There aren't multicollinearity problems because VIF scores are all within an acceptable range. F-scores indicate significant regressions suggesting the existence of a real effect of success as independent variables. The path coefficient between Strategic Awareness and Success was positive but not statistically significant ($\beta = 0.031$, $p > 0.05$). Thus, H1 was not supported. There was a significant positive relationship among Situation Analysis ($\beta = 0.154$, $p < 0.05$), Strategy Conception ($\beta = 0.224$, $p < 0.001$), Strategy Formulation ($\beta = 0.218$, $p < 0.001$), and Success, supporting H2, H3 and H4. This indicates that a higher level of Strategy Conception and Strategy Formulation can increase SISP Success. There was also a positive relationship between Strategy Implementation Planning and Success ($\beta = 0.338$, $p < 0.001$); thus, H5 was supported. This result indicates that managers' ability to efficiently implement strategic plans plays an important role in SISP success. Table 4 shows the results for individual paths and results (Fig. 2).

Table 3. Regression analysis between independent variables (strategic awareness, situation analysis, strategy conception, strategy formulation, strategy implementation planning) and dependent variable (Success). $*p < 0.05$, $**p < 0.01$, $***p < 0.001$.

Model	N	R^2	R^2 (adj.)	β	t-value	VIF	F-scores
	294	0.741	0.736				164.623
Strategic awareness				0.031	0.541	3.680	
Situation analysis				0.154	2.935	3.040	
Strategy conception				0.224	4.190	3.168	
Strategy formulation				0.218	3.985	3.337	
Strategy implementation planning				0.338	6.736	2.797	

Table 4. Structural estimates (hypotheses testing).

Hypothesized path	Results
H1: Strategic awareness positively affects SISP success	Not supported
H2: Situation analysis positively affects SISP success	Supported
H3: Strategy conception positively affects SISP success	Supported
H4: Strategy formulation positively affects SISP success	Supported
H5: Strategy implementation positively affects SISP success	Supported

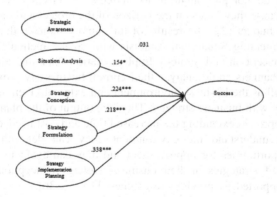

Fig. 2. Results for direct effects

Results indicate that IS executives are not aware of analyzing the external IT environment and evaluating opportunities for IS development. This finding is crucial because it confirms that senior executives in SMEs do not invest in emergent technologies and cannot fit with the strategic, structural, and environmental dynamics. Furthermore, an important obstacle is that managers do not focus on organizing the planning team. Employees who will participate in the development of IS should have IT skills, motivation to develop effective IS and cooperation skills. This finding is associated with the lack of management support and the lack of clear guidelines about the IS development. IS executives can define priorities, increase the cooperation among the IS team and provide guidelines regarding in order to support the effectiveness of IS plans and align them with business plans. These efforts are not implemented because IS executives do not focus on Strategic Awareness phase. These results confirm similar findings that have been discussed by previous researchers in the field of strategic alignment [24, 30].

In response to anticipated changes in business environment, companies are developing IS at an increasing rate. Therefore, IT investment has been a significant issue for CIOs, as it is crucial budget items in most businesses. However, senior executives do not formulate IT strategies and priorities, so they cannot anticipate risks and crises. As IT managers cannot identify problem areas, they cannot redesign business processes. Thus, IS that are developed are based on the existing business processes and they cannot be aligned with IS objectives. This finding confirms the negative consequences that SMEs face due to the lack of strategic planning. These results confirm similar findings that have been discussed by previous researchers in the field of strategic alignment [24, 30].

Management literature has shown results on the concentration of senior executives on Strategy Conception and Strategy Implementation. IT managers do not invest time on Strategic Awareness and Situation Analysis, as a result the implemented plans are not effective, successful and they do not meet business objectives [2, 8, 14, 15]. Furthermore, IT managers who only concentrate on the implementation of the process can achieve shorter SISP horizons but they cannot align strategic goals with IT ones. Senior executives do not pay attention to strategic objectives how IS can increase business value because they focus on the horizon of the project and on decrease of cost due to limited IT budget [2]. The results of this survey indicate that CIOs who pay attention to implementing Situational Analysis with greater meticulousness, they can apply Strategy Conception and Strategy Implementation Planning with greater agility rather than now. Planners could analyze their current business systems, organizational systems, IS, as well as the business environment and external IT environment in order to align IT strategy with business strategy. Thus, the output of the planning process can be significantly improved excluding the increased time and cost needed for the process. When executives understand the environment, they can determine important IT objectives and opportunities for improvement and they can evaluate them in order to define high-level IT strategies in their business' strategy conception These findings have also been supported by previous researchers [19, 33–36].

5   Conclusion

This paper examined the impact of IT and business strategy on IS planning success. The results of the analysis support research hypotheses that IS executives do not focus on Strategic Awareness and they are not aware of analyzing the external IT environment and evaluating opportunities for IS development. This finding is crucial because it confirms that senior executives in SMEs do not invest in emergent technologies and cannot fit with the strategic, structural, and environmental dynamics. Furthermore, an important obstacle is that IT managers do not focus on organizing the planning team.

Employees who will participate in the development of IS should have IT skills, motivation to develop effective IS and cooperation skills.

In response to anticipated changes in business environment, companies are developing IS at an increasing rate. Therefore, IT investment has been a significant issue for CIOs, as it is crucial budget items in most businesses. However, senior executives do not formulate IT strategies and priorities, so they cannot anticipate risks and crises. From a managerial perspective, they could be aware of the strategic use of IS planning in order to increase competitive advantage. Thus, senior executives have to choose the appropriate IT infrastructure (related to their organizational strategy and structure) in order to align business strategy with organizational structure.

Understanding those phases may help IS executives concentrate their efforts on organizations' objectives and recognize the greatest value of the planning process in their business. This paper suggests that IT appears to be an important issue in improving the alignment between IT strategy and organizational structure. Second, the results of this survey can increase their awareness of the phases of SISP. IS executives could be knowledgeable about the five phases and they could implement the tasks of each one with greater meticulousness in order to improve the coordination between IT and business strategy and increase firm performance. Finally, the findings contribute to IS executives in Greek SMEs who do not concentrate on strategic planning during the development of IS and they focus only on the technical issues. As a result, they could understand the significance of the SISP process in order to formulate and implement IS strategy which will be aligned with business objectives and increase the success of SMEs.

A limitation of this study stems from the fact that the survey was conducted only in Greece. Future researchers could examine and compare these results with relative ones from large companies and other countries. Apparently, future researchers may use different methodologies for data analysis, such as cluster analysis in order to compare the differences among organizations in different sectors during the implementation of the SISP process.

References

1. Brown, I.: Strategic information systems planning: comparing espoused beliefs with practice. In: ECIS 2010: Proceedings of 18th European Conference on Information Systems, South Africa, pp. 1–12 (2010)
2. Brown, I.T.J.: Testing and extending theory in strategic information systems planning through literature analysis. Inf. Resour. Manag. J. **17**(4), 20–48 (2004)
3. Giannacourou, M., Kantaraki, M., Christopoulou, V.: The perception of crisis by Greek SMEs and its impact on managerial practices. Procedia Soc. Behav. Sci. **175**(2015), 546–551 (2015)
4. Kamariotou, M., Kitsios, F.: Strategic information systems planning. In: Mehdi, K.-P. (ed.) Encyclopedia of Information Science and Technology, 4th edn, chap. 78, pp. 912–922. IGI Global Publishing, USA (2018)
5. Kamariotou, M., Kitsios, F.: An empirical evaluation of strategic information systems planning phases in SMEs: determinants of effectiveness. In: Proceedings of the 6th

International Symposium and 28th National Conference on Operational Research, Greece, pp. 67–72 (2017)

6. Kamariotou, M., Kitsios, F.: Information systems phases and firm performance: a conceptual framework. In: Kavoura, A., Sakas, D., Tomaras, P. (eds.) Strategic Innovative Marketing, Springer Proceedings in Business and Economics, pp. 553–560. Springer, Switzerland (2017). https://doi.org/10.1007/978-3-319-33865-1_67

7. Kamariotou, M., Kitsios, F.: Strategic information systems planning: SMEs performance outcomes. In: Proceedings of the 5th International Symposium and 27th National Conference on Operation Research, Greece, pp. 153–157 (2016)

8. Kitsios, F., Kamariotou, M.: Decision support systems and strategic planning: information technology and SMEs performance. Int. J. Decis. Support Syst. 3(1/2), 53–70 (2018)

9. Kitsios, F., Kamariotou, M.: Strategic IT alignment: business performance during financial crisis. In: Tsounis, N., Vlachvei, A. (eds.) Advances in Applied Economic Research, Springer Proceedings in Business and Economics, pp. 503–525. Springer, Switzerland (2017). https://doi.org/10.1007/978-3-319-48454-9_33

10. Lederer, A.L., Sethi, V.: Key prescriptions for strategic information systems planning. J. Manag. Inf. Syst. 13(1), 35–62 (1996)

11. Maharaj, S., Brown, I.: The impact of shared domain knowledge on strategic information systems planning and alignment: original research. S. Afr. J. Inf. Manag. 17(1), 1–12 (2015)

12. Mentzas, G.: Implementing an IS strategy - a team approach. Long Range Plan. 30(1), 84–95 (1997)

13. Mirchandani, D.A., Lederer, A.L.: "Less is more:" information systems planning in an uncertain environment. Inf. Syst. Manag. 29(10), 13–25 (2014)

14. Newkirk, H.E., Lederer, A.L., Srinivasan, C.: Strategic information systems planning: too little or too much? J. Strateg. Inf. Syst. 12(3), 201–228 (2003)

15. Newkirk, H.E., Lederer, A.L.: The effectiveness of strategic information systems planning under environmental uncertainty. Inf. Manag. 43(4), 481–501 (2006)

16. Newkirk, H.E., Lederer, A.L., Johnson, A.M.: Rapid business and IT change: drivers for strategic information systems planning? Eur. J. Inf. Syst. 17(3), 198–218 (2008)

17. Pai, J.C.: An empirical study of the relationship between knowledge sharing and IS/IT strategic planning (ISSP). Manag. Decis. 44(1), 105–122 (2006)

18. Kamariotou, M., Kitsios, F.: Critical factors of strategic information systems planning phases in SMEs. In: Themistocleous, M., Rupino da Cunha, P. (eds.) EMCIS 2018. LNBIP, vol. 341, pp. 503–517. Springer, Cham (2019). https://doi.org/10.1007/978-3-030-11395-7_39

19. Kitsios, F., Kamariotou, M.: Decision support systems and business strategy: a conceptual framework for strategic information systems planning. In: Proceedings of the 6th IEEE International Conference on IT Convergence and Security (ICITCS 2016), Prague, Czech Republic, pp. 149–153 (2016)

20. Merali, Y., Papadopoulos, T., Nadkarni, T.: Information systems strategy: past, present, future? J. Strateg. Inf. Syst. 21(2), 125–153 (2012)

21. Siakas, K., Naaranoja, M., Vlachakis, S., Siakas, E.: Family businesses in the new economy: how to survive and develop in times of financial crisis. Procedia Econ. Financ. 9(2014), 331–341 (2014)

22. Ullah, A., Lai, R.: A systematic review of business and information technology alignment. ACM Trans. Manag. Inf. Syst. 4(1), 1–30 (2013)

23. Zubovic, A., Pita, Z., Khan, S.: A framework for investigating the impact of information systems capability on strategic information systems planning outcomes. In: Proceedings of 18th Pacific Asia Conference on Information Systems, China, pp. 1–12 (2014)

24. Chatzoglou, P.D., Diamantidis, A.D., Vraimaki, E., Vranakis, S.K., Kourtidis, D.A.: Aligning IT, strategic orientation and organizational structure. Bus. Process Manag. J. **17**(4), 663–687 (2011)
25. Johnson, A.M., Lederer, A.L.: IS strategy and IS contribution: CEO and CIO perspectives. Inf. Syst. Manag. **30**(4), 306–318 (2013)
26. Wolf, C., Floyd, S.W.: Strategic planning research: toward a theory-driven agenda. J. Manag. **43**(6), 1754–1788 (2017)
27. Bourletidis, K., Triantafyllopoulos, Y.: SMEs survival in time of crisis: strategies, tactics and commercial success stories. Procedia Soc. Behav. Sci. **148**, 639–644 (2014)
28. Drechsler, A., Weißschädel, S.: An IT strategy development framework for small and medium enterprises. Inf. Syst. e-Bus. Manag. **16**(1), 93–124 (2018)
29. Queiroz, M.: Mixed results in strategic IT alignment research: a synthesis and empirical study. Europ. J. Inf. Syst. **26**(1), 21–36 (2017)
30. Street, C.T., Gallupe, B., Baker, J.: Strategic alignment in SMEs: strengthening theoretical foundations. Commun. Assoc. Inf. Syst. **40**(20), 420–442 (2017)
31. Kappelman, L., Johnson, V., Torres, R., Maurer, C., McLean, E.: A study of information systems issues, practices, and leadership in Europe. Europ. J. Inf. Syst. **28**(1), 26–42 (2019)
32. Spinelli, R., Dyerson, R., Harindranath, G.: IT readiness in small firms. J. Small Bus. Enterp. Dev. **20**(4), 807–823 (2013)
33. Arvidsson, V., Holmström, J., Lyytinen, K.: Information systems use as strategy practice: a multi-dimensional view of strategic information system implementation and use. J. Strateg. Inf. Syst. **23**(1), 45–61 (2014)
34. Burgelman, R.A., Floyd, S.W., Laamanen, T., Mantere, S., Vaara, E., Whittington, R.: Strategy processes and practices: dialogues and intersections. Strateg. Manag. J. **39**(3), 531–558 (2018)
35. Chen, D.Q., Mocker, M., Preston, D.S., Teubner, A.: Information systems strategy: reconceptualization, measurement, and implications. MIS Q. **34**(2), 233–259 (2010)
36. Marabelli, M., Galliers, R.D.: A reflection on information systems strategizing: the role of power and everyday practices. Inf. Syst. J. **27**(3), 347–366 (2017)
37. Peppard, J., Ward, J.: Beyond strategic information systems: towards an IS capability. J. Strateg. Inf. Syst. **13**(2), 167–194 (2004)
38. Kachigan, S.K.: Multivariate Statistical Analysis: A Conceptual Introduction, 2nd edn. Radius Press (1991)
39. Chan, Y.E., Reich, B.H.: IT alignment: what have we learned? J. Inf. Technol. **22**(4), 297–315 (2007)

Enterprise Computing: A Case Study on Current Practices in SAP Operations

Johannes Hintsch[✉] and Klaus Turowski

Very Large Business Applications Lab, Faculty of Computer Science,
Otto von Guericke University, Universitätsplatz 2, 39106 Magdeburg, Germany
{johannes.hintsch,klaus.turowski}@ovgu.de

Abstract. IT administrators are fundamental to effective IT operations but are challenged by outsourcing and technological as well as organizational change. This paper investigates how four companies in their operations of SAP-focused enterprise systems organize and carry out tasks. A literature-based frame of inquiry is used to gather information from four interviewees working in SAP administration and from two business representatives. This study sheds light on how current state-of-the-art operations concepts are applied in the day-to-day business of operating grown proprietary and hybrid (cloud) application system landscapes.

Keywords: IT System Operations · IT System Administration · Enterprise applications · Hybrid cloud computing

1 Introduction

Barrett et al. found that IT system administrators [2] experience substantial challenges in their daily work: broken tools, complex technical and social environments as well as a diversion from real work. Years later, efficient collaboration is still an important success factor in system administration [11]. Administration professionals are expensive and operations spendings significantly contributes to IT systems' total cost of ownership of [2]. Zarnekow et al. report that operating and enhancing an IT system makes up 80% of the system's total cost of ownership within the first five years [31].

Various challenges of IT system administration have been addressed: from a technical or tool perspective [5,14,26,28] as well as an organizational perspective [1,3,18]. Graduate coursework is being created to provide capable sysadmins [24]. Faced with increasing cost and innovation pressure, companies turned to cloud computing, and its adoption is steadily increasing [23]. Integrating applications running in the cloud, is a new challenge that sysadmins have to cope with [9]. Against the backdrop of these challenges, in this paper we investigate sysadmins. The goal is to contribute to the understanding of how sysadmins have integrated recent trends and recommendations into their daily work and what hinders them. A case study with four companies is conducted. This paper contributes by highlighting current challenges system administration teams face.

© Springer Nature Switzerland AG 2019
W. Abramowicz and R. Corchuelo (Eds.): BIS 2019 Workshops, LNBIP 373, pp. 124–135, 2019.
https://doi.org/10.1007/978-3-030-36691-9_11

The paper is structured as follows. The theoretical foundations are described in the following section. Thereafter, the research design a case study is outlined in Sect. 3. The study's results are presented in Sect. 4. The conclusion is presented in Sect. 5. The last section summarizes and presents the limitations as well as an outlook on further research.

2   Foundations

Operating software can be very case-specific. Different developers write software, usually with no common operating principles. For standard software, proprietary pieces of training can be booked to learn how to properly, in the eyes of the vendor, operate the software [19]. Open frameworks such as ITIL also find their way into proprietary operations - and vice versa [12].

Operating an SAP Netweaver application system, for example, includes the following areas: basic tooling knowhow (command line, graphical configuration), advanced tooling know-how (e.g., specific management software such as Solution Manager), maintaining system landscapes (transporting code from development into production, maintaining complex landscapes of development, test, production - including advanced deployment methods), rights and access management, monitoring, backup and recovery, and data management [12,25].

For enterprise system installations, past and current operations are still characterized by on-premise and a *full control* feeling of IT staff [10]. This feeling of *full control* over the IT stack is often particularly vivid in contrast to today's situation where a large part of the operations is performed either by dedicated outsourcers or in the cloud. An operator celebrating the *full control* feeling might positively remember the times where he could grab the person responsible for a misbehaving server in the infrastructure team. Such relationships often exist informally, or, operational service level agreements explicitly define them [22].

Different considerations play into the decision of outsourcing or keeping operations in-house. This can be related to attempted cost savings, problems of finding qualified personnel, or concentration on core competencies [21]. Often, the outsourcing client, retains personnel qualified to map business requirements with IT requirements. However, depending on preference and the specific situation, organizations may retain larger portions to oversee stable operations. The trend of retaining skilled staff in operations may be increasing again in times of digitalization, DevOps and the recognition that IT is crucial for a successful and thriving business [16].

Operations professionals' challenges stem from more than just organizational issues like staff shortage or cost considerations. Technical standardization and flexible deployment models of infrastructure and platform as a service have added challenges. Technical standardization on the infrastructure and platform layer give new room to custom software development in DevOps style [1]. Operators have to deal with these custom software extensions or standalone products, which usually have to be intertwined with legacy applications at some point in their lifecycle [17]. Meanwhile, software as a service is getting more common. Thus, operators also have to deal with landscapes where on-premise applications are replaced or augmented with software as a services [13].

In this changing environment, companies such as Google, Netflix, Microsoft, and Amazon are role models for technical and methodological excellence [3]. However, the applicability of their techniques and methodologies to large and heterogeneous application system landscapes of typical non-IT enterprises is uncertain. Such companies often operate proprietary software as well as a myriad of custom integrations or even full-fledged custom software. The reliance on external providers is often grown and change management is not trivial.

ITIL covers many IT service management processes, but insufficiently covers cloud and gives an insufficient guideline as to how to cope with these new situations. Some recent works have been paramount in the world of DevOps [18] and site reliability engineering, a term coined by Google [3], but also established works such as ITIL are still of great importance. In this paper, we use a literature-based structure for inquiry of the studied companies as shown in Table 1. Clear structuring of roles and responsibilities within IT is necessary. Cannon [4] propose roles within the general sphere of IT service management. However, more from an SAP-specific standpoint, Swonke proposes roles for SAP operations in an IT application system landscape that becomes an increasingly hybrid mix of on-premise enterprise software and cloud-based services. Kim et al. [18] describe how IT operations teams organization and coordination can be improved by the introduction of methods such as Kanban. Also obvious is the need for a service catalog to offer one's offerings in a scenario where all IT services are in questioned to be outsourced and where IT-business alignment is of great importance [15]. In order to keep up with innovation and propose competitive solutions to the business, operations should engage in active innovation management [3,27]. Beyer et al. [3] report that at Google, automation is incentivized with a simple principle. Operations professionals, or site reliability engineers, are asked to spent a portion of time on automating daily tasks and only spent the other portion of time on these daily tasks, thereby steadily increasing automation and efficiency. Automation technology is abundantly available on the open source software market and is pushed by large IaaS and PaaS providers such as Google, Amazon, or Microsoft [3,8,28]. Some of these technologies are available for enterprise software, but not all. Lastly, outsourcing is a well-known strategy in IT [21] and it remains to be a strategy to cope with requirements that cannot or shall not be fulfilled in-house [27].

Cloud computing is addressed in this paper from different perspectives. However, in literature [29] it has not sufficiently been addressed from the perspective of operators within enterprise software settings. Sysadmins that work in a highly very environment are often seen as craftsmen. However, some view their work increasingly as an academic discipline [24]. Therefore, this paper contributes by shedding light on the domain of operations in the enterprise systems domain in the time of the hybrid application system landscapes of 2018.

Table 1. Overview of areas for improvement within operation teams.

Area	Description	Sources
Roles and responsibilities	Clearly defined roles and responsibilities serve a smooth operation as well as communication with other departments	[4, 18, 27]
Service portfolio	A structured service portfolio services visibility of the operation team's offering and profile within the organization	[15]
Innovation	In order to keep up with increasing demands innovation is key, for instance through automation initiatives	[3, 27]
Automation	Automation promises to improve efficiency and quality of operations	[3, 8, 28]
Outsourcing	Benefits of outsourcing can range from cost-savings to added know-how	[21, 27]

3   Research Design

This research is aligned with case study methodology [6, 30]. Empirical research on the adoption of current operations practices is still rare. Although hypothesis testing research [6] might be adequate, it was decided to perform a case study first in order to get a better understanding of the domain [6]. Multiple cases were included in order to facilitate cross-case comparison [6]. In order to come to meaningful results, cases were sampled first [6]. Data was then collected, processed, and analyzed.

3.1   Case Sample

Four large[1] were sampled. All of these cases are client companies using SAP software. SAP software, predominately ERP software, is traditionally used by large clients [19]. Therefore, only large companies were sampled. Including differently sized companies would have aggravated cross-case comparison given the small sample size. Eisenhardt suggests a minimum of three and maximum of ten cases [6]. Contact with client companies was facilitated through the German SAP user group DSAG. The first author and interviewees from operations participated in a workshop series organized by SAP and DSAG. The workshop series started in early 2018 and sought to provide guidelines for operating hybrid SAP-focused IT system landscapes. The available workshop cases were further sampled based on the suitability of each case to contribute valuable insights to the study [6]. Suitability was subjectively judged by the author throughout three one-day workshop meetings. In order to enhance objectivity, business representatives were also sought to be interviewed. Two of the operations representatives (Beta and Delta)

---

[1] According to the company size definition by the European Union [7].

rejected providing a representative from the business. The operations manager of Delta gave as a reason that such an inquiry might be bad publicity for his team in the business departments. The interviewee from Beta did not get management approval to contact a business department for an interviewee. Table 2 provides an overview of the cases and what data sources were used for analysis. All cases operate a broad range of SAP application software. Application areas include enterprise resource planning, business intelligence, production planning and control, customer relationship management, webshop solutions as well as portal solutions. While Delta only uses one additional SAP SaaS offering, the other cases have two or more SAP SaaS and PaaS offerings in their portfolio. All of the companies also operate standard software by other vendors and use cloud services, including public IaaS offerings. The focus of the interviews and the interviewees' daily work, however, lies on SAP software and services.

Table 2. Case overview

Case	Description	Data
A	Business: Electronics manufacturer, Size: large, User location: international, Staff: 7, Supported Users: 14.000, Hosting: internal in one local data center	Interviews: Operator (1:15 h) and Business manager (0:36 h), Questionaire
B	Business: Medical equipment manufacturer, Size: large, User location: international, Staff: 6, Supported Users: 5.500, Hosting: external	Interviews: Operations manager (1:06 h), Questionaire
Γ	Business: Food precursor provider, Size: large, User location: international, Staff: 9, Supported Users: 3.000, Hosting: internal in three data centers	Interviews: Operations manager (1:02 h) and Business manager (0:40 h), Questionaire
Δ	Business: Electronics manufacturer Size: large, User location: national, Staff: x Supported Users: 650, Hosting: external	Interviews: Operations manager (0:40 h), Questionaire

3.2 Data Collection, Processing, and Analysis

Data were mainly collected through the means of interviews [20], which were conducted in November 2018 by telephone with one interviewer and one respondent. An additional questionnaire was handed out for more efficiency. It inquired as to the distribution of roles, the IT system architecture as well as some meta information. These questions could better be answered by writing than in an interview. The interview was structured with a previously created interview guideline. Both, guideline and questionnaire, were constructed on the basis of Table 1. A review of guideline and questionnaire was performed by a senior researcher and a senior domain expert with substantial operations experience. The review resulted in a small wording change in the questionnaire referring to a role description that could be perceived as evaluative, an addition of a question to the interview guideline as well as small wording changes for better understanding. All interviews were voice recorded after receiving the consent to do so from each interviewee and transcribed thereafter. German was the common language. The transcription process was semi-automatic. A SaaS offering[2] was used for automated transcribing.

4 Results

In the following subsection, the four main inquiry resut clusters are presented.

4.1 Coordination of Work

Alpha and Gamma report that most workload is handled internally. Both, Alpha and Gamma use cloud services. Gamma's procures consulting, as well as an external help desk service. Beta has subject matter experts and few internal sysadmin resources (approximately 10%). They rely to a great deal on the SAP basis services of a hosting provider. Beta's staff operates some application systems (above database layer) because the SAP-focused provider has no corresponding capability (e.g., different vendor's customer relationship management solution). Delta provides no internal delivery capabilities but reports that his team orchestrates between the different external providers who are responsible for all operational work. Capacity provided to the business is only limited by the business' budget to pay the provider. Delta's orchestration activities include contractual design, requirements and process definition, access rights definition and assignment as well as coordination between the stakeholders (different providers and business departments) and sporadic in-system work in case of incidents or change request to control fulfillment.

The perceived performance of external resources collaborating directly with the internal teams of the cases varies. While Gamma values the competence of an external integration developer for his cloud engagements, he is not satisfied with the limited availability of this resource. Delta reports satisfaction with most regular tasks of different roles taken up by external resources. For sysadmins, Delta is not satisfied with their ability to resolve complex issues. Subject matter experts, integration developers, and operations automation developers are limited in availability. Lastly, Delta would appreciate integration architects to contribute more to strategical issues.

---

[2] https://www.spext.co/ The service eased manual transcription effort when speakers spoke pronounced. The recognition rate significantly decreased when speakers spoke less pronounced or with dialect.

Interviewees were inquired about internal resources with bottleneck character and if strategies exist to cope with such situations. Alpha acknowledges very few instances of bottlenecks in his department, but points to inter-IT-departmental integration development where bottleneck situations occur more often. Beta strongly acknowledges the bottleneck problem and addresses it by creating an overview of his department's subject areas. For each subject area, he strives to have at least two of his staff to be able to substitute each other. Gamma reports no practices to deal with bottlenecks. He says that they occasionally occur, but that his small team is experienced and capable to cope with the situations and the negative business impact is neglectable. Delta reports that bottleneck situations are in most case not a problem because all operational work is performed by external providers.

Task distribution ranges from no formal distribution to defined basic operator tasks that have to be performed one to three times daily (e.g., checking system status reports). Skill-aligned distribution of reoccuring work is practiced. However, much reoccuring work is outsourced. Ticketing tools are used to handle incident, request, and change processes as well as smaller project-like tasks. Projects are handled using project management tools. Ticketing tools of external service providers are used where applicable.

Change requests are coming from the business units. Alpha and Beta are reporting the build-up of process experts in each business units that are capable of working with IT to translate their groups' business requirements into IT requirements. This build-up is ongoing. Business departments in the cases of Alpha, Beta, and Gamma rely on their IT department exclusively. Delta reports that their business departments either assisted or autonomous deal with external providers. Budgets are used for making IT investments. Alpha reports increasing professionalization in this area in line with the company's growth. An IT business and steering board approves planned changes. Gamma reports that the return on investment is hard to measure for making assessments for approval.

For interdepartmental communication, regular meetings take place (e.g., jour fix, weekly or every other week) amongst Alpha, Beta, and Gamma. Within these meetings activities such as upgrades which affect on other teams, for instance, infrastructure, are discussed. Regular meetings also are held with security and the external hosting providers (Beta). The conversation in the regular meetings with the service provider is also based on vendor-based recommendations as to how to improve the systems' performance. Some agile practices such as stand-up meetings are incorporated, but nothing agile was further (e.g., use of Kanban boards) reported.

4.2 Service Offering

The SAP basis teams do not have service catalogs. Gamma reports ordering is done via e-mail. Alpha and Beta state that service catalogs are planned to be introduced. Service catalogs, with service level agreements, are used from the external service providers providing infrastructure services. As there are no service catalogs, individual services also do not have explicit prices attached to them. IT costs are apportioned based on the sourced applications per department or business unit. Operational service agreements for interdepartmental account-ability do not exist in any of the four organizations. If the business requires new functionality no formal procedure exists for cases Alpha, Gamma, and Delta. Only case Beta has a predefined process. Their process includes checking of alternatives and price comparisons as well as operational considerations when integrating cloud applications. Integration of cloud applications is a challenge all of the organizations face. Problems that are faced include:

– effort estimations are difficult because cloud applications are new to staff
– identity management for on-premise and cloud applications is difficult to orchestrate
– skilled employees for these new products are rare
– network and firewall issues occur frequently
– user interface integration for seamless user experience is required but costly
– multi-provider scenarios: handling communication between different providers is costly

In terms of service provisioning, self-service is only limitedly available. All cases report self-service for standard functions such as password reset. In Alpha's and Beta's systems, emergency software transports for critical bug fixes are available. Cases Alpha, Beta, and Gamma state that self-service capabilities are planned.

4.3   Innovation

The interviewees were asked whether or not key performance indicators existed that incentivize efforts to increase operations automation. However, their per-formance was only measured in regards to incident resolution time. No explicit incentivization for automation of work in day-to-day operations, as proposed by Beyer et al., was reported. The interviewee of Beta points to a clear separation of duties between the build and run teams. Such operations automation tasks would fall to the build team. All respondents report the possibility and active support of training and conventions. No innovation management is reported by the respondents. Gamma uses the guidance of its vendor, SAP, for technical inno-vation. Delta points to a to zero budget for proofs-of-concept implementations. Therefore, he sees his department not in a position to make innovation sugges-tions but only reacting to business demands. Contrarily, the business respondent of Alpha expresses his wish to get more proactive support from the IT depart-ment. More business-aligned proposals originating in the IT department would be welcome in his view.

4.4   Standardization and Automation

Alpha, Beta, and Gamma use IT service management tools as well as system management tools (e.g., for system copy or profiling). Delta's SAP basis team operates no tool internally, but their providers use tools that they also use occasionally (e.g., to open incidents). Alpa, Beta, and Gamma report limited automation. Examples for automation in operations include operating system updates, backup, system copies, and software transports. Only software transports are integrated into IT service management workflows. Delta reports no automation and expresses no preference for manual or automated work as long as the work is done to a satisfactory degree by the provider. Provider performance is not monitored actively.

For their automation, the companies use scripts. Templates are used in operating system-level operation and for SAP transport automation. However, no community-shared repositories are tapped into. Monitoring solutions are in operation but often fragmented. Alpha reports on an initiative to centrally aggregate monitoring information. Gamma's monitoring is centralized. Alpha reports availability only for large business applications (e.g., ERP and data warehouse). Once a month, availability and performance reports are provided to management. Their cloud application reports response time. However, Alpha's interviewee states that these numbers often don't match the user experience. Beta and Delta report no metrics. Gamma's focus also lies on availability reporting. No artificial intelligence is used to recognize unanticipated phenomena.

Alpha reports that improvement is possible in terms of reducing false monitoring alerts by fine-tuning monitoring metrics. The interviewee criticizes low insight into cloud applications. Delta reports high coordination effort for troubleshooting because of the different providers involved.

All companies use cloud applications by SAP. Advantages are seen in the speed of implementation, easy scalability, standardized single-sign-on, and current software versions. From a business perspective, respondents appreciate more discipline to stick with the defined standard processes, high frequency of available innovative new features, and accessibility in terms of user interface and global availability. Business respondents criticize performance, strong dependence on the provider, relatively little customizability, as well as concerns about data security. Operators negatively mention no control over maintenance windows and negative effects of systems under maintenance on other systems, overwhelmed internal capabilities due to high innovation speed in the cloud, limited scalability, high efforts in configuring certificates, networks, and firewall, unclear support contacts, as well as limited influence in case of data problems (e.g., in case of bugs, data backups are more difficult to manage compared to on-premise).

5   Conclusion

The analysis of the four cases shows differences to the concepts presented in Sect. 2. Pure SAP basis administrator duties are shifting from internal IT to outsourced hosters where this has not already been the case. Internal operations staff is increasingly responsible for a multitude of technologies. Although their department's contribution to business continuity and innovative services is crucial, SAP basis teams almost in no case employ agile measures reported in the

DevOps and site reliability engineering paradigms. Beta, with still substantial internal staff, started addressing bottleneck situations. For Delta, this is not even necessary because all operational work is outsourced. Delta's respondent states that his application services do not have the highest availability or stability requirements. It is therefore questionable whether or not their approach is transferable to more critical areas like that of Beta. All external resources have availability as a major drawback. Coordination between departments is done routinely, but no agile planning tools like Kanban boards are employed.

Unlike the infrastructure or external services they use, the SAP basis teams have no service catalogs in place. Some initiative is on the way. Also, no operational service levels are implemented.

No innovation management is performed. Also, no incentivization for automation is in place. Both would be beneficial since the business requires assistance in defining innovative services and products, and freed up resources due to automation could assist in innovation projects.

Automation is performed almost exclusively for basic operating system level tasks and software logistics. Automation such as parameterized SAP ERP client deployment is not available. Also, unlike in operating system level configuration automation, no public or community repositories for configuration templates are used. Monitoring solutions are in place, but three of the cases do not have a consolidated picture available.

Cloud computing comes as a two-fold promise. It is easily accessible and has competitively priced innovative business functionality. Marketing claims that effort of internal IT operations shrinks. Expectations on IT operations remain the same in terms of stability as back when they used to operate purely on-premise. However, in reality, the effort of internal IT does not decrease. New problems arise and it becomes seemingly more complicated. Still business welcomes the cloud applications superior functionality and currentness and operations will have to cope with that.

6 Summary, Limitations, and Research Outlook

In this work, four companies, and specifically their SAP basis teams, were analyzed. Various differences compared to state-of-the-art operations principles where observed. Notably, no agile work coordination or automation incentivization is practiced. Former operators are increasingly required to become subject matter experts in various areas. Basic SAP basis work is outsourced to providers. One of the studied companies, without own SAP Basis resources, merely orchestrates between different providers doing the operational work.

Four cases were analyzed in the study. Only two of the cases allowed interviews with SAP basis and business representatives. Also, only four cases in total could be studied which has limitations in regards to generalizability.

In future work, we plan to conduct a quantitative study on the basis of what we learned. We want to gain a better understanding of how current practices from the DevOps and site reliability engineering paradigms are applied in proprietary enterprise-level systems administration and what hinders their application.

References

1. Alt, R., Auth, G., Kögler, C.: Innovationsorientiertes IT-Management - Eine Fallstudie zur DevOps-Umsetzung bei T-Systems MMS. HMD Praxis der Wirtschaftsinformatik **54**(2), 216–229 (2017)
2. Barrett, R., Kandogan, E., Maglio, P.P., Haber, E.M., Takayama, L.A., Prabaker, M.: Field studies of computer system administrators: analysis of system management tools and practices. In: Proceedings of the 2004 ACM Conference on Computer Supported Cooperative Work, CSCW 2004, pp. 388–395. ACM, New York, NY, USA (2004)
3. Beyer, B., Jones, C., Petoff, J., Murphy, N.: Site Reliability Engineering: How Google Runs Production Systems. O'Reilly Media, Newton (2016)
4. Cannon, D.: ITIL - Service Operation. The Stationery Office, Norwich (2011)
5. Delaet, T., Joosen, W., Van Brabant, B.: A survey of system configuration tools. In: van Drunen, R. (ed.) 24th Large Installation System Administration Conference. LISA, USENIX (2010)
6. Eisenhardt, K.M.: Building theories from case study research. Acad. Manag. Rev. **14**(4), 532–550 (1989)
7. European Commission: What is an SME? (2011). Accessed 23 Feb 2017
8. Forsgren, N., Durcikova, A., Clay, P.F., Wang, X.: The integrated user satisfaction model: assessing information quality and system quality as second-order constructs in system administration. CAIS **38**, 39 (2016)
9. Gholami, M.F., Daneshgar, F., Beydoun, G., Rabhi, F.: Challenges in migrating legacy software systems to the cloud - an empirical study. Inf. Syst. **67**, 100–113 (2017)
10. Gordon, A.: The hybrid cloud security professional. IEEE Cloud Comput. **3**(1), 82–86 (2016)
11. Haber, E.M., Kandogan, E., Maglio, P.: Collaboration in system administration. Queue **8**(12), 10:10–10:20 (2010)
12. Hagemann, S., Will, L., Mayr, R.: SAP NetWeaver AS ABAP - System administration. SAP Press (2015)
13. Heidt, M., Sonnenschein, R., Loske, A.: Never change a running system? How status quo-thinking can inhibit software as a service adoption in organizations. In: 25th European Conference on Information Systems, ECIS 2017, Guimarães, Portugal, 5–10 June 2017, p. 122 (2017)
14. Hernantes, J., Gallardo, G., Serrano, N.: It infrastructure-monitoring tools. IEEE Softw. **32**(4), 88–93 (2015)
15. Hunnebeck, L.: ITIL - Service Design. The Stationery Office, Norwich (2011)
16. Kappelman, L., Johnson, V., Maurer, C., McLean, E., Torres, R., David, A., Nguyen, Q.: The 2017 sim it issues and trends study. MIS Q. Exec. **17**(1), 53–88 (2018)
17. Keller, A.: Challenges and directions in service management automation. J. Netw. Syst. Manage. **25**(4), 884–901 (2017)
18. Kim, G., Behr, K., Spafford, K.: The Phoenix Project: A Novel about IT, DevOps, and Helping Your Business Win. IT Revolution Press, Portland (2013)
19. Klaus, H., Rosemann, M., Gable, G.: What is ERP? Inf. Syst. Front. **2**(2), 141–162 (2000)
20. Kromrey, H., Strübing, J.: Empirische Sozialforschung: Modelle und Methoden der standardisierten Datenerhebung und Datenauswertung. Uni-Taschenbücher, Lucius & Lucius, UTB für Wissenschaft (2009)

21. Lacity, M.C., Khan, S., Yan, A., Willcocks, L.P.: A review of the it outsourcing empirical literature and future research directions. J. Inf. Technol. **25**(4), 395–433 (2010)
22. Lloyd, V.: ITIL - Continual Service Improvement. The Stationery Office, Norwich (2011)
23. Ng, F., Nag, S., ling Lam, L., et al.: Forecast: Public Cloud Services, Worldwide, 2015–2021, 2017 Update. Technical report G00247462, Gartner Inc. (2017). Accessed 31 July 2014
24. Rowe, D.C., Moses, S., Wilkinson, L.: Systems administration at the graduate level: defining the undefined. In: Proceedings of the 16th Annual Conference on Information Technology Education, pp. 77–82. ACM (2015)
25. Schreckenbach, S.: SAP Administration - Practical Guide, 1st edn. SAP Press (2011)
26. Spring, J.: Monitoring cloud computing by layer, part 1. IEEE Secur. Priv. **9**(2), 66–68 (2011)
27. Swonke, C.: The SAP Basis Team of Tomorrow. Technical report, DSAG (2016)
28. Wettinger, J., Andrikopoulos, V., Leymann, F., Strauch, S.: Middleware-oriented deployment automation for cloud applications. IEEE Trans. Cloud Comput. **1**, 142–157 (2016)
29. Yang, H., Tate, M.: A descriptive literature review and classification of cloud computing research. Commun. Assoc. Inf. Syst. **31**, 35–60 (2012)
30. Yin, R.K.: Case Study Research: Design and Methods. Applied Social Research Methods Series. SAGE Publications, Los Angeles (2009)
31. Zarnekow, R., Scheeg, J., Brenner, W.: Untersuchung der lebenszykluskosten vonitanwendungen. WIRTSCHAFTSINFORMATIK **46** (2004)

Integration of Enterprise Modeling and Ontology Engineering as Support for Business/IT-Alignment

Kurt Sandkuhl[1,2(✉)], Holger Lehmann[1], and Tom Sturm[1]

[1] Chair of Business Information Systems,
University of Rostock, Rostock, Germany
{kurt.sandkuhl,holger.lehmann,
tom.sturm}@uni-rostock.de
[2] School of Engineering, University of Jönköping, Jönköping, Sweden

Abstract. To create viable digital products from business and technical perspective, stakeholders from different enterprise functions should be involved. The focus of the paper is on the use of modelling approaches, in particular ontologies and enterprise models, for specifying the requirements to new services or products. There are hardly any reports of ontology usage in business and IT-alignment efforts, although ontologies can be used to capture the shared understanding of important concepts between business and IT stakeholders. The paper aims to bridge the gap between representations adequate for business stakeholders and ontology representations. The integration of a (business-oriented) enterprise modeling method with an (IT-oriented) ontology construction method is proposed by developing a method component. The main contributions of the paper are (1) a method component integrating enterprise modeling and ontology construction procedures, (2) an application case motivating the method component and showing its usage, and (3) first experiences in using the method component.

Keywords: Enterprise modeling · Ontology construction · Method component · Business and IT-Alignment

1 Introduction

A challenge frequently experienced in the development of innovative digital products or services is the gap between methods, modelling approaches and viewpoints of the involved stakeholder groups in an enterprise [1]. In order to create viable digital products from business and technical perspective, stakeholders from different enterprise functions should be involved, including marketing, controlling, operations management, system design and human resource management. New products or services usually cause changes in many parts of an enterprise, as they will have to be integrated in the business processes, need qualified personnel, are part of the enterprise service structure. This gap has been addressed by research on Business and IT-alignment (BITA) [2] but is not fully covered yet. BITA is a continuous process aiming at

© Springer Nature Switzerland AG 2019
W. Abramowicz and R. Corchuelo (Eds.): BIS 2019 Workshops, LNBIP 373, pp. 136–149, 2019.
https://doi.org/10.1007/978-3-030-36691-9_12

aligning strategic and operational objectives and ways to implement them between the business divisions of an organization and the organization's information technology division.

The focus of the paper is on the use of modelling approaches, in particular ontologies and enterprise models, for specifying the requirements to new services or products. One of the most cited definitions of the term "ontology" was proposed by Gruber: "An ontology is the explicit formalization of a shared conceptualization" [3]. From a BITA perspective, the two words "shared conceptualization" are the most interesting ones as they indicate – according to Gruber – that an ontology establishes a joint understanding of the meaning of concepts among the stakeholders in a defined application domain. Such a joint understanding between business and IT stakeholders is an essential element of most BITA efforts: if concepts have different meanings for different stakeholder and if this remains unknown, agreeing on goals, strategies or implementation approaches might be difficult.

Despite this anticipated contribution of ontologies to BITA, there are hardly any reports of ontology usage in BITA efforts which might result from their "formal specification". Ontologies are represented in formal languages or graph-like structures difficult to understand by most business stakeholders as they require specific IT-competences in knowledge representation.

This paper sets out to bridge the gap between representations adequate for business stakeholders and ontology representations. More concrete, we propose the integration of a (business-oriented) enterprise modeling method with an (IT-oriented) ontology construction method. For this purpose, we propose a method component incorporating the required integration activities. The main contributions of the paper are (1) a method component integrating enterprise modeling and ontology construction procedures, (2) an application case motivating the method component and showing its usage, and (3) first experiences in using the method component.

The remaining part of the paper is structured as follows: Sect. 2 presents the theoretical background for our work. Section 3 introduces an industrial case in ontology engineering with a pragmatic approach for integrating enterprise modeling and ontology construction. Section 4 proposes the method component based on the experiences from the industrial case. Section 5 summarizes the work.

2   Theoretical Background

The theoretical background for our paper stems from the areas of enterprise modeling (Sect. 2.1) and ontology engineering (Sect. 2.2) which we aim to integrate, and the area of method engineering (Sect. 2.3) which provides the means to construct method components.

2.1   Enterprise Modelling

In general terms, enterprise modelling (EM) is addressing the systematic analysis and modelling of processes, organization structures, products structures, IT-systems or any other perspective relevant for the modelling purpose [4]. Enterprise models can be applied for various purposes, such as visualization of current processes and structures in an enterprise, process improvement and optimization, introduction of new IT solutions or analysis purposes. Approaches and methods for EM have been the subject of development during at least 30 years. Some of the many approaches proposed in this field are:

- Active Knowledge Modelling [6] supporting work in enterprises with executable solution enterprise models which can be updated while applying them.
- ARIS [7] includes the Event-Process-Chains (EPC) modelling technique and means for structuring different perspectives of an enterprise.
- ArchiMate [8] is an established standard of the Open Group for Enterprise Architecture modelling.
- MEMO [9] originates from information systems development and promotes the co-design of information systems as complex IT-artefacts.

Methodical integration of enterprise modeling and ontology construction was proposed by only a few authors in scientific literature, like, e.g., [20]. For the industrial case study presented in Sect. 3, we will apply the EM approach 4EM [5]. 4EM uses six interrelated sub-models that complement each other and capture different views of the enterprise. The sub-models are:

- Goals Model (GM) focuses on describing the goals of the enterprise and problems hindering the achievement of goals.
- Business Rule Model (BRM) is used to define explicitly formulated business rules, for example in the context of the Goals Model and the Business Process Model.
- Concepts Model (CM) is used to define the terminology and entity types used in the enterprise and in the other 4EM sub-models with attributes, and relationships.
- Business Processes Model (BPM) is used to define enterprise processes and how they handle information as well as material.
- Actors and Resources Model (ARM) is used to describe how different organizational units, actors and resources are related to each other.
- Technical Components and Requirements Model (TCRM) focuses on the technical systems (e.g. the IT architecture).

2.2   Ontology Engineering Methodologies

Ontology engineering is a complex task which to a large extent consists of modelling activities. Methods for ontology construction (OC) in general consist of two phases: the specification phase to acquire informal knowledge on the domain, and the conceptualization phase, which structures and represents this knowledge formally. An overview of OC methods can be found in [13, 14, 15].

The *Uschold and King's method* is an experience-based method which consists of four main stages [10]. The first stage identifies the purpose of the ontology development. The second step builds the ontology by capturing the key concepts in the domain of interest, formalizing the concepts or reusing existing ontologies. In the third step an evaluation follows checking if the ontology fulfills the requirements. The last step documents the development process. The most important project developed using this methodology is the Enterprise Ontology. Consequently this methodology is also referred as "Enterprise Ontology Methodology".

A methodology that proposes a set of activities based on artifact refinement is *METHONTOLOGY*, which was proposed by [11] and is referred to be one of the most mature and detailed methodologies. This methodology can be used for building up ontologies from scratch, reusing other ontologies as they are or reengineering them. In the first step the ontology development process is defined, i.e. which activities, e.g. scheduling, control, quality assurance etc. should be performed when building ontologies. Then the set of stages through which an ontology moves during its lifetime is identified, the relation of stages as well as the task to be performed in each stage are assessed. The final step defines the particular techniques to realize these tasks.

For the case study in Sect. 3, we apply the Noy & McGuinness method, which is an iterative ontology development process consisting of seven steps [12]:

- Domain and scope of the ontology: The development starts by defining its domain and scope in which several questions should be answered, i.e. "What is the domain that the ontology will cover?" or "for what we are going to use the ontology?" These questions should be populated and formed more specifically regarding the domain of interest in order to put together a list of "competency questions" (CQ).
- Consider reusing existing ontologies: For a particular domain and task it should be investigated, whether existing ontologies could be reused and how.
- Enumerate important terms in the ontology: A list of important terms should be written down.
- Define the classes and the class hierarchy: These terms should be organized as classes into a hierarchical taxonomy.
- Define the properties of classes: The internal structure of concepts should be specified.
- Define the facets of the slots: Slots are refined using slot cardinality, slot-value type as well as domain and range of a slot.
- Create instances: The last step is creating individual instances of classes in the hierarchy and filling in the slot values.

2.3   Method Engineering

The research area of method engineering offers a rich body of knowledge how to systematically develop, introduce and adapt "methods". Methods often are considered as prescriptive since they are supposed to provide guidance for problem solving or for performing complex tasks. This requires that a method includes what activities to perform, how to perform them (procedure), what results (artefacts) to develop and how to capture these results (notation) [2]. Different conceptualizations of the term "method" and related terms have been proposed. If there is a close link between procedure, notation, and concepts, the term method component is used. The concept of method component is similar to the concept method chunk [16] and the notion of method fragment [17].

The way methods and method components are described in Sect. 4 follows the method conceptualization proposed by Goldkuhl et al. [18]. Goldkuhl et al. state that a comprehensive method description should describe the perspective, framework, cooperation principles and all method components:

- Method components: A method component should consist of concepts, a procedure and a notation. The concepts specify what should be captured a model. The procedure describes in concrete terms how to identify the relevant concepts in a method component. The notation specifies how the result of the procedure should be documented, i.e. appropriate expressions or symbols for each concept.
- Framework: the method framework describes the relationships between the individual method components, i.e. which components are to be used and under what conditions, as well as the sequence of the method components (if any).
- Forms of cooperation: many modeling tasks require a range of specialist skills or cooperation between different roles. These necessary skills and roles must be described, along with the division of responsibilities between the roles.
- Perspective: every method describes the procedure for the modeling process from a particular perspective, which influences what is considered important.

3   Industrial Case Study

This section focuses on the case study which is used to illustrate the integration of a (business-oriented) enterprise modeling method with an (IT-oriented) ontology construction method. In Sect. 3.1, the case study methodology is briefly explained; Sect. 3.2 describes the case as such and Sect. 3.3 contains details of the use of enterprise models and ontologies.

3.1   Methodology

Qualitative case study is an approach to research that facilitates exploration of a phenomenon within its context using a variety of data sources [19]. This ensures that the subject under consideration is explored from different perspectives which allows for multiple facets of the phenomenon to be revealed and understood. The research question addressed in the industrial case in this work is: *In a project aiming at developing an ontology, how can business and IT stakeholders be integrated into the construction process?*

Within the case study, we used two different perspectives, which at the same time represent sources of data: We observed the activities during enterprise modeling and ontology construction and we analyzed documents from different phases of the development process. Yin differentiates various kinds of case studies [19]: explanatory, exploratory and descriptive. The case study presented in Sect. 3.2 has to be considered as exploratory, as it explores the process of integrated EM and OC in real-life context in which it occurs. Based on the case study results, we derive the proposal for a new method component presented in Sect. 4, which follows an argumentative-deductive research process.

3.2   Case Description

The industrial case is a small enterprise established some years ago in the area of electronic business. The company is located in the North of Germany and has an innovative business model combining media content and electronic commerce. First, movies or TV-programs are analyzed of their content. In a further step, the tagged video content can be used to offer commercial products visible in the video in a certain scene (i.e. in a defined period) to the audience. In addition, the tags can be applied to determine which commercials or advertisements would fit to the video content. This functionality meets the demand of marketing industries for dynamic, target-oriented marketing campaigns.

The focus of the case study is on implementing an automatic way of generating the tags for the video content. Instead of manual tagging, a combination of machine learning for object recognition in videos and situation detection with a tailor-made domain ontology is under development. The machine learning approach uses ready-made detectors for different classes of objects. In a first object recognition phase, only a (randomly selected) subset of all available detectors is applied in order to reduce computing workload. The objects detected in this first phase are mapped onto the ontology which returns candidates for additional objects which – based on the semantic relationships between the discovered objects from the first phase - might also be present in the video. In a second phase, the detectors for the objects recommended by the ontology are used to refine the tagging results. This second phase might be repeated several times.

Our approach used in the industrial case was to start with a participatory EM method as a means to involve the business stakeholders in actively defining required functionality and content of the ontology. More concrete, we used goal modeling from 4EM to first define business goals and concepts modeling to capture the concepts used during goal formulation. Participation of IT and business stakeholders during goal identification and definition supported a joint understanding of the overall goals to be achieved by developing the ontology. Concepts modeling was also meant to involve the IT-stakeholders in first steps to defining the concepts of the ontology.

When the business stakeholders were satisfied with the 4EM goal model and when the concepts model was completed from the perspective of the IT stakeholders, we derived competency questions from the goal in the goal model, we shifted attention towards the ontology but continued to work in a participatory way. Competency questions (CQ) are an established way in ontology engineering to specify what questions an ontology is supposed to answer, what minimal requirements to the content exists (cf. Sect. 3.2). We explained the purpose of the CQ to the business stakeholders as a definition what the ontology should contain. Most of the CQ surprisingly were only a more detailed rephrased version of the goal descriptions. More details are provided in Sect. 3.3.

3.3   Usage of Enterprise Modeling and Ontology Construction in the Case

The development of the domain ontology had to be performed in close interaction between business stakeholder and IT personnel because the ontology has to reflect the "situations" of interest for the customers from marketing industries whereas the structure of the ontology has to be kept in synchronization with the detector set from machine learning. In order to actively involve both stakeholder groups, business and IT, we used 4EM goal modeling and concept modeling (see Sect. 2.1). The business side decided to focus on videos and marketing customers in the area of fashion. The goal model was supposed to reflect the business goals of the enterprise and, more important, for what "fashion-related" situations the ontology was meant to provide support. The resulting goal model is shown in Fig. 1. Situations are visible in the lowest refinement level of the goals and turned out to be fashion for different occasions or cultural contexts.

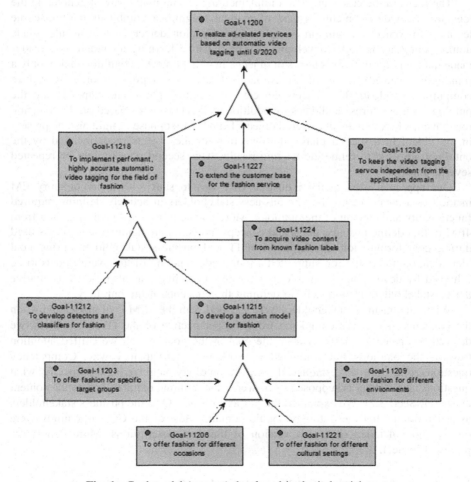

Fig. 1. Goal model (excerpt) developed in the industrial case

While developing the goal model, a number of terms were used which were captured in the concepts model. For some concepts model, attributes were identified. An excerpt of the resulting model is shown in Fig. 2.

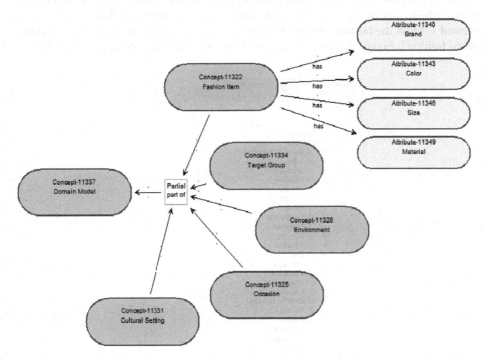

Fig. 2. Concepts model (excerpt) from the industrial use case

The contents of goal model and concepts model formed the starting point for the ontology development. We decided to use the Noy & McGuinness method (see Sect. 2.2) which recommends the definition of competency questions to specify the scope of an ontology. Since goals and requirements to the content of an ontology in our industrial case are closely related when considering the goals implying "situations", we rephrased the relevant goals into questions. Table 1 shows the resulting competency questions.

Table 1. Competency questions

No.	Competency question
QC1	What fashion items exist for defined target groups, such as women, men, boys, girls, etc.?
QC2	What fashion items exist for different occasions, such as weddings, funerals, parties, balls, etc.?
QC3	What fashion items exist for different genres, such as country style, city look, extreme leisure, etc.?
QC4	What fashion items exist for different environments, such as beach, maintain, snow, etc.?
QC5	What fashion items exist for certain cultural environments, such as Europe, Middle-East, etc.?
QC6	Which fashion items can be combined?

Starting from the competency questions, we were able to identify concepts in the concepts model which had to be included as classes in the ontology, because the reflect situations. However, as the situations do not specify fashion items as such, the development process of the ontology had to continue by structuring existing fashion items, which was by far more time consuming than the situations but could be performed without the business stakeholder who only defined the requirement to "include all of fashion". Figure 3 shows an excerpt from the resulting ontology in Protégé.

Fig. 3. Excerpt from domain ontology for fashion

4   Towards a Method Component for Integration EM and OE

With the experience from the use case presented in Sect. 3, we aim at developing a first version of a method component for bridging enterprise modeling and ontology construction methods. For the description of the method component (MC), we use the method conceptualization introduced in Sect. 2.3. All parts of the method conceptualization will be presented in the following.

Perspective. The method component is designed as a link between an EM method and OC which does not offer own views on EM and OC. However, the assumption is made that the applied EM method supports identification of goals and concepts as sources for transformation.

Framework. The MC consists of three method sub-components (MSC) which always have to be performed in the same sequence:

- MSC 0 (optimal): configure mapping. This step specifies what elements of the EM language are mapped onto what elements of an ontology. If the mapping has been configured (as for 4EM in the industrial case) the step is optional.
- MSC 1: transform goals. This step derives competency questions from goal descriptions.
- MSC 2: reuse concepts. This step creates an initial ontology based on the concepts in the enterprise model.

The different sub-components are described in the section on procedures (see below).

Table 2. Mapping of EM and ontology

EM meta-model	Ontology construction	Transformation
Goal	Competency question	Identify relevant goals and rephrase goal description
"support" relationship between goals	Competency question	Relate competency questions of sub-goals to other goals by incorporating the relation in the wording of the question
Concept	Class	Create one class for every concept
Attribute	Data property	Create data property for every attribute of a concept/class
"is_a" relationship between concepts	Class hierarchy	Create taxonomic relationship between classes who have a "is_a" relationship in concepts model
other relation-ship between concept and attributes	Object property	Create additional typed relationship between classes who have a relationship in concepts model

Cooperation Principles. To perform the method component, three sets of competences are required which usually are provided by two different persons/roles. The first competence required is expert knowledge in the source EM method. This is needed to identify relevant parts of the EM containing goals and concepts and to assist preparing these parts in cooperation with the business and IT stakeholders in the enterprise. The second set of competences is that of an ontology engineer to work on the future ontology. This second set usually also includes knowledge about model transformation or model mapping (which is the third competence set) because ontology engineering includes the reuse of existing taxonomies or of models in other representations.

Concepts. The concepts used in the method component and sub-components were identified in the industrial case and are enumerated in Table 2: goal, concept, class, data property, object property, taxonomic relation. As part of the MC, we defined a mapping between the relevant parts of the 4EM meta-model and the ontology structure, which is also shown in Table 2.

Procedures. The procedures to perform within the three sub-components are described in the following.

MC0 Configure Mapping:
- Identify concepts in EM representing goals (= goal-equivalent concepts) and representing concepts (= concept-equivalent concepts). This step is required because goals in some EM languages are represented in model component types, such as objective or aim, and concepts might not be modelled explicitly at all but represented in indicators or document
- Define a process for selecting all instances of goal-equivalent concepts from the enterprise model
- Define a process for selecting all instances of concept-equivalent concepts from the enterprise model

MC1 Transform Goals:
- Identify all goal-equivalent elements in the enterprise model based on the process defined in MC0
- For each goal, check suitability of the goal for capturing content in an ontology
- If the goal is suitable, rephrase the goal as competency question

MC2 Reuse Concepts:
- Identify all concept-equivalent elements in the enterprise model based on the process defined in MC0
- Identify position in the ontology's class hierarchy
- Insert concept as class in the ontology
- Create attributes of the concept (if existing) as data properties of the corresponding class in the ontology.

Notation. The MC does not define a separate notation for the MC. The notations of the EM language and the ontology representation used should be applied. For representing mapping steps and selected lists of elements, tables can be used.

Figure 4 summarize how the method component is creating a bridge between EM and OC. From EM, we use the goals and concepts to prepare OC. The proposed MC transforms goals into competency questions and concepts into classes. Afterwards, the OC process continues according to the selected method, which in the figure is the Noy & McGuiness method.

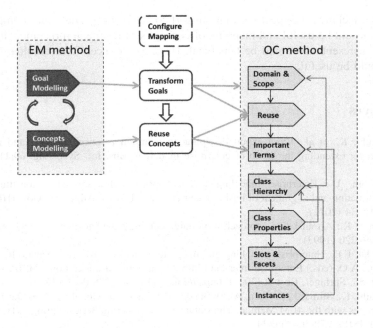

Fig. 4. Illustration of the overall approach

5   Discussion of Results and Conclusion

In this article we address the challenge of integrating methods, modelling approaches and viewpoints of different stakeholder groups in an enterprise. As a contribution to BITA, we connect a business stakeholder oriented way of specifying requirements (goal and concept modelling) with an IT-stakeholder oriented way to formally capture the specification (ontologies).

Based on the example from an industrial case, we defined an initial method component for an integrated use of EM and OC which transforms goals and concepts into competency questions and class hierarchies. This method component is illustrated in a case developing an ontology for the use in automatic object and situation recognition in videos. The biggest limitation of this work obviously is the missing validation of the method component. As the same case which inspired the development of the MC and provided the examples cannot be used for validating its utility, more work is needed to this end. Another limitation is that comparisons with other approaches were not made yet.

Future work is both technical and conceptual nature. From a conceptual perspective, the developed MC needs evaluation and refinement. More cases of ontology engineering are needed to verify the utility of the method. The three MSC need additional refinement and the practices should be added to all three of them.

From a technical perspective, tool support for converting goals into competency questions would be useful and mapping of concept sets from enterprise modeling into ontology representation could be beneficial. Here, experiences from ontology pattern design could be useful.

References

1. Sandkuhl, K., et al.: From expert discipline to common practice: a vision and research agenda for extending the reach of enterprise modeling. Bus. Inf. Syst. Eng. **60**(1), 69–80 (2018)
2. Seigerroth, U.: Enterprise modeling and enterprise architecture: the constituents of transformation and alignment of business and IT. Int. J. IT/Bus. Alignment Gov. (IJITBAG) **2**(1), 16–34 (2011)
3. Gruber, T.R.: A translation approach to portable ontology specifications. Knowl. Acquis. **5**(2), 199–220 (1993)
4. Vernadat, F.B.: Enterprise modelling and integration. In: Kosanke, K., Jochem, R., Nell, J. G., Bas, A.O. (eds.) Enterprise Inter- and Intra-Organizational Integration. ITIFIP, vol. 108, pp. 25–33. Springer, Boston (2003). https://doi.org/10.1007/978-0-387-35621-1_4
5. Sandkuhl, K., Stirna, J., Persson, A., Wißotzki, M.: Enterprise Modeling: Tackling Business Challenges with the 4EM Method. The Enterprise Engineering Series. Springer, Heidelberg (2014). ISBN 978-3662437247
6. Lillehagen, F., Krogstie, J.: Active knowledge models and enterprise knowledge management. In: Kosanke, K., Jochem, R., Nell, J.G., Bas, A.O. (eds.) Enterprise Inter- and Intra-Organizational Integration. ITIFIP, vol. 108, pp. 91–99. Springer, Boston (2003). https://doi.org/10.1007/978-0-387-35621-1_10
7. Scheer, A.-W., Nüttgens, M.: ARIS architecture and reference models for business process management. In: van der Aalst, W., Desel, J., Oberweis, A. (eds.) Business Process Management. LNCS, vol. 1806, pp. 376–389. Springer, Heidelberg (2000). https://doi.org/10.1007/3-540-45594-9_24
8. Josey, A.: ArchiMate® 2.1–A Pocket Guide. Van Haren, Zaltbommel (2013)
9. Frank, U.: MEMO organisation modeling language (1): focus on organisational structure. ICB-Research Report No. 48, University Duisburg-Essen (2011)
10. Uschold, M., King, M.: Towards a methodology for building ontologies. Artificial Intelligence Applications Institute, University of Edinburgh, Edinburgh (1995)
11. Fernandez-Lopez, M., Gomez-Perez, A., Juristo, N.: Methontology: from ontological art towards ontological engineering. In: Proceedings of the AAAI97 Spring Symposium, Stanford, USA, pp. 33–40 (1997)
12. Noy, N., McGuinness, D.: Ontology development 101: a guide to creating your first ontology. Development **32**(1), 1–25 (2000)
13. Öhgren, A., Sandkuhl, K.: Towards a methodology for ontology development in small and medium-sized enterprises (2005)
14. Corcho, Ó., Fernández-López, M., Gómez-Pérez, A.: Methodologies, tools and languages for building ontologies: where is their meeting point? Data Knowl. Eng. **46**(1), 41–64 (2003)
15. Fernández-López, M., Gómez-Pérez, A.: Overview and analysis of methodologies for building ontologies. Knowl. Eng. Rev. **17**(2), 129–156 (2002). https://doi.org/10.1017/s0269888902000462

16. Ralyté, J., Backlund, P., Kühn, H., Jeusfeld, M.A.: Method chunks for interoperability. In: Embley, D.W., Olivé, A., Ram, S. (eds.) ER 2006. LNCS, vol. 4215, pp. 339–353. Springer, Heidelberg (2006). https://doi.org/10.1007/11901181_26
17. Brinkkemper, S.: Method engineering: engineering of information systems development methods and tools. Inf. Softw. Technol. **1995**, 37 (1995)
18. Goldkuhl, G., Lind, M., Seigerroth, U.: Method integration: the need for a learning perspective. IEEE Proc. Softw. (Spec. Issue Inf. Syst. Methodol.) **145**(4), 113–118 (1998)
19. Yin, R.K.: Case Study Research: Design and Methods. Applied Social Research Methods Series, vol. 5, 3rd edn. Sage Publications Inc., Thousand Oaks (2002)
20. Karagiannis, D., Buchmann, R., Walch, M.: How can diagrammatic conceptual modelling support knowledge management? In: 25th European Conference on Information Systems (ECIS), Guimaraes (2017). http://aisel.aisnet.org

Towards Aligning IT and Daily Routines of Older Adults

Marite Kirikova[1(✉)], Ella Kolkowska[2], Piotr Soja[3], Ewa Soja[4],
and Agneta Muceniece[1]

[1] Department of Artificial Intelligence and Systems Engineering,
Riga Technical University, Riga, Latvia
Marite.Kirikova@rtu.lv, Agneta.Muceniece@edu.rtu.lv
[2] Center for Empirical Research in Information Systems (CERIS),
Örebro University School of Business, Örebro, Sweden
Ella.Kolkowska@oru.se
[3] Department of Computer Science, Cracow University of Economics,
Kraków, Poland
Piotr.Soja@uek.krakow.pl
[4] Department of Demography, Cracow University of Economics,
Kraków, Poland
Ewa.Soja@uek.krakow.pl

Abstract. Different IT solutions exist for supporting older adults. However, the ways in which these solutions are positioned usually concern only specific activities or specific problems. In this paper we analyze the current research state regarding activities of older adults, the contexts of their activities, and supportive IT solutions to create a background for further investigations regarding alignment of IT solutions and daily routines of older adults. The paper presents illustrative mapping between older adult activities and IT solution categories and derives therefrom some aspects that are to be taken into account for successful alignment between IT solutions and daily routines of older adults.

Keywords: Older adults · Context factors · IT solutions for older adults

1 Introduction

Better living conditions in many EU countries and other circumstances have caused a shift in age proportions towards a higher number of older adults (60+ year old citizens) as compared to those of a younger age. Simultaneously these citizens strive to maintain an independent and active life style. Different IT solutions, e.g. robots, are seen as one of the facilitating means to achieve this purpose. There are already a number of solutions proposed for older adults [1]. These solutions differ in their functionality, availability and usability. In this research in progress paper we will consider the following research question: "What are the alignment aspects to be taken into account in designing IT solutions for older adults regarding their daily routines".

© Springer Nature Switzerland AG 2019
W. Abramowicz and R. Corchuelo (Eds.): BIS 2019 Workshops, LNBIP 373, pp. 150–156, 2019.
https://doi.org/10.1007/978-3-030-36691-9_13

To answer this research question we will use the following approach: (1) Investigate examples of the activities of older adults; (2) Investigate contextual factors that have already been amalgamated in related works; (3) Investigate the existing IT solutions dedicated for older adults; and (4) Derive essential issues from the examples, published surveys and tool descriptions, focusing on IT alignment with daily routines of older adults.

While we are also currently performing an empirical analysis based on interviews and workshops, in this paper we will discuss only already published related works. We will focus on IT solutions which are dedicated to older adults, leaving the use of commonly known IT solutions, such as Skype, mobile phones etc., outside the scope of our attention unless these tools are parts of dedicated IT solutions.

In Sects. 2–5 of the paper we progressively discuss the results of the four steps of the above-mentioned research approach; in Sect. 6 we provide a brief conclusion.

2 Daily Activities of Older Adults

Authors of [2] (USA, 2017) have examined daily routines of 5 older adults using workflow analysis. They elaborated the list of 32 activities. The most frequent activities are sleeping, watching TV, having a meal, reading/writing, out of home (includes a spectrum of activities) and brushing teeth. To illustrate a significant difference, we can mention that the percentage of time watching TV was 12.7% of daily activities as compared to conversation, constituting only 0.5% of daily activities. This, to some extent, explains why social isolation is usually mentioned as one of the main problems of older adults [3]. The authors of [2] showed that there is a great level of heterogeneity in activity levels and space occupancy patterns amongst individuals, indicating that different people have different daily routine patterns. A routine means doing the same basic activities around the same time every day. This gives structure and a natural flow to the day [4] and this has been recognized as an important issue for the well-being of older adults.

The spectrum and popularity of activities depend not only on individuals' personal characteristics (e.g. health condition), but also vary across countries; for instance, the survey conducted in Japan showed reading and writing being the most frequent activity [5], but, in Europe, housekeeping was the second, after media [6]. In [7] six dimensions of routines of older adults are suggested, namely: Enjoy/dislike; Flexible/rigid; Minimal/extensive; Autonomy/dependence; Work/leisure; and People oriented/task oriented. These dimensions might well be important when designing IT solutions for supporting older adults regarding their wellbeing, which in [7] is characterized as follows (the survey considered women only): meet obligations; maintain activity level; maintain health; anticipate or look forward to things; maintain control; balance work, rest and play; accomplish and achieve; feel good about self; and provide continuity. These criteria do not contradict the quality of life indicators of Eurostat [8], and can be used to evaluate the impact of IT solutions on daily routines of older adults [9].

3 The Context of Usage of IT Solutions

There are many considerations that influence daily routines (and thus also the use of IT solutions) of older adults; for instance their neighborhoods [10]. The author of [7] points to the following factors: family values and goals; family structure; individuality; work outside the home; physical status; environment (includes neighborhoods mentioned above); others involved. In [11] community level factors are analyzed such as: (1) social environment including health and community support services, respect and recognition, and communication and information; and (2) physical environment that includes transportation, housing, accessibility, and meeting space.

The above-listed context factors are revealed in social science studies. In order for the context to be sensed by IT solutions, smaller granularity context factors are considered; such as medical history, residence layout, etc. [1]. For handling these factors, some situation modeling languages and ontologies have been developed [1].

4 State of the Art Regarding IT for Older Adults

There have been extensive research and development efforts made regarding IT solutions for older adults. However, the available surveys are quite fragmentary. The authors of [3] report on the ways by which *robotic technologies* can help older adults, showing that these technologies can address almost all problems of older adults. A survey of IT solutions developed by 2013 is available in [1]. This work groups the technologies into two classes: *smart homes* (defined there as regular homes which are augmented with various types of sensors and activators) and *mobile and wearable sensors*. It also points to a number of algorithms that support the tools, namely [1]: (1) activity recognition algorithms such as mobile activity recognition, ambient activity recognition, vision based activity recognition; (2) context modeling algorithms (basically for the data to be handled by sensors); (3) algorithms for anomaly detection that refer to the problem of finding patterns in data that do not conform to the expected behavior; (4) location and identity identification algorithms (such as for smart floor, WiFi based systems, ultrasonic systems etc.); and (5) planning algorithms (e.g. to create daily plans and daily reminders).

When the applications of IT solutions are classified, these classifications are mostly problem or specific activity based (they do not address daily routines – ordered sequences of activities – that we are focusing on in this paper). The authors of [1] classify the applications in: health and activity monitoring tools, wandering prevention tools, and Cognitive Orthotics (e.g. reminders). Demiris and Hense [11] distinguish between the following home assistive technologies: (1) physiological monitoring, (2) functional monitoring/emergency detection and response, (3) safety monitoring and assistance, (4) security monitoring and assistance, (5) social interaction monitoring and assistance, and (6) cognitive and sensory assistance. Authors of [12] show how a sympathetic design framework has been used for developing "Thinking of you Device", "Tag It Device",

"Altruist Device" (for socialization); "Forgetfulness Device", "Connect Device", "ShareLab Device", "Mokingbird Device", "DinnerClose", "Madeline Device", and "Onacom Device". These devices can be used in different activities of older adults, such as socialization, eating, and leisure activities; and also sharing the products they have made ("ShareLab"). There are also devices for games, e.g. full body motion interaction games [13], robotic pets [14], and much effort has been put into designing applications for health support and the support for financial activities [15]. One of the most comprehensive surveys of applications of IT solutions for older adults is provided by [16]. It divides IT solutions into the following groups: special purpose machines; virtual assistants; social networking; messaging services; intelligent environments; information services; health care such as remote care, assistive technology, rehabilitation, and care for active aging and healthy lifestyles. As we can see from the surveys discussed in this section, there are a plenty of IT solutions designed to support older adults. However, these solutions are targeted at specific activities and solving specific problems; it is not clear how well these tools may integrate into daily routines of older adults.

5 Daily Routines and IT Solutions

In Table 1 we represent the mapping between the daily activities reported in [2] and tool classifications available in [12] and [16].

The fact that a particular IT solution is mentioned in the activity row just means that the technology is available. It does not mean that it is always needed. If a symbol in the table is (–) – it does not mean that the technology does not exist; just that it was not found in [12] or [16]. Table 1 proves that almost each daily activity of an older adult can be supported by some already existing IT solutions. Activities that were not supported by any of the categories of [12] and [16], namely: have a break, dress, do personal care, watch TV, and do paperwork; are not shown in the table. On the other hand, not all technology types were mentioned in the table, which may mean that the daily routine with technologies may differ from the "ordinary daily routine". Also, the existence of the tools does not imply their availability, which depends on contextual factors mentioned in Sect. 3.

Table 1 shows IT solutions without consideration of the sequence of activities; however, the sequence of activities is what establishes the daily routine. Figure 1 shows a fragment of the daily routine, which is derived from data available in [2]. The fragment consists of three sequential activities each of which takes 10 min. So this part of a routine would take half an hour for an older adult without using specific IT solutions. But let us suppose that these technologies are used: assistant for brushing teeth, information services for reading/writing, and mockingbird for meditation. These three technologies have to be located, switched on, used, and switched off. That would require extra time in performing the activities. This observation leads to the assumption that the number of tools for a routine should be minimized.

154   M. Kirikova et al.

Table 1. IT solutions for daily activities of older adults.

Activity	IT solutions in [12]	IT solutions in [16]
Clean, fix, maintain	–	Special purpose machines, intelligent environments, virtual assistants
Exercise	–	Virtual assistants
Get in bed	–	Special purpose machines
Get from bed	–	Special purpose machines
Have a meal	Dinner Close Device	Virtual assistants
Have a coffee	Dinner Close Device	Virtual assistants
Do laundry	–	Special purpose machines
Prepare meal	–	Virtual assistants, intel. environments
Out of home	–	Healthcare (assistive technology)
Pray/meditate	Mokingbird	–
Read/write	–	Information services
Shower	–	Healthcare (assistive technology)
Sleep	–	Healthcare (assistive technology)
Brush teeth	–	Healthcare (assistive technology)
Use toilet	–	Healthcare (assistive technology)
Wash dishes	–	Special purpose machines
Wash face	–	Healthcare (assistive technology)
Use computer	C-Connect	Information services
Involve in conversation	Thinking of You, Tag It	Messaging service, Social networking
Drink water	–	Healthcare (assistive technology)
Prepare for going out	Altruist	Healthcare (active a. and healthy l. st.)
Sing	Mockinbird	–
Take medicine	Forgetfulness	Healthcare (assistive technology)
Make a phone call	–	Information services

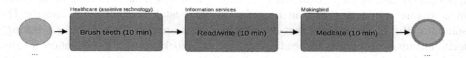

Fig. 1. An excerpt of a daily routine of older adult

Summarizing the information reflected in previous sections, we can list the following factors that are important in aligning IT and daily routines of older adults: (1) The possible routines should be well understood; also the difference between IT solution supported and non-supported routines must be understood. (2) The applicability of existing IT solutions for routine activities must be well understood (see the context factors discussed in Sect. 3); analysis of these factors may help to decide on applicability of the IT tools, also taking into account their affordability; and (3) The time and cost of tool usage have to be considered (minimized).

6   Conclusion

This paper provides an insight into issues that are relevant for achieving an alignment between IT solutions that are dedicated for older adults and their daily routines. So far the usage of the IT solutions has been considered only in the context of specific activities or problems. Daily routines, while seen as important for older adults, have not been documented so that their relevant patterns might be derived and IT solutions aligned with them. Therefore identification of these routines and analysis of their dependencies on context factors is one of the tasks for further research.

Acknowledgment. This work has been supported by Swenska Institutet, Sweden.

References

1. Rashidi, P., Mihailidis, A.: A survey on ambient-assisted living tools for older adults. IEEE J. Biomed. Health Inform. **17**(3), 579–590 (2013)
2. Chung, J., Ozkaynak, M., Demiris, G.: Examining daily activity routines of older adults using workflow. J. Biomed. Res. **71**, 82–90 (2017)
3. Shishehgar, M., Kerr, D., Blake, J.: A systematic review of research into how robotic technology can help older people. Smart Health **7**(8), 1–18 (2018)
4. Oasis Senior Advisors (2019). https://www.oasissenioradvisors.com. Accessed 29 Apr 2019
5. Samaio, P.Y.S., Ito, E.: Activities with higher influence on quality of life in older adults in Japan. Occup. Ther. Int. **20**, 1–10 (2012). https://doi.org/10.1002/oti.1333
6. Fortuijn, J.D., et al.: The activity patterns of older adults: a cross sectional study in six European countries. Popul. Space Place **12**, 353–369 (2006). https://doi.org/10.1002/psp.422
7. Ludwig, F.M.: How routine facilitates wellbeing in older women. Occup. Ther. Int. **4**(3), 215–230 (1997)
8. Quality of life indicators (2019). https://ec.europa.eu/eurostat/statistics-explained/index.php/Quality_of_life_indicators. Accessed 30 Apr 2019
9. Stockwell, S., et al.: Digital behavior change interventions to promote physical activity and/or reduce sedentary behavior in older adults: a systematic review and meta-analysis. Exp. Gerontol. **120**, 68–87 (2019). https://doi.org/10.1016/j.exger.2019.02.020. ISSN 0531-5565
10. Chaudhury, H., Campo, M., Michael, Y., Mahmood, A.: Neighbourhood environment and physical activity in older adults. Soc. Sci. Med. **149**, 104–113 (2016). https://doi.org/10.1016/j.socscimed.2015.12.011
11. Demiris, G., Hensel, B.K.: Technologies for an aging society: a systematic review of "smart home" applications. IMIA Schattauer GmbH **17**(1), 33–40 (2008)

12. Rebola, Cl.B.: Sympathetic devices: designing technologies for older adults. In: Proceedings of the ACM International Conference of Design of Communication, SIGDOC 2013, pp. 151–156 (2013)
13. Gerling, K., Livingston, I., Nacke, L., Mandryk, R.: Full body motion-based game interaction for older adults. In: Proceedings of the SIGCHI Conference on Human factors in Computing Systems, pp. 1873–1882. ACM (2012)
14. Lazar, A., Thompson, H., Piper, A.M., Demiris G.: Rethinking the design of robotic pets for older adults. In: Proceedings of the 2016 ACM Conference on Designing Interactive Systems, pp. 1034–1046 (2016)
15. Maqbool, S., Munteanu, C.: Understanding older adults' long-term financial practices: challenges and opportunities. In: DesignCHI'18 Extended Abstracts, 21–26 April 2018, Montreal, Paper no. LBW546 (2018)
16. Bastardo, R., Pavão, J., Martins, A.I., Queirós, A., Rocha, N.P.: The design for all paradigm in the development of applications to support older adults: a review. In: Proceedings of the 8th International Conference on Software Development and Technologies for Enhancing Accessibility and Fighting Info-exclusion, pp. 337–343 (2018)

Organizational Challenges of Digitalization Initiatives in Tourism Network Management Organizations

Susanne Marx[1,2(✉)]

[1] Stralsund University of Applied Sciences, Zur Schwedenschanze 15,
18435 Stralsund, Germany
susanne.marx@hochschule-stralsund.de
[2] Rostock University, Albert-Einstein-Str. 22, 18057 Rostock, Germany

Abstract. The tourism industry with mainly small and medium sized enterprises (SMEs) is strongly influenced by digitalization, though, confronting the actors with challenges. As network management organizations facilitate cross-cutting themes across their network, digitalization could be assumed to be one of them. In a case study approach this paper investigates the status and role of the Destination Management Organization (DMO) in digitalization initiatives, modes of stakeholder participation and related organizational challenges. The findings point to a tension between heterogeneity of the sector and required homogeneity of the touristic experience of the visitor. While the DMO's leadership role for digitalization is expected, it has not been fully embraced yet. The case study identifies a set of internal and external challenges impeding its implementation beyond single digital projects. The paper suggests collaborative portfolio governance for improved participation, flexibility and transparency. Limited by the single case study data, further research is recommended with additional case studies, quantitative data and incorporating findings from other network actors. Researching the operability and effects of the collaborative portfolio governance approach is subject to future research.

Keywords: Digitalization · Destination management organization · Portfolio governance

1 Introduction

After a decade of digitization and a decade of acceleration, tourism management is strongly impacted by information technology [1]. Digital transformation processes are inevitable, irreversible, fast and characterized by uncertainty [2]. However, organizations face challenges coping with digital transformation [3], with small and medium sized companies especially struggling e.g. with priority setting and sequencing [4].

The tourism sector is mainly constituted of companies with less than nine employees: In Germany in 2016, 72.2% of tourism enterprises were such micro enterprises [5]. The Digital Maturity Report 2017 [6] presents the lowest digital maturity for small organizations with below 50 employees.

© Springer Nature Switzerland AG 2019
W. Abramowicz and R. Corchuelo (Eds.): BIS 2019 Workshops, LNBIP 373, pp. 157–168, 2019.
https://doi.org/10.1007/978-3-030-36691-9_14

Digital transformation as a cross-cutting theme may be pushed and guided by network organizations across SMEs. Networks of various geographical scope characterize the tourism industry. Network organizations unite independent organizations that relate continuously and repeatedly across organizational boundaries [7]. In industries of vivid technological development like tourism [1], network organizations are especially valuable [8]. The destination management organization (DMO) is described as the network manager of a destination [9]. Their understanding has changed from marketing organizations in the past to 'destination developers' [10], although the World Tourism Organization [11] does not distinct when defining a "Destination Management/ Marketing Organization (DMO) is the leading organizational entity which may encompass the various authorities, stakeholders and professionals and facilitates tourism sector partnerships towards a collective destination vision". The understanding of the DMO as destination developers may include the responsibility for facilitating and leveraging digital transformation across the destination's network of tourism actors.

The main contribution of this paper is to identify digitalization challenges in tourism network organizations in a case study of a DMO and to develop a proposal of an organizational measure in participative portfolio governance to cope with these. The main findings are internal and external challenges hindering an expected front-runner role of the DMO for digitalization across the sector. Many of these challenges can be attributed to the nature of cooperation in the touristic network.

2   Literature Review

Digitization, digitalization and digital transformation are interpreted differently in the literature. Digitization is described as the transfer from analogue to digital [4, 12]. Other understanding is broader with information technology (IT) enabling and facilitating the interaction of objects [13, 14]. Digitalization can be understood as increased use of digital technology and its effect on humans [15]. Digital transformation is referred to as change caused by digital technology, however, in different perspectives, e.g. affecting life in general [16] or changing economic life, especially changes in business models that cause changes to various aspects of the organization [12, 17, 18]. Digital transformation shall be understood here in the sense of Hess et al. [18], p. 124: "Digital transformation is concerned with the changes digital technologies can bring about in a company's business model, which result in changed products or organizational structures or in the automation of processes."

Digital transformation is complex and continuous [18, 19]. Process aspects are part of the challenges in digital transformation [19]. Transformation management is one out of nine dimensions investigated in the digital maturity research of Hochschule St. Gallen [20], referring to new organizational structures and governance to phase digital projects. Organizing the implementation of digital transformation may include initiating multiple projects, coordinating them and monitoring them.

In inter-organizational networks, the network administrative organization might take over such tasks of a project management office (PMO) [21]. This would imply arrangements of project governance and governance of projects based on governmentality [22]. As resources in the network are provided from different partners, there are expectations how the network shall be governed. There are different perceptions of governing and supporting in portfolios run by complex ownership structures, as research on transformation portfolios found [23]. A network organization can be considered a complex ownership due to many actors providing resources, so varying perceptions of governing and supporting both the DMO and resulting portfolio implementation can be assumed to emerge.

The cooperation of various stakeholders is the very nature of network organizations. Stakeholder Management has gained considerable research attention in project management academia, however, looking at project governance research the focus has been mainly attributed to internal stakeholders [24]. The influence of external decision makers on governance in a broader project and portfolio context is not understood yet [24]. A changing perspective goes from management of stakeholders, to management for stakeholders [25]. Since authority in networks is both dynamic and polycentric with dynamic network boundaries [8, 26], an approach of management with stakeholders could open an additional perspective, though efficiency and participative decision making is identified as an area of mutual tension in network governance [27]. It can be questioned if this conclusion applies to portfolio governance in network organizations, that strongly rely on the cooperation of stakeholders. In a context of technological change, customer orientation increases the success of the portfolio [28]. From the perspective of DMOs, the stakeholders of the network could be regarded as customers, that are involved by repeated though dynamic relations.

Investigating project management literature for single organizations [24] revealed that external stakeholders are involved on corporate and project level, yet, the portfolio level lacks involvement, although the impact on these external stakeholders at this level is decisive. However, portfolio management methodologies (e.g. [29, 30]) suggest stakeholder engagement a task at portfolio level. Coming back to digital transformation and the requirement for agility, self-organization and cooperation [12] a continuous participation of stakeholders beyond single projects seems an opportunity for networks and network management organizations.

Specific challenges of digital transformation in touristic network organizations related to the portfolio and governance practices have not been researched yet.

3 Research Methodology

The research follows a case study strategy, suited for exploratory research towards developing research questions [31]. The strategy was chosen to gain in-depth understanding of one organization to identify a set of problems regarding digitalization initiatives and to prepare for further research. Primary data was collected by a semi-structured in-depth interview with the managing director of the case study DMO. The interview was recorded and transcribed, followed by a qualitative content analysis of transcribed interview text by building categories of themes. The finally resulting themes were chances and challenges of digitalization (Sect. 4.1), the role of the DMO in digital transformation of the industry (Sect. 4.2) and network governance related issues (Sect. 4.3) that were summarized. From data analysis a set of internal and external organizational challenges of digitalization initiatives of DMOs emerged (Sect. 4.4). Secondary data was retrieved from the DMO's website and internal documents.

The case DMO was chosen for the study as it looks back on a decade of intense cooperation, known as a best-practice example for voluntary sector cooperation in the tourism industry in Germany [36] and is thus as a unique case suited for a case study [37]. The DMO consists of two parts, which are intertwined and led by the same manager. One is a municipal body, both responsible for touristic responsibilities of local authorities, selected events and maintenance of infrastructure as well as public relations and marketing. It is supported by public funds. The second is a municipal company, also fully owned by the city, however, set up as a limited company. The latter is partly fed by public funds, but mainly by private funds from the tourism network. Private companies, e.g. accommodation providers, attractions, touristic services but also stores, join this tourism network contributing a yearly fee, that is invested in marketing and networking activities.

4   Findings and Discussion

The DMO was regarded taking only the first steps in the direction of digitalization, with internal (e.g. electronic time registration or document storage) and external projects (e.g. development of website and booking system) by the interviewee. However, the impact of digitalization and the need to embrace its opportunities is clearly identified as a major point of action, by the interviewee, though with the notion that the major development is yet to come. In the DMO's ten-year strategy conception 2022 digitalization played a minor role, only related to marketing activities.

4.1   Chances and Challenges of Digitalization and Digital Transformation

The interviewee identified chances for digitalization both for external and internal purposes. For external purposes, reaching out to and inspiring future customers with tailored information already before a decision for booking is made, appeared a main point. Internally, an increased efficiency and simplification of work processes were attributed to digitalization. The potential of facing lack of skilled workers by digital tools seemed another advantage. Opportunities for digitally enhanced cooperation within the network were considered though only after prompted by the interviewer.

Despite the opportunities, both technical and organizational prerequisites were identified lacking by the interviewee, e.g. the requirement of a data pool. The exploitation of data is also identified a starting point for digital transformation processes [2] in the literature. Though a data pool is fed in cooperation with the regional tourist organization, the effort to manage the various touristic service and thus data providers for data contribution is regarded high by the manager. Another challenge mentioned by the interviewee are global, open systems that also collect and provide such data. The interviewee stressed, "the DMO wants to keep control" and consciously steer the image of the destination. Global online businesses seem not only to compete on data, but also on services with the DMO (e.g. booking.com, HRS). Although aware of these challenges and the need for additional know-how, organizational limitations in municipal environment were perceived limitations by the manager. Another aspect was attributed to the network organization with heterogenous partners: "Different IT systems are difficult to synchronize".

Digitalization initiatives seem to be organized as separate projects. Despite a large proportion of DMO work being project-based (e.g. events, marketing activities, internal projects) there was no project management methodology in place. Instead it is accepted practice, that different people establish their own styles and approaches: "it is different from person to person". A central coordination across projects is maintained by the managing director by means of meetings in different layers of the organization. Although the manager attributes improvement in project delivery to this meeting system, it comes along with immense time efforts ("I dedicate a lot of time to this"), that consume considerable organizational resources. It can be assumed that his controlling system is fragile in case project quantity increases. Installing this meeting system was mainly based on former information gaps, with written briefings not meeting information needs of management levels in the organization. Thus, multiple project information is not transparently documented, but stored with the people involved.

With digital transformation defined as bringing about change to the business model of a company [18], the DMO is in the middle of such transformation, although not directly named as such in the interview. Despite the organizations being owned by the municipality, still income is generated by economic activities, both to increase the marketing budget and to gain flexibility outside of municipal decision making. This business model is changing by digitalization. In the past, the municipal body relied on commissions from accommodation services, but the market has changed completely in the past ten years, stated the interviewee, from face-to-face booking services in the tourist offices, that are still available today, towards own online booking interfaces. Now this income is threatened by global players, that have such dominance in the market, that the income of the DMO is at risk. "The strategy now changes from competing with the giants towards cooperating with them" claimed the interviewee, profiting from their omnipresence, accessibility and holistic representation of booking capacities, as e.g. hotels cannot afford to refrain from using these channels as it was the case with the DMO's own booking applications. The booking offer is broadened by the global players from accommodation to full touristic experiences with all sorts of transactions. The interviewee stresses, the DMO has to find ways to engage with these and so consistently to adapt its organizational structure and business case.

4.2 Role of the DMO in Digitalization of the Industry

The role of the DMO is perceived by the interviewee as a mediator between guests with their (future) needs and the touristic service providers. Cross-cutting themes like quality, infrastructure, internationalization are becoming prevailing tasks of the DMO, working with a network of touristic service providers, politicians, guests and also locals. The interviewee confirmed that digitalization is such cross-cutting theme, for which the network actors "like in other areas expect a trendsetting role" of the DMO. In this area more competition between destinations is expected for the future by the manager, however, he concludes, the DMO is in regard to digital transformation still "in its infancy".

The DMO relies on the cooperation within the network. "We have to engage the industry players, it is not enough that we as the DMO open up for new digital opportunities", stated the interviewee. Campaigns and new projects are largely initiated by the DMO, both with digital and in other projects, describing the DMO as the "frontrunner, who has to convince the other actors". However, when promoting certain (digital) services it raises the expectations of the visitor, which have to be finally met, even by the smallest tourist service provider for a holistic destination experience, confirms the interviewee. Thus, leveraging service levels across all actors in the destination is part of the DMOs work, which could also apply for digital services.

Though the DMO taking a trendsetter and project leadership role in other kinds of projects, it does not deliberately fill this role for digitalization initiatives, yet. However, it implements separate digital projects assuming a project management role across different actors. Despite expertise and initiative for digitalization is expected from the DMO by the partners, this cross-cutting theme seems to lag behind compared to others. Reasons could be the high frequency of change faced by static public service structures.

4.3   Governance and Participation

The collaboration with the network was identified as a basic requirement for the DMO's work in the case study, as it results into better acceptance of work, trust and a feeling of taking the players seriously in the opinion of the interviewee. Moreover, partners could withdraw if not satisfied and "the network and the company could vanish quickly".

Despite the DMO embracing participation as an overarching approach, it is still described as a continuous process of considerable effort from the DMO: "We are the ones who have to push". There seems to be a varying motivation of network members to engage. The interviewee attributed this mainly to external influences. In the beginning of the intensified work with the network, external threats were high, and engagement was large. Ever since the touristic figures have risen to great market success, in parallel a reduction of direct contribution of the network participants was observed by the interviewee. While the DMO has to prepare overarching topics for future threats and opportunities, digitalization could be one of them, the "partners seem to concentrate on their own business". The DMO has to argue continuously for individual added value to gain contribution according to the interviewee. The different background of the private industry and public body could be a reason for a remaining level of mistrust, despite all cooperation. While participation is expected by network actors, their practical engagement in enacting this participation varies.

At different governance layers, the participation of network actors differs. The municipal company with private industry partners, has an advisory board of industry representatives, set up during the foundation of the company and not changed since. The group "has no formal decision power", it is more a means of reporting and exchange with half-yearly meetings, "to give them a feeling we are doing a good work". Earlier on, "when trust was lower", meetings were held four times a year, states the interviewee. Projects are not discussed in detail in this body; it seems more a way to confirm compliance with the agreed long-term strategy and further building trust.

The development of the overarching decade strategy for the touristic destination, comparable to a corporate strategy, was realized in a participative approach, involving many partners, politicians and other stakeholders in an externally moderated process. While not having formal competency, the network members were given influence through this process. However, the resulting portfolio of projects is determined by the DMO within the framework of this strategy. Internally, departmental managers develop a yearly business plan for the DMO to be approved by the city parliament.

On individual project level, network actors are again involved for thematic expertise, on initiative of the DMO. For the large majority of network actors not involved in the advisory board, information is provided by a newsletter, the website or the annual report, all being retrospective, and in events, that focus on networking. Distribution of information via the advisory board cannot be taken for granted, "there is a barrier" confirms the interviewee. External stakeholders are not involved at portfolio governance level, only on corporate and project level. The current structure of participation is displayed in Fig. 1.

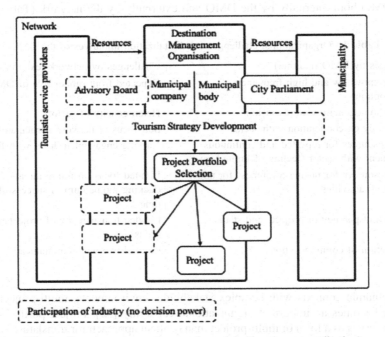

Fig. 1. Current structure of network participation (own contribution)

The requirements of building a 'connective destination vision' as defined by the World Tourism Organization (2016) seems a challenge, despite apparent participative processes in place in the case study DMO. "Cooperation with the network is the foundation of our work" claims the interviewee, however, "everybody is so busy with his/her own business". The question is if such joint understanding of the destination can be built by other forms of participation with formal impact and responsibility. Maybe even the nature of participation has to change over time, to prevent fading engagement and cooperation fatigue.

The DMO copes with heterogeneous interests of its partners, towards achieving a homogeneous experience of the visitor throughout his or her engagement with the destination. In the case study, the network increases both geographically and by involving additional kind of actors. Thus, ensuring transparency, participation and motivation across individual projects might be further challenged. With the network borders further blurred, instilling a joint vision and keeping momentum over time in changing (even favorable) environmental conditions can pose further challenges on the strength of the network. This challenge is framed by an apparent digital transformation of the industry that is, however, not strategically addressed across the network and further complicated by different experience levels and interests of actors.

4.4   Organizational Challenges and Future Research Directions

Organizational challenges regarding digitalization initiatives were identified in the case study DMO both internally by the DMO and externally by the network (Table 1).

Table 1. Organizational challenges for digitalization initiatives of the DMO

Challenges by DMO (internal)	Challenges by network (external)
Lacking knowhow and high frequency of change/options	Expected front-runner role of DMO
Needed homogeneity towards visitor	Heterogeneity of sector
Dependency on cooperation with sector	Self-focus of network participants
Bound resources for repeated and continuous engagement with sector (feeling of limited trust)	Varying engagement level with DMO
Bound resources for raising awareness for added value of all activities	Limited focus on future threats (lacking momentum in successful times)
Limited transparency of projects and status	Limited transparency of projects and status
Optimization of communication	Limited two-way communication

In dynamic contexts with complex stakeholder environments, multi-project management becomes an important organizational capability [32]. Project portfolio management serves as a form of multi-project management approach for translating strategy towards implementation initiatives (both programs and projects). It addresses resource allocation, sequencing of projects and readjusting priorities. Management is enacted within a frame of governance arrangements [33]. Such governance practices influence the identity of the project team and its relation to the organization [34]. It can be assumed that governance practices in networks impact the network identity and attitude of its (potential) members and thus impact future commitment and participation.

The involvement of stakeholders in portfolio governance (in Fig. 2 exemplified for project selection) might provide a solution for increasing engagement due to allowing higher influence. Participation is defined as collaborative decision making, sometimes referred to as collaborative governance [35]. Such proposal would challenge the view that external stakeholders are not involved at portfolio level [24]. It might invite further knowhow from the touristic network participants, ensure transparency and define modes of communication, both internally and externally. Portfolio governance mechanisms could be set up to both ensure agility and partner involvement.

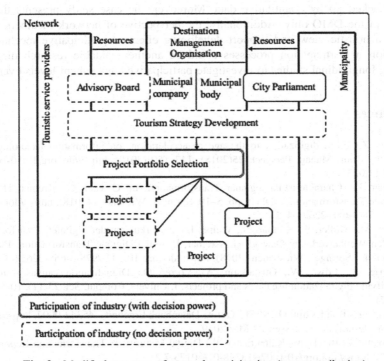

Fig. 2. Modified structure of network participation (own contribution)

5 Conclusion and Limitations

The case study confirmed, that also municipal organizations as tourism network management organizations are in a process of digital transformation, that brings about both externally and internally caused challenges. The case study points to digitalization initiatives being so far scattered projects. However, network participants are assumed to expect a leading role of the DMO in the cross-cutting topic of digital transformation. The collaboration with the tourism service providers and other stakeholders is crucial for the DMO. The main problem seems to be the tension of needed homogeneity towards the visitor and the apparent heterogeneity of the network participants. This touches both on technology used, but more so on interests, destination vision and required contribution from different actors. With a considerable number of projects, increasing numbers of stakeholders and varying motivation of engagement, changing the mode of participation could be a clue for facing the identified challenges. A future research question could address, if, how and by which tools a participative approach to portfolio governance could help develop continuous engagement of network stakeholders to provide the flexibility and joined competency for enabling the facilitating role of the DMO as a driving force for digital transformation of the sector.

Limited as a single instance source, the presented case study cannot be generalized. In further research, additional case studies could enhance the insights, that should be further backed up by quantitative data. Moreover, the case study presents the perspective of the DMO only. Additionally, the perspective of network members would provide a holistic view and support developing effective participative mechanisms. Motivation in participation processes could be another valuable research direction, requiring longitudinal studies to investigate participative engagement levels over time.

References

1. Xiang, Z.: From digitization to the age of acceleration: on information technology and tourism. Tour. Manag. Perspect. **25**(2018), 147–150 (2018). https://doi.org/10.1016/j.tmp. 2017.11.023
2. Krcmar, H.: Charakteristika digitaler Transformation. In: Oswald, G., Krcmar, H. (eds.) Digitale Transformation. INDITR, pp. 5–10. Springer, Wiesbaden (2018). https://doi.org/10. 1007/978-3-658-22624-4_2
3. Böhm, M., Müller, S., Krcmar, H., Welpe, I.: Auswirkungen der digitalen Transformation auf den Wettbewerb. In: Oswald, G., Krcmar, H. (eds.) Digitale Transformation. INDITR, pp. 35–47. Springer, Wiesbaden (2018). https://doi.org/10.1007/978-3-658-22624-4_4
4. Heberle, A., Löwe, W., Gustafsson, A., Vorrei, Ö.: Digitalization canvas – towards identifying digitalization use cases and projects. J. Univers. Comput. Sci. **23**(11), 1070–1097 (2017)
5. Statistisches Bundesamt: GENESIS-Online Datenbank Ergebnis - 45342-0002. https://www-genesis.destatis.de. Accessed 07 Mar 2019
6. Berghaus, S., Brack, A., Kaltenrieder, B.: Digital Maturity & Transformation Report 2017 (2017). https://doi.org/10.1007/s13398-014-0173-7.2
7. Moretti, A.: The Network Organization: A Governance Perspective on Structure Dynamics and Performance. Palgrave Macmillan, London (2017). https://doi.org/10.1007/978-3-319-52093-3
8. Sydow, J.: Editorial – Über Netzwerke, Allianzsysteme, Verbünde, Kooperationen und Konstellationen. In: Sydow, J. (eds.) Management von Netzwerkorganisationen, pp. 1–6. Gabler Verlag, Wiesbaden (2010). https://doi.org/10.1007/978-3-8349-8593-4_1
9. Volgger, M., Pechlaner, H.: Requirements for destination management organizations in destination governance: understanding DMO success. Tour. Manag. **41**, 64–75 (2014). https://doi.org/10.1016/j.tourman.2013.09.001
10. Presenza, A., Sheehan, L., Ritchie, J.B.: Towards a model of the roles and activities of destination management organizations. J. Hosp. Tour. Leisure Sci. **3**(1), 1–16 (2005). https://doi.org/10.1017/CBO9781107415324.004
11. World Tourism Organization (UNWTO): Conceptual Framework. http://www2.unwto.org/content/conceptual-framework-0. Accessed 30 Apr 2019

12. Fricke, H., Thiessen, T.: Mittelstand im Wandel - Wie ein Unternehmen seinen digitalen Reifegrad ermitteln kann, Berlin (2016)
13. Coreynen, W., Matthyssens, P., Van Bockhaven, W.: Boosting servitization through digitization: pathways and dynamic resource configurations for manufacturers. Ind. Mark. Manag. **60**(2017), 42–53 (2017). https://doi.org/10.1016/j.indmarman.2016.04.012
14. Schallmo, D., Reinhart, J., Kuntz, E.: Digitale Transformation von Geschäftsmodellen erfolgreich gestalten. Springer Gabler, Wiesbaden (2018). https://doi.org/10.1007/978-3-658-20215-6
15. Gimpel, H., Röglinger, M.: Digital transformation changes and chances – insights based on an empirical study, Augsburg/Bayreuth (2015)
16. Stolterman, E., Fors, A.C.: Information technology and the good life. In: Kaplan, B., Truex, D., Wastell, D., Wood-Harper, A.T., DeGross, J.I. (eds.) Information Systems Research. IIFIP, vol. 143, pp. 687–692. Springer, Boston (2004). https://doi.org/10.1007/1-4020-8095-6_45
17. Hess, T.: Digitalisierung. http://www.enzyklopaedie-der-wirtschaftsinformatik.de/wienzyklopaedie/lexikon/technologien-methoden/Informatik–Grundlagen/digitalisierung/. Accessed 21 Feb 2019
18. Hess, T., Benlian, A., Matt, C., Wiesböck, F.: Options for formulating a digital transformation strategy. MIS Q. Exec. **15**(2), 123–139 (2016). https://doi.org/10.1108/10878571211209314
19. Matt, C., Hess, T., Benlian, A.: Digital transformation strategies. Bus. Inf. Syst. Eng. **57**(5), 339–343 (2015). https://doi.org/10.1007/s12599-015-0401-5
20. Back, A., Berghaus, S.: Digital Maturity und Transformation Studie - Über das Digital Maturity Model. https://aback.iwi.unisg.ch/fileadmin/projects/aback/web/pdf/digitalmaturitymodel_download_v2.0.pdf. Accessed 30 Apr 2019
21. Braun, T.: Configurations for interorganizational project networks: the interplay of the pmo and network administrative organization. Proj. Manag. J. **49**(4), 53–61 (2018). https://doi.org/10.1177/8756972818781710
22. Müller, R., Zhai, L., Wang, A., Shao, J.: A framework for governance of projects: governmentality, governance structure and projectification. Int. J. Project Manag. **34**(6), 957–969 (2016). https://doi.org/10.1016/j.ijproman.2016.05.002
23. Kortantamer, D.: Governing major transformation portfolios in practice: illustrations from the UK central government. Int. J. Managing Proj. Bus. (2019). https://doi.org/10.1108/IJMPB-09-2018-0174
24. Derakhshan, R., Turner, R., Mancini, M.: Project governance and stakeholders: a literature review. Int. J. Proj. Manag. **37**(1), 98–116 (2019). https://doi.org/10.1016/j.ijproman.2018.10.007
25. Eskerod, P., Huemann, M.: Managing for stakeholders. In: Turner, R. (ed.) Handbook of Project Management, pp. 217–232. Gower, Surrey (2014)
26. DeFillippi, R., Sydow, J.: Project networks: governance choices and paradoxical tensions. Proj. Manag. J. **47**(5), 1–12 (2016)
27. Provan, K.G., Kenis, P.: Modes of network governance: structure, management, and effectiveness. J. Public Adm. Res. Theor. **18**(2), 229–252 (2007). https://doi.org/10.1093/jopart/mum015
28. Voss, M., Kock, A.: Impact of relationship value on project portfolio success - investigating the moderating effects of portfolio characteristics and external turbulence. Int. J. Proj. Manag. **31**(6), 847–861 (2013). https://doi.org/10.1016/j.ijproman.2012.11.005
29. Project Management Institute: The Standard for Portfolio Management – Fourth Edition. Project Management Institute (2017)

30. Directorate-General for Informatics (European Commission): PM^2 project management methodology guide - EU Law and Publications (2016). https://doi.org/10.2799/957700
31. Johannesson, P., Perjons, E.: An Introduction to Design Science. Springer, Cham (2014). https://doi.org/10.1007/978-3-319-10632-8
32. Martinsuo, M., Hoverfält, P.: Change program management: toward a capability for managing value-oriented, integrated multi-project change in its context. Int. J. Proj. Manag. 36(1), 134–146 (2018). https://doi.org/10.1016/j.ijproman.2017.04.018
33. Müller, R., Turner, J.R., Andersen, E.S., Shao, J., Kvalnes, O.: Governance and ethics in temporary organizations: the mediating role of corporate governance. Proj. Manag. J. 47(6), 7–23 (2017)
34. Toivonen, A., Toivonen, P.U.: The transformative effect of top management governance choices on project team identity and relationship with the organization - an agency and stewardship approach. Int. J. Project Manag. 32(8), 1358–1370 (2014). https://doi.org/10.1016/j.ijproman.2014.07.001
35. Newig, J.: Partizipation und neue Formen der Governance. In: Groß, M. (ed.) Handbuch Umweltsoziologie. Verlag für Sozialwissenschaften, Wiesbaden (2011). https://doi.org/10.1007/978-3-531-93097-8
36. Tourismus- und Heilbäderverband Rheinland-Pfalz e.V.: Nachhaltige Finanzierung kommunaler touristischer Aufgaben – eine Handlungshilfe, n.a, Koblenz
37. Saunders, M., Lewis, P., Thornhill, A.: Research Methods for Business Students. 9 Pearson Education, Harlow (2009)

A Configurational Approach
to Task-Technology Fit
in the Healthcare Sector

Patrick Mikalef[1,2(✉)] and Hans Yngvar Torvatn[1]

[1] SINTEF Digital, S. P. Andersens Veg 5, 7031 Trondheim, Norway
{patrick.mikalef,hans.torvatn}@sintef.no
[2] Norwegian University of Science and Technology,
Sem Saelands Vei 7-9, 7491 Trondheim, Norway

Abstract. In spite of strong investments in digital technologies in the health-care and medical services domain over the past couple of decades, one of the most pressing issues is that in many cases the technologies that are adopted to support the everyday tasks of professionals are often not used as intended, or even not used at all. A growing number of studies have also noted negative impacts in many circumstances when professionals such technologies them into their work tasks. This poses a major concern as investments in supporting technologies are often hindering efforts of professionals rather than enabling them. Following a task-technology fit approach we build on a sample of 445 health and medical service professionals working in Norway. This study explores the configurations of elements that lead to positive and negative impacts when using digital technologies to support work. To derive results, we utilize a fuzzy set qualitative comparative analysis (fsQCA) to showcase that there are several different configurations of tasks, technologies, and use practices that can either help produce positive impacts or create negative ones.

Keywords: Task-technology fit · fsQCA · Healthcare · Norway · Empirical

1 Introduction

In spite of heavy investments in digital technologies in the healthcare and medical services domain over the past couple of decades [1–3], one of the prevailing issues is that in many cases the technologies to support tasks of professionals are often not used as intended, or even not used at all [4]. In fact, several independent studies have documented that health and medical service professionals do not adopt newly introduced technologies, whether they are used to support core tasks [5], reporting and documenting [4], or for task coordination [6–8]. In particular when one factors in the large costs associated with developing and implementing such digital technologies in the healthcare sector, as well as their potential to significantly improve professionals work performance [9], it is a big surprise to see that there are still many professionals that chose to not adopt technologies in their work activities or report negative consequences [10]. In the last few years, a number of studies have delved into this issue, attempting to explore the reasons as to why health professionals either do not use

© Springer Nature Switzerland AG 2019
W. Abramowicz and R. Corchuelo (Eds.): BIS 2019 Workshops, LNBIP 373, pp. 169–180, 2019.
https://doi.org/10.1007/978-3-030-36691-9_15

supporting technologies, or to understand why they experience negative impacts from incorporating them in their work practices [11].

Despite a number of different approaches been utilized in examining such effects and their roots, a prominent perspective, that of task-technology fit, has been argued to be particularly suited in explaining how specific job-related tasks, aspects of the technology, as well as use practices coalesce to create fit, and subsequently positive impacts [12]. This theoretical framework examines alignment at the micro-level, looking into how individuals and their tasks are in fit with the used technologies. While the task-technology theory has received considerable attention in the broader IS domain, within the context of health and medical service professionals use of technology, studies have remained much sparser. Even more, the vast majority of studies applying this perspective to uncover key success factors to fit, adopt a methodological approach that does not account for the diversity of use patterns and requirements of varied tasks that professionals need to deal with in their everyday work [13]. Recent work in the field of health technology adoption, and within the more general IS domain, supports the idea that there may exist multiple different ways by which technology can produce positive impacts to employees [14]. The main rationale of such approaches is that individuals in their work are faced with different tasks that they must complete. This requires different approaches with regards to the use of technology, as well as specific adoption and diffusion practices to achieve expected outcomes.

The purpose of this study is to examine through a task-technology fit theoretical perspective, which are those combinations of tasks, technology, and individual use practices that fit together to contribute to positive impacts in the context of health and medical service professionals work. We draw on a recent large-scale empirical survey conducted with 445 professionals in the domain, and by applying the novel methodological approach fuzzy set qualitative comparative analysis (fsQCA) uncover several different configurations that lead to either positive or negative impacts. Through this way we are able to identify a series of different tasks, the aspects pertinent to technology that best fit task requirements, as well as individual use and adoption practices that facilitate optimal fit. Similarly, we highlight those that produce negative outcomes to professionals, as a means of demonstrating what should be avoided in practice. In the rest of the paper we discuss the background and related literature in the domain, introduce the method applied and the data that is analyzed, followed by the results and a discussion on their implications.

2   Background

To explore how different digital technologies can contribute to positive and negative impacts of work performance in the health and medical services sector we build on the task-technology fit theory [12]. The theory holds that digital technologies will have a higher probability of positively impact individual work performance when the capabilities they deliver can match the tasks individuals must perform. Since its inception the theory has been extended in several ways, with latest literature recognizing the fact that individual use characteristics and the design and training practices surrounding adoption play a significant role on performance impacts of technology use [15]. The task-technology fit theory has subsequently been used at various levels of analysis, examining effects on individuals and groups [16], as well as in many different contexts, from specific technologies [17] to effects on industries or particular professions [18]. Within the context of healthcare and medical services, there have been several studies that examine factors that contribute to task-technology fit, and as a consequence positive work-related impacts [19]. These studies have been increasing over the past few years seeing the growing use of digital technologies in the healthcare sector. Now, more than ever, health professionals are using digital technologies either due to governmental pressures, or to improve their work performance in a range of different tasks [7]. Yet, despite heavy investments and a strong move towards digitally-enhancing tasks of health professionals, there still many that state that such digital technologies are becoming more of an obstacle rather than an aid in improving work [20].

Configurational approaches which are grounded on the tenets of complexity theories have being growing in interest in the IS community over the past few years [21]. One of the main strengths of such approaches is that the allow for the possibility of multiple different paths, or solutions, that lead to an outcome of interest [22]. This means, that in the case of positive impacts of digital technology use in the health and medical services sector, it would be possible to detect several successful cases of using technologies to perform specific tasks, along with the individual use characteristics that describe them. The literature has documented some first studies following task-technology fit theory and configurational approaches in explaining optimal patterns for use of health and medical services technologies [23]. Nevertheless, there is still very limited research in exploring how the different aspects pertinent to task, technology, and individual use coalesce to drive fit, and as a result positive impacts in the workplace. While the bulk of research building on the task-technology fit theory has focused predominantly on the two main concepts (i.e. task and technology) [24], a growing stream of research incorporates in the investigation the role of individuals and how technologies are deployed and routinized in work activities [25]. In fact, more and more research is looking into the formal and informal mechanisms of adopting and routinizing the use of technologies in the workplace, acknowledging the fact that just as important as the technology itself to support a task are the practices through which they are embedded in work [26].

3   Method

3.1   Data Collection

To explore the configurations of elements pertinent to tasks, technology, and individual use context that lead to positive and negative impacts in the work environment, a survey instrument was developed. The survey-based approach is regarded as an appropriate method to accurately capture the use of technologies, and beliefs and attitudes of individuals in the work environment, and also specifically in the health sector [27]. According to Straub, Boudreau and Gefen [28]), the survey-based method is based suited in exploratory settings and predictive theory. To develop the respective constructs, we utilized a 5-point Likert scale, which is regarded as an appropriate method where no standard measures exist for quantifying notions such as attitudes and beliefs. To make sure that the measures were reliable and valid, a pilot study was conducted the year before the main study (i.e. in 2016) gathering responses from approximately 1000 individuals in Norway working in different sectors. This pilot study enabled us to assess the content validity of items, and to ensure that all questions were easily understood. For the main study, a representative population following the level 1 of NACE Classification Codes (Nomenclature des Activités Économiques dans la Communauté Européenne) was selected within Norway, and a list of individuals within each industry was constructed following a representative sample based on job type.

A professional data collection company was commissioned with conducting phone polls to individuals throughout Norway using a database of approximately 10.000 individuals in a variety of different industries, including those of health and medical services. The callers informed participants about the purpose of the study and asked respondents to answer a number of questions by giving an appropriate response. The data gathering process lasts roughly four months (May 2017–August 2017), and the average time for answering the questions of the survey was 23 min. A total of 445 complete responses were received from the health and medical services industry. From this sample, most responses came from the age-groups 30–44 years (34%) and 45–59 years (34%). In terms of gender distribution, the largest proportion of the sample consisted of female employees (74%) while men account for 26% of the sample. When looking at the educational background of respondents, most of them had as a highest academic qualification a degree from a university or other higher-education institution until 4 years (42.2%), while 36.6% had an educational background of over 4 years in higher education (equivalent to master's degree or Ph.D). Finally, when looking at leadership responsibilities, the vast majority of the sample stated that they did not have leadership responsibilities (74.4%), 8.8% noted that they had managerial responsibilities, 3.8% that they had personnel responsibilities, and 13.0% that they had both types of responsibilities. To examine the possibility of non-response bias in our sample, the profiles of the respondents from the mailing list were benchmarked against information about the health sector and the profiles of people employed from the central statistics bureau. Outcomes confirmed that there was no statistically significant difference between the two sub-groups and that the sample of respondents was representative of the population.

3.2 Measurements

To operationalize the different dimensions that are relevant in examining task-technology fit and individual use a number of different constructs were used to capture the greatest possible breadth of these categories of variables. All measures were based on prior empirical research and were therefore previously tested in empirical studies. In Appendix A we provide a full list of the questions asked.

When examining attributes relevant to the task itself, we utilized measures that included questions on the types of tasks in which digital technologies were used, the difficulty ad time-criticality of the task, if the level of non-routineness. The types of information we measured under the Task label followed relevant literature examining similar phenomena in IT use in the workplace [29, 30]. Specifically, we measured on a 5-point likert scale the frequency in which respondents used digital technology for core tasks, reporting and documentation tasks, and information/coordination [31]. To determine if they held positions that required leadership skills, we asked respondents to indicate if they had no leadership responsibilities, personnel, managerial, or both. For the purpose of this study, we aggregated as a dichotomous variable leadership with 1 denoting that they had at least one of personnel or managerial, or 0 if they didn't have any leadership responsibility. Finally, to assess the level of non-routineness, we asked respondents to indicate how often they were expected to work outside of paid work hours [32].

With regards to technology-related characteristics we followed a similar approach, looking at different aspects related to functionality and user-friendliness, while also incorporating specific types of devices in the questions tat are commonly used by health and medical professionals. More specifically, we captured the extent to which respondents believed that digital technologies they used in the jobs were functional and reliable, user-friendly, and flexible and adaptable [33]. Furthermore, we assessed the extent to which respondents need to use different types of devices to perform their work such as personal computers, mobile devices (e.g. smart phones, tablets and portable recording equipment), and wearables (smart glasses, smartwatch/bracelets), or augmented reality technologies [34].

In terms of individual use context, we tried to capture elements that were relevant to how individuals adopt and utilize novel digital technologies within their work place, as well as what types of support mechanisms are set up to facilitate such usage. In congruence with past empirical studies we include aspects that can affect how easily and well individuals utilize digital technology [12]. Specifically, we examine the degree tow which individual have a support network from colleagues when using digital technologies, the extent to which they have been trained to use the latest digital technologies in their organizations (e.g. courses, e-learning, self-education through reading), as well as the level to which they have been involved in the joined planning of introducing new digital technologies.

Finally, when it comes to examining the impacts of digital technology use in the healthcare and medical sector, we examine two opposing depending variables. On the one hand we capture the level to which digital technologies have a positive contribution to work performance. We operationalize this variable as the level to which the quality of work gets better, work is done fast, and the level to which the work performed relies on the use of digital technologies [35]. Since our aims is to also capture configurations that lead to decreased performance, we use separate measures to assess the negative consequences of using digital technologies. Specifically, we develop negative impacts by asking respondents to evaluate the level to which digital technologies have given them a greater workload. Have increased requirements for concentration in work, have resulted in greater time pressure, and have increased stress levels.

3.3 Measurement Model

Due to the fact that the model contains primarily formative or single-item constructs, we apply different assessment criteria to evaluate each. First-order formative constructs were assessed in terms of multicollinearity, weights and significance. Since we only had first-order constructs, these values were examined at the construct and item level respectively. All items had positive and significant association with their higher-order constructs. When examining for multicollinearity issues we looked at Variance Inflation Factor (VIF) values, with values above 3.3 being the cut-off threshold [36]. All first order variables had values below the threshold indicating an absence of multi-collinearity within our data.

4   Findings

To examine what configurations of task, technology, and use practice lead to lead to positive or negative work impact we utilize a fuzzy-set Qualitative Comparative Analysis (fsQCA) approach. FsQCA is a set-theoretic method that in based on Boolean algebra (i.e. set membership) to determine how configurations of elements are linked to specific outcomes. The technique follows the principles of complexity theories and allows for the examination of interplays that develop between elements of a messy and non-linear nature [22, 37]. What makes fsQCA different from other methods of analyzing data is that it supports the notion of equifinality. In essence, equifinality means that a specific outcome (e.g. positive or negative work impacts) may be a result of different configurations of elements, and that these configurations can deviate depending on context or individual use patterns. Applying such an approach is particularly relevant to the case of digital technology usage within the health and medical services context, since depending on the type of task, and characteristics of the individual, different digital technologies and use support mechanisms may be more or less relevant in producing positive impacts. Consequently, it is important to understand what configurations of tasks, technologies, and use practices yield most positive impacts, and which most negative ones. Conducting such analyses through FsQCA enables this identification as it is oriented towards reducing elements for each configuration to the fundamentally necessary and sufficient conditions. In addition, fsQCA supports the occurrence of causal asymmetry, which in short means that for an outcome to occur, the presence and absence of a causal condition depend on how this causal condition combines with one or more other causal conditions [22].

As a first step of performing the fsQCA analyses, it is necessary that we calibrate dependent and independent variables into fuzzy or crisp sets. Positive and negative impacts are set as the dependent variables of our study, while the independent variables that are used include those that fall under the categories of task, technology, and individual use context. The only crisp set we have in this analysis in the leadership responsibilities which are coded for 1 if there are is at least the requirement to handle personnel or other managerial matter, or 0 in the absence of such requirements. Contrarily, fuzzy sets in this analysis can range anywhere on the continuous scale from 0, which denotes an absence of set membership, to 1, which indicates full set membership. To calibrate continuous variables such as the ones we have utilized in the survey into fuzzy sets we followed the method proposed by Ragin [38]. Following this procedure, the degree of set membership is based on three anchor values. These include a full set membership threshold value (fuzzy score = 0.95), a full non-membership value (fuzzy score = 0.05), and the crossover point (fuzzy score = 0.50). Since this study uses a 5-point Likert scale to measure all continuous constructs, we follow the suggestions of Ordanini, Parasuraman and Rubera [39] to calibrate them into fuzzy sets. Following these guidelines, and based on prior empirical research (Fiss, 2011; Ragin, 2009), we computed percentiles for each construct so that the upper 25 percentiles serve as the threshold for full membership; the lower 25 percentiles for full non-membership; and the 50 percentiles represent the cross-over point.

4.1 Fuzzy Set Qualitative Comparative Analyses

To extract the configurations that lead to positive and negative impacts we relied on the software fsQCA 3.0. By conducting two separate analyses, the fsQCA algorithm produces truth tables of 2^k rows, where k is the number of predictor elements, and each row indicates a unique possible combination of elements. The fsQCA software then sorts all the 445 observations into each of these rows based on their degree of membership of all the causal conditions. An outcome if this is a truth table where some rows contain several observations while others just a few or even none depending on the collected data. As part of this step it is up to the researcher to reduce the number of rows according to two rules: (1) a row must contain a minimum number of cases, this value was set to a frequency threshold of 5 cases; and (2) selected rows must achieve a minimum consistency level of 0.80. Therefore, configurations that do not fit into these rules are excluded from the analyses. In order to obtain results that explain positive and negative impacts of digital technologies, we use the method proposed by Ragin and Fiss [40]. This method identifies core conditions that are part of both parsimonious and intermediate solutions, and peripheral conditions that are not detectable in the parsimonious solution and only appear in the intermediate solution [41]. Outcomes of the fuzzy set analyses for positive and negative impacts are presented in Table 1. The black circles (•) the presence of a condition, while the crossed-out circles (⊗) indicate the absence of it. Core elements of a configuration are marked with large circles, peripheral elements with small ones, and blank spaces are an indication of a don't care situation in which the causal condition may be either present or absent.

Table 1. Configurations leading to high and low performance

Configuration	Positive Impacts					Negative Impacts			
	P1	P2	P3	P4	P5	N1	N2	N3	N4
Task									
Core task			●		●	●			●
Reporting and documentation task		●	●	●			●		
Information/Coordination task	●	●		●				●	
Leadership	●	●	⊗	⊗	⊗	●	⊗	●	⊗
Non-Routineness	●		⊗	●	⊗		●	●	
Technology									
Reliability	●	●		●	●	⊗	⊗		
User-friendliness		●	●	●	●	⊗	⊗		
Adaptability/Flexibility	●	·			●			⊗	⊗
Personal computer		●	●	●		●	●	●	
Mobile devices	●			●				●	
Wearables					●				●
Use Context									
Colleague support			●	●	·	●	⊗	·	
Training		●	●		●		·	⊗	⊗
Planning participation	●				●	⊗		⊗	⊗
Consistency	0.913	0.907	0.892	0.917	0.873	0.943	0.908	0.874	0.870
Raw Coverage	0.216	0.221	0.184	0.194	0.131	0.131	0.092	0.106	0.118
Unique Coverage	0.192	0.186	0.144	0.139	0.088	0.122	0.073	0.899	0.101
Overall Solution Consistency	0.885					0.879			
Overall Solution Coverage	0.573					0.342			

The outcomes of the analysis for positive impacts produce five different solutions. The solutions are grouped into those that are oriented for leadership-related roles (P1–P2) and non-leadership (P3–P5). Solutions P1 and P2 present some commonalities but are based on use of different technologies. P1 produces positive impacts for use of mobile devices to perform information and coordination tasks that are characterized by non-routineness. For successful use of such systems a prerequisite is that the are above all reliable and adaptable, and that employees are contributors during the planning and introduction of such technologies. In P2 the utilized technologies are personal computers for reporting and documentation tasks and information/coordination. Again, reliability is found to be a core contributor to positive impacts of digital technology use, with user-friendliness being another core-condition, and adaptability playing a lesser important role. Successful adoption of such technologies is coupled with training. Solution P3 concerns personal computer use for core tasks and reporting and documentation. This solution corresponds to employees that do not undertake leadership tasks and their work is characterized by routine practices. Positive impacts in this case result from developing user-friendly technologies and providing support within the working environment and training for use. P4 on the other had refers to non-routinized work activities that necessitate tasks of reporting and documentation and information coordination. Here the used technologies include personal computer and mobile devices, with user-friendliness and reliability being core characteristics leading to positive impacts combined with support from colleagues. Finally, P5 refers to routinized work for core tasks using wearables. Here we find that for such technologies' reliability, user-friendliness and adaptability all have t co-exist in tandem with appropriate training and involvement in the planning and introduction of such digital technologies.

When looking into negative impacts we do not make the assumption that they will be the counter-situation to positive ones, since a series of different elements may coalesce to result in a negative outcome. We negative impacts are realized when for core tasks that are performed by employed with leadership responsibilities, there is an absence of user-friendliness and reliability for tasks done on personal computers, and where the preferred method of training is through collegial support and an absence of participation during planning and introduction. Similarly, in solution N3 when it comes to tasks that require information and coordination of a non-routinized nature performed on personal computers and mobile devices, an absence of flexibility combines with a lack of training and participation in planning lead to sub-optimal outcomes. In solution N2 which corresponds to personnel that do not have leadership responsibilities and use digital technologies for non-routinized reporting and documentation tasks on personal computers, the absence of reliability and user friendliness, along with low support within work on using such technologies leads to negative impacts. Finally, solution N4 concerns core tasks conducted by employees without leadership responsibilities utilizing wearable devices. In these cases, limited flexibility combined with no training and participation in the planning yields negative impacts.

5 Discussion

This study builds on the increased digitization of work practices within the healthcare and medical services sector and attempts to explore what configurations of tasks, technologies and individual use contexts lead to positive and negative impacts. This study is motivated by the increased embeddedness of work practices with digital technologies and the large amounts invested annually in improving operations by means of such technologies. Nevertheless, the value of such technologies is often questioned, and several studies pinpoint that a lack of any significant impacts, or even negative ones, are due to the fact that there is often a mismatch between what is required, how it is assimilated in operations, and how it is leveraged to support certain tasks. Even more, there are several reports that despite investments in digital technologies in the healthcare sector, there is a denial of use that can be attributed to several reasons, but primarily due to the fact that these technologies make work practices much more arduous and stressful rather than providing any value. While there has been some work on task-technology fit in the healthcare environment, the methodologies applied to date do not allow for the exploration of the diverse profile and patterns of use [42].

Specifically, our study contributes theoretically by expanding the perspective of task-technology fit and unshackling for research methods that can explain part of the picture. The use of configurational approaches such as that of fsQCA can enable researcher to uncover different configurations of conditions that lead to positive outcomes, providing a renewed, and more individual-specific perspective on how to optimally use digital technologies to enhance work and improve productivity. The findings demonstrate that there are unique combinations of critical factors that contribute to making technology work of healthcare and medical service professionals, and that these do not only relate to the technology, but also to its fit with specific tasks, the routinization of work, as well as how organizations plan and diffuse them. This raises the question of how organizations should plan such initiatives to prepare for pre-adoption, and to facilitate continued and optimal usage. From a practical point of view, the results of this study can be used by technology managers to formulate different strategies around digital technologies in the healthcare and medical sector. In particular, our results showcase something that is often mentioned by consultants, but that is hardly applied in practice; that there needs to be a greater degree of personalization when planning and deploying digital technologies to support work, particularly in a very information-sensitive, time-critical and low fault tolerant sector such as that of the healthcare. It is also quite striking to see that there are several ways in which digital technologies can produce negative impacts to professionals. Such results should prompt professionals to understand why heir digital solutions are creating more of a burden than helping those they were intended for and creating deployment practices that work towards positive impacts.

While the results of this research shed some light on the complex relationships between tasks in the healthcare sector, digital technologies, and individual usage characteristics, they must be considered under their limitations. First, the sample of our analysis consists of employees working in Norway. It is probable that individuals that work in other countries may have slightly different configurations of factors that positive impacts since there is likely a cultural effect that could play a role. Second, while we examine positive impacts, we do not look at them specifically. It may be likely that we have a mix of positive impacts and negative ones at the same time. An interesting future direction would see where the optimal balance between the two is and how to achieve that. It is very likely that positive impacts are also accompanied by some negative and more salient ones. Third, although fsQCA allows us to examine the configurations of factors that lead to positive and negative impacts in work performance, the process through which this is done is not well explained. A complementary study suing a qualitative approach would likely reveal more insight on the stages of use of technology, where major obstacles present themselves and how they are overcome.

References

1. Kohli, R., Devaraj, S., Ow, T.T.: Does information technology investment influences firm's market value? the case of non-publicly traded healthcare firms. MIS Q. **36**(4), 1145–1163 (2012)
2. Bardhan, I.R., Thouin, M.F.: Health information technology and its impact on the quality and cost of healthcare delivery. Decis. Support Syst. **55**, 438–449 (2013)

3. Mikalef, P., Batenburg, R.: Determinants of IT adoption in hospitals: IT maturity surveyed in an European context. In: Proceedings of the International Conference on Health Informatics, Rome, Italy (2011)
4. Ajami, S., Bagheri-Tadi, T.: Barriers for adopting electronic health records (EHRs) by physicians. Acta Inf. Med. **21**, 129 (2013)
5. Gagnon, M.-P., Ngangue, P., Payne-Gagnon, J., Desmartis, M.: m-Health adoption by healthcare professionals: a systematic review. J. Am. Med. Inf. **23**, 212–220 (2015)
6. Greenhalgh, T., Stramer, K., Bratan, T., Byrne, E., Russell, J., Potts, H.W.J.B.: Adoption and non-adoption of a shared electronic summary record in England: a mixed-method case study. BMJ **340**, c3111 (2010)
7. Mikalef, P., Kourouthanassis, P.E., Pateli, A.G.: Online information search behaviour of physicians. Health Inf. Libr. J. **34**, 58–73 (2017)
8. Kourouthanassis, P.E., Mikalef, P., Ioannidou, M., Pateli, A.: Exploring the online satisfaction gap of medical doctors: an expectation-confirmation investigation of information needs. In: Vlamos, P., Alexiou, A. (eds.) GeNeDis 2014. AEMB, vol. 820, pp. 217–228. Springer, Cham (2015). https://doi.org/10.1007/978-3-319-09012-2_15
9. Kellermann, A.L., Jones, S.S.: What it will take to achieve the as-yet-unfulfilled promises of health information technology. Health Aff. **32**, 63–68 (2013)
10. Pai, F.-Y., Huang, K.-I.: Applying the technology acceptance model to the introduction of healthcare information systems. Technol. Forecast. Soc. Change **78**, 650–660 (2011)
11. Walter, Z., Lopez, M.S.: Physician acceptance of information technologies: role of perceived threat to professional autonomy. Decis. Support Syst. **46**, 206–215 (2008)
12. Goodhue, D.L., Thompson, R.L.: Task-technology fit and individual performance. MIS Q. **19**(2), 213–236 (1995)
13. Willis, M.J., El-Gayar, O.F., Deokar, A.V.: Evaluating task-technology fit and user performance for an electronic health record system. Int. J. Healthc Technol. Manag. **11**(1), 327 (2009)
14. Kim, M.J., Chung, N., Lee, C.K., Preis, M.W.: Motivations and use context in mobile tourism shopping: applying contingency and task–technology fit theories. Int. J. Tourism Res. **17**, 13–24 (2015)
15. Aljukhadar, M., Senecal, S., Nantel, J.J.I.: Management: is more always better? investigating the task-technology fit theory in an online user context. Inf. Manag. **51**, 391–397 (2014)
16. Strong, D.M., Volkoff, O.: Understanding organization—enterprise system fit: a path to theorizing the information technology artifact. MIS Q. **34**, 731–756 (2010)
17. Furneaux, B.: Task-technology fit theory: A survey and synopsis of the literature. In: Dwivedi, Y., Wade, M., Schneberger, S. (eds.) Information systems theory, vol. 28, pp. 87–106. Springer, New York (2012). https://doi.org/10.1007/978-1-4419-6108-2_5
18. Cady, R.G., Finkelstein, S.M.: e-Health: task–technology fit of video telehealth for nurses in an outpatient clinic setting. Telemed. e-Health **20**, 633–639 (2014)
19. El-Gayar, O.F., Deokar, A.V., Wills, M.J..: Manag.: evaluating task-technology fit and user performance for an electronic health record system. In: AMCIS 2009 Proceedings, vol. 11, pp. 50–65 (2010)
20. Peute, L.W., Aarts, J., Bakker, P.J., Jaspers, M.W.: Anatomy of a failure: a sociotechnical evaluation of a laboratory physician order entry system implementation. Int. J. Med. Inf. **79**, e58–e70 (2010)
21. Mikalef, P., Pateli, A.: Information technology-enabled dynamic capabilities and their indirect effect on competitive performance: Findings from PLS-SEM and fsQCA. J. Bus. Res. **70**, 1–16 (2017)
22. Fiss, P.C.: Building better causal theories: a fuzzy set approach to typologies in organization research. Acad. Manag. J. **54**, 393–420 (2011)

23. Reyes-Mercado, P.: Adoption of fitness wearables: insights from partial least squares and qualitative comparative analysis. J. Syst. Inf. Technol. **20**, 103–127 (2018)
24. Or, C.K.L., Karsh, B.-T.: A systematic review of patient acceptance of consumer health information technology. J. Am. Med. Inf. **16**, 550–560 (2009)
25. Kim, D.: Adoption of personal information system: innovation diffusion theory and task-technology fit. In: Proceedings of the Allied Academies International Conference on Academy of Management Information and Decision Sciences, pp. 50, Jordan Whitney Enterprises, Inc. (2009)
26. Hamidi, H., Chavoshi, A.: Informatics: analysis of the essential factors for the adoption of mobile learning in higher education: a case study of students of the University of Technology. Telmatics Inf. **35**, 1053–1070 (2018)
27. Hikmet, N., Chen, S.K.: An investigation into low mail survey response rates of information technology users in health care organizations. Int. J. Med. Inf. **72**, 29–34 (2003)
28. Straub, D., Boudreau, M.-C., Gefen, D.: Validation guidelines for IS positivist research. Commun. Assoc. Inf. Syst. **13**, 63 (2004)
29. Gebauer, J., Shaw, M.J., Gribbins, M.L.: Task-technology fit for mobile information systems. J. Inf. Technol. **25**, 259–272 (2010)
30. Klopping, I.M., McKinney, E.: Extending the technology acceptance model and the task-technology fit model to consumer e-commerce. Technol. Learn. Perform **22**, 35–48 (2004)
31. Weiseth, P.E., Munkvold, B.E., Tvedte, B., Larsen, S.: The wheel of collaboration tools: a typology for analysis within a holistic framework. In: Proceedings of the 2006 20th Anniversary Conference on Computer Supported Cooperative Work, pp. 239–248. ACM (2006)
32. Cane, S., McCarthy, R.: Analyzing the factors that affect information systems use: a task-technology fit meta-analysis. J. Comput. Inf. Syst. **50**, 108–123 (2009)
33. Lin, T.-C.: Informatics, nursing: mobile nursing information system utilization: the task-technology fit perspective. CIN: Comput. Inf. **32**, 129–137 (2014)
34. Metcalf, D., Milliard, S.T., Gomez, M., Schwartz, M.: Wearables and the Internet of Things for health: Wearable, interconnected devices promise more efficient and comprehensive health care. IEEE Pulse **7**, 35–39 (2016)
35. Chung, S., Lee, K.Y., Kim, K.J.I.: Management: job performance through mobile enterprise systems: the role of organizational agility, location independence, and task characteristics. Inf. Manag. **51**, 605–617 (2014)
36. Petter, S., Straub, D., Rai, A.: Specifying formative constructs in information systems research. MIS Q. **31**, 623–656 (2007)
37. van de Wetering, R., Mikalef, P., Helms, R.: Driving organizational sustainability-oriented innovation capabilities: a complex adaptive systems perspective. Curr. Opin. Environ. Sustain. **28**, 71–79 (2017)
38. Ragin, C.C.: Qualitative comparative analysis using fuzzy sets (fsQCA). Config. Comp. Methods **51**, 87–121 (2009)
39. Ordanini, A., Parasuraman, A., Rubera, G.: When the recipe is more important than the ingredients: a qualitative comparative analysis (QCA) of service innovation configurations. J. Serv. Res. **17**, 134–149 (2014)
40. Ragin, C.C., Fiss, P.C.: Net effects analysis versus configurational analysis: an empirical demonstration. Redes. Soc. Inq.: Fuzzy Sets Beyond **240**, 190–212 (2008)
41. Mikalef, P., Boura, M., Lekakos, G., Krogstie, J.: Big data analytics and firm performance: findings from a mixed-method approach. J. Bus. Res. **98**, 261–276 (2019)
42. Hsiao, J.-L., Chen, R.-F..: Informatics, nursing: an investigation on task-technology fit of mobile nursing information systems for nursing performance. CIN: Comput. Inf. Nurs. **30**, 265–273 (2012)

Ontology-Based Fragmented Company Knowledge Integration: Multi-aspect Ontology Building

Nikolay Shilov[(✉)] and Nikolay Teslya

SPIIRAS, St. Petersburg, Russia
{nick, teslya}@iias.spb.su

Abstract. Early steps of ongoing digital transformation in companies is often driven by local business needs and results in usage of various information systems aimed at assisting in solving particular tasks. However, this leads to a dead end and further transformation is not possible without integration, what, in turn, requires interoperability support. The solution that seems to be the most simple is to use one complex system. However, various legacy systems used in various departments of companies have accumulated large volumes of corporate information and knowledge that are not easy to transfer into another system. Besides, spending time of specialists to learn different systems instead of those they are used to is not the best idea either. Though, the problem technical interoperability support is solved through usage of commonly accepted standards, the semantic interoperability is still an issue. In the previous paper, research results related to selection of the most appropriate solution for building a common information model enabling seamless knowledge exchange preserving existing information models was presented. This paper makes a step further through building a multi-aspect ontology taking into account differences between terminologies used in various information systems.

Keywords: Multi-aspect ontology · Interoperability · Knowledge management · Ontology building

1 Introduction

The forth industrial revolution (or Industry 4.0) and digitalization that are currently going on require intensive application of information and telecommunication technologies that are widely used at basically all companies' departments: engineering, design, production, sales, service and other.

This means that efficient application of such concepts requires a tight integration of software information systems along all the business processes of the company. But such integration is subject to multiple challenges arising due to the fact that different business processes in a company often have different goals, are aimed at solving different tasks, and apply different methods that assume application of different information models. These models have been developed as a result of multiple year experience and fit very well to the corresponding tasks, but usually they are not interoperable with each other.

W. Abramowicz and R. Corchuelo (Eds.): BIS 2019 Workshops, LNBIP 373, pp. 181–189, 2019.
https://doi.org/10.1007/978-3-030-36691-9_16

This was not a problem as long as they were dealing with their own pieces of information and until the IT system integration took place. However, the integration assumes that these information pieces often overlap and if one piece is modified as a result of a certain business process, this modification has to be taken into account in other processes. This causes a necessity to provide for interoperability support between various processes occurring in a company.

The research is motivated by a long-time collaboration with a worldwide provider of automation technology for factory and process automation with a wide assortments of products (more than 40 000 products of approximately 700 types, with various configuration possibilities) ranging from simple products to complex systems [1, 2].

During a number of years of collaboration, an eco-system of software tools aimed at support of various company business processes has been developed as shown in Fig. 1. Below, the elements of the figure are described in detail.

One of the first projects of the considered company related to this problem was launched in 2010 [3]. It was aimed at modification of work and information flows related to configuration of product combinations. The business process reorganization started with setting up a product ontology in a semi-automatic way originally aimed at product codification (order code scheme) by the NOC tool [3]. The resulting ontology (described in detail in [4]) consisted of more than 1000 classes organized into a four level taxonomy, based on the VDMA (Verband Deutscher Maschinen- und Anlagenbau/ Mechanical Engineering Industry Association) classification [5].

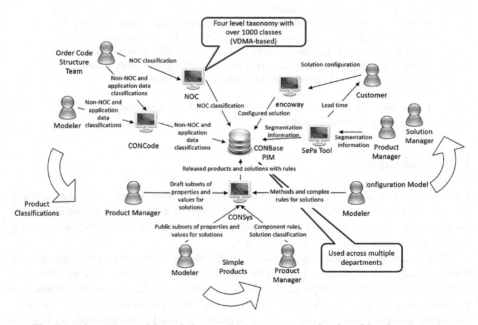

Fig. 1. Information and knowledge management systems developed by the moment.

The same taxonomy was used in the company's PDM (Product Data Management) and ERP (Enterprise Resource Planning) systems. The ontology structure enabled separation of various types of entities (e.g., physical products and software services) what made it possible to easily deal with it even though it was rather large. Different specialists could work with different parts of the ontology without the need to overview and manage the whole ontology at once (CONBase Product Information Management). Overall, application of the common ontologies in this particular project has proved itself as a convenient and reliable way of product and system knowledge organisation.

However, extension of the support of different processes has caused appearance of extensions of the central ontology aimed at particular processes (e.g., CONCode to support products, which have descriptions incompatible with the ontology). Complex product modelling and design system (CONSys tool) together with product segmentation policy definition tool (SePa) also introduced additional information to be managed. E.g., application data (an auxiliary component used for introduction of some additional characteristics and requirements to the product, for example, operating temperatures, certification, electrical connection, etc.) had to be added for marketing purposes and combined with other features through defined rules. Development of the product configuration tool (CONFig) was aimed at testing the possibility to configure systems based on the rules stored in the CONBase. The tool supported the configuration process in terms used within the company.

Business and information technology (IT) alignment (BITA) is aimed at developing models and methods for improvement of the interrelations between business and IT. In accordance with BITA alignment sequences presented in [6] this development would fall into the alignment sequence class of Functional Integration (Fig. 2). On the one hand this process is natural and evolutional, but on the other hand it leads to fragmentation of business processes and IT systems.

Although some integration results have been achieved in the area of complex product and system information management and configuration, still a lot has to be done to support the whole set of business-processes. One of the key tasks is to provide a coherent way of integration of different extensions into the common ontology. Ontologies are not only used in software tools but also often represent various aspects of enterprise architecture and business processes. As a result, they can help to shift the development approach of model-driven engineering to continuous alignment of business and IT [7].

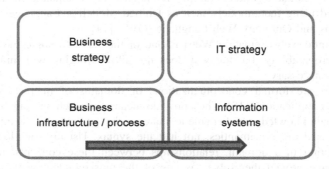

Fig. 2. Functional alignment prospective of BITA.

Having a number of ontologies is not an efficient way due to the necessity to continuously translate information and knowledge between them. However, plain integration is not possible either. For example, the customers are used to operate different terminology, which does not correspond one-to-one to that used within the company. Besides, customers from different industries also operate different terms.

Research results presented in this paper are aimed at solving this problem at the level of semantic interoperability. In the previously reported work [8] different approaches have been analyzed and the apparatus of describing fragmented company knowledge via multi-aspect ontology was selected. This paper describes the process of building a multi-aspect ontology. The paper is structured as follows Sect. 2 presents some existing efforts in the area of interoperability support. Section 3 describes the process of multi-aspect ontology building. The main results are summarized in the conclusion.

2 Interoperability Support

It is now widely recognized that knowledge sharing is a key enabler for most collaborative actions and the problem of interoperability support between independent heterogeneous information resources steps forward [9]. In Europe, this issue is currently receiving significant attention.

In the concept of a new European interoperability framework (New EIF [10, 11]), interoperability is defined as the "ability of organizations to interact towards mutually beneficial goals, involving the sharing of information and knowledge between these organizations, through the business processes they support, using the exchange of data between their ICT systems".

In Europe, the need for standardization and interoperable systems was recognized almost thirty years ago with the launch of the European Commission's CADDIA program in 1985, the IDABC program in 1995, the ISA program in 2009 (decision 2009/922/EC) and the creation of current compatibility solutions for European e-government services (ISA^2) in 2016 [12]. However, support for interoperability and integration of information resources into common ecosystems is still an unsolved interdisciplinary problem.

There are four levels of interoperability [11]: technical, semantic, organizational and legislative. Semantic interoperability is understood as semantic interpretation of data presented using meta-models such as Unified Modeling Language (UML [13]) class diagrams and Ontology Web Language (OWL [14]).

The semantic web (Semantic Web) is one of the ways to solve the problem of semantic interoperability, but today it does not allow working with information as seamlessly as necessary.

Ontologies are formal conceptualizations of domains of interests sharable by heterogeneous applications [15]. They provide means for machine-readable representation of domain knowledge and enable to share, exchange, and process information & knowledge based on its semantics, not just the syntax. Usually, ontologies include concepts existing in a domain, relationships between these concepts, and axioms. Ontologies have proved themselves as one of the most efficient ways to solve the problem of semantic interoperability support. Still there is a need for common ontologies of problem areas with supporting multiple modifications in a quick and simple way, as well as semantic queries in a given context, but applying ontologies to digital ecosystems is still a problem due to different terminologies and formalisms that the members of the ecosystems use.

It is generally accepted that models of specific problem areas (for example, configuration models of complex systems) can be obtained by inheriting or extending a common ontology. However, in systems with a dynamic structure this solution does not allow to achieve the required flexibility, since the expansion of the general ontology with the appearance of new information objects requires ontology matching. It should be noted that the automatic ontology matching methods are still not sufficiently reliable (except narrow domains), and manual ontology matching significantly reduces the efficiency.

3   Multi-aspect Ontology Building

The difficulty of supporting conciliated ontologies that capture different views on the same problem, as well as developing an ontology model for representation and processing of information used for solving problems of different nature, lies in the necessity to operate not only with different terminologies but also with different formalisms used to describe different domains; the terminologies and formalisms in turn depend on the tools used to effectively solve the domains' problems. In the previous publication [8] several paradigms of building multi-aspect ontologies have been analyzed and granular multi-aspect ontology proposed by [16] have been selected.

The next step was choosing the notation. The most progress in this direction is achieved by Hemam who in co-authorship with Boufaïda proposed in 2011 a language for description of multi-viewpoint ontologies - MVP-OWL [17] extended in 2018 with probability support [18].

In accordance with this notation, the OWL-DL language was extended in the following way (only some of the extensions are listed here; for the complete reference, please, see [17]). First, the viewpoints were introduced (in the current research they correspond to ontology aspects). Classes and properties were split into global (observed from two or several viewpoints) and local (observed only from one viewpoint). Individuals could only be local, however, taking into account the possibility of multi-instantiation, they could be described in several viewpoints and at the global level simultaneously. Also, four types of bridge rules were introduced that enable links or "communication channels" between viewpoints (only the bidirectional inclusion bridge rule stating that two concepts under different viewpoints are equal is used in the example below, indicated with the symbol $\overset{\equiv}{\leftrightarrow}$).

The presented below ontology is based on integration of several existing ontologies. The top-level ontology proposed in [19] was used as the basis. The described simplified but illustrative example Fig. 3 considers three aspects: *"Product Engineering"*, *"Sales"*, *"Strategic Planning and Production"* corresponding to different processes. The three aspects are aimed at different tasks (only one per aspect is considered in the example) and, as a result, they use different formalisms (below, these are described with references considering each of the aspects in detail). However, some of the concepts (e.g., "*Product*") are used across the viewpoints.

The task considered in the *Product Engineering* aspect is definition of a new product and its possible features [3]. The formalism used in this domain is OWL, and the example classes are "*Product Family*", "*Product Group*" (subclass of *Product Family*), "*Product*" (subclass of *Product Group*), and "*Feature*" (associated with the class *Product*). The product engineer needs a possibility to define new classes of products and new products with their possible features and feature attributes (e.g., *Cylinder XXX* is a subclass of *Pneumatic Cylinder* and has such features as "*diameter*", "*stroke*", "*lock in end position*", and others, that, in turn, have certain attributes). However, there still has to be a possibility to endure the consistency of product classes that is achieved via OWL and reasoning (the Pellet reasoner is currently used).

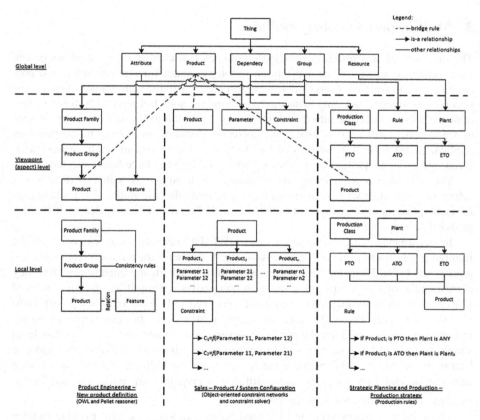

Fig. 3. Multi-aspect ontology for three viewpoints.

In the *Sales* aspect, the task is definition of functional dependencies between parameters of products and their processing when a product or an assembly of products are being configured by/for a customer [1]. There are three main classes in this aspect:

"*Product*", "*Parameter*" (product parameter such as "*mass*", "*power*", etc.), and "*Constraints*". The formalism of object-oriented constraint networks makes it possible to define functional dependencies (represented by constraints) between product parameters and then process these via a constraint solver when a particular product or a system is being configured. The "*Parameter*" in this aspect is not the same as "*Feature*" in the previous aspect. In certain cases they can coincide, however, generally this is not the case.

The third example aspect is *Strategic Planning and Production* where a production strategy is defined based on corresponding rules. The products are divided into three production classes: "*PTO*" (pick to order), "*ATO*" (assemble to order), and "*ETO*" (engineered to order) [20]. Based on this class the lead time for each product is defined together with the plant, where it is to be produced. As a result, the following classes are considered in this aspect: "*Production Class*", "*Product*", "*Plant*", "*Rule*", "*PTO*", "*ATO*", "*ETO*". In this view production rules ("if ... then ...") are used.

In accordance with [17] the following ontology elements have been defined:

Viewpoints (aspects): *Product Engineering, Sales, Strategic Planning and Production*

Global classes: *Thing, Product, Attribute, Dependency, Group, Resource.*

Local Classes:

> *Product Engineering: Product Family, Product Group, Product, Feature*
> *Sales: Product, Parameter, Constraint*
> *Strategic Planning and Production: Product, Production Class, Plant, Rule, PTO, ATO, ETO*

Bridge Rules:

> $Product \overset{\equiv}{\leftrightarrow} Product_{Sales}$
> $Product \overset{\equiv}{\leftrightarrow} Product_{ProductEngineering}$
> $Product \overset{\equiv}{\leftrightarrow} Product_{StrategicPlanningAndProduction}$
> i.e., the products from different viewpoints (aspects) are the same products.

When the viewpoints and bridge rules are defined, one can use any required formalism inside each of the viewpoints. Besides, the existing models can be integrated into such a multi-view ontology without significant modification.

4 Conclusion and Future Work

The paper considers the problem of interoperability support of different company business-processes and related IT tools with the help of an ontology. The problem of heterogeneity and overlapping of the knowledge and information models used in the various processes is addresses by application of different views (referred to as "aspects") within the same ontology. On one side, the multi-aspect ontology provides the common vocabulary what enables the interoperability between different company business-processes and supporting them IT systems. On the other side, the aspects preserve the internal notations and formalisms that have proved their efficiency for solving particular tasks (e.g., consistency checking, configuration, planning).

The presented ontology has been built using the OWL-MVP language that is aimed at support of different views (aspects) within the same ontology. The ontology is illustrated through an example from IT projects implemented during collaboration with the automation equipment producer including three aspects *"Product Engineering"*, *"Sales"*, *"Strategic Planning and Production"*), with each of them having one task.

The suggested approach can significantly facilitate the functional BITA alignment, where IT infrastructure development follows the evolution of business processes. Due to its capability to preserve most convenient information models for particular business processes, a seamless integration of different business processes in the part of information exchange can be achieved.

In the future, it is planned to extend the built ontology for other aspects and use it more intensively in real applications.

Acknowledgements. The reported study was partially funded by RFBR, project number 18-07-01203 (ontology-based representation of heterogeneous dynamically changing information) and State Research no. 0073-2019-0005 (studying information requirements of different user groups).

References

1. Smirnov, A., et al.: Knowledge management for complex product development framework and implementation. IFIP Adv. Inf. Commun. Technol. **409**, 110–119 (2013)
2. Smirnov, A., Shilov, N., Oroszi, A., Sinko, M., Krebs, T.: Changing information management in product-service system PLM: customer-oriented strategy. In: Ríos, J., Bernard, A., Bouras, A., Foufou, S. (eds.) PLM 2017. IAICT, vol. 517, pp. 701–709. Springer, Cham (2017). https://doi.org/10.1007/978-3-319-72905-3_62
3. Oroszi, A., Jung, T., Smirnov, A., Shilov, N., Kashevnik, A.: Ontology-driven codification for discrete and modular products. Int. J. Prod. Dev. **8**, 162–177 (2009). https://doi.org/10.1504/IJPD.2009.024186
4. Smirnov, A., Shilov, N.: Ontology matching in collaborative recommendation system for PLM. Int. J. Prod. Lifecycle Manag. **6**, 322–338 (2013). https://doi.org/10.1504/IJPLM.2013.063210
5. VDMA. German Engineering Federation (2018). http://www.vdma.org/en_GB/
6. Muñoz, L., Avila, O.: Business and information technology alignment measurement - a recent literature review. In: Abramowicz, W., Paschke, A. (eds.) BIS 2018. LNBIP, vol. 339, pp. 112–123. Springer, Cham (2019). https://doi.org/10.1007/978-3-030-04849-5_10
7. Hinkelmann, K., Gerber, A., Karagiannis, D., Thoenssen, B., van der Merwe, A., Woitsch, R.: A new paradigm for the continuous alignment of business and IT: combining enterprise architecture modelling and enterprise ontology. Comput. Ind. **79**, 77–86 (2016). https://doi.org/10.1016/j.compind.2015.07.009
8. Smirnov, A., Shilov, N.: Ontology-based fragmented company knowledge integration: possible approaches. In: Abramowicz, W., Paschke, A. (eds.) BIS 2018. LNBIP, vol. 339, pp. 30–37. Springer, Cham (2019). https://doi.org/10.1007/978-3-030-04849-5_3
9. Ordiyasa, I.W., Nugroho, L.E., Santosa, P.I., Kumorotomo, W.: Enhancing quality of service for eGovernment interoperability based on adaptive ontology. In: 2016 2nd International Conference on Science and Technology-Computer (ICST), pp. 102–107. IEEE (2016). https://doi.org/10.1109/ICSTC.2016.7877356

10. European Commission: Communication from the Commission to the European Parliament, the Council, the European Economic and Social Committee and the Committee of the Regions, European Interoperability Framework – Implementation Strategy. https://eur-lex.europa.eu/legal-content/EN/TXT/HTML/?uri=CELEX:52017DC0134&from=EN
11. European Commission: New European Interoperability Framework: Promoting seamless services and data flows for European public administrations. https://ec.europa.eu/isa2/sites/isa/files/eif_brochure_final.pdf
12. European Commission: ISA2 Interoperability solutions for public administrations, businesses and citizens. https://ec.europa.eu/isa2/home_en
13. Object Management Group (OMG): About the Unified Modeling Language Specification. Version 2.5. https://www.omg.org/spec/UML/2.5.1/
14. McGuinness, D.L., van Harmelen, F.: OWL Web Ontology Language Overview. W3C Recommendation. https://www.w3.org/TR/owl-features/
15. Gruber, T.R.: A translation approach to portable ontology specifications. Knowl. Acquis. **5**, 199–220 (1993). https://doi.org/10.1006/knac.1993.1008
16. Tarassov, V., Fedotova, A., Stark, R., Karabekov, B.: Granular meta-ontology and extended allen's logic: some theoretical background and application to intelligent product lifecycle management systems valery. In: Schwab, I., van Moergestel, L., Gonçalves, G. (eds.) The Fourth International Conference on Intelligent Systems and Applications, INTELLI 2015, pp. 86–93, St. Julians (2015)
17. Hemam, M., Boufaïda, Z.: MVP-OWL: a multi-viewpoints ontology language for the Semantic Web. Int. J. Reason. Intell. Syst. **3**, 147 (2011). https://doi.org/10.1504/IJRIS.2011.043539
18. Hemam, M.: An extension of the ontology web language with multi-viewpoints and probabilistic reasoning. Int. J. Adv. Intell. Paradig. **10**, 1 (2018). https://doi.org/10.1504/IJAIP.2018.10003857
19. Borsato, M., Estorilio, C.C.A., Cziulik, C., Ugaya, C.M.L., Rozenfeld, H.: An ontology building approach for knowledge sharing in product lifecycle management. Int. J. Bus. Syst. Res. **4**, 278 (2010). https://doi.org/10.1504/IJBSR.2010.032951
20. Smirnov, A.V., Shilov, N., Oroszi, A., Sinko, M., Krebs, T.: Changing information management for product-service system engineering: customer-oriented strategies and lessons learned. Int. J. Prod. Lifecycle Manag. **11**, 1–18 (2018). https://doi.org/10.1504/IJPLM.2018.091647

BSCT Workshop

BSCT 2019 Workshop Chairs' Message

The Second Workshop on Blockchain and Smart Contract Technologies (BSCT 2019) took place on June 28–29, 2019, in Sevilla, Spain. The event was co-organized with the 22nd International Conference on Business Information Systems (BIS 2019). This volume is the aftermath of its participants' research effort as well as discussions that took place during the workshop. Now, it is our privilege as BSCT chairs – to present the selected papers to the wide audience of Springer's LNBIP readers. This year the number of submissions was lower than the year before. Usually, this kind of statement sounds disappointing. But, this is not the case, as we must remember that the previous workshop was by far outstanding in terms of figures. Regardless, the second edition was still on a very decent level of 24 papers. All these articles were carefully reviewed by the dedicated members of Program Committee (PC). The team of reviewers prepared in total 70 thoughtful opinions. On this basis we were able to select a set of the most promising study descriptions. Together, they totalled to 10 papers accepted for publication after additional editorial review. Consequently, the rate of acceptance in this year's edition rose to 44%. We perceive the organization of the second workshop as a great success.

In fact, the mentioned success of the event exceeded the wildest expectations of the organizers. When we planned the organization of this new workshop we knew that there was an urgent and growing need from the researchers as well as from a business perspective to meet on common ground in order to facilitate and accelerate the exchange of ideas and knowledge in the area of the workshop. In our conservative estimates we presumed the number of submissions to be around 15. The submission system showed this number one week before the deadline. However, two days before the deadline the number doubled. Ultimately the process ended with 46 submissions, tripling the initial anticipations. On the one hand we were really excited with the level achieved, but on the other hand we were full of doubts as to whether we would be able to live up to the high quality organizational characteristics that we were all accustomed to. As one may expect such an abundance gives rise to numerous organizational issues.

The workshop covered a wide area of topics. There are also many challenges appearing on the horizon as the blockchain technologies are in a phase of swift advancement. Despite some turbulences on the cryptocurrencies markets we are certain that the blockchain and smart contract will thrive, develop, and continue to emerge in many new usages. That is why we are strongly convinced that the workshop as a platform for discussion and thought sharing will be even more important in the years to come.

As a final point, the chairs would like to express their heartfelt gratitude to all the participants and especially authors whose attendance and contribution allowed us to organize this very successful event. We believe that the workshop is all about community. Therefore the voice of the participants is of the utmost importance to us. The role of the PC members is always undervalued. That is why we would like to express our deepest thanks to them. It is only thanks to their knowledge, sound judgment, and kind support that the workshop took place in its final shape. Without this hard work from the PC, the organizers would not have been able to make the selection of the best works.

Finally, as usual we would like to direct our sincere appreciation to the organizers of the hosting conference (BIS 2019). Without any doubts their organizational know-how and assistance was one of key factors for success. The next BIS conference will take place in Colorado Springs, Colorado, USA, which for sure will be the venue of the third edition of BSCT as well. Thus we would like to invite all this year participants, submitters, and newcomers to the planned event in 2020.

Saulius Masteika
Erich Schweighofer
Piotr Stolarski

Organization

Chairs

Saulius Masteika   Vilnius University, Lithuania
Erich Schweighofer   University of Vienna, Austria
Piotr Stolarski   Poznan University of Business and Economics, Poland

Program Committee

Emmanuelle Anceaume	Irisa, France
Jan Beinke	University of Osnabrück, Germany
François Charoy	Université de Lorraine, LORIA, Inria, France
Nicolas T. Courtois	University College London, UK
Stefan Eder	Benn-Ibler Rechtsanwälte GmbH, Austria
Ernestas Filatovas	Vilnius University, Lithuania
Adrian Florea	Lucian Blaga University of Sibiu, Romania
Vladislav V. Fomin	Vilnius University, Lithuania
Jaap Gordijn	Vrije Universiteit Amsterdam, The Netherlands
Ralf-Christian Härting	Hochschule Aalen, Germany
Aquinas Hobor	National University of Singapore, Singapore
Constantin Houy	Institute for Information Systems at DFKI (IWi), Germany
Monika Kaczmarek	University Duisburg Essen, Germany
Kalinka Kaloyanova	University of Sofia, Bulgaria
Salil S. Kanhere	The University of New South Wales, Australia
Gary Klein	University of Colorado Boulder, USA
Saulius Masteika	Vilnius University, Lithuania
Raimundas Matulevicius	University of Tartu, Estonia
Massimo Mecella	Sapienza University of Rome, Italy
Remigijus Paulavičius	Vilnius University, Lithuania
Cristina Pérez-Solà	Universitat Autònoma de Barcelona, Spain
Kouichi Sakurai	Kyushu University, Japan
Erich Schweighofer	University of Vienna, Austria
Piotr Stolarski	Poznan University of Economics, Poland
Davor Svetinovic	Masdar Institute of Science and Technology, UAE
Herve Verjus	Universite de Savoie, LISTIC, Polytech'Savoie, France
Hans Weigand	Tilburg University, The Netherlands
Netherlandsainer Alt	Leipzig University, Germany
Edgar Weippl	SBA Research, Austria
Jakob Zanol	Working Group Legal Informatics, Austria

Comparing Market Phase Features for Cryptocurrency and Benchmark Stock Index Using HMM and HSMM Filtering

David Suda[(✉)] and Luke Spiteri

Department of Statistics and Operations Research, University of Malta,
Msida MSD2080, Malta
{david.suda,luke.spiteri.13}@um.edu.mt

Abstract. A desirable aspect of financial time series analysis is that of successfully detecting (in real time) market phases. In this paper we implement HMMs and HSMMs with normal state-dependent distributions to Bitcoin/USD price dynamics, and also compare this with S&P 500 price dynamics, the latter being a benchmark in traditional stock market behaviour which most literature resorts to. Furthermore, we test our models' adequacy at detecting bullish and bearish regimes by devising mock investment strategies on our models and assessing how profitable they are with unseen data in comparison to a buy-and-hold approach. We ultimately show that while our modelling approach yields positive results in both Bitcoin/USD and S&P 500, and both are best modelled by four-state HSMMs, Bitcoin/USD so far shows different regime volatility and persistence patterns to the one we are used to seeing in traditional stock markets.

Keywords: Hidden Markov Models · Hidden Semi-Markov Models · Cryptocurrencies · Filtering · Nowcasting

1 Introduction

The relatively short history of Bitcoin and other cryptocurrencies is filled with numerous events that have drastically affected its value. The following three reasons justify the intense volatility experienced by cryptocurrencies: (i) cryptocurrency wealth distribution is more disproportionate than that of traditional financial assets, (ii) public understanding is subjective and highly divided, and lastly (iii) regulation from governments, for and against cryptocrurrencies, has greatly impacted their value. Some important events are mentioned hereafter. In 2015, the U.S. Commodity Futures Commission declared that cryptocurrencies essentially are not considered as currencies, but more as a commodity, and hence could not be regulated. 2017 saw Japan pass a law to accept Bitcoin as a legal form of payment, Bitcoin was split into two derivative digital currencies (the Bitcoin chain BTC and the Bitcoin cash chain BCH), and China's government ceased

© Springer Nature Switzerland AG 2019
W. Abramowicz and R. Corchuelo (Eds.): BIS 2019 Workshops, LNBIP 373, pp. 195–207, 2019.
https://doi.org/10.1007/978-3-030-36691-9_17

domestic exchanges. In 2018, South Korea prohibited anonymous cryptocurrency trading, social media platforms such as Facebook and Twitter banned cryptocurrency advertisements, and the UK's Financial Conduct Authority (FCA) issued advice on the high risks of investing in the unregulated market of cryptocurrencies. While 2017 was, generally, a bull year for cryptocurrencies, 2018 has seen much decline in their value and some cryptocurrencies have even been wiped out. Presently, however, the value of one Bitcoin is on the rise again and worth more than $9000.

The aim of this paper is that of identifying market regimes - mainly bull and bear market phases - of cryptocurrencies through the use of hidden Markov models (HMMs) and hidden semi-Markov models (HSMMs). We shall implement mock investment strategies on test data, and compare to a buy-and-hold approach, to determine how well these regimes are identified. When prices are on the rise for a relatively long period of time, the market condition is said to be a bull market, and when prices fall steeply with respect to recent highs, the market condition is referred to as a bear market. Two other phases which may be detected in the process are corrections and rallies, with the former being a period of steady decrease amid a bull market, and the latter being a period of slow increase within a bull or bear market. It is possible that HMMs and HSMMs may struggle to distinguish between these two states due to the fact that neither is associated with a steep change. Our research allows for the mean, and not just the volatility, to depend on the states - this is at times ignored in the literature. Due to high correlation between cryptocurrency dynamics, we consider the daily closing prices of Bitcoin/USD (BTC/USD), for the dates ranging from 01/01/2016 to 28/01/2019 for a total of 1124 trading days. Bitcoin is around 50% of the crypto market. Since traditionally, positive trends with low volatility and negative trends with high volatility have respectively been labelled as bull and bear markets, we shall compare and contrast our findings with a de facto standard stock market - the 'S&P 500' where the dates considered are 01/01/2000 – 28/01/2019. This can be invested in collectively via the S&P 500 Index Fund.

The following is a review of existent literature related to cryptocurrencies and the use of HMMs and HSMMs to model financial assets. Starting with the former, [7] fit various parametric distributions on cryptocurrency returns. Furthermore [2, 4, 8, 13, 18] fit generalised autoregressive conditional heteroscedastic (GARCH) models and its variants in their single-regime form. [14] look at the application of Markov switching autoregressive models to Bitcoin. Recent publications which involve the modelling of Bitcoin volatility dynamics at multiple regimes are [1, 3, 6] - though different approaches were used for modelling in these papers with slightly varying results, in all cases, multi-regime dynamics within a heteroscedastic framework was detected. The following, on the other hand, are examples of literature using HMMs and HSMMs to model different phases of financial asset price movements. [17] show that a normal-HMM is capable of reproducing most of the stylised facts for daily S&P 500 return series established by [9, 10]. However, they only allow the standard deviations to vary by the state, while the means are fixed at zero. Recently, [16] applied a four-state HMM for stock trading by predicting monthly closing prices of the S&P 500, showing that the HMM is superior to the buy-and-hold strategy as it yields larger percentage profits under different training and testing periods. Modelling literature on financial time series using HSMMs is, on the other hand, quite limited. [15] implemented a three-state HSMM to describe the dynamics of the Chinese stock market index (CSI 300) returns. The authors assumed normal state-dependent distributions with logarithmic dwell-time distributions, and also implemented a profitable trading strategy. In the next section, we discuss the modelling approach implemented in this paper.

2   General Methodology

The daily adjusted close prices of BTC/USD and S&P 500 were obtained for suitably chosen time periods, not equal in length, which encapsulate the swings the financial instrument goes through. Log returns of the daily adjusted close prices were taken, and the HMM and HSMM models were then fitted on the log returns. Mathematically, an m-state HMM consists of two processes: (i) an unobserved (hidden) discrete-time m-state Markov chain, $(Z_n)_{n\in\mathbb{N}}$, taking values in a finite state-space, $\mathcal{S} = 1, 2, \ldots, m$, and (ii) a state-dependent process, $(Y_n)_{n\in\mathbb{N}}$, whose outcomes (observations) are assumed to be generated by one of m distributions corresponding to the current state of the underlying discrete-time Markov chain (DTMC). The distribution of Y_n is assumed to be conditionally independent of previous observations and states, given the current state Z_n. For a thorough review of HMMs, refer to [20]. One drawback of basic HMMs is due to the one time lag memory of the underlying first order DTMC which is inherently geometric. One possible way to circumvent this problem is to consider general state (possibly not geometric) dwell-time distributions, $d_i(r)$, leading to the HSMM framework. Thus, HSMMs generalise HMMs by explicitly modelling state persistence and state switches separately. This is achieved by considering a discrete-time semi-Markov chain (DTSMC), $(S_n)_{n\in\mathbb{N}}$ with state-space $\mathcal{S}$. For a thorough account of HSMMs, refer to [10] and references therein.

   Since the log returns take values in the real space $\mathbb{R}$, we assume the HMM specification $a_{ij} = \mathrm{P}(Z_n = j | Z_{n-1} = i)$ and $Y_n | Z_n = i \sim N(\mu_i, \sigma_i)$ where a_{ij} are the transition probabilities, and the state-dependent distributions are assumed to be normal with mean μ_i and standard deviation σ_i, for each hidden state i. Similarly, the HSMM specification assumes $q_{ij} = \mathrm{P}(S_n = j | S_{n-1} = i, S_n \neq i)$, $q_{ii} = 0$, $d_i(r) \sim NBinom(v_i, p_i)$ and $Y_n | S_n = i \sim N(\mu_i, \sigma_i)$ - here model state switches are denoted by q_{ij}, $d_i(r)$ models state persistence via negative binomial dwell-time distributions (of which the geometric distribution is a special case) with parameters v_i and p_i, while we once again assume normal state-dependent distributions as for HMMs. Parameter estimation of HMMs can be carried out by either direct numerical maximisation (DNM) of the likelihood via Newton-type methods or by the Expectation-Maximisation (EM) algorithm. Both methods are described in [20]. HSMMs are usually fitted via the EM algorithm as described in [11]. For state inference, the Viterbi algorithm in [19] can be applied for both HMMs and HSMMs to obtain a sequence of most likely hidden states.

The daily log return series are then analysed as follows: (i) suitable HMMs and HSMMs on the complete time series are fitted by varying the number of assumed states; (ii) the optimal model based on the Akaike information criterion (AIC), Bayesian information criterion (BIC), and Hannan-Quinn information criterion (HQC) is chosen; (iii) the chosen time period is split into mutually exclusive training and testing periods; (iv) an expanding window method is implemented by first fitting the optimal model on the training set, and then iteratively adding one time point from the test set (until testing period is exhausted) to the training period and applying the Viterbi algorithm as a filtering procedure to nowcast the current most likely hidden state after parameter re-estimation; and (v) finally, investment strategies based on the model features arising from the Viterbi algorithm are applied to determine models' success at determining market phases. The data analysis presented next is carried out in RStudio by using the packages *HiddenMarkov* of [12] and *hsmm* of [5]. In the next section, we look at the modelling of the different market phases of both BTC/USD and S&P 500, and also draw comparisons.

3   Estimation and State Inference for HMM and HSMM Models

This section is divided into two parts, where first we present the model fit on the complete series and state inference outputs using the Viterbi algorithm for BTC/USD, and this is followed by the same for S&P 500. A comparison of the properties of the two series will ensue. Not more than four states were considered as the algorithms experienced numerical issues for five states or more.

3.1   BTC/USD

In Table 1, we see the relevant goodness-of-fit criteria for 2-, 3- and 4-state HMMs and HSMMs. It can be seen that the homogeneous 4-state normal-HSMM provides the best fit throughout for all information criteria.

Table 1. Goodness-of-fit of stationary normal-HMMs and homogeneous normal-HSMMs for 2, 3 and 4 states based on the entire series of daily log returns of BTC/USD.

	Likelihood	AIC	BIC	HQC
2-state HMM	2924.454	5860.980	5891.056	5872.302
3-state HMM	2872.646	5769.292	5829.587	5792.078
4-state HMM	2846.546	5737.093	5837.586	5775.070
2-state HSMM	2887.872	5779.743	5789.793	5783.541
3-state HSMM	2857.086	5720.171	5735.245	5725.868
4-state HSMM	**2837.926**	**5683.852**	**5703.950**	**5691.447**

For brevity, we present the parameter estimates for the best model (4-state HSMM) only. The parameter estimates (ordered by increasing volatility), obtained via the EM algorithm, are given by,

$$\hat{\mathbb{Q}} = \begin{pmatrix} 0 & 0.831 & 0.000 & 0.169 \\ 0.901 & 0 & 0.000 & 0.099 \\ 0.000 & 0.270 & 0 & 0.730 \\ 0.006 & 0.769 & 0.225 & 0 \end{pmatrix}, \hat{\boldsymbol{\delta}}(1) = (1,0,0,0)),$$

$$\hat{\boldsymbol{v}} = (0.351, 0.204, 10.573, 0.143), \hat{\boldsymbol{p}} = (0.180, 0.126, 0.170, 0.031),$$

$$\hat{\boldsymbol{\mu}} = (0.099, 0.603, 0.376, -0.702), \hat{\boldsymbol{\sigma}} = (0.617, 2.135, 4.162, 7.376),$$

where $\hat{\mathbb{Q}}$ contains estimates of the state switches q_{ij}, $\hat{\boldsymbol{v}}$ and $\hat{\boldsymbol{p}}$ contain estimates of the negative binomial parameters for the dwell-times of the different states, while $\hat{\boldsymbol{\mu}}$ and $\hat{\boldsymbol{\sigma}}$ contain estimates of the normal distribution parameters for the different states. Finally $\hat{\boldsymbol{\delta}}(1)$ is the initial distribution of the DTSMC, which suggests that the series starts from state 1. The normal state-dependent parameters allow us to attach the following interpretations. State 3 can be associated with a bull market due to the moderately high mean, common occurrence and strong persistence. State 4 can be associated with a bear market due to the large (and only) negative mean with relatively weak persistence. Both states exhibit very high volatility, though the bear state exhibits a stronger drift and volatility. Attaching interpretations to state 1 and 2 can be a bit more tricky, as both have weak persistence. State 1 appears to be a market correction/rally state due to its low drift and volatility, while state 2 appears to be an additional bull state with stronger drift, smaller volatility and weak persistence.

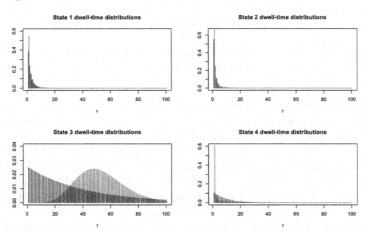

Fig. 1. BTC/USD: state dwell-time distributions for the homogeneous 4-state normal-HSMM (red) and for the stationary 4-state normal-HMM (black) (Color figure online).

The dwell-time distributions for the 4-state HSMM are compared with the equivalent geometric dwell-time distribution of the 4-state HMM in Fig. 1. For states 1 and 2, the geometric and negative binomial distributions closely resemble each other and show a lack of persistence in these states. The HSMM

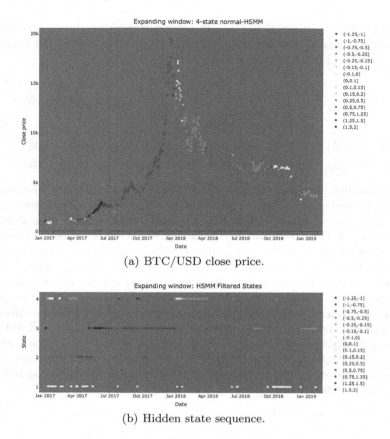

(a) BTC/USD close price.

(b) Hidden state sequence.

Fig. 2. Expanding window: 4-state normal-HSMM filtering via the Viterbi algorithm on BTC/USD. The colours vary by the mean, while the sizes vary by the volatility .

dwell-time distribution for state 3, however, is clearly non-geometric as it shows an extremely high persistence with a modal run length of 47 time steps until a state-switch. For state 4, the HMM geometric distribution shows a higher persistence than the negative binomial dwell-time distribution of the HSMM.

We next employ the expanding window procedure for BTC/USD, where we take the training period to be 01/01/2016 – 31/12/2016 and the testing period to be 01/01/2017 – 28/01/2019. Figure 2 shows that the 4-state HSMM, based on a filtering method, can capture the hidden economic regimes pertaining to bull and bear market phases quite well, since upward (positive) trends are generally a shade of blue while sharp downward (negative) trends are generally orange to red in colour. Observe that the Viterbi algorithm assigns most of the test period in the third state - the bull state. Then, at the start of 2018 the value of one Bitcoin starts plummeting, which is identified early by the Viterbi algorithm as state 4 - the bear state. Moreover, the last days of the testing period switch between states 1 and 2. Ultimately, the 4-state normal-HSMM seems to perform fairly well in detecting the changing market conditions.

3.2   S&P 500

We shall now fit the same models to S&P 500. It is typically more common to see HMM-type models implemented on S&P 500, due to the fact that the features most commonly associated with financial time series can be found here. We can thus also use this stock market index as a benchmark for comparison. Also for this case, a homogeneous 4-state normal-HSMM with negative binomial dwell-time distributions was found to be the best, and the following parameter estimates were obtained,

$$\hat{\mathbb{Q}} = \begin{pmatrix} 0 & 0.998 & 0.002 & 0.000 \\ 0.973 & 0 & 0.023 & 0.004 \\ 0.000 & 0.767 & 0 & 0.233 \\ 0.000 & 0.000 & 1.000 & 0 \end{pmatrix}, \ \hat{\boldsymbol{\delta}}(1) = (0,0,1,0)),$$

$$\hat{\boldsymbol{v}} = (0.079, 0.112, 7.755, 0.455), \ \hat{\boldsymbol{p}} = (0.028, 0.044, 0.119, 0.015),$$

$$\hat{\boldsymbol{\mu}} = (0.107, 0.000, -0.068, -0.270), \ \hat{\boldsymbol{\sigma}} = (0.449, 0.970, 1.540, 3.385),$$

where the initial distribution suggests that the series starts from state 3. Note that the parameter estimates for the negative binomial parameters show clear deviations from geometric distributions. Hence, the following interpretations were considered: (i) state 1 can be associated with a bull market due to a large positive mean with low volatility and an eventual highly likely switch to state 2, (ii) state 4 can be associated with a bear market due to the large negative mean and high volatility with an eventual and almost certain switch to state 3, and (iii) states 2 and 3 can both be interpreted as market correction/rally phases, where the former is characterised by an almost zero mean with low volatility, while the latter has a negative mean with larger volatility. Note that the less volatile correction state, i.e. state 2, is likely to transition to the bull state or to the more volatile correction state, i.e. state 3, while the latter can transition to the bear state or to the other correction state.

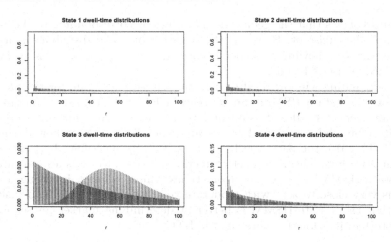

Fig. 3. S&P 500: state dwell-time distributions for the homogeneous 4-state normal-HSMM (red) and for the stationary 4-state normal-HMM (black) (Color figure online).

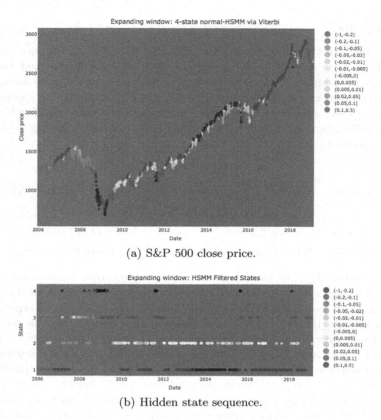

(a) S&P 500 close price.

(b) Hidden state sequence.

Fig. 4. Expanding window: 4-state normal-HSMM filtering via the Viterbi algorithm on S&P 500. The colours vary by the mean, while the sizes vary by the volatility.

Figure 3 shows that the geometric distributions corresponding to the 4-state HMM are all persistent. However, the negative binomial distributions assume different shapes, showing high persistence in states 3 and 4, while a lack of persistence in states 1 and 2.

The expanding window results using the Viterbi algorithm for the S&P 500 series for the 4-state HSMM can be seen in Fig. 4. In this case, our method can more accurately identify bull and bear markets since upward trends are generally blue while downward trends are generally red. Note how during the period 2010–2015, the S&P 500 Index is on the rise with few short periods of drops in price highlighting market corrections. These instances are captured by the 4-state HSMM as very pale (sometimes white) colours, implying a mean which is very close to zero with moderate volatility (state 2). In conclusion, it seems that the 4-state HSMM is better at determining market phases for the S&P 500 than it is for the more volatile BTC/USD.

3.3 Comparison of Results for BTC/USD and S&P 500

Given the previous outputs, we now compare and contrast the features for both BTC/USD and S&P 500. The 4-state HSMMs in both cases reveal two states indicative of bull and bear behaviour, with two "in-between" states. However, while Bitcoin has had strong and persistent bull phases with savage and weakly persistent bear phases, for most part S&P 500 tended to switch between bull and stable/bull correction phases with rare but persistent bear phases. Also, BTC/USD can exhibit higher volatility in comparison to S&P 500, as it is more novel and prone to external events. Indeed, both bull and bear markets for BTC/USD are volatile, while for S&P 500 only bear markets are volatile. For this reason, cryptocurrencies have often been remarked to be excessively volatile and subject to speculation and hence not, as yet, currency-like in their behaviour.

Secondly, BTC/USD states are less interpretable in terms of market phases than S&P 500. While our models seem to perform well in detecting the bear states, for BTC/USD it is harder to distinguish between bull phases and more stable ones. For S&P 500, on the other hand, steep upward trends are associated with the lowest volatility while steep downward trends tend to be the most volatile. Ultimately, the 4-state HSMM appears to be an effective modelling framework for both BTC/USD and S&P 500. Therefore, we shall implement two mock model-based investment strategies using filtered states on both the 4-state HSMM and 4-state HMM equivalent, with the aim of assessing the suitability of HSMMs, and whether they are an improvement of HMMs for determining market phases.

4 Using Investment Strategies to Assess Model Adequacy

In order to analyse the success of HMMs and HSMMs in determining bull and bear features, we devise two mock investment strategies and apply them with the expanding window procedure on both BTC/USD and S&P 500, using the buy-and-hold as a benchmark. For simplicity the following assumptions were made for each strategy: (i) the actions (buy or sell) are not subject to transaction costs; (ii) the testing period is entered with an initial capital of \$20,000; (iii) the first action is to buy on the first day of the testing period; (iv) if a buy signal is given, financial assets are bought only if enough capital is at hand, in which case, the maximum possible amount of capital is invested (v) if a sell signal is given, financial assets are sold in their entirety if and only if they are owned. The investment strategies are defined hereafter.

Strategy 1 - Buy-and-Hold: This is a naive investment strategy which is used for comparative purposes only. It is defined by the following two actions: (i) buy on the first day of the testing phase and, (ii) sell on the last day of the testing phase.

Strategy 2 - Regime: This strategy is based on the way we arbitrarily associate the states obtained via the Viterbi algorithm, under the expanding window procedure (see earlier explanations for more detail). At each state change, apply the following actions: (i) if state i^*_{n-1} is associated with a bear market and state i^*_n is associated with a bull market then buy as many financial positions as possible at time n; (ii) if state i^*_{n-1} is associated with a bull market state and state i^*_n is associated with a bear market then sell all financial positions at the close price of time n; otherwise (iii) do nothing. For Bitcoin we shall consider state 3 as a bull state and state 4 as a bear state, while other states will not be labelled since they are ambiguous and infrequent. For S&P 500, on the other hand, we shall consider states 1 and 2 as bull states and states 3 and 4 as bear states, based on the probabilities in $\hat{\mathbb{Q}}$ connecting them.

Strategy 3 - Drift: This strategy is based on the drift of the states obtained via the Viterbi algorithm, under the expanding window. Given arbitrary $\epsilon \geq 0$, at each state change, apply the following actions: (i) if $\hat{\mu}_{n-1} < 0$ and $\hat{\mu}_n > \epsilon$ then buy as many financial positions as possible at time n; (ii) if $\hat{\mu}_{n-1} > 0$ and $\hat{\mu}_n < -\epsilon$ then sell all financial positions at the close price of time n; otherwise (iii) do nothing.

For each strategy we shall record: (i) the number of actions (NOA), (ii) the last sell date (LSD), (iii) the final cumulative amount (FCA), and (iv) the return on investment (ROI) which is the profit/loss made as a percentage of initial capital. With regards to strategy 3, only that ϵ which returned the highest ROI out of the possible grid values is shown. The following grid values for ϵ, based on empirical evidence, were taken: $\epsilon = 0, 0.2, 0.4, 0.6, 0.8, 1.0$ and $\epsilon = 0, 0.005, 0.01, 0.02, 0.03, 0.1$, for BTC/USD and S&P 500, respectively.

Table 2 compares the investment strategies considered for the BTC/USD exchange rate for testing period 01/01/2017 – 28/01/2019. As can be observed, the buy-and-hold strategy is the most inferior of all strategies considered over the given period. Strategy 2 works marginally better for the 4-state HMM model, but for 4-state HSMM model and taking $\epsilon = 0$, Strategy 3 by far outperforms Strategy 2. Furthermore, the 4-state HSMM is superior to the 4-state HMM under all model-based investment strategies, and also yields less actions which, as mentioned, would incur more transaction costs.

Table 2. Investment strategies during the testing period 01/01/2017 – 28/01/2019 for BTC/USD.

Strategy	ϵ	NOA	LSD	FCA ($)	ROI (%)
1 (Buy-and-Hold)	n/a	2	28/01/2019	69,384.79	245.92
2 (Regime/HMM)	n/a	60	10/10/2018	71,967.73	259.84
3 (Drift/HMM)	0	82	19/11/2018	71,299.09	256.50
2 (Regime/HSMM)	n/a	22	20/12/2018	113,540.75	467.70
3 (Drift/HSMM)	**0**	**36**	**20/12/2018**	**147,203.48**	**636.02**

On the other hand, the results for S&P 500 are summarised in Table 3 for testing period 01/01/2006 – 28/01/2019. As can be observed, the buy-and-hold

Table 3. Investment strategies during the testing period 01/01/2006 – 28/01/2019 for S&P 500.

Strategy	ϵ	NOA	LSD	FCA ($)	ROI (%)
1 (Buy-and-Hold)	n/a	2	28/01/2019	40,625.75	103.13
2 (Regime/HMM)	n/a	38	11/10/2018	45,275.13	126.38
3 (Drift/HMM)	0.005	46	11/10/2018	32,789.96	63.95
2 (Regime/HSMM)	n/a	46	10/10/2018	41,505.15	107.53
3 (Drift/HSMM)	**0.02**	**16**	**22/03/2018**	**47,898.68**	**139.49**

strategy works fairly well for the long testing period, outperforming Strategy 3 for the 4-state HMM. Strategy 2 for the 4-state HMM, however, works better. For the 4-state HSMM, both Strategy 2 and Strategy 3 work better, with Strategy 3 taking $\epsilon = 0.02$ being the most profitable under the assumed circumstances for the S&P 500 Index.

Upon comparing, Tables 2 and 3 yield some noteworthy revelations. Firstly, the naive buy-and-hold strategy for the considered testing periods works fairly well for S&P 500 while it is the least profitable for BTC/USD. Secondly, the HSMM framework provides a clear improvement over the standard HMM methodology in both cases. Thirdly, it must be noted that Strategy 3 surpassed Strategy 2 for the better performing 4-state HSMM model, indicating that allowing the interpretations of the states to adjust at each step according to the mean of the state can have its advantages. Also, despite high return in the best of strategies, we note that there were periods of huge gains and periods of considerable losses for BTC/USD. However, for S&P500, market phases were more appropriately identified. Finally, had we considered transaction costs, it is very likely that the HSMM framework using Strategy 3 could still result in being the most profitable due to its superior performance with relatively smaller number of transaction costs.

5   Conclusion

In this paper we propose that a more desirable approach for modelling both BTC/ USD and S&P 500, and capturing effectively the dynamics of bull and bear market regimes, is a 4-state normal-HSMM with negative binomial dwell-time distributions. When implementing investment strategies, it has proven to be considerably superior to a buy-and-hold approach for our data, while this was not always the case for HMMs, which constrained dwell-times to be geometric. Indeed, by allowing dwell-time distributions on the states with larger modes, the number of buy/sell actions is greatly reduced in comparison. Although in the case of BTC/USD, the states of the 4-state HSMM model are not as interpretable as in the case of S&P 500, it still provides a good basis for further improvement and future research. On a concluding note, one must pinpoint that S&P 500 is a much older financial instrument with consistent long-term behaviour. On the other hand, inference on BTC/USD behaviour is based on a much shorter history and, as the asset matures, consistent long-term features may also develop.

Acknowledgements. The research work carried out, was partially funded by the European Social Fund/ENDEAVOUR Scholarships Scheme.

References

1. Ardia, D., Bluteau, K., Reude, M.: Regime changes in Bitcoin GARCH volatility dynamics. Finan. Res. Lett. (2018, in press)
2. Baur, D.G., Dimpfl, T., Kuck, K.: Bitcoin, gold and the dollar - a replication and extension. Finan. Res. Lett. **25**, 103–110 (2018)
3. Bonello, A., Suda, D.: Volatility regime analysis of bitcoin price dynamics using Markov switching GARCH models. In: Proceedings of the European Simulation and Modelling Conference, pp. 213–218 (2018)
4. Bouri, E., Azzi, G., Dyhrberg, A.H.: On the return-volatility relationship in the Bitcoin market around the price crash of 2013. Econstor Economics Discussion Papers, 2016-41 (2018)
5. Bulla, J., Bulla, I.: hsmm: Hidden Semi-Markov Models. R package version 0.4. http://CRAN.R-project.org/package=hsmm. Accessed 12 Mar 2019 (2013)
6. Chappell, D.-R.: Regime heteroskedasticity in Bitcoin: A comparison of Markov switching models. MPRA paper 90682, University Library of Munich, Germany (2018)
7. Chan, S., Chu, J., Nadarajah, S., Osterrieder, J.: A statistical analysis of cryptocurrencies. J. Risk Finan. Manage. **10**(12), 1–23 (2017)
8. Chu, J., Chan, S., Nadarajah, S., Osterrieder, J.: GARCH modelling of cyprtocurrencies. J. Risk Finan. Manage. **10**(17), 1–15 (2017)
9. Granger, C.-W., Ding, Z.: Some properties of absolute return: an alternative measure of risk. Annales d'Economic et de Statistique **40**, 67–91 (1995a)
10. Granger, C.-W., Ding, Z.: Stylized facts on the temporal and distributional properties of daily data from speculative markets. San Diego, unpublished paper, Department of Economics, University of California (1995b)
11. Guédon, Y.: Estimating hidden semi-Markov chains from discrete sequences. J. Comp. Graph. Statist. **12**, 604–639 (2003)
12. Harte, D.: R package 'HiddenMarkov', version 1.8-1. http://homepages.maxnet.co.nz/davidharte/SSLIB/. Accessed 12 Mar 2019 (2014)
13. Katsiampa, P.: Volatility estimation for Bitcoin, a comparison of GARCH models. Econ. Lett. **158**, 3–6 (2017)
14. Kodama, O., Pichl, L. and Kaizoji, T.: Regime change and trend prediction for Bitcoin time series data. In: Proceedings of the CBU International Conference on Innovations in Science and Education vol. 5, pp. 384–388 (2017)
15. Liu, Z., Wang, S.: Decoding Chinese stock market returns: tThree-state hidden semi-Markov model. Pac. Basic Finan. J. **44**, 127–149 (2017)
16. Nguyen, N.: Hidden Markov model for stock trading. Int. J. Finan. Stud. **6**, 1–17 (2018)
17. Rydén, T., Teräsvirta, T., Åsbrink, S.: Stylized facts of daily return series and the hidden Markov model. J. Appl. Econ. **13**, 217–244 (1998)
18. Stavroyiannis, S.: Value-at-risk and related measures for the Bitcoin. J. Risk Finan. **19**(2), 127–136 (2018)

19. Viterbi, A.J.: Error bounds for convolutional codes and an asymptotically optimal decoding algorithm. IEEE Trans. Inf. Theor. **13**, 260–269 (1967)
20. Zucchini, W., MacDonald, I.L., Langrock, R.: Hidden Markov Models for Time Series: An Introduction Using R, 2nd edn. Chapman & Hall/CRC, Boca Raton (2016)

Contagion in Bitcoin Networks

Célestin Coquidé[1], José Lages[1], and Dima L. Shepelyansky[2(✉)]

[1] Institut UTINAM, OSU THETA, Université de Bourgogne Franche-Comté, CNRS,
Besançon, France
{celestin.coquide,jose.lages}@utinam.cnrs.fr
[2] Laboratoire de Physique Théorique, IRSAMC, Université de Toulouse, CNRS,
UPS, 31062 Toulouse, France
dima@irsamc.ups-tlse.fr

Abstract. We construct the Google matrices of bitcoin transactions for all year quarters during the period of January 11, 2009 till April 10, 2013. During the last quarters the network size contains about 6 million users (nodes) with about 150 million transactions. From PageRank and CheiRank probabilities, analogous to trade import and export, we determine the dimensionless trade balance of each user and model the contagion propagation on the network assuming that a user goes bankrupt if its balance exceeds a certain dimensionless threshold κ. We find that the phase transition takes place for $\kappa < \kappa_c \approx 0.1$ with almost all users going bankrupt. For $\kappa > 0.55$ almost all users remain safe. We find that even on a distance from the critical threshold κ_c the top PageRank and CheiRank users, as a house of cards, rapidly drop to the bankruptcy. We attribute this effect to strong interconnections between these top users which we determine with the reduced Google matrix algorithm. This algorithm allows to establish efficiently the direct and indirect interactions between top PageRank users. We argue that this study models the contagion on real financial networks.

Keywords: Markov chains · Google matrix · Financial networks

1 Introduction

The financial crisis of 2007–2008 produced an enormous impact on financial, social and political levels for many world countries (see e.g. [1,2]). After this crisis the importance of contagion in financial networks gained a practical importance and generated serious academic research with various models proposed for the description of this phenomenon (see e.g. Reviews [3,4]). The interbank contagion is of especial interest due to possible vulnerability of banks during periods of crisis (see e.g. [5,6]). The bank networks have relatively small size with about $N \approx 6000$ bank units (nodes) for the whole US Federal Reserve [7] and about $N \approx 2000$ for bank units of Germany [8]. However, the access to these bank networks is highly protected that makes essentially forbidden any academic research of real bank networks.

© Springer Nature Switzerland AG 2019
W. Abramowicz and R. Corchuelo (Eds.): BIS 2019 Workshops, LNBIP 373, pp. 208–219, 2019.
https://doi.org/10.1007/978-3-030-36691-9_18

However, at present the transactions in cryptocurrency are open to public and the analysis of the related networks are accessible for academic research. The first cryptocurrency is bitcoin launched in 2008 [9]. The first steps in the network analysis of bitcoin transactions are reported in [10,11] and overview of bitcoin system development is given in [12]. The Google matrix analysis of the bitcoin network (BCN) has been pushed forward in [13] demonstrating that the main part of wealth of the network is captured by a small fraction of users. The Google matrix G describes the Markov transitions on directed networks and is at the foundations of Google search engine [14,15]. It finds also useful applications for variety of directed networks described in [16]. The ranking of network nodes is based on the PageRank and CheiRank probabilities of G matrix which are on average proportional to the number of ingoing and outgoing links being similar to import and export in the world trade network [17,18]. We use these probabilities to determine the balance of each user (node) of bitcoin network and model the contagion of users using the real data of bitcoin transactions from January 11, 2009 till April 10, 2013. We also analyze the direct and hidden (indirect) links between top PageRank users of BCN using the recently developed reduced Google matrix (REGOMAX) algorithm [19–23].

Table 1. List of Bitcoin transfer networks. The BCyyQq Bitcoin network corresponds to transactions between active users during the qth quarter of year 20yy. N is the number of users and N_l is the total amount of transactions in the corresponding quarter.

Network	N	N_l	Network	N	N_l	Network	N	N_l
BC10Q3	37818	57437	BC11Q3	1546877	2857232	BC12Q3	3742174	8381654
BC10Q4	70987	111015	BC11Q4	1884918	3635927	BC12Q4	4671604	11258315
BC11Q1	204398	333268	BC12Q1	2186107	4395611	BC13Q1	5997717	15205087
BC11Q2	696948	1328505	BC12Q2	2645039	5655802	BC13Q2	6297009	16056427

2   Datasets, Algorithms and Methods

We use the bitcoin transaction data described in [13]. However, there the network was constructed from the transactions performed from the very beginning till a given moment of time (bounded by April 2013). Instead, here we construct the network only for time slices formed by quarters of calendar year. Thus we obtain 12 networks with N users and N_l directed links for each quarter given in Table 1. We present our main results for BC13Q1.

The Google matrix G of BCN is constructed in the standard way as it is described in detail in [13]. Thus all bitcoin transactions from a given user (node) to other users are normalized to unity, the columns of dangling nodes with zero transactions are replaced by a column with all elements being $1/N$. This forms S matrix of Markov transitions which is multiplied by the damping factor $\alpha = 0.85$ so that finally $G = \alpha S + (1 - \alpha)E/N$ where the matrix E has all elements being unity. We also construct the matrix G^* for the inverted direction of transactions and then following the above procedure for G. The PageRank vector P is the right eigenvector of G, $GP = \lambda P$, with the largest eigenvalue $\lambda = 1$ ($\sum_j P(j) = 1$). Each component P_u with $u \in \{u_1, u_2, \ldots, u_N\}$ is positive and gives the probability to find a random surfer at the given node u (user u). In a similar way the CheiRank vector P^* is defined as the right eigenvector of G^* with eigenvalue $\lambda^* = 1$, i.e., $G^* P^* = P^*$. Each component P_u^* of P^* gives the CheiRank probability to find a random surfer on the given node u (user u) of the network with inverted direction of links (see [16, 24]). We order all users $\{u_1, u_2, \ldots, u_N\}$ by decreasing PageRank probability P_u. We define the PageRank index K such as we assign $K = 1$ to user u with the maximal P_u, then we assign $K = 2$ to the user with the second most important PageRank probability, and so on ..., we assign $K = N$ to the user with the lowest PageRank probability. Similarly we define the CheiRank indexes $K^* = 1, 2, \ldots, N$ using CheiRank probabilities $\{P_{u_1}^*, P_{u_2}^*, \ldots, P_{u_N}^*\}$. $K^* = 1$ ($K^* = N$) is assigned to user with the maximal (minimal) CheiRank probability.

The reduced Google matrix G_R is constructed for a selected subset of N_r nodes. The construction is based on methods of scattering theory used in different fields including mesoscopic and nuclear physics, and quantum chaos. It describes, in a matrix of size $N_r \times N_r$, the full contribution of direct and indirect pathways, happening in the global network of N nodes, between N_r selected nodes of interest. The PageRank probabilities of the N_r nodes are the same as for the global network with N nodes, up to a constant factor taking into account that the sum of PageRank probabilities over N_r nodes is unity. The (i, j)-element of G_R can be viewed as the probability for a random seller (surfer) starting at node j to arrive in node i using direct and indirect interactions. Indirect interactions describes pathways composed in part of nodes different from the N_r ones of interest. The computation steps of G_R offer a decomposition into matrices that clearly distinguish direct from indirect interactions, $G_R = G_{rr} + G_{pr} + G_{qr}$ [20]. Here G_{rr} is generated by the direct links between selected N_r nodes in the global G matrix with N nodes. The matrix G_{pr} is usually rather close to the matrix in which each column is given by the PageRank vector P_r. Due to that G_{pr} does not bring much information about direct and indirect links between selected nodes. The interesting role is played by G_{qr}. It takes into account all indirect links between selected nodes appearing due to multiple pathways via the N global network nodes (see [19, 20]). The matrix $G_{qr} = G_{qrd} + G_{qrnd}$ has diagonal (G_{qrd}) and non-diagonal (G_{qrnd}) parts where G_{qrnd} describes indirect interactions between nodes. The explicit mathematical formulas and numerical computation methods of all three matrix components of G_R are given in [19, 20, 22, 23].

Following [18, 22, 23], we remind that the PageRank (CheiRank) probability of a user u is related to its ability to buy (sell) bitcoins, we therefore determine the balance of a given user as $B_u = (P^*(u) - P(u))/(P^*(u) + P(u))$. We consider that a user u goes to bankruptcy if $B_u \leq -\kappa$. If it is the case the user u ingoing flow of bitcoins is stopped. This is analogous to the world trade case when countries with unbalanced trade stop their import in case of crisis [17, 18]. Here

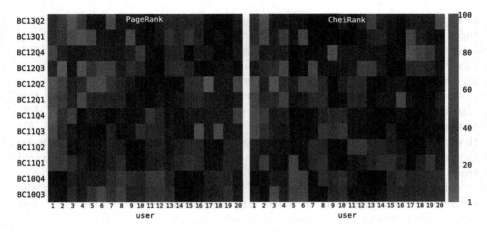

Fig. 1. Twenty most present users in top100s of BCyyQq networks (see Table 1) computed with PageRank (left panel) and CheiRank (right panel) algorithms. In horizontal axis the twenty users labeled from 1 to 20 are ranked according to the number of occurrences in the time slice top100s. The color ranges from red (user is ranked at the 1st position, $K = 1$ or $K^* = 1$) to blue (user is ranked at the 100th position, $K = 100$ or $K^* = 100$). Black color indicates a user absent from the top100 of the corresponding time slice. (Color figure online)

κ has the meaning of bankruptcy or crisis threshold. Thus the contagion model is defined as follows: at iteration τ, the PageRank and CheiRank probabilities are computed taking into account that all ingoing bitcoin transactions to users went to bankruptcy at previous iterations are stopped (i.e., these transactions are set to zero). Using these new PageRank and CheiRank probabilities we compute again the balance of each user, determining which additional users went to bankruptcy at iteration τ. Initially at the first iteration, $\tau = 1$, PageRank and CheiRank probabilities and thus user balances are computed using the Google matrices G and G^* constructed from the global network of bitcoin transactions (*a priori* no bankrupted users). A user who went bankrupt remains in bankruptcy at all future iterations. In this way we obtain the fraction, $W_c(\tau) = N_u(\tau)/N$, of users in bankruptcy or in crisis at different iteration times τ.

3   Results

The PageRank and CheiRank algorithms have been applied to the bitcoin networks BCyyQq presented in Table 1. An illustration showing the rank of the twenty most present users in the top 100s of these bitcoin networks is given in Fig. 1. We observe that the most present user (#1 in Fig. 1) was, from the third quarter of 2011 to the fourth quarter of 2012, at the very top positions of both the PageRank ranking and of the CheiRank ranking. Consequently, this user was very central in the corresponding bitcoin networks with a very influential activity of bitcoin seller and buyer. Excepting the case of the most present user (#1 in Fig. 1), the other users are (depending of the year quarter considered) either top sellers (well ranked according to CheiRank algorithm, $K^* \sim 1 - 100$) or top buyers of bitcoins (well ranked according to PageRank algorithm, $K \sim 1 - 100$). In other words excepting the first column associated to user #1 there is almost no overlap between left and right panels of Fig. 1.

From now on we concentrate our study on the BC13Q1 network. For this bitcoin network, the density of users on the PageRank-CheiRank plane (K, K^*) is shown in Fig. 2a. At low K, K^*, users are centered near the diagonal $K = K^*$ that corresponds to the fact that on average users try to keep balance between ingoing and outgoing bitcoin flows. Similar effect has been seen also for world trade networks [17].

The dependence of the fraction of bankrupt users $W_c = N_u/N$ on the bankruptcy threshold κ is shown in Fig. 2b at different iterations τ. At low $\kappa < \kappa_c \approx 0.1$ almost 100% of users went bankrupt at large $\tau = 10$.

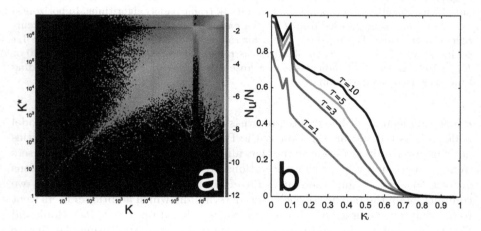

Fig. 2. Panel a: density of users, $dN(K, K^*)/dKdK^*$, in PageRank–CheiRank plane (K, K^*) for BC13Q1 network; density is computed with 200×200 cells equidistant in logarithmic scale; the colors are associated to the decimal logarithm of the density; the color palette is a linear gradient from green color (low user densities) to red color (high user densities). Black color indicates absence of users. Panel b: fraction N_u/N of BC13Q1 users in bankruptcy shown as a function of κ for $\tau = 1, 3, 5,$ and 10.

Indeed, Fig. 3 shows that the transition to bankruptcy is similar to a phase transition so that at large τ we have $W_c = N_u/N \approx 1$ for $\kappa < \kappa_c \approx 0.1$, in the range $\kappa_c \approx 0.1 < \kappa < 0.55$ there are only about 50%–70% of users in bankrupcy while for $\kappa > 0.55$ almost all users remain safe at large times.

The distribution of bankrupt and safe users on PageRank–CheiRank plane (K, K^*) is shown in Fig. 4 at different iteration times τ. For crisis thresholds $\kappa = 0.15$ and $\kappa = 0.3$, we see that very quickly users at top $K, K^* \sim 1$ indexes go bankrupt and with growth of τ more and more users go bankrupt even if they

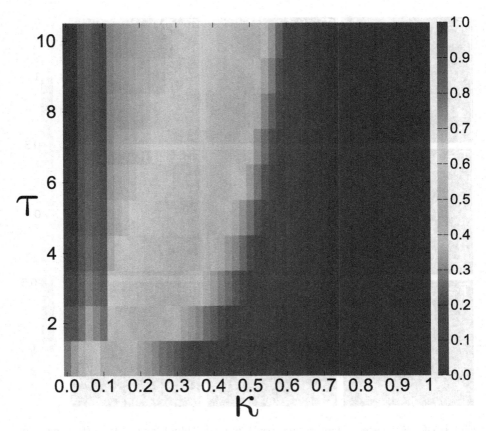

Fig. 3. Fraction N_u/N of BC13Q1 users in bankruptcy as a function of κ and τ. (Color figure online)

are located below the diagonal $K = K^*$ thus having initially positive balance B_u. However, the links with other users lead to propagation of contagion so that even below the diagonal many users turn to bankruptcy. This features are similar for $\kappa = 0.15$ and $\kappa = 0.3$ but of course the number of safe users is larger for $\kappa = 0.3$. For a crisis threshold $\kappa = 0.6$, the picture is stable at every iterations τ, the contagion is very moderate and concerns only the white region comprising roughly the same number of safe and bankrupt users. This white region broadens moderately as τ increases. We note that even some of the users above $K = K^*$ remain safe. We observe also that for $\kappa = 0.6$ about a third of top $K, K^* \sim 1$ users remain safe.

Figure 5 presents the integrated fraction, $W_c(K) = N_u(K)/N$, of users which have a PageRank index below or equal to K and which went bankrupt at $\tau \leq 10$. We define in a similar manner the integrated fraction of CheiRank users $W_c(K^*) = N_u(K^*)/N$ being bankrupts. From Fig. 5 we observe $W(K) \approx K/N$ and $W(K^*) \approx K^*/N$. Formal fits $W_c(K) = \mu^{-1}K^\beta$ of the data in the range

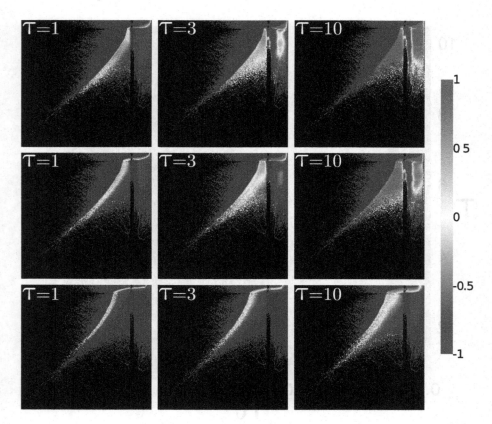

Fig. 4. BC13Q1 users in bankruptcy (red) and safe (blue) for $\kappa = 0.15$ (top row), for $\kappa = 0.3$ (middle row), and for $\kappa = 0.6$ (bottom row). For each panel the horizontal (vertical) axis corresponds to PageRank (CheiRank) indexes K (K^*). In logarithmic scale, the (K, K^*) plane has been divided in 200×200 cells. Defining N_{cell} as the total number of users in a given cell and $N_{u,\text{cell}}$ as the number of users who went bankrupt in the cell until iteration τ, we compute, for each cell, the value $(2N_{u,\text{cell}} - N_{\text{cell}})/N_{\text{cell}}$ giving $+1$ if every user in the cell went bankrupt (dark red), 0 if the number of users went bankrupt is equal to the number of safe users, and -1 if no user went bankrupt (dark blue). Black colored cells indicate cell without any user. (Color figure online)

$10 < K < 10^5$ give ($\mu = 5.94557 \times 10^6 \pm 95, \beta = 0.998227 \pm 1 \times 10^{-6}$) for $\kappa = 0.15$ and ($\mu = 5.65515 \times 10^6 \pm 231, \beta = 0.99002 \pm 4 \times 10^{-6}$) for $\kappa = 0.3$. Formal fits $W_c(K^*) = \mu^{-1}K^{*\beta}$ of the data in the range $10 < K^* < 10^5$ give ($\mu = 1.03165 \times 10^7 \pm 3956, \beta = 1.02511 \pm 3 \times 10^{-5}$) for $\kappa = 0.15$ and ($\mu = 1.67775 \times 10^7 \pm 1.139 \times 10^4, \beta = 1.05084 \pm 6 \times 10^{-5}$) for $\kappa = 0.3$.

The results of contagion modeling show that PageRank and CheiRank top users $K, K^* \sim 1$ enter in contagion phase very rapidly. We suppose that this happens due to strong interlinks existing between these users. Thus it is interesting to see what are the effective links and interactions between these top PageRank

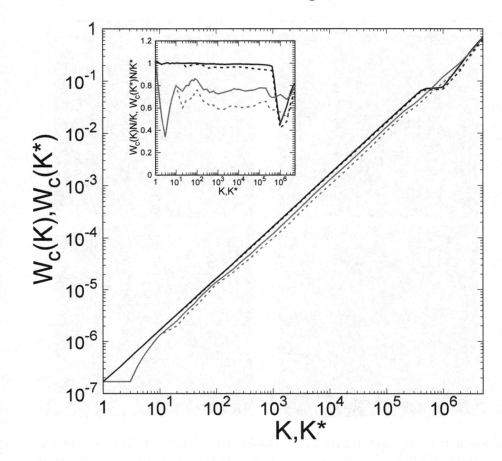

Fig. 5. Integrated fractions, $W_c(K)$ and $W_c(K^*)$, of BC13Q1 users which went bankrupt at $\tau \leq 10$ for $\kappa = 0.15$ (solid lines) and for $\kappa = 0.3$ (dashed lines) as a function of PageRank index K (black lines) and CheiRank index K^* (red lines). The inset shows $W_c(K)N/K$ as a function of K and $W_c(K^*)N/K^*$ as a function of K^*. (Color figure online)

and top CheiRank users. With this aim we construct the reduced Google matrix G_R for the top 20 PageRank users of BC13Q1 network. This matrix G_R and its three components G_{pr}, G_{rr} and G_{qrnd} are shown in Fig. 6. We characterize each matrix component by its weight defined as the sum of all matrix elements divided by $N_r = 20$. By definition the weight of G_R is $W_R = 1$. The weights of all components are given in the caption of Fig. 6. We see that W_{pr} has the weight of about 50% while W_{rr} and W_{qr} have the weight of about 25%. These values are significantly higher comparing to the cases of Wikipedia networks (see e.g. [20]). The G_{rr} matrix component (Fig. 6 bottom left panel) is similar to the bitcoin mass transfer matrix [13] and the (i, j)-element of G_{rr} is related to direct

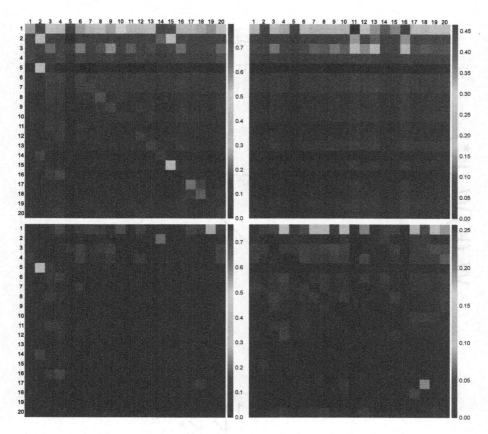

Fig. 6. Reduced Google matrix G_R associated to the top 20 PageRank users of BC13Q1 network. The reduced Google matrix G_R (top left) has a weight $W_R = 1$, its components G_{rr} (bottom left), G_{pr} (top right), and G_{qrnd} (bottom right) have weights $W_{rr} = 0.29339$, $W_{pr} = 0.48193$, and $W_{qr} = 0.22468$ ($W_{qrnd} = 0.11095$). Matrix entries are ordered according to BC13Q1 top 20 PageRank index.

bitcoin transfer from user j to user i. As $W_{rr} = 0.29339$, the PageRank top20 users directly transfer among them on average about 30% of the total of bitcoins exchanged by these 20 users. In particular, about 70% of the bitcoin transfers from users $K = 5$ and $K = 14$ are directed toward user $K = 2$. Also user $K = 5$ buy about 30% of the bitcoins sold by user $K = 2$. We observe a closed loop between users $K = 2$ and $K = 5$ which highlights between them an active bitcoin trade during the period 2013 Q1. Also 30% of bitcoins transferred from user $K = 19$ were bought buy user $K = 1$. The 20×20 reduced Google matrix G_R (Fig. 6 top left panel) gives a synthetic picture of bitcoin direct and indirect transactions taking into account direct transactions between the $N \sim 10^6$ users encoded in the global $N \times N$ Google matrix G. We clearly see that many bitcoin transfers converge toward user $K = 1$ since this user is the most central in the bitcoin network. Although the G_{rr} matrix component indicates that user $K = 1$ obtains about 10% to 30% of the bitcoins transferred from its direct partners, the G_{pr} matrix component indicates that indirectly the effective amount transferred from direct and indirect partners are greater about 10% to more than 45%. In particular, although no direct transfer exists from users $K = 11$ and $K = 16$ to user $K = 1$, about 45% of the bitcoins transferred in the network from users $K = 11$ and $K = 16$ converge indirectly to user $K = 1$. Looking at the diagonal of the G_R matrix we observe that about 60% of the transferred bitcoins from user $K = 1$ returns effectively to user $K = 1$, the same happen, e.g, with user $K = 2$ and user $K = 15$ with about 30% of transferred bitcoins going back. The G_{qr} matrix component (Fig. 6 bottom right panel) gives the interesting picture of hidden bitcoin transactions, i.e., transactions which are not encoded in the G_{rr} matrix component since they are not direct transactions, and which are not captured by the G_{pr} matrix component as they do not necessarily involve transaction paths with the most central users. Here we clearly observe that 25% of the total transferred bitcoins from user $K = 15$ converge indirectly toward user $K = 2$. We note that this indirect transfer is the result of many indirect transaction pathways involving many users other than the PageRank top20 users. We observe also a closed loop of hidden transactions between users $K = 17$ and $K = 18$.

4 Discussion

We performed the Google matrix analysis of Bitcoin networks for transactions from the very start of bitcoins till April 10, 2013. The transactions are divided by year quarters and the Google matrix is constructed for each quarter. We present the results for the first quarter of 2013 being typical for other quarters of 2011, 2012. We determine the PageRank and CheiRank vectors of the Google matrices of direct and inverted bitcoin flows. These probabilities characterize import (PageRank) and export (CheiRank) exchange flows for each user (node) of the network. In this way we obtain the dimensionless balance of each user B_u ($-1 < B_u < 1$) and model the contagion propagation on the network assuming that a user goes bankrupt if its dimensional balance exceeds a certain bankruptcy threshold κ ($B_u \leq -\kappa$). We find that the phase transition takes place in a vicinity of the critical threshold $\kappa = \kappa_c \approx 0.1$ below which almost 100% of users become bankrupts. For $\kappa > 0.55$ almost all users remain safe and for $0.1 < \kappa < 0.55$ about 60% of users go bankrupt. It is interesting that, as house of cards, the almost all top PageRank and Cheirank users rapidly drop to bankruptcy even for $\kappa = 0.3$ being not very close to the critical threshold $\kappa_c \approx 0.1$. We attribute this effect to strong interconnectivity between top users that makes them very vulnerable. Using the reduced Google matrix algorithm we determine the effective direct and indirect interactions between the top 20 PageRank users that shows their preferable interlinks including the long pathways via the global network of almost 6 million size.

We argue that the obtained results model the real situation of contagion propagation of the financial and interbank networks.

Acknowledgments. We thank L.Ermann for useful discussions. This work was supported by the French "Investissements d'Avenir" program, project ISITE-BFC (contract ANR-15-IDEX-0003) and by the Bourgogne Franche-Comté Region 2017-2020 APEX project (conventions 2017Y-06426, 2017Y-06413, 2017Y-07534; see http://perso.utinam.cnrs.fr/~lages/apex/). The research of DLS is supported in part by the Programme Investissements d'Avenir ANR-11-IDEX-0002-02, reference ANR-10-LABX-0037-NEXT France (project THETRACOM).

References

1. Financial crisis of 2007–2008. https://en.wikipedia.org/w/index.php?title=Financial_crisis_of_2007%E2%80%932008&oldid=882711856. Accessed Apr 2019
2. Three weeks that changed the world, The Guardian Dec 27 (2008). https://www.theguardian.com/business/2008/dec/28/markets-credit-crunch-banking-2008. Accessed Apr 2019
3. Gai, P., Kapadia, S.: Contagion in financial networks. Proc. R. Soc. A **466**, 2401 (2010). https://doi.org/10.1098/rspa.2009.0410
4. Elliott, M., Golub, B., Jackson, M.: Financial networks and contagion. Am. Econ. Rev. **104**(10), 3115 (2014). https://doi.org/10.1257/aer.104.10.3115
5. Anand, K., Craig, B., von Peter, G.: Filling in the blanks: network structure and interbank contagion. Quant. Finan. **15**(4), 625 (2015). https://doi.org/10.1080/14697688.2014.968195
6. Fink, K., Kruger, U., Meller, B., Wong, L.-H.: The credit quality channel: modeling contagion in the interbank market. J. Fin. Stab. **25**, 83 (2016). https://doi.org/10.1016/j.jfs.2016.06.002
7. Soramaki, K., Bech, M.L., Arnold, J., Glass, R.J., Beyeler, W.E.: The topology of interbank payment flows. Phys. A **379**, 317 (2007). https://doi.org/10.1016/j.physa.2006.11.093
8. Craig, B., von Peter, G.: Interbank tiering and money center banks. J. Finan. Intermediation **23**(3), 322 (2014). https://doi.org/10.1016/j.jfi.2014.02.003
9. Nakamoto Satichi: Bitcoin: A Peer-to-Peer Electronic Cash System (2008). https://bitcoin.org/bitcoin.pdf. Accessed Apr 2019
10. Ron, D., Shamir, A.: Quantitative analysis of the full bitcoin transaction graph. In: Sadeghi, A.-R. (ed.) FC 2013. LNCS, vol. 7859, pp. 6–24. Springer, Heidelberg (2013). https://doi.org/10.1007/978-3-642-39884-1_2
11. Biryukov, A., Khovratovich, D., Pustogarov, I.: Deanonymisation of clients in Bitcoin P2P network. In: Proceedings of 2014 ACM SIGSAC Conference on Computer and Communications Security (CCS 2014), p. 15. ACM, N.Y. arXiv:1405.7418v3 [cs.CR] (2014). https://arxiv.org/abs/1405.7418
12. Bohannon, J.: The Bitcoin busts. Science **351**, 1144 (2016). https://doi.org/10.1126/science.351.6278.1144
13. Ermann, L., Frahm, K.M., Shepelyansky, D.L.: Google matrix of Bitcoin network. Eur. Phys. J. B. **91**, 127 (2018). https://doi.org/10.1140/epjb/e2018-80674-y
14. Brin, S., Page, L.: The anatomy of a large-scale hypertextual web search engine. Comput. Netw. ISDN Syst. **30**, 107 (1998). https://doi.org/10.1016/S0169-7552(98)00110-X
15. Langville, A.M., Meyer, C.D.: Google's PageRank and beyond: the science of search engine rankings. Princeton University Press, Princeton (2006)

16. Ermann, L., Frahm, K.M., Shepelyansky, D.L.: Google matrix analysis of directed networks. Rev. Mod. Phys. **87**, 1261 (2015). https://doi.org/10.1103/RevModPhys.87.1261
17. Ermann, L., Shepelyansky, D.L.: Google matrix of the world trade network. Acta Physica Polonica A **120**, A158 (2011). https://doi.org/10.12693/APhysPolA.120.A-158
18. Ermann, L., Shepelyansky, D.L.: Google matrix analysis of the multiproduct world trade network. Eur. Phys. J. B **88**, 84 (2015). https://doi.org/10.1140/epjb/e2015-60047-0
19. Frahm, K.M., Shepelyansky, D.L.: Reduced Google matrix, arXiv:1602.02394 [physics.soc] (2016). https://arxiv.org/abs/1602.02394
20. Frahm, K.M., Jaffres-Runser, K., Shepelyansky, D.L.: Wikipedia mining of hidden links between political leaders. Eur. Phys. J. B **89**, 269 (2016). https://doi.org/10.1140/epjb/e2016-70526-3
21. Lages, J., Shepelyansky, D.L., Zinovyev, A.: Inferring hidden causal relations between pathway members using reduced Google matrix of directed biological networks. PLoS ONE **13**(1), e0190812 (2018). https://doi.org/10.1371/journal.pone.0190812
22. Coquidé, C., Ermann, L., Lages, J., Shepelyansky, D.L.: Influence of petroleum and gas trade on EU economies from the reduced Google matrix analysis of UN COMTRADE data. Eur. Phys. J. B **92**, 171 (2019). https://doi.org/10.1140/epjb/e2019-100132-6
23. Coquidé, C., Lages, J., Shepelyansky, D.L.: Interdependence of sectors of economic activities for world countries from the reduced Google matrix analysis of WTO data arXiv:1905.06489 [q-fin.TR] (2019). https://arxiv.org/abs/1905.06489
24. Chepelianskii, A.D.: Towards physical laws for software architecture. arXiv:1003.5455 [cs.SE] (2010). https://arxiv.org/abs/1003.5455

Towards Blockchain and Semantic Web

Juan Cano-Benito$^{(\boxtimes)}$, Andrea Cimmino$^{(\boxtimes)}$, and Raúl García-Castro$^{(\boxtimes)}$

Universidad Politécnica de Madrid, Madrid, Spain
{jcano,cimmino,rgarcia}@fi.upm.es

Abstract. Blockchain has become a pervasive technology in a wide number of sectors like industry, research, and academy. In the last decade a large number of tailored-domain problems have been solved thanks to the blockchain. Due to this reason, researchers expressed their interest in combining the blockchain with other well-known technologies, like Semantic Web. Unfortunately, as far as we known, in the literature no one has presented the different scenarios in which Semantic Web and blockchain can be combined, and the further benefits for both. In this paper, we aim a providing an in-depth view of the beneficial symbiotic relation that these technologies may reach together and report the different scenarios that we have identified in the literature to combine Semantic Web and blockchain.

Keywords: Blockchain · Semantic Web · Semantic blockchain

1 Introduction

In the last decade the blockchain technologies have become a pervasive in our world [1]. Sectors like finance, security, IoT, or public services have benefited from the quantum leap that block chain has brought [2]. The wide range of domains in which this technology has been used has led researchers to elicit and analyse the problems and challenges related to the use of blockchain technologies [3].

One of the interests that researchers have shown lately is to combine the Semantic Web and blockchain technologies [4, 4, 5]. The reason of this interest relies on the symbiotic relationship that enhances both technologies, and the potential that can be reached combining them [6]. As far as we known current literature focuses mainly in applications that rely on blockchain and Semantic Web, with the exception of English et al. who presented the only article that analyses the benefits of combining these technologies [7]. The work of English et al. provides an overview of what the Semantic Web can do for the blockchain and vice-versa, nevertheless their work focuses on covering a large number of topics, and not only the benefits, and thus, they lack of an in-depth analysis of the benefits and the scenarios in which both technologies are combined.

In this paper we aim to extend the work of English et al. [7], by providing an in-depth analysis of the benefits that blockchain may find by relying on Semantic Web and vice-versa. In addition, our goal is to provide an overview

© Springer Nature Switzerland AG 2019
W. Abramowicz and R. Corchuelo (Eds.): BIS 2019 Workshops, LNBIP 373, pp. 220–231, 2019.
https://doi.org/10.1007/978-3-030-36691-9_19

of the different scenarios and approaches to combine blockchain with Semantic Data by analysing the advantages and disadvantages of the different scenarios.

The rest of this article is organised as follows: Sect. 2 introduces the key concepts of the blockchain and the Semantic Web. Thirdly, Sect. 3 presents the different benefits that both technologies may offer to the other. After that, Sect. 4 introduces the different scenarios that we have identified to combine blockchain and Semantic Web. Finally, Sect. 5 recaps our conclusions.

2   Preliminaries

In this section we aim at introducing the key-concepts of the blockchain and the Semantic Web, as well as, the main characteristics of both. Our goal is not to provide an in-depth description, instead we aim at describing only the key-concepts to later explain on top of these the benefits and the scenarios.

2.1   Blockchain

The blockchain counts with several implementations each of which has some differences, e.g. Bitcoin or Ethereum. Nevertheless, all these implementations follow a common bottom line. The blockchain can be seen as a shared database among several peers who validate its content without the intervention of a third part. Some of the key concepts of blockchain are the following ones:

Definition 1 (Chain). *The chain is a list of blocks. When a peer aims at adding a new block a specific procedure has to be followed: the hash of the new block is computed relying on the hash of the last block in the chain, then the block is forwarded to all the peers who share the chain, and is included only when the rest of the peers validate the new block. In addition, when something is included in the chain it becomes immutable, and thus, that information is no longer modifiable by anyone.*

Definition 2 (Block). *The blocks are the minimal storage unit of the blockchain. They have some meta-data, like the hash of the previous block and the current hash, and the actual data, i.e., their content. The content can be expressed in multiple formats regardless if another block in the same chain used a different one. Depending on the current implementation the meta-data may change. In addition, the content of a block is limited to a maximum amount of data that may change depending on the implementation, e.g., Bitcoin supports up to 80 bytes [8] whereas Ethereum supports only 32 bytes [9].*

Depending on the peers and the grants to read/write in the chain that they have, three types of blockchains are distinguished:

– Public blockchain: any peer is able to read in the chain, even anonymously, and write blocks in such chain.

- Consortium blockchain: peers may only read the chain if an administrator invites them, however, once invited, all the peers are able to write new blocks in the chain.
- Private blockchain: peers may only read the chain if they received an invitation from an administrator, in addition, further permissions must be granted in order to write in the chain.

On the one hand, a well-known drawback in blockchain is its scalability, blocks with large amount of data entails that a larger storage space is required, and thus, the propagation of the block to the rest of the peers in the network will be slower [2]. On the other hand, since the chain is shared by several peers and the blocks are build relying on the previous ones the blockchain is more secure than other data stores [10].

2.2   Semantic Web

The Semantic Web is an alternative to the classic Web of Documents that counts with a stack of bespoke technologies [11]. The collection of Semantic Web technologies is large, following we present the more relevant ones and the key capabilities that Semantic Web technologies support.

Definition 3 (RDF). *The W3C has promoted a standardised formal language called Resource Description Framework (RDF) [12], which allows to describe data regardless the format used to express it. Data is expressed in form of triplets in which the first and the second elements are known as subject and predicate, respectively, and are URIs, and the third element is known as object, which can be either a URI referencing a subject or a literal. The data expressed in RDF is modelled as a graph.*

Definition 4 (Virtual RDF). *Data expressed in RDF is usually stored in a file or a triple store. In the literature there are several proposals that relying on that stored RDF produce on the fly new RDF data, which is called virtual RDF. Another approach to generate virtual RDF is publishing RDF from heterogeneeus datasources relying on specifications provided by users [13, 14].*

Definition 5 (Linked Data). *The RDF data published following the principles proposed by Tim Berners-Lee [15] is known as Linked Data. These principles refer to a set of data quality requirements that the data must meet:*

1. *Use URIs as names for resources*
2. *Use HTTP URIs so that people can look up those names*
3. *When someone looks up a URI, provide useful information using the standards (RDF, SPARQL)*
4. *Include links to other URIs so that they can discover more things*

According to this principles two features must be remarked, on the one hand, the resources are identified relying on URIs which are dependant on the domain name space (DNS) used to publish the data. This means that if the DNS changes the name space provided, then the resources will no longer be identified by these URIs nor retrievable. On the other hand, the data is stored following a decentralised approach, however when consuming such data it will appear as an unique dataset thanks to the links between datasets and the online availability of the resources.

Definition 6 (RDFs and OWL). *The W3C has promoted two formal languages to model data [16, 17], i.e., RDFs and OWL. The use of this languages aim at defining ontologies that are formal models. One of the characteristics of the ontologies is the fact that they support reasoning over the data they model. They allow to validate the consistency of data, or generate new data that is not explicitly defined or stored by using reasoning mechanisms. There are multiple standard ready-to-use ontologies in the literature for a wide range of domains [18].*

Definition 7 (Ontology mappings). *Linked data allows to store data in different datasets, and, at the same time, thanks to the links consuming such data as a whole. Ontologies have a similar mechanism known as mappings that allow to relate one ontology to another [19], meaning that even if a local ontology is used to define some data if the mappings exists the same data can be automatically modelled according to another ontology referenced by the mappings.*

Definition 8 (SPARQL). *The W3C has promoted a formal language to query data express in RDF following an ontology [20], i.e., SPARQL. Assuming there is an engine that reads all the data, then SPARQL allows to query and consume the data from one dataset, or several datasets at once, i.e., SPARQL federation [21].*

Definition 9 (Data shapes). *In order to validate RDF data against a set of constraints the W3C promoted a new language known as Shapes Constraint Language [22], also known as data shapes. This language allows to specify a wide range of constraints, from the structure that data should follow to how literals should look like according to a regular expression. In addition, the data shapes allow to define some so-called SPARQL definitions that create virtual RDF.*

3   Benefits

The work presented by English et al. [7] introduced namely one benefit that Semantic Web offers to the blockchain, i.e., by using ontologies to model the meta-data of the blocks practitioners may perform queries using SPARQL. Unfortunately, such approach does not query the content of the blocks since their data was not expressed in RDF, as pointed out by the authors. On the other hand, the benefit that Semantic Web may find by using blockchain according to English et al. is the following one: IRIs to identify resources in Semantic Web depend on a DNS, by using blockchain technologies the identification of resources can be relayed on the hashes of a blockchain that will point to their related properties, achieving decentralise the domain name system (DNS).

However, after analysing both technologies we have reached a richer and detailed list of benefits. Considering the Semantic Web technologies, the blockchain may find the following benefits:

1. **One language multiple formats:** RDF is not bounded to a specific format therefore the data described following this standard can be expressed in multiple formats, e.g., RDF/XML, JSON-LD, TURTLE. Blockchain may rely on RDF to write the content of the blocks, using the format that suits better a specific domain problem.

2. **Model data following well-known standards:** Semantic Web technologies like RDF, SPARQL, RDFs, or OWL are well-known W3C standards. This entails that there is a global consensus which makes them reliable and trustworthy. In addition, there is a large amount of standard ontologies ready-to-use to describe the data of multiple domains easing the modelling task for a given problem.

3. **Linking of data:** one of the properties that promotes RDF is to reference data from other datasets by relying on links, obtaining as a result a global view of the data although the storage of the different fragments is distributed through the web. Linking data is a well-known, and largely address, challenge in the Semantic Web community [23]. Blockchain may benefit from this feature by linking the content of the blocks with external datasets, or even with the content of other blocks in the same or in a different chain.

4. **Multiple data models:** ontologies count with mappings to relate their properties and classes to other ontologies. This feature means that when a blockchain relies on an ontology that has mappings to another ontology, the data described with the former ontology can be translated to the model of the latter automatically. This is specially suitable when data must be modelled at the same time differently depending on who is consuming such data.

5. **Search over blockchain:** assuming the blockchain relies on ontologies and RDF to describe their meta-data and their content, then, practitioners may use SPARQL to query the chain. However, this capability requires a third part service that reads the blockchain and executes the queries.

6. **Blockchain data and meta-data validation:** once a chain relies on ontologies and RDF it may benefit from the shapes to validate its data and meta-data. The shapes report the errors in the model and the content of a specific RDF document.

7. **Blockchain consistency validation:** the Semantic Web counts with reasoning engines that allow to check the consistency of the data. In this case the blockchain should count with a third-party service to perform the reasoning and have its meta-data expressed relying on an ontology.

8. **Virtual RDF:** data expressed in RDF is not always stored, instead sometimes such data is generated on the fly. This generated RDF is known as virtual RDF. One approach consist in using reasoning engines, which infer new data. An alternative approach is to infer virtual RDF relying on data shapes. Finally, another approach relies on graphs embedding that anal-

yse the current data and create new knowledge relying on machine learning proposals [24].

9. **Virtual RDF services:** Semantic Web counts with some engines that relying on specifications are able to translate on the fly data from heterogeneous datasources into RDF [13,14]. A blockchain may benefit from this kind of engines, known as virtual RDF services, by storing data in non-RDF formats and relying on these third-party services to generate at the same time their content in RDF.

10. **Interoperability:** relaying on semantic web technologies, and using standard ontologies to model data, both meta-data and content, the blockchain becomes interoperable. Been interoperable means that an information system is able to transparently interact with other interoperable systems, e.g., other blockchains, databases, or services. In addition, third-party systems can discover interoperable systems and know how to access their data automatically.

The benefits that Semantic Web may find by using blockchain are:

1. **Data decentralisation:** on the one hand, the Semantic Web aims at storing data following a decentralised approach, on the other hand, blockchain is a decentralised data store. Therefore, Semantic Web may benefit from the decentralised nature of the blockchain in order to store the data. In addition, the fact that the chain is shared by several peers increases the data availability, which normally depends only on one service.

2. **Identifiers for RDF resources:** one of the well-known benefits that blockchain brings to the Semantic Web is the generation of identifiers that do not depend on a DNS [7], e.g., Ethereum Name Service (ENS).

3. **Data immutability:** Semantic Web has been adopted by several public entities to provide open, accessible, and transparent data, e.g., open government initiatives [25]. These scenarios require that data published and its provenance can be trusted. One of the well-known properties of blockchain is that once data is published it cannot be modified. This makes blockchain the perfect technology to be used in these scenarios. For instance, a Danish political party in 2014 relayed on the immutability that blockchain offers to perform its internal elections [1].

4. **Data transparency and privacy:** since blockchain counts with different reading and writing permissions, the data stored is immutable, and information is shared and decentralised. Thus, applications of Semantic Web that aim at promoting transparency with privacy policies find in blockchain the perfect technology to rely on. A clear scenario that may benefit from this is the clinical data in which data is sensitive and must follow strict privacy policies [26].

5. **Crowdsourcing data:** a large number of Semantic Web applications rely on the participation of external entities, humans or machines. Public blockchains bring the perfect technology for this kind of applications, since external entities will be able to publish data and at the same time, provenance, trust, and transparency will be guaranteed.

4 Semantic Web and Blockchain Scenarios

The Semantic Web consists of a set of technologies that focus on data, i.e., how is described, modelled, and linked. On the other hand, the blockchain is a technology that aims at storing data and share such data among a set of peers, who validate the content without the intervention of a third-party services. It is clear that blockchain will benefit by storing or expressing its data using the Semantic Web technologies, and on the other way around, the Semantic Web will benefit from the blockchain due to the decentralisation and the data immutability that this technology offers.

As far as we know, there is only one article that address some preliminary ideas about how to combine these technologies, i.e., Ugarte [27], who presented three scenarios in which Semantic Web and blockchain could be combined. Starting from this article and analysing the state of the art, we have identified a total of six different scenarios, which we explain in the following sub-sections.

4.1 Blockchain with Semantic Meta-data

This scenario is the first step to integrate Semantic Web and blockchain technologies. This show-case depicted in Fig. 1 consists of a chain of blocks in which the meta-data is expressed following an ontology, and the content of the blocks is expressed in a non-RDF format. Some ontologies have been proposed for this purpose [28], however none is a standard yet.

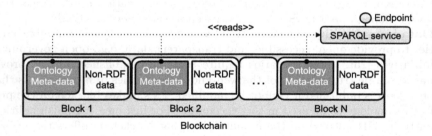

Fig. 1. Blockchain with meta-data referencing an ontology

The main benefit of this scenario is that practitioners may perform search queries considering the meta-data of the blocks. However this benefit requires to have an external service that reads the blockchain and is able to process SPARQL queries. For instance, with this benefit an user could search all the blocks which hash follows a provided regular expression.

The main drawback of this approach is that only the meta-data of the blocks is expressed using Semantic Web technologies. Therefore, in this scenario executing SPARQL queries over the meta-data is the only feasible benefit from our list.

4.2   Blockchain with RDF Content

In this show-case the approach to combine Semantic Web and blockchain relies on storing data in the blocks using RDF, as shown by Fig. 2. This scenario is complementary to the previous one. The content of the blocks may be expressed in any format that RDF supports, e.g., JSON-LD or XML/RDF.

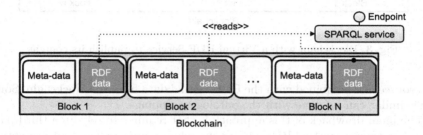

Fig. 2. Blockchain with RDF data

Assuming there is an external service that reads the blockchain and is able to process SPARQL queries, then, in this scenario the blockchain obtains all the benefits of our list. On the one hand, practitioners can execute SPARQL queries over the content of the blocks and their meta-data, which were described using an ontology. On the other hand, in case of having links to other data sources or ontologies these links should be stored the chain.

The main drawback of this scenario has not been studied yet, as far as we know. RDF formats like RDF/XML, JSON-LD, or TURTLE, are very verbose and require large number of characters. On the contrary, the amount of data that can be stored in each block is limited to a small amount of characters. As a result, using RDF entails that the chain will contain a larger amount of blocks to express the same information that could be expressed with a non-RDF format. Having a large number of blocks that contain large amount of data may drop the blockchain efficiency. As far as we know, authors have not presented a research work that relies this scenario or analyses its feasibility in terms of efficiency.

4.3   Blockchain and Virtual RDF

This scenario consists in a blockchain and a virtual RDF service. Virtualisation services take as input a data source, i.e., the blockchain, and generate RDF as depicted by Fig. 3. Some services publish the data as a dataset and count with a SPARQL query endpoint, others only generate an RDF dump that must be stored in a triple store in order to query the data.

This approach counts with all the benefits that we reported without the problem that entails storing directly RDF in the blockchain. Most of the virtual RDF services offer the capability of linking data and combining several data sources. Therefore, links between data can be generate on the fly, or stored in another

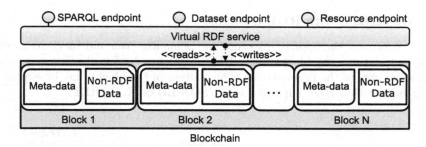

Fig. 3. Blockchain with a Virtual RDF Service to publish its content

data source and combined with the RDF virtual data from the blockchain. Something similar can be done with the ontology mappings.

The main drawback of this approach is that requires to rely on a third-party service to generate virtual RDF. As far as we know, authors have not presented a research work that presents the results of any third-party service that generates virtual RDF from a blockchain.

4.4   Blockchain with External Pointers

In this scenario there is a blockchain and an RDF dataset as depicted by Fig. 4. The bottom line is to rely on the blockchain to uniquely identify fragments of data from the RDF dataset, avoiding in this case the DNS problem. Set of triplets from the RDF dataset that share the same subject will be related to a hash from the blockchain [29], which will be an alternative identifier independent from the DNS used to identify the URI of such subjects.

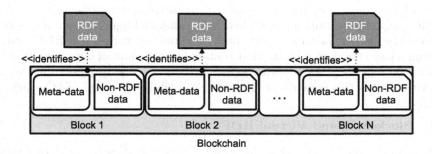

Fig. 4. Blockchain providing DNS-free identifiers for RDF fragments

In this scenario the blockchain does not obtain any benefit from the Semantic Web technologies. On the other hand, the Semantic Web technology is the one that benefits from the blockchain. The RDF data in this scenario has an alternative identifier that is independent from the DNS, entailing that resources are uniquely identified even if the DNS changes over time.

4.5   Blockchain Referencing Another Blockchain

In this scenario there are two blockchains as depicted by Fig. 5. One chain is used to identify RDF resources that are stored in the other chain following any of the approaches reported in this section. As a result, in this scenario RDF data will be immutable, transparent, and double identified (by the URIs and the hashes of the first blockchain).

In this scenario the Semantic Web counts with all the benefits that we reported from the blockchain.

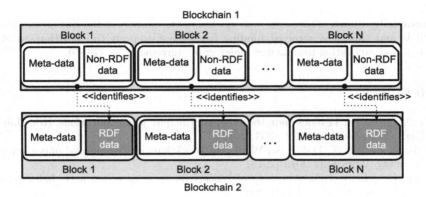

Fig. 5. Blockchain providing identifying the RDF stored in another chain

4.6   Semantic Blockchain

This scenario consists of a forked blockchain implementation that is meant to use Semantic Web technologies from the beginning, as depicted in Fig. 6. As far as we known, there is no such implementation yet but considering the relevance of the benefits that Semantic Web offers to the blockchain and vice-versa is likely that one implementation will be proposed.

This approach will count with all the benefits that we reported, the ones that the Semantic Web offers to blockchain, and the other way around.

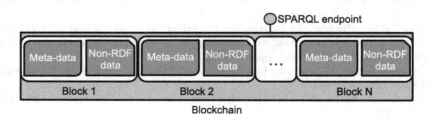

Fig. 6. Blockchain implementation relaying on Semantic Web

5   Conclusions

Recently blockchain as become a relevant technology to solve a wide-range of problems in different domains. Some researchers have expressed their interest in combining blockchain with Semantic Web, since the former offers special features to store data, and the latter is used to model and publish data. In this paper we analysed the benefits that blockchain may offer to the Semantic Web technologies, and vice-versa. In addition, we reported six different scenarios that show how these two technologies can be combined, considering which benefits they will gain and which drawbacks will have.[1]

Acknowledgement. This paper was written in the context of the European project DELTA, and thus, has received funding from the European Union's Horizon 2020 research and innovation programme under grant agreement No 773960.

References

1. Pilkington, M.: 11 blockchain technology: principles and applications. Res. Handb. Digit. Transform. **225**, 225–253 (2016)
2. Zheng, Z., Xie, S., Dai, H.N., Wang, H.: Blockchain challenges and opportunities: A survey. Work Pap.-2016 (2016)
3. Lin, I.C., Liao, T.C.: A survey of blockchain security issues and challenges. IJ Netw. Secur. **19**(5), 653–659 (2017)
4. Ruta, M., Scioscia, F., Ieva, S., Capurso, G., Di Sciascio, E.: Semantic blockchain to improve scalability in the internet of things. Open J. Internet Things (OJIOT) **3**(1), 46–61 (2017)
5. Panarello, A., Tapas, N., Merlino, G., Longo, F., Puliafito, A.: Blockchain and iot integration: a systematic survey. Sensors **18**(8), 2575 (2018)
6. Sikorski, J.J., Haughton, J., Kraft, M.: Blockchain technology in the chemical industry: machine-to-machine electricity market. Appl. Energ. **195**, 234–246 (2017)
7. English, M., Auer, S., Domingue, J.: Block chain technologies & the semantic web: a framework for symbiotic development. In: Lehmann, J., Thakkar, H., Halilaj, L., Asmat, R. (eds.) Computer Science Conference for University of Bonn Students, pp. 47–61 (2016)
8. Bartoletti, M., Pompianu, L.: An analysis of bitcoin op_return metadata. FC 2017. LNCS, vol. 10323, pp. 218–230. Springer, Cham (2017). https://doi.org/10.1007/978-3-319-70278-0_14
9. Wood, G., et al.: Ethereum: a secure decentralised generalised transaction ledger. Ethereum Proj. Yellow Pap. **151**, 1–32 (2014)
10. Maly, R.J., Mischke, J., Kurtansky, P., Stiller, B.: Comparison of centralized (client-server) and decentralized (peer-to-peer) networking. Semester thesis, ETH Zurich, Zurich, Switzerland, pp. 1–12 (2003)
11. Berners-Lee, T., Hendler, J., Lassila, O., et al.: Semant. Web. Scientific american **284**(5), 28–37 (2001)
12. Brickley, D., Guha, R.V., McBride, B.: RDF schema 1.1. W3C recomm. **25**, 2004–2014 (2014)

---

[1] https://www.delta-h2020.eu/.

13. Lefrançois, M., Zimmermann, A., Bakerally, N.: A SPARQL extension for generating RDF from heterogeneous formats. In: Blomqvist, E., Maynard, D., Gangemi, A., Hoekstra, R., Hitzler, P., Hartig, O. (eds.) ESWC 2017, Part I. LNCS, vol. 10249, pp. 35–50. Springer, Cham (2017). https://doi.org/10.1007/978-3-319-58068-5_3
14. Dimou, A., Vander Sande, M., Colpaert, P., Verborgh, R., Mannens, E., Van de Walle, R.: RML: A generic language for integrated RDF mappings of heterogeneous data. In: LDOW (2014)
15. Bizer, C., Heath, T., Berners-Lee, T.: Linked data: the story so far. In: Semantic Services, Interoperability and Web Applications: Emerging Concepts, pp. 205–227. IGI Global (2011)
16. McGuinness, D.L., Van Harmelen, F., et al.: Owl web ontology language overview. W3C Recomm. **10**(10), 2004 (2004)
17. Nejdl, W., Wolpers, M., Capelle, C., Wissensverarbeitung, R., et al.: The RDF schema specification revisited. In Modelle und Modellierungssprachen in Informatik und Wirtschaftsinformatik, Modellierung 2000 (2000)
18. Vandenbussche, P.Y., Atemezing, G.A., Poveda-Villalón, M., Vatant, B.: Linked open vocabularies (LOV): a gateway to reusable semantic vocabularies on the web. Semant. Web **8**(3), 437–452 (2017)
19. Uschold, M.: Achieving semantic interoperability using RDF and OWL-v4, 2005 (2013)
20. Harris, S., Seaborne, A., Prud'hommeaux, E.: Sparql 1.1 query language. W3C Recomm. **21**(10), 778 (2013)
21. Buil-Aranda, C., Arenas, M., Corcho, O.: Semantics and optimization of the SPARQL 1.1 federation extension. In: Antoniou, S., et al. (eds.) ESWC 2011, Part II. LNCS, vol. 6644, pp. 1–15. Springer, Heidelberg (2011). https://doi.org/10.1007/978-3-642-21064-8_1
22. Knublauch, H., Kontokostas, D.: Shapes constraint language (SHACL). W3C Candidate Recomm. **11**(8) (2017)
23. Nentwig, M., Hartung, M., Ngonga Ngomo, A.C., Rahm, E.: A survey of current link discovery frameworks. Semant. Web **8**(3), 419–436 (2017)
24. Lin, Y., Liu, Z., Sun, M., Liu, Y., Zhu, X.: Learning entity and relation embeddings for knowledge graph completion. In: Twenty-Ninth AAAI Conference on Artificial Intelligence (2015)
25. Sidoroff, T., Hyvönen, E.: Semantic e-goverment portals-a case study. In: Proceedings of the ISWC-2005 Workshop Semantic Web Case Studies and Best Practices for eBusiness SWCASE05, vol. 7 (2005)
26. Nugent, T., Upton, D., Cimpoesu, M.: Improving data transparency in clinical trials using blockchain smart contracts. F1000Research **5** (2016)
27. Ugarte, H.: A More Pragmatic Web 3.0: Linked Blockchain Data. Bonn, Germany (2017)
28. Pfeffer, J., et al.: Ethon-an Ethereum Ontology (2016)
29. García-Barriocanal, E., Sánchez-Alonso, S., Sicilia, M.-A.: Deploying metadata on blockchain technologies. In: Garoufallou, E., Virkus, S., Siatri, R., Koutsomiha, D. (eds.) MTSR 2017. CCIS, vol. 755, pp. 38–49. Springer, Cham (2017). https://doi.org/10.1007/978-3-319-70863-8_4

Detecting Brute-Force Attacks
on Cryptocurrency Wallets

E. O. Kiktenko[1]([✉]), M. A. Kudinov[1,2], and A. K. Fedorov[1]

[1] Russian Quantum Center, Skolkovo, Moscow 143025, Russia
{e.kiktenko,akf}@rqc.ru
[2] Bauman Moscow State Technical University, Moscow 105005, Russia
mishel.kudinov@gmail.com

Abstract. Blockchain is a distributed ledger, which is protected against malicious modifications by means of cryptographic tools, e.g. digital signatures and hash functions. One of the most prominent applications of blockchains is cryptocurrencies, such as Bitcoin. In this work, we consider a particular attack on wallets for collecting assets in a cryptocurrency network based on brute-force search attacks. Using Bitcoin as an example, we demonstrate that if the attack is implemented successfully, a legitimate user is able to prove that fact of this attack with a high probability. We also consider two options for modification of existing cryptocurrency protocols for dealing with this type of attacks. First, we discuss a modification that requires introducing changes in the Bitcoin protocol and allows diminishing the motivation to attack wallets. Second, an alternative option is the construction of special smart-contracts, which reward the users for providing evidence of the brute-force attack. The execution of this smart-contract can work as an automatic alarm that the employed cryptographic mechanisms, and (particularly) hash functions, have an evident vulnerability.

Keywords: Blockchain · Cryptocurrency · Brute-force attack

1 Introduction

Recently, peer-to-peer payment systems based on the blockchain technology, so-called cryptocurrencies, attracted a significant deal of interest [1]. The crucial feature of cryptocurrencies is their possibility to operate without a central authority that governs the system. This becomes possible thanks to the use of specific cryptographic tools inside blockchains, such as digital signatures and hash functions [2]. This type of cryptographic primitives is based on so-called one-way functions. These are believed to be straightforward to run on a conventional computer but difficult (or practically impossible) to calculate in reverse [3]. For example, multiplying two large prime numbers is easy, but finding the prime

Supported by the Russian Foundation for Basic Research (18-37-20033).

W. Abramowicz and R. Corchuelo (Eds.): BIS 2019 Workshops, LNBIP 373, pp. 232–242, 2019.
https://doi.org/10.1007/978-3-030-36691-9_20

factors of a given product is hard. Existing algorithms based on such a paradigm are known already more than 40 years, but their security remains unproven.

A particular element of blockchain is a cryptographic hash function, which is a compressive transformation that takes a string of arbitrary length and reduces it to one of predefined finite length [4]. It is assumed that the task of inverting hash function is extremely difficult for modern computers [5]. Specifically, the mechanism of hash functions enables achieving consensus in the concept know as proof-of-work, which is used in Bitcoin [6] and other cryptocurrencies [7]. Another use-case for hash functions in the Bitcoin network for additional security of wallets that are used by network members for collecting assets.

However, the security status of cryptographic tools may change with time. In particular, quantum computing, which is a tool for information processing with the use of quantum phenomena such as superposition and entanglement, allows solving particular classes of tasks more efficient than with the use of existing classical algorithms. These tasks include integer factorization and discrete logarithm problems [8] or searching for an unsorted database [9]. From the viewpoint of blockchain security [10], the latter can be used for achieving a quadratic speedup in calculating the inverse hash function [9]. We note that the security of Bitcoin from the viewpoint of attacks from quantum computers has been considered in Ref. [11]. Large-scale quantum computers that enable to realize such an algorithm, however, are not yet available. Meantime, significant efforts of the community are concentrated on the distributed brute-force-type analysis of hash function, for example, in the Large Bitcoin Collider (LBC) project [12] (for a survey on the blockchains security issues arising from the classical computing see [13,14]). It is then important to consider possible practical attacks on hash function in a middle-term horizon.

In our work we consider a particular attack on cryptocurrency wallets based on brute-force search for digital signature secret keys that match addresses of existing wallets. Our goal was to figure out whether it is possible to detect the presence of such a successful attack in the blockchain network due to an appearance of two colliding public keys corresponded to a particular address. The motivation behind this study relates to the crypto-agility paradigm: if there is as convincing evidence that some cryptographic primitive became insecure, then this primitive has to be exchanged with some new one as soon as possible. Here we show that the success of the attack can be proven with high probability and provide a lower bound for this probability. We also suggest a modification of cryptocurrency networks that makes such an attack unprofitable and also consider a mechanism that motivates users to announce the fact of hacking their wallets by brute-force-type attack. These methods can be employed for creating an additional security level for cryptocurrency network with the possibility to reveal and prove the fact of specific types of malicious transactions. Our ideas are applicable for a general cryptocurrency model, however, we restrict our consideration to the Bitcoin network. We expect that the generalization for other cryptocurrencies can be rather straightforward.

The paper is organized as follows. In Sect. 2, we describe a brute-force-type attack on cryptocurrency wallets. In Sect. 3, we demonstrate that if the attack has been processed successfully then the fact of the brute-force-type attack can be revealed with high probability. We also obtain a lower bound for the probability of proving the attack (obtaining the 'evidence of the attack'). In Sect. 4, we suggest a modification of consensus rules that makes such an attack unprofitable. The proposed mechanism is based on 'freezing' potentially stolen assets. In Sect. 5, we demonstrate that it is possible to create a specific type of altruistic transactions and corresponding smart-contract allowing honest users to collect assets if he/she proofs that the assets from the wallet have been stolen in the result of the brute-force-type attack. This creates a mechanism that motivates users to announce the fact of hacking wallets by brute-force-type attacks in the blockchain network. We then conclude in Sect. 6.

2   Brute-Force Attack on Bitcoin Wallets

We start our consideration of a brute-force attack with brief revising the construction of Bitcoin wallets. Each Bitcoin wallet could be considered a set of *addresses*, which are unique identifiers that are assigned to the possession of certain funds. The ownership of an address by a person corresponds to his knowledge of the secret (also known as private) key that is used for the construction of a corresponding address. We note that one person can have unlimited addresses. Moreover, for the security reasons it is recommended to generate new address after each withdrawing funds from an existing address.

2.1   Address Generation

The construction of Bitcoin addresses is presented in Fig. 1. It is based on employing elliptic curve digital signature algorithm (ECDSA) [15] defined with secp256k1 standard [16]. The address construction begins with a random generation of a secret key, which is a random string of 256 bits length. Despite a small restriction on possible secret keys values, almost every 256-bit string corresponds to a valid ECDSA secret key. Thus, the total number of possible secret keys is given by $N_{\text{sec}} \simeq 2^{256} \approx 1.16 \times 10^{77}$. Then the public key is calculated using the given secret key that is a computationally simple task for modern computing devices. We note that the reverse operation of obtaining a secret key from the corresponding known public one is assumed to be computationally infeasible for existing computers.

The compressed version of the public key, that is a 268-bit string, then goes through irreversible operations of hashing first with SHA-256 and then with RIPEMD-160 cryptographic hash functions. As a result, one obtains a 160-bit string that is an essence of Bitcoin address. In practice, this hash is concatenated with 4 bytes of a checksum (obtained with doubled SHA-256) and an additional version byte, and then the 25-byte (200 bit) result is represented with

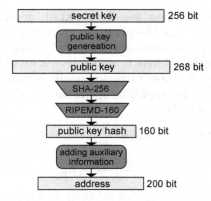

Fig. 1. Basic algorithm of the Bitcoin address generation.

Base58Check encoding [17] to obtain a final Bitcoin address. We note that the transition between RIPEMD-160 hash and 200-bit address can be easily reversed.

Due to the intrinsic proprieties of cryptographic hash functions, which make them operates as pseudo-random functions [4], the effective size of the address space is given by $N_{\mathrm{addr}} \simeq 2^{160} \approx 1.46 \times 10^{48}$ that is far less than space size of the possible keyspace N_{sec}. This feature plays a central role in our consideration. Also, we remind that the security of employed cryptographic hash functions must make it computationally infeasible to find *any* valid public key which gives a particular 160-bit hash [4].

In what follows we consider only Pay-to-PublicKey Hash (P2PKH) transactions. The idea behind this kind of transactions is that if a user would like to transfer some funds to a particular address, he/she publishes a transaction of a special form with an output containing the given address. In order to redeem the funds, the owner of the address has to create another transaction with input containing a public key, which hashes to the given address, and a signature, which is created by using the secret key and corresponding public key. This signature serves as a proof to the system that the author of the transaction is indeed the owner of the address.

2.2   Attack Description

Here we consider a particular type of a brute-force-type attack. The considered attack is based on the exhaustive search strategy for the signature forgery attack that is performed by an adversary intended to steal bitcoins from honest users.

1. The adversary makes a list AddrList of all the Bitcoin addresses which posses some funds, using the current set of unspent transaction outputs (UTXO) corresponded to the current state of the Bitcoin blockchain (we remind that we consider P2PKH transactions only).
2. The adversary chooses a subset SKList in the space of all secret keys. This subset is then used for checking over.

3. The adversary takes a secret key from SKList, generates a corresponding address, and looks whether the obtained address is inside the set AddrList. If it is the case, then the adversary publishes a transaction which transfers available funds from this address to some pre-generated address owned by the adversary. In the result, these funds, originally belonged to some legitimate user, end up with the adversary. The operation in the current step is repeated for all the secret keys in SKList.

The average rate of finding valid secret keys by the considered attack can be calculated as follows:

$$R = \frac{|\mathsf{AddrList}|}{N_{\mathrm{addr}}} R_0, \tag{1}$$

where $|\mathsf{AddrList}|$ stands for the size of AddrList and R_0 is the rate of repeating the step 3 of the attack algorithm.

We note that here we described only a general idea of the attack. Some additional steps including updates of AddrList can be also considered. Also, we would like to point out that this attack is implemented against all the users possessing bitcoins rather than a particular user or address. From Eq. (1) one can see that this fact increases the probability of the success in $|\mathsf{AddrList}|$ times, that is at least a total number of people having Bitcoins at the current moment.

3   Proving the Fact of a Successful Attack

We consider a scenario, where an adversary succeeded in implementing the brute-force attack considered above and transferred funds from an address of a legitimate user to some another address. We claim that this scenario drastically differs from a scenario, where an adversary succeeded in stealing funds by unauthorized access to the secret key of a legitimate user. The reason is a huge difference between the sizes of secret key space N_{sec} and address space N_{addr}. It turns out that the same address can be generated to approximately $N_{\mathrm{sec}}/N_{\mathrm{addr}} \sim 10^{29}$ different secret keys. Due to the fact that legitimate users (commonly) choose their secret keys at random, in the case of successful attack with very high probability, the secret key chosen by adversary will be different from the one belonging to the legitimate user. This fact, in turn, leads to the difference between corresponding public keys. Finally, a successful brute-force attack yields a revealing of collision for RIPEMD-160(SHA-256($\cdot$)) function (see illustration in Fig. 2).

The important point is that the stealing transaction, which transfers funds from the legitimate user address, essentially includes a public key that hash gives this address. That is why the legitimate user, possessing another public key, can in principle prove the fact of the successful brute-force by publishing his alternative public key together with the already published public key from the stealing transaction. The observation of such the collision any user can make sure that there was someone in the network who spent a huge amount of computational resources in order to find a valid secret key for the existing address. We call the alternative public key, which gives the same address as some another public key, the *evidence of the brute-force attack* (or the evidence for short).

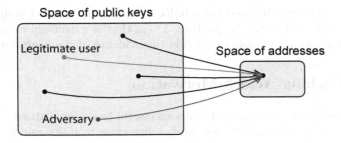

Fig. 2. Basic idea behind the providing an evidence of successful brute-force attack: With a high probability the public key of legitimate user will be different from the presented public key of an adversary.

Let us derive a rigorous estimation on the probability that in case of the successful brute-force attack the evidence could be constructed. In our consideration, we use the following assumptions. The first is that a legitimate user's secret key is generated with uniformly random distribution over the whole secret keyspace. The second is that the action of RIPEMD-160(SHA-256($\cdot$)) hashing satisfies the random oracle assumption [18]: Calculating a hash for every new argument can be considered to be equivalent to a generation of a uniformly random variable in the space of 160-bit strings.

We then consider an address and a corresponding subspace of secret keys, which gives this address. Under the assumptions described above, the size of this space is given by a random variable as follows:

$$N \sim \mathrm{Bin}(N_{\mathrm{sec}}, 1/N_{\mathrm{addr}}), \tag{2}$$

where $\mathrm{Bin}(n, p)$ stands for the binomial distribution with number of trials n and success probability p. The probability ε to obtain the same secret key as the original secret key during the brute-force attack is as follows:

$$\varepsilon = \sum_{n=0}^{N_{\mathrm{sec}}} \frac{1}{n} \Pr[N = n] < \Pr[N \le n_0] + \frac{1}{n_0} \Pr[N > n_0] < \Pr[N \le n_0] + \frac{1}{n_0}, \tag{3}$$

where n_0 is some positive integer less than expectation value $N_{\mathrm{sec}}/N_{\mathrm{addr}}$. We then consider n_0 in the form $n_0 := kN_{\mathrm{sec}}/N_{\mathrm{addr}}$ with $k < 1$. According to Ref. [19], the following upper bound on the binomial cumulative distribution function can be used:

$$\Pr[n \le N_0] \le \frac{N_{\mathrm{sec}} - kN_{\mathrm{sec}}/N_{\mathrm{addr}}}{N_{\mathrm{addr}}(N_{\mathrm{sec}}/N_{\mathrm{addr}}(1-k))^2} < \frac{N_{\mathrm{addr}}/N_{\mathrm{sec}}}{(1-k)^2}. \tag{4}$$

By substituting Eq. (4) into Eq. (3) and choosing $k := 0.36$ providing an extremum value of RHS of Eq. (3), we obtain the following expression:

$$\varepsilon < 5.22 \times N_{\mathrm{addr}}/N_{\mathrm{sec}} < 7 \times 10^{-29} < 10^{-28}. \tag{5}$$

One can see that the obtained value indeed is negligibly small. Finally, we conclude that with probability larger than $1 - \varepsilon$, that is extremely close to 1, the legitimate user would be able to provide the evidence of the brute-force attack.

4   Diminishing Attack Motivation

As we discussed above, the presence of a successful brute-force attack, considered in Sect. 2, can be proven with the probability close to unity under reasonable assumptions about the employed cryptographic hash functions and users behavior. However, there is a particular issue about evidencing the attack presence. The problem is that there is no straightforward way to figure out whose of two colliding public keys belongs to the adversary, and whose belongs to a legitimate user. From the viewpoint of other users in the network both of the public keys seem to be equivalent. We note that a time order in which these keys appear also does not resolve the problem. One can think, that the first appeared public key is a forged one, but the second, shown as evidence, belongs to the legitimate user. However, the adversary can wait until the legitimate user publishes his transaction and then disclose his public key as the evidence and claim that he suffered from the attack.

Here we consider a solution which aims not to distinguish between legitimate user and adversary, but to diminish the whole motivation of the brute-force attack. This can be achieved by freezing funds transfer after an appearance of the evidence of the brute-force attack related to these funds. The solution is based on introducing two modification of the current Bitcoin protocol. The first modification consists of introducing a new transaction type which contains evidence of brute-force attack. We call it an *evidence transaction*. The second modification is an introducing of timeout requirement between publishing a transaction and spending funds from its outputs. This requirement is necessary to have enough time to publish the evidence transaction to the blockchain before the stolen funds will be spent (transferred to other probably legitimate users). Let us consider the proposed modification in more detail.

4.1   Evidence Transaction

The aim of the evidence transaction is to provide a possibility to present an alternative valid public key to another public key used to transfer funds from some P2PKH transaction(s) output(s). By alternative public key, we understand a public key which hashes to the same address which we call a *disputed address*. In contrast to standard cryptocurrency transactions, evidence transactions refer not to the outputs, but to the P2PKH inputs of related transactions, which call as *suspect transactions*. The outputs of the suspect transaction have to be unspent, that should be provided by the second proposed modification. The evidence transaction should contain alternative a public key corresponding to the published key in related inputs of suspect transactions, and also provide an auxiliary address, whose purpose will be discussed later.

If the evidence transaction got into blockchain, then the following operations should be performed.

1. All the transactions that (i) contain P2PKH inputs with public key colliding to public key presented in evidence transaction, and (ii) published in blocks appeared not earlier than the oldest block containing suspect transactions given in the evidence transaction, started to be considered as suspect transactions.
2. All the outputs of the suspect transactions and all the outputs containing the disputed address are removed from UTXO.
3. Outputs of the transactions related to the inputs of the suspect transactions, which do not contain a disputed address, turn back into an unspent state (move back to UTXO).
4. An extra output is added to UTXO, which contains a number of bitcoins given by the sum of funds on all the inputs of suspect transactions that have a colliding public key and fees of the suspect transactions. These funds should be able to be spent by publishing a transaction signed with the secret key corresponded to the public key in the suspect transaction (giving a disputed address), but can be only transferred to the auxiliary address given in the evidence transaction.

The first three operations ensure that the funds taken from addresses which were not hacked continue their circulation in the system. At the same time, the funds from disputed address will be frozen, and the only way how they can continue their circulation is their transfer by the author of suspect transactions to the address given by the author of the evidence transaction. This scenario can be realized if the author of the suspect transaction is "white hacker", whose aim is only to demonstrate the vulnerability of the system, but not to steal funds.

An important issue related to evidence transaction is its fee to miners. Since the legitimate author of the evidence transaction probably no longer has any coins after the suspect transaction is published, we propose to introduce an extra reward for miners to add evidence transactions to the blocks (the evidence transaction itself should bot contains any fee). The reward could be calculated as a median value of total transaction fees in the last six blocks, and should be added to the number of coins emitted in the current block.

4.2 Timeout Requirement

Since the outputs of a suspect transaction should not be spent by the time an evidence transaction is published, one need to introduce a timeout between publishing a transaction and spending its outputs in subsequent transactions. This timeout is necessary for providing the opportunity for the legitimate user to react on unauthorized funds transfer and publish the evidence transaction.

In the Bitcoin network, it is recommended to wait until five blocks appear on top of the block containing a particular transaction in order to be (almost) sure that this transaction will not be removed from the blockchain. From this perspective, the considered timeout can be selected at the same level of six blocks. This choice, arguably, does not lead to a noticeable decrease in network performance.

Finally, we would like to emphasize that the considered approach of introducing an evidence transaction is applicable only in the case of the brute-force attack presented in Sect. 2. It is not valid in the case, where the adversary is able to find two valid secret keys giving a particular address at once.

5   Rewarding the Collision Detection

Another option for dealing with brute-force attacks, which does not require any changes in the present consensus, is introducing a reward for finding colliding public keys. Obtaining the reward can be realized in automatic fashion by means of creating a corresponding smart contract. It turns out that the Bitcoin script language allows creating such kind of rewarding.

Consider the following Bitcoin output script (scriptPubKey):

```
OP_OVER OP_OPVER OP_EQUAL OP_NOTIF OP_OVER OP_HASH160
OP_SWAP OP_HASH160 OP_EQUALVERIFY OP_CHECKSIG OP_ELSE
OP_RETURN OP_ENDIF
```

It can be interpreted as follows: "The funds from the output can be redeemed by presenting a triple (sig_1, $pubkey_1$, $pubkey_2$), where $pubkey_1$ and $pubkey_2$ are two different public keys which give the same address, and sig_1 is a valid signature under the public key $pubkey_1$. The fund from this output could be redeemed a legitimate user, whose funds were stolen, or by the adversary, who obtained some alternative public key.

The rewarding transaction can be published by anyone, who would like to participate in the project of detecting the brute-force attack. Of course, the information about the presence of rewarding transaction has to be somehow spread among the community.

We also note that in presence of such rewards the adversary could include in his list of addresses for which he would try to find a valid secret key (AddrList) all the addresses without funds but with public keys published in the blockchain. Unfortunately, if there were some funds on address whose public keys were published, then the adversary could both steal the funds and obtain the reward.

Finally, we would like to make some remarks about why this kind of rewarding is valuable for the whole Bitcoin blockchain system. The first reason is providing some automatic compensation for a person who suffered from a successful brute-force attack. The second and more important one is that in the case when someone redeems this reward, the whole network will obtain an important signal, that the employed cryptography (particularly) hash functions have an evident vulnerability or there is some participant (e.g. pool) which possess incredible computational resources.

6   Conclusion

Here we summarize the main results of our work. We have considered a brute-force attack on Bitcoin wallet which consists of finding secret keys for existing addresses. We have demonstrated that if this attack succeeds then with a probability higher than $1 - 10^{-28}$ the legitimate user will be able to prove that it was the brute-force attack. However, we also have shown that there is difficulty determining who is a legitimate user and who is an adversary.

We have considered two possible approaches to dealing with a possible brute-force attack. The first approach involves modifications in present consensus and allows to freeze stolen funds transfer. This approach allows diminishing attack motivation since even if the adversary will succeed in implementing the attack, with very high probability he will not be able to use the stolen funds. This method may be used in developing a new cryptocurrency system.

The second approach does not involve any modification in the present Bitcoin consensus, but propose to create special reward transaction, which allows getting some coins as compensation to a person who suffered from brute-force attack. More importantly, the fact of obtaining of this reward will serve as undeniable evidence the cryptography employed in the current blockchain network has some vulnerabilities. This kind of reward transaction could be added by any person who wants to donate his coins to the project of detecting brute-force attacks.

References

1. Swan, M.: Blockchain: Blueprint for a New Economy. O'Reilly Media Inc., Sebastopol (2015)
2. White, J.H.: The blockchain: a gentle four page introduction, arXiv:1612.06244
3. Bernstein, D.J., Lange, T.: Post-quantum cryptography. Nature **549**, 188–194 (2017)
4. Schneier, B.: Applied Cryptography. John Wiley & Sons, New York (1996)
5. Gilbert, H., Handschuh, H.: Security analysis of SHA-256 and sisters. In: Matsui, M., Zuccherato, R.J. (eds.) SAC 2003. LNCS, vol. 3006, pp. 175–193. Springer, Heidelberg (2004). https://doi.org/10.1007/978-3-540-24654-1_13
6. Nakamoto S.: Bitcoin: A Peer-to-Peer Electronic Cash System (2008)
7. Miraz, M.H., Ali, M.: Applications of blockchain technology beyond cryptocurrency. AETiC **2**, 1–6 (2018)
8. Shor, P.W.: Algorithms for quantum computation: discrete log and factoring. SIAM J. Comput. **26**, 1484 (1997)
9. Grover, L.K.: A fast quantum mechanical algorithm for database search. In: Proceedings of 28th Annual ACM Symposium on the Theory of Computing, p. 212. ACM, New York (1996)
10. Fedorov, A.K., Kiktenko, E.O., Lvovksy, A.I.: Quantum computers put blockchain security at risk. Nature **563**, 465–467 (2018)
11. Aggarwal, D., Brennen, G.K., Lee, T., Santha, M., Tomamichel, M.: Quantum attacks on Bitcoin, and how to protect against them. Ledger **3**, 68–90 (2018)
12. Large Bitcoin Collider. https://lbc.cryptoguru.org/. Accessed 14 Apr 2019

13. Li, X., Jiang, P., Chen, T., Luo, X., Wen, Q.: A survey on the security of blockchain systems. Future Gener. Comput. Syst. (2017). https://www.sciencedirect.com/science/article/pii/S0167739X17318332?via=ihub
14. Moubarak, J., Filiol, E., Chamoun, M.: On blockchain security and relevant attacks. In: IEEE Middle East and North Africa Communications Conference (MENACOMM), Jounieh, 2018, pp. 1–6 (2018)
15. Vanstone, S.: Responses to NIST proposal. Commun. ACM **35**, 50–52 (1992)
16. Secp256k1 standard for ECDSA. https://en.bitcoin.it/wiki/Secp256k1. Accessed 11 Apr 2019
17. Base58Check encoding description. https://en.bitcoin.it/wiki/Base58Check_encoding. Accessed 11 Apr 2019
18. Koblitz, N., Menezes, A.J.: The random oracle model: a twenty-year retrospective. Des. Codes Cryptogr. **77**, 587–610 (2015)
19. Feller, W.: An Introduction to Probability Theory and Its Applications, vol. 1, 3rd edn. Wiley, USA (1968)

Analyzing Transaction Fees
with Probabilistic Logic Programming

Damiano Azzolini[✉], Fabrizio Riguzzi, and Evelina Lamma

University of Ferrara, Via Saragat 1, 44122 Ferrara, Italy
{damiano.azzolini,fabrizio.riguzzi,evelina.lamma}@unife.it

Abstract. Fees are used in Bitcoin to prioritize transactions. Transactions with high associated fee are usually included in a block faster than those with lower fees. Users would like to pay just the minimum amount to make the transaction confirmed in the desired time. Fees are collected as a reward when transactions are included in a block so, on the other perspective, miners usually process first the most profitable transactions, i.e. the one with higher fee rate. Bitcoin is a dynamic system influenced by several variables, such as transaction arrival time and block discovery time making the prediction of the confirmation time a hard task. In this paper we use probabilistic logic programming to model how fees influence the confirmation time and how much fees affect miner's revenue.

Keywords: Bitcoin · Blockchain · Probabilistic logic programming

1 Introduction

In the last year, the terms *blockchain* and *bitcoin* started to gain more and more popularity. The absence of a centralized third party, the security and the opportunity to develop new cryptocurrencies where all transactions are stored in a distributed ledger are only a few of the features of blockchain systems. Research on blockchain involves several different research areas, among them: distributed systems to maximize and improve the connections between peers, cryptography to ensure data consistency, economy to study the behaviour of the cryptocurrencies and game theory to model the interaction between interacting parties.

According to [32], blockchains have evolved over time: starting from version 1.0, where, thanks to Bitcoin [19], people were allowed to trade monetary value, Ethereum [7] extended the use cases, allowing users to define the so-called *smart contracts*. Nowadays, we are witnessing the birth of blockchains 3.0 with solutions like Lighting Network [23], that increases substantially the number of processed transactions.

Despite the availability of many different blockchains such as Ethereum [7, 34], EOS.IO [11], Hyperledger [14] and Cardano [8], Bitcoin still has the highest market capitalization of all[1].

---

[1] https://coinmarketcap.com/.

© Springer Nature Switzerland AG 2019
W. Abramowicz and R. Corchuelo (Eds.): BIS 2019 Workshops, LNBIP 373, pp. 243–254, 2019.
https://doi.org/10.1007/978-3-030-36691-9_21

A probabilistic analysis can be particularly useful to determine how miners, peers and users interact, even when non determinism and randomization are not allowed by the various blockchain protocols. The intrinsic uncertainty of these processes requires a probabilistic analysis to be fully understood and predicted.

Probabilistic (Logic) Programming [10] has been applied to model several real world domains [20] including the Bitcoin protocol [3].

In particular starting from measures of average block size, average number of transactions in a block and average fee rate, we created two probability models: one for computing how transaction fees affect the average profit of a miner and one to analyze how fee rates in Bitcoin affect the confirmation time. For both experiments we used *likelihood weighting* to see how the observation of a certain event, such as the confirmation of a transaction with a certain fee rate or an increase of the average fee rate, modifies the probability of confirmation of the following transactions.

The paper is structured as follows: in Sect. 2 we give a brief overview of blockchain in general, Bitcoin and fees. Section 3 shows basic concepts of probabilistic logic programming. Section 4 explains how we conducted the experiments shown in Sect. 5. Section 6 concludes the paper with a discussion about the existing literature and some future works.

2   Blockchain, Bitcoin and Fees

The first idea to use cryptography to secure timestamping digital data goes back to 1991 [13]. In 2008 Satoshi Nakamoto published his paper [19] and shortly after Bitcoin and Blockchain were born. In brief, a blockchain is a sequence of blocks linked together using cryptography functions in order to guarantee data integrity and data consistency. The whole blockchain is maintained by a set of peers. All the peers can see the same data, in particular, all the blocks in the same order, thanks to a so-called *consensus* algorithm: in the case of Bitcoin, this involve solving a computationally hard problem that, once solved, can be easily checked by anyone in the network. This algorithm, called *proof-of-work*, allows also the system to function without a centralized third party. To increase the probability of success, peer usually group themselves into mining pools to share the computing power and split the revenues in case of success. Find a solution to the PoW allows the solver to append a new block to the blockchain. After that he will receive a reward in bitcoin for his work. Users in the system can send transactions, transfers of value (bitcoin) among two or more users. Each block is composed by a set of transactions. Each transaction is also attached to an amount of bitcoin as a reward for the miner who includes it into a block. One of the most interesting features is the possibility, starting from block number 0 (called *genesis block*), to reconstruct in a fully deterministic way the whole history of blocks and transactions, allowing everyone to have access to the same data.

The miner who solves the PoW receives, in addition to an amount of bitcoin, the sum of all the fees of the transactions in a block trough a special transaction called *coinbase* transaction. Thus the miner is incentivised to include the most profitable transactions into a block. However, due to the max block size limit (1 Mb, a very discussed threshold[2]), and the difficulty of the PoW puzzle (set to be solved in 10 min of average), transactions usually wait several minutes in the so-called *mempool*, waiting to be included in a block and confirmed.

To reduce the time spent in the mempool, users can attach a high fee to a transaction. This option, however, triggers a high competition situation where peers keep increasing the fees to prioritize transactions. On the other hand, increasing the average fees can potentially reduce the number of users, since they may be unwilling to pay such a high amount of fees for the transfer of a little amount. Users are therefore incentivised to find an equilibrium between the priority of the transaction, its size, its associated fees and the *fee rate* (amount of fees, usually measured in *satoshi*, per byte where 1 satoshi = 10^{-8} bitcoin).

A common scenario which complicates the optimal fee rate estimation is the presence of dependent transactions in the same block. According to the Bitcoin consensus rule, all peers must see all blocks and all transactions in a block in the same sequential order. Moreover, bitcoin cannot be spent before being received. This means that, if A sends an amount X to B and B wants to send X to C, the transaction where A sends X to B must appear earlier in the sequence than the one used by B to send X to C. With this constraint, a miner cannot simply order the transaction in a descending fee rate value order but he needs to take into account dependencies: if B has a high associated fee rate and spends the output of A, A must be included before B even if A has a low associated fee rate. This situation con be used to force a transaction confirmation and it is known as *Child Pay for Parent*[3].

For all the previous reasons, fee estimation is a hard task. In addition, the number of transactions received by the network during a certain time span is unpredictable as well as is block discovery time.

There are several methods to estimate the optimal fee rate. One of the most used Bitcoin client, Bitcoin Core[4], offers a command called *estimatesmartfee* to estimate the optimal fee rate to attach to a transaction in order to have it confirmed with high probability in N blocks, where N is chosen by the user and can be up to 1008. The algorithm, as described in the Bitcoin Core source code[5], works as follow: instead of tracking every single fee rate, which is too expensive both for storage and computation, Bitcoin Core groups transactions into exponentially spaced *buckets*. Transactions in the same bucket have similar fee rate. The algorithm then tracks the number of transactions that enters in each bucket and the number of transactions successfully included into the blockchain within the target. Moreover, to make the prediction more accurate, the algorithm gives more importance to recent blocks than to older blocks.

---

[2] https://en.bitcoin.it/wiki/Block_size_limit_controversy.
[3] https://en.bitcoin.it/wiki/Miner_fees.
[4]   https://bitcoin.org/en/download.
[5]   https://github.com/bitcoin/bitcoin/blob/master/src/policy/fees.h.

3   Probabilistic Logic Programming

In this paper we consider Probabilistic Logic Programming under the distribution semantics, as proposed in [26,31], which is capable of representing several domains [1,2,27]. A probabilistic logic program defines a probability distribution over logic programs called *worlds*. To define the probability of a query, this distribution is extended to a joint distribution of the query and the worlds. Consequently, the probability of the query is obtained from the joint distribution by summing out the worlds in a process called *marginalization*.

Each sentence of a logic program is called *clause* composed by a *head* and a *body*. An example of clause is: $tails(Coin) :- toss(Coin)$, where $tails(Coin)$ is called head and $toss(Coin)$ body. The previous clause can be read as: "if a *Coin* is tossed then the *Coin* lands tails". In these experiments we consider Logic Programs with Annotated Disjunctions (LPADs) [33] with no function symbols (if function symbols are allowed see [25]). Alternatives are expressed with disjunctive heads of clause where each atom is annotated with probability. An LPAD is composed by one or more clauses C_i. The general form of a clause is: $h_{i1} : \Pi_{i1}; \ldots; h_{iv_i} : \Pi_{iv_i} :- b_{i1}, \ldots, b_{iu_i}$, where $h_{i1}, \ldots, h_{iv_i}$ are logical atoms, $b_{i1}, \ldots, b_{iu_i}$ are logical literals and $\Pi_{i1}, \ldots, \Pi_{iv_i}$ are real numbers in the interval $[0,1]$ that sum to 1. $b_{i1}, \ldots, b_{iu_i}$ is indicated with $body(C_i)$. Clauses where $\sum_{k=1}^{v_i} \Pi_{ik} < 1$ are also allowed: in this case the head of the annotated disjunctive clause implicitly contains an extra atom *null* that does not appear in the body of any clause and whose annotation is $1 - \sum_{k=1}^{v_i} \Pi_{ik}$. An example of LPAD can be:

$$heads(Coin) : 0.5; tails(Coin) : 0.5 :- toss(Coin), \setminus + biased(Coin).$$
$$heads(Coin) : 0.6; tails(Coin) : 0.4 :- toss(Coin), biased(Coin).$$
$$fair(Coin) : 0.9; biased(Coin) : 0.1.$$
$$toss(coin).$$

This program can be read as: if we toss a *Coin* that is not $(\setminus+)$ biased then it lands heads with probability 0.5 and tails with probability 0.5. If we toss a *Coin* that is biased then it lands heads with probability 0.6 and tails with probability 0.4. The third clause states that a *Coin* is fair with probability 0.9 and biased with probability 0.1. The last clause assert that a *coin* is certainly tossed.

Evaluating the probability of a query, a task called *inference*, is one of the main challenges in probabilistic (logic) programming. There are two types of inference: approximate inference and exact inference. Exact inference is used when the problem has to be solved exactly. Several tools that performs exact inference have been presented, such as PITA [28,29]. The main disadvantage of exact inference is that it is, in general, #P-complete [16] so it is not usable for large domains. A possible alternative to exact inference is *approximate* inference. Both types of inferences are implemented in *cplint* [27], accessible also online[6].

---

[6] http://cplint.eu/.

3.1   Conditional Approximate Inference

Approximate inference in cplint is performed using Monte Carlo algorithms [6, 24]. Each algorithm is usually composed by the following steps: (1) sampling a world by sampling each ground probabilistic fact, (2) checking if the query is true in the world, (3) compute the probability p of the query as the fraction of samples where the query is true and (4) repeat the process for a fixed number of times or until convergence. This process is still very expensive for large programs because the generation of a world requires sampling many probabilistic facts. To reduce the number of calculations, usually samples are evaluated lazily, i.e., the sampling of probabilistic facts is performed only when required by a proof [26].

Using Monte Carlo methods, it is also possible to compute the probability of a query given a certain evidence, using algorithms such as rejection sampling or Metropolis-Hastings Markov Chain Monte Carlo (MCMC). In the case that the evidence is on atoms that have continuous values as argument, *likelihood weighting* must be used [21]. In likelihood weighting, each sample has an associated weight based on the evidence. The total probability of the query is then computed summing all the weights of the samples where the query is true and then dividing this value by the total sum of the weights of the samples.

In cplint, (conditional) approximate inference can be done using the module MCINTYRE [24]. cplint also allows the definitions of continuous random variables using the syntax A:Density:- Body. In particular, g(X):gaussian(X,0, 1) states that argument X of $g(X)$ follows a Gaussian distribution with mean 0 and variance 1. The following example shows how to model a mixture of two Gaussians: a biased coin is toss. With probability 0.6 it lands heads, with probability 0.4 it lands tails. If it lands heads, X in $mix(X)$ is sampled from a Gaussian with mean 0 and variance 1. If it lands tails, X is sampled from a Gaussian with mean 5 and variance 2.

$$heads : 0.6; tails : 0.4.$$
$$g(X) : gaussian(X, 0, 1).$$
$$h(X) : gaussian(X, 5, 2).$$
$$mix(X) :- heads, g(X).$$
$$mix(X) :- tails, h(X).$$

Using cplint, we can take N samples of X in $mix(X)$ by querying mc_sample_arg (mix(X),N,X,L0) or we can take N samples of X in $mix(X)$ given that *heads* was true by querying mc_mh_sample_arg(mix(X),heads,N,X,L0).

4   Modelling Transaction Fee with Probabilistic Logic Programming

Transaction fee are a hot topic in Bitcoin. As said above, miners are interested in selecting only the most profitable transactions while users are interested in minimizing the cost for a transaction. There are several sources of uncertainty that makes the computation of the optimal value a complicated task. One of them is block discovery time [5]. Its probability distribution can be described with a Poisson distribution with rate (usually indicated with λ) 10 since all the events are independent i.e., the discovery time of a block does not give information about the next block and blocks are discovered every 10 min on average. To keep the block production rate constant, the *target* value, that conditions the block discovery time, is dynamically updated every 2016 blocks, based on the time it took to find the last 2016 blocks.

Other sources of uncertainty, just to name a few, are: the number of transactions broadcast every minute, the average size of them and the average size of a block. All of them can be modelled with a Normal (also known as Gaussian) distribution. This distribution is characterized by two parameters, *mean* (μ) and *variance* (σ^2) and is well suited to model data that tends to be around a central value. Moreover, thanks to the Central Limit Theorem, the Poisson distribution with mean λ can be approximated with a Gaussian distribution with mean and variance λ, i.e., $Possion(\lambda) \approx Gaussian(\lambda, \lambda)$.

5   Experiments

In this paper we use probabilistic programming to model two real world scenarios: computing the amount of fees collected by a miner over time and computing the Bitcoin transaction fees trend.

In the first experiment, we are interested in computing how transaction fees affect the average profit of a miner. Nowadays most of the revenues of miners come from blocks reward: each miner that appends a block to the blockchain receives a certain amount of bitcoin. However, the Bitcoin block mining reward halves every 210,000 blocks so, the more blocks will be appended to the main chain, the less will be the miner's revenue be. Currently, the revenue is 12.5 bitcoin but approximately by the end of 2020 it will be halved. Therefore, in the future, transaction fees will have a central role in supporting the miners activity.

In this experiment we modelled the number of transactions in a block (N_{tx}), and the transaction reward R as Gaussian distributions. For both, the mean of the distribution is sampled from another Gaussian distribution. The obtained fees are $N_{tx} * R$. The model is shown in Listing 5-1:

```
mean_r(M):gaussian(M,18,2).
mean_b(M):gaussian(M,700,25).
revenue(_,M,R):gaussian(R,M,2).
block_size(_,M,S):gaussian(S,M,25).

val_r(I,V):- mean_r(M), revenue(I,M,V).
val_b(I,V):- mean_b(M), block_size(I,M,V).

obtained_fees(I,O):- val_r(I,R), val_b(I,B), O is R*B/100000.
```

Listing 5-1. Example of a model.

The predicates `val_b/2` and `val_r/2` compute the average size of a block and the average fee rate. Finally, `obtained_fees/2` computes the amount of fees received for creating one block. The output value is divided by 10^5 to get the value in bitcoin, since the average fee rate is in satoshi/byte and the block size in kilobyte. To compute the results, we used the predicates `mc_expectation/4` and `mc_lw_expectation/5` from the cplint package. The signature of the first predicate is the following: `mc_expectation(+Query:atom,+N:int,?Arg:var,-Exp: float)`. It takes N samples of `Query` and sums up the value of `Arg` for each sample. The overall sum is divided by N to give `Exp`. The second predicate has one more argument, the evidence. The difference with respect to the previous one is that each sample is weighted by the likelihood of evidence in the sample, according to likelihood weighting. The results are shown in Fig. 1, where we observed `val_r/2` with V variable according to the legend and in Fig. 2 where we observed `val_b/2` with V variable according to the legend. For both experiments we used 1000 samples.

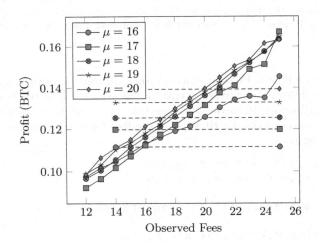

Fig. 1. The graph shows how a variation in the average bitcoin fee rate can influence the miner profit. The data are computed by setting the parameters for the Gaussian distribution for block size as $\mu = 700$ and $\sigma^2 = 700$ and for rewards as $\sigma^2 = 5$ and μ according to the legend. The straight lines represent the values computed without observations (obtained with `mc_expectation/3`).

In the second experiment, we want to understand how transaction fees may vary over time. In particular, we want to know what is the probability that a transaction with a certain fee rate is confirmed after a given number of blocks. We start by defining the probability distributions of the involved variables. Looking at Bitcoin data from blockchain.com, we retrieved the average number of transactions in a block, the average block discovery time and the average number of transactions added to the mempool per second. All these variables can

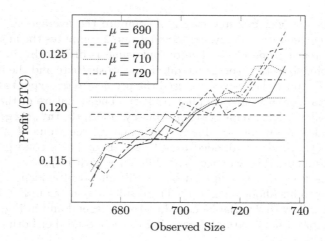

Fig. 2. The graph relates the block size with the average profit obtained from fees. The parameters for the distribution for block size are $\sigma^2 = 700$ and μ variable and for the reward $\mu = 17$ and $\sigma^2 = 2$. Straight lines represent the values computed without observations.

be assumed to follow a Poisson distribution that can be approximated with a Gaussian distribution. The average transaction fee rate is also modelled with a Gaussian distribution. However, because this value often varies over time, we re-sample the mean of the distribution of the fees for every iteration. The model is shown in Listing 5-2.

```
average_fee(_,M):uniform(M,15,25).
compute_fee(_,M,F):gaussian(F,M,4).

fee(I,F):- average_fee(I,M), compute_fee(I,M,F).

compute_time(F,M,V):gaussian(F,M,V).
number_of_tx_in_block(_,N):gaussian(N,1600,1600).
block_discovery_time(_,N):gaussian(N,500,500).
tx_per_second(_,N):poisson(N,5).

generate_pool(N,N,[]):-!.
generate_pool(I,N,[F|T]):- I < N, fee(I,F), I1 is I+1,
    generate_pool(I1,N,T).

get_len(A,B,B):- A >= B, !.
get_len(A,B,A1):- A < B, A1 is A-1.

loop_pool(FeeRate,I,NBlocks,Pool):- I =< NBlocks,!,
    number_of_tx_in_block(I,N), N11 is round(N),
    length(Pool,LP), get_len(LP,N11,N1),
    length(L,N1), append(L,RemPool,Pool),
```

```
loop_pool_check(FeeRate,I,RemPool,NBlocks).

loop_pool_check(_,_,[],_):- !.
loop_pool_check(FeeRate,_,[H|_],_):- H < FeeRate,!.
loop_pool_check(FeeRate,I,RemPool,NBlocks):- !,
    I1 is I+1, block_discovery_time(I,Time),
    tx_per_second(I,T), NNewTx is T*Time,
    NT1 is round(NNewTx),
    generate_pool(0,NT1,NewArrived),
    append(NewArrived,RemPool,NewPool),
    sort(0, @>=, NewPool, PoolSorted),
    loop_pool(FeeRate,I1,NBlocks,PoolSorted).

included(_I,FeeRate,NBlocks):-
    loop_pool_check(FeeRate,0,[FeeRate],NBlocks).
```

Listing 5-2. Example of model.

The program creates an initial pool of N transactions by sampling N times a value from a Gaussian distribution using the predicates **generate_pool/3** and **fee/2**. To compute how many blocks we need to wait to confirm a transaction with associated fee rate F, we sort the pool, compute the average number N_b of transactions in a block, the average block discovery time T and the average number of transactions per second N_{txs} (predicates **loop_pool/4** and **loop_pool_check/4**). We then compute $N_{txs} * T = N_{ta}$, the number of transactions arrived during the last block creation. To simulate the inclusion of N_{ta} transactions in a block we removed the best N_b transactions from the mempool (we suppose the miner acts as expected, i.e., he includes only the most profitable transactions). If the transaction with the best fee rate in the remaining mempool has a value less than F, this means that the transaction we consider has been successfully included in a block and the iteration stops. Otherwise, we simulate the arrival of N_{ta} new transactions to the mempool with **generate_pool/3** and repeat the process. In this case, we compute the results using both **mc_sample/3** and **mc_lw_sample/4** provided by the cplint package. The first one samples the goal a certain number of times and computes the probability of success. The second one works in a similar way but, in addition, performs likelihood weighting: each sample is weighted by the likelihood of the evidence in the sample. Results are shown in Fig. 3. The used parameters are shown in Listing 5-2 and $NBlocks$ was set to 1 (next block). For instance, if $\phi = 16$ the query is: ?- **mc_lw_sample(included(1,16,1),included(0,ObservedFees,1), NSamples, Probability)**. As expected, the confirmation probability decreases as the observed fees increase. ϕ represents the fees associated to a transaction. The experiments were executed computing 250 samples. Value of observed fees less than ϕ gives probability = 1 and so are not reported in the graph.

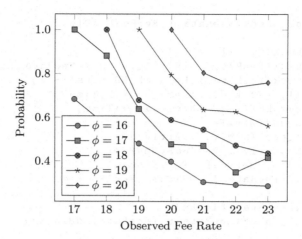

Fig. 3. The graph shows how transaction fees influence the probability of confirmation in N blocks. We selected a value of fee rate (ϕ) for the transaction under consideration and then computed how probability changes according observed fee rate.

6   Conclusion

In this paper we show how to model blockchain fees using probabilistic logic programming. Starting from real world data, we try to model how transaction fees influence the confirmation time and how transaction fees contribute to miners revenue. Despite being a relatively new technology, Bitcoin has attracted a lot of interest in research. There are several papers that study Bitcoin behaviour such as [3,22,30] where the authors study the so-called double spending attack. A game theoretic analysis can be found in [18] where Bitcoin is analyzed in a situation where all the participants behave according to their incentives. However, there are only few works in the literature concerning Bitcoin fees. In particular, in [15,17] the authors proposed a method based on queuing theory to model how fees effect the confirmation time. To avoid price fluctuation, authors in [4] proposed a new method to computes fees. An analysis on how block reward, transaction fees and their ratio influences the Bitcoin ecosystem can be found in [9].

To extend our work, decision theory and game theory models can be used to deeply analyze miner's behaviour and understand how they can optimally select transactions based on several profit variables. Another interesting direction could be the usage of deep learning models [12] to analyse historical data and predict the evolution of the system.

References

1. Alberti, M., Bellodi, E., Cota, G., Riguzzi, F., Zese, R.: cplint on SWISH: probabilistic logical inference with a web browser. Intell. Artif. **11**(1), 47–64 (2017). https://doi.org/10.3233/IA-170105
2. Alberti, M., Cota, G., Riguzzi, F., Zese, R.: Probabilistic logical inference on the web. In: Adorni, G., Cagnoni, S., Gori, M., Maratea, M. (eds.) AI*IA 2016. LNCS (LNAI), vol. 10037, pp. 351–363. Springer, Cham (2016). https://doi.org/10.1007/978-3-319-49130-1_26
3. Azzolini, D., Riguzzi, F., Lamma, E., Bellodi, E., Zese, R.: Modeling bitcoin protocols with probabilistic logic programming. In: Bellodi, E., Schrijvers, T. (eds.) Proceedings of the 5th International Workshop on Probabilistic Logic Programming, PLP 2018, Co-located with the 28th International Conference on Inductive Logic Programming (ILP 2018), Ferrara, Italy, 1 September 2018, CEUR Workshop Proceedings, vol. 2219, pp. 49–61. CEUR-WS.org (2018). http://ceur-ws.org/Vol-2219/paper6.pdf
4. Basu, S., Easley, D., O'Hara, M., Sirer, E.G.: Towards a functional fee market for cryptocurrencies. CoRR abs/1901.06830 (2019). http://arxiv.org/abs/1901.06830
5. Bowden, R., Keeler, H.P., Krzesinski, A.E., Taylor, P.G.: Block arrivals in the bitcoin blockchain. CoRR abs/1801.07447 (2018). http://arxiv.org/abs/1801.07447
6. Bragaglia, S., Riguzzi, F.: Approximate inference for logic programs with annotated disjunctions. In: Frasconi, P., Lisi, F.A. (eds.) ILP 2010. LNCS (LNAI), vol. 6489, pp. 30–37. Springer, Heidelberg (2011). https://doi.org/10.1007/978-3-642-21295-6_7
7. Buterin, V.: A next-generation smart contract and decentralized application platform (2014). https://github.com/ethereum/wiki/wiki/White-Paper. Accessed 14 Feb 2019
8. Cardano. https://whycardano.com/
9. Carlsten, M., Kalodner, H., Weinberg, S.M., Narayanan, A.: On the instability of bitcoin without the block reward. In: Proceedings of the 2016 ACM SIGSAC Conference on Computer and Communications Security, pp. 154–167. ACM (2016)
10. De Raedt, L., Kimmig, A.: Probabilistic (logic) programming concepts. Mach. Learn. **100**(1), 5–47 (2015)
11. Eosio - an introduction by ian grigg. https://eos.io/introduction
12. Goodfellow, I., Bengio, Y., Courville, A.: Deep Learning, vol. 1. MIT Press, Cambridge (2016)
13. Haber, S., Stornetta, W.S.: How to time-stamp a digital document. In: Menezes, A.J., Vanstone, S.A. (eds.) CRYPTO 1990. LNCS, vol. 537, pp. 437–455. Springer, Heidelberg (1991). https://doi.org/10.1007/3-540-38424-3_32
14. Hyperledger. https://www.hyperledger.org/
15. Kasahara, S., Kawahara, J.: Priority mechanism of bitcoin and its effect on transaction-confirmation process. CoRR abs/1604.00103 (2016). http://arxiv.org/abs/1604.00103
16. Koller, D., Friedman, N.: Probabilistic Graphical Models: Principles and Techniques. Adaptive Computation and Machine Learning. MIT Press, Cambridge (2009)
17. Koops, D.T.: Predicting the confirmation time of bitcoin transactions. CoRR abs/1809.10596 (2018). http://arxiv.org/abs/1809.10596
18. Kroll, J.A., Davey, I.C., Felten, E.W.: The economics of bitcoin mining, or bitcoin in the presence of adversaries. In: Proceedings of WEIS, vol. 2013, p. 11 (2013)

19. Nakamoto, S.: Bitcoin: A peer-to-peer electronic cash system (2008)
20. Fadja, A.N., Riguzzi, F.: Probabilistic logic programming in action. In: Holzinger, A., Goebel, R., Ferri, M., Palade, V. (eds.) Towards Integrative Machine Learning and Knowledge Extraction. LNCS (LNAI), vol. 10344, pp. 89–116. Springer, Cham (2017). https://doi.org/10.1007/978-3-319-69775-8_5
21. Nitti, D.: Hybrid Probabilistic Logic Programming. Ph.D. thesis, KU Leuven (2106)
22. Pinzón, C., Rocha, C.: Double-spend attack models with time advantange for bitcoin. Electr. Notes Theor. Comput. Sci. **329**, 79–103 (2016). https://doi.org/10.1016/j.entcs.2016.12.006
23. Poon, J., Dryja, T.: The bitcoin lightning network: Scalable off-chain instant payments (2016). https://lightning.network/lightning-network-paper.pdf
24. Riguzzi, F.: MCINTYRE: a Monte Carlo system for probabilistic logic programming. Fund. Inform. **124**(4), 521–541 (2013). https://doi.org/10.3233/FI-2013-847
25. Riguzzi, F.: The distribution semantics for normal programs with function symbols. Int. J. Approx. Reason. **77**, 1–19 (2016). https://doi.org/10.1016/j.ijar.2016.05.005
26. Riguzzi, F.: Foundations of Probabilistic Logic Programming. River Publishers, Gistrup (2018). http://www.riverpublishers.com/book_details.php?book_id=660
27. Riguzzi, F., Bellodi, E., Lamma, E., Zese, R., Cota, G.: Probabilistic logic programming on the web. Softw.-Pract. Exp. **46**(10), 1381–1396 (2016). https://doi.org/10.1002/spe.2386
28. Riguzzi, F., Swift, T.: Tabling and answer subsumption for reasoning on logic programs with annotated disjunctions. In: ICLP TC 2010. LIPIcs, vol. 7, pp. 162–171. Schloss Dagstuhl - Leibniz-Zentrum fuer Informatik (2010). https://doi.org/10.4230/LIPIcs.ICLP.2010.162
29. Riguzzi, F., Swift, T.: The PITA system: tabling and answer subsumption for reasoning under uncertainty. Theor. Pract. Log. Prog. **11**(4–5), 433–449 (2011). https://doi.org/10.1017/S147106841100010X
30. Rosenfeld, M.: Analysis of hashrate-based double spending. CoRR abs/1402.2009 (2014). http://arxiv.org/abs/1402.2009
31. Sato, T.: A statistical learning method for logic programs with distribution semantics. In: Sterling, L. (ed.) ICLP 1995, pp. 715–729. MIT Press (1995)
32. Swan, M.: Blockchain: Blueprint for a New Economy. O'Reilly Media Inc., Newton (2015)
33. Vennekens, J., Verbaeten, S., Bruynooghe, M.: Logic programs with annotated disjunctions. In: Demoen, B., Lifschitz, V. (eds.) ICLP 2004. LNCS, vol. 3132, pp. 431–445. Springer, Heidelberg (2004). https://doi.org/10.1007/978-3-540-27775-0_30
34. Wood, G.: Ethereum: a secure decentralised generalised transaction ledger. Ethereum Proj. Yellow Pap. **151**, 1–32 (2014)

An On-Chain Method for Automatic Entitlement Management Using Blockchain Smart Contracts

Timothy Nugent[1], Fabio Petroni[2]([✉]), Benedict Whittam Smith[1], and Jochen L. Leidner[1,3]

[1] Refinitiv Labs, Refinitiv, London, UK
{tim.nugent,benedict.whittamsmith,jochen.leidner}@refinitiv.com
[2] Facebook, London, UK
petronif@acm.org
[3] University of Sheffield, Sheffield, UK

Abstract. Managing the entitlements for the compliant use of digital assets is a complex and labour-intensive task. As a consequence, implemented processes tend to be slow and inconsistent. Automated approaches have been proposed, including systems using distributed ledger technology (*blockchains*), but to date these require additional off-chain sub-systems to function. In this paper, we present the first approach to entitlement management that is entirely *on-chain*, *i.e.* the functionality for matching the digitally encoded rights of content owners (expressed in ODRL) and the request for use by a customer are checked for compliance in a smart contract. We describe the matching algorithm and our experimental implementation for the Ethereum platform.

Keywords: Entitlement management · Digital rights management · Smart contracts · Blockchain · ODRL · Ethereum

1 Introduction

As the global demand for information products and services continues to accelerate, the efficient management of digital rights becomes an ever more critical business function. In the absence of technical mechanisms designed for intellectual property (IP) protection, digital information such as financial data, text content such as books or news archives, music and video content is easily used in ways that do not comply with license contracts. This can result in a sharp decline in the product value over time, creating an incentive for compliance solutions that protect the rights of data suppliers, data consumers, and data aggregators. As the importance of digital rights management increases, so too does both its quantity and complexity – to the point at which we now require automated systems to better understand, manage, and enforce our rights and obligations.

F. Petroni—This work was carried out while the author was working at Refinitiv Labs.

W. Abramowicz and R. Corchuelo (Eds.): BIS 2019 Workshops, LNBIP 373, pp. 255–266, 2019.
https://doi.org/10.1007/978-3-030-36691-9_22

There is a desire for financial regulators to improve trust and transparency around exchange data towards a mode of operation that permits the easier review of the collection, distribution and sale of market data by exchanges [1]. These factors create an opportunity to address some of the key objectives in entitlements management, namely *(i)* lowering auditing costs, *(ii)* increasing transparency, and *(iii)* enhancing enforcement. The use of blockchain smart contracts present a potential technical solution to some of these challenges.

A blockchain acts as a distributed database which maintains a continuously growing list, or *ledger*, of transaction records [11]. These transactions are organized into blocks using consensus algorithms, allowing untrusted parties to agree on a common state while ensuring tamper resistance. Block validators verify a transaction's digital signature and the correctness of the resulting state change, providing cryptographically irrefutable evidence of both the provenance and existence of a record at a given point in time. Blockchains typically provide a scripting language which provides additional functionality; the Bitcoin platform has a rudimentary stack-based language [18], while Ethereum [3,24] supports a Turing-complete language and isolated (*i.e.* no access to network or file system) run-time environment, the Ethereum Virtual Machine (EVM), therefore defining a platform for decentralized applications. Such applications are typically referred to as *smart contracts* due to their trusted execution, though they bear a closer resemblance to objects in object-orientated languages (encapsulation of state, constructors and functions to manage state) than contracts in the legal sense.

Our goals in this paper are to define an entitlement management system that allows multiple parties to independently verify compliance between multiple digital product licenses, with the requirement that such licenses and the verification process can be proven to be tamper resistant. We evaluate the use of smart contracts for this purpose due to the trustless execution characteristics of such blockchain platforms. We first describe an ODRL-based (Open Digital Rights Language) schema for representing data licenses which can be stored in and retrieved from a smart contract RDF (Resource Description Framework) triple-store. We then define an algorithm within another smart contract that can validate that agreements between a data aggregator and data supplier (Supplier Agreement) and between a data aggregator and data consumers (Product Offer) are both compatible and compliant. Such a system represents a novel application of verifiable computing that should help to increase trust and compliance between data aggregator, suppliers and consumers, while providing a secure, transparent and auditable method for managing the entitlements for digital data assets.

2   Related Work

2.1   Entitlement and Rights Management

ODRL [12,13,21] is an open standard for describing entitlements[1], which we make use of in this paper. For example, [21] shows how it can be applied to

---

[1] Version 2.2 is the current version, c.f. https://www.w3.org/ns/odrl/2/.

linked open data, and [6] apply it to Web services. [15] is a revision of XrML 2.0, another rights language specifically targeting movie content. The PRISM specification [14] defines a name-space for digital rights management. DALICC [9,19] is a framework for making the consumption of data assets more compliant[2]. The system, like the approach in this paper, uses ODRL, but uses an answer set reasoner instead of a smart contract to check license compatibility. [8] implement their own contract layer on top of ODRL, and they present their REL interpreter for such contracts. [23] describes REAP, an access protocol for intellectual property, and ADEPT, a distributed version of the Alexandria digital library. [5] present the PARMA (Pervasive Application Rights Management Architecture), a rights management architecture focused in particular on software application assets in pervasive environments. [7] present PLANE (Platform to Assist Negotiation), a platform for buying and selling digital assets. Compared to our work, PLANE is positioned more as a market-making platform, whereas we focus on the entitlement validation problem. The use of Natural Language Generation (NLG) has been championed in [4] for the generation of rights descriptions understandable by humans; our work extends the state-of-the-art on the input side; our templates are used not to generate natural language descriptions, but ODRL specifications that correspond to human intentions selected by making choices expressed in natural language. [16] is an excellent review of the challenges in the field of rights/entitlement specifications as well as a description of the history. [17] is a more recent and comprehensive review that covers specifically RDF-based approaches for the time period 2002 to 2014. Two important problems with rights expression languages and digital rights management systems overall are adoption and interoperability.

The past work acknowledges these issues, but no solution to these challenges have been provided to date. Our approach attempts to address both by embedding entitlement validation into an existing smart contracts platform rather than proposing yet another system which risks not gaining traction. The work that most closely resembles ours is that of Herbert *et al.* [10], who also proposed a blockchain based system for entitlement management. However, their method runs partially off-chain. In contrast, to the best of our knowledge, our proposal is the first to be fully computed on-chain and therefore defines a novel verifiable computation scheme.

3   Methods

In this section, we first introduce our ODRL-based representation of product data licenses. We then describe our proposed system and introduce the core smart contracts, before providing a description of the compliance check algorithm.

---

[2] https://dalicc.net (accessed 2019-02-18).

3.1   Data Representation

We represent policies using ODRL 2.1[3], a W3C[4] standardized policy expression language that provides a flexible and interoperable information model, vocabulary, and encoding mechanisms for representing statements about the usage of content and services. In the ODRL Core Model, the *Policy* is the central entity that holds a set of ODRL Rules together. There are three types of Rules in ODRL: *Permissions*, *Duties* (entitlements and obligations to do something) and *Prohibitions* (i.e. negative obligations: call to refrain from doing something).

A Permission allows a particular Action to be executed on a specified Asset. Figure 3 shows part of a Policy (of type Product) that offers a single Permission allowing a display Action to be taken over the example information. The Party that grants this Permission is linked to it with the Role assigner, while the Party that is granted the Permission is linked to it with the Role assignee, e.g. "assigner (e.g. Deutsche Boerse AG) grants the Permission to assignee Aggregator (e.g. Thomson Reuters Corporation)". Additionally, a Permission may be linked to Duty rules. When a Duty is associated with a Permission it states that a certain Action must be executed by the Party with the Role assignee for the Permission to be valid, e.g. "JP Morgan must pay 5 EUR in order to exercise the Permission to display the real-time equity data". The Prohibition entity is used in the same way as Permission, with the two differences that it does not refer to Duties and that it forbids the Action.

A Policy can collect multiple Permissions, Prohibitions, and Duties together. As such, Policies can be used to represent complex agreements between Parties of the sort frequently found in the licenses controlling the use of digital assets in the data supply chain. We use Supplier Agreement Policies to represent the assignments between data suppliers and data aggregators, and Product Offer Policies to represent the assignments between data aggregators and date consumers. We can then check that the Product Offer Policies offered to consumers are compliant with the Supplier Agreements offered by suppliers.

In this model, suppliers can circumscribe the Permissions which an aggregator can offer in their products by placing a Duty on the aggregator that specifies a Policy that must subsume those Permissions. Effectively, they offer a set of "template" Permissions within which the aggregator must operate. These Duties are represented by subgraphs (PR1: PR1-P1-D1, PR1-P1-D2, PR1-P2-D1, and PR1-P2-D2; SA1: SA1-P1-D1 and SA1-P2-D1) in the Directed Acyclic Graph (DAG) representations of the Policies shown in Figs. 1 and 2, which point to either Constraints or Policies and their associated Permissions. We can now check whether the product Permissions PR1-P1 and PR1-P2 are compliant with any of the supplier Permissions SA1-P1, SA1-P2, and SA1-P3, and their associated template permissions. If not, they cannot be offered to data consumers as that would lead to non-compliance.

---

[3] https://www.w3.org/TR/odrl-model (accessed 2019-02-18).
[4] https://www.w3.org (accessed 2019-02-18).

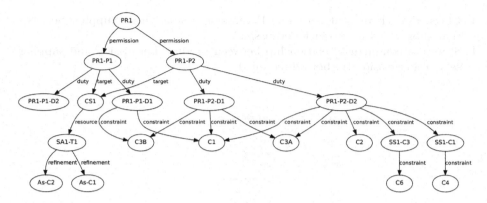

Fig. 1. ODRL licenses are tree structured. Here, a Product Offer, represented by an ODRL tree with root PR1, allows data aggregators to offer data consumers the entitlement to use an asset, subject to a set of Permissions (the ability to perform an action over an Asset, PR1-P1 and PR1-P2), Duties (obligations to perform actions, PR1-P1-D1, PR1-P1-D2, PR1-P2-D1, and PR1-P2-D2), and Constraints (conditions applicable to a policy rule) on the target Asset.

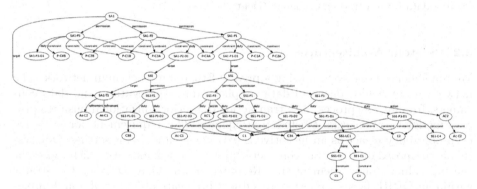

Fig. 2. An ODRL license representing a Supplier Agreement, with root SA1, allowing a data supplier to offers permissions to a data aggregator to distribute the asset subject to a set of Permissions (SA1-P1, SA1-P2, and SA1-P3), Duties and Constraints. Our compliance check algorithm takes the root SA1, along with the Product Offer root PR1 from Fig. 1, and performs tree traversal operations on both trees to ensure that all assets in the Product Offer match at least an asset in the Supplier Agreement, while ensuring that all permissions and constraints are satisfied.

In general, the compliance check procedure can be characterized by the following four steps:

1. Trace the underlying resources of each content service targeted by the product Permission.
2. For each resource, identify the Permissions in the supplier service that controls it.

3. Check that there is at least one Permission among those Supplier Services that subsumes the Product Permission.
4. Store the compliance relationship between product Permission and supplier service Permission (in both directions).

```
:S-P1    a                odrl:Permission ;
         odrl:assigner    <https://permid.org/1-4298007872 > ;
         odrl:assignee    <https://permid.org/1-4295861160 > ;
         odrl:action      rbim:distribute ;
         odrl:target      <https://permid.org/X-123 > .

:V-P1    a                odrl:Permission ;
         odrl:assigner    <https://permid.org/1-4295861160 > ;
         odrl:action      rbim:display ;
         odrl:target      <https://permid.org/X-123 > .
```

Fig. 3. Top: Sample Permission (Policy fragment S-P1): An example permission from a trading exchange (Deutsche Boerse AG) to an aggregator to distribute equity prices (Thomson Reuters Corporation). Bottom: View Permission (Policy fragment V-P1): An example permission from an aggregator which entitles its customers to display trading data from a trading exchange (Deutsche Boerse AG).

3.2   System Architecture

We implemented our system using a private Ethereum blockchain network. The network users would consist of data suppliers, data aggregators, and data consumers, framing the process as a transactional inter-organizational business process model between semi-trusted participants. The requirement for a native cryptocurrency to act as an incentive is extraneous under this setting. Our system is composed of three core contract types: *(i)* node contracts which represent the individual Policy Element, i.e. Resource, Permission, Duty or Constraint within an ODRL license; these store subject-predicate-object triples and implement functions to set and retrieve these values, *(ii)* a registry contract which provides look-ups for node contracts based on their subject or address, and *(iii)* the license compatibility check contract which takes the root nodes of two ODRL licenses as arguments and determines whether or not they are compliant.

Our implementation used the Ganache[5] development environment of Ethereum for all experiments and the Python Web3 API[6] to interact with it. Contracts were written in the Solidity[7] smart contract programming language. The system is initiated by deploying the registry contract. ODRL licenses are then parsed and node contracts are created for each Policy Element via a separate transaction; the node contract constructor function additionally registers the node address with the registry contract. Further transactions are used to

---

[5] https://github.com/trufflesuite/ganache (accessed 2019-02-18).
[6] https://github.com/ethereum/web3.py (accessed 2019-02-18).
[7] https://github.com/ethereum/solidity (accessed 2019-02-18).

append each subject-predicate-object triple to a container within the corresponding node. Once all triples have been added, the entire ODRL tree can be reconstructed by querying the registry contract using the root node subject and the address of the license creator (*i.e.* msg.sender), allowing the addresses of all child nodes to be retrieved.

3.3 Compliance Check Algorithm

The input of the compliance check algorithm are two ODRL license tree roots, one for the Product Offer (T_O) and one for the Supplier Agreement (T_{SA}). We consider all external nodes (i.e., nodes that do not have child nodes) of an ODRL tree as attributes of the parent node. The main idea is to perform specific tree traversal operations on both trees to check that all assets in the offer match at least an asset in the supplier agreement while complying with all the permissions on it.

Algorithm 1 refers to the pseudo-code implementation of the compliance check. The first step consists of retrieving the set of all assets in the Product

---

Algorithm 1. Compliance check

Require: T_O and T_{SA}, ODRL license trees for the offer and the supplier agreement, respectively.

Ensure: A boolean value that indicates if T_O is compatible with T_{SA}

```
 1: A_O ← getAssets(T_O)
 2: A_SA ← getAssets(T_SA)
 3: for all x ∈ A_O do
 4:     P_O ← getPermissions(T_O, x)
 5:     for all y ∈ A_SA do
 6:         found ← True
 7:         if checkAttributes(x, y) then
 8:             P_SA ← getPermissions(T_SA, y)
 9:             for all q ∈ P_O do
10:                 comp ← False
11:                 for all w ∈ P_SA do
12:                     comp ← checkPermissions(q, w)
13:                     if comp then
14:                         break
15:                 if ¬comp then
16:                     found ← False
17:                     break
18:         else
19:             found ← False
20:         if found then
21:             break
22:     if ¬found then
23:         return False
24: return True
```

Offer tree (A_O - line 1) and in the Supplier Agreement tree (A_{SA} - line 2). This is achieved with a simple tree traversal operation *getAssets*, where all nodes of type *asset* are returned. Next, for each asset $x \in A_O$, we first retrieve all the permissions P_O for x through the *getPermission* function (line 4). Again, this operation is straightforward; it can be achieved by performing a tree traversal over the sub-graph under the node for the asset x, looking for nodes of type *permission*. We then iterate over all assets y in the Supplier Agreement tree (line 5), and we check the attributes between x and y through the *checkAttributes* function (line 7). This function inspects the attributes of nodes x and y and checks their compliance; this operation is application specific and depends on the particular ontology defined over the data. For instance, the ontology might indicate that *timelinessOfDelivery eq realTime* is incompatible with *timelinessOfDelivery eq bestEffort*, but the inverse might be true (i.e., *realTime* is compatible with *bestEffort*). If the attributes for x and y are compatible, we retrieve all the permissions P_{SA} for y (line 8). Finally, the algorithm checks if all permissions $q \in P_O$ for the offer asset x match with at least one permission $winP_SA$ for the Supplier Agreement asset. This compliance check between permissions is performed through the *checkPermissions* function (line 12).

The key idea of this function is that the sub-tree under the Product Offer permission q should be contained in the sub-tree under the Supplier Agreement permission w, that is, for each node in the first sub-tree we should find a node in the second sub-tree with compatible type[8] (e.g., Duty, Constraint etc.) and attributes. This can be achieved combining a tree traversal operation with the *checkAttributes* function. Finally, we return *False* if the algorithm was unable to find a compatible permission or asset (line 23), or *True* otherwise (line 24).[9]

4   Evaluation

We parsed a broad range of ODRL licences of varying complexity and represented them on-chain as described above. For the most complex licenses, a few hundred transactions were required (*i.e.* one per RDF triple) with a typical transaction requiring ~85,000 units of gas. Gas is the execution fee for every operation made on Ethereum and reflects the computational overhead in performing the state update. For reference, a typical transaction that transfers native tokens between accounts might require 21,000 gas. This suggests that the majority of licenses could be quickly and easily deployed within a few blocks. Given that data licenses typically span multiple years and so will not be issued frequently, this indicates that our system is both scalable and relatively inexpensive to deploy given current Ethereum gas prices. Reconstruction of full ODRL license trees can be achieved quickly by querying the registry contract using *view* functions

---

[8] Note that the type is an attribute of the node, therefore the *checkAttributes* function will consider it.

[9] The idea behind this sub-tree containment is similar to the subsumption check conducted as part of the unification algorithm [20]; however, in computational terms, run-time complexity benefits from the flat nature of the Policy DAGS.

(*i.e.* constant or read-only) in such a way that data provenance and integrity can be ensured. The timestamp at which each RDF triple was appended can be retrieved, as can the Ethereum address of the entity which submitted the transaction. This creates a high quality, tamper-resistant, and standardized digital audit trail, which is in stark contrast to the often paper-based workflows that currently exist.[10]

We then tested the compliance check algorithm using a selection of ODRL licenses. The checking function is again a *view* function and so can be called offline without the need for a transaction. For debugging purposes, we modified our code to create EVM *events* (equivalent to logs) so we could identify precisely where the compliance check failed in the case of license incompatibility. Since functions that generate *events* cannot be *view* functions (*events* are stored within transaction receipt hashes inside blocks), we invoked the checking function using transactions and monitored gas usage. Gas usage varied considerably from ~1,000,000 gas for relatively simple licenses (up to ~10 ODRL tree nodes) to over 8,000,000 gas for more complex examples (up to ~50 ODRL tree nodes). While this indicates that it would not be possible to evaluate two licenses of high complexity within a single public Ethereum block (which currently has a gas limit of ~8,000,000), this is not necessarily a concern given we can revert to a *view* function. A greater issue is actually the compute time for the calculation which ranged from a few seconds for simple licenses, to over a minute for more complex ones. Here, we regularly encountered issues with remote procedure call (RPC) timeouts to the Ethereum node we were using (confirmed using the Geth[11] and Parity[12] clients, as well as Ganache), at which point the function call would terminate. Without modification to the underlying client code bases to address this issue, this places a limit on the size and complexity of license that our system is currently able to validate. Where the function call did not exceed the timeout, we were able to successfully verify compliance (or lack thereof) with EVM *events* indicating the exact reason in the case of a violation. Again, this enhances the digital audit trail and allows all parties to independently verify their own compliance.

5   Discussion and Conclusions

In this paper, we have proposed a system of smart contracts for entitlement management which can verify compliance between multiple digital product licenses that are stored on-chain. To do so, we implemented an RDF triple-store and a compliance checking algorithm in the Solidity smart contract programming language. While we have demonstrated the system can successfully verify compatibility between licenses of medium complexity, it is clear that we are close

---

[10] In particular, using a blockchain avoids the existence of inconsistent states between the producer and consumer of data assets.
[11] https://github.com/ethereum/go-ethereum (accessed 2019-02-18).
[12] https://github.com/paritytech/parity-ethereum (accessed 2019-02-18).

to the computational limits of the EVM. Currently, the majority of smart contracts deployed on the public Ethereum blockchain concern the relatively simple (in terms of gas usage) exchange and movement of digital tokens; here, we implement a costly tree search algorithm that is ultimately limited by the compute time of the EVM and the RPC timeout of our Ethereum client. Future enhancements to the EVM, for example—the move to Ethereum WebAssembly[13] for code execution—may enable more complex operations to be efficiently performed. However, alternative approaches that could be applied here include the use of Trusted Execution Environments (TEEs) and verifiable off-chain computation.

Methods based on TEEs utilize hardware-based secure enclaves to verify data integrity. Such approaches include Intel's SGX[14] (Software Guard eXtensions), AMD's Secure Execution Environment[15], and ARM's TrustZone[16]. SGX guarantees data integrity, ensuring that applications running within an enclave are protected against tampering by both the CPU and any other process. SGX also offers applications confidentiality, ensuring that the state is opaque to other processes when run inside the enclave, and allows attestation by generating a digitally signed proof that an application (identified by a hash of its build) is actually running within an enclave. By verifying this digital signature, it would be possible to verify that the license compliance algorithm is running securely within a SGX enclave, proving that the instance has not been tampered with, and that output is therefore authentic.

Approaches for verifiable off-chain computation employ a system of solvers and verifiers to perform computations and verification of their correctness. If a solution is challenged, an iterative "verification game" on subsets of the problem commences on-chain. This proceeds through a series of rounds, recursively checking smaller and smaller subset of the computation. The final round is sufficiently trivial such that the judges – block validators (*i.e.* miners) – can make a final on-chain ruling on whether the challenge was justified. TrueBit [22] is an example of such a system; it allows decentralized applications to pay for scalable verifiable computation to be performed outside of the network, but relies on the Ethereum protocol to enforce the "verification game". In theory, this enables smart contracts to securely perform a broad range of computationally intensive tasks.

An area we have *not* covered in this work is the issue of data privacy. Currently, data written to the Ethereum blockchain is visible to all parties, thus our system provides no privacy guarantees for license data. While recent improvements to the Ethereum protocol have focused on methods such as zero-knowledge proofs to verify transaction while maintaining data privacy, such techniques are not currently applicable to state variables such as the RDF triple data which

---

[13] https://github.com/ewasm/design (accessed 2019-02-18).

[14] https://software.intel.com/en-us/sgx (accessed 2019-02-18).

[15] https://www.amd.com/en/technologies/security (accessed 2019-02-18).

[16] https://developer.arm.com/technologies/trustzone (accessed 2019-02-18).

our compliance check algorithm operates upon. Alternative blockchain protocols may be a more appropriate solution here. Quorum[17] is an Ethereum-based protocol which offers full transaction and contract privacy, in addition to some novel consensus mechanisms and significant performance improvements compared to Geth. Quorum enables both private transactions and private contracts by separation of public and private state. It also utilizes peer-to-peer encrypted message exchange, allowing direct transfer of private data to network participants. Migrating our system to Quorum should be straightforward as it is fully compatible with the EVM. Other protocols which support varying degrees of privacy and are well suited to enterprise use-cases include Hyperledger Fabric [2] and Corda[18].

In summary, we have demonstrated that smart contracts running on the Ethereum blockchain can be used in principle to enhance the management of entitlements for digital data assets. While we believe the reported work shows significant potential, there is clearly still some way to go before current protocols offer full data privacy and are sufficiently performant to allow a more comprehensively decentralized alternative to existing legacy systems.

References

1. Costly data battle heats up between traders and equity exchanges. https://www.ft.com/content/785092ec-33d8-11e6-ad39-3fee5ffe5b5b. Accessed 06 May 2019
2. Androulaki, E., et al.: Hyperledger fabric: a distributed operating system for permissioned blockchains. In: Proceedings of the Thirteenth EuroSys Conference, EuroSys 2018, pp. 30:1–30:15. ACM, New York, NY, USA (2018). https://doi.org/10.1145/3190508.3190538
3. Buterin, V.: Ethereum: A next-generation smart contract and decentralized application platform (2014). https://github.com/ethereum/wiki/wiki/White-Paper. Accessed 22 Aug 2016
4. Cabrio, E., Aprosio, A., Villata, S.: These are your rights: a natural language processing approach to automated RDF license generation. In: Proceedings of ESWC, pp. 255–269 (2014)
5. Dusparic, I., Dahlem, D., Dowling, J.: Flexible application rights management in a pervasive environment. Technical report, Trinity College Dublin (2005)
6. Gangadharan, G., D'Andrea, V., Iannella, R., Weiss, M.: ODRL/L(S): A Language for Service Licensing. Technical report. DIT-07-027, Department of Information and Communication Technology, University of Trento, Povo, Trento, Italy (2007)
7. Guedes, R., Laurentino, M., Dias, C., Brito, A.: PLANE: a platform for negotiations of multi-attribute multimedia objects. Artif. Intell. Interact. Multimed. **2**(4), 81–86 (2013). https://doi.org/10.9781/ijimai.2013.2410
8. Guth, S., Neumann, G., Strembeck, M.: Experiences with the enforcement of access rights extracted from ODRL-based digital contracts. In: Proceedings of DRM (2003)

---

[17] https://github.com/jpmorganchase/quorum (accessed 2019-02-18).
[18] https://www.r3.com/corda-platform/ (accessed 2019-02-18).

9. Havur, G., et al.: DALICC: A framework for publishing and consuming data assets legally. In: Khalili, A., Koutraki, M. (eds.) Proceedings of the Posters and Demos Track of the 14th International Conference on Semantic Systems Co-located with the 14th International Conference on Semantic Systems (SEMANTiCS 2018), Vienna, Austria, 10–13 September 2018, CEUR Workshop Proceedings, vol. 2198. CEUR-WS.org (2018). http://ceur-ws.org/Vol-2198

10. Herbert, J., Litchfield, A.: A novel method for decentralised peer-to-peer software license validation using cryptocurrency blockchain technology. In: Proceedings of the 38th Australasian Computer Science Conference, ACSC 2015, pp. 27–35 (2015)

11. Herlihy, M.: Blockchains from a distributed computing perspective. Commun. ACM **62**(2), 78–85 (2019). https://doi.org/10.1145/3209623

12. Ianella, R.: Open Digital Rights Language (ODRL). Version: 1.1. Technical report. IPR Systems Pty Ltd. (2002)

13. Iannella, R., Guth, S. (eds.): Proceedings of the First International ODRL Workshop, 22–23 April 2004 (2004)

14. IDEA Alliance: IDEA: The PRISM Rights Language Namespace. PRISM Specification: Modular: Version 1.2. Technical report. International Digital Enterprise Alliance Inc. (2005)

15. ISO: Motion Picture Experts Group (MPEG)/ISO: ISO/IEC 21000–5 - MPEG-21 Part 5, Rights Expression Language. International standard, International Organization for Standardization (2003)

16. Jamkhedkar, P., Heileman, G.: A formal conceptual model for rights. In: Proceedings of DRM, pp. 29–38 (2008)

17. Kirrane, S., Mileo, A., Decker, S.: Access control and the resource description framework: a survey. Semant. Web Interoperability, Usability, Appl. **7**, 1–42 (2016)

18. Nakamoto, S.: Bitcoin: A peer-to-peer electronic cash system. http://bitcoin.org/bitcoin.pdf

19. Pellegrini, T., Mireles, V., Steyskal, S., Panasiuk, O., Fensel, A., Kirrane, S.: Automated rights clearance using semantic web technologies: the DALICC framework. In: Hoppe, T., Humm, B., Reibold, A. (eds.) Semantic Applications, pp. 203–218. Springer, Heidelberg (2018). https://doi.org/10.1007/978-3-662-55433-3_14

20. Robinson, J.A.: Computational logic: the unification computation. Mach. Intell. **6**, 63–72 (1971)

21. Steyskal, S., Polleres, A.: Defining expressive access policies for linked data using the ODRL ontology 2.0. In: Proceedings of the 10th International Conference on Semantic Systems, SEM 2014, pp. 20–23. ACM, New York, NY, USA (2014). https://doi.org/10.1145/2660517.2660530

22. Teutsch, J., Reitwießner, C.: A scalable verification solution for blockchains (2017). https://people.cs.uchicago.edu/teutsch/papers/truebitpdf

23. Vestavi, Ø.: REAP: a system for rights management in digital libraries. In: Proceedings of the First International ODRL Workshop, pp. 79–85 (2004)

24. Wood, G.: Ethereum: A secure decentralised generalised transaction ledger EIP-150 revision (759dccd - 2017–08–07) (2017). https://ethereum.github.io/yellowpaper/paper.pdf. Accessed 01 Mar 2018

Study of Factors Related to Grin Cryptocurrency Mining Efficiency with GPUs

Paulius Danielius$^{(\boxtimes)}$ ⓘ, Tomas Savenas, and Saulius Masteika

Vilnius University Kaunas Faculty, Muitines St. 8, 44280 Kaunas, EU, Lithuania
paulius.danielius@mif.vu.lt, {tomas.savenas,
saulius.masteika}@knf.vu.lt

Abstract. Grin cryptocurrency is one of the most recent implementations of Mimblewimble – specific stripped-down blockchain design as basis for strong privacy and good scalability features, which are complementing each other. Considering recent Grin inception and ongoing development there is a lack of research providing guidelines for optimizing mining efficiency in Grin's network. In this study we aimed to experimentally test the influence of some factors on GPU mining efficiency, which should be taken into account. We have found, that choosing the right combination of mining software and GPU specific parameters are among them. In general, NVIDIA and AMD GPUs were comparably effective. The results may be relevant for creators of alternative cryptocurrencies, for which GPU mining is a part of design.

Keywords: Blockchain · Cryptocurrency · Grin · Mimblewimble · GPU · Mining efficiency · Cuckaroo29

1 Introduction

Year 2019 marked the birth of two next generation cryptocurrencies with the premise of security and scalability – Grin and Beam, which are different implementations of specific blockchain design with peculiar name Mimblewimble. The distinct identity of the transaction construction model it uses is the inherent focus on privacy and scalability [3, 12]. Furthermore, in Grin's case there is announced list of what it will not do, like "no addresses" and "no visible amounts", which is quite contrary to the ongoing trends in cryptocurrency market [2, 6]. Further development of these projects has the potential to bring unique innovations in the field of blockchain and cryptocurrencies.

One of the aspects by which cryptocurrencies try to distinguish themselves from the rest is monetary policy. In this regard, Grin uses a linear emission rate of 1 grin/second and does not have maximum supply cap. This results in high inflation rate at start, which diminishes over time falling close to 1% in a couple of decades, but never reaching zero [9]. Such model is better suited to stabilize currency value and grants more equal ground for early miners and newcomers.

Another important aspect, especially for new cryptocurrencies is ensurement of decentralization. In this regard, GPU mining is crucial, because being affordable, it allows for broad and distributed user community. This would be impossible to achieve

© Springer Nature Switzerland AG 2019
W. Abramowicz and R. Corchuelo (Eds.): BIS 2019 Workshops, LNBIP 373, pp. 267–273, 2019.
https://doi.org/10.1007/978-3-030-36691-9_23

with only ASIC mining. Moreover, the creation of ASICs is practical only when cryptocurrency gets broader adoption and popularity.

In this study we aimed to get some insight in what factors may influence Grin mining efficiency on Mimblewimble blockchain network, as previous research on Ethereum mining [4] has shown that choosing right equipment and tweaking its settings, like memory clock frequency and core voltage, for optimized performance is not trivial. For such young project like Grin there is a lack of works, which tried to answer these questions in experiment-backed way.

Our main questions in this study were following: (1) what impact on mining efficiency has different mining software, (2) how different GPU architectures may influence mining efficiency.

The results of this study might be interesting for researchers working in blockchain field, cryptocurrency developers and currency mining researchers.

The paper is organized in following way: Sect. 2 introduces dual Proof of Work algorithm system used in Grin blockchain. Section 3 provides details on experiment organization. Section 4 describes experiment results. Section 5 concludes.

2 Grin Mining Algorithms

Proof of Work (PoW) is the consensus mechanism for accepting newly created blocks with transactions used by major part of cryptocurrencies.

The basis for Grin's PoW system is the Cuckoo Cycle algorithm. Because it is primarily memory bound (that means solution time is bound by memory bandwidth rather than CPU or GPU speed), mining should be viable on most commodity hardware [7].

Cuckoo Cycle algorithm is designed to find cycles (set of connected nodes which starts and ends on the same node) in randomly generated *bipartite* graph, whose nodes (vertices) are members of one from two separate node groups. So, Cuckoo Cycle PoW is concerned with finding cycles of a certain length within such random graph.

Adjusting the number of edges relative to the number of nodes changes the difficulty of cycle finding, and that means mining process difficulty.

The paper of John Tromp, initial proposer of this algorithm, describes Cuckoo Cycle in detail [11].

In order to prevent rapid creation of and mining with ASICs (highly efficient application-specific integrated circuits) shortly after the launch of Grin's blockhain network and thus gaining control of a large percentage of the hash rate, dual PoW system is employed consisting of primary algorithm Cuckatoo31+ and secondary algorithm Cuckaroo29. The difference between them is such that Cuckaroo29 is ASIC resistant – this means that difficulty of blocks mined with it is calculated differently in a way, which does not allow ASICs to mine significantly better than GPUs. Cuckatoo31 + is ASIC friendly, allowing ASICs to gain huge efficiency improvements over GPU by utilizing faster SRAM memory [1, 8]. The Grin mining process is organized in such way, that at the beginning Cuckatoo31+ will contribute to 10% of all mined blocks and Cuckaroo29 – 90%, giving GPU owners a good headstart. Over 2-year timespan the ratio of both algorithms will gradually change in favor of primary algorithm, and after two years Grin will be 100% mined with Cuckaroo31+ accepting inevitable creation of ASICs [5].

In our work we focus on Cuckaroo29 algorithm to test mining efficiency with GPUs.

3 Experimental Setup

For our experiment we used computing machine (GPU rig) with four different GPUs.

The list of hardware used in the experiment

1. SAPPHIRE Ellesmere RX 580, 8 GB, BIOS 113-1E3870U-O49
2. AMD Ellesmere RX 480, 8 GB, BIOS 113-D0090101-100
3. ASUS Strix Ellesmere RX 480, 8 GB, BIOS 115-D000PIL-100
4. ASUS NVIDIA GeForce GTX 1070 Ti, 8 GB, BIOS 86.04.85.00.B9.

Power Supply: EVGA SuperNOVA 1600 T2, 80+ TITANIUM

Motherboard: Gigabyte X99-UD4-CF

CPU: 12 x Intel(R) Core(TM) i7-5820K, 3.30 GHz

RAM: 8 GB KINGSTON DDR4

Disk drive: KINGSTON SV300S37A240G, 250 GB

Software installed on the GPU rig:

Operating system: Ubuntu 18.04.2 LTS (Bionic Beaver) Server version.

AMD Radeon headless driver version – 18.30-641594

NVIDIA headless driver version 410 and Cuda 10.1

Tested mining software: Bminer 15.3, GrinPro 1.2, Grin-miner 1.0.2.

Mining pool: we have chosen Grin-Pool.org, because of best response time and no fees.

Note: by default AMD and NVIDIA card drivers do not have high-performance computational support needed for mining activity, therefore additional utility software has to be installed, and specific settings have to be provided during driver installation as presented in guidelines [10]. All RX 480 cards were applied with "one click timing patch" using Polaris Bios Editor 1.7.

We used GPS (graphs per second) provided by mining software for mining performance measurement. To compare different GPU efficiency regarding power consumption we used GPS/W (GPS per watt).

As in experiment [4] it was found that tweaking certain GPU hardware settings might yield better efficiency, we made some pre-tests to find optimal parameters in similar way for further use in experiment. However, for AMD cards we were able to change only GPU core speed through *rocm-smi* utility. As the performance of RX 480 GPUs was the same for different core speeds, while RX 580 GPU has shown minor improvement of GPS/W on lower core speeds, we have chosen slightly lower than default, 1194 MHz core clock speed for all three AMD GPUs, which caused less heat up.

We were not able to change any settings For NVIDIA GPU and used default setup with 3802 MHz core clock speed and 1873 MHz memory clock speed.

The Experiment was Performed in Following Way
Hardware and software were prepared and installed beforehand, and during experiment no additional installations or configurations were made.

For our working paper we have run several test cases. During individual case different GPU was activated through mining software, and for every GPU mining performance with each mining software was measured separately. Measurements were taken by 10 s intervals for 10 min, after initial 5 min period of initialization and mining performance stabilization. Data was gathered from miner software and respective GPU driver utility (*nvidia-smi* and *rocm-smi*). Average values of GPS and watts were calculated for each GPU.

To ensure accuracy of measured data and to eliminate mistakes we repeated entire experiment several times.

4   Experiment Results

As Bminer support for Cuckaroo29 on AMD cards (RX 480 and RX 580) added recently in version 15.1.0 is still experimental, we tested it only with NVIDIA GPU. Grin-Miner and GrinPro were tested with all GPUs. Performance data is presented in Table 1.

Table 1. GPU performance with different mining software

	NVIDIA 1070 Ti	AMD RX 480	ASUS RX 480	SAPPHIRE RX 580
Grin-Miner1.0.2				
GPS	2.8	1.5	1.55	1.6
Watts	150	82	83	90
GPS/Watt	0.0187	0.0183	0.0187	0.0178
GrinPro 1.2				
GPS	4.02	1.94	1.96	2.1
Watts	155	86	86	120
GPS/Watt	0.0259	0.0226	0.0228	0.0175
Bminer 15.3				
GPS	5.02	N/A	N/A	N/A
Watts	154			
GPS/Watt	0.0326			

For NVIDIA card Bminer 15.3 is clear leader with 0.0326 GPS/W. While with three of cards GrinPro is the second, its result with fourth – RX 580 was slightly worse than Grin-Miner's. With the rest three cards, Grin-miner was the last (Fig. 1).

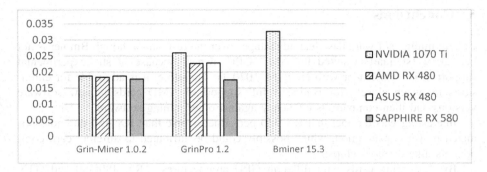

Fig. 1. Miner software efficiency, GPS/Watt

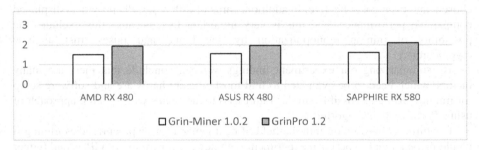

Fig. 2. RX series GPU mining performance by pure GPS

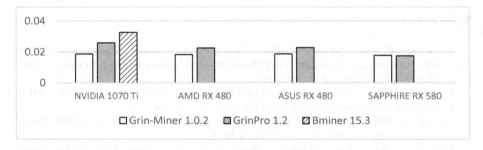

Fig. 3. GPU cards efficiency, GPS/Watt

While looking at pure GPS, RX 580 seemed to perform slightly better (Fig. 2), actually its efficiency was worse than RX 480 GPUs when considering GPS per Watt (Fig. 3).

Comparing NVIDIA GTX performance with all AMD RX cards we can notice that looking at pure GPS the difference may seem to be almost twofold in favor of GTX GPU (Table 1). However, when we recalculate efficiency in GPS per Watt, the difference is significantly less impressive, and RX 480 cards with GrinPro may even surpass GTX with Grin-Miner (Fig. 1).

5 Conclusions

Certain mining software has clear advantages over the rest, and although Bminer is not yet (2019 1st quarter) suited for AMD GPU owners because of still experimental support, it is clear leader with NVIDIA 1070 Ti. Therefore, it is advisable for enthusiasts to watch closely for Bminer's full support of AMD cards in new software versions and then compare its efficiency against other mining software.

Interesting was the fact that RX 580 performed worse than RX 480 due not optimized power consumption, which possibly could be attributed to different card components, like memory chips.

By comparing cards with different GPU architectures – RX 480/580 and GTX 1070–ti cards, we can say that Grin mining with tested RX cards, which already are considered legacy, might be perfectly viable, especially if proper miner software is chosen, and even cost-effective. In addition, cards of different GPU providers displayed comparable performance, and this is very important fact, because this excludes the possibility of mining monopolization by one brand and raises trust in new cryptocurency.

By summarizing our experiment findings, we can conclude that there are many factors, which need to be evaluated to find most efficient hardware and software setup for mining Grin and possible similar future cryptocurrencies with specific approach of using *Proof of Work* algorithms.

For further contribution into the field of next generation cryptocurrencies mining it would be beneficial to perform experiment with newest generation of GPUs and bigger sample of different cards.

References

1. CryptoNewsReview: Cudo targets GPU rigs as it brings GUI mining to Grin for the first time (2019). https://cryptonewsreview.com/cudo-targets-gpu-rigs-as-it-brings-gui-mining-to-grin-for-the-first-time. Accessed 15 Apr 2019
2. Curran, B.: What is Grin Coin & MimbleWimble? Complete Beginner's Guide (2019). https://blockonomi.com/grin-mimblewimble. Accessed 15 Apr 2019
3. Curran, B.: What is the BEAM Coin? Mimblewimble & Grin vs Beam (2019). https://blockonomi.com/beam-coin-guide. Accessed 15 Apr 2019
4. Danielius, P., Savenas, T., Masteika, S.: Research of ethereum mining hash rate dependency on GPU hardware settings. In: Abramowicz, W., Paschke, A. (eds.) BIS 2018. LNBIP, vol. 339, pp. 223–228. Springer, Cham (2019). https://doi.org/10.1007/978-3-030-04849-5_20
5. GitHub: https://github.com/mimblewimble/docs/wiki/How-to-mine-Grin. Accessed 15 Apr 2019
6. GitHub: https://github.com/mimblewimble/docs/wiki/No-this,-no-that. Accessed 15 Apr 2019
7. GitHub: https://github.com/mimblewimble/grin/blob/master/doc/pow/pow.md. Accessed 15 Apr 2019
8. Le Sceller, Q.: An Introduction to Grin Proof-of-Work (2018). https://blog.blockcypher.com/an-introduction-to-grin-proof-of-work-103aaa9f66ce. Accessed 15 Apr 2019

 9. Medium: (2019). https://medium.com/@CryptoProfG/grin-money-explained-3-supply-and-monetary-properties-of-grin-aa753fdb91b8. Accessed 15 Apr 2019
10. Savenas, T.: Installing NVIDIA and AMD GPU Driver on Linux server (2019). https://medium.com/@tomas_savenas/installing-nvidia-and-amd-gpu-driver-on-linux-server-4f1f1d4360d. Accessed 15 Apr 2019
11. Tromp, J.: Cuckoo cycle: a memory bound graph-theoretic proof-of-work (2019). https://github.com/tromp/cuckoo/blob/master/doc/cuckoo.pdf. Accessed 15 Apr 2019
12. Van Wirdum, A.: Battle of the Privacycoins: What We Know About Grin and Beam's Mimblewimble (2018). https://bitcoinmagazine.com/articles/battle-privacycoins-what-we-know-about-grin-and-beams-mimblewimble. Accessed 15 Apr 2019

Towards Blockchain-Based
E-Voting Systems

Chiara Braghin[1(✉)], Stelvio Cimato[1], Simone Raimondi Cominesi[1],
Ernesto Damiani[1,2], and Lara Mauri[1]

[1] Dipartimento di Informatica, Università degli Studi di Milano, Milan, Italy
{chiara.braghin,stelvio.cimato,simoneraimondi.cominesi,
lara.mauri}@unimi.it
[2] EBTIC Laboratory, Khalifa University, Abu Dhabi Campus,
PO Box 127788, Abu Dhabi, UAE
ernesto.damiani@ku.ac.ae

Abstract. Electronic voting is one of the most challenging crypto-graphic problems, since the developed system should guarantee strong and sometimes contrasting security properties. Blockchain technology can be of help providing for free some important guarantees such as the immutability and transparency of the votes using a distributed ledger. In this paper we propose a blockchain based e-voting system, which is lightweight, since it does not rely on strong cryptographic primitives, and efficient, since it improves over previous proposals in terms of both execution time and associated cost for the required infrastructure. We provide the description of a proof of concept system together with the cost and performance analysis.

Keywords: Cryptographic protocol · Blockchain · Ethereum · E-Voting

1 Introduction

Elections play a vital role within the context of a democratic society. In particular, systems for electronic voting (e-voting) are a pivotal technology currently subject of research, opening new opportunities for the development of e-democracy. As a matter of fact, e-voting can help increase the level of citizen participation in the decision-making process by reaching a wider public and allowing individuals to express their opinion more easily. For example, compared to traditional paper-based systems, it has the obvious benefit of making long-distance voting easier, especially for armed forces and other voters overseas, and of improving accessibility for elderly and physically impaired, thus increasing the voter turnout. The approach to voting through digital systems is a continuous evolving domain with the overall goal to make the entire election procedure secure, verifiable and transparent. A second but not secondary purpose is also to increase efficiency, minimise the negative factor of human error and reduce cost of elections.

© Springer Nature Switzerland AG 2019
W. Abramowicz and R. Corchuelo (Eds.): BIS 2019 Workshops, LNBIP 373, pp. 274–286, 2019.
https://doi.org/10.1007/978-3-030-36691-9_24

In general, e-voting protocols rely on the existence of a public bulletin board to support verifiability, since all voters can transparently access and check the correct submission and counting of the votes [7]. E-voting is a natural area where blockchain technology has been exploited since its first appearance. Most of the proposals adopt blockchain framework as an immutable centralised database where votes can be stored ensuring a number of security guarantees.

Currently, there are several commercial remote e-voting protocols, namely BitCongress, FollowMyVote, and TIVI; some of them have been applied for informal and consultative voting, some others have been deployed for city or national voting [8]. Recently, online voting has been adopted in the USA, where West Virginian residents serving overseas were able to cast federal election ballots using a smartphone app [14]. Voters registered by taking a photo of their government-issued identification and a selfie, and then uploaded them via an app that has been developed by Voatz, a Boston company in charge of the development of the voting infrastructure. Using facial recognition software, voters used the app to cast their ballots, that were anonymised and stored on the blockchain.

The proposals above have some scalability and performance issues, restricting the number of participants, or requiring strong cryptographic primitives that are computationally expensive. In all cases, the resulting system fits to small scale elections or has lower performance in terms of time and/or cost. Debate on the advantages coming from the replacement of traditional balloting and on the potential risks of mobile voting technology is still ongoing [17].

However, we think that most of the issues can be well addressed by proposing simple voting frameworks where usability and security guarantees are well balanced, using the technical resources available. To this aim, in this paper we propose a remote e-voting system based on the deployment of standard cryptographic techniques, in particular we adopt chameleon hash as a means to add coercion-resistance property to the resulting system.

Our contribution

- We propose a lightweight and efficient contract-based e-voting framework and discuss the security properties it satisfies. Our proposal is implemented using a single smart contract and can be scaled to manage from small community to country-wide elections.
- As a proof of concept, we describe a prototype implementation relying on the Ethereum blockchain. For this purpose, we describe the implementation on Ganache, a local blockchain framework, and give a detailed representation of the associated costs for generic elections, evaluating also the performance in comparison with previous proposals.

2   Related Works

Since their first appearance, blockchain frameworks have revolutionised the financial sector creating a large number of crypto-currencies available in place of traditional currencies, and paving the way for deep transformation in the digital economy [15]. The success of blockchain is mostly derived from the possibility to remove the role of the banks that usually play the role of the central authority managing a financial ledger and ensuring the correctness of all the financial transactions. On the contrary blockchains provide a distributed ledger managed by a peer-to-peer network where all the members interact and where a consensus mechanism gives the possibility to verify the transactions and validate the state of the shared ledger [9]. Taking advantage of the distributed consensus mechanism, practical applications of blockchain technology beyond the financial sector have been started in different fields such as health, science, government, culture and art [1].

Several digital voting systems have been proposed to improve the public electoral process in terms of costs and time efficiency, and achieve more direct form of democracy. Recently, different proposals consider blockchain frameworks as a means to get transparency and security guarantees. Some proposals use smart contracts to perform the voting phases.

Mc Corry et al. in [10] present an implementation of the Open Vote Network over the Ethereum blockchain. Open Vote Network [5] is a decentralized two-round protocol designed for supporting small-scale boardroom voting, where in the first round registrations of the voters are collected, while in the second round all voters can cast their vote. The system allows voting yes/no by collecting zero-knowledge proofs according to the Cramer et al. technique [2]. In the Ethereum implementation, two smart contracts are deployed, one for the voting and one for the cryptography computations devoted to the creation and the verification of zero knowledge proofs needed in the protocol. It is worth to notice that the current limitation in the Ethereum platform and the cost of the deployed contracts limit the usability of this approach to yes/no elections including a restricted number of voters (less than fifty).

In [3], the Broncovote framework for university-scaled elections is presented. The system is deployed on the Ethereum blockchain and relies on the Paillier homomorphic encryption to achieve voters' privacy. The implementation include three contracts: one for setting up the ballot and defining the candidates for the election; the second is the Registrar contract used by the administrator to allow potential voters to register; the third contract allow voters to cast their votes using homomorphic encrypted ballots. To encrypt the votes and to update the vote count, Broncovote interacts with an external server which perform the needed operations. Also in this case, considerations on the costs in terms of gas needed to perform the transactions limit the adoption of the system to elections involving a small number of participants (about thirty).

The implementation of a national e-voting system (examining the characteristics of Iceland, home country of the authors) based on blockchain has been considered in [6]. Different roles for the actors have been distinguished, and different blockchain frameworks analysed for the implementation, among Exonum, Quorum and Geth. The presented election scheme requires each voter to go at a voting district and makes use of a private Ethereum blockchian.

3 Background

3.1 Blockchain and Smart Contracts

A blockchain system [13] is a distributed peer-to-peer framework where participants are involved in transactions without trusting themselves, not relying on any trusted intermediary, but still having a way to verify the exchanges. Transactions are registered in a *distributed ledger* that does not need a central repository of information, but realises a distributed data structure replicated and shared among all the members of the network. All transactions that have been finalised in the blockchain are registered in a permanent and verifiable way. In a blockchain, each block is connected to the rest of the chain using the cryptographic hash of the previous blocks, being in this way resistant to any modification, since once recorded, the data in any given block cannot be altered retroactively without alteration of all subsequent blocks. Transactions are verified and inserted in the chain by special nodes which are called *miners*. Their work consists in checking the sender and the content of the transaction and in generating a new block of transactions only after that a computationally expensive task, the so called *Proof of Work*, has been solved. The generated block can be then propagated to the rest of network where the other nodes can validate its correctness.

Some blockchain framework give the possibility to define and execute *smart contracts*, that are executable pieces of code stored and running on the blockchain to facilitate, execute and enforce the terms of an agreement. A smart contract executes independently and automatically according to the data that was included in the triggering transaction, and the blockchain network acts as a distributed VM.

3.2 Chameleon Hash

Chameleon hash functions are particular kinds of collision resistant hash functions which allow the existence of a trapdoor. We will use them to allow voters to check if their vote has been recorded correctly in the blockchain (see Sect. 4), avoiding coercion. If the trapdoor is not known, the function has the same security properties of ordinary collision-resistant hash functions, while the user can use the the trapdoor to easily find a collision.

A *chameleon hash function* is composed by three procedures:

- Gen takes as input a security parameter $1k$ and outputs the evaluation key ek
- CH takes as input the evaluation key ek, a message m and a random value r and outputs a hash value h
- CH^{-1} takes as input the trapdoor tk, two messages m, m' and a random value r and returns a value r', such that $CH(ek, m, r) = CH(ek, m', r')$.

Here, we use the instantiation of chameleon hash based on the discrete logarithm problem similarly to what reported in [4]. The procedure Gen selects a group G of prime order q of elements in Z_p^* with generator g. After selecting an element x in Z_q and computing the value $h = g^x$ the evaluation key ek is defined as $ek = (G, g, h)$ and the trapdoor key tk is defined as $tk = (ek, x)$. The procedure CH is defined for a message m and the random value r to output $ch = g^m * h^r$. The procedure $\mathsf{CH}^{-1}(m, r, m')$ outputs the value r' such that $r' = (m - m') * x^{-1} + r$.

4   A Blockchain-Based E-Voting System

In this section, we describe the architecture of a blockchain-based remote e-voting system, abstracting from the blockchain on which it is based on. The only assumptions made on the actual system are that smart contracts are supported and that users own a registered account to the system, with an associated public key. In this way, the security issues discussed in Sect. 4.1 remain valid in any scenario.

The main actors of the proposed framework are the *administrator* and the *voter*. The administrator represents the institution organising the election, thus in charge of configuring ballots with the list of candidates, registering eligible voters, deciding the lifetime of the election, and deploying the smart contract. An eligible voter, to cast her vote, just needs an Internet connection and a registered account to the blockchain system used (e.g., Ethereum or Bitcoin).

By following the classical high-level models of election systems, we focus on the three major phases of an e-voting process: *(i) Pre-election Phase*, in which candidates and eligible voters are registered; *(ii) Election Phase*, the actual voting phase in which only eligible voters are able to cast ballots from any location that is accessible through the Internet; and *(iii) Post-election Phase*, in which votes are published.

In our framework, the election process consists of the following steps:

1. *Election set-up - Phase I*: Each municipality configures the election ballots and includes in a white-list all the eligible voters.
2. *Voter registration*: An eligible voter must register with her municipality the public key of the blockchain account she will use to vote. The voter authenticates herself by presenting some personal data, such as social security number, ID number and address. The voter also deposits the evaluation key ek, keeping secret the element x needed to compute the trapdoor key. At the end of the registration phase, the voter is given an url that will be active during the election period (a sort of a virtual polling place), and that she will use to vote.
3. *Election set-up - Phase II*: Each municipality deploys a contract containing the list of the public keys associated with each voter, the list of candidates and an associated integer value representing the votes obtained by the candidate (and set to zero at the beginning). The contract also contains a *voting function* that is triggered only when the eligible voter casts her vote from the url she has been given during the registration phase.

4. *Voting*: The voter goes to the url and casts her vote by selecting the candidate from the (closed) list of candidates available for her municipality. The *voting function* checks if the voter is eligible and has not voted yet, then, if the candidate is valid, it records that the voter has voted and it increments the voting count (without connecting the vote with the voter). Moreover, it provides as receipt the result of the chameleon hash function computed using the evaluation key, a random value and the message containing the details of the vote she cast.
5. *Publication of Results*: At the end of the voting phase, the results are published, reporting the vote count for each candidate and the vote receipts as computed in the previous step.

4.1   Security Issues

Every voting system, either online voting or traditional paper-based voting, should satisfy specific security requirements. In this section, we list the major desirable security properties and discuss if and how properties are held. Since our system uses the blockchain to record vote counts and voting operations, the system inherits some of the properties "out of the box".

- *Eligibility:* only voters with the right to vote are allowed to cast a vote. This property states that only legitimate persons can vote and every vote cast must be counted only once.
  In our framework, only eligible voters will cast a vote: before recording the vote, the smart contract checks if the public key associated to the private key used to sign the voting transaction is the one presented to the administrator during the registering phase (thus recorded in the contract).
- *Correctness:* every valid vote cast is counted. This property implies that in order to correctly count submitted votes, those submitted by unauthorised or unauthenticated voters must be classified as invalid and hence not counted.
  In our framework, the smart contract (and the votes) are recorded in the blockchain, which is resistant to modification of data by construction.
- *Uniqueness:* no voter is able to vote more than once.
  In our system, double voting is prevented by the fact that the contract records (and checks) if a voter has already voted before counting the vote as valid.
- *Integrity:* no one should be able to modify, forge, or delete votes without detection.
  In our system, the votes (and the smart contract) are recorded in the blockchain, which is resistant to modification of data by construction.
- *Vote anonymity:* neither election administrators nor anyone should be able to determine how any individual voted.
  In our system, no individual vote is traceable back to the voter since the fact that a person has voted and the value of her vote are two separate pieces of information.
- *Auditing:* every voter can check whether his vote has been counted or not. This property refers to the ability of the voter to verify that his ballot choice

has been really counted, thus implying trust in the vote tallying process by all parties involved.

In our system, the voter can check if the receipt of her vote (computed using the chameleon hash) is registered in the vote count in order to be sure that her vote has been correctly recorded.

- *Coercion-resistance:* this requirement ensures that the voter can deceive a coercer into thinking that he has voted for some designated choices as instructed, when the voter has in fact cast a ballot according to her own opinion.

  In our system, although the usage of the chameleon hash function allows the voter to check (and eventually prove) her vote, the coercer is not able to determine or not the targeted voter behaved as instructed.

5   Implementation

In this section, we describe *Chaincracy*, an Ethereum-based prototype implementation of the framework described in the previous section. It aims at reaching the highest number of eligible voters, since also users who cannot reach their polling places for different reasons, will be enabled to cast their vote by accessing a user-friendly web page showing the election ballot of his municipality.

5.1   Environment and Tools

At the moment, Ethereum is one of the most popular public blockchain platform for developing smart contracts, since it provides a built-in high-level Turing-complete language called Solidity (resembling common languages such as C++, Python and JavaScript). Accounts represent the main *entities* in Ethereum, since their configuration defines also the state of the Ethereum network. It is possible to distinguish between two types of accounts: *externally owned accounts* (EOAs), and *contract accounts*. The first category represents users interacting via transactions with the blockchain, while the second category represents the interactions due to the execution of smart contracts. A contract can change the state of the network on the basis of the transaction it receives, and usually can read or write data to its private storage, or store money into its account balance, or send/receive money from other users or other contracts, or, finally, send messages to other contracts to trigger their execution.

More in detail, for the implementation of our system prototype, we used Truffle web framework to write, compile and debug Solidity smart contracts; Ganache, a local Ethereum blockchain, to deploy the smart contract and run tests; and MetaMask to manage voters' accounts and to transact with a smart contract deployed on the blockchain from inside a JavaScript and a web application.

Truffle web framework [16] is a development environment, a testing framework and an asset pipeline for Ethereum, offering automated contract testing and some kind of debug feature.

Ganache is a local blockchain RPC server to test and develop against, integrated into Truffle and available both as a desktop application, as well as a command-line tool. It provides ten initial accounts pre-funded with 100 Ether along with a twelve-word seed phrase for re-generating those accounts. The seed phrase can be used to initialize a MetaMask client with the same accounts. The interface shows: the accounts generated and their balances, each block as mined on the blockchain, along with gas used and transactions, a list of all transactions run against the blockchain, and the logs for the server.

MetaMask [11] is a browser's plugin available for Chrome, Firefox, Opera and Brave allowing a user to access the Ethereum network. The plugin injects a JavaScript library developed by the Ethereum core team called web3.js into the namespace of each page loaded, thus providing the browser with APIs to make read and write requests on the Ethereum blockchain from regular websites. As a consequence, it allows users to make Ethereum transactions through regular websites, interacting with a local or remote Ethereum node, using a HTTP or IPC connection, without running a full Ethereum node. The tool also provides users with a secure identity vault, working as an Ethereum wallet, which allows anyone to manage identities across different websites and use them to sign blockchain transactions. Keys are stored encrypted on the browser, not on a remote server. So far, MetaMask has proven to be quite secure and there have been no successful hack attacks that have resulted in currency losses.

5.2   Implementation Details

In this section, we describe the most important components of the e-voting system we implemented, that are the Solidity smart contract, the web page presented to the voter, and the JavaScript file interacting with the server and the system to communicate data and update the status of the voter (see Fig. 1).

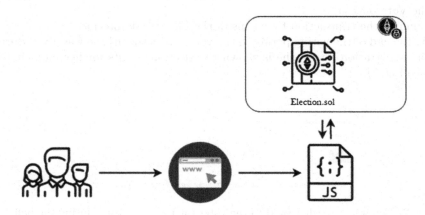

Fig. 1. *Chaincracy* voting framework.

More in detail:

- Election.sol: It is the (only) smart contract file, where the election candidates, the voters' public keys and the vote counters are recorded. Moreover, it contains a set of functions doing the vote count, controlling the eligibility of the voter, the correctness of the whitelist and of the candidates, avoiding double voting, etc.
- Index.html: This file represents the virtual polling place. It is the file requested by the url given to the voter after the registration phase. If requested during the election time, it calls the App.js file that retrieves the data from the blockchain and shows it to the voter.
- App.js: The file contains the configuration of web3 library, retrieves the candidates list and loads it in the web page displayed to the users. The file updates the page according to the status of the voter, for example showing a new page without the ability to vote if the voter has already cast her vote.

In the prototype implementation, from the point of view of the user, to participate to the voting process, each user should follow these steps:

1. Download and install the MetaMask plugin in her browser.
2. Either create an external user Ethereum account, or import an existing one from another wallet.
3. Before the election phase, register the public key of the chosen account to her municipality and record the voting url.
4. During the election period, visit the url she was given. The page (see Fig. 2) shows the list of candidates of her municipality retrieved from the blockchain thanks to the functions contained in the App.js file and her public key. In case she has already voted, she sees a page telling her that double voting is not permitted.
5. Select the candidate she wants to vote for, and cast her vote by clicking over the Vote button.
6. Confirm the transaction by means of the MetaMask interface.
7. At the end of the voting period, if the voter visits the url she was given during the registration phase, she is shown the election results for her municipality (see Fig. 3).

Make your choice:

Alice   ⇕

Vote

Your account: 0xb044c012bd4920d84f65e527c9fcb108fed73435

Fig. 2. The web page displayed to the voter (at her first visit), during the ballot.

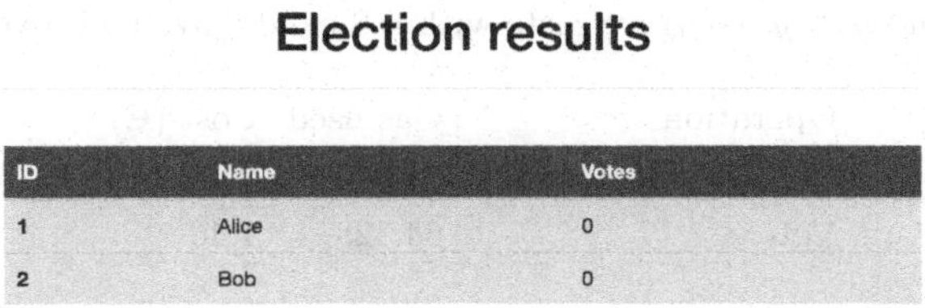

Election results

ID	Name	Votes
1	Alice	0
2	Bob	0

Fig. 3. The web page displayed to the voter when the voting phase is finished.

Extracts of the Contract. In the contract, the most important part is the vote function, where some controls are executed before incrementing the vote counter of the voted candidate.

In particular, the contract checks:

– that the voter has not voted yet (and updates her status after the vote):

```
mapping(address => bool) public voters;
...
require(!voters[msg.sender]);
...
voters[msg.sender] = true;
```

In Solidity, mappings act as hash tables which consist of key types and corresponding value type pairs. A mapping is defined like any other variable type: here, we create a mapping called voters associating a unique Ethereum address with a boolean. It allows us to look up a specific voter with his Ethereum address, and check if he has voted or not.

– that the ballot time is still valid (in the fragment the starting time is set to December, 1st 2018 and the ballots lasts 24 hours):

```
// using unix timestamp
require (block.timestamp > 1543622400 &&
block.timestamp < 1543708800);
```

– that the public key of the voter is included in the contract list of eligible voters' public keys:

```
require(0x225f8F1c8 == msg.sender || ... )
```

This means that the public key has been registered by an eligible voter during the registration phase at her municipality.

5.3 Cost Analysis of the System

The currency used within Ethereum network is called *Ether* (ETH). Computation within the blockchain and the EVM are repaid in ETH, although the execution fee is computed in terms of *gas*. In general, one unit of gas corresponds to the execution of one computational step and gas and ETH are deliberately

Table 1. *Chaincracy*: contract costs with a 8 candidates and 6 voters ballot.

Operation	Gas used	Cost (€)
Contract deployment	91,000	2.08
Vote	64,328	1.46

decoupled, such that fluctuation of the price of ETH is caused by external market forces, while the cost of gas is directly related to the computation costs.

A *transaction* in Ethereum defines the data that are signed by the entity starting the exchange and contains a message sent from an account to another account on the blockchain. Also contracts can send *messages* to other contracts, where each contract canbe conceived as *function calls*. The content of transactions and messages is similar: both contain a recipient, a value field indicating the amount of wei (1 *ether* is 1e18 *wei*) to transfer from the sender to the recipient, an optional data field hat is the actual input data to the contract, a gasLimit field representing the maximum number of computational steps the transaction or code execution is allowed to take to be used to compute the cost of the computation. A transaction contains also a gasPrice field, representing the fee the sender is willing to pay for gas.

The execution of a contract is triggered by a message or another transaction and every instruction is then executed on every node of the network. For every executed operation there is a specified cost, expressed in a number of gas units and each transaction has a maximum ether cost that is then equal to gasLimit ∗ gasPrice.

In Table 1, we show the *gas* costs and the corresponding prices in € for the deployment of the contract and for the voting operation. At the time of carrying out the experiments, November 2018, the *ether* exchange rate was 1 ETH = € 114.35, and the median gasPrice was approximately 0.0000002 ETH (20 Gwei).

We considered a small ballot with 8 candidates and 6 voters in order to make a precise comparison with BroncoVote (see Table 2). Notice that the contract deployment cost is fixed, whereas the cost of the voting operation is per person. In Italy, this voting system could help the government to save money: in 2013, the government spent 389,50 million of Euros for national elections (including regional and local elections), with 46,905,154 eligible electors (and 35,271,541 effective voters). If we consider an average cost of around € 40 every 20 people (i.e., € 2 per person) and about 50 million eligible voters, Chaincracy could save near 300 million Euros.

Observe that the cost of the voting operation is charged to the voter within her MetaMask account. A possible solution could be to distribute at the end of the registration phase € 1.5 to each voter's MetaMask account, using the public keys listed in the voters' white-list. However, due to the floating value of Ethereum currency, the price should not be fixed, but computed running the contract locally to check the actual price. Another solution could be the usage of tokens.

Comparison with Other Systems. In Table 2, we report the *gas* costs and the corresponding prices in € for the deployment of the contracts and for the voting operation for BroncoVote, the only alternative to our system with an available cost analysis. The cost values in *gas* are taken from [3] by merging the cost of the three different contracts used by the system. Notice that the usage of our simplified architecture gives a higher performance: € 51 vs € 2.

To encrypt the votes and to update the vote count, BroncoVote interacts with an external server which perform the needed operations. The operations are not counted in Table 2 since they are done externally to the contract, however they should also be take in consideration. Moreover, the server, being a trusted centralised server, may be subject to the classical form of attacks, such as DoS.

Table 2. *BroncoVote*: contract costs with a 8 candidates and 6 voters ballot.

Operation	Gas used	Cost (€)
Contracts deployment	2,263,132	51.75
Vote	813,977	18.60

6 Conclusions

To date, several e-voting protocols have been developed and used in various forms. However, in order to achieve a wide adoption of such systems it is necessary to improve their resilience against potential faults due to programming errors, hardware problems and malicious behaviours that are hardly detected.

Blockchain technology seems well positioned to address many issues related to digitalisation of voting process and provide enhanced security features without affecting usability, efficiency and reliability. In this paper, we proposed a simple and efficient e-voting system based on the Ethereum blockchain. We also described a prototype implementation, evaluating its performance in terms of costs, efficiency and scalability.

The framework improves over the previous proposals, and is scalable for country-wide elections, as the analysis of the associated costs has proved. Future works will address the formal evaluation of the security properties of these protocols, and the analysis of the trust assumptions needed during the whole voting process.

References

1. Braghin, C., Cimato, S., Damiani, E., Baronchelli, M.: Designing smart-contract based auctions. In: Yang, C.-N., Peng, S.-L., Jain, L.C. (eds.) SICBS 2018. AISC, vol. 895, pp. 54–64. Springer, Cham (2020). https://doi.org/10.1007/978-3-030-16946-6_5
2. Cramer, R., Damgård, I., Schoenmakers, B.: Proofs of partial knowledge and simplified design of witness hiding protocols. In: Desmedt, Y.G. (ed.) CRYPTO 1994. LNCS, vol. 839, pp. 174–187. Springer, Heidelberg (1994). https://doi.org/10.1007/3-540-48658-5_19

3. Dagher, G. G., Marella, P. B., Milojkovic, M., Mohler, J.: Broncovote: secure voting system using ethereum's blockchain. In: [12], pp. 96–107 (2018)
4. Guasch, S., Morillo, P.: How to challenge *and* cast your e-vote. In: Grossklags, J., Preneel, B. (eds.) FC 2016. LNCS, vol. 9603, pp. 130–145. Springer, Heidelberg (2017). https://doi.org/10.1007/978-3-662-54970-4_8
5. Hao, F., Ryan, P.Y., Zielinski, P.: Anonymous voting by two-round public discussion. IET Inf. Secur. **4**(2), 62–67 (2010)
6. Hjalmarsson, F. P., Hreioarsson, G. K., Hamdaqa, M., and Hjalmtysson, G.: Blockchain-based e-voting system. In: 11th IEEE International Conference on Cloud Computing, CLOUD 2018, San Francisco, CA, USA, 2–7 July 2018, pp. 983–986. IEEE Computer Society (2018)
7. Kiayias, A., Yung, M.: Self-tallying elections and perfect ballot secrecy. In: Naccache, D., Paillier, P. (eds.) PKC 2002. LNCS, vol. 2274, pp. 141–158. Springer, Heidelberg (2002). https://doi.org/10.1007/3-540-45664-3_10
8. Kshetri, N., Voas, J.: Blockchain-enabled e-voting. IEEE Softw. **35**(4), 95–99 (2018)
9. Mauri, L., Cimato, S., Damiani, E.: A comparative analysis of current cryptocurrencies. In: [12], pp. 127–138 (2019)
10. McCorry, P., Shahandashti, S.F., Hao, F.: A smart contract for boardroom voting with maximum voter privacy. In: Kiayias, A. (ed.) FC 2017. LNCS, vol. 10322, pp. 357–375. Springer, Cham (2017). https://doi.org/10.1007/978-3-319-70972-7_20
11. Metamask (2018). Metamask. https://metamask.io/
12. Mori, P., Furnell, S., Camp, O. (eds.) Proceedings of the 4th International Conference on Information Systems Security and Privacy, ICISSP. SciTePress (2018)
13. Nakamoto, S.: Bitcoin: A Peer-to-Peer Electronic Cash System, p. 9 (2008)
14. O'Sullivan, D.: West Virginia to introduce mobile phone voting for midterm elections (2018)
15. Swan, M.: Blockchain: Blueprint for a New Economy. O'Reilly Media Inc., Newton (2015)
16. Truffle. Truffle suite: Sweet tools for smart contracts (2018). https://truffleframework.com/
17. Yurieff, K.: Can this technology modernize how we vote? (2018)

Internet of Things and Blockchain Integration: Use Cases and Implementation Challenges

Kelechi G. Eze[✉], Cajetan M. Akujuobi, Matthew N. O. Sadiku, Mohamed Chouikha, and Shumon Alam

The Center of Excellence for Communication Systems Technology Research (CECSTR), Systems to Enhance Cybersecurity for Universal Research Environment (SECURE), Cybersecurity Center of Excellence, Department of Electrical Engineering, Prairie View A&M University, Prairie View, TX 77446, USA
kelechigodwin9@gmail.com, {cmakujuobi,mfchouikha,shalam}@pvamu.edu,
sadiku@ieee.org

Abstract. Research on blockchain (BC) and Internet of things (IoT) shows that they can be more powerful when combined or integrated together. However, the technologies are still emerging and face a lot of challenges. The paper focuses on Internet of things integration with the blockchain technology. We reviewed these technologies and identified some use cases of their combination and key issues hindering their integration. These issues are scalability, interoperability, inefficiencies, security, governance and regulation. While these issues are inherent in the current generations of blockchain such as Bitcoin and Ethereum respectively, with a well-designed architecture, the majority of these issues can be solved in the future generation. This work is inspired by the rapid growth in the number of connected devices and the volume of data produced by these devices and the need for security, efficient storage and processing.

Keywords: Blockchain · Security · Internet of Things · Smart contracts · Artificial intelligence · Cloud computing

1 Introduction

Blockchain and Internet of Things (IoT) are emerging Internet-based technologies that will have a tremendous disruptive effect in all disciplines, industries and economies [1]. Blockchain (Distributed Ledger Technology, (DLT)) is a decentralized network that constitutes of nodes or parties where all nodes in the network maintain a copy of the blockchain (i.e. have the same data, keeps a history of the transactions and receive the same transaction). The blockchain uses cryptography and consensus algorithm to make transaction secure and records immutable in a distributed fashion. Blockchain technology started with Bitcoin in 2008 which is referred to as the first generation blockchain. Today, we have

© Springer Nature Switzerland AG 2019
W. Abramowicz and R. Corchuelo (Eds.): BIS 2019 Workshops, LNBIP 373, pp. 287–298, 2019.
https://doi.org/10.1007/978-3-030-36691-9_25

the second generation blockchain like the Ethereum blockchain, NEO blockchain and Waves blockchain with smart contract support, a feature that makes it programmable. The property of programmability makes the second generation blockchain adaptable to a whole lot of application beyond Bitcoin, especially in the area of Internet of thing.

Applications of blockchain beyond bitcoin include IoT security, management of IoT devices and service provision in IoT, data management, data security, greater efficiency etc [2–6,9–17]. Blockchain has gained so much attention from the private and public sector, especially in the financial industry. The major attractions for the blockchain technology are its distributed nature, security (immutability) and applicability to a whole lot of domains.

While this paper is focused on IoT integration with blockchain, AI and the cloud will have a crucial role to play in this integration. While IoT devices produce enormous quantity of data, these data are usually aggregated for computation and processing in the cloud and AI applied to further turn these big data into actions and insights. Accordingly, IoT, AI, and blockchain can be considered as interconnected organic processes where IoT plays the role of sensing, AI handles reasoning and the blockchain acts as the memory [18].

Blockchain technology converged with Internet of things, artificial intelligence (AI) and cloud computing will bring solutions to problems, leading to greater trust and reliability as well as extended advantages within these technologies. Efficient and secure integration of emerging technologies and IT systems of diverse types, needed to build smart industrial, city and home applications and services, remains the greatest challenge to overcome today. This paper investigates current issues in blockchain technology with respect to its application and integration in the Internet of things, while considering AI and the cloud as a vital components of this integration.

The rest of this paper is organized as follows. Section 2 presents an overview of the technological components of blockchain and Internet of things (IoT). The Integration of blockchain and IoT, that is bringing blockchain and IoT to function together is discussed in Sect. 3. Section 4 is a summary of the use cases of integrating blockchain and IoT. The issues we found to be the major issues hindering blockchain and IoT integration are presented and analyzed in Sect. 5 and lastly our conclusion and future directions is presented in Sect. 6.

2   Overview of the Basic Concepts

In this section we give a brief overview of the basic concepts of blockchain, Internet of Things and associated technologies.

2.1   Blockchain Technology

Blockchain refers to a decentralized network of databases in the form of blocks capable of holding and transferring digital assets or data in a tamper-proof manner. Blockchain is designed with the properties of immutability, no central authority, irreversibility, time-stamping, replication and cryptography. It uses elliptic curve cryptography (ECC) and various hashing schemes like KECCAK-256 and secure hashing algorithms (e.g. SHA-256) for security, business logic and replicated ledger [14,19]. Figure 1 is a simplified structure of the blockchain. Each block in a blockchain is linked cryptographically to the previous blocks to maintain immutability as shown in Fig. 1 (i.e. the parentHash of any block must be same as the hash of the previous block). The genesis block (first block) has index of 0, timestamp of 0, parentHash of 0 and a preassigned nonce value while the second block derive most of its values computationally or cryptographically from the genesis block and so on. The nonce is a 32 bit random number taken into account during consensus process. The consensus algorithm is used to reach decision on a single version of the data to get stored in the blockchain. Transactions are events allowed to take place within the blockchain protocol such as sending and receiving data (e.g. cryptocurrency) from one node to another and are stored in blocks.

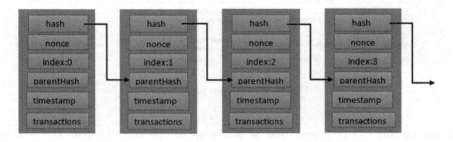

Fig. 1. Basic structure of blockchain.

Some examples of blockchain are Bitcoin, Ethereum, Corda, Hyperledger, Komodo etc. We have prepared a list of popular blockchain platforms as shown in Fig. 2. The blockchains are categorized as private or permissioned, public blockchains or unpermissioned blockchain and consortium blockchain [6]. A public blockchain are free to the public to join without restrictions but the private blockchain are restricted and can only be connected to with valid credentials. An example of permissioned blockchain are Hyperledger fabric and Ethereum is an example of permissioned blockchain.

2.2 Smart Contracts

Smart Contract is an executable code representing a set of promises or agreements that automatically runs on the blockchain and is self-enforced [20]. Just like a computer program, a smart contract is written in a smart contract language (Solidity) or general-purpose language (Java, Go or node.js), compiled and run on a blockchain. The smart contract is compiled into two separate parts, the application binary interface (ABI) and the bytecode [9]. The bytecode is the

Popular Blockchain Platforms	Major Application Areas	Unique Selling Points	Consensus
Ethereum	Cryptocurrency, IoT	smart contract support, public, open source	Proof of Work (PoW)
Waves	Dapps, Tocken Exchange	smart contract, open source	Proof of Stake(PoS)
Cardano	Cryptocurrency, evolving for many other applications	smart contracts, open source, sidechains, interoperability	Proof of Stake(PoS)
Hyperledger	Supply Chain, Healtcare, Energy, Transport	private, smart contract support (chaincode), modulrity, enterprise focused	Pluggable Consensus (PC)
Komodo	Cryptocurrency	multichain interoperability, smart contract support	delayed Proof of Work (dPoW)
IOTA (Tangle)	IoT, Smart Energy	open source, support for smart contracts	Tangle/Coordination
Enigma	AI, Data Marketplace, Healthcare, IoT	privacy, scalability	Proof of Stake (PoS)
Corda	Financial services , Energy and Governement	open source, business focused, smart contract support	Pluggable Consensus(PC)
Stella	Cryptocurrency	interoperability, micropayments	Stella Consensus
Nxt, Ardor	Cryptocurrency	blockchain-as-a-service, smart contract support, public	Proof of Stake (PoS)
Qtum	Crptocurrency	smart contracts	Proof of Stake (PoS)
ICON	Crytocurrency, AI, Healthcare, Education	private, smart contract support, applied to many use cases	Loop Fault Tolerance (LFT)
NEM	Cryptocurrency	smart contract support. private or public	Proof of Importance (PoI)
Openchain	Cryptocurrency , Commodities and Securities	modularity, smart contract support, support for many use cases	Partitioned Consensus (PC)
Tezos	Platform for Dapps	smart contract support (support for Dapps)	Proof of Stake (PoS)
Wanchain	Finance	connects other blockchains together, smart contract support, builds on ethereum	Proof of Stake (PoS)
Origintrail	Supplychain, Crytocurrency	interoperability, smart contract support, diverse use cases	Zero knowledge Proof (ZKP)
Bitcoin	Cryptocurrency	payment processing	Proof of Work (PoW)

Fig. 2. Blockchain platforms.

actual machine instructions that is made up of opcodes; whereas the ABI is data formatted in JavaScript Object Notation (JSON) that describes the various functions (methods) in the smart contract. ABI also provides a convenient way to interact with the smart contracts.

Smart contract is a feature of blockchain that makes it programmable and therefore possible to develop flexible and decentralized applications on blockchain. These applications run on blockchain when predefined conditions are met and are tamper proof, secure and transparent [20]. A typical smart contract specifies the parties involved in a transaction, what the transaction should do and the state transitions in the blockchain. Therefore, the smart contract removes the need for a trusted third party in a blockchain technology. Most blockchains supports smart contracts.

2.3   Internet of Things

Internet of things (IoT) is simply the enabling of non-traditional computing devices for Internet connectivity. IoT refers to anything (e.g cars, smart devices, objects, wearables, etc.) enabled to communicate (send and receive data) using the Internet network. Edge devices in Internet of things paradigm are often limited in memory and computational capability and thus uses specialized protocols MQTT, CoAP, ZigBee, Bluetooth, LoRaWan etc. for communication and are inherently distributed. Internet of things thus involves devices of various types, sizes and capabilities that are distributed [10].

The rapid growth of Internet of things poses serious challenge to the centralized or the client-server model which involves having these many IoT devices connected to a single server with high computational and storage resources for management and control. The centralized model is expensive and suffers from single point of failure when compromised by cybersecurity attacks (e.g. Denial of Service (DoS) and ransomware attacks) [11, 14, 21]. A solution to this problem is a decentralized model for IoT where nodes will share the computational power as well as the storage resources required in the network and can tolerate faults [11].

Internet of Things (IoT) are widely being adopted in industries such as manufacturing, healthcare, finance, logistics, energy etc where it helps in making automation of industrial processes a lot more efficient. The IoT also empowers flexible information and resource sharing in the industry as well as enhanced collaborations. The IoT is therefore very essential for expanding growth and productivity in Industrial sector.

3   Blockchain and IoT Integration

The centralized architecture where a central server provides services to clients on the network has downsides of high maintenance costs, poor interoperability and single point of failures from security threats [4]. A decentralized architecture on the other hand will eliminate the disadvantages of the centralized architecture. A rising decentralized management platform for IoT is blockchain. By design, the blockchain network operates in a decentralized fashion where network nodes can communicate in a peer-to-peer fashion.

Blockchain and Internet of things integration will strengthen the security of the future Internet as this integration will incorporate the security features of blockchain. Requirements for the implementation of the aforementioned integration will depend on hosting platform (cloud or fog), use case and choice of blockchain platform (such as Ethereum, Hyperledger etc.) [7]. We have shown this integration where Internet of things integrates the cloud and AI for extended advantages in Fig. 3.

The Internet of things in the block diagram (Fig. 3) contains the actors in the network such as user applications and IoT devices and communicate to the cloud network using the gateways. The cloud network aggregates sensor data in the cloud storage for computation and analytics using built-in AI capabilities. The capabilities of the cloud network and smart contracts efficiently monitors raw telemetry data (sensor data), converts it to the appropriate format and routes it to the blockchain. IoT devices are also able to receive services (e.g. secure updates) from the blockchain on a regular basis as the case may be. The block diagram also shows that the cloud network houses Application Programming Interface (APIs) or access layer that give enterprises and cloud providers access into the blockchain. Also note that from Fig. 3, the gateway functions as a node

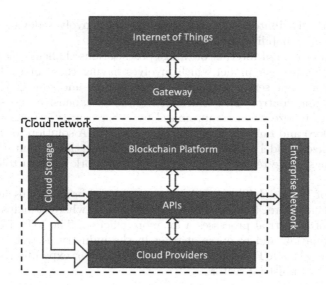

Fig. 3. Block diagram of blockchain and IoT integration.

on the blockchain (external to the cloud network but local to the IoT devices) and therefore decentralized.

4 Use Cases of Converging Blockchain and IoT

Many industries today are using blockchain to solve most IoT issues such as security and identity management. Extended advantages are also derived by combining these two technologies. The following are the use cases of combining blockchain and Internet of Things [8].

- *Access Control and Identity Management*: Using smart contracts, features of a blockchain can be extended to adapt to a variety of use cases. A contract for access control will enforce access control of the various resources on the blockchain network and a smart contract for identity management will enhance the identity management capability of the blockchain for various IoT devices on the network [15].
- *Secure Update of Edge Devices in IoT*: Blockchain combined with Internet of things can be used to provide firmware or software update in scenarios like the smart cities and smart homes. Here, smart contracts are used to define the update conditions and the secure nature of blockhain make them resistant to cyberattacks.
- *Logistics and Supply Chain Management*: In IoT-enabled supply chain where vehicles and cargoes are equipped with sensors, combining blockchain and Internet of things enables near real time access to status information regarding shipment, increasing visibility and reliability within the supply chain.

- *Automobile Industry*: Automobiles are becoming highly equipped with sensors and Internet capabilities making them part of the IoT ecosystem. Connecting smart cars to the blockchain network will enable trusted exchange of information, improved connectivity and security as well as accurate vehicle records (e.g. trip information, service, fault information etc.).
- *Sharing Economy*: As the sharing economy is rapidly growing in adoption, blockchain can enable a decentralized application on shared economy, making the exchange of value, goods and services seamless at reduced cost.
- *Healthcare Industry*: Blockchain by enabling transparency and traceability in pharmaceutical supply chain can drastically reduce the problem of fake medicines (one such application is mediledger project). Also patients using monitoring healthcare devices connected to the blockchain can choose who to share their data and be guaranteed that only healthcare professional responsible for their care can have access to such data.
- *Agriculture*: Sensor data from farms stored on the blockchain can provide useful information regarding provenance of products, improved transparency in agricultural supply chain and informed decision making for farmers and customers.
- *Micropayments*: Micropayments in IoT will involve either machine to machine or person to machine transactions using crypto currencies without involving centralized third parties like the banks. Examples are a smart connected electric vehicle making payment to a charging station and a person making payment for a product from a connected vending machine. Micropayment enables faster and cheaper payment among the parties involved.
- *Data Integrity in IoT*: Combining IoT and Blockchain will ensure IoT data integrity automatically using the digital signature and hashing technique that are inbuilt by design on the blockchain. This is especially very useful in scenarios where multiple parties are involved like the smart energy grid to eliminate fraud and rip-offs by the participants in energy trading.

5   Major Blockchain and IoT Integration Issues

Blockchain has a number of technological limitations as well as non-technological limitations, although it is a very powerful technology. We have reviewed and identified the major problems that hinders blockchain integration with Internet of things as shown in Fig. 4. They are scalability, interoperability, inefficient consensus algorithm, security, privacy, governance and regulations.

5.1   Issue with Scalability

A major issue in the integration of blockchain with Internet of things is scalability [4]. The problem of scalability in the context of blockchain integration with Internet of things is caused mainly by ubiquitous nature of IoT [22] and the limitations inherent in a typical IoT device. An optimal blockchain solution must be scalable with the number of IoT devices or gateways (i.e. nodes on the

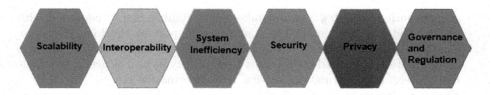

Fig. 4. Internet of things and blockchain integration challenges.

blockchain network) and be able to handle high transaction rates. The block size and block generation interval will vary with the number of IoT devices and will reach a maximum set size at a point. The transaction throughput or performance increases with the number of IoT devices up to a maximum while the block generation interval decreases as the number of IoT devices increase up to an optimal point [4]. The blockchain is initialized with the genesis block and grows according to the configuration settings for the genesis file, e.g. the gas limit, mining difficulty, etc. In bitcoin, however the block size determines the rate of growth. In each case, a high number of transactions will result in a corresponding decrease in throughput. The number of transactions per second is governed by: (i) the block generation time, (ii) the number of transaction that a block can hold, and (iii) the time it takes to reach a consensus.

"Blockchain pruning" (i.e., erasing unnecessary record to avoid holding the entire blockchain on a single node) is a possible solution to the ever-growing blockchain [23]. With the help of AI, federated learning, a new decentralized machine learning system can also be used along with other techniques such as sharding technique to make the blockchain system more efficient.

5.2   Issue with Interoperability

Interoperability is the ability to transact and share data across blockchain and non-blockchain systems. Today, interoperability is a big issue facing the integration of blockchain with other systems such as Internet of things, AI and cloud computing. Blockchain was originally designed to operate with computers with high computational powers on the Internet. Internet of things (edge devices/sensors) on the other hand has low computational powers by design. IoT and blockchain are therefore mismatch in computational powers. IoT sense and transmit enormous data in Terabytes while the blockchain is limited by design on storage capacity. This is another important bottleneck that need to be addressed.

AI and cloud computing when combined with this integration will play a huge role in solving the interoperability issue faced with Blockchain and IoT. While the AI will help reduce this data to a form that can be handled by blockchain through techniques such as data compression, data normalization, data smoothing etc. [24], cloud computing will provide a suitable computation environment for these data.

5.3   System Inefficiency

Blockchain is slow in running codes and smart contracts on traditional computing devices. This is because the process of mining in blockchain requires a lot of computational power. Therefore, miners or special hardware are required to carry out mining in a typical blockchain solution. This could lead to inefficiencies and extra investment.

Popular consensus algorithm used in a blockchains today are modified Proof of Work (PoW), Practical Byzantine Fault Tolerance and Binary consensus [11]. Major concerns about these consensuses are the high computational power consumed in the mining process and the time taken (high latency) to reach consensus [11,25]. The Proof of Work is also vulnerable to majority hash rates or the 51% attack which makes it possible for someone to reverse transaction history and prevent incoming transaction from confirmation by controlling most of the networks hash rate. Examples of where this attack has occurred are Bitcoin Gold, Verge, ZenCash, and other POW-based cryptocurrencies [5]. Other consensus protocol used in blockchain are Proof of Stake and (PoS), Proof of Burn (PoB), Proof of Activity, Proof of Capacity (PoC), Proof of Elapsed Time (PoET), Proof of Authority (PoA), Proof of Importance (PoI) [17,26]. These consensus algorithms have issues to be addressed as well.

5.4   Issue with Security

Blockchain is said to be immutable and hack resistant. In scenarios such as Decentralized Autonomous Organization (DAO) and Bitfinex [27], where extra layers of applications are involved however, security could be a major concern. This will also be the case when blockchain is integrated with other technology like the Internet of things, AI and the cloud.

The security of blockchain rests upon two one-way cryptographic technologies: cryptographic hash functions and digital signatures. Most blockchain platforms generate this digital signature using the elliptic curve public-key cryptography (ECDSA) or the large integer factorization algorithm (RSA) [27]. Unfortunately, what determines the security of these algorithm is the computational complexity of some mathematical algorithms. Unfortunately computers like the quantum computers could solve these algorithms thereby making underlying digital signature algorithm vulnerable to attack. The Grover search algorithm for example could lead to the 51% attack by enabling a quadratic speedup in calculating the reverse hash function used in blockchain.

Another security concern in blockchain is smart contracts. Smart contracts cannot access data outside of their network without the use of external third-party services. This third-party service uses what is known as oracles, a data feed or an agent that communicate real world occurrences to the blockchain. Effective implementation of an oracles come with huge security challenges because third party data sources cannot be fully reliable for trustless execution in a blockchain network. Data from oracles should therefore be properly authenticated using appropriate methods. Finally, a smart contract should be developed following best practices in software engineering to ensure code security and quality. A poorly written smart contract may contain a bug or security hole that attacker may leverage to compromise the system.

5.5 Issue with Privacy

An important feature of the blockchain is transparency where transactions can be audited, traced back and verified from the first transaction. In fact, all data in a blockchain is public by default and this means no privacy. Trust is maintained in the blockchain by keeping data transparent in this way. This situation directly raises the issue of privacy in blockchain and it becomes even more serious with the Internet of things when it involves a privacy sensitive information such as smart home devices and smart medical devices.

The current anonymity features in blockchain is not be enough to protect privacy and it is highly recommended that more efforts should be made to provide stronger pseudonyms [9] as the data in a blockchain can be accessed by anyone [30]. In order to solve the problem of privacy in blockchain, homomorphic encryption can be used on blockchain data. Homomorphic encryption is the ability to perform compute operations directly on encrypted data. Blockchain like Enigma is able to perform computation on data without exposing the raw data to the nodes of the network by encrypting data and then splitting the data in the network. Zerocash [30] improves upon user privacy by hiding user attributes such as identity, transaction activities and account balances from public access.

5.6 Issue with Governance and Regulation

Governance and Regulation is very important for blockchain standards, interoperability, integration, and architecture. Work in this area has been slow probably due to the complexity of blockchain technology and early stages of its development. According to [6], standard making bodies such as IEEE, NIST and ITU are making progress towards standardizing blockchain. Regulating blockchain is not going to be easy because of the nature of the technology as it was designed with no regulation in mind. However, some level of regulation in form of private and consortium blockchains are currently present [9].

A new set of regulations has to be made to guide the integration of blockchain with other technologies such as IoT, AI and Cloud computing. This could help set standards for the security features that these technologies must have in order to operate.

6 Conclusion

In this work, we reviewed Blockchain technology and identified its integration issues with Internet of things and the need to further extend this integration to include AI and cloud computing. We introduced current state of affairs in the blockchain space and how blockchain is being adopted in areas such as healthcare, government, supply chain management etc. with the Internet of things. We have an integration diagram for blockchain in action with IoT, AI and the cloud. The issues discussed in this paper must be solved to achieve a successful integration of Blockchain and IoT. We summarized major blockchain implementations taking the consensus algorithm used into consideration. There are significant improvements on the Proof of Work (PoW) consensus seen in early blockchains like the bitcoin and Ethereum in form of Proof of Stake (PoS), Proof of Space (PoS), Proof of Burn (PoB), Proof of Importance (PoI) etc. However, the consensus layer still remains an open research issue to be solved in the upcoming generations of blockchain. Other open issues are scalability, interoperability, security, privacy, efficiency and regulation. These issues are currently standing on the way of a successful integration of blockchain and Internet of Things and may take a while to fully resolve.

References

1. Sadiku, M.N.O.: Emerging Internet-Based Technologies. CRC Press, Boca Raton (2019)
2. Zheng, Z., et al.: An overview of blockchain technology: architecture, consensus, and future trends. In: Proceedings of the IEEE 6th International Congress on Big Data, pp. 557–564 (2017)
3. Miller, D.: Blockchain and the Internet of Things in the industrial sector. IEEE IT Prof. 20(3), 15–18 (2018)
4. Sagirlar, G., et al.: Hybrid-IoT: hybrid blockchain architecture for Internet of Things-PoW sub-blockchains, pp. 1–10 (2018). https://arxiv.org/pdf/1804.03903.pdf
5. Dinh, T.N., Thai, M.T.: AI and blockchain: a disruptive integration. IEEE Comput. 51(9), 48–53 (2018)
6. Salah, K., Rehman, M.H., Nizamuddin, N., Al-Fuqaha, A.: Blockchain for AI: review and open research challenges. IEEE Access 7, 1–23 (2019)
7. Samaniego, M., Deters, R.: Blockchain as a service for IoT. IEEE International Conference on Internet of Things and Green Computing and Communications, pp. 433–436 (2016)
8. Opportunities and Use Cases for Distributed Ledger Technologies in IoT (2018). https://www.gsma.com/iot/wp-content/uploads/2018/09/Opportunities-and-Use-Cases-for-Distributed-Ledgers-in-IoT-f.pdf
9. Reyna, A., et al.: On Blockchain and Its integration with IoT. Future Gener. Comput. Syst. 88, 173–190 (2018)
10. Novo, O.: Blockchain meets IoT: an architecture for scalable access management in IoT. IEEE Internet of Things J. 5(2), 1184–1195 (2018)
11. Zoican, S., Zoican, R., Vochin, M., Galatchi, D.: Blockchain and consensus algorithms in Internet of Things. In: Proceeding of the International Symposium on Electronics and Telecommunications (ISETC), pp. 1–4 (2018)
12. Pahl, C., El Ioini, N., Helmer, S.: A decision framework for blockchain platforms for IoT and edge computing. In: International Conference on Internet of Things, Big Data and Security (2018)

13. Biswas, S., Sharif, K., Li, F., Nour, B., Wang, Y.: A scalable blockchain framework for secure transactions in IoT. IEEE Internet of Things J. 1–10 (2018)
14. Almadhoun, R., Kadadha, M., Alhemeiri, M., Alshehhi, M., Salah, K.: A user authentication scheme of IoT devices using blockchain-enabled fog nodes. In: Proceedings of the IEEE/ACS 15th International Conference on Computer Systems and Applications, Jordan, Aqaba, pp. 1–8 (2018)
15. Zhang, Y., Kasahara, S., Shen, Y., Jiang, X., Wan, J.: Smart contract-based access control for the Internet of Things. IEEE Internet of Things J. 1 (2018)
16. Ølnes, S., Ubacht, J., Janssen, M.: Blockchain in government: benefits and Implications of distributed Ledger Technology for information sharing. Gov. Inf. Q. **34**, 355–364 (2017)
17. Sadiku, M.N.O., et al.: Blockchain technology in healthcare. Int. J. Adv. Sci. Res. Eng. **4**(5), 154–159 (2018)
18. Oracle: Transformational Technologies Today How IoT, AI, and blockchain will revolutionize business. http://www.oracle.com/us/solutions/cloud/tt-technologies-white-paper-4498079.pdf
19. Cachin, C., et al.: Blockchain. Cryptography and Consensus, IBM Research (2017)
20. Sadiku, M.N.O., et al.: Smart contract: a primer. J. Sci. Eng. Res. **5**(5), 538–541 (2018)
21. Uddin, M.A., et al.: An efficient selector miner consensus protocol in blockchain oriented IoT smart monitoring (2018). https://www.researchgate.net/publication/329235620_An_Efficient_Selective_Miner_Consensus_Protocol_in_Blockchain_Oriented_IoT_Smart_Monitoring
22. Dwivedi, A.D., et al.: A decentralized privacy-preserving healthcare blockchain for IoT. Sensors **19**(2), 326 (2019)
23. Corea, F.: AI and blockchain. In: Corea, F. (ed.) An Introduction to Data. SBD, vol. 50, pp. 69–76. Springer, Cham (2019). https://doi.org/10.1007/978-3-030-04468-8_11
24. Alasadi, S.A., Bhaya, W.S.: Review of data preprocessing techniques in data mining. J. Eng. Appl. Res. **12**, 4102–4107 (2017)
25. Ali, M.S., Dolui, K., Antonelli, F.: IoT data privacy via blockchains and IPFS. In: Proceedings of the 7th International Conference on the Internet of Things. ACM, New York (2017)
26. King, S., Nadal, S.: PPCoin: peer-to-peer crypto-currency with proof-of-stake, vol. 19 (2012). https://decred.org/research/king2012.pdf
27. Bitfinex: The world Largest Cryptocurrency platform. https://www.bitfinex.com
28. Kiktenko, E.O., et al.: Quantum-secured blockchain. Quantum Sci. Technol. **3**(3), 1–7 (2018)
29. Ellul, J., Pace, G.J.: AlkylVM: a virtual machine for smart contract blockchain connected Internet of Things. In: Proceedings of the 9th IFIP International Conference on New Technologies, Mobility and Security, pp. 1–4 (2018)
30. Ben-Sasson, E., et al.: Zerocash: decentralized anonymous payments from bitcoin. In: Proceedings of IEEE Symposium on Security & Privacy, pp. 459–474 (2014)

Wikipedia as an Information Source on Cryptocurrency Technology

Piotr Stolarski$^{(\boxtimes)}$ ⓘ and Włodzimierz Lewoniewski ⓘ

Poznań University of Economics and Business,
al. Niepodległości 10, Poznań, Poland
{Piotr.Stolarski,
Wlodzimierz.Lewoniewski}@ue.poznan.pl

Abstract. The paper is an initial study that aims to analyze relations between Wikipedia as an unbiased source of information and cryptocurrency technologies. The purpose of the research is to explore how diversified decentralized cash systems are presented and characterized in the largest open-source knowledge base. Additionally, the interactions between information demand in different language versions are elaborated. A model is proposed that allows to assess the adoption of cryptocurrencies in a given country on the basis of the mentioned knowledge. The results can be used not only for the analysis of popularity of blockchain technologies in different local communities, but also can show which country has the biggest demand on particular cryptocurrency, such as Bitcoin, Ethereum, Ripple, Bitcoin Cash, Monero, Litecoin, Dogecoin and other.

Keywords: Wikipedia · Cryptocurrencies · Bitcoin · Information demand

1 Introduction

Wikipedia has been for long time criticized for its lack of reliability as a source of information. Nevertheless, for the period of its existence this negative attitude and unfavorable opinions about its credibility have partially changed. At the same time, Wikipedia is one of the most important web portals on the modern Internet, which makes it potentially interesting when modeling Internet users' behaviors.

Cryptocurrencies are yet another trend of Internet era. The idea which was introduced in 2009 as a peer-to-peer digital cash analogue within 10-years became a thriving economical ecosystem, which valuation surpasses many national economies. In the meantime, this single digital cash system commenced to replicate in evolutional fashion, so that currently the number of potential cryptocurrencies that can be chosen from to use is immense. However, majority of them is of marginal importance.

Wikipedia has rich sets of information on almost every specialized issue. This encyclopedia reflects – to limited degree - the state of scientific knowledge and may claim to have some potential to influence scientific community [1, 2]. Currently, this encyclopedia has over 50 million articles in over 300 language versions [3]. The broad topic of cryptocurrencies is no exception. In fact, a limited number of studies which used Wikipedia and a limited number of other Internet knowledge sources in

© Springer Nature Switzerland AG 2019
W. Abramowicz and R. Corchuelo (Eds.): BIS 2019 Workshops, LNBIP 373, pp. 299–308, 2019.
https://doi.org/10.1007/978-3-030-36691-9_26

connection with a few chosen cryptocurrencies have been already successfully conducted. Although, the character of the mentioned researches (e.g. [4, 5]) is different as to their approaches and purposes than the one presented herein.

This study examines information about cryptocurrencies using data from Wikipedia. Especially, we introduced the novel popularity model for cryptocurrencies in different countries. This model can help to answer the research question: how the popularity of the selected cryptocurrency depends on the geographical location? Additionally, we investigated how well decentralized cash systems are presented and characterized in the largest multilingual, collaboratively written, web-based knowledge base. Particularly, we focused on quality assessment of information about cryptocurrencies.

A model is proposed that allows to assess the adoption of cryptocurrencies in given country on the basis of all the mentioned knowledge.

2 Related Works

In general, Wikipedia is frequently used as an object of research. Especially when it comes to examine the concepts related with quality or credibility of information source. Wikipedia has been used in two-stage study which identifies the factors in making judgments about believability of the content [6]. Authors of [7] reveals that students frequently use Wikipedia during their study courses. Moreover, they argue that the behavior of additional verification of the information presented in the on-line free encyclopedia is a rather unpopular task.

The perception of Wikipedia as a reliable source of knowledge has been topic of inquiry by [8]. The author assessed that about 33% of students employed Wikipedia in order to find facts and relevant information. The further study by [9] showed that participants of a college group were able to develop a critical approach toward Wikipedia articles.

In [4] the dependencies between Bitcoin, which is the first P2P digital currency, and statistics derived from Wikipedia are subject of study. Additionally, these data are mixed with information that comes from Google Trends (open-access SEO tool).

The aim of [10] is to test numerous hypothesis about possible correlation between several time-series datasets representing market factors. Part of the data describe Bitcoin behavior in the market and the other part is to reflect the traditional economy. This way the authors strive to find interrelationships between the real and crypto economy. A robust research [11] is conducted in a similar spirit as the one previously mentioned. In the study both the traditional determinants of currency value, e.g., supply and demand for the currency as well as causes specific only for digital currencies are considered. The additional and distinctive aspect of the paper is the inclusion of a widely accepted economic model, namely Barro's model for gold.

The result reported in [5] is that Bitcoin parallelly exemplifies a very specific blend of typical financial assets properties and speculative features. Three types of factors that have feasible influence on Bitcoin value are examined in the article. The three groups encompasses technical, fundamental and speculative causes.

To sum up the analysis of related literature, one may conclude that the interesting relationships between broad range of online information media and the cryptocurrency market has been already noticed by previous researchers. Wikipedia has been perceived as one of these influential medium. Furthermore, although the quality of articles and the credibility of Wikipedia is questionable, it is now much more believable as a source of knowledge than it used to be in the past. However, in the context of cryptocurrencies the issues of information quality or credibility have not been analyzed in any way before.

3   Wikipedia as Information Source

From our perspective, Wikipedia may be treated as a three-fold source of information. On the one hand, there is a content layer. Wikipedia is a well-categorized, semi-structured source of lexical units on a chosen topic [12, 13]. On the other hand, there is a statistical data layer about visits, editions and aspects of use [3]. Finally, there is a measures layer which is partially artificial, meaning it can be induced from the first two layers of information [14].

The structured content of the articles that are part of the open encyclopedia gives opportunities for using sophisticated techniques in order to provide interesting ana-lytical insight. The texts are divided into named sections and are associated with quotes and references. Moreover thematic information is aggregated in the form of infoboxes, which contains values for properties that characterize the entity that is being described. This kind of setting calls for using information extraction, text mining, semantic or sentiment analysis.

The foundation hosting all Wikipedia projects make periodically available almost all data concerning many aspects of how the project is performing. The data as well as all the public content are publicized in the form of large dump files [14, 15]. The information that can be obtained in this way contains among others: all pages metadata, subjects templates, media/file descriptions, category trees and articles revision information.

4   Analysis of Cryptocurrencies Knowledge from Wikipedia

4.1   Standards

The main approach of Wikipedia is that it is open to be edited by any volunteering party. At the same time, all the content is expected to meet some quality expectations, which are reflected in rules. For example, Wikipedia articles must be written with the appropriate style and present facts from a neutral point of view [14].

The creation and work on articles is based on assumption that the editors will strive to obtain a stable version by reaching consensus. The more technical side of Wikipedia in order to enforce certain behaviors or omissions uses extensive article security sys-tem. The system is independent in each language version. The same applies to policies on encouraging improvement in quality of content.

4.2   Measures

The access and analysis of knowledge gathered on Wikipedia as well as data provided by its administrators allow to generate plentiful range of measures and indicators [14, 16]. Together they make possible objective assessment of each aspect of functioning of the platform.

In the context of cryptocurrencies one may examine topics as well as single articles that discuss certain decentralized cash systems. In order to receive a list of articles on a specific area, Wikipedia categories as well as data from semantic knowledge bases, such as DBpedia and Wikidata can be used [3, 17, 18]. This method has been employed in order to obtain all the interesting Wikipedia entries in all languages for the research.

Quality of the Wikipedia articles can be measured using synthetic measure in a scale from 0 to 100 [3]. This kind of measure is used in WikiRank service [19]. In Wikipedia, 77 cryptocurrency systems are described in at least one language version as separate article. The average quality of the article about cryptocurrency in English version is 41.6 (100 units is the maximum). This is 178% higher than the average quality of all articles in this language version. The quality values will be discussed at later point. Figure 1 depicts the temporal distribution of events of creation of particular cryptocurrency encyclopaedic entries. The vertical axis represents the level of quality of subsequent articles. As can be seen Bitcoin entry has the highest excellence, and its level far exceeds other cryptocurrencies described in Wikipedia.

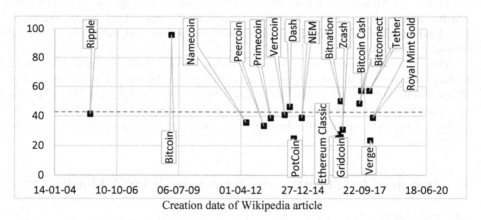

Fig. 1. Chronology of appearance of selected cryptocurrency articles in English Wikipedia.

4.3   Rankings

Wikipedia is an open knowledge base, and everyone can contribute it. However, not any arbitrary content can be placed in this encyclopedia – notable articles must contain verifiable and sourced statements. Additionally, the articles should describe only recognized and undisputed subjects. These quality requirements are obviously the cause of rather limited number of articles that deals with the crypto-economy.

The mentioned WikiRank can be used to assess and compare quality and popularity of the Wikipedia articles in various language versions. Table 1 shows list of the selected articles in English Wikipedia about cryptocurrencies together with values of their quality scores.

Table 1. Simple ranking using WikiRank quality score based on English Wikipedia.

Name	Quality score
Bitcoin	95.91
Ripple (payment protocol)	93.84
Ethereum	88.62
Dogecoin	77.67
Namecoin	64.44
Peercoin	64.25
Devcoin	61.16
Petro (cryptocurrency)	59.82
NeuCoin	57.58
Bitcoin Private	54.46

Data presented in Table 2 blends several rankings in one place. The table lists top 10 cryptocurrencies described in Wikipedia articles according to the number of language versions of any given article available. This number of language versions is given in the second column. Third column contains data on aggregated number of monthly visits of given article. Forth column represents the language chapter which is the most popular. Another column possess the information about the language edition of the article which can be observed as model because it has highest quality rank of all the internationalized versions. Finally, the last column shows overall number of unique authors in all language versions of particular cryptocurrency during one month.

The WikiRank quality score [19] for each Wikipedia article has been used in column fifth of the table. The algorithm is language agnostic and has been computed for any national edition of particular article related to cryptocurrency.

As can be seen in the table, in terms of the cumulative number of views, Bitcoin is the most popular. Consequently, Ethereum and Ripple are on distinguished positions whereas the rest of ranked articles do not have significant popularity level. However, this order is slightly different when it comes to number of articles language versions. Here, Ethereum falls at third place giving way to Litecoin. Ripple is only the sixth behind Dodgecoin and Monero.

In the case of all cryptocurrency articles, the most often visited language edition is English. Nonetheless, this is not always the case when one looks at the sequence according to quality level. This column of the table is relatively differentiated. For example, Bitcoin - contrary to appearances – has the most excellent description in Russian, whereas Litecoin in German, while Ethereum article has the top content in Chinese.

Table 2. Varied rankings of cryptocurrencies articles on international editions of Wikipedia.

Name	Number of languages	Popularity in all lang. (sum)	The most popular language	The most "quality" lang.	Wikipedians interest in all languages
Bitcoin	96	577 813	en	ru	124
Litecoin	41	22 721	en	de	63
Ethereum	40	89 085	en	zh	55
Dogecoin	32	20 315	en	en	53
Monero	27	20 396	en	zh	36
Ripple	22	35 956	en	uk	26
Dash	18	9 906	en	uk	21
Bitcoin Cash	20	25 412	en	es	32
Zcash	12	7 316	en	zh	16
Namecoin	10	3 587	en	pt	14

The order according to the ranking in last column is similar to the first one. It means that the interest of Wikipedians in all languages reflects the number of language editions for a given cryptocurrency article.

5   Cryptocurrencies Popularity Model

In this section a simple model is given which allows to estimate the information demand for an article that concerns given cryptocurrency based on number of statistical data from Wikipedia. All the data are open and accessible through different means described earlier.

Before the model has been created few assumptions were made about the use of Wikipedia and cryptocurrencies. These assumptions are formulated as follow:

- popularity is at least proportional to number of visits in given period,
- if more than one nationality use the same national language then proportional division of visits is assumed,
- population of a given nationality use in general their national language (the rest that not obey to this rule is negligible),
- the ratio of visits of users from given territory to all visits of the certain language version is constant in time.

The model is represented by the following equation:

$$P(c)_t = \sum_{lang=1}^{N} \alpha(t)_{lang} * V(c)_{lang} \qquad (1)$$

In the above model:

- P is the popularity estimate of certain cryptocurrency c in a given territory (country) t,
- α represents the coefficient indicating the ratio of visits of users from country t to all visits of the certain Wikipedia language version,
- V is the overall number of monthly views of selected cryptocurrency article in a given Wikipedia language version,
- N is the total number of analyzed Wikipedia internationalized editions.

During the course of the study all Wikipedia internationalized editions were taken into account. The processing of data also encompassed large majority of all countries in the world and every article concerned with whatever cryptocurrency described in any edition. Exemplary values of α coefficient are presented in Table 3. Columns show particular language versions of the Wikipedia. Rows depict selected states.

Table 3. Ratio of visits of users from selected countries to all visits of the certain Wikipedia language version.

Country	Language version									
	de	en	es	fr	it	ja	pl	pt	ru	zh
BR	.0006	.0064	.0029	.0014	.0015	.0003	.0002	.7961	.0027	.0004
CA	.0013	.0456	.0015	.0529	.0024	.0012	.0024	.0015	.0028	.0191
DE	.7648	.024	.0049	.0124	.0091	.0027	.0191	.0049	.0175	.0096
FR	.0089	.012	.0092	.6733	.012	.0012	.0046	.0039	.0142	.0071
GB	.0037	.0993	.0054	.0066	.0057	.0012	.0182	.0024	.004	.0126
IN	.0005	.0808	.0004	.0007	.0004	.0003	.0004	.0004	.0053	.0008
IT	.0053	.0075	.0024	.0041	.9088	.0004	.0018	.0016	.0034	.0026
JP	.0011	.005	.0006	.0024	.001	.9603	.0005	.0015	.0018	.0302
RU	.002	.0076	.0014	.0023	.0013	.0013	.0016	.0012	.6054	.0065
US	.019	.4117	.0462	.0372	.0122	.0126	.0124	.0576	.0182	.1022

The values of the α coefficient are used according to Eq. 1 in order to calculate the estimated popularity $P(c)_t$. The popularity can be determined in one of two forms. The integral form is the number of users from a given territory anticipated to have visited the cryptocurrency article in the assumed period. The percentile form is the fraction composed of users from particular country divided by total number of citizens of this country which have access to internet. The excerpt from the matrix of popularity values in the integral form are placed in Table 4.

Table 4. Page views of 7 most popular cryptocurrencies for 15 selected countries.

Country	Cryptocurrency						
	Bitcoin	Etherium	Ripple	Bitcoin Cash	Monero	Litecoin	Dogecoin
AU	7500	1236	573	447	278	328	619
BR	23758	1827	974	474	303	563	521
CA	13442	2147	999	769	484	567	1000
DE	47160	7312	3587	3166	1736	1760	1663
ES	10541	1722	557	649	291	442	406
FR	24453	3792	1654	1246	808	882	800
GB	25601	3948	1927	1467	914	1086	2085
ID	11276	866	162	121	76	312	413
IN	24233	3029	1530	1138	715	881	1666
IR	25247	1282	796	692	314	478	786
IT	21054	3154	1234	154	566	754	555
JP	17723	3403	2286	1184	532	447	474
MX	7253	1251	408	495	194	300	297
NL	8923	996	367	245	158	403	303
PL	14441	1385	458	516	66	392	125

5.1 Model Estimation

In order to estimate whether the model works appropriately the results generated by the model were checked against popularity indicators published by Hypestat [20], Alexa [21], and other SEO tools, which can help to indicate trust and reputation of the online services [22]. The comparison involved the importance of users from a particular country within the all visits in tested period. The order of importance taken from the model reflected total number of visits of users from given territory. The SEO tools provided us with alternative ranking of ratio of users from specific states. The results of this assessment are shown on the basis of example of Wikipedia Bitcoin article and SEO data of bitcoin.org portal. The effect of the process is depicted on Fig. 2.

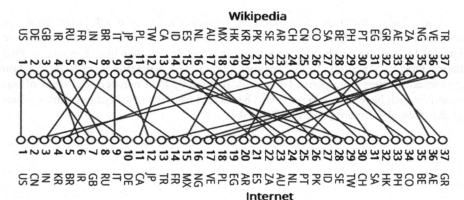

Fig. 2. The comparison of SEO tools and Wikipedia rankings of Bitcoin visitors

On the picture one can see two sequences of country codes. The numbers represent their position within the sequences. The US is in the first place in both rankings. According to the model Germany is on the second place while SEO tools indicate that this place is reserved for China. These two countries are in the alternative ranking accordingly on 10th (DE) and 25th (CN) position.

The Spearman's Rank coefficient was used to estimate the relevance of connection of both orderings. The value of the coefficient r_s was at the level of 0.56235 whereas p (2-tailed) = 0.00029. Such results indicate that by usual standards the association between the values of analyzed two datasets is statistically significant.

6 Conclusions

In the paper we have concentrated on the Wikipedia as an important knowledge base in the global Internet. Although criticized for long time since its deployment, Wikipedia became one of the most important information portal in the modern world. Surely, it is a trustworthy source in comparison to other social or collaborative platforms of content creation.

The article research on measures and statistics that allow to evaluate the information demand and in consequence relative popularity of enumerated cryptocurrencies in Wikipedia. Moreover, as Wikipedia has language versions in almost any world language the data were used to combine a model that permit to extrapolate the information demand of particular language users group. We estimate our findings by comparing the results of the model with some indirect data which should indicate the estimated popularity of cryptocurrency-related web pages.

In future work we plan to extend number of the considered measures in order to improve obtained model. Particularly, inclusion of measures related to content quality in this model looks promising. We also plan to combine data from Wikipedia with other open data sources which provides information about cryptocurrency and various economic indicators.

References

1. Thompson, N., Hanley, D.: Science is shaped by Wikipedia: evidence from a randomized control trial. MIT Sloan Research Paper No. 5238-17, 13 February 2018. SSRN: https://ssrn.com/abstract=3039505 or http://dx.doi.org/10.2139/ssrn.3039505
2. Jemielniak, D., Aibar, E.: Bridging the gap between Wikipedia and academia. J. Assoc. Inf. Sci. Technol. **67**, 1773–1776 (2016)
3. Lewoniewski, W., Węcel, K., Abramowicz, W.: Multilingual ranking of Wikipedia articles with quality and popularity assessment in different topics (2019)
4. Kristoufek, L.: BitCoin meets Google trends and Wikipedia: quantifying the relationship between phenomena of the internet era. Sci. Rep. **3**, 3415 (2013)
5. Kristoufek, L.: What are the main drivers of the Bitcoin price? Evidence from wavelet coherence analysis. PLoS ONE **10**, e0123923 (2015)
6. Rowley, J., Johnson, F.: Understanding trust formation in digital information sources: the case of Wikipedia. J. Inf. Sci. **39**, 494–508 (2013)

7. Menchen-Trevino, E., Hargittai, E.: Young adults' credibility assessment of Wikipedia. Inf. Commun. Soc. **14**, 24–51 (2011)
8. Lim, S.: How and why do college students use Wikipedia? J. Am. Soc. Inf. Sci. Technol. **60**, 2189–2202 (2009)
9. Lim, S., Simon, C.: Credibility judgment and verification behavior of college students concerning Wikipedia. First Monday **16**(4–4) (2011). https://firstmonday.org/ojs/index.php/fm/article/view/3263/2860
10. Georgoula, I., Pournarakis, D., Bilanakos, C., Sotiropoulos, D., Giaglis, G.M.: Using time-series and sentiment analysis to detect the determinants of BitCoin prices. SSRN 2607167 (2015)
11. Ciaian, P., Rajcaniova, M., Kancs, A.: The economics of BitCoin price formation. Appl. Econ. **48**, 1799–1815 (2016)
12. Zesch, T., Müller, C., Gurevych, I.: Extracting lexical semantic knowledge from Wikipedia and Wiktionary. In: LREC (2008)
13. Horn, C., Manduca, C., Kauchak, D.: Learning a lexical simplifier using Wikipedia. In: Proceedings of the 52nd Annual Meeting of the Association for Computational Linguistics, Short Papers, vol. 2 (2014)
14. Lewoniewski, W.: Measures for quality assessment of articles and infoboxes in multilingual Wikipedia. In: Abramowicz, W., Paschke, A. (eds.) BIS 2018. LNBIP, vol. 339, pp. 619–633. Springer, Cham (2019). https://doi.org/10.1007/978-3-030-04849-5_53
15. Wikimedia: Wikimedia Downloads (2019). https://dumps.wikimedia.org/. Accessed 22 Apr 2019
16. Warncke-Wang, M., Cosley, D., Riedl, J.: Tell me more: an actionable quality model for Wikipedia. In: WikiSym 2013 (2013)
17. Erxleben, F., Günther, M., Krötzsch, M., Mendez, J., Vrandečić, D.: Introducing Wikidata to the linked data web. In: Mika, P., et al. (eds.) ISWC 2014. LNCS, vol. 8796, pp. 50–65. Springer, Cham (2014). https://doi.org/10.1007/978-3-319-11964-9_4
18. Lehmann, J., et al.: DBpedia–a large-scale, multilingual knowledge base extracted from Wikipedia. Semant. Web **6**, 167–195 (2015)
19. WikiRank: Quality and popularity assessment of Wikipedia articles (2019)
20. HypeStat: Main page (2019)
21. Alexa: The top 500 sites on the web (2019)
22. Najafi, I., Kamyar, M., Kamyar, A., Tahmassebpour, M.: Investigation of the correlation between trust and reputation in B2C e-commerce using Alexa ranking. IEEE Access **5**, 12286–12292 (2017)

DigEX Workshop

DIGEX 2019 Workshop Chairs' Message

It is with great pleasure that we present the post-proceeding papers of the First International Workshop on Transforming the Digital Customer Experience (DigEx 2019) that was organized in Sevilla, Spain, in conjunction with the 22nd International Conference on Business Information Systems (BIS 2019). It was the first edition of the workshop that responded to an increasing need from the scientific and business communities to find a space to exchange ideas and knowledge in this emerging area. Indeed, the workshop was at the corner between technological and business progresses by focusing on how the mix of new technologies and new organizational models can help in developing services to improve the experience for the digital customer. The workshop embraced concepts from Computer Science, Information Systems, and Business Administration areas. The workshop had 12 submissions in all, among them 5 were accepted for presentation after the reviewing process. Each article was reviewed by four reviewers. The authors were allowed to revise the papers with the reviewers' comments and the discussions of the presentation so that there was a second stage of reviewing before including them in the conference proceedings. Concerning the Program Committee, it included 24 outstanding researchers representing 14 countries from 5 continents. Their evaluation of the submitted papers by using the highest scientific standards enabled us to ensure the workshop quality in terms of the value of the scientific contributions, the excellence of the presentations, and the pertinence of the discussion. We would like to thank the authors of the submitted papers, the members of the Program Committee, the members of the Systems and Computing Engineering Department of Los Andes University that participated and helped in any way to promote the workshop, and the organizers of the BIS 2019 conference belonging to the Poznan University of Economics and Business and the University of Seville. Without their efforts, it would have been impossible to organize this academic event.

Oscar Avila
Virginie Goepp

Organization

Chairs

Oscar Avila	Universidad de los Andes, Colombia
Virginie Goepp	INSA Strasbourg, France

Program Committee

Oscar Avila	Universidad de los Andes, Colombia
Sonia Camacho	Universidad de los Andes, Colombia
Beatriz Helena Díaz	Universidad Nacional de Colombia, Colombia
Hector Florez	Universidad Distrital Francisco José de Caldas, Colombia
Lauri Frank	University of Jyväskylä, Finland
Virginie Goepp	INSA Strasbourg, France
Oscar Gonzalez-Rojas	Universidad de los Andes, Colombia
Laura Gonzalez	Universidad de la República, Uruguay
Paul Grefen	Eindhoven University of Technology, The Netherlands
Olga Kalimullina	The Saint-Petersburg State University of Telecommunications, Russia
Francois Kiefer	INSA Euro-Mediterranee, Morocco
Richard Lackes	TU Dortmund, Germany
Andres Moreno	Universidad de los Andes, Colombia
Patrick Mikalef	Norwegian University of Science and Technology, Norway
Leonardo Muñoz	Universidad de los Andes, Colombia
Christina Pakusch	University of Applied Sciences, Germany
Michaël Petit	Université de Namur, Belgium
Chelsea Phillips	Queensland University of Technology, Australia
Camille Salinesi	Université Paris Sorbonne, France
Mario Sanchez	Universidad de los Andes, Colombia
Markus Siepermann	TU Dortmund, Germany
Sagar Sen	Simula Research Lab, Norway
Mathupayas Thongmak	Thammasat Business School, Thailand

Towards Analyzing High Street Customer Trajectories - A Data-Driven Case Study

C. Ingo Berendes[✉]

Paderborn University, 33098 Paderborn, Germany
ingo.berendes@upb.de

Abstract. Nowadays, many high streets face the problem of declining attractiveness. City management and high street retailers hardly know their customers. Therefore, they can scarcely react to the customers' needs and wishes to make the customer experience more attractive. We aim at studying how customers behave in high streets using a data-driven approach by recording and evaluating customer trajectories with modern positioning technology. For doing so, we carry out a pilot test in order to check whether our approach is suitable for recognizing customer behavioral patterns. The result obtained by a cluster analysis reveals five clusters in the analyzed customer trajectories.

Keywords: High street retail · Shopping motives · Customer behavior · Customer trajectories · Case study

1 Introduction

The high street is one of the main attractions of almost every city for hundreds of years [38]. In the times of digitalization [35], however, a change has taken place that has led to a decline in the significance and economic importance of the high street, which is particularly evident in the diminishing number of visitors [11,21]. The decline in visitor numbers has, in turn, led to a decrease in the attractiveness of the high streets as such, as retailers are dependent on the attractiveness of the high street [15]. Additionally, digitalization is increasingly affecting the visiting intention, shopping behavior, and other habits of high street visitors [11,25].

Digitalization has created new opportunities to learn more about customer behavior in high streets. While customers in a high street are unknown for the retailers, online retailers are situated with detailed knowledge about their customers on the basis of earlier purchases and customers that have bought similar products in the past [28]. Furthermore, they can track the behavior of customers on their shopping website and can learn from what their customers are interested in and how they behave during their online shopping trip to create customer profiles [28]. This gives online retailers the opportunity to provide personalized, tailored offers by recommendation systems [29,43] and thereby the opportunity to actively support their customers' decision-making processes [30]. Retailers in high streets lack similar mechanisms and similar precise knowledge

© Springer Nature Switzerland AG 2019
W. Abramowicz and R. Corchuelo (Eds.): BIS 2019 Workshops, LNBIP 373, pp. 313–324, 2019.
https://doi.org/10.1007/978-3-030-36691-9_27

about customer behavior. Knowledge about customer behavior in high streets, about which businesses they visit, and how long can help both city management and retailers to improve the customer experience and to strengthen local high streets. This knowledge may further be utilized for e.g., high street recommender systems, which recommend personalized offers, new retailers, or even activities of interest to customers in the high streets [8].

Research on customer shopping behavior revealed that customers follow different motives on their shopping trips [38] that can be subsumed in hedonic and utilitarian shopping motives [39]. Most studies, however, have aimed at studying customer behavior in high streets by using surveys or interviews [2, 10, 12, 34]. An observation of customer behavior during a shopping trip in a high street with modern tracking technology such as beacon positioning and Global Positioning System (GPS) positioning has never been done before, although tracking customers using beacons, which broadcast Bluetooth Low Energy (BLE) signals within a range of approximately 10–20 m autonomously [37], is shown to work [46]. Since a customer may interact with several groups of actors in the high street, above all retailers, pubs, and restaurants, who function as service providers [42], we use the term business for all groups of actors.

Inspired by online retailing, our research endeavor aims at analyzing customer behavior in high streets from a data-driven perspective to close the gap between a customer journey in the high street and known shopping motivations from marketing discipline. Therefore, we plan to digitize a medium-sized German city, namely Paderborn, by equipping retailers and points of interest with beacons. A tracking application for mobile phones provided, we track the behavior of customers in the high street during their shopping trip. Following Bhattacherjee's approach [9], we conduct a pilot test first based on GPS prior to equipping the high street with beacons. This pilot test with a smaller amount of customers is performed as it gives us an idea of whether the gathered data at all can be used to analyze customer behavior with beacons in high streets. This paper reports on the results from the pilot test. The research question of our research project is as follows: *To what extent can the behavior of high street visitors be derived from analyzing their shopping trajectories?*

The remainder of this paper is structured as follows. The next chapter provides theoretical background knowledge. Then, we present the research approach of our pilot study and depict first results. Afterward, we discuss the limitations of our research and give an outlook on how we plan to proceed in our main case study to collect data.

2   Theoretical Background

2.1   Customer Experience and Customer Journeys in High Streets

To understand how customers behave in high streets, we draw from theory on both customer journeys [42] and customer experience [26, 41].

While a customer visits the high streets of a city, he/she may interact with different groups of actors, such as other customers, retailers, or service providers [42]. The high street customer journey is the time-logical sequence of touchpoint instances a customer has with other actors "along prepurchase, purchase and postpurchase situations" [20, p.384]. In this context, a touchpoint instance is defined as a discrete interaction between a customer and a service offering actor [47]. In a high street, these situations occur when the customer enters the high streets until he/she leaves it. Customer experience is described as an "evolvement of a person's sensorial, affective, cognitive, relational and behavioral responses to a [service offering] by living through a journey of touchpoints along prepurchase, purchase and postpurchase situations and continually judging this journey against response thresholds of co-occurring experiences" [20, p.384]. Individual customer experience can be generated by offering value propositions and by encouraging interactions [18].

In addition to retail stores, numerous companies and service providers are located in the high street. Besides the "convenience aspect to minimize shopping endeavours in a multi-purpose shopping trip" [39, p.384], a high street offers entertainment [40], such as cultural offerings, municipal offices, restaurants and cafés, and public squares. In contrast to shopping malls, high streets are located in the city center and do not exclusively pursue a commercial/retailing goal [13]. Consequently, there are numerous reasons for individuals to visit the high street, which leads to more diverse customer journeys (and trajectories).

2.2   Shopping Motivation and Customer Behavior

How people shop is a question, research is paying attention to since decades (e.g., [38]). Customers behave depending on their shopping motivation and shopping goal [34]. Research on shopping motives, however, showed that different motives impact customer journeys by inducing customers to shop and visit stores [38].

To learn more about customer behavior, their activities during a shopping trip and their visited stores, researchers use different approaches [2,3,19,31–34]. These studies distinguish between two main shopping values: hedonic and utilitarian shopping values.

A utilitarian shopping value is mainly created by the efficiency of a shopping process [23,24], by an optimal ratio between process input (e.g., resources such as time) and process output (e.g., desired product and low price) [40]. In contrast, a hedonic value arises above all from the benefit that the customer achieves through the shopping trip [3,23]. Learning about the latest trends [38], also referred to as "idea shopping" [2], "adventure shopping" [2] or exploring shopping by so-called "browsers" [22] inter alia "produce hedonic shopping value" [2, p.80].

To learn more about customer behavior, their activities during a shopping trip and their visited retailers, researchers use different approaches. Some studies opt for customer trajectories to describe customer behavior during shopping trips (e.g., [10,33,34]). These studies assemble customers' trajectories by asking customers which businesses they have visited, which activities they have pursued and how much time they have spent in the business and for the activities, respectively. There are no studies observing and analyzing customers' behavior in a real-life context, i.e. high street, yet.

3   Research Approach

Our research aims at closing the gap between a customer journey in the high street and known shopping motivations from marketing discipline. To perform a mapping between theoretical shopping motivations and data-driven customer journeys, we record and analyze the behavior of customers in the high street from a customer journey perspective.

We follow Bhattacherjee's research approach [9] consisting of the three research execution stages *pilot testing*, *data collection*, and *data analysis*, which are carried out sequentially. In this paper, we report on the pilot test as an excerpt from the research process we have conducted prior to proceeding to the data collection stage.

3.1   Pilot Testing Case Description

We designed our pilot test as a case study [44] to detect potential problems in our research design and research instrumentation [9, p.23]. In this pilot test, we do not aim at evaluating the tracking algorithm and technology as such but at finding out whether data about customer trajectories is at all suitable for analyzing customer behavior. This gives us an idea whether our research project is viable. The pilot case study takes place within a real-life context [44] to understand the nature and complexity [5,16] of customer behavior in high streets. To test the viability, we selected a subset of our targeted study participants (test customers) and developed a mobile application for Android mobile devices that tracks how our test customers move within the high street using GPS signals. We already knew that beacons can be used for positioning and tracking purposes both indoor and outdoor [7,14,46]. But for the pilot test, we chose GPS as it does not require any investment into beacons or winning and participation of businesses and other service providers since a success of our research endeavor was not guaranteed. Pilot testing was conducted between July and September 2018 in the city center of Paderborn. In accordance with the official definition of the town planning department [36], we define the high street in the city to be within the inner traffic circle. We regard Paderborn as a representative example of about 40 cities in Germany, which are home for 100.000–200.000 residents and are characterized by similar high street structures containing a variety of small and medium-sized enterprises (SMEs) and branches of large retail chains.

Forty-eight test customers took part in the pilot test. Nineteen of them were male, 29 female. At the time of the pilot test, all test customers ranged between 18 and 62 years, 40 test customers were between 18 and 40 years old.

When a test participant enters the defined high street area, he/she starts the recording mechanism in the app. The app then locates the GPS position every 20 seconds. We chose this recording interval, as we found out in various, previously run tests that it keeps the power consumption at an acceptable level while the behavior of our test customers in the high streets can – for our purposes – still be reliably tracked. In that case, the app loses the connection (e.g., the user has entered a building such as a store, bar, shopping mall where GPS signals are not available), it records empty values until a new GPS position can be received. This is to later sort out faulty customer trajectories and to be able to interpret the missing values as visiting a store, bar, shopping mall, respectively. Before the recording is started, the participant is asked to answer a survey which asks for the goal of the upcoming shopping trip. When the customer is about to leave the high street, the participant stops his/her shopping trip and is asked to confirm his/her shopping goal or to enter a new shopping goal in case, it has changed during the shopping trip. The following shopping goals are derived from scholar on shopping motives presented in Sect. 2.2 and were eligible for the participants: *looking for cheap prices, looking for particular product, looking for a present, social interaction, request for consultation, having an adventure, looking for diversion, entertainment, relaxation, reward,* and *hunting bargains.* Additionally, we added *traversing the high street* as participants can enter the high street without shopping intention. Furthermore, the participants were asked to select their gender, their age range, and whether they are accompanied.

The pilot testing stage with the mobile app was conducted in strict accordance with the General Data Protection Regulation (GDPR). The mobile app was designed to manage without any personal information (except age range and gender) and could be used anonymously. After the recording mechanism has been stopped, the app shows the recorded trajectory in a map and enables the user to destroy the recorded data or to send it to our servers for our research endeavor.

3.2 Data Transformation and Data Analysis

The results from pilot testing need then to be transformed to extract the information about where the trip was started, which trajectories a customer followed, which business he/she visited and how long he/she stayed there. For pilot testing, we chose GPS technology for recording customer trajectories. The results, however, tracked by using GPS were expected to differ from those tracked by beacons in the main data collection setting in the main study. While GPS enables exact positioning (deviation of a few meters possible) [45], beacons send out a BLE signal continuously within a small range allowing deriving an approximate distance between beacon and receiver [46].

As these two recording mechanisms differ, a transformation of the gathered data was required to simulate the dataset that will be collected with beacons in the main data collection stage. To transform the gathered data, we applied a data schema that corresponds to event-based customer journey touchpoint data [6] derived from beacon contacts as we argue that a touchpoint is a discrete interaction between the customer and a service provider [47]. Touchpoints in a time-logical sequence in a purchase process are described as customer journey [42].

For the transformation process, we borrowed some of Berendes, Bartelheimer, Betzing, and Beverungen's [6] customer journey event types: *Customer has entered the high street area, Customer has left the high street, Customer has entered service provider's vicinity, Customer has left service provider's vicinity,*

Customer has entered service provider's entrance area, Customer has left service provider's entrance area, and *Customer's position has been tracked.* In case, a customer spends some time in a park, this period of time would be transformed as a sequence of "Customer's position has been tracked" events within the park area. In the main data collection stage, these events will be triggered by beacons we placed on points of interest.

After data had been transformed, we checked whether the transformed data can be used to analyze customer behavior in high streets. We opted for cluster analysis. For clustering journeys, we used data such as the event type, the sort of business, the business' position, and the duration of the event. Additionally, we examined the time span between events. We paid particular attention to the time span between the events *Customer has entered service provider's vicinity* and *Customer has left service provider's vicinity* as well as *Customer has entered service provider's entrance area* and *Customer has left service provider's entrance area.* By doing so, we could infer both that a customer strolls through the high street or that he/she is on the way to a predefined business and that he/she entered the business and interacted with the business.

Based on the explanation of [10,12] and [34], we derived the following variables for a cluster analysis based on customer's trajectories: *duration of shopping trip, duration of walking within high street, distance walked within high street, duration of leisure or touristic activities, duration in drugstores, duration in electrical stores, duration in furniture/decoration stores, duration for financial services, duration in grocery stores, duration in clothing stores, duration in restaurant/pubs/cafés, duration in other stores,* and *amount of visited stores.* These variables are used for clustering customers by their shopping behavior in high streets. Each customer journey needs to be converted into values for these variables. The upcoming cluster analysis will be applied on these values.

For building clusters, we applied a two-stage approach similar to the approach proposed by Milligan and Sokol [27]. In the first stage, we used the ward method, also known as minimum variance method, to build initial cluster centroids and to determine the optimal amount of clusters. After that, we applied the k-means method for optimization in the second stage.

4   Pilot Test of Customer Trajectories Analysis

The recorded data consists of 265 customer trajectories, of which 208 trajectories are regarded as being valid for the cluster analysis. Fifty-seven customer trajectories have been sorted out as they were not complete (e.g., recording started too late or stopped too early) or due to recording failure after having lost the GPS signal. The remaining 208 customer trajectories were used to build event-based customer journeys, which then were converted to quantitative values for the variables. Table 1 shows an excerpt from one recorded customer trajectory after conversion to an event-based customer journey. The position of the business (service provider) was left out and retailer names were replaced by synonyms on account of data protection.

Table 1. Excerpt from one selected customer trajectory from the pilot test

Event type	Retailer information	Sector	Timestamp (hh:mm:ss)
Customer enters high street			10:02:31
Customer's position tracked			10:02:41
Customer enters vicinity	Bob's bakery	Grocery store	10:03:23
Customer leaves vicinity	Bob's bakery	Grocery store	10:03:35
Customer enters vicinity	Charly's cocktail bar	Pub	10:04:13
Customer leaves vicinity	Charly's cocktail bar	Pub	10:04:25
Customer enters vicinity	Clare's clothes	Grocery store	10:05:13
Customer leaves vicinity	Clare's clothes	Grocery store	10:05:30
Customer enters vicinity	Adam's coffee shop	Café	10:06:02
Customer has entered stores's entrance area	Adam's coffee shop	Café	10:06:08
Customer conducts purchase	Adam's coffee shop	Café	10:09:24
Customer has left stores's entrance area	Adam's coffee shop	Café	10:42:16
Customer leaves vicinity	Adam's coffee shop	Café	10:42:31
Customer's position tracked			10:42:54
Customer enters vicinity	Emily's tea house	Café	10:44:23
Customer leaves vicinity	Emily's tea house	Café	10:44:58
Customer's position tracked			10:46:03
[...]			
Customer leaves high street			14:48:41

The applied cluster analysis showed five clusters that are presented in table 2. Additionally, the table shows the shopping goals, which were selected for the shopping trip after the recording was stopped, and the percentage of the selection. Those goals that made up less than 5% of the mentions in each cluster were left out. The trajectories grouped in the clusters are distinct from each other, which can be seen above all in the shopping goals mentioned by the study participants. A look at the shopping trajectories reveals that the shopping goals of high street visitors are reflected in the trajectories and that high street visitors behave according to their shopping goals during their shopping trip.

Taking a closer look at the shopping trips in the respective clusters, it reveals that the clusters clearly show either a hedonic or a utilitarian character (except for cluster *three*). A comparison with the mentioned shopping goals confirms this impression. Shopping trips in the *first* cluster are almost exclusively utilitarian. They were mainly carried out to search for a particular product and to obtain advice if necessary. In contrast, shopping trips in cluster *two*, *four*, and *five* are predominantly hedonic. These three clusters differ in the way of how the

Table 2. Built clusters with description of main characteristics

	Description of main characteristics	Mainly mentioned shopping goals
1	This cluster summarizes mainly trajectories recorded by male customers. The trajectories mainly show visits in clothing stores and drugstores. It is noticeable that the time spent in the high street is the lowest in all clusters. By comparing walking distance and time spent in the high street, it can be assumed that these trajectories show a shopping trip that had a predefined goal, namely, looking for a specific product	looking for particular product (74%), request for consultation (9%)
2	Cluster 2 aggregates trajectories showing an opposite behavior. These trajectories include visited businesses from all kind of stores and bars. The amount of visited stores is the highest of all clusters	Looking for diversion, entertainment, relaxation, reward (67%), social interaction (14%)
3	The third cluster contains trajectories with no specific shaping. The different kinds of businesses were approximately equally visited with a slight focus on clothing stores	(shoppings goals nearly mentioned equally)
4	Trajectories in the forth cluster are characterized by a high duration in the high street with relatively few walked meters in the high street. These customers have mainly spent time in public areas, such as parks. The amount of visited businesses is low. A clear majority of trajectories in this cluster was recorded by female customers	Looking for diversion, entertainment, relaxation, reward (36%), social interaction (31%), looking for present (15%)
5	The fifth cluster mainly summarizes customer trajectories with a relatively high duration spent in restaurant, cafés or bars. Short visits to drugstores and grocery stores can also be observed. Again, a clear majority of trajectories in this cluster was recorded by female customers	Looking for diversion, entertainment, relaxation, reward (41%), social interaction (40%), looking for particular product (6%)

hedonic customer experience is generated. The *second* cluster summarizes all those shopping trips that feature the typical pattern of strolling through the high streets, both alone and accompanied. Contrary to this cluster, those shopping trips are grouped in the *fourth* and *fifth* cluster that are characterized by very few contacts to businesses. The hedonic customer experience in these clusters is mainly created by spending time on public squares and parks (cluster *four*) or in restaurants/cafés/bars (cluster *five*). In some cases, short visits are made to cafés, ice cream parlors, and drugstores, respectively. Shopping trips in the *third* cluster are too diverse to generalize their characteristics.

5   Contribution, Limitations, and Outlook

The pilot test revealed five clusters that could be built based on customer trajectories in high streets. We could show that high street visitors behave according to their shopping goals during their shopping trip. Verification of the results in the upcoming main study provided, we assume that the shopping goals, vice versa, can be derived from the customers' behavior in the high streets. For our upcoming main study, we expect that analyzing customer trajectories based on beacon signals is a possible way to study customer behavior in high streets.

In this pilot study, we used event-based trajectories to simulate data that is gathered when using beacons. Our transformation, however, does not take possible problems into account when capturing beacon signals, e.g., missing values if a customer passed a business too quickly without the app being able to recognize him/her. GPS tracking has advantages in regards to how a customer behaves in high streets. Strolling through the high street or having a designated target is easier to recognize as GPS allows to capture the customer's position whenever it is required. But it is also accompanied by drawbacks, such as missing data protection and the feeling of being observed all the time. Additionally, our participants knew that they were taking part in a case study. This fact may have led them to behave differently than they would under normal circumstances. We, however, believe that this effect – mainly known as the Hawthorne effect [1] – has little or no impact on our results for two reasons: Firstly, all study participants and their trajectories remain completely anonymous. We cannot associate a trajectory with a study participant. Secondly, recorded trajectories can be deleted by the participants afterward. This leads to the fact that the data may not fully contain all trajectories, but the remaining ones are to be regarded as real. Furthermore, the number of customer trajectories examined is quite low. The amount, however, is still sufficient for pilot testing in order to determine whether analyzing customer trajectories based on beacon data is a suitable approach to study customer behavior in high streets before equipping the city with beacons. Beyond these limitations, we are aware that customer behavior in high streets depends on many factors. This could include different shopping cultures in different countries and regions, sociological aspects, but also the connection with (public) transport and whether it is a city with tourist appeal, etc. Possible effects of these factors have not been considered in this pilot study.

After pilot testing has been successfully completed, we instantiate a digital community platform (see [4] for more details) that serves as the primary data source for our endeavor of studying customer shopping behavior. On this platform, we use beacons for our tracking purpose. The beacon technology makes outdoor tracking and indoor navigation and positioning possible [14]. We equip the participating businesses within the inner city circle with at least two beacons in order to track whether a customer is passing or entering a business and how long he/she remains in that business. Additionally, we equip lanterns with beacons to achieve a higher beacon coverage in the high street and better data quality. We plan to call up some additional information to understand what a customer actually did during his/her high street visit as it sometimes remains unclear by only interpreting the events in a customer journey.

The following data analysis can aim at enhancing theory on customer shopping motives and customer behavior in high streets from a data-driven perspective. Future research could test existing theory on customer shopping types and contribute a novel model describing customer shopping types based on recorded customer trajectories.

Retailers in a high street can use the behavior classification to target only a specific group of high street visitors for their marketing campaigns. As utilitarian customers have a predefined goal for their high street shopping trip (e.g., looking for a particular product) [17], they might be addressed differently than hedonically motivated customers that are possibly more sensitive to product recommendations [20]. City managers could use the knowledge to monitor whether both hedonic and utilitarian shopping motives are satisfied to maintain the attractiveness of a city's high streets. We believe that the attractiveness of a high street can be strengthened digitally. To provide digital services in a high street context, knowledge about customers and their behavior in high streets is necessary. One step to do so is towards analyzing high street customer trajectories.

Acknowledgements. This paper was developed in the research project *smartmarket²*, which is funded by the German Federal Ministry of Education and Research (BMBF), promotion sign 02K15A073. The authors thank the Project Management Agency Karlsruhe (PTKA).

References

1. Adair, J.G.: The Hawthorne effect: a reconsideration of the methodological artifact. J. Appl. Psychol. **69**(2), 334 (1984)
2. Arnold, M.J., Reynolds, K.E.: Hedonic shopping motivations. J. Retail. **79**(2), 77–95 (2003)
3. Babin, B.J., Darden, W.R., Griffin, M.: Work and/or fun: measuring hedonic and utilitarian shopping value. J. Consum. Res. **20**(4), 644–656 (1994)
4. Bartelheimer, C., Betzing, J.H., Berendes, I., Beverungen, D.: Designing multisided community platforms for local high street retail. In: 26th European Conference on Information Systems, ECIS 2018, Portsmouth, UK (2018)
5. Benbasat, I., Goldstein, D.K., Mead, M.: The case research strategy in studies of information systems. MIS Q. **11**(3), 369–386 (1987)
6. Berendes, C.I., Bartelheimer, C., Betzing, J.H., Beverungen, D.: Data-driven customer journey mapping in local high streets: a domain-specific modeling language. In: 39th International Conference on Information Systems, ICIS 2018, San Francisco, CA, USA (2018)

7. Betzing, J.H.: Beacon-based customer tracking across the high street: perspectives for location-based smart services in retail. In: 24th American Conference on Information Systems, AMCIS: New Orleans, p. 2018, LA (2018)
8. Betzing, J.H., Bartelheimer, C., Niemann, M., Berendes, C.I., Beverungen, D.: Quantifying the impact of geospatial recommendations: a field experiment in high street retail. In: 27th European Conference on Information Systems, ECIS 2019, Stockholm, SE (2019)
9. Bhattacherjee, A.: Social science research: principles, methods, and practices. Global Text Project (2012)
10. Bloch, P.H., Ridgway, N.M., Dawson, S.A.: The shopping mall as consumer habitat. J. Retail. **70**(1), 23–42 (1994)
11. Bollweg, L., Lackes, R., Siepermann, M., Weber, P.: Carrot-or-stick: how to trigger the digitalization of local owner operated retail outlets? In: 51st Hawaii International Conference on System Sciences, HICSS 2018, pp. 3811–3820, Big Island (2018)
12. Borgers, A., Timmermans, H.: A model of pedestrian route choice and demand for retail facilities within inner-city shopping areas. Geogr. Anal. **18**(2), 115–128 (1986)
13. Bromley, R.D.F., Thomas, C.T.: Small town shopping decline: dependence and inconvenience for the disadvanged. Int. Rev. Retail Distrib. Consum. Res. **5**(4), 433–456 (1995)
14. Cay, E., Mert, Y., Bahcetepe, A., Akyazi, B.K., Ogrenci, A.S.: Beacons for indoor positioning. In: 2017 International Conference on Engineering and Technology (ICET), pp. 1–5 (August 2017)
15. Eichholz-Klein, S., Preißner, M., Lerch, C., Brylla, T.: Stadt, land, handel 2020. Technical report, IFH Institut für Handelsforschung Köln, Cologne, Germany (2015)
16. Gable, G.G.: Integrating case study and survey research methods: an example in information systems. Eur. J. Inf. Syst. **3**(2), 112–126 (1994)
17. Ghose, A., Li, B., Liu, S.: Mobile targeting using customer trajectory patterns. Manag. Sci. forthcoming, 1–51 (2018)
18. Grönroos, C., Voima, P.: Critical service logic: making sense of value creation and co-creation. J. Acad. Mark. Sci. **41**(2), 133–150 (2013)
19. Hirschman, E.C., Holbrook, M.B.: Hedonic consumption: emerging concepts, methods and propositions. J. Mark. **46**(3), 92–101 (1982)
20. Homburg, C., Jozić, D., Kuehnl, C.: Customer experience management: toward implementing an evolving marketing concept. J. Acad. Mark. Sci. **45**(3), 377–401 (2015)
21. Köln, I.F.H.: Vitale innenstädte 2016. Technical report, IFH Institut für Handelsforschung Köln, Cologne, Germany (2017)
22. Jarboe, G.R., McDaniel, C.D.: A profile of browsers in regional shopping malls. J. Acad. Mark. Sci. **15**(1), 46–53 (1987)
23. Jones, M.A., Reynolds, K.E., Arnold, M.J.: Hedonic and utilitarian shopping value: investigating differential effects on retail outcomes. J. Bus. Res. **59**(9), 974–981 (2006)
24. Kim, Y.-K.: Consumer value: an application to mall and internet shopping. Int. J. Retail Distrib. Manag. **30**(12), 595–602 (2002)
25. Kumar, V., Anand, A., Song, H.: Future of retailer profitability: an organizing framework. J. Retail. **93**(1), 96–119 (2017)
26. Lemon, K.N., Verhoef, P.C.: Understanding customer experience and the customer journey. J. Mark. **80**(6), 69–96 (2016)

27. Milligan, G.W., Sokol, L.M.: A two-stage clustering algorithm with robust recovery characteristics. Educ. Psychol. Meas. **40**(3), 755–759 (1980)
28. Miyazaki, A.D., Fernandez, A.: Consumer perceptions of privacy and security risks for online shopping. J. Consum. Aff. **35**(1), 27–44 (2001)
29. Park, Y.-J., Chang, K.-N.: Individual and group behavior-based customer profile model for personalized product recommendation. Expert Syst. Appl. **36**(2), 1932–1939 (2009)
30. Ricci, F., Rokach, L., Shapira, B.: Recommender systems: introduction and challenges. In: Ricci, F., Rokach, L., Shapira, B. (eds.) Recommender Systems Handbook, pp. 1–34. Springer, Boston, MA (2015). https://doi.org/10.1007/978-1-4899-7637-6_1
31. Rintamäki, T., Kanto, A., Kuusela, H., Spence, M.T.: Decomposing the value of department store shopping into utilitarian, hedonic and social dimensions: evidence from Finland. Int. J. Retail Distrib. Manag. **34**(1), 6–24 (2006)
32. Rintamäki, T., Kuusela, H., Mitronen, L.: Identifying competitive customer value propositions in retailing. Managing Serv. Qual. Int. J. **17**(6), 621–634 (2007)
33. Ruiz, J.-P., Chebat, J.-C., Hansen, P.: Another trip to the mall: a segmentation study of customers based on their activities. J. Retail. Consum. Serv. **11**(6), 333–350 (2004)
34. Saarloos, D., Joh, C.-H., Zhang, J., Fujiwara, A.: A segmentation study of pedestrian weekend activity patterns in a central business district. J. Retail. Consum. Serv. **17**(2), 119–129 (2010)
35. Seeger, G., Bick, M.: Mega and consumer trends - towards car-independent mobile applications. In: International Conference on Mobile Business (2013)
36. Stadt Paderborn - Stadtplanungsamt. Innenstadtverkehrskonzept endbericht, June 2013
37. Stephen Statler. Beacon Technologies: The Hitchhiker's Guide to the Beacosystem. Apress (2016)
38. Tauber, E.M.: Why do people shop? J. Mark. **36**(4), 46–49 (1972)
39. Teller, C.: Shopping streets versus shopping malls - determinants of agglomeration format attractiveness from the consumers' point of view. Int. Rev. Retail Distrib. Consum. Res. **18**(4), 381–403 (2008)
40. Teller, C., Reutterer, T., Schnedlitz, P.: Hedonic and utilitarian shopper types in evolved and created retail agglomerations. Int. Rev. Retail Distrib. Consum. Res. **18**(3), 283–309 (2008)
41. Verhoef, P.C., Lemon, K.N., Parasuraman, A., Roggeveen, A., Tsiros, M., Schlesinger, L.A.: Customer experience creation: determinants, dynamics and management strategies. J. Retail. **85**(1), 31–41 (2009)
42. Voorhees, C.M., et al.: Service encounters, experiences and the customer journey: defining the field and a call to expand our lens. J. Bus. Res. **79**, 269–280 (2017)
43. Xiao, B., Benbasat, I.: E-commerce product recommendation agents: use, characteristics, and impact. MIS Q. **31**(1), 137–209 (2007)
44. Yin, R.K.: Case study research design and methods third edition. Appl. Soc. Res. Methods Ser. **5** (2003)
45. Yoshimura, T., Hasegawa, H.: Comparing the precision and accuracy of GPS positioning in forested areas. J. Forest Res. **8**(3), 147–152 (2003)
46. Yoshimura, Y., Amini, A., Sobolevsky, S., Blat, J., Ratti, C.: Analysis of pedestrian behaviors through non-invasive Bluetooth monitoring. Appl. Geogr. **81**, 43–51 (2017)
47. Zomerdijk, L.G., Voss, C.A.: Service design for experience-centric services. J. Serv. Res. **13**(1), 67–82 (2010)

How Are Negative Customer Experiences Formed? A Qualitative Study of Customers' Online Shopping Journeys

Tiina Kemppainen[1]([✉]) [iD] and Lauri Frank[2] [iD]

[1] Faculty of Information Technology and School of Business and Economics, University of Jyvaskyla, Jyväskylä, Finland
tiina.j.kemppainen@jyu.fi
[2] Faculty of Information Technology, University of Jyvaskyla, Jyväskylä, Finland

Abstract. This study investigates how negative customer experiences are formed during customers' online shopping journeys. A qualitative, in-depth dataset collected from 34 participants was employed to identify negatively perceived touchpoints that contribute to the customer experience in a negative way. The findings reveal that negative touchpoints are experienced during customers' entire journeys, particularly after a purchase is completed. We identified 152 negative touchpoints from the data, of which 53 were experienced during search and consideration, 35 when finalizing a purchase, 33 during delivery, and 31 during after-sales interactions with the company. Within these four main categories, 20 subthemes describing the touchpoints and formation of customers' negative experiences were identified therein. The findings highlight the importance of understanding the holistic customer experience formation, including the before- and after-purchase phases of the online shopping journey. In practice, the findings can be utilized in online service design and improvement.

Keywords: Negative customer experience · Customer journey · Touchpoints · Online shopping · E-Commerce · Service design

1 Introduction

The rapidly evolving consumption field, wherein customers are gaining more control and additional consumption opportunities, has created a significant need for researchers and firms to more thoroughly understand the customer experience and its formation. Understanding the customer experience has been assessed as "critical" [1] and placed at the core of a company's offering because top-quality interactions between a customer and a company are becoming increasingly expected along every step of the customer journey.

While the customer experience has been a frequently discussed topic in marketing and information systems research as well as management practice, the collective understanding of the customer experience nevertheless remains limited and fragmented, especially in the online consumption context [2, 3]. Researchers have argued that, while

© Springer Nature Switzerland AG 2019
W. Abramowicz and R. Corchuelo (Eds.): BIS 2019 Workshops, LNBIP 373, pp. 325–338, 2019.
https://doi.org/10.1007/978-3-030-36691-9_28

the customer management discussion has strongly focused on the service provider perspective [4] and exploratory attempts to conceptualize and measure customer experience outcomes [1], the customer-oriented perspectives have attracted less attention. Therefore, it remains unclear what constitutes an experience from a customer's point of view [2] and how customers construct their experiences. Specifically, marketing researchers have recently called for a more thorough understanding of customer perspectives [4, 5] and are increasingly recognizing the need to understand the holistic nature of the customer experience. Overall, understanding the customers' views including their wants and needs plays an important role in all kinds of businesses [6].

In the online context, the majority of past studies have consistently focused on examining customers' positive perceptions toward and beliefs about [7] online shops. Negative customer experience formation has been a scantly researched topic, although previous studies have sufficiently demonstrated the consequences of a negative customer experience, particularly in physical service environments; studies have, for example, indicated that customers' negative experiences can cause substantial damage to a company's reputation and relationship with their customers [8]. Negative experiences have also been demonstrated to affect customer loyalty [9] and influence complaining behaviors [10], repurchase intentions [11], and customers' attitudes toward a company [12]. Negative customer experiences are also frequently communicated to other customers [8], which increases the potential damage caused by a poor experience; today, online channels and social media specifically provide customers with opportunities for sharing their experiences in a fast and easy way. Hence, as the role of online consumption is becoming increasingly important, a more thorough understanding of the incidents that negatively contribute to a customer experience is vital for improving and designing online services that meet the needs of today's consumers.

To address the gaps in the customer experience literature, this paper investigates negative customer experience formation through a customer's lens. A qualitative, in-depth dataset collected from 34 participants is employed to identify negatively perceived touchpoints during customer journeys in an online shopping context. As this study highlights a customer's primary role as an experience constructor, and as experience formation is investigated through a customer journey perspective, this study contrasts with the dominant provider-led approaches that typically study the customer experience during a main service encounter (e.g., a store visit).

This study is structured as follows. First, the study's theoretical background is discussed, which includes both the customer experience and the customer journey. The study's methodology and findings are subsequently presented and, to conclude, the study's contributions and managerial implications are discussed.

2 Theoretical Background

2.1 Customer Experience

The customer experience has been a popular research topic in marketing since the 1990s. Due to the advances in technology and the rise of e-commerce, this experience research has expanded from physical environments to online environments. While marketing researchers have investigated experience from the online consumption perspective [13], information systems research has discussed similar issues with a technological lens by, for instance, paying attention to the use of technology and the user experience [14, 15]. As the word *experience* is both a noun and a verb in the English language, experience has been studied as both an outcome and as a process [16]. In this study, we regard customer experience as an outcome; as a summary of all the meanings customers construct through their customer journeys, during which they interact with a firm or multiple firms through various touchpoints. Negatively perceived touchpoints generate negative meanings and add negative tones to the customer experience, while positively perceived touchpoints have the opposite effect.

It is commonly assumed in the marketing literature that firms can orchestrate an experience to its customers. Therefore, the key elements regarding a customer experience have often been studied with quantitative, predefined, firm-led attributes that measure customers' reactions (e.g., satisfaction) to service environment stimuli. In an online context, the antecedents and consequences of customers' online encounters have been sufficiently identified in various studies, and several models and measurements have been developed to understand the influence of specific firm actions and factors on the customer experience as an outcome [17, 18]. Furthermore, many studies have investigated the interaction between online service providers and their customers [19, 20] during the main service encounter, at which point the customer is directly interacting with the company.

However, despite great interest in the customer experience, researchers have argued that customer experience research nevertheless remains limited and fragmented in both online and offline contexts [3, 5] due to the dominance of provider-oriented and quantitative approaches. According to Heinonen and Strandvik [4], consumption can include many other important activities and meanings other than those that are visible to the company through direct interactions with their customers. Therefore, when applying firm-based measurements to the customer experience, a limited understanding of the total customer experience is obtained, as it provides no information on how the customer experience is influenced by other actors and factors beyond the firm's control [21]. Thus, understanding how customer experiences are constructed through the entire customer journey—including the prepurchase and postpurchase stages—should constitute each company's main interest.

2.2 Customer Journey

The customer journey represents the different phases that characterize an individual's interaction with a service, product, or brand in a certain context. The customer journey is formed through various touchpoints, which are incidents an individual perceives and consciously relates to a given firm or brand. Touchpoints allow customers to construct their experiences with a service, brand, or product because their opinions and perceptions are largely influenced by the contact that is made through touchpoints in different channels. Although customer journeys are interpreted in different ways in the literature and can be described by various scopes, a customer journey is typically characterized as a customer's flow his/her (1) prepurchase actions to the actual

(2) purchase and further to the (3) postpurchase stage. As Lemon and Verhoef [1] explain, prepurchase actions include need recognition, search, and consideration. The purchase phase includes a customer's interactions with the selected company during the purchase event and is characterized by actions such as choice, ordering, and payment. The postpurchase phase covers the interactions after making a purchase that relate in some way to the product or service itself. The postpurchase phase typically includes behaviors such as usage, consumption, and service requests.

Despite the widespread agreement that the customer journey must be understood across all touchpoints, most research has focused on parts of the journey in isolation [22]. The purchase phase has attracted significant attention in the marketing literature, as the influence of marketing activities and the servicescape on one's purchase decision has been of special interest to marketing researchers [1]. However, the proliferation of different channels has led to an explosion in the number of different touchpoints within the customer journey. Therefore, understanding the effects of diverse touchpoints in an equivalent manner is needed in order to holistically understand the customer journey. Today, customers operate in multichannel retail environments, which means they can interact with various companies through various channels during their customer journeys. Information is searched through one channel, purchase is executed through another channel, and the product is retrieved through a third channel. Tynan and McKechnie [23] note that managing the customer experience through its whole lifespan —including the before and after stages—is of great importance, and in-depth knowledge of customers is required to exert such efforts. Studying services from a customer's perspective is beneficial because it provides insights into customers' value creation processes and helps identify the important elements that affect the customer experience within the service context [21].

3   Methodology

As this study's purpose was to gain insights into the customer perspective in online shopping, a qualitative and interpretive research design was applied during data collection. Interpretive methods make sense of human experiences by collecting and analyzing narratives. To collect a versatile set of narratives, individual interviews (N = 7), small-group interviews (N = 9, two to three participants per group), and written essays (N = 18) were used as data. The interview participants were recruited through mailing lists targeted to University of Jyvaskyla's stakeholders, student groups, and staff, and the 500–1000-word essays were collected during a marketing course. The sample included Finnish consumers, 24 of whom were women and 10 of whom were men. The participants' ages varied from 21 to 68 years, but the majority (73.5%) were young adults under 30 years. Most were students (79%), which is explained by the chosen recruitment channels. Most participants visited online stores at least monthly (77%) and made online purchases on a monthly basis (65%). Therefore, the participants can be described as rather accustomed online shoppers, as is typical for Finnish consumers. The respondents' descriptive statistics are reported in Appendix 1.

Individual interviews and group interviews lasted for approximately 60 min and were subsequently recorded and transcribed. Open-ended questions were asked to capture the participants' real-life experiences. All participants were asked to describe themselves as online shoppers and then recall and reflect their own experiences in online shopping by describing their positive and negative experiences as well as their emotions during their online shopping journeys. Because the participants retrospectively reflected on their experiences, the data describes real-life experiences and touchpoints that have remained in these customers' minds and can thus be regarded as important and meaningful events from the customer's perspective.

The data was analyzed with a thematic analysis alongside an inductive coding and analysis process. The analysis was performed with the NVivo software and was grounded in empirical data expressions, wherein the analysis unit was a sentence or statement articulated by a participant. The negatively perceived touchpoints were categorized following a multistep, iterative process wherein all the statements made by participants that described unpleasant and irritating situations during their customer journeys were collected from the data as well as grouped and regrouped multiple times based on their content. The final categorizations and findings are discussed in the following section.

4 Findings

The findings demonstrate that customers face various negatively perceived touchpoints throughout their entire online shopping journeys. Overall, 152 negatively perceived touchpoints were identified from the data. These touchpoints were grouped into four main categories based on the customer journey phases, including: (1) search and consideration (53 references), (2) finalizing the purchase (35 references), (3) delivery (33 references), and (4) after-sales interaction with the company (31 references). Within the main categories, 20 subthemes that describe the touchpoints were identified. The negative customer journey touchpoints are summarized in Appendix 2 and analyzed in detail in the following sub-sections.

4.1 Search and Consideration

Search and consideration is a significant step in the customer journey. During this phase, customers compare various options and search for the best deal. Negatively perceived touchpoints can easily drive the customer to a competitor who is merely a couple clicks away in an online environment. Lack of information (27 references) and navigation difficulties (26 references) in online stores were identified as the main themes contributing to customer experience during the search and consideration phase.

Lack of information was strongly connected to inadequate product descriptions and was experienced on many levels. Undetailed written and pictorial descriptions as well as incorrect information were among the negative touchpoints. As online shoppers rely on product descriptions and pictures to understand what they are buying, copying product information from competitors' webpages, providing outdated information, and exclusively providing limited product information were all perceived as laziness and as signs of a poorly managed online store. The lack of information was considered as a significant buying barrier. The participants reported negative experiences when their wrong impression had led to unpleasant surprises upon receiving their orders, which were not as expected in terms of, for instance, material quality or product dimensions. Overall, the negligent product descriptions reduced customers' trust toward the online store, and some considered inadequate product information the greatest mistake an online store can make.

> *"If there's almost nothing told about the product, it's a sign of unreliability. It tells me about the shopkeeper's attitude towards his business." (Male, 49)*

In addition to product-related content, lack of information was linked to communication with the company. Negative touchpoints were experienced specifically in situations wherein customers were unable to find contact information or receive a response from an online store. Such situations were determined critical in terms of customers' willingness to continue the shopping process with a particular online store. Some customers reported their use of simple e-mail questions as a tool to evaluate a store's service quality and trustworthiness; before ordering from a new shop, this was considered a useful practice for checking whether or not the store actually existed and provided decent customer service. The online store's inability to answer a customer's questions sufficiently or quickly on different channels was perceived as annoying. Chat services were commonly experienced as negative touchpoints because they had failed to provide answers to customers' questions in the expected timeframe.

> *"I don't have any good experiences. It's time consuming, as the same person is probably taking care of ten different chats at the same time." (Male, 26)*

Navigation difficulties were explained by a store's confusing layouts and poor technical functionality. As online shoppers are accustomed to the same general patterns of navigation from their experiences on the online retail sites they regularly use, negatively perceived online stores were described as "messy," "recondite," "structurally confusing," and "difficult to use." Due to customers' high expectations toward the user interface, poor technical functionality, including download slowness, technical errors, and mobile incompatibility, was considered annoying and even unforgivable. Furthermore, distractions such as pop-ups, ads, and music were among the negative touchpoints that disturbed the shopping process.

> *"Those ads, all the flashing ads around...I'm so irritated! They are particularly annoying." (Female, 40)*

Online stores' attempts to communicate with their customers during store visits were perceived as unwanted surprises and espionage. Pop-up chat boxes specifically aroused feelings of discomfort; "I feel I'm under espionage," and "it feels intrusive" were typical customer viewpoints regarding pop-up chats. As many customers considered an online chat similar to dealing with a real person, rejecting the chat aroused discomfort and feelings of impoliteness.

4.2 Finalizing the Purchase

Finalizing the purchase is a critical phase during the customer journey, as the customer has made a purchase decision and is willing to close the deal. The findings demonstrate that the checkout process is a key touchpoint of the online shopping journey. Negatively perceived touchpoints and the interruption of the purchase process at the "late stage" can cause the customer great disappointment due to his/her loss of both the desired product and the time spent on the shopping process. Negative incidents included unpleasant surprises, such as unexpected details concerning an order (e.g., lack of information and payment options). Unexpected terms of delivery (e.g., high shipping costs and service charges, destinations) were a typically negative touchpoint, especially when dealing with foreign online shops. The participants reported feeling betrayed on such occasions as well as being misled to desire something that could not ultimately be reached.

"Sometimes you find out at the end that they do not deliver to Finland. Then you feel betrayed."
(Female, 27)

Identification procedures (e.g., including registration and passwords) were experienced as "frustrating," "time consuming," and "too complicated," touchpoints. Much of this annoyance was connected to pressure caused by different sign-ins, as users today must remember many different usernames and passwords. Registration was also associated with spam mail and, as such, was avoided.

"The number of different passwords is overwhelming. I don't want to create a single account anymore." (Female, 34)

Technical errors at checkout were recalled as highly annoying; typical incidents of this nature included a store not accepting payment information or other details provided by a customer. For many customers, payment success was a threshold issue, and payment failure often led to termination of the customer–firm relationship.

"If I have problems with payment, I'll never go back to that store." (Male, 27)

Furthermore, invalid discount codes at checkout caused puzzlement and anger; "the code does not apply to these products," "the code cannot be combined with other offers," and "this code is valid only for purchases over X euros" were typical unpleasant experiences depicted by the participants.

4.3 Delivery

From a customer's perspective, delivery is often the last mile of the customer journey that ultimately concludes the purchase process. Delivery is also the stage when the online shopping purchase becomes concrete on a physical level and requires some actions from the customer. The findings indicate that negative touchpoints at this stage can have a strong impact on the overall customer experience. Delivery speed and ease of pick-up were identified as especially meaningful to the participants. Slow shipping was reported as a factor that may "ruin the whole shopping experience," especially if shipping is delayed. Overall, fast shipping and various shipping options were expected.

"I'm very annoyed, especially with Finnish companies, as they don't provide immediate delivery...that a taxi brings it to me, no matter what it costs." (Male, 49)

The convenience of delivery was found to be important because the customers wanted to receive their parcels without exerting special effort or wasting time, preferably in locations that were close to their everyday routes. Being forced to pick up the delivery from an unpleasant or inconvenient location and dealing with pricy customs were considered irritating potential side effects of delivery.

> *"The origin of a store itself does not matter as long as I do not have to pay high shipping costs or deal with customs. I am so stingy and lazy that these are threshold issues." (Female, 23)*

A lack of shipping information was also experienced negatively. The participants expressed that they desired transparency—that is, visibility into the size and status of a package throughout the whole delivery process. Some participants specifically linked the negative touchpoints to courier services, which were considered annoying due to their service processes. During these processes, the customer must make special arrangements, such as by setting up an appointment for the delivery or impatiently waiting for the delivery during a workday.

4.4   After-Sales Interaction with the Online Store

After-sales interaction continues a customer's relationship with a firm after a purchase has been completed. In this study, aggressive after-sales marketing, deficiencies in customer service, and complicated or expensive return procedures were identified as negative touchpoints of the customer journey.

Among the interviewed participants, aggressive after-sales marketing was considered damaging to the customer–firm relationship. Being on companies' contact lists was considered annoying, and "not being able to get rid of a store," "too many advertisements sent by e-mail," and "too many newsletters" surfaced as typical causes for irritation. "Only for you" advertisements caused special irritation among the young adults. As these were considered marketing tricks, companies sending such advertisements were interpreted as "underestimating the customer's intelligence." Overall, many participants depicted the receipt of too many e-mails and advertisements from online stores as well as the spamming of customers as foolish and amateur.

> *"It should be pretty self-evident that no one likes it if they get e-mails [from the same firm] several times a week." (Female, 24)*

Contacting customer service after delivery was conveyed as displeasing, troublesome, and a measure that was exclusively taken when absolutely necessary. Some participants reported communication problems with customer service staff due to the staff's lack of knowledge and language skills. Poor translations and spelling mistakes in customer–firm communications were considered a sign of negligence, laziness, and poor service.

> *"There were spelling mistakes on my airline ticket. I got very nervous! I think it is totally incomprehensible to have errors on your airline ticket." (Male, 23)*

Online stores' inappropriate communication styles also caused irritation. Downplaying customers' problems and offering no apology when customers were disappointed stirred up negative emotions among the participants. When returning purchases, complicated returning procedures were identified as negative touchpoints. Thus, online shopping returns were an issue that participants carefully considered before finalizing a purchase, and the availability of cost-free returns was a considerable incentive to make a purchase.

5 Conclusions and Managerial Implications

This study's purpose was to increase the understanding of the customer experience formation in the online shopping context by examining negatively perceived touchpoints during customers' online shopping journeys. This study contributes to the existing literature by addressing the calls for understanding the customer's viewpoint alongside the holistic customer experience [4, 24]. As previous research has dominantly studied the customer experience with provider-led approaches and while favoring customer experience measurements [17, 18, 25], the present study provides new insights by examining customer experience formation through multiple customers' viewpoints, as depicted by customers themselves. Our study adds to the small number of studies [2, 26] that have focused on the customer experience from a customer's perspective in the online shopping context. Furthermore, this study contrasts earlier studies, which have focused on examining customers' positive perceptions and beliefs [7] of online shops. Investigating customer experience formation through customers' lenses provides important knowledge for academics and practitioners, as it helps us more thoroughly understand how customers make sense of services and what they find truly meaningful in a certain context. In this study, the customers retrospectively recalled their negative online shopping experiences. Therefore, the findings demonstrate what kinds of touchpoints during the customers' online shopping journeys generally remain in customers' minds. Understanding what these touchpoints are and how customers interpret them is useful due to their potential effect on customers' future choices regarding online shopping and online stores. Investigating the negative contributors to the customer experience is especially important, as the negative consequences of customers' negative experiences are sufficiently demonstrated in the existing literature [10, 11, 27].

This study's findings demonstrate that, from a customer's perspective, customer experience in online shopping context is built during the entire customer journey and not merely during an online store visit. Customers actively evaluate the entire path with a particular purchase, from the product search to the delivery and onward to other after-purchase activities. During the prepurchase phase, many negative incidents were expectedly related to the online store's appearance, technical functionality, and provided information. In line with previous literature [15], the findings highlight the importance of a finalized and clear user interface as well as carefully created content (e.g., product descriptions). As the aesthetic quality and functional designs of online stores continuously rise alongside customers' expectations of those stores, the provision of an attractive website design plays a key role in successful online sales and a firm's survival in the intensifying competition among online stores. During the purchase phase, the terms of delivery and a smooth checkout process were important touchpoints for determining the customer experience. Closing the sale is every retailer's ultimate goal as well as an important "moment of truth" for a customer because this stage finalizes the consideration process, which may at times last for days or even weeks. This study's findings, as do those of previous studies [28], highlight the convenience of the checkout stage; all the complicated touchpoints that potentially dissuade the customer from completing the purchase should be identified and eliminated by the online store.

Whereas the previous literature has highlighted the phase during which the customer interacts with the main provider [1] (e.g., the online store), this study's findings indicate that partner companies may also play an important role in forming the customer experience. The findings demonstrate the importance of the delivery process, as a considerable amount of customer irritation in the participants' online shopping experiences was caused by shipping processes as well as unawareness and inconvenience related to those processes. In line with previous research [29], the findings reveal that the choice of delivery subcontractors as well as the ease of delivery are significant from the customer's perspective, as poor touchpoints (e.g., delivery delay) cause customer dissatisfaction [30]. Due to the technical advancements and rising standards in online consumption, customers are increasingly expecting quick and easy delivery solutions from online retailers despite the product they order or the industry to which the company belongs. In addition, customers' negative experiences with delivery are often attributed to the online shop from which a purchase is made, as the shop determines which options or services a customer can choose for the later stages of his/her customer journey. As depicted by this study's participants, partner companies are important when selecting the place of purchase. Hence, online stores should carefully choose their subcontractors (e.g., delivery partners). Furthermore, the after-sales communication between the online store and the customer plays an important role in forming the customer experience, as excessively aggressive advertising and return persuasion may negatively influence that experience.

Finally, this study demonstrates that the customer experience in online shopping does not purely occur "online". As negative incidents and touchpoints were linked to both online and offline touchpoints during the entire online shopping journey, online stores are advised to holistically consider their customers' journeys. It is important to understand how customers utilize the multiple service channels available to them, manage conflicts, and come to rely on particular service providers. Understanding the entire customer journey and the most important negative and positive, online and offline touchpoints therein is a key factor for the successful design and management of e-commerce services. Service design methods (e.g., customer journey mapping, including the depiction of customer activities, emotions, pain points, etc.), provide useful tools for online stores seeking to improve their services [31].

The customer insights gained through this study can be utilized and further investigated in research and practice aiming to more thoroughly understand online shopping behavior and customer experiences therein. The formation of customer experiences in the online context should be further studied within different customer groups, through various methods and in diverse service settings. Furthermore, the postpurchase phase of the customer journey specifically requires more attention from both practitioners and academics.

Appendix 1. The Descriptive Statistics of the Respondents (N = 34)

	N = 34	%
Gender		
Male	10	29.4%
Female	24	70.6%
Age		
21–29 years	25	73.5%
30–39 years	4	11.8%
40–49 years	3	8.8%
50–59 years	1	2.9%
60–69 years	1	2.9%
Status		
Student	27	79.4%
Employee	6	17.6%
Retired	1	2.9%
On average, how often do you visit online stores?		
Daily	1	0.5%
Weekly	13	25.1%
Monthly	16	51.6%
Yearly	4	20.5%
Less than yearly	0	2.3%
On average, how often do you make online purchases?		
Daily	0	0.0%
Weekly	3	8.8%
Monthly	19	55.9%
Yearly	12	35.3%
Less than yearly	0	0.00%

Appendix 2. Negative Touchpoints During Customers' Online Shopping Journeys

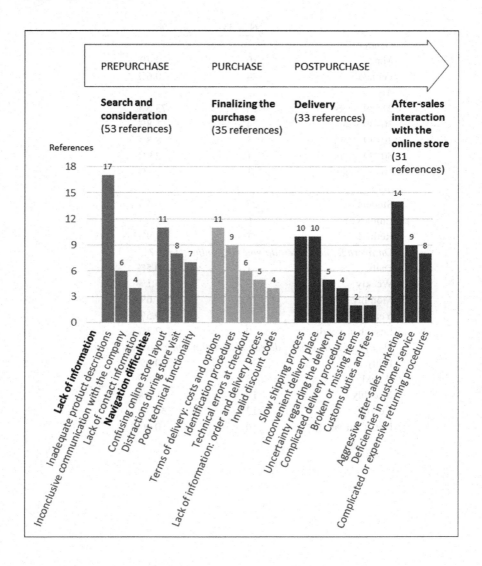

References

1. Lemon, K.N., Verhoef, P.C.: Understanding customer experience throughout the customer journey. J. Mark. **80**(6), 69–96 (2016)
2. Kawaf, F., Tagg, S.: The construction of online shopping experience: a repertory grid approach. Comput. Hum. Behav. **72**, 222–232 (2017)
3. McLean, G., Wilson, A.: Evolving the online customer experience... is there a role for online customer support? Comput. Hum. Behav. **60**, 602–610 (2016)
4. Heinonen, K., Strandvik, T.: Reflections on customers' primary role in markets. Eur. Manag. J. **36**(1), 1–11 (2018)
5. McColl-Kennedy, J.R., Zaki, M., Lemon, K.N., Urmetzer, F., Neely, A.: Gaining customer experience insights that matter. J. Serv. Res. **22**(1), 8–26 (2019)
6. Kettunen, E., Kemppainen, T., Lievonen, M., Makkonen, M., Frank, L., Kari, T.: Ideal types of online shoppers: a qualitative analysis of online shopping behavior. In: MCIS Proceedings (2018)
7. Hasan, B.: Perceived irritation in online shopping: the impact of website design characteristics. Comput. Hum. Behav. **54**, 224–230 (2016)
8. Svari, S., Slåtten, T., Svensson, G., Edvardsson, B.: A SOS construct of negative emotions in customers' service experience (CSE) and service recovery by firms (SRF). J. Serv. Mark. **25**(5), 323–335 (2011)
9. Roos, I., Friman, M., Edvardsson, B.: Emotions and stability in telecom-customer relationships. J. Serv. Manag. **20**(2), 192–208 (2009)
10. Stephens, N., Gwinner, K.P.: Why don't some people complain? A cognitive-emotive process model of consumer complaint behavior. J. Acad. Mark. Sci. **26**(3), 172–189 (1998)
11. Grewal, D., Levy, M., Kumar, V.: Customer experience management in retailing: an organizing framework. J. Retail. **85**(1), 1–14 (2009)
12. Davidow, M.: Organizational responses to customer complaints: what works and what doesn't. J. Serv. Res. **5**(3), 225–250 (2003)
13. Bilgihan, A., Kandampully, J., Zhang, T.: Towards a unified customer experience in online shopping environments: antecedents and outcomes. Int. J. Qual. Serv. Sci. **8**(1), 102–119 (2016)
14. Hassenzahl, M., Tractinsky, N.: User experience-a research agenda. Behav. Inf. Technol. **25**(2), 91–97 (2006)
15. Nielsen, J.: Designing Web Usability: The Practice of Simplicity. New Riders Publishing, Indianapolis (1999)
16. Helkkula, A.: Characterising the concept of service experience. J. Serv. Manag. **22**(3), 367–389 (2011)
17. Cho, N., Park, S.: Development of electronic commerce user-consumer satisfaction index (ECUSI) for internet shopping. Industrial Management & Data Systems **101**(8), 400–406 (2001)
18. Novak, T.P., Hoffman, D.L., Yung, Y.: Measuring the customer experience in online environments: a structural modeling approach. Mark. Sci. **19**(1), 22–42 (2000)
19. Constantinides, E.: Influencing the online consumer's behavior: the web experience. Internet Res. **14**(2), 111–126 (2004)
20. McLean, G., Osei-Frimpong, K.: Examining satisfaction with the experience during a live chat service encounter-implications for website providers. Comput. Hum. Behav. **76**, 494–508 (2017)
21. Trischler, J., Zehrer, A., Westman, J.: A designerly way of analyzing the customer experience. J. Serv. Mark. **32**(7), 805–819 (2018)

22. Baxendale, S., Macdonald, E.K., Wilson, H.N.: The impact of different touchpoints on brand consideration. J. Retail. **91**(2), 235–253 (2015)
23. Tynan, C., McKechnie, S.: Experience marketing: a review and reassessment. J. Mark. Manag. **25**(5–6), 501–517 (2009)
24. Ordenes, F.V., Theodoulidis, B., Burton, J., Gruber, T., Zaki, M.: Analyzing customer experience feedback using text mining: a linguistics-based approach. J. Serv. Res. **17**(3), 278–295 (2014)
25. Rose, S., Clark, M., Samouel, P., Hair, N.: Online customer experience in e-retailing: an empirical model of antecedents and outcomes. J. Retail. **88**(2), 308 (2012)
26. Izogo, E.E., Jayawardhena, C.: Online shopping experience in an emerging e-retailing market: towards a conceptual model. J. Consum. Behav. **17**(4), 379–392 (2018)
27. Bougie, R., Pieters, R., Zeelenberg, M.: Angry customers don't come back, they get back: the experience and behavioral implications of anger and dissatisfaction in services. J. Acad. Mark. Sci. **31**(4), 377–393 (2003)
28. Jiang, L., Yang, Z., Jun, M.: Measuring consumer perceptions of online shopping convenience. J. Serv. Manag. **24**(2), 191–214 (2013)
29. McKinnon, A.C., Tallam, D.: Unattended delivery to the home: an assessment of the security implications. Int. J. Retail Distrib. Manag. **31**(1), 30–41 (2003)
30. Liao, T., Keng, C.: Online shopping delivery delay: finding a psychological recovery strategy by online consumer experiences. Comput. Hum. Behav. **29**(4), 1849–1861 (2013)
31. Teixeira, J., Patrício, L., Nunes, N.J., Nóbrega, L., Fisk, R.P., Constantine, L.: Customer experience modeling: from customer experience to service design. J. Serv. Manag. **23**(3), 362–376 (2012)

A Model to Assess Customer Alignment Through Customer Experience Concepts

Leonardo Muñoz[✉] and Oscar Avila

Department of Systems and Computing Engineering, School of Engineering,
Universidad de los Andes, Bogotá, Colombia
{l.munozm, oj.avila}@uniandes.edu.co

Abstract. Business and Information Technology alignment has been one of the main concerns for IT and Business executives due to its importance to the overall company performance. In the Business and IT alignment area, there is a lack of research works and approaches to measure the organizations' alignment level with external customers. However, this alignment level is today relevant as customers have become more exigent and digitally connected and they have increased their negotiation power. To fulfil this lack, this paper presents the design and application of a maturity model for customer alignment measurement. The originality of our approach is that the model embraces digital transformation concepts aimed at measuring the experience level that the organization is offering to customers through the customer lifecycle.

Keywords: Information system · Strategic alignment · Capability model · User experience · Marketing · Sales · Service · Digital transformation

1 Introduction

The organizational context is characterized today by fast and unexpected changes that force organizations to adapt their internal operation and relationship with the environment in order to be according to evolving issues, needs and requirements. Following this operational and strategical transformations, new technologies have been introduced as the main lever to generate new business capabilities and transform the business model. In this context, Business and Information Technology Alignment is a key process for the performance of the organizations in a fast changing and highly demanding market [1, 2].

This process must be approached from three different levels [3]: (i) the "classical" internal level that consists in aligning IT services with business processes; (ii) the alignment with the environment that concerns the alignment of the organization with external actors, issues and needs; (iii) the alignment with uncertain evolutions that relates the alignment of the organization with external and internal overcoming events and changes. Due to the importance of Business and Information Technology Alignment in last 25 years, its measurement has become important in order to get insight about the current maturity level of companies' capabilities allowing them to align IT and Business domains. Such picture makes possible to identify and correct gaps in the

© Springer Nature Switzerland AG 2019
W. Abramowicz and R. Corchuelo (Eds.): BIS 2019 Workshops, LNBIP 373, pp. 339–351, 2019.
https://doi.org/10.1007/978-3-030-36691-9_29

progress made in both domains and to identify the impact of organizational and digital transformation initiatives.

A literature review looking for contributions in alignment measurement at the three before mentioned levels [4], showed that the wide research work is focused on the measurement of the internal alignment level with great advances and many approaches. This analysis showed as well that there is an absence of measurement models for the alignment with the external environment and uncertain evolutions. However, these two levels are increasingly becoming relevant in the business world, because of the emerging importance of actors, such as customers, competitors and suppliers that generate pressure for change on the environment in which companies compete.

Keeping in mind this gap, this work focuses on the alignment with the external environment and specifically in the alignment with customers. We delimit the scope of our work to customer alignment assessment when considering the complexity of the subject and the fact that customers have become more exigent and digitally connected and have increased their negotiation power. It is not a surprise thus that for many companies today customers have become the central point of their strategies [5]. We adopt additional concepts in the Digital Transformation (DT) arena [6] because to address new challenges related to customer alignment, companies are today trying to improve the customer experience by profiting of new disruptive technologies and implementing DT projects. In this work, DT frameworks are taken as a basis in conjunction with existing assessment models in order to propose a maturity model for measuring the strategic alignment with customers.

This article is structured as follows: Sect. 2 presents related work in customer alignment and digital transformation, Sect. 3 presents our model for measuring the maturity of organizations' alignment with customers, Sect. 4 presents the model application methodology, Sect. 5 describes a case study on which the proposed model was applied and last, Sect. 6 presents the conclusions and future work.

2   Customer Alignment and Digital Transformation

According to [4] it is evident the lack of research works addressing the alignment of organisations with external environment actors, and specifically with customers. We define customer alignment as the fit between the company's strategy and operation and the customer lifecycle. This lifecycle is composed by the following stages: customer needs discovering, customer attracting, purchasing process monitoring and, finally, post-sale support [7]. For aligning the customer lifecycle with the company strategy and processes, it is very important to focus on the customer experience through the whole lifecycle. The better the customer experience, the more client attraction, effective sales and faithful clients are likely to be [8]. Our underlying conception is therefore that the better is the customer experience, the more aligned is the company with its customers. To improve customer experience, the companies must know better their customer's needs, tastes and behaviour to be agile and flexible in the decision-making process. It reinforces the idea of technology as the main tool in the business models to enable new capabilities in the companies to align to their customers and improve the performance.

In this context, we consider as fundamental to include DT concepts as a base for the development of our approach considering that DT frameworks generally include the customer experience as one of their main pillars [6, 9, 10]. Moreover, according to [11] customers are generating new and faster requirements that must be solved through customer experience initiatives. This work argues it is necessary to use disruptive technologies to understand the customer and external context, improve and maximize the physical experience with digital tools and focus on smart investments in digital channels [11].

3 Design of the Maturity Measurement Model

As indicated earlier, alignment with customers is about closing the gaps between the strategies and operation of the organization and the preferences, needs and tastes of its customers through all the customer lifecycle [7].

In this context, for defining the maturity measurement model, we consider the "Customer Experience" development pillar of the DT framework proposed in [6], which is one of the first and more used frameworks in DT. This pillar focuses on the transformation of the relationships with users and customers through digital tools and capabilities. Our contribution is intended to measure customer experience capabilities through all the customer lifecycle, from the pre-sale stage, going through sales process, to post-sale services.

3.1 Model Proposal Methodology

For structuring the maturity model, we propose the steps described below. Application of steps 2 to 4 is presented in next subsections.

1. *Structure definition:* we design the maturity model by using a two-dimensional structure (measurement criteria and maturity levels) which is very common in maturity models designed in the academy and the industry [12]. We also adopt the structure of the Strategic Alignment Maturity Model (SAMM) [13] which develops measurement criteria in terms of business practices.
2. *Measurement criteria definition:* we define business practices for each measurement criterion from the elements that constitute the "Customer Experience" development pillar of the DT Framework [6] (see Fig. 1). We complemented then such practices with concepts from the related work presented in Sect. 2.
3. *Maturity levels definition:* we define the maturity levels that conforms the measurement scale from the Likert scale used in the SAMM model and in most of the maturity models [12]. It is composed of 5 maturity levels which will be evaluated for each business practice.
4. *Reference states definition:* according to the structure adopted, it is proposed a reference state description in the intersection of each business practice and each maturity level, which can help us as a comparative reference during the evaluation process. These reference states are proposed from the experience of several experts that were interviewed during the development of the model.

3.2   Measurement Criteria Definition

Measurement criteria were defined from the activities that the organization needs to carry out in order to tackle with the customer life-cycle. Such activities typically include customer understanding, marketing, sales and post-sales activities. Corresponding business practices were defined from the "Customer Experience" pillar defined in [6] (see Fig. 1). This pillar includes three building blocks: *customer understanding, top line growth and customer touch points*. Each building block possesses desired capabilities, for instance, the *customer touch points* building block includes three capabilities: *customer service, cross-channel coherence* and *self-service capabilities*. We used such capabilities to propose the business practices of our model. For example, by understanding and interpreting the *cross-channel coherence* capability we propose four business practices belonging to two measurement criteria: use of digital sales channels, use of digital marketing channels, use of digital service channels, and coherence between communication channels practices (see Fig. 1). In order to validate criteria and practices, we organize several meetings with a group of 4 experts conformed by IT and business consultants as well as sales and service managers. Validation meetings also served to revise the reference states defined for the maturity levels of each business practice. Below we describe in detail each evaluation criterion.

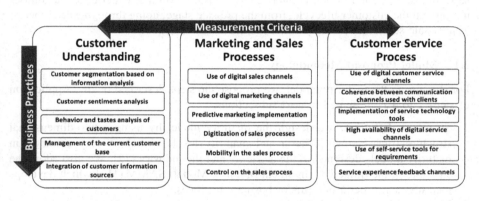

Fig. 1. The maturity measurement model for customer alignment

Customer Understanding. The objective of this criterion is to evaluate the maturity of the processes to obtain customer information, improve understanding of customer preferences, behaviors and tendencies, and enable customization of the products and service offers. This criterion groups the following practices:

- *Customer segmentation based on information analysis:* this practice assesses the use of technological tools such as databases and business intelligence applications to classify customers according to information obtained from internal and external sources.

- *Customer sentiments analysis:* this practice aims at evaluating the ability to obtain and analyze customer sentiments and opinions about company's products, services, brands and image by using technological tools.
- *Behavior and taste analysis:* this practice assesses the ability to create profiles of current and prospective customers that include their tastes, behaviors and preferences by using technological tools.
- *Management of the current customer base:* this practice is intended to assess the gathering, storage, analysis and management through computer tools of the information of the current customers, which can be vital for company operation and decision making.
- *Integration of customer information sources:* this practice evaluates the level of maintenance, management and consolidation of multiple customer information sources by using technological tools such as centralized data warehouses.

Marketing and Sales Processes. This criterion aims at assessing the use of different technological tools to transform the company's revenue channels and their related processes. In addition, the use of customer attraction and retention tools is also assessed. The practices grouped within this criterion are described as follows:

- *Use of digital sales channels:* this practice evaluates the implementation and proper use level of digital sales channels, as well as their integration with traditional channels.
- *Use of digital marketing channels:* this practice evaluates the implementation and proper use level of digital marketing channels, as well as their integration with traditional marketing channels.
- *Predictive marketing implementation*: it assesses the level of use of business intelligence in marketing processes for forecasting analysis.
- *Digitization of sales processes:* within this practice, the use of technological assistance or automation tools to support the activities of sales managers and staff is evaluated to make it much more agile and effective for customers.
- *Mobility in the sales process:* in this practice the objective is to assess the availability level of sales tools in different mobile devices, which facilitate the relationship with the customer during the sales process.
- *Control on the sales process:* it evaluates the visibility and control level of sales process and data allowing customers to have a personalized and secure experience.

Customer Service Process. This criterion aims to evaluate the improvement in speed and effectiveness to solve service or post-sale requirements through new digital channels and associated processes. The practices of this criterion are described as follows:

- *Use of digital customer service channels:* this practice aims at evaluating the use of different digital channels to respond to customers after-sales requirements in a flexible and agile way.
- *Coherence between communication channels:* in this practice, the integration level between the customer service channels is evaluated.

- *Implementation of simple and agile service technology tools:* this practice evaluates the level of simplicity and efficiency of customer service tools. It is not enough to implement technological tools, but they must be friendly and agile to guarantee the best possible experience.
- *High availability of digital service channels:* within this practice, the continuity and availability of service channels serving as customer touch points is evaluated.
- *Use of self-service tools for requirement management:* it assesses the existence of platforms that allow customers to have control and obtain response to their requirements by their own.
- *Service experience feedback channels:* this practice evaluates the availability of feedback channels to get information from the customer about her experience through the customer life-cycle.

3.3 Maturity Levels Definition

It is proposed to assess measurement criteria under the following 5 maturity levels:

1. *Initial/Ad-hoc process:* the practice is not implemented or not conceived to help organizations align with customers.
2. *Committed process:* the organization has plans to implement and/or improve the practice.
3. *Focused and stabilized process:* the practice is established but external alignment with customers is still lacking.
4. *Improved/Managed Process:* within the practice digital and disruptive technologies are conceived as a value element towards the alignment with customers.
5. *Optimized Process*: the practice has been entirety implemented, it is flexible in face of external market changes and helps the organization gain competitive advantages.

3.4 The Maturity Model and Reference States Definition

Specific reference states are established for each practice within each maturity level, which will serve as a guide for the maturity assessment. The complete maturity model is presented in Table 1.

4 Maturity Model Application Methodology

For the application of the model, it is necessary to define an evaluation team made up of business and IT managers and executives, who are in charge of answering and discussing the maturity level that fit the best to the current state of the company in each business practice. This group also identifies gaps and possible actions to close them from the results. The specific steps for the application of the measurement model take as reference the methodology of the SAMM model [13, 14], that includes the following 4 steps:

Table 1. Maturity model for customer alignment

C	Practice	Level 1	Level 2	Level 3	Level 4	Level 5
Customer understanding	Customer segmentation based on information analysis	There is no segmentation of the customer base	Clients are inaccurately segmented from incomplete information, however, there are plans to improve the information sources and analysis tools	Clients are segmented based on local data analysis. Analysis tools are obsolete, or sources are limited	Clients are segmented based on local data analysis. CRM tools are used	Clients are segmented based on analysis of local and external data. CRM tools and business intelligence are used
	Customer sentiments analysis	There are no tools or data sources for customer sentiment analysis	Manual monitoring and analysis are carried out from a single source of information	Monitoring and semi-automatic analysis of several sources with isolated tools for each source	Semi-automatic monitoring and analysis is performed consolidating data from multiple sources	Automatic monitoring and analysis are performed consolidating data from multiple sources, using filters and artificial intelligence
	Behavior and tastes analysis	There are no tools or data sources for analysis of behavior and preferences	Manual monitoring and analysis are done with local and limited data sources	Semi-automatic monitoring and analysis is done with some data capture by tools in web portals and social networks	Automatic monitoring and analysis are done with centralized tools and multiple web sources of information	Automatic monitoring and analysis are done with centralized and intelligent tools and multiple web and IoT sources
	Management of the current customer base	There is no database of current customers	Clients are managed with an outdated database	Clients are managed in a local database with occasional updates	Clients are managed within a CRM system with little adoption and inadequate use	Clients are managed within an updated CRM system in real time through mobile and local tools
	Integration of customer information sources	There is no integration strategy for information sources	There are isolated sources of information and plans for future integration	The information sources are partially integrated and updated with low frequency	There is a central data bank that is frequently updated with information from a limited number of sources	There is a central data bank that is updated in real time with customer information from multiple channels
Marketing and sales processes	Use of digital sales channels	There are no digital sales channels	There is a catalog of products within a web portal	The web portal implements an online sales platform with some products and a complex process	The web portal implements an online sales platform and a complete product portfolio	There are multiple integrated digital sales channels such as social networks and web portal, among others
	Use of digital marketing channels	There are no digital marketing channels	There are plans to implement digital marketing media, emails and web pages	The email is used to send marketing material to customers. There is no monitoring of its effectiveness	Email and social networks are used as marketing channels and there is a manual monitoring of effectiveness	Consolidation tools of digital marketing channels are used and full monitoring of the effectiveness of campaigns is made
	Predictive marketing implementation	There is no predictive marketing	Marketing is based on limited customer information	Marketing is based on full local customer information	Marketing is based on trends of local and external customer information	Marketing is based on predictive models in artificial intelligence tools and by using local and external customer information
	Digitalization of sales processes	Completely manual sales processes	Manual sales process with digitization plans in progress	Partially digitized sales process with digital payment	Digitized sales process with paper support documents	Sales process completely digital and connected to the company's information systems

(continued)

Table 1. (*continued*)

C	Practice	Level 1	Level 2	Level 3	Level 4	Level 5
	Mobility in the sale process	There are no sales tools for mobile devices	There are digital sales tools and implementation plans for mobile tools	There are sales tools for mobile devices, but they are not adequately used	Sales tools have mobile access implemented	Sales tools have mobile access implemented and real-time connection to information systems
	Control on the sales process	The sales process is not visible to the customer	The sales process is partially visible to the customer	The sales process is visible to the customer in its entirety without granting control to the client. (tracking)	The client has visibility and partial control of the sales process. (e.g. times and delivery places)	The sales process is visible and customizable for the client. (e.g. shopping channels, offers, times, deliveries)
Customer service process	Use of digital customer service channels	There are no digital channels for customer service	There is an implementation plan of the customer service channel by email	Customer service is provided through the contact section of the web portal	Customer service is provided through different digital channels such as social networks and web portal	There is a centralized management platform for customer service through social networks and a web portal with information available to customers
	Coherence between communication channels	The communication channels with customers do not share information between them	There is a plan to integrate information from traditional communication channels such as email and web portal	Traditional communication channels share information with low frequency	Traditional communication channels are integrated and coherent. The new channels have a partial integration	Traditional communication channels are integrated with new channels such as social networks. The IT area has visibility and total control
	Implementation simple and agile service technology tools	There are no technological tools for customer service	There are plans to implement traditional technological tools for customer service	There are obsolete technological tools for customer service with high levels of complexity	There are agile customer service technology tools with multi-channel integration	There are advanced customer service tools and with some level of autonomy
	High availability of digital service channels	Customer service channels do not have high availability strategies	There is a project to implement high availability strategies in service channels	The main service channel has high availability, but is not implemented for all customer service channels	Traditional customer service channels have high availability. No new service channels are contemplated	It has high availability for traditional service channels and is integrated with channels in the cloud as social networks
	Use of self-service tools for requirement management	No self-service requirements tools are implemented	The requirements request tools have a projection for the implementation of self-service modules	Requirement request tools allow self-service partially for clients	There is a complete self-service platform for customer requirements with occasional assistance by the service team	There is a complete self-service platform for customer requirements assisted by intelligent systems. Minimum human assistance
	Service experience feedback channels	Service experience feedback channels are not implemented	There is a basic survey on unconsolidated paper. There is a plan to implement digital channels	A service comment box is available through a web portal or email	The service tools implement digital feedback channels associated with the requirements. (online forms)	There is multi-channelity for the feedback of the service experience. The channels are integrated and relate to the requirements of each client

1. *To conform the evaluation team:* The number of business and IT executives conforming the evaluation team varies depending on the size of the company and whether a business unit or the entire organization will be evaluated.
2. *To gather information:* The defined team must evaluate each of the business practices. This can be done in three ways by using:
   a. Meetings in which team members work together.
   b. Surveys responded by each one of the members and then organizing a discussion to consolidate results.
   c. Combining both methods in case that some of the members have difficulties to assist to the meetings proposed in the first method.
3. *To decide the individual scores:* The team must reach an agreement to assign a score to each one of the evaluated practices, highlighting gaps and possible steps to solve them. The reference score for each of the criteria will be the average of the scores of the practices that it groups.
4. *To decide the overall alignment score:* The team must achieve a consensus of the general maturity score to be assigned to the current alignment state of the company. The average score of each criterion will guide this consensus, but the team can adjust the total score if it considers that according to the industry context certain practices may have more or less weight within the company than others.
5. *To present an executive report:* After consolidating the partial scores and the total score, it is recommended to prepare an executive summary of the evaluation for the board of directors, which includes the obtained levels, found gaps and potential improvement strategies. It is proposed to use a general evaluation consolidation format as a reference.

5 Case Study

The case study involves the business area of a multinational technology and services company responsible for carrying out pre-sale and sale activities of business technology solutions, serving around 20.000 corporate clients throughout the Latin-American region. This business area has about 200 employees working in services and product industrial sectors in several countries of the region. This case study is not intended to characterize the company or its market, but only to document the experience of applying the model in a real business environment.

5.1 Application of the Measurement Model

For the application of the proposed model, the company defined an evaluation team conformed by the sales director, 3 sales managers, the business development manager and the pre-sales manager of the region. According to the application methodology, there are two stages in obtaining results, the first involves defining the average results of the individual evaluations made by the members of the evaluation team, and the second consists in consolidating the results under consensus of the entire evaluation team and the identification of gaps and potential future strategies. In this article we will only present the second staged, i.e., the consolidated results.

Results by Consensus of the Evaluation Team. After obtaining the results of the evaluations carried out individually by each member of the assessment team, the company proceeded to hold an evaluation meeting in which the maturity levels obtained in each criterion and evaluated practice were discussed and adjusted.

Table 2 presents the consolidated results of the company with the weights assigned to each criterion. Below the most important gaps that were identified within the evaluation process.

Main Gaps Identified. In the *customer understanding* criterion, the evaluation team identified that, although the company uses advanced CRM tools for information management, all the functionalities available in such tools are not used in a full and adequate manner. Problems of information quality and source integration were also identified.

In the *sales and marketing processes* criterion, the team identified that, despite of having a Business to Business (B2B) model, it should be desirable to implement more agile technological tools to allow final customers to enter and track purchase orders. Mobile tools for sales exist, but their full and adequate use is not achieved due to the lack of initiative and management of the direction level. There are plans to implement artificial intelligence within the marketing processes, but it is not yet available for use within the business area under study.

In the *customer service process* criterion, it was identified that technological tools lack self-service options and there are problems of resource availability to respond quickly to post-sales requirements. In addition, there is no user experience feedback channel. The implementation of artificial intelligence was identified as an improvement option to assist customers in the post-sales support process.

Analysis of the Results. The team members maintained the average scores obtained from the individual evaluations made. Regarding the weight of the evaluated practices, relevance to customer sentiment analysis was removed as the team members argued that within a B2B business model, it is not of vital importance. The remaining practices maintained an equal ponderation.

As a business area of a multinational technology company with a presence and a long history throughout Latin-America, its operating characteristics are quite mature and this unit possesses a very good technology adoption level which was established by the last years implementation of its business strategy. Even so, there are significant gaps in the alignment with customers as observed in the results obtained, for this reason a maturity level of 3.4 was assigned to this company, what is somewhat higher than 3 (focused and stabilized processes level). The unit has practices to use technological tools with a higher level in customer understanding and the sales process aspects, what positions the company, in general, in a very good range of maturity.

Among the proposals for customer experience improvement, one of the most important is the evaluation and projection of using new and disruptive technology such as artificial intelligence, as well as implementing information systems integration processes. This would help the company reach a maturity level of 4 in the alignment with customers.

Table 2. Results by consensus of evaluating team of Company.

Criterion	Practice	Average level	Weighting in%	Average by criterion
Customer understanding	Segmentation of clients based on information analysis	4,2	25%	3,54
	Analysis of customer sentiments	2,2	0%	
	Analysis of the behavior and tastes of potential clients	2,8	25%	
	Management of current customer base with computer systems	3,8	25%	
	Integration of information sources of current and prospective clients	3,3	25%	
Sales and marketing processes	Use of digital sales channels	3,3	16,67%	3,3
	Use of digital marketing channels	4,0	16,67%	
	Predictive marketing implementation	2,7	16,67%	
	Digitization of sales processes	3,5	16,67%	
	Mobility in the sale process	3,7	16,67%	
	Visibility of sales processes to the client	2,8	16,67%	
Customer service process	Use of digital channels for customer service	4,0	16,67%	3,3
	Coherence between the communication channels used with clients	2,8	16,67%	
	Implementation of simple and agile service tools	3,5	16,67%	
	High availability of digital service channels	3,2	16,67%	
	Use of self-service tools of requirements	4,0	16,67%	
	Service experience feedback channels	2,5	16,67%	
General	**3,4**			

6 Conclusions and Future Work

For improving strategic alignment with customers by improving the overall experience through the customer life-cycle, companies are today making many efforts and investing resources in the adoption of new technologies.

In this research, a qualitative model was developed to assess customer alignment maturity based on the SAMM model and a leading DT framework. From the application of this model in a company in the IT services sector, it was concluded that: (i) although the measurement model has reference states at each level for each of the evaluated practices, they cannot cover all the business models, scenarios and industries in a generic way due to the high complexity that each context implies. Additionally, the qualitative nature of the maturity measurement model possesses a certain level of subjectivity in the evaluation, which needs to be mitigated through discussion meetings of the evaluation team. (ii) Although the company's maturity level is medium due to the lack of formality in customer alignment processes, the company was aware of its importance thanks to this study. (iii) To make the evaluation process more precise, it is necessary to include an external business consultant or business architect in order to generate a more neutral environment during the assessment process, further reducing the subjectivity of the application of the model. (iv) Despite being a model with some subjectivity level, its application may allow companies to carry out a structured and guided evaluation of their alignment with customers as well as define a base roadmap to reach a higher maturity level. This exercise would be very difficult to undertake without a structural model.

The following important topics were identified for future work: (i) Research work and approaches for measuring alignment with external environment actors, in addition to the clients, are necessary. An example of this is the alignment with suppliers, business partners, competitors, etc. (ii) It is necessary to validate and adjust the maturity model for customer alignment by applying it to different industries and obtaining feedback in order to adjust evaluation criteria and practices. It is also possible to propose methodological complements to the measurement model in order to avoid subjectivity and make it more faithful with respect to the produced results. (iii) It is still necessary to propose strategies to allow companies to go from a current maturity state to the next one.

References

1. Luftman, J., Derksen, B.: Key issues for IT executives 2012: doing more with less. MIS Q. Exec. **11**, 207–218 (2012)
2. Luftman, J., Derksen, B., Dwivedi, R., Santana, M., Zadeh, H.S., Rigoni, E.: Influential IT management trends: an international study. J. Inf. Technol. **30**, 293–305 (2015)
3. Avila, O., Goepp, V., Kiefer, F.: Understanding and classifying information system alignment approaches. J. Comput. Inf. Syst. **50**(1), 2–14 (2009)
4. Muñoz, L., Avila, O.: Business and information technology alignment measurement - a recent literature review. In: Abramowicz, W., Paschke, A. (eds.) BIS 2018. LNBIP, vol. 339, pp. 112–123. Springer, Cham (2019). https://doi.org/10.1007/978-3-030-04849-5_10

5. MIT Sloan Management Review and Google: RESEARCH REPORT Leading With Next-Generation Key Performance Indicators. Massachusetts Institute of Technology (2018)
6. MIT Center for Digital Business and Capgemini Consulting: Digital Transformation: a roadmap for Billion-Dollar Organizations. MIT Center for Digital Business and Capgemini Consulting (2011)
7. Buttle, F.: Customer Relationship Management, Concepts and Tools. Elsevier Butterworth-Heinemann, Oxford (2004)
8. Morgan, B.: Forbes - Breathing New Life Into The Customer Lifecycle, 24 April 2017. https://www.forbes.com/sites/blakemorgan/2017/04/24/breathing-new-life-into-the-customer-lifecycle/#4f0d19014294. Accessed 19 Sept 2018
9. Reis, J., Amorim, M., Melão, N., Matos, P.: Digital transformation: a literature review and guidelines for future research. In: Trends and Advances in Information Systems and Technologies, WorldCIST 2018. Advances in Intelligent Systems and Computing, vol. 745, pp. 411–421 (2018)
10. Harvard Business Review Analytic Services: The Digital Transformation of Business. Harvard Business School Publishing (2015)
11. Bonnet, D., Buvat, J., Subrahmanyam, K.V.J.: Rewired: crafting a compelling customer experience. Digital Transformation Review, no. 6 (2014)
12. Becker, J., Knackstedt, R., Pöppelbuß, J.: Developing maturity models for IT management. Bus. Inf. Syst. Eng. 1(3), 213–222 (2009)
13. Luftman, J.: Strategic alignment maturity. In: vom Brocke, J., Rosemann, M. (eds.) Handbook on Business Process Management 2. IHIS, pp. 5–43. Springer, Heidelberg (2015). https://doi.org/10.1007/978-3-642-45103-4_1
14. Luftman, J.: Assessing it/business alignment. Inf. Syst. Manag. 20(4), 9–15 (2003)
15. Henderson, J.C., Venkatraman, N.: Strategic alignment: leveraging information technology for transforming organizations. IBM Syst. J. 32(1), 4–16 (1993)
16. Vandermerwe, S.: How increasing value to customers improves business results. MIT Sloan Manag. Rev. 42(1), 27–37 (2000)

Understanding Users' Preferences for Privacy and Security Features – A Conjoint Analysis of Cloud Storage Services

Dana Naous[(⊠)] and Christine Legner

Faculty of Business and Economics (HEC), University of Lausanne,
1015 Lausanne, Switzerland
{dana.naous,christine.legner}@unil.ch

Abstract. Digital transformation has produced different applications and services for personal use. In an interconnected world, privacy and security concerns become main adoption barriers of new technologies. IT companies face an urgent need to address users' concerns when delivering convenient designs. Applying conjoint analysis (CA) from consumer research, we explore users' preferences and willingness-to-pay for privacy preserving features in personal cloud storage. Our contributions are two-fold: For research, we demonstrate the use of CA in understanding privacy tradeoffs for the design of personal ICTs. For practice, our findings can inform service designers about preferred privacy and security options for such services.

Keywords: IS design · Privacy · Security · Preference · Tradeoffs · Willingness-to-pay · Conjoint analysis · Cloud storage

1 Introduction

With the emerging digital age, new technologies such as mobile, cloud and internet-of-things have changed the way people communicate, work, learn and live. Normal citizens are transformed into information citizens that use a plethora of applications and services consuming and producing tremendous amounts of data. In such an interconnected world, privacy and security concerns become main adoption barriers of new technologies. Based on a survey of 12,355 Internet users, 70% of users are concerned about personal data theft and unauthorized use, and 65% are worried about data security practices of companies holding personal or financial information [1]. Users are confronted with multiple ICT offerings that they need to evaluate against various performance levels, business models and security options. As a result, IT companies and service providers face an urgent need to address users' concerns when delivering convenient designs. This calls for a clear understanding of users' attitudes and preferences for their selected and accepted services.

Cloud computing has contributed to the digital transformation through its provisioning model that facilitates access to IT resources for end-users [2]. Among the widely adopted cloud services is personal cloud storage, such as Dropbox, Google Drive and SecureSafe. These services offer infrastructure resources to users for storing

© Springer Nature Switzerland AG 2019
W. Abramowicz and R. Corchuelo (Eds.): BIS 2019 Workshops, LNBIP 373, pp. 352–365, 2019.
https://doi.org/10.1007/978-3-030-36691-9_30

data with sharing privileges and access from various devices. Price and storage capacity were traditionally among the most important features to users of such services [3]. However, 44% of users store sensitive data on their devices and wouldn't want anyone to access it [1]. On the other hand, highly secure cloud storage services have had difficulties in establishing sustainable business models, as underpinned by the shut down of the highly secure cloud service Wuala in 2015 (Wuala.com). This triggers questions regarding users' attitudes towards the use of secure personal cloud storage and their implications for personal cloud storage design. Accordingly, we ask: *How do users value privacy and security features in personal cloud storage services?*

In this study, we opt for the conjoint analysis (CA), a popular market research technique, to study privacy tradeoffs in the context of cloud services and perform willingness-to-pay (WTP) simulations. CA provides insights into user preferences for the formation of services that fit users' expectations [4], and could be useful in understanding the privacy tradeoffs for designing personal ICTs [5]. We aim for empirical insights on users' preferences of privacy and security features that allow service providers to better design or adjust their offerings to market needs. Our results are interesting for academia and practice: They inform research on personal ICTs by demonstrating that privacy and security concerns are not uniform among users. For practice, they imply that providers need to address different segments of varied preferences.

The remainder of this paper is structured as follows: We start by elaborating on personal cloud storage services and their secure design. Next, we motivate our research approach and present the essential steps in applying the CA method and WTP simulations. Then, we present key findings from the conjoint survey. We conclude with a synthesis of our findings and implications.

2   Background: Secure Design of Personal Cloud Storage

By providing IT resources as a service over the Internet [2], cloud computing has introduced a paradigm shift from ownership to usage of IT resources. The software as a service (SaaS) cloud model was the main driver for the personal use of cloud computing. In this model, individual users are able to access and use application software through a web interface [6]. Whereas positive outcomes include lower cost, accessibility and reliability, cloud services are associated with security and privacy risks that influence individual adoption. Among the main privacy concerns for cloud users are the unauthorized secondary use of data, improper access and control of information [6]. This suggests that cloud service providers should address these concerns through providing the necessary security and privacy features that meet user expectations.

The most commonly used cloud service targeting individuals is personal cloud storage. It is accessible from various devices (i.e. PCs, smartphones and tablets) and enables users to store, archive and share information such as personal documents and media (i.e. photos and videos). The business model mostly applied for such services is the "freemium" model, where a certain level of consumption is provided for free and revenues are made based on superior features such as additional storage or increased encryption [7]. Hence, users' privacy concerns are not addressed and cloud service providers consider additional security and privacy protection features as premiums.

To address privacy concerns of cloud users and design secure personal cloud storage, it is necessary to understand which security and privacy features these services should have. In [8], five goals for secure cloud computing applications are identified: (1) availability for use at any time and any place which entails backup; (2) confidentiality of user's data through applying necessary encryption techniques before saving it in the cloud; (3) data integrity through protection against loss and unauthorized users; (4) control through regulating the use of the system; and (5) audit through monitoring system use and access. In addition to that, [9] highlights security and privacy protection issues in the data lifecycle due to the openness and multi-tenancy of the cloud. This involves granularity of shared data, and user authorization for the transformation of data. Also, [10] discusses cloud security challenges of authentication and authorization, backup and recovery as well as encryption of data. Moreover, the issue of resource locality is emphasized since end-users of cloud services are unaware where their data is physically stored. The multi-location aspect of cloud raises additional privacy issues due to the fact that the applicable legal regulations depend on the location of the data and which country it resides in [8]. This increases the importance of having data protection laws that are relevant to the cloud scenario to ensure legal compliance and impose restrictions on the use of personal data in cloud services. In addition, [11] discusses the importance of a rigorous identity infrastructure (authentications) to achieve security and privacy goals in cloud service design.

While most studies in the information systems (IS) field focus on explaining information privacy, few are prescribe designs or actions [14]. This calls for research on the design of services that address privacy concerns and enable the protection and control of information. From our literature review, we are able to map users' privacy concerns [6] into security and privacy features of personal cloud storage (Table 1).

Table 1. Security and privacy features of personal cloud storage services

Privacy concerns	Security and privacy features	References
Unauthorized secondary use of data	Encryption	[8, 9, 12]
	Data segregation	[9, 12]
	Location of servers	[8–10]
	Legal compliance	[8–10, 12]
Improper access	System audit or monitoring	[8–10]
	Sharing	[8–10]
	Authorization	[8, 9, 12]
	Authentication	[9–11]
Control	Backup	[8–10]
	Recovery	[8–10]
	Availability	[8–10]
	Accessibility	[9]
	User control	[8, 12, 13]
	Feedback process	[12, 13]

3 Methodology: Conjoint Analysis

3.1 Selection of Research Approach

Conjoint analysis, from market research, allows investigating the monetary value of privacy and exploring user preferences when using online technologies through WTP. A recent literature review on CA in IS research by [4] emphasizes that CA is a very suitable method to inform IS design through an empirical analysis of user preferences. Among IS studies that use CA for privacy tradeoffs are [15, 16] that explore the cost for revealing personal information online and [17] that also estimates the monetary value that users associate to their own information on social networks. This motivates our research, where we employ CA to explore user preferences and tradeoffs regarding privacy and security features of personal cloud storage.

CA provides insights on user preferences for different product features based on a complete product evaluation [18], which enables the estimation of a preference structure applying the utility concept. Deriving a utility function from consumer evaluations of product features (i.e. attributes and levels), CA provides evidence on the most influencing factors on the consumer's choice of a product. This method is increasingly used for investigating user preferences in the cloud domain. [19] performed choice-based CA (CBCA) on consumers' preferences for cloud services relying on rank order of product profiles, and [20] investigated through adaptive CBCA preferences for emerging cloud platforms. Moreover, [3] investigated with CBCA consumers' choice decisions for cloud archiving services. Their study reveals price and storage capacity among the most important features, confirming a commoditization assumption.

We apply Adaptive Choice-based Conjoint Analysis (ACBCA) [21]. In this CA variant, we ask participants to choose among a set of profiles (or stimuli) after a self-explicated task where they rate attributes to exclude unacceptable attribute levels from the evaluation to reduce the choice burden. ACBCA was selected as it has been suggested for studies of a large number of attributes, which is typically the case when we speak about the design of IS. Moreover, the approach allows estimating utilities using a small sample size with less than 100 participants [4]. Part-worth utilities and relative importance measures are calculated using the Hierarchical Bayes (HB) [22]. We use specialized commercial software, Sawtooth Software, to administer the online survey.

3.2 Data Analysis

CA provides part-worth utility estimation for product attributes and levels, which can be translated into a relative importance score for the different attributes. Based on the data provided, other analysis techniques can be applied including market simulations [23]. To better understand customer tradeoffs with respect to security and privacy features, we opt for users' WTP simulation. We follow the procedure suggested by [24]. This involves comparing the utility of a certain product configuration with the utility of a reference product. The respondent's WTP denotes the maximum price at which the product's utility is still above the reference product's utility. Only one attribute is altered at a time, and the difference in the WTP between the new config-uration and the reference corresponds to the WTP for the changed attribute level. The WTP estimation model based on the conjoint data is the following:

$$u_{it|\sim p} + u_i(p) \geq u_i * + \varepsilon. \qquad (1)$$

where u_i* corresponds to individual i's utility of the reference product, $u_{it|\sim p}$ corre-sponds to the part-worth utility of the non-price attributes of product t with the changed attribute level and $u_i(p)$ is the part-worth utility due to the price attribute of t. ε is an arbitrarily small positive number.

4   CA for Cloud Storage Services

4.1   Attributes and Levels Selection

The most challenging step in CA is the determination of relevant attributes and levels that would be evaluated by users. For that, we followed a mixed method approach [4] based on three stages: (1) A literature review on cloud storage services (Sect. 2) with a focus on security and privacy aspects. We identified an initial list of 14 attributes (Table 1). (2) A market analysis of existing services to examine the presence of attributes from literature and identify attribute levels. Our analysis included 13 products that we selected based on reviews of cloud vendors from comparison websites (e.g., cloudwards.net). The list is composed of: big market players (Google Drive, DropBox, Microsoft One Drive and Amazon Drive), secure cloud storage services (Tresorit, SpiderOak and SecureSafe), and mid-sized players (Sync, Pcloud, Carbonite, Sugar-Sync, Elephant Drive, Box and Mozy). We identified 10 attributes with their levels based on the analysis. (3) We finally organized a focus group of 7 researchers who are experienced cloud storage users and privacy-oriented. From the discussions among participants, we identified relevant attributes and eliminated ones that less contributing to the security and privacy perceptions of the participants.

The three phases contributed to the formation of our final list of attributes and levels with 7 security and privacy features (Table 2) in addition to storage and price.

4.2   Study Setup

We started our online survey by introducing personal cloud storage services and asked the participants for their demographic and professional background (gender, age, country, industry sector, and income). This was followed by questions on personal cloud storage use, i.e., purpose of use, use of paid services, and types of files stored. The survey then was based on three sections in the following order:

Section 1 – Build Your Own: In this section, participants are asked to build the most preferred configuration of cloud storage services. They select among the list of levels available given a summed price to be considered when they build their product. The base price was centered on the storage space and premiums were added on enhanced

Table 2. List of attributes and levels for personal cloud storage

Attribute	Attribute description	Attribute levels (from basic to enhanced)
Accessibility	Options of devices supporting the service	(1) Website only, (2) website and desktop application, and (3) website, desktop application and mobile
File sharing	Methods for sharing files with other parties	(1) Link sharing, (2) link sharing with password, and (3) sharing with managed permissions
Authentication	Methods in which credentials are provided for accessing the storage service	(1) Password only, (2) 2-steps authentication, and (3) zero-knowledge authentication (provider has no access to the unencrypted form)
Location of cloud servers	Location of the servers that the service provider deploy to store user data	(1) Worldwide, (2) worldwide (non-US), (3) countries with high data protection and privacy standards (e.g., Switzerland, Iceland, Canada), and (4) own country
Encryption	Transformation of the customer data to cipher text using different encryption algorithms	(1) Server-side encryption, and (2) end-to end encryption (encryption and decryption are done on the client-side with a private key)
File recovery	Data restore and recovery in case of disasters such as data loss or deletion	(1) Not available, (2) limited to 30 days, (3) limited to 90 days, and (4) Unlimited
File change history	File versioning and system monitoring depending on the provider's policies	(1) Not available, (2) limited to 10 versions, and (3) full history with "Access and Activity" log
Storage space	Capacity of the file storage	(1) 5 GB, (2) 50 GB, (3) 100 GB, (4) 500 GB, and (5) 1 TB
Price	A summed price attribute, which is set based on incremental prices for attributes obtained from a market analysis	Varies between 0\$ to 29\$/month depending on the selected attribute levels

security and privacy features. Based on their answers, the following sections concentrate on the product concepts that evolve around the respondent's preferred levels.

Section 2 – Screening: At this stage, respondents are asked to evaluate product profiles that were generated as possibilities for them to purchase or not. Based on our number of attributes, we presented 7 screening tasks with three options. In line with the self-explicated task in adaptive studies, respondents were asked on must-have or unacceptable features when their answers showed uniform decisions for certain attributes. Once these features were identified, they are not further displayed.

Section 3 – Choice Task Tournament: This is the final and central component of the survey where respondents evaluate product profiles and choose among them. We present a maximum of 10 choice tasks to respondents where they need to select the most convenient service among three options for estimation of preferences.

4.3 Study Sample

In line with [25], we selected Amazon's Mechanical Turk (MTurk), an online crowdsourcing platform, as a channel to hire participants of cloud storage users. MTurk is widely used in behavioral studies since it provides a fast, inexpensive and convenient sampling method and is appropriate for generalizing studies [26]. It is a suitable platform for our study as it allows us to obtain a diversified sample. Aiming for high quality of responses, we restricted the participation in the survey to current cloud storage service users. We used a qualification test to eliminate non-users and also prevented multiple participation of one respondent by controlling MTurk IDs. We compensated 1.50$ per response, which is an average price for a 10 min survey similar to ours. As MTurk participant's attention span might drop during complex tasks or bots might be used [27], we excluded responses that took less than 5 min.

5 Results

5.1 Sample Background

We received a total of 188 responses from which 144 were included in the analysis. Among the respondents, 57.64% are males and 42.36% females. The majority was between 25 and 45 years old (77.08%). Most respondents are from the US (76.39%). They came from different industries among them IT (18.75%), education (14.58%), manufacturing (11.81%) and healthcare (11.11%). In terms of income, 23.61% have low income, 71.53% average, and only 4.86% have high income.

As for their actual use of cloud storage services, 81.94% use free plans. The main use purposes were storing files (93.75%), sharing (72.92%) and collaboration (33.33%). They mainly store.pdf files (77.08%), official documents (45.14%) e.g., IDs and contracts, editable files (65.28%) for collaboration, and media (86.11%).

5.2 User Preferences for Personal Cloud Storage Services

In the "build your own" section, respondents were able to build their concepts by selecting preferred options simulating a real purchase scenario. They were presented a summed price, where additional storage or security and privacy features required incremental prices. They mainly selected basic features, which was reflected in the users' preferences (Table 3). However, there was a major agreement on unlimited recovery (88.89%). Also for accessibility, majority (72.22%) require the presence of different channels. This is expected from the screening section, where the full accessibility was seen as a must-have (7.64%) and no recovery was unacceptable (19.44%).

Table 3. User preferences and part-worth utilities of personal cloud storage attribute levels

Attribute	Attribute levels	Average utilities	Standard deviation	Distribution for BYO section (%)
Storage space	5 GB	−6.87	104.60	35.42
	50 GB	24.74	64.91	31.94
	100 GB	5.48	27.98	14.58
	500 GB	−5.25	60.89	9.03
	1 TB	−18.10	91.49	9.03
Accessibility	Website only	−30.90	23.43	13.19
	Website and desktop	0.89	19.95	14.58
	Website, desktop and mobile	30.01	32.03	72.22
File sharing	Sharing link	2.12	28.99	51.39
	Sharing link with password	2.59	17.39	24.31
	Sharing with managed permissions	−4.70	28.16	24.31
Authentication	Password only	10.12	36.93	57.64
	2-step authentication	3.86	28.84	32.64
	Zero-knowledge authentication	−13.98	27.15	9.72
Location of servers	Own country	−8.00	36.37	27.78
	Countries with high privacy standards	3.93	26.16	15.97
	Worldwide (non-US)	−12.19	18.39	4.17
	Worldwide	16.26	36.68	52.08
Encryption	Server-side	4.20	25.07	63.19
	End-to-end encryption	−4.20	25.07	36.81
Recovery	Not available	−28.93	27.49	1.39
	Limited to 30 days	−7.95	21.18	6.25
	Limited to 90 days	−8.12	24.60	3.47
	Unlimited	45.00	39.18	88.89
File change history	Full history with log	13.58	36.88	40.97
	Limited to10 versions	−3.21	16.73	16.67
	Not available	−10.36	35.82	42.36
Price	0 $	79.27	123.88	–
	29 $	−79.27	123.88	–

Through an HB estimation, we were able to derive part-worth utilities for the attribute levels of personal cloud storage services (Table 3). The part-worth utilities are normalized HB, where positive utilities correspond to prefered levels and negative utilities correspond to less desired levels. As suggested by [20], we assess the "goodness of fit" using percentage certainty (PC) and root likelihood (RLH). The data show PC mean of 0.482, indicating acceptable results of fit. RLH valued 0.646, which is considered more fit than the chance level given we have three choice tasks.

Based on the part-worth utilities, ACBCA provides relative importance measures of attributes (Fig. 1). The results show price (28%) as the most important attribute for users of personal cloud storage, thereby underlining price-sensitivity. This is followed by storage space (21%) as the main functionality of the service. In terms of security and privacy features, recovery ranked third with an importance of 10%, which can be related to the data loss concern of personal cloud storage users. Location of servers and access followed (8%). Then, change history and authentication (7%). Less importance was given to file sharing (6%) and encryption (5%).

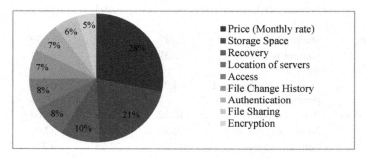

Fig. 1. Relative importance of personal cloud storage attributes

5.3   Customer Segments

CA allows for determining customer segments based on individual part-worth utilities. The segmentation could be based on demographic and professional background information, which proved to be insignificant in our case. It could also be achieved through clustering analysis. Using k-means, we optimally find three customer segments of contrasting preferences towards information privacy concerns (Table 4).

All three clusters expose similar preferences for accessibility and recovery attributes, but differ with regards to other attributes. The first customer segment consists of 38 users that prefer basic privacy and security features with least storage options; they are the "unconcerned users". Surprisingly, these users have positive utility for higher prices, which means they are generally insensitive to price. The second segment is the largest with 77 users; they are the "privacy-rights advocates". These users prefer enhanced privacy and security features but with a positive utility for low prices. They require secure personal cloud storage services and believe privacy is a right without the need to pay for it. Finally, the third customer segment consists of 29 users; they are the "privacy-concerned users". This segment requires enhanced security and privacy options but have a positive utility for higher prices, which means they are aware of the cost of their privacy and the need of additional requirements to achieve that.

Table 4. Identified clusters with preferences based on customer segmentation

	Cluster 1	Cluster 2	Cluster 3
Number of participants	38	77	29
Privacy characterization	Unconcerned users	Privacy-rights advocates	Privacy-concerned users
Preferences			
Storage space	5 GB–50 GB	100 GB–500 GB	500 GB–1 TB
Accessibility	Website, desktop application and mobile	Website, desktop application and mobile	Website, desktop application and mobile
File Sharing	Sharing link	Sharing link with password	Sharing with permissions
Authentication	Password only	2-step authentication	2-step authentication
Location of servers	Worldwide	Own country or Countries with high privacy standards	Countries with high privacy standards or Worldwide
Encryption	Server-side encryption	End-to-end encryption	End-to-end encryption
Recovery	Unlimited	Unlimited	Unlimited
File change history	Not available	Full history	Full history
Price	High	Low	High

5.4   Willingness-to-Pay

To understand price-sensitivity for security and privacy features, we perform market simulation using Sawtooth Software to study WTP. Our study uses a reference product that is a status quo in the market and widely adopted by users. It corresponds to 100 GB storage with basic security and privacy features except for recovery, access and file change history for 2$. The WTP estimation involves calculating the utility of various price points for the compared product. Our ACBCA provides utilities estimation of summed prices from 0$ to 29$, the utilities of additional price points are estimated using linear interpolation [24]. The change in utility from the reference product and a compared product with varied attribute level was reported as ΔWTP. A negative change was observed for all security and privacy attribute levels, thus negative WTP. However, this varies among different attributes. A difference of 2.00$ (in Table 5) implies zero WTP for the product configuration with the new changed level, which was the case for most levels. File sharing was among the attributes that users are willing to pay for with less than 2$: 1.80$ for the password option and 1$ for managed permissions, even if it is more secure. Similarly, users are willing to pay 1$ for the same configuration but with 2-steps authentication and no WTP for the zero-knowledge option. Results also show difference of 1.70$ for the secure location of servers in countries with high data protection and privacy standards. Moreover, end-to-end encryption is worth 1$ only. No compromise was given for recovery; all levels resulted with 0 WTP. As for file change history, users were willing to pay less amount (0.50$) for limited versioning capabilities.

Table 5. Willingness-to-pay for changing attribute levels (monthly rate)

Attribute	Base level	Changed attribute level	ΔWTP ($)
Accessibility	Website, desktop and mobile	Website and desktop	−2.00
		Website, desktop and mobile	−2.00
File sharing	Sharing link	Sharing link with password	−0.20
		Sharing with managed permissions	−1.00
Authentication	Password only	2-step authentication	−1.00
		Zero-knowledge authentication	−2.00
Location of servers	Worldwide	Own country	−2.00
		Countries with high privacy standards	−1.70
		Worldwide (non-US)	−2.00
Encryption	Server-side	End-to-end encryption	−1.00
Recovery	Unlimited	Limited to 90 days	−2.00
		Limited to 30 days	−2.00
		Not available	−2.00
File change history	Full history with "Access & Activity" log	Limited to 10 versions	−1.50
		Unavailable	−2.00

6   Discussion and Implications

In this paper, we employ ACBCA to study preference measures for privacy and security features in personal cloud storage. Thus understanding privacy tradeoffs of users and informing design of these services. Our overall results comply with the assumption of commoditized personal cloud storage services [3], where price and storage space are most important to users. For privacy and security measures, we have seen that recovery comes first. There is a consensus on its significance as an essential security aspect in cloud. Interestingly, location of servers is not of a concern for cloud users although there is a huge debate on the importance of data protection laws and regulations. Moreover, secure authentication and sharing as less critical features raises questions on the complexity of the security mechanisms that users are willing to adopt. Finally, having encryption as the least important attribute with preference towards server-side encryption shows that users are not aware of the data confidentiality issues in the cloud and secondary use of information. It can also indicate that users are not willing to do efforts for securing their data with private keys.

In line with the relative importance of attributes, our WTP simulation shows that users are unwilling to pay for additional security and privacy protection features. The freemium model of personal cloud storage provides basic functions that users take advantage of for free. Thus, users' satisfaction with basic configurations might influence their WTP for additional features [7]. We also find that among the security and privacy attributes, the participants valued most the enhanced sharing option with password where they would pay a comparable price (1.80$) to the status quo product. This might be driven by the sensitivity of the data stored and users' concerns of improper access and unauthorized use [6]. Moreover, having no WTP for "zero-knowledge" products explains the difficulties for security-driven vendors to survive.

All these aspects could also be related to the fact that our sample is not necessarily privacy concerned. The risk factors associated to personal cloud storage services are influenced by how trustworthy is the service vendor [28]. In [29], the authors explain that establishing a trust relationship with cloud providers can mitigate information privacy concerns. The users in this study might have low risk perceptions of the use of cloud storage service based on their current experiences. Another explanation to these results can be established by the privacy paradox phenomenon [30]. Accordingly, individuals expressing privacy concerns can still behave contradictory to it based on their assessment of the cost and benefit for information privacy.

However, our segmentation shows that there are no uniform preferences among cloud storage users. We identified three user segments with different preference structures. The first segment represents traditional users of basic personal cloud storage services who do not have specific privacy concerns. However, their positive price part-worth utility characterizes them as price insensitive. These users target other premiums than privacy and security (e.g., storage). The second segment represents a majority of users who are concerned about privacy and security, but would not pay for it. These customers believe privacy is a right and services should be designed accordingly. The last segment represents customers who seek security features and are willing to pay for them. Their attitude can be explained based on the privacy calculus [31]; they estimate a cost for their benefit of reduced privacy risks when their service is secure and privacy protective enough.

Our findings have implications for both research and practice. For research, we demonstrate a method for understanding user tradeoffs for privacy and security aspects to inform the design of personal ICTs. CA has been applied in previous research for estimating privacy tradeoffs in monetary value, but is not fully exploited for secure design studies. We suggest adopting market research techniques, specifically CA, as an approach for understanding user preferences in mass-market scenarios. CA techniques can be leveraged to study preferences based on utility functions, perform segmentation and run market simulations. Our empirical results show that there are no uniform preferences among personal cloud storage users. This should be further investigated in future research that can thoroughly study the identified segments' characteristics. In addition, other CA studies can be performed to assess the users' privacy concerns in different sample populations and their willingness-to-pay for secure options. Our sample is majorly from the US, which is a limitation to this study. An opportunity for research would be to apply similar CA studies to a wider sample from different backgrounds, especially with the current general data protection regulation in the European Union, for better generalizability of results.

For practice, the segmentation presented in this paper could be very useful in future development of cloud storage services or refinement of existing ones. Service providers should keep in mind users' privacy concerns and their WTP for privacy and security features to be able to deliver offerings that meet users' needs. Our results with multiple segments imply that service providers should build product bundles that take into consideration the different user preferences. Whereas the freemium model based on storage capacity can be interesting to some users, privacy-rights advocates and concerned users have other requirements. From our sample, we observe that most users underestimate the risks of privacy invasion, which should not be exploited by service providers. Users should have a better understanding of the security features provided by cloud services before deciding on its use; this is a starting point and should be treated by service providers when marketing their offerings. Concerned users should have the option to control their privacy settings at low cost.

Acknowledgment.   The research reported in this manuscript was supported by the Swiss National Science Foundation (SNSF) under the grant number 159951.

References

1. Statista: Consumer confidence about personal online data security 2015 | Statistic. https://www.statista.com/statistics/296700/personal-data-security-perception-online/
2. Rimal, B.P., Jukan, A., Katsaros, D., Goeleven, Y.: Architectural requirements for cloud computing systems: an enterprise cloud approach. J. Grid Comput. **9**, 3–26 (2010)
3. Burda, D., Teuteberg, F.: Understanding the benefit structure of cloud storage as a means of personal archiving - a choice-based conjoint analysis. In: ECIS (2014)
4. Naous, D., Legner, C.: Leveraging market research techniques in IS–a review of conjoint analysis in IS research. In: ICIS (2017)
5. Mihale-Wilson, C., Zibuschka, J., Hinz, O.: About user preferences and willingness to pay for a secure and privacy protective ubiquitous personal assistant. In: ECIS (2017)
6. Gashami, J.P., Chang, Y., Rho, J.J., Park, M.-C.: Understanding the trade-off between privacy concerns and perceived benefits in SaaS individual adoption. In: PACIS (2014)
7. Trenz, M., Huntgeburth, J.: Understanding the viability of cloud services: a consumer perspective. In: ECIS (2014)
8. Zhou, M., Zhang, R., Xie, W., Qian, W., Zhou, A.: Security and privacy in cloud computing: a survey. In: International Conference on Semantics Knowledge and Grid (SKG), pp. 105–112. IEEE (2010)
9. Chen, D., Zhao, H.: Data security and privacy protection issues in cloud computing. In: Computer Science and Electronics Engineering (ICCSEE), pp. 647–651. IEEE (2012)
10. Rai, R., Sahoo, G., Mehfuz, S.: Securing software as a service model of cloud computing: issues and solutions. ArXiv Prepr. (2013)
11. Cavoukian, A.: Privacy in the clouds. Identity Inf. Soc. **1**, 89–108 (2008)
12. Pearson, S.: Taking account of privacy when designing cloud computing services. In: ICSE Workshop on Software Engineering Challenges of Cloud Computing, pp. 44–52. IEEE Computer Society (2009)

13. Itani, W., Kayssi, A., Chehab, A.: Privacy as a service: privacy-aware data storage and processing in cloud computing architectures. In: International Conference on Dependable, Autonomic and Secure Computing, pp. 711–716. IEEE (2009)

14. Bélanger, F., Crossler, R.E.: Privacy in the digital age: a review of information privacy research in information systems. MISQ **35**, 1017–1042 (2011)

15. Hann, I.-H., Hui, K.-L., Lee, S.-Y.T., Png, I.P.L.: Overcoming online information privacy concerns: an information-processing theory approach. JMIS **24**, 13–42 (2007)

16. Hann, I.-H., Hui, K.-L., Lee, T., Png, I.: Online information privacy: measuring the cost-benefit trade-off. In: ICIS (2002)

17. Krasnova, H., Hildebrand, T., Guenther, O.: Investigating the value of privacy in online social networks: conjoint analysis. In: ICIS (2009)

18. Green, P.E., Rao, V.R.: Conjoint measurement for quantifying judgmental data. J. Mark. Res. **8**, 355–363 (1971)

19. Koehler, P., Anandasivam, A., Dan, M., Weinhardt, C.: Customer heterogeneity and tariff biases in cloud computing. In: ICIS (2010)

20. Giessmann, A., Stanoevska, K.: Platform as a service – a conjoint study on consumers' preferences. In: ICIS. AIS Electronic Library (AISeL), Orlando (2012)

21. Green, P.E., Srinivasan, V.: Conjoint analysis in consumer research: issues and outlook. J. Consum. Res. **5**, 103–123 (1978)

22. Howell, J.: CBC/HB for beginners. Sawtooth Softw. Res. Pap. **98382**, 1–5 (2009)

23. Giessmann, A., Legner, C.: Designing business models for cloud platforms. ISJ **26**, 551–579 (2016)

24. Kohli, R., Mahajan, V.: A reservation-price model for optimal pricing of multiattribute products in conjoint analysis. J. Mark. Res. **28**, 347–354 (1991)

25. Pu, Y., Grossklags, J.: Using conjoint analysis to investigate the value of interdependent privacy in social app adoption scenarios. In: ICIS (2015)

26. Jia, R., Steelman, Z.R., Reich, B.H.: Using mechanical turk data in IS research: risks, rewards, and recommendations. Commun. AIS **41**, 14 (2017)

27. Downs, J.S., Holbrook, M.B., Sheng, S., Cranor, L.F.: Are your participants gaming the system? Screening mechanical turk workers. In: SIGCHI Conference on Human Factors in Computing Systems, pp. 2399–2402. ACM (2010)

28. Li, Y., Chang, K.: A study on user acceptance of cloud computing: a multi-theoretical perspective (2012)

29. Ermakova, T., Baumann, A., Fabian, B., Krasnova, H.: Privacy policies and users' trust: does readability matter? (2014)

30. Pavlou, P.A.: State of the information privacy literature: where are we now and where should we go? MISQ **35**, 977–988 (2011)

31. Dinev, T., Hart, P.: An extended privacy calculus model for e-commerce transactions. ISR **17**, 61–80 (2006)

The Role of Location Dependent Services for the Success of Local Shopping Platforms

Lars Bollweg[1], Richard Lackes[2], Markus Siepermann[2(✉)] ⓘD,
and Peter Weber[1]

[1] South Westphalia University of Applied Sciences, 59494 Soest, Germany
lars-bollweg@gmx.de, weber.peter@fh-swf.de
[2] Technische Universität Dortmund, 44221 Dortmund, Germany
{richard.lackes,markus.siepermann}@tu-dortmund.de

Abstract. Competitors and customers put Local Owner-Operated Retail Outlets (LOORO) under digitalization pressure. Local Shopping Platforms (LSP) seem to offer a promising approach to overcoming the manifold e-commerce adoption barriers for LOOROs. However, the business model of LSPs focuses on services that support the online Point of Sale (PoS). Therefore, it is crucial for LOOROs to know if customers will accept and use LSPs and what are the main drivers. This paper presents a survey of customers of a medium-sized town in Germany investigating these factors. Results show that location dependent services are crucial for the success of LSPs.

Keywords: Location-dependent services · Location-enabled services · Location-based services · Local shopping platforms · E-marketplaces

1 Motivation

The digital transformation of all parts of the society and of the retail industry in particular poses tremendous challenges to local owner-operated retail outlets (LOOROs), which are characterized by a small-sized store area, a limited number of staff and high owner-involvement in the day-to-day business operations [7]. Although the overall retail market is growing, the share of LOOROs in Germany constantly declined and hardly reached 18% anymore in 2015 [18]. Forecasts are even more worrying and predict a decline in revenue of up to 50% within the next ten years [19, 23, 43]. Besides strong price and service competition induced by (new) online competitors, reasons for this development are the changing shopping habits of customers, who are getting accustomed to online shopping and services more and more [22, 45], and the strategic turnaround of online and offline competitors. While formerly pure online players begin to conquer the cities with physical stores [20, 31], big-box retail outlets and chain stores are digitalizing their business models and offer multichannel sales and services to their local customers [17]. All of these factors pressure LOOROs to rethink and adapt their traditional business models [8].

However, studies show that LOOROs, like other small- and medium-sized enterprises (SME), still hesitate to adopt e-commerce channels (e.g. their own online shops) [42] as well as to participate in electronic marketplaces (e.g. eBay or Amazon) [46].

© Springer Nature Switzerland AG 2019
W. Abramowicz and R. Corchuelo (Eds.): BIS 2019 Workshops, LNBIP 373, pp. 366–377, 2019.
https://doi.org/10.1007/978-3-030-36691-9_31

So-called Local Shopping Platforms (LSP) which act as intermediaries between LOOROs and customers aim at filling this gap and are currently spreading in German cities (e.g. Atalanda.com, Lozuka.de) [32]. Like electronic marketplaces, (1) they match (local) buyers and sellers, (2) they enable the exchange of information, and (3) they facilitate transaction and fulfillment services [4, 44]. While in big e-market-places like Amazon or eBay, national boundaries blur [36], in LSPs, a counter-development takes place. LSP implement location-dependent self-restrictions into their business models. They either limit the cooperation with retailers or with customers from a certain area, or both. LSPs use these location-dependent self-restrictions as their unique selling proposition. They sell the existing offer of merchandise of LOOROs via their platform and try to reach time advantages in delivery and service through the use of local shops as decentralized storage places near the households of their local customers [38].

On the one hand, this approach seems to be promising for LOOROs because it helps them to overcome many of the e-commerce adoption barriers by outsourcing the digitalization challenge to the LSP [42, 46]. LSPs serve as digital service providers and release LOOROs from the burden of building up their own digital infrastructures and hiring specially educated staff. Furthermore, LSPs enable cooperation among competitors, which could lead to high savings through synergy effects. For example, LSPs can spread the development costs of the platforms infrastructure (IT, logistics) among the connected shops, which makes it favorable for LOOROs to participate as it does not require high investments [21]. Finally, and this is probably one of the most important factors, LSPs offer LOOROs a platform to make use of their location advantages in the digital world [30]. LSPs facilitate the offer of location dependent services. That means with the locational proximity between LOOROs and their customers, new services like same-day-delivery, click & collect, or special discounts for people shopping in the city can be installed.

On the other hand, this approach seems to be problematic for LOOROs as they find themselves in a self-reinforcing spiral of ubiquitous online price competition on LSPs resulting in lower online sales prices [36]. Additionally, LOOROs are charged with transaction fees by the LSPs which even reduces the profit margin. LOOROs can try to compensate this by charging their customers additional fees for certain services like same day delivery. But it is uncertain whether customers will accept those fees as well as an electronic marketplace that is limited to the offers of local vendors [9]. Finally, LSPs focus on services that support the online Point of Sale (PoS) and neglect the local stores as PoS. It is not certain if such platforms can help LOOROs to sustain their threatened core business, namely, their physical store. Therefore, it is crucial to know for LOOROs if their customers would honor the effort of joining a LSP and maintaining the shop with its product data. If customers are not interested in using an LSP, the resources used by LOOROs for the LSP can be spent better. However, LSPs have been neglected by research so far. Accordingly, this paper aims to close the existing research gap with answering the following research questions:

RQ1: Do customers accept LSP?
RQ2: Which are the main factors for using LSPs and what role do the provided services play?

To answer these research questions, a survey was conducted among 284 consumers. The remainder of this paper reports this empirical study and is organized as follows. In the next section, the role of location for retailers is investigated. Two different kinds of location-dependent services are identified. These are used in explaining factors in the research model that is developed in Sect. 3. Section 4 describes the survey conducted and provides the statistical analysis. The paper closes with a discussion of the results, implications, and limitations.

2 Location-Dependent Services

Before the e-commerce era, the location of a shop was believed to be the most important success factor for retailers [11]. Even for the best retailers, a poor location was an insurmountable obstacle [1]. However, with the advent of e-commerce, the importance of the location choice seems to vanish [24]. Many pure players built big warehouses outside the cities to enable the efficient implementation of the fulfillment promises they made to their customers [50].

Table 1. Identified location-dependent services on LSP [5]

No.	Location-Enabled Services (LES)	No.	Location-Based Services (LBS)
Information services		*Information services*	
1.	Map with store locations	1.	Location-based product consultation
2.	Information about local news	2.	Barcode scanner
3.	Information about local events	3.	Location-based map with store locations
4.	Information about product availability (In-Store)	4.	Location-based map with closest product location
5.	Information about store opening hours	*Communication services*	
6.	Information about store contact data	5.	Location-based support
Communication services		6.	Location-based advertisement
7.	Support at home	7.	Location-based loyalty program
8.	Face to face support	8.	Location-based price-draws
9.	Local loyalty card	9.	Location-based discounts
10.	Customer integration (Customer feedback on store services)	*Navigation services*	
11.	Community integration	10.	In-store navigation
Logistics services		11.	Outdoor navigation
12.	Same day delivery	12.	Location-based shopping tour
13.	Same hour delivery	*Payment and billing services*	
14.	Click & return	13.	Location-based self-checkout
15.	Click & collect		
16.	Reserve & collect		

But recently, the location is becoming more and more important again in the retail sector due to the rising service competition between pure e-commerce players and stationary retailers who offer location-dependent services like same day delivery or even same hour delivery [3, 33]. In this regard, transportation costs that are directly affected by distance are growing and receive high attention [29]. Even in an environment with near zero trade cost, physical distance matters [6] and especially location-dependent service are essential to attract and retain customers in multi-channel retail environments [34, 40]. Furthermore, these location-dependent services, like logistics services and especially express delivery services are positively correlated with repurchases and the loyalty of customers [29].

Table 2. Differentiation location-independent and location-dependent services

Location-independent services	Location-dependent services	
Standard web-services	Location-enabled services	Location-based services
All Services provided on e-marketplaces and not related to location	Services that are feasible if the location of the retailer is close to the households of the customers	Services that are feasible if the customers are close to the store location

Hence, retailers who orchestrate their locational advantages may finally reach a competitive advantage [47]. In general, two factors can be distinguished (see Table 2): First, the location of the vendor enables so-called location-enabled services (LES). If the vendor's location is close to households of the customers, short distance services with low transportation costs are feasible like Click & Collect, same day delivery etc. [26, 28]. Secondly, if customers are close to the vendor, location-based services (LBS) can be implemented. These services aim to utilize foot-traffic at popular places like main streets, parks, etc. using location-awareness information systems and devices, like smartphones and wearables [10, 35, 37, 41]. An overview of existing location-enabled and location-based services is given in Table 1.

3 Conceptual Model

To analyze the factors that influence the acceptance of customers towards LSP, we use the two kinds of location-dependent services identified in the previous section, namely location-enabled and location-based services. As we are not able to measure the behavioral actions of customers on LSPs directly, we will measure the customers' intention to buy via LSPs accordingly. Many theories in the field of psychology and social science describe the relation between beliefs, attitudes, behavioral intention, and, finally, behavioral actions. The Theory of Reasoned Action (TRA), its successors the Theory of Planned Behavior (TPB) and the Reasoned Action Approach (RAA) are worth noting. All share the conviction that an individual's behavior is determined by the individual's intention to carry out his or her behavior and that behavioral intention is affected by the person's attitudes and subjective norms, related to the target behavior

[2]. Critics of the TRA and its successors claim that the investigated behavioral intention is often interpreted as, but is not equal to, the subjective probability of future behavior [27]. We follow this assessment and interpret the measured behavioral intention accordingly as determination to act in a certain way or, in other words, as potential behavior. Considering the theory discussed, we define the construct "Attitude towards LSP" as the general stance of users towards LSPs in terms of attractiveness, helpfulness, and enrichment [51] and the "Intention to buy via LSP" as the future willingness of customers to shop via an LSP [48]. Hence, we hypothesize:

H1: A positive attitude towards Local Shopping Platforms has a positive influence on the intention to buy on a Local Shopping Platform.

The TRA and its successors further postulate that the effect of external variables on the intention is mediated by key beliefs [12]. Derived from the Cost-Benefit Paradigm, "Perceived Usefulness" is a well-established key belief. However, the Cost-Benefit Paradigm from Behavioral Decision Theory explains people's choices in terms of a cognitive trade-off of expected effort and expected result. As per the Cost-Benefit Paradigm, we decided to evaluate this trade-off with regards to its positive forms of expression: perceived low cost (in terms of effort) and perceived high benefits. To measure these perceived advantages, we have decided on a twofold approach. First, we evaluate the perceived usefulness of LSP, location-enabled services (LES) and location-based services (LBS), and, second, we evaluate if the perceived advantage of LES and LBS are high enough to have an impact on the customers' willingness to pay extra for such services. Accordingly, we define three constructs to measure the usefulness. The first construct is called "Perceived Usefulness of Local Shopping Platforms". It is based on Davis [12] and measures how advantageous customers assess the characteristics of LSPs. In line with Davis [12], we hypothesize:

H2: The Perceived Usefulness of Local Shopping Platforms has a positive influence on the attitude towards LSPs.

While the "Perceived Usefulness of LSPs" measures the overall usefulness of an e-commerce platform with a locational focus, it does not explicitly consider the different services provided. Therefore, we use two further constructs that reflect the importance of the locational proximity and the two different kinds of services that are enabled thereby. They are called "Perceived Usefulness of Location-Enabled Services", measuring how advantageous the different LES are perceived as, and "Perceived Usefulness of Location-Based Services", measuring how advantageous customers perceive the various LBS. We hypothesize:

H3: The perceived usefulness of Location-Enabled Services has a positive influence on the perceived usefulness of Local Shopping Platforms.
H4: The perceived usefulness of Location-Based Services has a positive influence on the perceived usefulness of Local Shopping Platforms.

Despite the increasing service competition, services like same day delivery can hardly be offered for free. Therefore, the construct "Willingness to Pay" is defined as the customers' readiness to pay for the new convenient services. Accordingly, we finally hypothesize:

H5: The willingness to pay for Location-Dependent Services has a positive influence on the intention to buy on a Local Shopping Platform.

The research model is depicted in Fig. 1 together with the results and the questionnaire in Table 3.

4 Analysis

4.1 Data Collection

We conducted the survey among potential customers of LSPs in the city center of a medium-sized town in Germany. The questionnaire, containing 34 questions measured in a 5-point-Likert-Scale, was answered by 228 participants over an online form and by 56 participants on paper. The participation in the research study was voluntary. Participants have been informed about the purpose of the study. All special terms used in the survey have been briefly introduced to the participants. In sum, 284 questionnaires

Table 3. Questionnaire

Construct	Item	Question	Source
Usefulness of location-enabled services	ULE1	How useful is same day delivery for you?	Table 1 [12]
	ULE2	How useful is information about product availability (in-store) for you?	
	ULE3	How useful is click & collect for you?	
	ULE4	How useful is click & return for you?	
	ULE5	How useful is a local loyalty card for you?	
	ULE6	How useful is face to face support for you?	
Usefulness of location-based services	ULB1	How useful is location-based product information for you?	Table 1 [12]
	ULB2	How useful are location-based advertisements for you?	
	ULB3	How useful are location-based discounts for you?	
	ULB4	How useful are location-based navigation services for you?	
	ULB5	How useful are location-based loyalty services for you?	
	ULB6	How useful are location-based price-draws for you?	
Usefulness of LSP	U1	How useful is a broad overview of offers from local retailers for you?	[12]
	U2	How useful is a local store nearby, when buying online, for you?	
	U3	How useful is it to meet as yet unknown local shops online for you?	
	U4	How useful is it to support local stores while buying online for you?	
Attitude towards LSP	A1	I think a joint platform with local shops is an attractive idea	[51]
	A2	I think LSPs are helpful for me	
	A3	I think LSPs enrich the shopping environment of my city	
Willingness to pay	W1	I would be willing to pay more for location-based information services	Table 1
	W2	I would be willing to pay more for location-based navigation services	
	W3	I would be willing to pay more for same day delivery	
	W4	I would be willing to pay more for click and collect	
	W5	I would be willing to pay more for click and return	
	W6	I would be willing to pay more for face to face support	
Intention to buy	I1	I want to buy via local shopping platforms	[48]
	I2	I will think about buying on a LSP	
	I3	I want to buy as soon as possible on a LSP	

have been answered and 275 containing full data sets could be used for the analysis. For the analysis of the collected data and the evaluation of the research model, we used SmartPLS [39]. Bootstrapping was done with 5000 samples and 275 cases, determining the significance of weights, loadings and path coefficients. For the multicollinearity tests of the formative constructs, we used SPSS.

4.2 Measurement Model

The research model is composed of two reflective ("Intention to buy", "Attitude towards LSP") and four formative constructs ("Usefulness of Location-Enabled Services", "Usefulness of Location-Based Services", "Usefulness of LSP", "Willingness to Pay for Location-Dependent Services") that have to be analyzed differently [14]. The significance of the constructs' indicators is assessed by their loadings (reflective constructs) that should be greater than 0.7 or weights (formative constructs) that should be greater than 0.1 [25] and their t-values. An indicator is significant if its t-value is greater than 1.65. This corresponds to a significance level of 10%. In order to reach a significance level of 5% (1%), the t-value must be greater than 1.96 (2.57) [25]. Table 3 shows the t-values as well as the corresponding loadings/weights for all indicators of our model, and also indicates the result with regards to the calculated significance. Significant indicators are depicted in black, not significant indicators in grey. Concerning the reflective constructs, all indicators are significant. Each *AVE* (Average Variance Extracted) is above 0.7 (minimum > 0.5), and the composite reliabilities are above 0.8 (minimum 0.7) so that the model fits to the convergence criteria. The discriminant validity of the constructs is also given. The model complies with the Fornell-Larcker criterion: With 0.4, its highest squared construct correlation is below the maximum of 0.5, and the loadings of the reflective indicators are significantly higher than their cross loadings as compared to the other constructs. The internal consistency is given as both reflective constructs exceed the critical value of 0.7 for Cronbachs' alpha ("Intention to buy": 0.853, "Attitude towards LSP": 0,796) [16]. The prediction validity Q^2 is higher than 0 for both constructs [15].

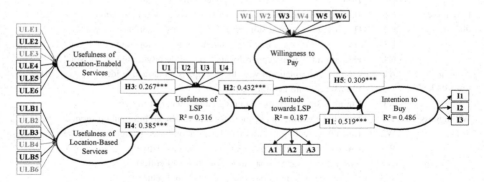

Fig. 1. Research model and results of the PLS algorithm

The results of the formative constructs are as follows (see Table 4): For the construct, "Usefulness of Location-Enabled Services", four (ULE2, ULE4, ULE5, ULE6)

of the six indicators have significant positive influences. The construct, "Usefulness of Location-Based Services", includes three of the six significant indicators: ULB1, ULB3, ULB5. In the construct, "Usefulness of Local Shopping Platforms", all four indicators are significant. For the construct, "Willingness to Pay", three of the six indicators are significant: W3, W5, W6. In addition to the significance of indicators, the discriminant validity of the formative constructs must be verified. The highest correlation between the latent variables is given for the constructs "Attitude towards LSP" and "Intention to Buy via LSP" with a value of 0.519. This does not go beyond the set maximum of 0.9 so that the criterion concerning the discriminant validity is met [15]. The analysis conducted using SPSS with regard to multicollinearity showed that all indicators of the models are sufficiently different and independent of each other [15].

Table 4. Results of the measurement model

	Indicator	Loading/weight	t-statistics	Significance	VIF
Usefulness of location-enabled services	ULE1	0.220	1.589	ns	1.618
	ULE2	0.502	3.656	***	
	ULE3	0.011	0.102	ns	
	ULE4	0.251	1.765	*	
	ULE5	0.297	2.058	**	
	ULE6	0.277	1.814	*	
Usefulness of location-based services	ULB1	0.572	4.309	***	1.612
	ULB2	0.017	0.176	ns	
	ULB3	0.321	2.507	**	
	ULB4	0.059	0.683	ns	
	ULB5	0.236	1.739	*	
	ULB6	0.158	1.295	ns	
Usefulness of LSP	U1	0.492	3.861	***	1.435
	U2	0.219	1.802	*	
	U3	0.377	3.626	***	
	U4	0.408	3.458	***	
Attitude towards LSP	A1	**0.873**	41.030	***	1.751
	A2	**0.840**	19.177	***	
	A3	**0.815**	21.811	***	
Willingness to pay	W1	0.096	0.867	ns	1.335
	W2	−0.052	0.514	ns	
	W3	0.557	4.997	***	
	W4	−0.107	0.863	ns	
	W5	0.435	2.685	***	
	W6	0.309	2.133	**	
Intention to buy	I1	**0.881**	44.578	***	1.792
	I2	**0.880**	39.110	***	
	I3	**0.876**	35.307	***	

ns = not significant; *p < 0.10 (1.65); **p < 0.05 (1.96); ***p < 0.01 (2.57)

4.3   Structural Model

In order to validate the model, the constructs were assessed using the variance inflation factor ($VIF=1/(1 - R^2)$) as to potential multicollinearity [49]. The VIF is lower than the required level of 3.33, which shows that there is no multicollinearity here either [13]. The value of R^2 represents the coefficient of determination, which indicates a substantial influence if the value exceeds 0.67. Above the value of 0.33, a moderate influence of a latent independent variable on the dependent latent variable can be assumed. A weak influence is indicated by an R^2 value of higher than 0.19 [48]. Concerning the hypotheses, all path coefficients are greater than 0.1 and have t-values greater than 2.7 so that all hypotheses can be confirmed at the 1% level [14].

5   Discussion

Local shopping platforms are spreading in Germany. Their business model is still lacking proof of concept, but LSPs' location-dependent business approach seems to be promising. To answer our research questions, we conducted a survey among 284 end consumers in a medium-sized German town. The results of the study are promising. More than 75% of all interviewees have a positive attitude towards LSP and can imagine to shop via LSPs (70%). With the help of our research model, we were able to prove the positive impact of Location-Dependent Services in general and of Location-Enabled and Location-Based Services specifically on the customers' intention to buy via LSPs. All hypotheses could be confirmed. The coefficient of determination R^2 shows a moderate level for the constructs "Intention to Buy" and "Usefulness of LSP" and misses the weak level for the construct "Attitude towards LSP" only very slightly.

With a view to the performance of the examined Location-Dependent indicators, we can determine that LES have a high usefulness for customers; only Same Day Delivery and the Click & Collect Service have not performed as expected. The indicator "Information about in-store product availability" performed best for LES. There is also a high perceived usefulness of LBS, although we can determine that Location-Based Advertisements, Price-Draws and Navigation Services have not performed as expected. Our findings show high perceived usefulness for Location-Based Discounts, Loyalty Services and Information Services. A willingness to pay is visible for LES, as long as they include clear time advantages like Same Day Delivery and Click and Return or individual services like Face to Face support. However, there is no willingness to pay for Click & Collect Services, nor for Location-Based Information and Navigation Services.

As a result, Location-Dependent Services have a positive impact on the customers' perceived value of an LSP. Additionally, channel integrations open doors for new revenue streams, like affiliation fees. For LSPs this is an opportunity to expand their business model. Our examination showed that customers highly appreciate information about the availability of in-store merchandise. If LOOROs would share information about merchandise availability via LSPs or their own web presence, they could make use of the Research Online, Purchase Offline Effect (ROPO I) and lead more customers into the stores. According to these findings, we suggest a circular omnichannel service infrastructure for LOOROs and LSPs:

1. Location-Enabled Services leverage local stores as showrooms and decentralized storage and pull customers to the online PoS.
2. LSPs serve as digital services and logistics providers and introduce Location-Based Services to push customers to the offline PoS.

A successful implementation of such an omnichannel service infrastructure could help LOOROs to overcome their digitalization barriers, make use of their location advantages, trigger effects like ROPO, and lead to a sustainable business relationship between LOOROs and LSPs. Without offline-sales support, LOOROs will not be able to escape the self-reinforcing spiral of online price competition and will still be threatened in their very existence.

As always, also this study is not without limitations. The survey was only conducted in a small region of Germany. Future studies should carry out investigations among a greater region and other countries. In addition, only a subset of Location-Enabled and Location-Based Services was used in the research model. This view should also be broadened in future research.

References

1. Achabal, D.: MULTILOC: a multiple store location model. J. Retailing **58**(2), 5–25 (1982)
2. Ajzen, I., Fishbein, M.: Understanding Attitudes and Predicting Social Behavior. Prentice-Hall, Englewood Cliffs (1980)
3. Allen, J., et al.: Under-standing the impact of e-commerce on last-mile light goods vehicle activity in urban areas: the case of London. Transport Res. D-Tr. E. 61(No. Part B), pp. 325–338 (2018)
4. Bakos, Y.: The emerging role of electronic marketplaces on the internet. Commun. ACM **41**(8), 35–42 (1998)
5. Bärsch, S., Bollweg, L., Lackes, R., Siepermann, M., Weber, P., Wulfhorst, V.: Local shopping platforms – harnessing locational advantages for the digital transformation of local retail outlets: a content analysis. In: Internationale Tagung Wirtschaftsinformatik (2019)
6. Blum, B., Goldfarb, A.: Does the internet defy the law of gravity? J. Int. Econ. **70**(2), 384–405 (2006)
7. Bollweg, L.M., Lackes, R., Siepermann, M., Weber, P.: Mind the gap! Are local retailers misinterpreting customer expectations regarding digital services? IADIS Int. J. WWW/Internet **13**(1), 17–29 (2015)
8. Bollweg, L.M., Lackes, R., Siepermann, M., Sutaj, A., Weber, P.: Digitalization of local owner operated retail outlets: the role of the perception of competition and customer expectations. In: Pacific Asia Conference on Information Systems (PACIS) (2016)
9. Brynjolfsson, E., Hu, Y.J., Rahman, M.S.: Competing in the age of omnichannel retailing. MIT Sloan Manag. Rev. **54**(4), 23 (2013)
10. Cabri, G., Leonardi, L., Mamei, M., Zambonelli, F.: Location-dependent services for mobile users. IEEE Trans. Syst. Man Cybern. **33**(6), 667–681 (2003)
11. Craig, C.S., Ghosh, A., McLafferty, S.: Models of the retail location process: a review. J. Retailing **60**(1), 5–36 (1984)

12. Davis, F.D.: Perceived usefulness, perceived ease of use, and user acceptance of information technology. MIS Q. **13**(3), 319–340 (1989)
13. Diamantopoulos, A., Siguaw, J.A.: Formative versus reflective indicators in organizational measure development. Br. J. Manag. **17**(4), 263–282 (2006)
14. Fornell, C., Bookstein, F.L.: Two structural equation models: LISREL and PLS applied to consumer exit-voice theory. J. Mark. Res. **19**(4), 440–452 (1982)
15. Hair, J.F., Hult, G., Ringle, C., Sarstedt, M.: A Primer on Partial Least Squares Structural Equation Modeling (PLS-SEM). Sage Publications, Thousand Oaks (2014)
16. Hair, J.F.: Multivariate Data Analysis, 6th edn. Prentice-Hall, Englewood-Cliffs (2006)
17. HDE - Retail Federation Germany: Brief Profile. HDE – Retail Federation Germany (2017). https://einzelhandel.de/images/presse/Graphiken/HDE_Presentation_eng.pdf
18. HDE, Retail Federation Germany: Deutschlands Innenstaedte drohen zu veröden (2016). https://www.welt.de/wirtschaft/article165248634/Deutschlands-Innenstaedte-drohen-zu-veroeden.html
19. Heinemann, G.: Online-Handel gräbt stationärem Einzelhandel das Wasser ab – bereits 15 Prozent Anteil in 2013 erwartet (2013). http://www.hs-niederrhein.de/forschung/eweb-researchcenter/aktuelles
20. Holden, R.: Amazon's 'no Line, no Checkout' Grocery Stores are Still in Beta. Forbes Magazine, 22 May 2017. https://www.forbes.com/sites/ronaldholden/2017/05/22/amazons-no-line-no-checkout-groceries-are-still-in-beta/#40fe7a0169ed
21. Huber, B., Sweeney, E., Smyth, A.: Purchasing consortia and electronic markets. Electron. Mark. **14**(4), 284–294 (2004)
22. Köln, I.F.H.: Vitale Innenstädte 2016. IFH Köln, Köln (2016)
23. IFH Köln: Stadt, Land, Handel 2020. http://www.ifhkoeln.de/News-Presse/Fast-jedes-zehnte-Ladengeschaeft-von-Schliessung-bedroht–all
24. Iyer, K.N., Germain, R., Frankwick, G.L.: Supply chain B2B e-commerce and time-based delivery performance. Int. J. Distr. Log. **34**(8), 645–661 (2004)
25. Jarvis, C.B., Mackenzie, S.B., Podsakoff, P.M.: A critical review of construct indicators and measurement model misspecification in marketing and consumer research. J. Consum. Res. **30**(2), 199–218 (2003)
26. Jensen, C.S.: Research challenges in location-enabled m-services. In: Mobile Data Management, pp. 3–7 (2002)
27. Jonas, K., Doll, J.: Eine kritische Bewertung der Theorie überlegten Handelns und der Theorie geplanten Verhaltens. Z. für Sozialpsychologie **27**(1), 18–31 (1996)
28. Jones, M., Mothersbaugh, D., Beatty, S.: The effects of locational convenience on customer repurchase intentions across service types. J. Serv. Mark. **17**(7), 701–712 (2003)
29. Kim, T.Y., Dekker, R., Heij, C.: Cross-border electronic commerce: distance effects and express delivery in European Union markets. Int. J. Electron. Commer. **21**(2), 184–218 (2017)
30. Navickas, V., Krajňáková, E., Navikaite, A.: Paradigm shift of small and medium-sized enterprises competitive advantage. Eng. Econ. **26**(3), 327–332 (2015)
31. Liebmann, W.: Online retailers moving into offline shopping – fast. Forbes Magazine, 13 May 2013. http://www.forbes.com/sites/wendyliebmann/2013/05/30/online-goes-offline-fast/
32. Location Insider. http://locationinsider.de/atalanda-und-buy-local-wollen-mehr-lokale-online-marktplaetze-aufbauen/
33. Lösch, A.: The Economics of Location. Yale University Press, Yale (1954)
34. Massad, N., Heckman, R., Crowston, K.: Customer satisfaction with electronic service encounters. Int. J. Electron. Commer. **10**(4), 73–104 (2006)

35. Mennecke, B., Strader, T.: Where in the world on the web does location matter? A framework for location based services in m-commerce. In: AMCIS 2001 Proceedings, p. 90 (2001)
36. Pan, X., Shankar, V., Ratchford, B.T.: Price competition between pure play versus bricks-and-clicks e-tailers. Adv. Appl. Microecon. 11, 29–61 (2002)
37. Pura, M.: Linking perceived value and loyalty in location-based mobile services. Manag. Serv. Qual.: Int. J. 15(6), 509–538 (2005)
38. Reimann, E.: David gegen Goliath: Wie der lokale Handel gegen Amazon kämpft. http://www.heise.de/newsticker/meldung/David-gegen-Goliath-Wie-der-lokale-Handel-gegen-Amazon-kaempft-2552842.html
39. Ringle, C., Wende, S., Will, A.: SmartPLS 2.0.M3. SmartPLS, Hamburg (2005)
40. Saeed, K.A., Grover, V., Hwang, Y.: The relationship of e-commerce competence to customer value and firm performance: an empirical investigation. J. Manag. Inf. Syst. 22(1), 223–256 (2005)
41. Sahai, A., Machiraju, V.: Enabling of the ubiquitous e-service vision on the internet. E-Service 1(1), 5–19 (2001)
42. Sandberg, K.W., Håkansson, F.: Barriers to adapt ecommerce by rural microenterprises in Sweden: a case study. Int. J. Knowl. Res. Manag. E-Commer. 4(1), 1–7 (2014)
43. Siemssen, S.: Oliver Wyman Retail Journal German. Oliver Wyman (2017). http://www.oliverwyman.de/content/dam/oliverwyman/europe/germany/de/insights/publications/2017/Feb_2017/2017_Oliver_Wyman_Retail_Journal_German.pdf
44. Standing, S., Standing, C., Love, P.E.: A review of research on e-marketplaces. Decis. Support Syst. 49(1), 41–51 (2010)
45. Statista – Statistisches Bundesamt: Verteilung der Konsumausgaben der privaten Haushalte in Deutschland nach Verwendungszwecken von 1970 bis 2016. Statista - Das Statistik-Portal (2017)
46. Stockdale, R., Standing, C.: Benefits and barriers of electronic marketplace participation: an SME perspective. J. Enterp. Inf. Manag. 17(4), 301–311 (2004)
47. Strandskov, J.: Sources of competitive advantages and business performance. J. Bus. Econ. Manag. 7(3), 119–129 (2006)
48. Van der Heijden, H., Verhagen, T., Creemers, M.: Understanding online purchase intentions. Eur. J. Inf. Syst. 12(1), 41–48 (2003)
49. Weiber, R., Mühlhaus, D.: Strukturgleichungsmodellierung. Eine anwendungsorientierte Einführung in die Kausalanalyse. Springer, Berlin (2010). https://doi.org/10.1007/978-3-642-35012-2
50. Weltevreden, J.W.: B2C E-commerce logistics: the rise of collection-and-delivery points in The Netherlands. Int. J. Distr. Log. 36(8), 638–660 (2008)
51. Xu, H., Teo, H.H.: Alleviating consumers' privacy concerns in location-based services: a psychological control perspective. In: ICIS 2004 Proceedings, p. 64 (2004)

iCRM Workshop

ICRM 2019 Workshop Chairs' Message

Today, more than 3.4 billion people are actively using social media [1]. Businesses aim to connect with this "digital population" by establishing presences in the social web while seeking for competitive advantages in this environment. Integrated Social Customer Relationship Management (Social CRM) focuses on exploiting the potentials of social media for business processes in marketing, sales, and customer services [2]. The notion of integration implies that not only the digital social media platforms, which are typically operated outside the company, need to be aligned with the world of CRM within companies. In particular, adopting Social CRM is merely a technological undertaking, but requires to align business strategies and processes as well as information systems [3]. Accompanied by an increasing interest of research regarding related methods, effect, and technologies (e.g. [4–7]) a variety of software applications ranging from social analytic tools, workflow management systems, or content management have become available. Businesses have been built upon these resources and demonstrated numerous potential use cases since Social CRM spread some ten years ago. However, they also face challenges, such as the automated extraction of knowledge from user-generated content (UGC) or measuring the effects of Social CRM activities, which still need to be solved. The 4th iCRM workshop aimed to shed light on current research efforts, from a technical and economical perspective, targeting the development and implementation of integrated Social CRM solutions. The setup was interdisciplinary and invited researchers and professionals from different fields (e.g. marketing and relationship management, information systems design, computational intelligence) gave talks on the topic. The two papers of this year's workshop deepen the understanding of the market through social media analysis and about the stakeholders in Social CRM projects. The first paper "Social Network Advertising Classification Based on Content Categories" demonstrates a method for social media content analysis with machine learning that helps businesses to classify postings according to their marketing intention. The implementation of such methods supports the development of processes and functionalities, which provide marketing departments with new means to differentiate a company from its competitors, as well as to monitor common practices in the market. While the first paper focuses on technological aspects, the second paper "Social CRM Services in Digital Marketing Agencies: A Preliminary Study on Outsourcing Practices in German SMEs" sheds light on potential services of digital marketing agencies for the realization of integrated Social CRM approaches. Although agencies already provide services dedicated to the use of Social CRM, the low support of Social CRM-related tasks limits the options for companies to build on external support in the realization of integrated Social CRM. Thus, it points towards a potential barrier that hinders an increasing adoption of Social CRM. Both studies point out to relevant practical implications that may support businesses in establishing processes and strategies according to the potentials of technology and provisions of services related to Social CRM. The workshop was a community effort and the contribution of all authors, as well as Program Committee members, was highly appreciated.

Rainer Alt
Olaf Reinhold
Fabio Lobato

References

1. We are social: Digital in 2019. https://wearesocial.com/global-digital-report-2019 (2019) Accessed on 2019-08-28
2. Alt, R., Reinhold, O.: Social customer relationship management (social crm): Application and technology. Business & information systems engineering 4(5) (2012) 287–291
3. Alt, R., Reinhold, O.: Social Customer Relationship Management: Fundamentals, Applications, Technologies. Springer Nature (2019)
4. Greenberg, P.: CRM at the Speed of Light: Social CRM Strategies, Tools, and Techniques for Engaging Your Customers. The McGraw-Hill Companies (2009)
5. Choudhury, M.M., Harrigan, P.: Crm to social crm: the integration of new technologies into customer relationship management. Journal of Strategic Marketing 22(2) (2014) 149–176
6. Trainor, K.J., Andzulis, J.M., Rapp, A., Agnihotri, R.: Social media technology usage and customer relationship performance: A capabilities-based examination of social crm. Journal of Business Research 67(6) (2014) 1201–1208
7. Sigala, M.: Implementing social customer relationship management: A process framework and implications in tourism and hospitality. International Journal of Contemporary Hospitality Management 30(7) (2018) 2698–2726

Organization

Chairs

Rainer Alt   Leipzig University and Social CRM Research
                                        Center, Germany
Olaf Reinhold   Leipzig University and Social CRM Research
                                        Center, Germany
Fabio Lobato   Federal University of Western Pará, Brazil

Program Committee

Antônio Jacob Jr.   State University of Maranhão, Brazil
Cristiana Fernandes De Muylder   FUMEC University, Brazil
Douglas R. Cirqueira   Dublin City University, Ireland
Emílio Arruda   FUMEC University and University of Amazon,
                                        Brazil
Flavius Frasincar   Erasmus University Rotterdam,
                                        The Netherlands
Julio Viana   Social CRM Research Center, Germany
Nino Carvalho   IPOG Instituto de Pós-graduação, Brazil, and
                                        IPAM Instituto Português de Administração
                                        de Marketing, Portugal
Omar Andres Carmona Cortes   Instituto Federal do Maranhão, Brazil
Rafael Geraldeli Rossi   Universidade Federal do Mato Grosso do Sul,
                                        Brazil
Renato Fileto   Federal University of Santa Catarina, Brazil
Sandra Turchi   Digitalents, Brazil

Social CRM Services in Digital Marketing Agencies: A Preliminary Study on Service Offerings in Germany

Julio Viana[1]([✉]) [iD], Maarten van der Zandt[2], Olaf Reinhold[2] [iD],
and Rainer Alt[2] [iD]

[1] Social CRM Research Center, Leipzig, Germany
julio.viana@scrc-leipzig.de
[2] Leipzig University, Leipzig, Germany
maarten.vandz@gmail.com,
olaf.reinhold@wifa.uni-leipzig.de,
rainer.alt@uni-leipzig.de

Abstract. Outsourcing of Digital Marketing services is a commonly adopted strategy in the market. The increasing importance of the Social CRM topic and its data analysis feature sheds light on specific changes that might occur on how Digital Marketing Agencies offer their services, as well as on outsourcing practices. This work analyzes the Social CRM services provided by these agencies and validates them according to the German market. It focuses on a preliminary phase within the research process, which aims at discovering outsourcing practices within German SMEs. The results support the adaptation and validation of the Social CRM services according to the German Digital Marketing Agencies. Additionally, it provides an overview on the types of service German agencies provide, as well as the practical implications for these companies.

Keywords: Social CRM outsourcing · Digital marketing · German agencies

1 Introduction

The concept of Customer Relationship Management (CRM) has been discussed in the literature and practices for decades. It combines people, processes and technology throughout an organization to understand its customers [1, 2]. CRM's main goal is to provide an infrastructure to support companies defining and increasing customer value, as well as motivate valuable customers to stay loyal [3]. CRM has evolved as new Information Technologies (IT) emerged [1]. Following these advances and the rise of the Web 2.0, the concept of Social CRM surged to discuss how social media engagement affects CRM [4, 5]. Meanwhile, scholars began to study how to integrate the large amount of data into CRM systems [6], as well as the application of IT techniques to analyze this data in companies [7].

Aligned with its interdisciplinary approach, Social CRM converges with the latest discussions on digital marketing strategies due to its social media strategy to engage and build relationship with customers and prospects [8]. Hence, this scenario might

© Springer Nature Switzerland AG 2019
W. Abramowicz and R. Corchuelo (Eds.): BIS 2019 Workshops, LNBIP 373, pp. 383–395, 2019.
https://doi.org/10.1007/978-3-030-36691-9_32

influence how Digital Marketing Agencies (DMAs) define their services as the search for integrating and analyzing customer data increases [9, 10].

Although marketing activities related to advertising and campaign promotion have been outsourced for a long time, companies have been increasingly outsourcing operational and analytical tasks as well [11]. It gives room for multi-vendor strategies, envisioning different service providers within a company's value chain, as well as adopting a close relationship to one specific provider [12].

Considering the aforementioned factors, this study is part of a research project that aims at exploring the digital marketing outsourcing panorama among SMEs in Germany. This paper, however, focuses on the validation of a service catalogue that consists of Social CRM services offered by German DMAs, as well as on preliminary analysis of service offerings from these companies. Thus, this study seeks to answer the following research questions:

- What are the Social CRM services provided by German DMAs?
- How are these services described by the state-of-practice in the German market?

Figure 1 introduces the complete research agenda, highlighting the focus of this paper.

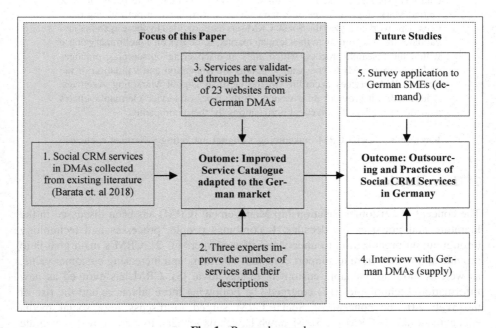

Fig. 1. Research agenda

Previous research on the topic analyzed the literature and classified the services according to the main categories within the Social CRM framework [13]. Following the research agenda, we analyzed and improved these services and their descriptions according to inputs from experts in the field. The improved catalogue with 27 services was then validated to align these services and descriptions to the digital marketing industry in Germany. The result is an initial analysis of the service offerings from German DMAs and a comprehensive service catalogue adapted to this market. The remainder of this paper is organized as follows: introduction to the applied methodology, results that support the improvement of the service catalogue, results regarding implications for businesses and conclusions.

2   Methodology

The following subchapters describe the methodology for the preparation phase and validation process of the service catalogue. The first step consisted of improving an existing service catalogue based on review from experts in the field. Consequently, German DMAs were selected according to the service description available on their website. The validation process took place by contrasting the information collected from DMAs with the existing catalogue improved by experts.

2.1   Services from Existing Literature and Expert Contribution

The validation process requires an initial catalogue of Social CRM services provided by DMAs, as well as services and descriptions specifically from the German market, indicating possible improvements and adaptations. This initial catalogue was developed based on the list provided by [13]. The items from the previous study on Social CRM services provided by DMAs consisted of 22 services divided into the following categories: Analysis (ten services); Interaction (ten services); and Management (two services). The initial catalogue was used as starting point for the analysis with experts.

Three experts in the field of Social CRM and digital marketing analyzed the services. They were selected according to recent research on the topic, their current positions and availability to participate on the study. It resulted on sessions with two experts from the academic sector and one from the industry.

These experts analyzed the existing services and suggested improvements for their names and descriptions. After reviewing the services and descriptions, the sessions resulted in an improved catalogue of 27 services. Despite improvements, the Social CRM categories provided by [6] were maintained (Analysis, Interaction, and Management/Integration).

2.2   The German DMAs

In order to select the German DMAs, we took into consideration an agency database that ranks digital marketing agencies according to a network of professionals. The page Top Interactive Agencies provided a ranking of 48 DMAs located in Germany [14] and was accessed between March and June, 2019. The DMAs were later selected according to the following filters:

- Filter 1 (F1): The agencies provided comprehensive definitions for their services.
- Filter 2 (F2): The agencies provided a detailed description for each of these services.

Many agencies do not provide a catalogue of well-described services, focusing rather on their campaign portfolio. Some of the agencies were able to define their services, but did not provide a detailed description for them. The table below shows the selection process indicating the agencies that provided a good definition and description of services according to the filters (Table 1).

Table 1. Application of filters for selecting German DMAs

Agency	F1	F2	Agency	F1	F2	Agency	F1	F2
Artificial Rome			Battalion	X		VCCP	X	X
SinnerSchrader			RWATGG			Wivern Digital		
Nolte & Lauth			SYZYGY	X	X	Die Webstars	X	X
Sholtz & Volkmer	X	X	Spyke Media			Fairwalk Design		
Elespacio			Serviceplan			Exozet		
Ming Labs			Thinkmoto			Ape Unit		
Adwise & Co			Aperto			Awesome Dev.	X	X
Demodern	X		& Revenue	X	X	Entermedia		
Byte Park	X	X	Vivid Binaries			Uhura	X	X
Ufomammoot			Mothership	X	X	Innomative	X	X
Kubikfoto			KKLD			D&B Interactive	X	X
Stink Studios	X	X	Interone	X	X	Moccu	X	X
MoreSleep			Lucid	X		Gyro		
Delasocial	X		Mobiteam			Tribal		
Hy.am Studios	X	X	UX&I	X		Slash Digital	X	X
Goldener Westen			NUISOL	X	X	R/GA		
Number of DMAs	6	4		8	5		8	8
Total	17							

Hence, we selected 17 companies that were able to provide a definition and detailed description of their services. However, due to the low number of agencies, another ranking was used to improve these numbers and provide a better analysis. The Clutch database catalogues and ranks agencies across the globe, indicating the German agencies with the highest ranking according to client reviews, past work, market presence, and specialization [15]. Following this ranking and filters, six extra agencies were selected: Edelman, MediaBoostr, Ketchum, Studio Humm, Radish Lab and Quisma. The table below indicates all the 23 analyzed agencies and their references (Table 2).

Table 2. Selected German DMAs

DMA	Agency name	Ref.	DMA	Agency name	Ref.
A01	Sholz und Volkmer	[22]	A13	Uhura	[29]
A02	Byte Park	[16]	A14	Innomative	[24]
A03	Stink Studios	[18]	A15	D&B Interactive	[26]
A04	Hyam	[20]	A16	Moccu	[37]
A05	Syzygy	[28]	A17	Slash Digital	[34]
A06	& Revenue	[32]	A18	Edelman	[17]
A07	Mothership	[23]	A19	MediaBoostr	[19]
A08	Interone	[30]	A20	Ketchum	[21]
A09	NUISOL	[31]	A21	Studio Humm	[25]
A10	VCCP	[35]	A22	Radish Lab	[27]
A11	Die Webstars	[36]	A23	Quisma	[33]
A12	Awesome Developers	[20]			

2.3 Validation Process

The services found on the websites from German agencies were analyzed and compiled according to their suitability to Social CRM. They were then compared with the existing services improved by three experts.

The expert sessions concluded in an improved service catalogue, which supported the validation process, essential to improve the service descriptions. The review on the websites from German DMAs also supported the preliminary analysis of the current offerings from these companies in Germany. The service names were used as keywords for analyzing how many companies are offering them. For example, when searching for services, such as "Conversion Rate Comparison" and "Omnichannel Interaction", the first one resulted only in few hits, while the second resulted in several hits. The full catalogue, as well as further improvements, are presented in the next section.

3 Improvements in the Service Catalogue

The expert sessions and validation process contributed significantly to enhancements in the existing service catalogue. Table 3 introduces the improved catalogue and indicates the changes.

Of the 27 existing services descriptions, 25 could be assigned to suitable services on the website from agencies, resulting in a successful validation of approximately 92% of the catalogue. The services S09 and S23 did not match the services described on the websites. This result indicates that either German DMAs do not offer these services or their definitions and descriptions are not in line with the offerings of the agencies.

Moreover, services S08, S10, S15, S18 and S21 were validated only by one or two agencies. These services are related to either lead management or data integration to CRM tools, indicating a niche opportunity for DMAs willing to integrate concepts of

Table 3. Expert-improved services catalogue and validation

Service	Description	DMAs
Interaction		
S01. Content Production/Copywriting	Produce different content and formatting for social media	A01, A02, A03, A04, A05, A06, A08, A10, A11, A13, A14, A15, A16, A17, A20, A21, A22, A23
S02. Interaction with blogging community and forums* *- New Service Name:* **S02. Community Management**	**Produce specific content for collaboration on blogs and forums of the same niche of the company or with a similar audience**	**A01, A04, A08, A11, A13, A18, A22, A23**
S03. Social Media General Interaction	Interact and reply to clients through posts, mentions, comments or direct messages according to brand management guidelines	A04, A07, A08, A10, A11, A13, A18
S04. Crisis Management*	Use predefined engagement and conversation templates to guide marketers on how to proceed during crises. **- New Description: Use pre-defined guidelines and discussion templates to help marketers anticipate, tackle and resolve crises.** **- Quote from DMA:** [A08] *"...we can identify possible problems and critical issues at an early stage and counteract storms."*	**A08, A11, A18, A20**
S05. Setup of Services within Social Platforms	Provide applications such as games and chatbots using social media APIs to improve customer interaction	A03, A11, A14
S06. Omnichannel Interaction	Communicate the brand and its products/services across different means to improve customer experience and optimize the number of visitors, integrating content from social media and other online platforms	A02, A04, A07, A08, A10, A11, A15, A16, A17, A18, A19, A20, A23
S07. Product/Service Offerings	Share service or product offerings from client companies through social media campaigns	A02, A05, A07, A08, A09, A11, A14, A17, A23
S08. Traffic Increase to Landing Pages	Increase traffic to landing pages by using Social Media as a redirection tool	A11

(continued)

Table 3. (*continued*)

Service	Description	DMAs
Analysis		
S09. Brand Mention Search	Search for brand mentions and discussions through major social web platforms (e.g., Facebook, Instagram, Twitter, and YouTube) and/or other sources (e.g., websites, blogs)	–
S10. Social Web General Search	Search relevant and up-to-date content and topics on the internet, as well as connections among people, groups, organizations, and influencers for marketing purposes	A11
S11. Competition and Segment Analysis* - *New Service Name:* **S11. Competition Analysis**	**Analyze content, reputation and brand positioning from competing segments through social web**	**A07, A14, A21, A22, A23**
S12. Keyword Analysis	Indicate keywords to improve the company's SEO and SEM results based on segment data analysis	A04, A05, A07, A14, A15, A22
S13. Trends, Insights, and Content Identification* - *New Service Name:* **S13. Trend Monitoring and Detection**	**Use the data from social media sources to decode information that can identify trends, patterns and specific characteristics of particular audiences**	**A14, A16, A18, A20, A23**
S14. Analysis of Brand and Campaign Impact	Classification of social media data to monitor companies' impact and reputation, as well as analyze the reach and relevance of campaigns	A03, A04, A05, A07, A08, A09, A14, A15, A14, A17, A18, A20
S15. Lead Opportunity, Detection, and Classification*	Indicate and classify possible prospects, opportunities to contact, and customer needs. **- New Description: Identify and classify possible prospects and contact opportunities through social media.** **- Quote from DMA:** A19 *"...convert your visitor into active users that engage with your content or purchase your products...", "...identify behavior patterns and optimize each step of the journey."*	**A19**
S16. Data Analysis Reports	Provision of insights in the form of reports, summaries and/or charts based on customer data analysis	A05, A06, A07, A08, A14, A18, A19, A20, A23

(*continued*)

Table 3. (*continued*)

Service	Description	DMAs
Management/Integration		
S17. Communication Strategy and Budget* - *New Service Name:* **S17. Development of a Communications Strategy**	Develop strategies and allocate the appropriate budget for online communication (marketing campaigns, brand management, persona identification, and creative direction). **- New Description: Develop and implement online communication strategy.** **- Quotes from DMAs:** A05 *"Consumer & Market Insights, Brands and CRM-Strategies."* A20 *"Strategy Development."*	**A05, A06, A07, A09, A10, A11, A15**
S18. Integration of CRM and Social Media Data	Integrate CRM information from companies to social media data analysis to support communication processes and customer classification	A12, A22
S19. Feedback and Complaint Management	Manage customers' feedback and complaints within social platforms	A01, A04, A08, A11, A18
S20. Social Media Accounts Management	Set up social media accounts across different online platforms according to communication strategies. **- New Description: Set up of accounts and company representation on different social media platforms.** **- Quotes from DMAs:** A06 *"...set up accounts and campaigns..."* A10 *"...ensure that your company is represented on the social media channels relevant to your target group..."*	**A06, A08, A11, A12, A17, A18**
S21. Track and Monitor Leads/Prospects through Social Media	Track and monitor prospect's progress and location within the sales funnel (attract, convert, close, delight) through social media to indicate actions	A14, A19
S22. Conversion Rate Comparison	Compare conversion rates based on traffic source and social media. It can understand where conversions are stronger and weaker on the online contact points and develop strategies from this	A11, A14, A19
S23. Establishment of Process Roadmap for Customer Interaction	Define workflows to guide and optimize the intern organization and the interaction process with customers	–

(*continued*)

Table 3. (*continued*)

Service	Description	DMAs
S24. Educational Trainings on Data Integration	Provide training to support companies in the integration process of CRM and social media data	A09, A17, A23
S25. Software Development and/or Setup	Develop and/or provide to companies a management software and applications to improve their interaction and monitoring of customers	A11, A12, A13, A14, A16, A22
S26. Information Architecture and Design	Develop intuitive, clear and engaging pages in social media for a better navigation experience	A11, A14, A18, A21, A22
S27. Digital Influencer Marketing	Selection and management of appropriate digital influencers to produce sponsored content about the brand for their followers and develop brand awareness	A04, A05, A07, A08, A17, A18, A20

information systems and CRM to their service portfolio. On the contrary, services S01, S06, S07, S14 and S16 had a strong matching with the services on the websites, suggesting a stronger focus from DMAs on content production and dissemination, as well as analysis of campaigns results.

Some descriptions were modified to improve the matching with the terminologies used by DMAs. After the analysis of the offered services and the comparison with the existing service description, the main use of the services was highlighted to fit the business-to-business (B2B) environment. The original service description of service four focused on the possibilities of support in the event of a crisis that had already occurred. However, the DMA services focused on the early identification of problems and the anticipation and counteraction of any crises. Regarding service 17, the DMAs did not refer to budget allocation. Therefore, this item was removed to avoid misunderstandings in future studies. Lastly, the description from service 20 was modified to include the brand representation on social media.

The review of service descriptions also supported the simplification and revision of some service names. Community Management was the most common used term to describe the management of blogs, forums and other alike services. In the same direction, the term "segment" was removed from service S11, as well as the term "insights" and from service S13, to simplify and facilitate the understanding of the core service. Following the change on the description from service 17, the term "budget" was also removed from the service name. This adaptation is important to make sure that research and industry terms are aligned to support the use of the final catalogue in further studies.

4   Service Offerings and Their Implications for Businesses

As seen on the results of the validation, most of the analyzed DMAs do not provide services in regarding the integration of social media monitoring and data analysis to CRM systems. The categorization of the services follows the proposed method by [13], based on [6] depicted in Fig. 2.

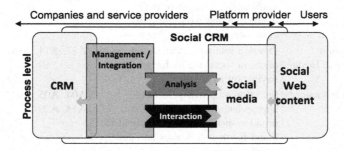

Fig. 2.   Categorization of services based on [6]

The proposed Social CRM model support the understanding of how social media presence can be integrated to CRM activities. However, the initial analysis of the offerings from German DMAs shows that agencies do not follow this model, concentrating on activities related to content development, management of social media accounts and analysis of campaign results. The total of agencies providing services in the categories are: interaction (22 DMAs), analysis (17 DMAs) and management/ interaction (21 DMAs). However, as indicated on Fig. 2, interaction was the category with the highest number of matches, followed by analysis and management/integration. This analysis, took into consideration the number of agencies offering specific services within the category.

Additionally, the results indicate that many agencies specializes on specific services. The company &Revenue, for example, claim to focus on pay-per-click and email marketing, while the agency Mediaboostr focuses on Facebook and Instagram marketing. In this specialization trend, companies would need hire different companies in order to have access to all needed services. However, small and medium-sized companies (SMEs) might have limited resources for outsourcing digital marketing services from different specialized agencies and would rather focus on a close relationship with a single provider.

In addition, results show a lack in the market for agencies aligned with the evolving integration of information systems (e.g. software and app development) to social media activities. Therefore, offerings regarding the integration of social media marketing with CRM systems is low. Nonetheless, CRM data is usually detained by the client companies, which can either decide to share this data with the agencies or are forbidden to do so, due to legal restrains.

Thus, these preliminary results support a future study with German DMAs to deeply understand their offerings, as well as the design of an effective survey aiming at understanding the outsourcing practices from small and medium-sized companies in Germany.

5 Conclusions and Further Work

This paper discusses the results of a preliminary study on service offerings within German DMAs as part of a research project. It provides an extensive Social CRM service catalogue adapted to German DMAs. The validation process of this catalogue suggests practical implications related to the type of services German DMAs offer in the market. Additionally, this phase grounds further research on outsourcing activities of Digital Marketing services by German SMEs.

The results successfully answers the proposed research questions by providing an extensive catalogue of Social CRM services, as well as a detailed description for each service adapted to the German market. Additionally, it provides an initial analysis on the offerings from German DMAs. Services with low or missing validation indicate areas that are not yet explored by the analyzed agencies, as well as opportunities for German DMAs to broaden their service portfolio. Software development, lead management and integration of social media data and campaigns to CRM systems are not well explored, suggesting an opportunity for improving services related to information systems within the agencies. The results of the validation strongly contributes to the next phase of the research, which seeks to analyze further the offerings from the agencies and the outsourcing demands from German SMEs. A cross-study with insights from supply and demand sides on Digital Marketing services can support DMAs to detect market opportunities and SMEs to improve their outsourcing strategies.

Further works could adapt the catalogue to different markets in order to analyze different variables regarding Digital Marketing and Social CRM services. Additionally, further improvements could take place by incorporating the opinions and suggestions of more experts in the field.

References

1. Chen, I.J., Popovich, K.: Understanding customer relationship management (CRM). Bus. Process Manag. J. **9**(5), 672–688 (2003). https://doi.org/10.1108/14637150310496758
2. Brown, S.A.: Customer Relationship Management: A Strategic Imperative in the World of e-Business. Wiley, Toronto, Chichester (2000). Brown, S.A. (Editor and contributor)
3. Dyché, J.: The CRM Handbook. Addison-Wesley, Harlow (2001)
4. Malthouse, E.C., Haenlein, M., Skiera, B., et al.: Managing customer relationships in the social media era: introducing the social CRM house. J. Interact. Mark. **27**(4), 270–280 (2013). https://doi.org/10.1016/j.intmar.2013.09.008
5. Greenberg, P.: CRM at the Speed of Light: Social CRM Strategies, Tools, and Techniques for Engaging Your Customers, 4th edn. McGraw-Hill, New York (2010)
6. Alt, R., Reinhold, O.: Social-customer-relationship-management (Social-CRM). Wirtschaftsinformatik **54**(5), 281–286 (2012). https://doi.org/10.1007/s11576-012-0330-6

7. Chagas, B.N.R., Viana, J.A.N., Reinhold, O., et al.: Current applications of machine learning techniques in CRM: a literature review and practical implications. In: 2018 IEEE/WIC/ACM International Conference on Web Intelligence (WI), pp. 452–458. IEEE (2018)
8. Faase, R., Helms, R., Spruit, M.: Web 2.0 in the CRM domain: defining social CRM. IJECRM **5**(1), 1 (2011). https://doi.org/10.1504/ijecrm.2011.039797
9. Jobs, C.G., Aukers, S.M., Gilfoil, D.M.: The impact of big data on your firms marketing communications: a framework for understanding the emerging marketing analytics industry. Acad. Mark. Stud. J. **19**(2), 81–92 (2015)
10. Woodcock, N., Green, A., Starkey, M., et al.: Social CRM as a business strategy. J. Database Mark. Customer Strategy Manag. **18**(1), 50–64 (2011). https://doi.org/10.1057/dbm.2011.7
11. McGovern, G., Quelch, J.: Outsourcing marketing. Harvard Bus. Rev. **83**, 22–26 (2005)
12. Alt, R., Reitbauer, S.: Towards an integrated architecture and assessment model for financial sourcing. In: Rabhi, F.A., Veit, D.J., Weinhardt, C. (eds.) Second International Workshop on Enterprise, Applications and Services in the Finance Industry, pp. 67–74. IEEE, Regensburg (2005)
13. Barata, G.M., Viana, J.A., Reinhold, O., et al.: Social CRM in digital marketing agencies: an extensive classification of services. In: 2018 IEEE/WIC/ACM International Conference on Web Intelligence (WI), pp. 750–753. IEEE (2018)
14. Top Interactive Agencies (2019). https://www.topinteractiveagencies.com/about-us/. Accessed 20 Mar 2019
15. Clutch: Clutch Research Methodology (2019). https://clutch.co/methodology. Accessed 20 Mar 2019
16. Byte Park (2019). https://www.bytepark.de/en/about-us/. Accessed 31 Mar 2019
17. Edelman: Expertise (2019). https://www.edelman.com/expertise. Accessed 21 Mar 2019
18. Stink Studios (2019). https://www.stinkstudios.com/about. Accessed 31 Mar 2019
19. MediaBoostr (2019). https://www.mediaboostr.com/?utm_source=clutch&utm_medium=referral#aboutus. Accessed 21 Mar 2019
20. Hyam: Social Media (2019). https://hyam.de/social-media. Accessed 21 Mar 2019
21. Ketchum: Trending Solutions (2019). https://www.ketchum.com/reach-approach/. Accessed 21 Mar 2019
22. Sholz & Volkmer: Agentur (2019). https://www.s-v.de/de/agentur/. Accessed 31 Mar 2019
23. Mothership: What We Do Best (2019). https://mothersh1p.de/. Accessed 31 May 2019
24. Innomative: What We Do (2019). http://www.innomative.com/WhatWeDo.php. Accessed 31 Mar 2019
25. Studio Humm: From discovery to design and development (2019). https://www.studiohumm.com/services. Accessed 31 Mar 2019
26. D&B Interactive: Die Agentur (2019). https://d-b-interactive.com/dieagentur/. Accessed 21 Mar 2019
27. Radish Lab: Services (2019). https://radishlab.com/services/. Accessed 31 Mar 2019
28. Syzygy: Agentur (2019). https://www.syzygy.net/germany/de/agentur. Accessed 21 Mar 2019
29. Uhura: Agentur-Profil und Kompetenzen (2019). https://www.uhura.de/kompetenzen/. Accessed 31 Mar 2019
30. Interone: Was Wir Machen (2019). https://interone.de/leistungen. Accessed 21 Mar 2019
31. NUISOL: What We Do (2019). https://nuisol.com/services/. Accessed 31 May 2019
32. & Revenue: What We Do (2019). https://andrevenue.com/what-we-do/. Accessed 21 Mar 2019
33. Quisma: Unsere Leistungsübersicht (2019). https://quisma.com/leistungen/. Accessed 31 Mar 2019

34. Slash Digital: What We Do (2019). https://slash.digital/social-media-agency/. Accessed 21 Mar 2019
35. VCCP: Unsere Kompetenzen (2019). http://vccp.de/capabilities/. Accessed 21 May 2019
36. Die Webstars: Was wir so machen (2019). https://diewebstars.de/. Accessed 21 May 2019
37. Moccu: Services (2019). https://www.moccu.com/services/. Accessed 21 May 2019

Social Network Advertising Classification Based on Content Categories

Gustavo Nogueira de Sousa[2,3](✉) ⬚, Gustavo R. Almeida[1] ⬚,
and Fábio Lobato[1,3](✉) ⬚

[1] Engineering and Geoscience Institute,
Federal University of Western Pará (UFOPA), Santarém, Brazil
sougusta@gmail.com, gr.almeida00@gmail.com,
fabio.lobato@ufopa.edu.br
[2] Social CRM Research Center (SCRC), Leipzig, Germany
[3] State University of Maranhão, São Luís, Brazil

Abstract. Social media usage is expanding in different sectors of society. As a consequence, a large amount of User-Generated-Content is produced every day. Due to its different effects on users, content management is essential for business advertising on these platforms. However, in view of social media's large volume of content, measuring the effect on users entails high costs and effort. This paper examines the use of machine learning techniques to reduce the cost and effort of this kind of analysis. To this end, an automatic document classification is employed to check its viability by testing it in the companies publications in Facebook. The results show that the machine learning classifier obtained has an excellent potential to measure effectiveness and analyze a significant amount of content with more efficiency. The classifier has practical implications since it allows an extensive competitor analysis to be conducted and is also able to influence social media campaigns.

Keywords: Social network · Advertising · Engagement · Machine learning · Data-driven decision making

1 Introduction

Social media usage is growing steadily [4]. In 2019 it is estimated that these platforms have around 2.77 billion users, with Facebook as the leading platform with 2.3 billion users [19]. In addition, other platforms feature a large number of users, such as Youtube with 1.9 billion, Twitter with 330 million and Instagram with 1 billion [21, 22]. Due to their ease of use, users can create, interact, collaborate, and share contents with others through these media [13, 15]. This phenomenon has resulted in a significant improvement in communication and social interaction. Hence, it has had a significant impact on the relationship between companies and their customers [2, 17].

Having a facility to share information through these platforms has triggered a phenomenon called electronic Word-of-Mouth (eWoM), which has transformed consumers into active actors [2]. The eWoM can be understood as the act of creating and sharing information about brands, products, and services in the digital media [18]. This

© Springer Nature Switzerland AG 2019
W. Abramowicz and R. Corchuelo (Eds.): BIS 2019 Workshops, LNBIP 373, pp. 396–404, 2019.
https://doi.org/10.1007/978-3-030-36691-9_33

means that social media has become a place with a significant power to share these types of contents [1].

The information derived from eWoM allows a comparison to be made between brands, products, or services [11]. By applying community detection methods on social media data, for instance, it is possible to provide useful insights about some of the dynamics and phenomena that take place in such systems [20]. Moreover, it is directly related to the sector of tourism, since a large number of tourists select their destination, hotel, tours, and restaurants with the aid of eWoM content, such as photos, video, reviews, and feedback scores [10, 16]. This can be described as Smart Tourism (ST), which is defined as an omnipresent customer service for tourist information, and is characterized by the provision, management, and sharing of services and experiences during the tourists' journey [8, 12].

The transformations and changes brought about by the use of ST can be leveraged through the integration of Customer Relationship Management (CRM) systems and social media strategy planning [6]. This reduces the risks involved in decision-making and leads to transparency and trust in the contacts with clients [6, 23]. The impact of eWoM is not restricted to ST. The energy sector is also applying social network analysis to understand how people's conversations might influence their energy practices and attitudes to energy conservation [9]. Another example is given by [14], in which the authors are making social networks a means to save energy, by using Twitter as a communication channel for eco-aware appliances to share their usage patterns.

Bearing in mind the importance of eWoM for the market, in this paper we focused on Social Network Advertising (SNA) with regard to (a) its forms of content that are created by brands and disseminated by the social media; and (b) the Digital Content Engagement (DCE) - the psychological state induced from interactions with the brand identity in a digital environment. Seven SNA content categories and three levels of DCE are defined by [7], which can be correlated by the analysts to determine their effectiveness. Given the large amount of SNA content in the social media, high costs and a considerable effort are required to assess their impact on DCE [13]. In light of this, the following research question needs to be defined:

- Is it possible the automatic posts classification according to the SNA Content Categories presented by [7]?

For answering this research question, we tested machine learning methods to develop an automatic SNA content classifier based on the categories outlined by [7]. The automatic data classification method was developed and tested in publications on tourism published in Facebook. Moreover, practitioners validated the model and discussed its practical implications. For example, it is possible to use the classifier in the automation of competitor analysis, in the deployment of marketing strategies by evaluating the SNA content and its engagement, and in the development of a decision support system to predict user engagement based on the post contents.

The remainder of this study is structured as follows: Sect. 2 outlines the methodology employed in the study. The results are analyzed and discussed in Sect. 3. Finally, the conclusions are summarized in Sect. 4.

2   Methodology

In this section, the research question is answered by means of a dataset description, followed by the SNA categories DCE levels, and establishing the Experimental Framework.

2.1   Dataset Description

In this work, we used data that was taken from publications of several companies related to tourism in Facebook. This complied with the following selection criteria: (i) they had to have profiles in a social network; and (ii) they had been active in the last six months. Facebook was chosen as a platform for data collection, because of its popularity and large number of users. The data extraction was carried out through the official API of Facebook from January to June 2018.

The selection criteria were defined on the basis of [15]. In total, data from 93 companies were collected from a wide range of sectors. Altogether there was a total of 10,925 publications drawn on during the extraction period, and the data for each publication are described in Table 1.

Table 1. Description of the data extracted.

Data	Format	Description
Post ID	Numeric	Identification of each publication in the social network
Text	String	Textual content of each publication
Type	String	Publication type – it is made clear if the publication is a 'photo', 'video', 'status' and/or 'link'
Link	URL	Post link
Publication date	Date	Publication date in the social network
Reactions	Emoticons	Reactions from users on post – these reactions are: 'Likes', 'Hahas', 'Loves', 'Wows', 'Sads', 'Angrys', 'Special'
Shares	Numeric	Number of times that the publication was shared

2.2   SNA Categories and DCE Levels

This paper focuses on Social Network Advertising with the levels of Digital Content Engagement outlined by [7]. Table 2 shows the content categories with their respective descriptions. In the same way, Table 3 shows the levels of DCE with an evaluation of their degree of influence on its effectiveness and the description of each level.

Table 2. SNA categories adopted from [7].

Category	Label	Description
None	None	Publications that do not belong to any of the other categories
New product announcement	NP	Publications highlighting the announcement of new products and/or services
Current product display	CP	Publications that highlight the current product establishment or the return of a product
Sweepstakes and contents	SW	Publications with information about sweepstakes, rules and regulations
Sales	SA	Publications that advertise sales or promotion of a product, including discount information and vouchers
Consumer feedback	CF	Publications requesting customers to provide information such as product rating, evaluation or problems
Infotainment	IT	Publications that provide new, useful, educational or interesting information
Organization branding	OB	Publications that highlight the organization or brand (through logos, captions, general company information, organizational attributes, store network and employees)

Table 3. DCE Categories described by [7].

Category	Degree	Description	Metrics
Positive filtering	Moderate	Response showing positive emotional attitudes toward content	Reactions (likes, loves, wows, haha, sads, angrys, special)
Cognitive and affective processing	Moderate to Strong	Co-creation in the brand environment	Comments
Advocacy	Strong	Strong cognitive and emotional investment, value co-creation, publishing, self-expression	Shares

2.3 Experimental Framework

The experimental framework adopted for the study is described in Fig. 1. This consists of the following steps: (i) data acquisition process (raw data); (ii) data pre-processing; (iii) manual annotation of a significant data sample (iv) classification of the remaining of the publications through a machine learning algorithm; (v) measurement of accuracy and validation of the classifier obtained in step 4; (vi) correlation of the SNA categories with the levels of DCE; (vii) validation of the obtained results.

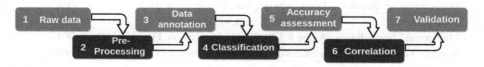

Fig. 1. Overall workflow of the experiments.

The first stage described in Fig. 1 is the raw data acquisition, which was carried out with the Facebook API. The automated classification process involves preparing and annotating the data to build a classification model. The second stage was the application of pre-processing methods in the texts for each publication aiming to reduce the noise; this entailed removing URLs, stopwords, numbers, accentuation, emoticons and special characters, as well as reducing the length of the words with stemming. This approach was based on the work of [5].

The third stage of the workflow refers to the manual data annotation according to the SNA categories mentioned before. The data annotation was undertaken by two independent annotators. The reliability of the annotations was assessed by means of Cohen's Kappa coefficient and only the data with concordance between the annotators were retained. In other words, only when the two reviewers assigned the same label to a post, the post was included in the training dataset.

Some machine learning algorithms used for classification were tested to answer the previously defined research questions, namely, K-Nearest Neighbors (KNN), Gaussian Naïve Bayes, Support Vector Machine (SVM), Multinomial Naïve Bayes, and Random Forest. These algorithms are available in the scikit-learn framework. The algorithm parameterization was conducted using GridSearch for SVM and KNN. For the others, the default parameters were used. In Table 4 the algorithms and parameters adopted are given.

The following performance measurements were used: Accuracy, Precision, Recall, and F1-measure (weighted), and the data were stratified through cross-validation (10-fold). The F1-Measure (weighted) was adopted instead of micro/macro because of it takes into account label imbalance. In light of the best performance measurements, the SVM algorithm was adopted (Table 4).

The correlation of the SNA categories with the metrics that determine the levels of DCE is also carried out to determine the content effectiveness [7]. The validation was carried out considering a real-world scenario related to smart tourism, in which two practitioners that are working in this sector conducted a qualitative evaluation of the results obtained in the previous steps.

The evaluation process consisted of a random selection of some classified publications and verify its reliability. Moreover, we also applied a topic modeling algorithm for the entire classified dataset, presenting the results (per class) for the practitioners. They analyzed if the topic summarization was consistent with the proposed classes.

Table 4. List of algorithms and their best parameterization considering the classification accuracy.

Algorithms	Parameters	Accuracy
KNN	k = 9, distance = 'cosine'	73%
Gaussian Naive Bayes	Priors = None, Var_smoothing = 10^9	71%
SVM	C = 10000, Kernel = 'sigmoid'	80%
Multinomial Naive Bayes	Alpha = 1.0, Class prior = None, Fit prior = True	68%
Random Forest	n estimators = 7, min samples split = 9	79%

3   Results and Discussions

Considering the amount of publications collected, 628 publications were needed to obtain a confidence interval of 99% with a 5% margin of error. However, since it was possible that the annotators failed to match the same label for the same data, in this work, 1020 publications were extracted for manual annotation.

As mentioned in the Methodology Section, the annotations were evaluated using Cohen's Kappa coefficient and obtained the value of 0.5, which means there is a moderate level of agreement between the annotations. These data initially represented 9% of the total number of publications, although only the data classified with the same label were maintained, which resulted in 680 publications, or about 6%, more than that required by the confidence interval and error defined previously. All the data were randomly extracted, annotated, and processed.

Several pre-processing stages were followed on the training dataset, to clear and remove all unnecessary information, e.g., URLs and stopwords. In the SVM classifier, the publications that had been manually annotated were submitted to the training of the algorithm, and the results obtained an Accuracy of 80.87%, Precision of 77.03%, Recall of 80.87% and F1-measure of 78.17%. The performance measurements can also be seen in Fig. 2, which was normalized for providing a better data visualization.

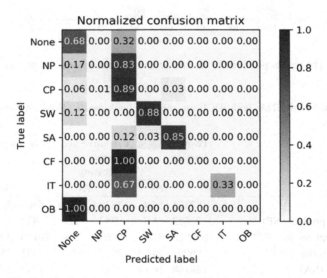

Fig. 2. Confusion matrix related to DCE categories considered.

As a means of proving that the automatic classification of publications can obtain similar results to a manual classification, the trained classifier was applied to the rest of the dataset, (about 94% of the data). The results were promising, the distribution of the categories in the results in Fig. 3 support the use of machine learning techniques as an effective way of reducing the labeling effort of the task to measure the effectiveness of

SNA in DCE. Furthermore, it makes it possible to analyze large amounts of data, and convincingly demonstrate how it is better to engage the users with the content of SNA [7].

Table 5 was designed on the basis of the results of the automatic classification, and a correlation can be observed between the SNA categories and the metrics of the DCE levels proposed by [7]. In these the SW categories have a greater appeal to the DCE in accordance to the average of Likes, comments and shares in each publications.

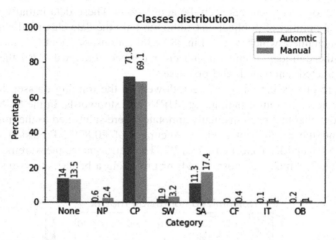

Fig. 3. The results provided by automatic and manual annotations per categories.

Table 5. Relation of SNA with DCE in the Facebook posts. Note: AV = Average and F = Frequency.

	Positive filtering		Cognitive and affective processing		Advocacy	
	F	Av	F	Av	F	Av
None	87175	54.4	3820	2.3	5508	3.4
New product (NP)	23523	36.7	947	5.5	472	1.7
Current product (CP)	604910	81.5	39367	5.3	26194	3.5
Sweepstakes (SW)	66005	244.4	42617	157.8	7455	157.8
Sales (SA)	128148	100.9	3571	2.8	1742	1.3
Customer feedback (CF)	331	16.5	27	1.35	4	0.2
Infotainment (IT)	1977	34	160	2.75	99	1.7
Organization branding (OB)	7406	68.5	459	4.2	219	2

4   Conclusions

This research investigated the use of machine learning techniques to reduce the cost and effort of evaluating Social Network Advertising strategies. To do so, we adopted the Digital Content Engagement categories proposed by [7] and Facebook data. Based on extensive experiments, we evaluated several machine learning classifiers, namely, K-Nearest Neighbors (KNN), Gaussian Naïve Bayes, Support Vector Machine (SVM), Multinomial Naïve Bayes, and Random Forest. The results show that the SVM classifier has an excellent potential to measure the effectiveness of SNA categories at the DCE level, since it is able to analyze a large amount of content with greater efficiency and less cost/effort. Hence, in proportional terms, the automatic classifier can achieve similar results to those obtained by manual annotation.

The classifier results were evaluated and validated by practitioners. Based on the findings, some practical implications were visualized: (i) it is possible to follow-up the competitors by analyzing their social media advertising content automatically; (ii) the classifier can be embedded in a decision support system, helping in the measurement of user engagement and in the development of new marketing strategies; (iii) the classifier can also support the analysis of user engagement according to current market demands for community management in the energy and other sectors. These are well-known services provided by digital marketing agencies [3], which can be enhanced by the obtained classifier.

However, there are some limitations in our study which need to be tackled in future studies. First, our dataset only included tourism data, and thus resulted in an unbalanced dataset. Second, since only two annotators were used, there was a low confidence interval in the results. In view of this, in future work, we would like to expand our dataset to other market sectors and to include a third annotator to improve the reliability of the research. Moreover, we are planning to include techniques that deal with imbalanced datasets or to improve classification performance.

Acknowledgments. The authors gratefully acknowledge the financial support for this research by the Federal University of Western Pará (PMAI), German Academic Exchange Service (DAAD, SCRM-SPECS) and the Federal Ministry for Economic Affairs and Energy (BMWI, SMECS) and the Maranhão Foundation for the Protection of Research and Scientific and Technological Development (FAPEMA).

References

1. Ahmad, S.N., Laroche, M.: Analyzing electronic word of mouth: a social commerce construct. Int. J. Inf. Manag. **37**(3), 202–213 (2017)
2. de Almeida, G.R.T., Lobato, F., Cirqueira, D.: Improving Social CRM through electronic word-of-mouth: a case study of ReclameAqui. In: XIV Workshop de Trabalhos de Iniciação Científic (2017)
3. Barata, G.M., Viana, J.A., Reinhold, O., Lobato, F., Alt, R.: Social CRM in digital marketing agencies: an extensive classification of services. In: 2018 IEEE/WIC/ACM International Conference on Web Intelligence (WI), pp. 750–753 (2018)

4. Bello-Orgaz, G., Jung, J.J., Camacho, D.: Social big data: recent achievements and new challenges. Inf. Fusion **28**, 45–59 (2016)
5. Cirqueira, D., Pinheiro, M.F., Jacob, A., Lobato, F., Santana, A.: A literature review in preprocessing for sentiment analysis for Brazilian Portuguese social media. In: 2018 IEEE/WIC/ACM International Conference on Web Intelligence (WI), pp. 746–749. IEEE (2018)
6. Colomo-Palacios, R., García-Peñalvo, F.J., Stantchev, V., Misra, S.: Towards a social and context-aware mobile recommendation system for tourism. Perv. Mob. Comput. **38**, 505–515 (2017)
7. Gavilanes, J.M., Flatten, T.C., Brettel, M.: Content strategies for digital consumer engagement in social networks: why advertising is an antecedent of engagement. J. Advertising **47**(1), 4–23 (2018)
8. Gretzel, U., Werthner, H., Koo, C., Lamsfus, C.: Conceptual foundations for understanding smart tourism ecosystems. Comput. Hum. Behav. **50**, 558–563 (2015)
9. Hamilton, J., Hogan, B., Lucas, K., Mayne, R.: Conversations about conservation? Using social network analysis to understand energy practices. Energy Res. Soc. Sci. **49**, 180–191 (2019)
10. Harrigan, P., Evers, U., Miles, M., Daly, T.: Customer engagement with tourism social media brands. Tour. Manag. **59**, 597–609 (2017)
11. Hussain, S., Guangju, W., Jafar, R.M.S., Ilyas, Z., Mustafa, G., Jianzhou, Y.: Consumers' online information adoption behavior: motives and antecedents of electronic word of mouth communications. Comput. Hum. Behav. **80**, 22–32 (2018)
12. Li, Y., Hu, C., Huang, C., Duan, L.: The concept of smart tourism in the context of tourism information services. Tour. Manag. **58**, 293–300 (2017)
13. Lobato, F., Pinheiro, M., Jacob, A., Reinhold, O., Santana, Á.: Social CRM: biggest challenges to make it work in the real world. In: Abramowicz, W., Alt, R., Franczyk, B. (eds.) BIS 2016. LNBIP, vol. 263, pp. 221–232. Springer, Cham (2017). https://doi.org/10.1007/978-3-319-52464-1_20
14. López-de-Armentia, J., Casado-Mansilla, D., López-de-Ipiña, D.: Making social networks a means to save energy. J. Netw. Comput. Appl. **59**, 237–246 (2016)
15. Maiz, A., Arranz, N., Juan, J.C.: Factors affecting social interaction on social network sites: the Facebook case. J. Enterp. Inf. Manag. **29**(5), 630–649 (2016)
16. Oliveira, B., Casais, B.: The importance of user-generated photos in restaurant selection. J. Hosp. Tour. Technol. **10**, 2–14 (2018)
17. Pradiptarini, C.: Social media marketing: measuring its effectiveness and identifying the target market. J. Undergrad. Res. **14**, 1–11 (2011)
18. Schmäh, M., Wilke, T., Rossmann, A.: Electronic word-of-mouth: a systematic literature analysis. In: Lecture Notes in Informatics (LNI), p. 147 (2017)
19. Shiau, W.L., Dwivedi, Y.K., Lai, H.H.: Examining the core knowledge on Facebook. Int. J. Inf. Manag. **43**, 52–63 (2018)
20. Silva, W., Santana, Á., Lobato, F., Pinheiro, M.: A methodology for community detection in Twitter. In: Proceedings of the International Conference on Web Intelligence, pp. 1006–1009 (2017)
21. Statista: Facebook users worldwide 2018—Statista (2018)
22. Statista: Global social media ranking 2019—Statistic (2019)
23. Del Vecchio, P., Mele, G., Ndou, V., Secundo, G.: Creating value from social big data: implications for smart tourism destinations. Inf. Process. Manag. **54**(5), 847–860 (2018)

iDEATE Workshop

Ideate 2019 Workshop Chairs' Message

With big data and business analytics now becoming increasingly more prevalent in contemporary enterprises, there is a growing interest on how such technologies can be leveraged to provide a competitive edge. Recent commentaries, reports, and empirical studies highlight that many attempts to deploy big data analytics in the organizational fabric fail for reasons other than the technology itself or the data used to generate insight. It is now becoming increasingly more apparent that big data analytics is an organizational effort and requires changes in multiple levels in order to result in any measurable business value. Another critical issue is how exactly can the value of big data analytics be measured, and through what means are such targets realized. We often hear about big data analytics contributing towards innovation, increased business efficiency, reducing time and cost of processing data, and even in aiding or replacing human decision-making. Yet, despite such claims we still know very little about how big data analytics projects need to be planned, what aspects need to be taken into consideration when piloting projects, how such projects can be matured and scaled up, as well as how they can be benchmarked with regard to performance outcomes.

While we now know more about the key organizational aspects that influence outcomes of big data projects, such as, the level of human skills in technical and business roles, the culture surrounding big data analytics, governance practices, data-driven decision-making structures and processes, as well as key hindrances. Nevertheless, the quest on how to differentiate from competition in leveraging big data analytics still remains open. There is considerable work to be done on how big data analytics should be employed to drive strategy, and how a difficult to imitate digital strategy building on should be developed and deployed. In addition, we have seen in the last few years the emergence of some companies that put forth innovative business models which build on the power of big data analytics, yet there is still limited research on the viability and emergence of such new forms of conducting business. Our belief is that the opportunities enabled though big data analytics and other emerging technologies will have a significant impact on how digital strategies and developed and how companies and public organizations think of developing digital capabilities for sustained performance.

The aim of this workshop was to bring together people who have an interest in how big data analytics changes the way business is conducted and seek to explore mechanisms in which this can be achieved. We have had an open call for papers and invited researchers and practitioners from both industry and academia to submit original results of their completed or ongoing projects. The scope of our call has been broad in order to include all relevant aspects relating to big data analytics, organizational transformation, and business value. We have encouraged the submission of empirical work and innovative studies. The workshop received nine submissions, of which the Program

Committee selected five for presentation at the workshop. We would like to thank all members of the Program Committee, authors, and local organizers for their efforts and support.

Patrick Mikalef
Ilias O. Pappas
Michail N. Giannakos
John Krogstie
Rogier van de Wetering

Organization

Chairs

Patrick Mikalef	Norwegian University of Science and Technology, Norway
Ilias O. Pappas	University of Agder, Norway
Michail Giannakos	Norwegian University of Science and Technology, Norway
John Krogstie	Norwegian University of Science and Technology, Norway
Rogier van de Wetering	Open Universitat, The Netherlands

Program Committee

Anastasia Griva	Athens University of Economics and Business, Greece
Konstantina Spanaki	Loughborough University, UK
Milena Strozyna	Poznan University of Economics and Business, Poland
Björn Johansson	Lund University, Sweden
Mikael Berndtsson	University of Skövde, Sweden
George Lekakos	Athens University of Economics and Business, Greece
Demetrios Sampsons	Curtin University, Australia
Johan Versendaal	Hogeschool Utrecht, The Netherlands

Developing an Artificial Intelligence Capability: A Theoretical Framework for Business Value

Patrick Mikalef[1,2(✉)], Siw Olsen Fjørtoft[1], and Hans Yngvar Torvatn[1]

[1] SINTEF Digital, S.P. Andersens Veg 5, 7031 Trondheim, Norway
patrick.mikalef@sintef.no
[2] Norwegian University of Science and Technology (NTNU),
Sem Sælands Vei 7-9, 7034 Trondheim, Norway

Abstract. Despite the claim that Artificial Intelligence (AI) can revolutionize the way private and public organizations do business, to date organizations still face a number of obstacles in leveraging such technologies and realizing performance gains. Past studies in other novel information technologies argue that organizations must develop a capability of effectively orchestrating and deploying necessary complementary resources. We contend that if organizations aim to realize any substantial performance gains from their AI investments, they must develop and promote an AI Capability. This paper theoretically develops the concept of an AI capability and presents the main dimensions that comprise it. To do so, we ground this concept in the resource-based view of the firm and by surveying the latest literature on AI, we identify the constituent components that jointly comprise it.

Keywords: Artificial Intelligence · Organizational capability · Resource-Based View · Theoretical framework

1 Introduction

Artificial Intelligence (AI) can be defined as a set of technologies that simulate human cognitive processes, including reasoning, learning, and self-correction. Following the rapid growth of data and processing power. AI has re-emerged on the stage as a key technology that will likely play a central role in realizing performance and competitive value for firms [1]. The main value proposition of AI is that it can perform a large number of manual tasks with greater speed, accuracy, and detail compared to humans, therefore enabling the human work force to engage in activities that require competences that are distinctively human [2]. While a large proportion of the discussion has centered around the role of AI in replacing certain human tasks, there is also a growing debate regarding the potential symbiosis between humans and machine, enabling in such a way the core strengths of each in a complimentary manner [3]. Nevertheless, while traditionally AI has been talked about in technical terms, the renewed interest in the tools and techniques that underpin AI have given rise to a new type of focus, i.e.

© Springer Nature Switzerland AG 2019
W. Abramowicz and R. Corchuelo (Eds.): BIS 2019 Workshops, LNBIP 373, pp. 409–416, 2019.
https://doi.org/10.1007/978-3-030-36691-9_34

how AI can be leveraged in business and how organizations should prepare for harnessing its potential.

This shift in the focus regarding AI use in the organizational setting has raised concerns about the areas where organizations should focus their efforts. As with other emerging technologies and information systems, it is widely acknowledged that adopting and leveraging such technological innovations is a firm-wide effort and requires significant attention in several key areas [4]. Building on this perspective of leveraging emerging technologies as a key organizational capability, Bharadwaj [5] argued that firms need to develop an Information Technology (IT) capability in order to be able to effectively utilize new and emerging technologies. The concept has been adapted in recent years and been narrowed down to specific technologies [6, 7]. Most notably, there has been a stream of research examining the ability of firms to utilize their big data investments, giving rise to the notion of a big data analytics capability [8, 9]. Similar to big data analytics, AI requires that organizations develop a plan that enables them to leverage the full potential of such technologies. Nevertheless, to date there is still no theoretical framework to define the important dimensions and aspects that are critical to realize business value.

The purpose of this study is to take a theoretically grounded approach in developing an Artificial Intelligence Capability and its main dimensions. We define an AI capability as *the ability of a firm to orchestrate organizational resources and apply computer systems able to engage in human-like throughout processes such as learning, reasoning, and self-correction towards business tasks*. This definition adopts a broader perspective on AI taking into account the fact that in order to be able to deploy such technological innovations and for them to be applied to business tasks a firm-wide effort is required. We adopt the theoretical underpinnings of the Resource-Based View (RBV) and through a review of existing literature review the core dimensions that are relevant in the context of AI [10, 11]. The purpose of this study is to develop a theoretical framework through which the maturity of organizations AI capability can be assessed and benchmarked. From a practical perspective this instrument can be used to identify areas that have been neglected and to formulate roadmap in order to streamline deployments and increase business value.

The rest of the paper is structured as follows. I the next section we introduce the RBV and overview the existing studies on AI and business value. Next, in Sect. 3 we define the dimensions of an AI capability and briefly discuss what each encompasses. Finally, in Sect. 4 we discuss about the ways future research can extend this theoretical framework and how practice can apply it to formulate an adoption plan. We close the paper with the conclusions that can be draw as well as some key limitations.

2 Background

2.1 The Resource-Based View (RBV)

The Resource-Based View (RBV) of the firm has been one of the most influential theoretical frameworks to describe the types of IT resources firms need to consider when deploying their investments in the organizational context [12]. The main premise upon which the RBV is based is that the competitive position of organizations depends on the types of resources they posses or have under their control [13]. According to this view, not all resources can generate equal value, but rather, the competitive positions that firms are able to achieve as a result of utilizing their resources depends on certain characteristics of the resources themselves. Specifically, resources that are valuable, rare, non-inimitable, and not easily transferable can be the source of business value if leveraged appropriately [14]. One of the main assumptions that the RBV builds on is that these resources will be orchestrated and deployed in an optimal manner, thus enabling firms to outperform their competitors. Despite this underlying assumption, the RBV is a strong theoretical framework as it unites several dissimilar resources, which in turn can be combined to generate a competitive advantage [15].

The RBV provides an appropriate theoretical basis since knowledge about what AI specific resources a firm has to manage is a core part of attaining a competitive advantage. Furthermore, the ability to integrate the frameworks with other theoretical perspectives (e.g. dynamic capabilities, absorptive capacity) makes the RBV an attractive approach to explain business value stemming from IT investments [9, 16]. Past research in the broader IS domain has applied the RBV extensively. For example, Melville, Kraemer and Gurbaxani [17] recognize that the RBV can allow empirically testable hypotheses, which help advance our knowledge regarding the role of IS resources in organizational performance. Similarly, Gupta and George [8] recognize that it is an appropriate theoretical framework to categorize the different types of resources relevant to big data analytics. Overall, the RBV is a well-established theory for theoretically and empirically examining the relationship between different types of organizational resources and performance. Since the objective of this study is to isolate several key resources that will enable organizations to create AI capabilities, which in turn will result in performance gains, the choice of the RBV as the theoretical framework for this study is deemed as appropriate.

2.2   Towards the Development of an Artificial Intelligence (AI) Capability

Despite the fact that published research on AI is still very limited, there are several studies that have identified challenged associated with the success of AI projects. These studies range from large-scale empirical research studies, to case studies and surveys with industry professionals published in practitioner journals. We use the distinction provided by the RBV to categorize types of resources into three main types, tangible (e.g. physical resources and data), intangible (e.g. organizational culture), and human skills and knowledge (e.g. employees competencies and skills) according to Grant [18]. Regarding the first type of resources, i.e. tangible, literature on AI places a heavy emphasis on the data required to enable AI and the technology to support it [19]. Data is widely regarded as the foundation for AI, with the quality of data being the key aspect in regard to the value of the AI it is applied towards [20–22]. According to a study by Ransbotham, Gerbert, Reeves, Kiron and Spira [23] pioneers in the use of AI develop more sophisticated data management systems and decentralized data lakes. Furthermore, being able to integrate data from several channels and streamlining operations of sharing and cleansing data so that it can be readily used in AI applications is repeatedly noted as being a key element [24]. Nevertheless, being able to perform such operations regarding data sharing, cleansing, and processing to support advanced AI techniques also requires that there is an appropriate technological infrastructure to support it. Such infrastructure includes cloud-based technologies for processing data [25], computational power by state-of-the-art CPUs and GPUs [26], as well as enterprise networks that support efficiency and scale.

Apart from the tangible resources related to AI, there has also been considerable focus on the human factor [23]. This discussion revolves typically around two areas, the human skills required to develop and train AI applications, and the foresight and managerial capacity to apply such methods to business problems [27]. This issue about the importance of skills in the AI landscape is also noted by public bodies including amongst others the European Commission, that has placed increased emphasis on the importance of developing such skills. Wilson, Daugherty and Bianzino [28] in an influential article highlight the different jobs AI will create in the near future. These include three main profiles, and several other sub-profiles, with roles such as trainers, explainers, and sustainers. Trainers will be needed to teach AI systems how they should perform, Explainers, will be required to bridge the gap between technologists and business leaders by providing clarity, while Sustainers will be in charge of making sure AI systems operate as designed and that unintended consequences are addressed appropriately.

The final category of resources revolves around intangible elements that require firm-wide development. Specifically, several studies note that developing an AI-oriented culture is a key part of succeeding [29]. In fact, in a recent study conducted by Ransbotham, Gerbert, Reeves, Kiron and Spira [23] one of the main barriers to AI adoption was the cultural resistance to AI approaches, as well as the competing investments priorities. These results indicate that embracing an AI culture and developing a strategy to support it are critical resources in realizing performance gains. Adding to the AI-oriented culture, several researchers also indicate that promoting organizational learning is important in the age of AI. Being able to search, acquire, assimilate and exploit new knowledge as it emerges is key in being capable to be within the group of pioneers and outperforming competition [30]. Collectively, these resources comprise a firm-wide AI capability and require that attention is attributed to each. This necessitates that there is a strategy regarding AI deployment and use and a roadmap for such deployments.

3   A Research Framework for AI and Business Value

Building on the foregoing discussion around the constituent elements of an AI capability and the emerging literature regarding the business value of such technologies in the organizational context, the question is to examine if an AI capability can lead to business value and through what mechanism that can be realized. Overall, literature recognizes that AI can produce value in four different ways, (1) *Automation*, (2) *Decision support*, (3) *Marketing* and (4) *Innovation*. By automatizing several manual tasks AI can enable the human workforce to perform other activities that require more creative skills and critical thinking. For instance, the use of chatbots to interact with customers or citizens, or applying AI to perform checks on reports, documents and financial statements can significantly increase the efficiency of organizations. Nevertheless, AI can also be used to enhance the judgement and decision-making of humans in a stream termed augmented intelligence [31]. The main premise here is that AI can help humans sense external stimuli and assist in decision-making by enabling analysis and offering advice and implementation support [32]. In terms of marketing, AI has been applied to identify unique personas of customers, and offer tailored-made marketing campaigns, or even special offers and services. In this way, AI replaces human action in developing marketing approaches as it bases selection of methods and approaches on fine-grained information and can improve its precision based on different performance metrics [33]. Finally, many creative professions are now deploying AI to support innovation projects, as for instance biomedical applications or uses of AI to help in design or creativity. For instance, many designers now use input provided by AI to come up with new ideas for their work-related activities [34]. The figure below presents a schematic representation of the business value-adding relationships that underpin AI. The objective of this research framework is to provide a structure to the internal organizational resources that need to be leveraged in order to generate value, and to comprehend the areas where AI can be applied to realize such performance gains (Fig. 1).

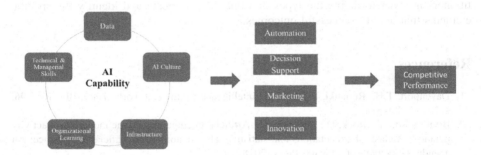

Fig. 1. AI Capabilities and competitive performance framework

4 Discussion

While AI is still at an early stage of deployment in organizations, it has already become a topic of discussion regarding implementation and use in the business realm. Several studies have already started to look at potential business cases for AI and have explored what challenges and opportunities executives perceive during such attempts. Despite the research still being quite fragmented and scarce, a consensus is developing around the areas that firms must take into account if they want to realize performance gains from such investments. Building on the increasing rate of AI use in private and public organizations, this study sought to examine what elements contribute to developing a firm-wide AI capability. This notion is argued to be critical for contemporary firms in order to avoid costly investments without any actual competitive or financial returns.

The objective of this study was to develop a theoretically grounded definition of an AI capability and to extract the core resources that comprise it. We built on the RBV of the firm as an appropriate theoretical framework and distinguished between resources based on the classification of Grant [18]. Guided by this categorization and based on relevant literature we defined and discussed the dimensions and what aspects of them are important in realizing business value from AI investments. Similar to past empirical studies looking at IT investments within the organizational sphere, our goal was to examine what aspects managers should consider when deploying AI solutions. Having defined then the constituent components of an AI capability, we proceeded to identify the business areas through which AI can produce value and competitive performance gains [35]. Our analysis revealed that AI can produce value in four different ways, through automation, decision-support, marketing, and innovation. We expanded briefly on each of these and how AI can be used to support them.

While this study is still on a theoretical level proposing a framework for analysis and performance gains, it is a first attempt to do so in a theoretically guided way. The next steps in this research will be to develop a set of items to quantitatively assess the maturity of all the underlying dimensions and as a result the total level of AI capability. By doing so we can examine if AI produces business value, and if so through what mechanisms [36]. The research framework can also be used by academics and practitioners in order to define the types of value AI can create and identify the specific elements that lead to successful outcomes.

References

1. Davenport, T.H., Ronanki, R.: Artificial intelligence for the real world. Harv. Bus. Rev. **96**, 108–116 (2018)
2. Brynjolfsson, E., Rock, D., Syverson, C.: Artificial intelligence and the modern productivity paradox: A clash of expectations and statistics. The economics of artificial intelligence: An agenda. University of Chicago Press (2018)
3. Jarrahi, M.H.: Artificial intelligence and the future of work human-AI symbiosis in organizational decision making. Bus. Horiz. **61**, 577–586 (2018)
4. Pavlou, P.A., El Sawy, O.A.: From IT leveraging competence to competitive advantage in turbulent environments: the case of new product development. Inf. Syst. Res. **17**, 198–227 (2006)
5. Bharadwaj, A.S.: A resource-based perspective on information technology capability and firm performance: an empirical investigation. MIS Q. 169–196 (2000)
6. Mikalef, P., Boura, M., Lekakos, G., Krogstie, J.: Big data analytics capabilities and innovation: the mediating role of dynamic capabilities and moderating effect of the environment. Br. J. Manag. **30**, 272–298 (2019)
7. Mikalef, P., Boura, M., Lekakos, G., Krogstie, J.: Big data analytics and firm performance: findings from a mixed-method approach. J. Bus. Res. **98**, 261–276 (2019)
8. Gupta, M., George, J.F.: Toward the development of a big data analytics capability. Inf. Manag. **53**, 1049–1064 (2016)
9. Mikalef, P., Boura, M., Lekakos, G., Krogstie, J.: Big data analytics capabilities and innovation: the mediating role of dynamic capabilities and moderating effect of the environment. Br. J. Manag. (2019, in press)

10. Mikalef, P., Krogstie, J., Pappas, I.O., Pavlou, P.: Exploring the relationship between big data analytics capability and competitive performance: the mediating roles of dynamic and operational capabilities. Inf. Manag. (2019)
11. Mikalef, P., Pappas, I.O., Krogstie, J., Giannakos, M.: Big data analytics capabilities: a systematic literature review and research agenda. Inf. Syst. e-Bus. Manag. **16**, 1–32 (2018)
12. Wade, M., Hulland, J.: The resource-based view and information systems research: review, extension, and suggestions for future research. MIS Q. **28**, 107–142 (2004)
13. Barney, J.B.: Resource-based theories of competitive advantage: a ten-year retrospective on the resource-based view. J. Manag. **27**, 643–650 (2001)
14. Lockett, A., Thompson, S., Morgenstern, U.: The development of the resource-based view of the firm: a critical appraisal. Int. J. Manag. Rev. **11**, 9–28 (2009)
15. Palmatier, R.W., Dant, R.P., Grewal, D.: A comparative longitudinal analysis of theoretical perspectives of interorganizational relationship performance. J. Mark. **71**, 172–194 (2007)
16. Sirmon, D.G., Hitt, M.A., Ireland, R.D., Gilbert, B.A.: Resource orchestration to create competitive advantage: breadth, depth, and life cycle effects. J. Manag. **37**, 1390–1412 (2011)
17. Melville, N., Kraemer, K., Gurbaxani, V.: Information technology and organizational performance: an integrative model of IT business value. MIS Q. **28**, 283–322 (2004)
18. Grant, R.M.: The resource-based theory of competitive advantage: implications for strategy formulation. Calif. Manag. Rev. **33**, 114–135 (1991)
19. Varian, H.: Artificial intelligence, economics, and industrial organization. National Bureau of Economic Research (2018)
20. Maddox, T.M., Rumsfeld, J.S., Payne, P.R.J.J.: Questions for artificial intelligence in health care. JAMA **321**, 31–32 (2019)
21. Mikalef, P., Framnes, V.A., Danielsen, F., Krogstie, J., Olsen, D.H.: Big data analytics capability: antecedents and business value. In: Pacific Asia Conference on Information Systems (2017)
22. Mikalef, P., Pappas, I.O., Krogstie, J., Giannakos, M.: Big data analytics capabilities: a systematic literature review and research agenda. Inf. Syst. e-Bus. Manag. 1–32 (2017)
23. Ransbotham, S., Gerbert, P., Reeves, M., Kiron, D., Spira, M.: Artificial intelligence in business gets real. MIT Sloan Manag. Rev. (2018)
24. Balaraman, V., Brown, S., Duggirala, M., Moore, S., Nie, J.-Y.: Complexity sciences and artificial intelligence for improving lives through convergent innovation. In: Academy of Management Proceedings, pp. 17958. Academy of Management Briarcliff Manor, NY (2018)
25. Li, B.-H., Hou, B.-C., Yu, W.-T., Lu, X.-B., Yang, C.-W.: Applications of artificial intelligence in intelligent manufacturing: a review. Front. Inf. Technol. Electron. Eng. **18**, 86–96 (2017)
26. Lemley, J., Bazrafkan, S., Corcoran, P.: Deep learning for consumer devices and services: pushing the limits for machine learning, artificial intelligence, and computer vision. IEEE Consum. Electron. Mag. **6**, 48–56 (2017)
27. Sousa, M.J., Rocha, Á.: Skills for disruptive digital business. J. Bus. Res. **94**, 257–263 (2019)
28. Wilson, H.J., Daugherty, P., Bianzino, N.: The jobs that artificial intelligence will create. MIT Sloan Manag. Rev. **58**, 14 (2017)
29. Bloomfield, B.P.: The culture of artificial intelligence. In: The Question of Artificial Intelligence, pp. 59–105. Routledge (2018)
30. Brynjolfsson, E., Mcafee, A.: The business of artificial intelligence. Harv. Bus. Rev. (2017)
31. Zheng, N.-N., Liu, Z.-Y., et al.: Hybrid-augmented intelligence: collaboration and cognition. Front. Inf. Technol. Electron. Eng. **18**, 153–179 (2017)

32. Shortliffe, E.H., Sepúlveda, M.J.: Clinical decision support in the era of artificial intelligence. Jama **320**, 2199–2200 (2018)
33. Sterne, J.: Artificial Intelligence for Marketing: Practical Applications. John Wiley & Sons (2017)
34. Heer, J.: Agency plus automation: Designing artificial intelligence into interactive systems. Proc. Nat. Acad. Sci. **116**, 1844–1850 (2019)
35. Mikalef, P., Pateli, A.: Information technology-enabled dynamic capabilities and their indirect effect on competitive performance: findings from PLS-SEM and fsQCA. J. Bus. Res. **70**, 1–16 (2017)
36. Mikalef, P., Van de Wetering, R., Krogstie, J.: Big data enabled organizational transformation: the effect of inertia in adoption and diffusion. In: Business Information Systems (BIS) (2018)

Measuring Qualitative Performance Criteria with Fuzzy Sets

Harry Martin[1,2(✉)]

[1] Open University Netherlands, Valkenburgerweg 177, Heerlen,
The Netherlands
Harry.martin@ou.nl
[2] KU Leuven, Heverlee, Leuven, Belgium

Abstract. In this work-in-progress paper the use of a fuzzy set controller is explored as a measurement instrument for qualitative performance criteria in a context in which organizations have a strategic partnership. Organizations struggle to get a grip on qualitative performance criteria, such as trust, information transparency, etc., to monitor the health of their relationships. First steps, i.e. the development of specialized tooling and actual field experiments will be discussed, some challenges and future directions will be presented.

Keywords: Fuzzy set theory · Strategic cooperation · Measurement · Qualitative performance criteria

1 Introduction

For quite some time, performance measurement has had significant scientific interest as well as in many organizations (e.g. Santos et al. [9]). Performance measurement is the cornerstone to quality management in general and in specific areas of management control such as the management of strategic cooperation between different organizations (e.g. Niesten et al. [7]). In particular, in the latter case problems can arise, many times cumulating in the premature break-up of a cooperation (e.g. Spekman et al. [12]). Then, often not only the envisioned results of the cooperation will not materialize, but also other kinds of damage are a net result, triggering legal and financial disputes.

Arguably, inadequate monitoring of the performance of strategic cooperations may contribute to a cooperation failure. It seems, still a lot is to be gained according to Lambe et al. [3]. Although, much effort may be spent on the preparation of formal partnership contracts, many issues may not be easily formalized accurately, or may be even entirely unknown beforehand. Such a situation can pose a substantial risk and need be dealt with in scrutiny. In this paper, the focus is on qualitative performance criteria, which are complicated, usually subjective and difficult to understand, to convey and therefore difficult to measure. Mutual behavioral expectations fall in this category and are frequent subjects in scientific discussions (e.g. de Man and Roijakkers [5]). Sometimes, some claims on desirable partner behavior are made in contracts, but usually it is less than clear how performance in this area will be monitored and assessed.

In this paper, some explorative intermediate progress made in this area will be reported, discussed and future directions for further research will be presented. Since

© Springer Nature Switzerland AG 2019
W. Abramowicz and R. Corchuelo (Eds.): BIS 2019 Workshops, LNBIP 373, pp. 417–423, 2019.
https://doi.org/10.1007/978-3-030-36691-9_35

qualitative performance criteria are difficult to quantify, fuzzy set theory has been used for the quantification of qualitative measures and first experiments in actual organizational strategic cooperations have been carried out. Fuzzy set theory seems a suitable approach for measurement of qualitative performance criteria (see next section), but may not be easy in practice. So far, the main goal in research is to identify obstacles and opportunities in the practical application of fuzzy sets in this context. The findings of these first case studies will be presented and analyzed to formulate future directions of research in this area.

In essence, this study underpins the importance of having meaningful qualitative data and to be able to transform it, to monitor the health of strategic cooperations in a comprehensive way.

2 Why Using Fuzzy Sets

To understand the measurement problem of qualitative performance criteria, it is worthwhile discussing some typical qualitative criteria first and then, dive deeper into measurement issues. In practice, when a strategic cooperation seems desirable most consideration goes into the development of the formulation of the primary goals of a cooperation. The variety of goals that can be taken up in a contract between partners can be practically limitless, but usually hard to quantify (see Vosselman et al. [14]). Verstegen [13] describes an interesting case where a hospital outsources its energy supply to a specialist energy provider. Despite the numerous conceivable safeguards that seem vital in ensuring a smooth operation of the hospital at all times, not much was specified concerning (financial) liabilities. Rather, continuous good partnership behavior was demanded from the energy provider. The cost of energy provisioning was clearly of second nature. The problem with such behavior-centered contracts is the qualitative nature of things like "good behavior". What is "good behavior", and just as important, how can we measure it? Numerous publications address the behavioral aspects of a strategic relationship between organizations. An extensive discussion of numerous behavioral performance criteria is outside the scope of this paper. For the sake of the argument we will limit ourselves to the aspect of "Transparency of information ex-change" (Reynaers [8]), seen by many as a significant contributor to trust in a professional relationship.

According to Schnackenberg [10], transparency is determined by the (timely) availability of information, the accuracy and clarity of information. Interestingly, these three factors, although still rather vague, are much more understandable then "transparency". So, instead of estimating a value for transparency in a particular situation directly, one can expect that an estimation of the separate three factors would be slightly easier and perhaps would yield more accurate and trustworthy estimates. Of course, a relationship between the three factors and transparency must be stipulated.

A common practice is to construct some kind of score-model in which a weighted sum is proposed for all three factors, adding up to some measure for transparency. However, despite the simplicity of this computation, it has some serious drawbacks. First and foremost, measuring information availability, accuracy and clarity are measured on different measurement scales, because these are entirely different entities, irrespective that units of measure for any of those factors haven't been found yet, they appear to be unitless. Adding up estimates of these factors would be like adding up degrees Celsius, kilometers and hours. Using score models is so commonplace that many forget about the potential incompatibilities with units of measure. Also, to a lesser extent, score models are prone to manipulation. It is very easy for humans to predict a favorable outcome for transparency by providing, perhaps unintended, biased estimates of the contributing factors.

Using a fuzzy set controller as a measuring mechanism could be a means to avoid these problems (Zadeh [15], Smithson [11]). The fuzzy set controller uses a transformation algorithm based on preset membership functions and fuzzy rules to interpret the contributing factors (i.e. the linguistic variables), to construct a new measurement scale for transparency (i.e. the consequent). Thus, creating a systematic construct between heterogenous factors, forcing the model builder to carefully formalize his view on "how to measure qualitative things". This transformation algorithm respects the respective measurement scales of the individual linguistic variables, yet it is too mathematically intensive to be easily manipulated manually. Fuzzy set controllers are originally developed to control devices and mimic human judgement, and are used in this study not to produce control signals but measurement values.

3   Tooling

Clearly, the application of a fuzzy set controller (=FSC) in real situations does require software support geared towards the measurement of qualitative variables. From the outset it was planned not to use FSC in artificial laboratory conditions with technical experts. At this stage of the research project the focus was set on how actual potential users would respond to this type of measurement, rather than that deep theoretical issues in fuzzy set theory were investigated.

In essence, a windows software program was developed with some special features built in to visualize the behavior of fuzzy sets, which have been input by a user and shown in several graphs. Users can define with visual support their own linguistic variables, the membership functions and the fuzzy rules, asses the relative impact of the variables on the consequent and the shape and range of the consequent. The program can be used to determine consequent values with proper input linguistic variables values.

Special care was taken to avoid unnecessary mathematical knowledge in using the FSC by practitioners. In addition, a short introductory manual was written to assist newcomers to the idea of using a fuzzy set controller to measure qualitative factors and how to use the software.

4   Experimenting with Fuzzy Sets

The FSC software was primarily targeted to experienced practitioners in the field facing actual challenges in monitoring the quality of strategic cooperations, and who are well aware that soft factors are important to achieve a complete picture. Several master thesis students from the Dutch Open University (OU) volunteered to assist and observe practitioners and experiment with FSC for measurement by using the FSC software tool described in the previous section. Typically, OU students are relatively senior individuals with several years of business experience, i.e. having a job whilst studying part-time at the OU. They are expected to have a scientific mindset and have developed analytical skills, whilst understanding the business context they working in very well. Usually, these students scan their employer organization for suitable cases of strategic cooperation in their business environment and know the context very well. To give some idea on the scope and range of the contexts that have been studied so far, the following cases were studied:

1. A Dutch government owned shared service center having a (mandatory) strategic cooperation with the Office of Foreign Affairs, covering the provisioning of housing for Dutch Embassy staff internationally. The study focused on transparency issues.
2. An investigation into the so-called strategic fit (based on theory of Naessens [6]) between two large secondary schools willing to cooperate in sharing resources. Several factors associated with determining a "fit" were measured.
3. A case study on the long-term relationship of an IT-supplier and two clients, with a focus on their trust and risk perceptions (based on theory of McEvily [4]).
4. 4 case studies of the general measurement of qualitative performance criteria in Agile software development for client organizations and the qualitative assessment of strategic communal budget plan.
5. A strategic partnership between a midsized manufacturing company and several of its suppliers with the focus on trustworthiness (based on theory of McEvily [4]).

Several other case studies are in the pipeline. All case studies looked for possible problems and opportunities in the application of FSC for measurement from a user's perspective. In all situations the students have constructed the FSC model with varying consultation of the envisioned problem owners, i.e. the practitioners in the respective organizations.

5   Preliminary Findings

The purpose of the preliminary case studies was to get a first impression on how actual business users would respond to this type of measurement. Several issues were discovered validating further research:

1. The difficulty to measure qualitative performance criteria systematically has been widely recognized and tooling support was welcomed. Managers struggle in general in dealing with soft factors and seem to prefer numerical KPI-style of performance reporting. Typically, managers state: "with time several things happened, improvement activities have been carried out, with varying effects. But, at the end of the day the question remains, did we improve on trusting our partners or not?".
2. It is difficult for most practitioners to grasp the concept and purpose of membership functions and fuzzy rules and therefore they feel quite uncertain about the outcome of such measurements.

3. Practitioners expect and in fact prefer rational scale measurement. Because an FSC measurement uses an interval scale, several measurements are needed to get some idea on what is deemed a better or worse performance. E.g. a single measurement on "mutual trust" is meaningless, unless the value can be compared with other values measured with the same fuzzy model.
4. Practitioners also have trouble in trusting an outcome they cannot explain easily. In general, managers are much more accustomed to output in its own right. A direct relation between input and output values cannot be deduced intuitively. Instead, faith can only be derived from the development process of membership functions and appropriate fuzzy rules. A "gold standard" for output values simply doesn't exist.
5. Practitioners with a background in science have much less trouble understanding the underlying principles and are sometimes even excited about FSC measurements.
6. It seems that if partners construct a measurement model jointly, a much better understanding is established about each other's interests, stakes and risks and, consequently, the acceptance of actual measurements improves.
7. If more than 4 linguistic variables are used, the model requires an unmanageable large number of fuzzy rules to establish a refined consequent profile. E.g. in one situation, a special rule generator was programmed to generate nearly 88000 fuzzy rules. Clearly, several and largely unverified assumptions had been made for the generation of these rules. Larger FSC models are getting overwhelmingly large and unwieldy rather quickly.
8. Although the primary goal is to use FSC model for performance measurement in strategic partnerships, no principal reason has been discovered against the use of measurement of qualitative factors in other types of contexts.

6 Looking Ahead

In general, we can conclude that the first experiments with FSC measurements are promising, but require a good deal of further attention. Although, no actual show-stoppers have been encountered, fuzzy set logic clearly is a demanding undertaking, even though the mathematics are shielded from view of users. Abstractions of human judgement in the form of variables (antecedents), membership functions and rules are difficult to grasp. Moreover, practitioners are not readily able to accept the idea that by a careful development process of the FSC model, they have to automatically trust the measurement outcomes. In short, they have to accept that the quality of model construction process is the only valid basis for trusting the measurement outcomes. Future research will much more focus on the FSC construction process in which the practitioner's perspective is critical.

Furthermore, despite all FSC logic, input data still depends for the most part on human judgement. This urges for specific selection and training of those providing estimates (the so-called calibration of the estimators). Perhaps, special selection, training and testing programs can help in this matter.

A structural problem emerges if more complicated measurement logic with numerous linguistic variables and fuzzy rules are deemed necessary and overwhelm the model builders. Sometimes, the situation can be alleviated somewhat by introducing a hierarchical structure of linguistic variables, in which some variables are aggregated to consequents, which in turn, constitute input variables for higher order consequents, and so forth. In this manner, the number of rules per level can be reduced substantially. Also, critical review of variables may show some correlation, which could make certain variables redundant or to cluster them. Finally, it may be worthwhile to investigate the potential of automatic rule generation based on learning data (e.g. Chen and Chen [1], and Cintra et al. [2]).

Acknowledgements. This research owes gratitude to the following (former) master students: Doortje Kerpershoek, Erwin de Jong, Fleur Muit, Eddy van Baal, Arjan Valstar, Jean-Pierre Linkens, Joost van Bree and Jos van Dijk. I would like to thank my colleagues Lianne Cuijpers, Ben Roelens and Rogier van de Wetering for their comments and suggestions.

References

1. Chen, S.-M., Yung-Chou, C.: Automatically constructing membership functions and generating fuzzy rules using genetic algorithms. Cybern. Syst. Int. J. **33**, 841–862 (2002)
2. Cintra, M.E., Camargo, H.A., Monard, M.C.: Genetic generation of fuzzy systems with rule extraction using formal concept analysis. Inf. Sci. **349–350**, 199–215 (2016)
3. Lambe, C.J., Spekman, R.E., Hunt, S.D.J.: Alliance competence, resources, and alliance success: Conceptualization, measurement, and initial test. J. Acad. Mark. Sci. **30**(2), 141–158 (2002)
4. McEvily, B.: Tortoriello, M: Measuring trust in organizational research: Review and recommendations. J. Trust Res. **1**(1), 23–63 (2011)
5. De Man, A.P., Roijakkers, N.: Alliance governance: balancing control and trust in dealing with risk. Long Range Plann. **42**(1), 75–95 (2009). https://doi.org/10.1016/j.lrp.2008.10.006
6. Naessens, K., Gelders, L., Pintelon, L.: A swift response framework for measuring the strategic fit for a horizontal collaborative initiative. Int. J. Prod. Econ. **121**, 550–561 (2009)
7. Niesten, E., Jolink, A.: The impact of alliance management capabilities on alliance attributes and performance: a literature review. Int. J. Manage. Rev. **17**, 69–100 (2015). British Academy of Management
8. Reynears, A.M., Grimmelikhuijsen, S.: Transparency in public-private partnerships: not so bad after all? Public Adm. **93**(3), 609–626 (2015)
9. Santos, S.P., Belton, V., Howick, S., Pilkington, M.: Measuring organizational performance using a mix of OR methods. Technol. Forecast. Soc. Change **131**, 18–30 (2017). Elsevier
10. Schnackenberg, A.K., Tomlinson, E.C.: Organizational transparency: a new perspective on managing trust in organization-stakeholder relationships. J. Manage. 1–27 (2014)
11. Smithson, M., Verkuilen, J.: Fuzzy Set Theory; Applications in the Social Sciences. Quantitative Applications in the Social Sciences. SAGE Publications, London (2006)
12. Spekman, R., Davis, E.: The extended enterprise: a decade later. Int. J. Phys. Distrib. Logist. Manage. **46**(1), 43–61 (2016)
13. Verstegen, B.H.J., Olink, H., Vosselman, E.G., Martin, H.: Dynamic links between three realms of transactional relationships. In: Working Paper Series Social Science Research Network. http://ssrn.com/abstract=931625

14. Vosselman, E., Verstegen, B., Olink, H., Martin, H.: Organizational structure, operational coordination and relational signals: how voluntary actions by organizations lead to format control structures. Int. J. Manage. **29**(3), 137 (2012). Part1
15. Zadeh, L.A.: Fuzzy sets. Inf. Control. **8**(3), 338–353 (1965). https://doi.org/10.1016/s0019-9985(65)90241-x

SmartM: A Non-intrusive Load Monitoring Platform

Xiufeng Liu(✉), Simon Bolwig, and Per Sieverts Nielsen

Technical University of Denmark, 2800 Kongens Lyngby, Denmark
xiuli@dtu.dk

Abstract. Real-time energy consumption monitoring is becoming increasingly important in smart energy management as it provides the opportunity for novel applications through data analytics, including anomaly detection, energy leakage, and theft. This paper presents a smart non-intrusive load monitoring approach for residential households, collecting fine-grained energy consumption data and disaggregating the data of appliances. The paper describes the implementation of the monitoring system, the data set, load disaggregation, and the challenges for future work.

Keywords: Non-intrusive load monitoring · Disaggregation · Platform · Data set

1 Introduction

With the rapid urbanization, energy and sustainability have become one of the greatest challenges of our society. Saving energy and using renewable energy raise an increasing interest. An integral part is to measure household energy consumption and to provide real-time feedback to the customers in order to save energy. This is because residential energy consumption is one of the biggest energy-consuming sectors. For example, in Denmark residential electricity consumption is a comparatively large part of the electricity sector, which accounts for about 30% of the total electricity consumption [1]. The previous study [2] has shown that the availability of fine-grained energy consumption information can stimulate households to take effective measures to save more energy, e.g., reducing the use or turning off some unnecessary appliances. In addition, detailed energy consumption information can also allow utilities to design demand-response programs, introduce dynamic pricing schemes, and provide personalized services to their customers. Also, the value of consumption data allows politicians to make new energy policies and evaluate the effectiveness of existing energy-saving policies. Fine-grained energy consumption can be obtained through load monitoring that measures real-time consumption and activities of turning on and off appliances over a period of time [3]. Load monitoring can be achieved in an intrusive or non-intrusive way. The intrusive load monitoring (ILM) requires attaching

© Springer Nature Switzerland AG 2019
W. Abramowicz and R. Corchuelo (Eds.): BIS 2019 Workshops, LNBIP 373, pp. 424–434, 2019.
https://doi.org/10.1007/978-3-030-36691-9_36

individual sensors to the appliances to be monitored, while non-intrusive load monitoring (NILM) does not have this requirement. NILM collects aggregated energy information using a sensor attached to the entry point of energy into a household, but the consumption can be discomposed through analyzing the turning on-and-off signals of appliances [4]. To date NILM becomes more popular as no additional devices are needed for energy auditing, thus, the method does not introduce any inconvenience to customers.

In this paper, we present a smart non-intrusive load monitoring platform called *SmartM*. In this work, we not only present a complete load monitoring solution that supports data extraction, processing, load and analysis in real time, but also investigate the disaggregation solution for recorded energy consumption. We have collected the data from five residential households for over a one-year period and preprocessed the data according to conforming to NILMTK data format so that it can be analyzed by the existing NILM analytic tools. In addition, we describe the detected appliances of the monitored household and show the case of load disaggregation.

The rest of this paper is organized as follows. Section 2 surveys the related works. Section 3 describes the implementation of the SmartM platform. Section 4 describes the load disaggregation algorithm used in this paper. Section 5 describes the data set, and Sect. 6 concludes the paper and provides the direction for future work.

2 Related Work

Buildings are the main consumers of energy and contributors to carbon emission. For example, in Denmark buildings accounts for 41% of total final energy consumption, residential up to 30% [16]. NILM is one of the effective measures for understanding and optimizing energy consumption, and received growing attention in recent years. An increasing number of public data sets and tools have been collected and developed.

Among them, the following NILM open data sets were found, including REDD [17], AMPds [18], Dataport [19], COMBED [20], and iAWE [21]. These data sets contain the household's total consumption data and sub-metering consumption data, which can be used to evaluate the load disaggregation algorithms. In this paper, we developed SmartM to collect NILM data sets for Danish residential households in order to assess building performance, retrofit effects and user consumption behavior in specific Nordic countries with similar building infrastructure.

In the field of energy disaggregation, various tools and algorithms have been developed. The most popular one is NILMTK [14], which facilities load disaggregation and comparison of different NILM data sets and algorithms. The current version is NILMTK v0.2, developed by Kelly et al. [22], which supports any size of a data set, e.g., those that do not fit into memory. In addition, it provides off-the-shelf converters to convert many existing NILM datasets into a unified NILMTK data format, as well as the API for implementing the converter for a new NILM data set. Moreover, the algorithms for disaggregation

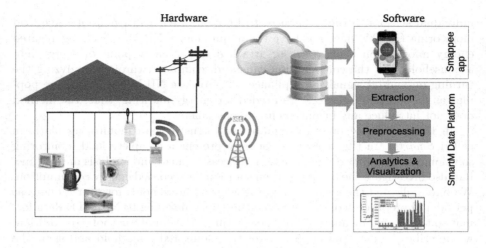

Fig. 1. SmartM hardware and software implementation

have been extensively investigated in [4]. The algorithms for load disaggregation can be divided into two broad categories, including supervised and unsupervised learning algorithms. Supervised learning algorithms require labeled data to train models, such as CO-based [15], while unsupervised learning algorithms can use events, labeled data, or other prior information. The latest trend is of using unsupervised learning algorithms [4], such as FHMM, which has also been used in this paper. To improve the accuracy and reduce complexity, an occupancy-aided load disaggregation approach was proposed in [13]. In order to achieve the real-time capability, Nguyen et al. [23] implement a NILM system by the optimizing hardware platform which uses System on Chip (SoC) integrating with Field-programmable Gate Array (FPGA); Welikala et al. [24] instead use an optimizing software platform that combines a fast deconvolution-based technique for load disaggregation. In comparison, SmartM uses the open source software stack to achieve real-time capability, using the technologies including Apache Zeppelin, PostgreSQL, and MADlib. It is highly flexible and easy for implementation and deployment.

3   SmartM Platform

The implementation of SmartM consists of the hardware setup and the software implementation for real-time monitoring and consumption disaggregation, which are shown in Fig. 1.

3.1   Hardware Platform

The hardware implementation of SmartM provides real-time, non-intrusive load monitoring for a household. We use Smappee as the smart monitoring and processing device. The installation of Smappee is rather simple, i.e., the current

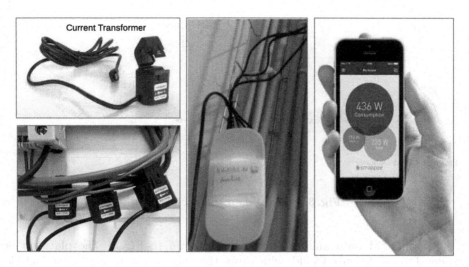

Fig. 2. The monitor Smappee and its mobile app

transformer sensors are simply attached to the three-phase power lines at the entrance of a household (see Fig. 2). The current flowing into a household is measured in real time and the signal events when using appliances are recorded. The sensor's readings are transmitted to the Cloud via a WiFi connection to the Internet. In our setup, we use the LTE connection instead (see Fig. 1), as the power cables for the monitored households are laid in the wall. In Denmark, it is rather challenging to find suitable households with exposed cable lines, as well as with a WiFi connection at the installation site.

3.2   Software Platform

SmartM software platform consists of two components in the following: Smappee app and the SmartM data platform. In the mobile app, users can monitor their real-time aggregated energy consumption, consumption history and the events of using appliances. The SmartM data platform is developed in this project, which provides advanced features for data analytics and visualization. The app and the data platform both use the Smappee cloud database as the data source. The captured data are stored in the Smappee cloud database, and the cloud database manages the data using gradual data aggregation approach according to time granularity [5]. This approach does the following: 5 min interval data is stored for 15 days, hourly interval data for 90 days, daily interval data for 1 year and monthly interval data for 3 years. This approach saves data-storage space by assuming that data will lose value over time. Therefore, we build the SmartM data platform to keep all the finest granular data in our private Science Cloud [6], and do the advanced data analysis including load disaggregation. In the following, we focus on the introduction of the SmartM data analysis platform.

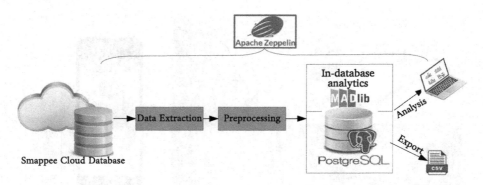

Fig. 3. SmartM data analytic platform

The SmartM data analysis platform is shown in Fig. 3. The platform is deployed in our Science Cloud, which uses the open-source technologies, including Apache Zeppelin [7], PostgreSQL [8] and the in-database analysis library MADlib [9]. We use Zeppelin for data extraction, data pre-processing, visualization and scheduling jobs. Zeppelin is a web-based notebook that provides pluggable layers of integrating different programming languages and data processing systems in its backend. The current version v0.18 supports over 20 data processing systems, including Spark, PostgreSQL, Hive, Hadoop, Cassandra; and the script languages including Scala, SQL, Python, R, Markdown, and more. It enables interactive data analysis and facilitates collaboration. SmartM extracts the real-time data from the Smappee cloud database, transforms the extracted JSON-format data into relational format data, and saves them into PostgreSQL database. Zeppelin schedules the job for data extraction and preprocessing to run every 5 min. Zeppelin user interface is shown in Fig. 7 in Appendix A. The processing pipeline has the following sequential steps: extraction, preprocessing, loading and visualization, which are run as dependent paragraphs in Zeppelin. The data extracted from the Smappee cloud include electricity data, the aggregated consumption and the events of using appliances, i.e., turning on and off. The time-series data are stored in PostgreSQL, and MADlib is used for manipulating data and doing analytics in the database. The reason of using MADlib is to achieve better performance for in-database analytics compared with ordinary analytic approaches, which requires moving the data out of the database [10]. Therefore, we can query analytic results by executing simple SQL statements and visualize them directly on Zeppelin, which can greatly ease the use.

4   Load Disaggregation

NILM uses a single point of a sensor to record aggregated consumption of a household, which is much easier to set up by comparing with ILM. However, NILM is less accurate and more challenging for identifying the consumption for separate appliances of a whole property [11]. This requires algorithms for

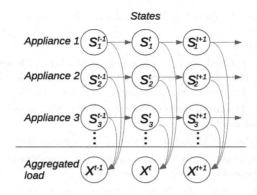

Fig. 4. Graphic representation of FHMM, reproduced from [17]

identifying the signatures of appliances from the aggregated consumption that correlates individual appliance states [12]. In this paper, we are not to present a new method, but rather to demonstrate using the state-of-the-art algorithm for the load disaggregation and present the challenges for future work.

In the following, we introduce the load disaggregation method used in SmartM, called *Factorial Hidden Markov Model* (FHMM) [13]. The method can be formalized as follows. Suppose that a household has many appliances, defined as a set, M. For an appliance $i \in M$, it may have multiple working modes corresponding to different operational states. For example, an LCD lamp has three modes (ON, Standby, and OFF), and a washing machine or a dish waster has different functionalities for working corresponding to different states. The FHMM model disaggregates the load by taking into account the change of states between time instances. The graphic representation of FHMM is depicted in Fig. 4. In this figure, the states are simplified as an OFF state and a number of discrete ON states. The ON/OFF states are formalized as $S = \{0, 1\}$. The state of an appliance i at the time t is formalized as $s_i^t \in S$. The consumption power of an appliance is distributed at $[\mu_i^t - \delta_i^t, \mu_i^t + \delta_i^t]$, with a average of μ_i^t and a variance of δ_i^t. The model for load disaggregation can, therefore, be formulated as

$$\hat{s}_i^t = \arg\min_{\hat{s}_i^t} \sum_{t=1}^{|\mathcal{T}|} (x^t - \hat{x}^t)^2 \tag{1}$$

where x^t is the aggregated load at the time t, $\hat{x}^t$ is the sum of the load of all appliances at the time t, $\hat{x}^t = \sum_{i=1}^{|M|} \mu_i^t s_i^t$, and $|M|$ is the number of appliances of a household, and $|\mathcal{T}|$ is the number of occupied periods.

The power information of the appliances under consideration is measured by observing the changes of power change between on and off events.

Table 1. The identified appliances of each household

Household	Appliances
H1	Air dryer, Cloth dryer, Coffee maker, Cooker, Dish washer, Electric shaver, Hair dryer, Iron, Stove, Laptop, Lights, Microwave, Play station, Fridge, Toaster, Vacuum, Washing machine, Kettle
H2	Cooker, Dryer, Hair dryer, Kettle, Lights, Microwave, Oven, Fridge, Washing machine
H3	Kettle, Lights, Microwave, Oven, Play station, Fridge, TV, Vacuum
H4	Blinder, Coffee maker, Dishwasher, Electronic Shaver, Iron, Lights, Microwave, Oven, Fridge, Stove, TV
H5	Cooker, Coffee maker, Dish washer, Kettle, Lights, Laptop, Oven, TV, Washing machine, Vacuum

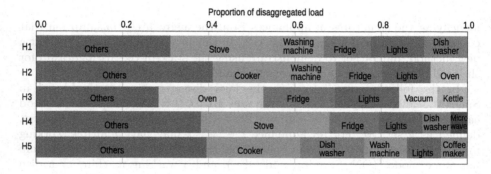

Fig. 5. Top-5 disaggregated load for the five households

5   The NILM Data Set

In this section, we describe the collected NILM data and disaggregate the data using the method presented in Sect. 4. We use the NILMTK [14] as the load preprocessing and disaggregation tool. NILMTK provides several off-the-shelf functions for analyzing NILM data, including data availability, sub-metered energy usage, and top-k appliances of energy consumption.

Smappee can detect most of the events that occur when appliances are used and their energy consumption of appliances. However, there are still some unaccounted parts in the aggregated consumption that are classified into others. Smappee reports aggregated consumption at irregular intervals ranging a few seconds to minutes. Therefore, we preprocess the data into a regular time series format so that it can be processed by the NILMTK disaggregation function. The missing values of the time series are interpolated by the preprocessing functions offered by NILMTK.

We first present the detected appliances of each household in Table 1. As shown, different types of appliances were detected by Smappee for each house-

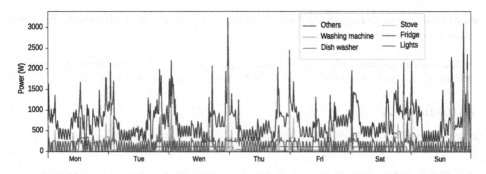

Fig. 6. FHMM load disaggregation for a typical one-week data of household H_1

hold. Ideally, the consumption of a household will be disaggregated for all detected appliances. However, this will complicate the disaggregation model significantly. Therefore, it is often better to model top-k appliances rather than all of them [14]. The top-k appliances have the greatest values for load disaggregation, while the rest can be considered as noise only, which can reduce the model complexity. In this study, we choose $k = 5$ and describe the proportion of appliance load as a horizontal stacked bar chart in Fig. 5. The proportion of *others* accounts for the parts of the undetected appliances and the appliances that are not within the top five.

Figure 6 shows an example time series of one week for the top five appliances of the household, H_1, disaggregated by the FHMM algorithm. The NILMTK provides a *model* module that encapsulates the results of the training module required by the disaggregation algorithm. But, note that NILMTK also provides another disaggregation algorithm, called *Combinatorial Optimisation (CO)* [15]. In this study the FHMM is used since this method does not require sub-metered data for training.

6 Conclusions and Future Work

Load monitoring is an effective approach to optimizing building energy consumption. In this paper, we have presented a NILM platform, SmartM, and the data set that contains detailed consumption of appliances. We have also demonstrated the technologies used for NILM and described the load disaggregation algorithms. In addition, we have presented a show-case of load disaggregation for our platform.

There are several directions for future work. First, we would like to improve the load disaggregation algorithm by augmenting time-use survey data in order to improve its accuracy, therefore a time-use survey platform will be developed. Second, it is interesting to conduct a comprehensive benchmarking study for the load disaggregation algorithms with the available NILM data sets. Third, we would like to use the disaggregated data to optimize household energy consumption, make personalized energy-saving suggestions, and ultimately lead to consumer behavior changes.

Acknowledgements. This research was supported by the Røskilde Smart Monitoring Household Project (No: 82568), and the CITIES project (No: 1035-0027B).

Appendix A

See Fig. 7.

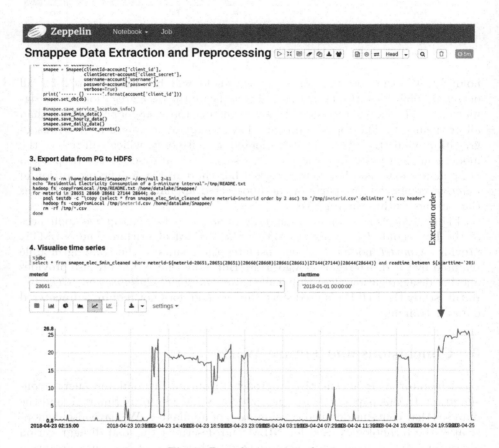

Fig. 7. Zeppelin user interface

References

1. Kitzing, L., Katz, J., Schroder, S.T., Morthorst, P.E., Andersen, F.M.: The residential electricity sector in Denmark: a description of current conditions. Technical University of Denmark, Lyngby (2016)

2. Ayres, I., Raseman, S., Shih, A.: Evidence from two large field experiments that peer comparison feedback can reduce residential energy usage. J. Law Econ. Organ. **29**(5), 992–1022 (2013)
3. Zeifman, M., Roth, K.: Nonintrusive appliance load monitoring: review and outlook. IEEE Trans. Consum. Electron. **57**(1), 76–84 (2011)
4. Najafi, B., Moaveninejad, S., Rinaldi, F.: Data analytics for energy disaggregation: methods and applications. In: Big Data Application in Power Systems, pp. 377–408 (2018)
5. Iftikhar, N., Pedersen, T.B.: Using a time granularity table for gradual granular data aggregation. In: Catania, B., Ivanović, M., Thalheim, B. (eds.) ADBIS 2010. LNCS, vol. 6295, pp. 219–233. Springer, Heidelberg (2010). https://doi.org/10.1007/978-3-642-15576-5_18
6. Liu, X., Nielsen, P. S., Heller, A., Gianniou, P.: SciCloud: a scientific cloud and management platform for smart city data. In: Proceedings of DEXA Workshop, pp. 27–31 (2017)
7. Apache Zeppelin. https://zeppelin.apache.org/ as of 2019-06-01
8. PostgreSQL. https://www.postgresql.org/ as of 2019-06-01
9. Hellerstein, J.M., et al.: The MADlib analytics library: or MAD skills, the SQL. Proc. VLDB Endow. **5**(12), 1700–1711 (2012)
10. Liu, X., Golab, L., Golab, W., Ilyas, I.F., Jin, S.: Smart meter data analytics: systems, algorithms and benchmarking. ACM Trans. Database Syst. **42**(1), 2 (2016)
11. Berges, M.E., Goldman, E., Matthews, H.S., Soibelman, L.: Enhancing electricity audits in residential buildings with nonintrusive load monitoring. J. Ind. Ecol. **14**(5), 844–858 (2010)
12. Chalmers, C., Fergus, P., Montanez, C., Sikdar, S., Ball, F., Kendall, B.: Detecting activities of daily living and routine behaviours in dementia patients living alone using smart meter load disaggregation (2019). arXiv preprint arXiv:1903.12080
13. Tang, G., Ling, Z., Li, F., Tang, D., Tang, J.: Occupancy-aided energy disaggregation. Comput. Netw. **117**, 42–51 (2017)
14. Batra, N., et al.: NILMTK: an open source toolkit for non-intrusive load monitoring. In: Proceedings of the 5th International Conference on Future energy systems, pp. 265–276 (2014)
15. Suzuki, K., Inagaki, S., Suzuki, T., Nakamura, H., Ito, K.: Noninstrusive appliance load monitoring based on integer programming. In: Proceedings of SICE, pp. 2742–2747 (2008)
16. Santin, O.G., Itard, L., Visscher, H.: The effect of occupancy and building characteristics on energy use for space and water heating in Dutch residential stock. Energy Build. **41**(11), 1223–1232 (2009)
17. Kolter, J.Z., Johnson, M.J.: REDD: a public data set for energy disaggregation research. In: Proceedings of Workshop on SIGKDD, vol. 25, pp. 59–62 (2011)
18. Makonin, S., Popowich, F., Bartram, L., Gill, B., Bajic, I.V.: AMPds: a public dataset for load disaggregation and eco-feedback research. In: Proceedings of Electrical Power and Energy Conference, pp. 1–6 (2013)
19. Parson, O., et al.: Dataport and NILMTK: a building data set designed for non-intrusive load monitoring. In: Proceedings of GlobalSIP, pp. 210–214 (2015)
20. Batra, N., Parson, O., Berges, M., Singh, A., Rogers, A.: A comparison of non-intrusive load monitoring methods for commercial and residential buildings. arXiv preprint arXiv:1408.6595 (2014)
21. Batra, N., Gulati, M., Singh, A., Srivastava, M.B.: It's different: insights into home energy consumption in India. In: Proceedings of the 5th ACM Workshop on Embedded Systems For Energy-Efficient Buildings, pp. 1–8 (2013)

22. Kelly, J., et al.: NILMTK v0.2: a non-intrusive load monitoring toolkit for large scale data sets: demo abstract. In: Proceedings of the 1st ACM Conference on Embedded Systems for Energy-Efficient Buildings, pp. 182–183 (2014)
23. Nguyen, T.K., Dekneuvel, E., Jacquemod, G., Nicolle, B., Zammit, O., Nguyen, V.C.: Development of a real-time non-intrusive appliance load monitoring system: an application level model. Int. J. Electr. Power Energy Syst. **90**, 168–180 (2017)
24. Welikala, S., Thelasingha, N., Akram, M., Ekanayake, P.B., Godaliyadda, R.I., Ekanayake, J.B.: Implementation of a robust real-time non-intrusive load monitoring solution. Appl. Energy **238**, 1519–1529 (2019)

Towards a Digitized Understanding of the Skilled Crafts Domain

Maximilian Derouet$^{(\boxtimes)}$, Deepak Nagaraj$^{(\boxtimes)}$, Erik Schake$^{(\boxtimes)}$, and Dirk Werth$^{(\boxtimes)}$

AWSi, 66123 Saarbrücken, Germany
{maximilian.derouet, deepak.nagaraj, erik.schake,
dirk.werth}@aws-institut.de

Abstract. Skilled workers are over-proportionally exposed to physical stress and hazards, which often means that their work is characterized by high physical demands. In this paper we deal with a proof of concept, which uses wearable sensors to monitor the movement of workers to automatically identify working gestures and poses which result in high physical stresses. Based on a rating system a real-time alerting on unhealthy positions is initiated. Apart from solutions concerning individual persons, time series data from all the workers at the site can be used to create a smart schedule optimizing the process flow and minimizing individual physical stresses. Altogether, we use the interrelations between everyday behavior and health problems to approach one of the greatest common goals of both employers and employees – the goal of "staying healthy".

Keywords: Preventive healthcare · Machine learning · IoT · Wearables · Automated scheduling · Real-time

1 Introduction

Due to immense physically stressful tasks in the construction sector, the rate of work-related accidents is enormous, while preventive actions are only taken by approximately half of all businesses [1]. In addition, only 12.9% of employers perform a complete risk assessment process, which must be made manually and requires a post-operations effectiveness check. This culminates in a gross loss of 5.9 billion Euros in the German construction sector [1].

In order to lower these numbers, the German ministry for labor and social affairs has started an initiative in 2002 aiming at reducing the number of Musculoskeletal Disorders (MSDs) at the workplace. However, in recent years, there has been nearly no change in the number of instances of these disorders [1]. This indicates that the present preventive health measures have not made much difference, therefore new technologies need to help to further increase safety and well-being at the construction site.

Tools that are predominantly used to determine the liability of construction workers to MSDs are ergonomic assessment sheets (e.g. OWAS by Karhu, Kansi, and Kuorinka [2]), which identify situational poses a worker has to suffer that lead to high stress and tension. Although it is possible to point out undesired poses by using these sheets, they

© Springer Nature Switzerland AG 2019
W. Abramowicz and R. Corchuelo (Eds.): BIS 2019 Workshops, LNBIP 373, pp. 435–444, 2019.
https://doi.org/10.1007/978-3-030-36691-9_37

are not appropriate for operational tasks, since they rely only on manually obtained input [3], which is error-prone and naturally precludes a real-time-capability. To overcome these problems, several techniques based on motion capturing systems have been used to provide better, more efficient and automatically generated input data. In motion capturing, tools such as sensors or cameras in conjunction with markers are used to track the motion of a person and represent it digitally.

The German institute for occupational safety developed a system named CUELA that allows an evaluation of musculoskeletal stress during physically demanding movements. It can be worn at the construction site and is designed not to interfere with normal execution of tasks, however it is a very massive system that restricts the freedom of movement enormously [4] (see Fig. 1). By using such a system, it is possible to detect body angles in real-time and alert the user instantaneously whenever a bad posture is detected [5].

In PREFLOW, a project aimed at alerting workers in logistics domain of bad postures and also establishing an interface to a company's workflow-management in order to ergonomically optimize it, intelligent clothes track the worker's motion and use this data to perform an ergonomic assessment [6].

A different approach is presented by Alwasel et al. [8]. Their system utilizes magneto resistive sensors to track shoulder angles and deduct stressful positions of the arms by setting ergonomically reasoned threshold values. However, the system does not consider all the body parts and corresponding stresses, therefore it's use is limited.

Another interesting approach by Brandl et al. [9] completely renounces body worn sensors and instead uses cameras for marker less motion capturing. From that, a skeleton model is generated which allows for body angles to be calculated and an ergonomic assessment sheet such as the OWAS method can be used. Workers are not impaired by any extra clothes or sensors they have to wear, however, cameras are mostly installed statically and objects in the field of vision may block some parts of the

Fig. 1. Floor Tiler wearing the CUELA system. [7]

worker being analyzed. Additionally, many cameras have to be installed to track the tasks effectively, which induces a financial overhead. As described in the above instances, recent projects show promising results in automatically analyzing body postures and alerting the user whenever necessary. However, all the methods still pose many disadvantages, mainly impracticability in wearing the sensors, restrictions to only parts of the body and camera occlusion, that do not allow for application as permanent companion at work.

This project – called BauPrevent (refer to Sect. 6 for more details), as briefly introduced in this paper – aims at developing a wearable sensor-based system that is lightweight and can therefore be used at work without major impairments, thus making it worker-friendly. At the same time, it should still produce reliable results and support construction workers in raising their ergonomic health awareness. In operational use, the system warns a worker in real-time whenever an unhealthy position is taken. In addition, a smart planner uses the recorded movements of the workers to create a smart schedule so that the overall physical stress can be significantly lowered and process flow at the site can be optimized.

The following content is organized as follows. Section two gives an overview of the different types of physical stress a human can suffer and how these can be identified. Afterwards, our concept of sensor placement for effectivity and practicability is presented, that allows for real-time alerting of unhealthy postures. In section four we discuss our approaches for ergonomically optimizing the daily schedule at the construction site before we conclude our work in section five.

2   Types of Physical Stress

The daily work in a typical construction labor causes stresses in various parts of the body. Painters for instance often need to raise one of their arms above their heads to paint the upper parts of a wall or the ceiling. This leads to an increased risk of suffering tension in their lower back [10]. Floor tilers, on the other hand, spend most of the time in a kneeling or crouching position, causing tensions and fatigue. Every craft in this sector has a unique range of physical hazards [11] which together contribute to the high number of work-related injuries in that field.

Manual techniques to limit risks and overall stress on workers has been researched for a long time [12, 13] and has also been a focus point of the German employer's liability insurance association [11]. This association – called BG Bau – has published various documents aiming at helping employers identify the risks at their professions and supporting them in implementing helpful ergonomic solutions. This field of ergonomics is defined in the work of Jaffar et al. as the "relationship between humans, machine systems, job design and the work environment" [14]. All those parts must be properly coordinated in order to assure a long-lasting and healthy professional life.

Besides the physical stress factors, other risks can be identified. These include psychological and social stress (e.g. being put under pressure by a superior) and stresses caused by the direct environment (e.g. noises, dangerous substances). However, we address only physical stresses in this project as it constitutes the major part [15].

Jaffar et al. [14] consider seven ergonomic risk factors: namely bad posture, forceful work, highly repetitive work, vibration, high static loading, contact stress and extreme temperature. One-time exposure to one of these risks may not cause fatal consequences directly, furthermore it cannot be completely prevented. However, constant or frequently repeated exposure can lead to MSDs such as sprains, strains and cumulative trauma disorders [16, 17]. A wide range of ergonomic tools exist in the industry, that reduce some of these stress factors or abandon them completely [11].

A huge problem however is to identify situations in which some of the above-mentioned stress factors take effect. Therefore, several ergonomic tools based on the analysis of numeric evaluation of a working posture have been developed. However, most of them rely on input obtained through manually performed observation. OWAS [2] is probably the most used tool worldwide. It distinctly assesses the postures of the spine, arms and legs numerically together with a value for the carried load. The result is a combination of four numbers, the OWAS code, that is subsequently classified into one of four categories depicting whether or not the posture is musculo-skeletally harmful [2] and requires sanctions.

In Germany, the so-called "Leitmerkmalmethode" is very popular for evaluating stress factors for certain tasks. It also focuses on the posture and carried weights, and additionally considers the frequency of a motion and certain restrictions on the freedom of movement. A numeric value is derived based on these four features that determines a measure for stress factors and consequently helps to decide whether any action is required or not. Other companies and organizations have developed similar methods [18, 19]. In most of the cases the posture is manually estimated and categorized in order to obtain the physical stress level.

In practice, these methods are applied mostly to pictures of body postures taken during actual construction activities. Analysis of those observations is very vague, inefficient and time-consuming due to the loss of the three-dimensional information as well as the human resource that is required. This causes the assessment to be imprecise and done infrequently. They therefore do not allow an evaluation of stress over a complete working day, but only several distinct instances. Some systems have been developed in order to automate the entire evaluation process [3, 4, 8, 9, 16], however none of them are suitable for daily application at the construction site, but rather require a laboratory or specific conditions to produce reasonable results.

3 Sensors and Real-Time Alerting

Position tracking and physical load recognition are implemented using a wide variety of methods, where many of them include sensors or even visual systems. In a simple system, sensors of a smartphone strapped to the back of an user monitors the trunk bending angle and notifies whenever a threshold value is exceeded [5]. Another more complex approach utilizes no sensors but only a camera. Using the raw video data, an algorithm then detects the position of several body parts, deducts angles and subsequently applies the OWAS method in order to evaluate the corresponding posture [9].

Most commonly, sensor based direct measurement methods use IMUs (Inertial Measurement Units)[1] [16]. First tests showed that these devices are suitable for activity recognition and detecting body angles. We therefore follow this widespread approach. Apart from the position we also take the carried weights into account. To do so we use sensors to measure the pressure applied to the shoe-soles.

We want to consider the effects of the workload on the whole body, which naturally requires a distribution of the IMUs to all body areas. Frequently used approaches apply approximately twenty IMUs (see Fig. 2, [20]) in this context, which facilitates to analytically calculate kinetics and kinematics[2] given the underlying body model, which is a mathematical description on the degrees of freedom a human body has.

The usual analytic approach to calculate physical stress out of kinetics and kinematics is computationally very expensive and can therefore not easily be done in real-time. Furthermore, applying so many sensors restricts the freedom of movement enormously leading to a lower practicability and general acceptance.

Therefore, one of the aims of this project is to use as few IMUs as possible to maintain a good balance between the practicability and accuracy of state estimation. However, using a lower number of sensors leads to information loss. Models that can evaluate current stress levels using approximately 17 sensors already exist [20]. To make the system lighter we plan to predict the value of neglected sensors (corresponding to red dots in Fig. 2) with only the data obtained from the seven IMUs (corresponding to green dots in Fig. 2); the sensors attached to the head, arms, back, pelvis and feet can be integrated into accessories such as headbands/helmets, smart watches, trunk belts and work shoes respectively. To achieve this, different machine learning approaches will be tested and evaluated concerning their respective effectiveness. Bidirectional recurrent neural networks [24] can be one of the probable models for this application [26]. If this proves to be non-practical, we plan to increase the number of sensors and test the effectiveness iteratively.

Apart from raw sensor data from the IMUs and from the pressure soles, only dimensions of different body parts parameterizing the whole body are the features considered for calculating stresses using machine learning. This makes the system easily generalizable to new workers. Further, the trained model can be applied to an unknown worker when the corresponding body dimensions are known. Additionally, a provision can be made to also include respective health conditions of an individual in the process planning phase. This is necessary in order to identify body parts that are particularly vulnerable to certain movements leading to higher stress values for some tasks. It is therefore necessary to periodically check the workers' physical state.

The detection of physical stress using the proposed set of sensors deals as foundation for the real-time alerting. Once the system is capable of performing this detection for each individual body-segment a comparison with a threshold can be used to warn the person who takes unhealthy positions. The general idea is simple, but in order to obtain satisfying results, in addition to information about physical stress at an

---

[1] IMU is a device consisting sensors like accelerometer, gyroscope, magnetometer etc.

[2] Kinetics refers to the study of motion and angles while kinematics also takes the underlying forces into account.

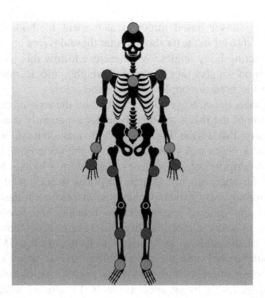

Fig. 2. [21] IMUs placed on the body (green dots: planned to be used in BauPrevent; red dots: usually used but planned to be neglected in this project). (Color figure online)

isolated moment, the current physical health of that person including the health history must also be taken into account.

4 Smart Scheduling

An optimized schedule for every project determines an important part of a business' very economic foundation. The typical parameters to develop such a schedule are not limited to just the tasks themselves. Besides, every task needs to be defined with specified time length along with consumption of resources that may or may not be renewable. Workers performing a given task can be mathematically modeled as a vector pertaining to their characteristics. Once the available workers are assigned to a given task at a time, they can be considered for the next task only upon completion of the present task. The overall objective then is to assign starting times to each task, such that the total lead-time of the project is minimized. This so-called resource constrained project scheduling problem has been a subject of various researches for a long time [25].

   Conventionally, this problem is formulated mathematically as a Mixed Integer Linear Programming problem with the goal to minimize an objective function. But it unfortunately poses a problem of NP-hardness[3] and therefore cannot be solved in efficient polynomial time. It is essential to introduce heuristics in order to find a good solution which will be quicker than the search for the best overall schedule. However,

---

[3] Non-deterministic Polynomial-time hardness: Probably not solvable in polynomial time.

to reduce physical stress for all workers, other factors must be considered. A matrix can be introduced assigning a stress value to each worker-task combination. The higher the value, the more harmful the task is if performed by that particular worker. This value could for instance be calculated by considering the health history of the individual worker. Taking these numbers into account, the overall objective function should consider minimizing the total lead-time as well as the total physical stress of all workers at the site. This makes the problem even more complex and requires problem specific heuristics to be applied. Multi-objective scheduling has been found to yield satisfying results in such cases [22].

Another approach to solve this constrained optimization problem is to use artificial intelligence to find a solution in the solution space. The basic idea is that an algorithm searches a search tree containing all possible sequences of actions aiming at finding the cost optimal path through the solution space. Using an HTN-planner[4] for instance [23], the problem of finding a (near) optimal solution can be modeled very realistically. Tasks are formulated that consist of subtask which themselves can consist of further subtasks and so forth.

It is thereby possible to model the project precisely consisting of tasks with all subtasks, while assigning time and resource constraints only to higher level tasks. Many search algorithms have been proposed with varying performances on different domains [23]. The flexibility to adapt to different objectives and simplicity of modeling a problem makes this approach very favorable.

The real challenge, however, is to create the cost matrix shown illustratively in Table 1 with the goal of finding characteristics of tasks that cause strain to certain parts of the human body. Workers then have to be assessed in order to find tasks that are particularly harmful for them. One way to do this is to create body profiles manually beforehand and deduct probable unhealthy movements conflicting with a person's health and body characteristics. But this approach is very time-consuming and requires specialists for examination. The second approach uses a learning algorithm to find these values. However, much data is needed for this approach and reliable values can therefore only be found over time. For our Information and Communications Technology-system (ICT-system) one of the core components consists of an HTN-planner. Interfaces to an ERP-system and to the sensor data guarantee that necessary information is available. The information from the ERP-system includes tasks to be performed and their dependencies, available resources as well as the skills required to perform the tasks. The sensor-platform on the other hand provides time series of the physical stress of the skilled workers. The simplified architecture of the system with corresponding data flows between each component is depicted in Fig. 3. Considering these aspects, a schedule can be generated which reduces the overall physical stress of the construction site. This schedule particularly considers the individual history and additionally assures that certain constraints such as the completion of high priority tasks are met. Physical stress can thus be avoided before it even occurs.

---

[4] Hierarchical Task Network.

Table 1. A worker-task matrix with numbers in range 0–10. In this example carrying heavy loads is particularly harmful for worker 1 while drilling is rather harmless for worker 2.

Tasks workers	Hammering	Drilling	Carrying
Worker 1	5	2	9
Worker 2	3	1	4
Worker 3	8	7	3

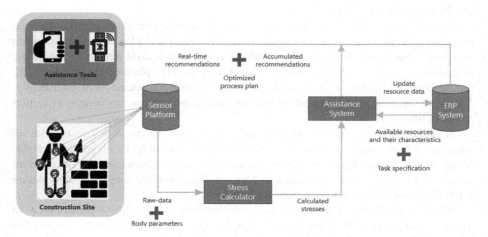

Fig. 3. System architecture.

5 Implications and Concluding Remarks

The Preventive Health system that is designed in the context of BauPrevent not only poses technical questions but also has to be evaluated in a socio-economic and ethical sense. For the socio-economic part it is important that the system is not too cost-expensive and accepted by both those who apply it and by those on whom it is applied. Both criteria are considered in BauPrevent due the fact that mainly easily available sensors are used and that an acceptance study is carried out at the end of the project. To make the system more attractive to employers the activity tracking might be used to automatically generate timesheets from an activity tracking. The ethical acceptability is guaranteed by an ethic commission which eventually will evaluate the project. This is necessary since the information coming from the sensors especially after being mapped to activities could be misused if the system does not take care of preventing it. Apart from just focusing on the skilled crafts domain and physical stress, the BauPrevent concept could in the future also be adapted to other domains like the back-office and psychic stress for instance to prevent burnouts. The presented paper conceptually shows a way on how the BauPrevent project implements a preventive health system for the skilled crafts domain. This is done by introducing lightweight sensors and thereby becoming capable of performing real-time alerting and generating smart schedules to improve the overall health level.

In the current phase of the project, we are examining two datasets that were recorded in order to figure out how the system has to be shaped eventually to be well-suited for the use cases painter- and stuccoer-craftsmanship. In the first set, twelve painters performed strictly defined tasks such as lifting and carrying weights under the observation of two sports therapists (for evaluating automatically generated stresses) in a clinic. The workers were fully equipped with 17 IMUs and pressure measuring shoe-soles and were filmed by two cameras for reference. The second data set corresponds to three stuccoers, who were monitored with the same setup as for the other sensor set, but performing tasks like painting and plastering in a natural way at an actual construction site. Both datasets are being used to build a model which allows to reduce the number of sensors (imputation of missing sensors values). Eventually activity detection and stress calculation will be carried out. Apart from implementing/training the algorithms as mentioned, research is also being made for defining balancing exercises for unhealthy body postures. Here our approach is to use the concept of agonists and antagonists in order to figure out which muscles have to be trained at the end of the day depending on the tasks performed by a given worker.

Acknowledgements. This work is based on BauPrevent, a project partly funded by the German ministry of education and research (BMBF) and the European Social Fund (ESF) as part of the "Zukunft der Arbeit: Mittelstand - innovativ und sozial" program, reference number 02L17C011. The authors are responsible for the content of this publication.

References

1. BAuA (Bundesanstalt für Arbeitsschutz und Arbeitsmedizin). Sicherheit und Gesundheit bei der Arbeit – Berichtsjahr 2016 - Unfallverhütungsbericht Arbeit Sicherheit und Gesundheit (2017)
2. Karhu, O., Kansi, P., Kuorinka, I.: Correcting working postures in industry: a practical method for analysis. Appl. Ergon. **8**, 199–201 (1977)
3. Kivi, P., Mattila, M.: Analysis and improvement of work postures in the building industry: application of the computerised OWAS method. Appl. Ergon. **22**, 43–48 (1991)
4. Ellegast, R.: Messung von Muskel-Skelett-Belastungen mit dem CUELA-Messsystem. Aus der Arbeit des IFA 50–51 (2013)
5. Lietz, R.: CUELA-Feedback: Körperhaltungs-Check mit dem Smartphone (2016)
6. Gräbener, T., Horn, U.: PREFLOW Abschlussbericht Uni Kassel (2006)
7. DGUV Fliesenleger mit CUELA-Messsystem. https://www.dguv.de/ifa/fachinfos/ergonomie/kniebelastende-taetigkeiten/index.jsp. Accessed 7 Feb 2019
8. Alwasel, A., Elrayes, K., Abdel-Rahman, E.M., Haas, C.: Sensing Construction Work-Related Musculoskeletal Disorders (WMSDs), pp. 164–169 (2011). https://doi.org/10.22260/ISARC2011/0027
9. Brandl, C., Bonin, D., Mertens, A., et al.: Digitalisierungsansätze ergonomischer Analysen und Interventionen am Beispiel der markerlosen Erfassung von Körperhaltungen bei Arbeitstätigkeiten in der Produktion. Z Arbeitswiss **70**, 89–98 (2016). https://doi.org/10.1007/s41449-016-0016-9
10. Bau, B.G.: Betriebsärztlicher Gesundheitsbericht für Maler

11. Bau, B.G.: Ergonomie am Bau Damit es leichter geht Damit es leichter geht (2013)
12. Koningsveld, E.A.P., der Molen, H.F.: History and future of ergonomics in building and construction. Ergonomics **40**, 1025–1034 (1997)
13. Schneider, S., Susi, P.: Ergonomics and construction: a review of potential hazards in new construction. Am. Ind. Hyg. Assoc. J. **55**, 635–649 (1994)
14. Jaffar, N., Abdul-Tharim, A.H., Mohd-Kamar, I.F., Lop, N.S.: A literature review of ergonomics risk factors in construction industry. Procedia Eng. **20**, 89–97 (2011). https://doi.org/10.1016/j.proeng.2011.11.142
15. DGUV. Arbeitsbedingte Gesundheits gefahren (2015)
16. Wang, D., Dai, F., Ning, X.: Risk assessment of work-related musculoskeletal disorders in construction: state-of-the-art review. J. Constr. Eng. Manage. **141**, 04015008 (2015). https://doi.org/10.1037/a0021167
17. Killough, M.K., Crumpton, L.L.: An investigation of cumulative trauma disorders in the construction industry. Int. J. Ind. Ergon. **18**, 399–405 (1996)
18. Plus E A Step-by-Step Guide Rapid Upper Limb Assessment (RULA)
19. Plus E A Step-by-Step Guide Rapid Entire Body Assessment (REBA)
20. Inc. XNA (2019). XSENS. https://www.xsens.com/. Accessed 16 Apr 2019
21. Skeleton, M.J.
22. Kulcsár, G., Erdélyi, F.: A new approach to solve multi-objective scheduling and rescheduling tasks. Int. J. Comput. Intell. Res. **3**, 343–351 (2007)
23. Norvig, P., Russel, S.: Artificial Intelligence - A Modern Approach
24. Schuster, Mike, Paliwal, Kuldip K.: Bidirectional recurrent neural networks. IEEE Trans. Signal Process. **45**(11), 2673–2681 (1997)
25. Hannun, A., et al.: Resource-constrained project scheduling problem: review of past and recent developments. J. Proj. Manage. **3**, 55–88 (2018). https://doi.org/10.5267/j.jpm.2018.1.005
26. Cao, W., Wang, D., Li, J., Zhou, H., Li, L., Li, Y.: BRITS: Bidirectional Recurrent Imputation for Time Series. In: NeurIPS (2018)

Competing for Amazon's Buy Box: A Machine-Learning Approach

Álvaro Gómez-Losada$^{(\boxtimes)}$ and Néstor Duch-Brown

Joint Research Centre, European Commission, Seville, Spain
alvaro.gomez.losada@gmail.com,
nestor.duch-brown@ec.europa.eu

Abstract. A key feature of the Amazon marketplace is that multiple sellers can sell the same product. In such cases, Amazon recommends one of the sellers to customers in the so-called 'buy-box'. In this study, the dynamics among sellers for occupying the buy-box was modelled using a classification approach. Italy's Amazon webpage was crawled during ten months and features from products analyzed to estimate the more relevant ones Amazon could consider for a seller occupy the buy-box. Predictive models showed that the more relevant features are the ratio between consecutive prices in products and their number of assessment received by customers.

Keywords: Buy-box · Amazon · Machine learning · Classification · Data science

1 Introduction

Amazon is currently the leading online e-commerce platform in Europe [1] and attracts exceptionally large public interest. In this platform, Amazon acts as a re-seller of some products and also as a marketplace that enables independent sellers to sell new or used products. Sellers have the possibility to use the platform's different services, including among others management of inventories, advertisement of products and the *Fulfilled by Amazon* program, by which Amazon handle logistics for independent sellers' products. A key feature of the Amazon marketplace is that multiple sellers can offer the same product. In such cases, Amazon recommends one of the competing sellers to customers in the so-called 'buy-box' [2]. This box is placed on every product detail page so customers can begin the purchase process by adding items to their shopping carts directly.

One of the main challenges in Amazon marketplace operation is the lack of understanding of the empirical mechanisms adopted by sellers for market competition. To the best to the authors' knowledge, just one study has focused on studying mechanisms that sellers adopt to gain exposure to consumers in Amazon marketplace from a machine learning perspective. Chen et al. [3] explored algorithmic pricing strategies from sellers in Amazon marketplace by obtaining products and seller characteristics. These authors examined the empirical behavior of the buy-box to understand relevant features by which Amazon selects a given seller among competitors to occupy the buy-box. These authors studied sellers' and products' characteristics and

W. Abramowicz and R. Corchuelo (Eds.): BIS 2019 Workshops, LNBIP 373, pp. 445–456, 2019.
https://doi.org/10.1007/978-3-030-36691-9_38

estimated that the product price related characteristics are the most relevant for winning the buy-box.

In this study, the dynamics of competition among sellers for occupying the buy-box was modeled using a predictive approach based on classification. After scraping Italy's Amazon webpage, longitudinal datasets were created for selected products describing over time the different default sellers selected by Amazon to sell such products (i.e., to occupy the buy-box). The classification models built on each longitudinal dataset aimed to predict when a change of seller for a product occurs at the buy-box.

The objective of this work is twofold. First, we aim to contribute to the empirical understanding of the Amazon's buy-box algorithm, detecting the more relevant features that explain that a given seller is featured to occupy the buy-box. Second, we offer a characterization of the more representative sellers according to these features. The remainder of this study is organized as follow. In Sect. 2, the methodology applied to estimate the more relevant features from sellers for becoming buy-box eligible is described. A discussion about these estimated features is provided in Sect. 3, together with the characterization of sellers according to them. Finally, in Sect. 4, the main conclusions are presented.

2   Research Methodology

The methodology used in this study is illustrated in Fig. 1 which summarize: (i) the characteristics of the database obtained, (ii) the creation of a longitudinal dataset for every analyzed product, (iii) the creation and selection of features in each dataset,

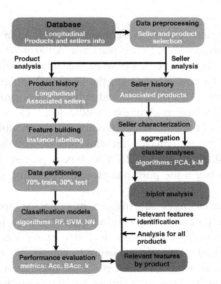

Fig. 1. Methodology and analyses performed. Blue boxes indicate the main obtained results (RF: random forest; SVM: support vector machine; NN: neural network; Acc: Accuracy; BAcc: Balanced accuracy; k: kappa statistic; PCA: Principal component analysis, k-M: k-means). (Color figure online)

(iv) the modeling step using three different classifiers, (v) the estimation of relevant features for winning the buy-box by analyzing all the individual results from products, and (vi) the clustering of sellers considering these latter features.

2.1   Data Collection

Data for this study was obtained using a crawler that navigated through 26 categories of new products in Italy's Amazon webpage, over the course of 10 months, beginning on April 4, 2018. These categories were selected according to the results from a previous crawling experiment to detect the more dynamic ones in terms of products' price changing and presence of sellers offering the same products (some digital categories including apps for Android, *Kindle* or products offered primarily by Amazon like videos were not considered). For each category, just the details from most popular products were extracted. The interest focused on the most demanded ones which are likely to describe seller's strategies for maximizing benefits, and therefore providing more information and easing the modeling process. Due to Amazon's strategic commercial reasons, the number of most popular products displayed for each category varied along the crawling period (*top*-20, *top*-50 or *top*-100) causing the frequency of crawling cycles to differ ($\approx$1 h to complete the crawling of *top*-20 products displayed for each category). Each time the crawler visited a product page, it recorded the time of crawling, the characteristics of the product and those from the seller featured in the buy-box. An example of product characteristics and the buy-box is illustrated in Fig. 2. To consider the time the crawler extracted information from products through navigation allowed for obtaining a longitudinal approach for each of them.

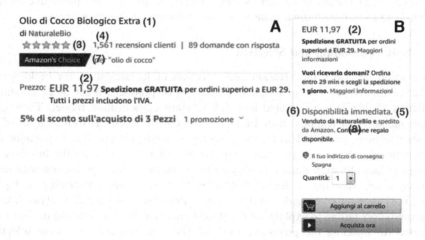

Fig. 2. Characteristics from a given product (**A**) and buy-box in Italy's Amazon webpage (**B**). Numbers in brackets are explained in Table 1.

Table 1. Features from products extracted during the crawling process.

Feature	Description
Product	Unique identifier of the product (ASIN code)
Price	Seller price for the product
Ratings	Customers rating of the product
Assessments	Number of assessments (opinions) the product received by customers
Fulfilled	Fulfilment of the product by Amazon
Stock	Availability of the product
Choice	Recommended product by Amazon (Amazon's choice)
Seller	Unique identifier of the seller selected by Amazon to sell the Product
Time	Time instant the product was crawled

2.2   Longitudinal Datasets for Products

Once semi-structured data from crawling was processed, an indexed-by-time database containing the products' and sellers' characteristics was obtained. Such database was filtered by products, obtaining an independent longitudinal dataset for each of them. The aim was to describe the change over time of characteristics of products featured in Table 2, and importantly, to monitor the different sellers that have sold each product. For modelling purposes a total of 461 products were selected to be studied. These products fulfilled a double criterion. Firstly, each product was offered by more than three sellers, and secondly, information from products by crawling was obtained a minimum of 110 occasions. This latter threshold was stablished according to the one in five ratio of examples (instances) per predictor variable [4, 5], considering that a maximum of 21 candidate predictors were considered to build the predictive models (Table 2) in each longitudinal dataset. These predictors are analyzed next.

2.3   Feature Building and Selection

This section describes the creation and selection of features used for building the predictive models. For every longitudinal dataset of products, a set of 21 candidate predictors (Table 2) were created to build a binary classification model. These predictors included all features from Table 1 (except ASIN code) as well as a set of 13 dynamic features generated from price, aiming to study the possible implications of product prices' trends and variations applied by sellers for winning the buy-box. In order to reduce the high dimensionality in these datasets, those predictors with near-zero variance, showing a linear dependency or correlated (Pearson's r higher than ± 0.8) were removed. Additionally, using a Principal Component Analysis (PCA), those predictors failing to explain a 95% of the variance in the longitudinal dataset were excluded for building the predictive models. These techniques for feature selection were used in each longitudinal dataset from products. To detect variables with variance close to zero, correlated or showing linear dependency, the *nearZeroVar*, *findLinearCombos* and *findCorrelation* functions from the *caret* package [6, 7] in *R* [8] were used, respectively. PCA for feature selection was applied with the *preProcess* function from the same package.

Labelling. For each instance in every longitudinal dataset, a positive or negative class was assigned according to the next criteria. The first time a new seller was selected to occupy the buy-box for selling a product, the value "1" was assigned to the instance (representing the positive class), and "0" otherwise. An example of the labeling process is illustrated in Fig. 3. In this study, the selection by Amazon of a new merchant to occupy the buy-box is considered the more decisive instant to understand the algorithm that performs such selection. It is assumed that once a new merchant is selected, its continuity in time by winning the boy-box does not provide conclusive information, since this could be achieved simply by either inactivity (e.g., out of stock) or unknown strategic decisions from other competing sellers.

2.4   Classification

Three well-known classifiers, namely, random forest (RF), support vector machine (SVM) and neural networks (NN), were used independently to predict if a competing seller is likely to replace the current one occupying the buy-box. It is important to remind that the purpose of this predictive approach is not to identify the seller likely to win the buy-box among others offering the same product, but to estimate if the current merchant selling a product is going to be replaced by another competing seller also offering the same product. For each longitudinal dataset from products, such classification models were built and the prediction accuracy evaluated. Once accomplished this prediction exercise, the relative importance of the involved predictors (after the feature selection process) was estimated.

Product	Seller	Label
1	A	1
1	A	0
1	A	0
1	B	1
1	B	0
1	C	1
1	D	1
1	D	0

Fig. 3. Example of positive and negative class assignments ("1": positive class) in a longitudinal dataset.

Model Building. Longitudinal datasets from each product were split in training and test sets following a 70:30 proportion, respectively. For tuning parameters of classifiers, ten trials were carried out using the training data, repeated three times, following a 10-fold cross-validation (CV) resampling scheme. Every tuned classifier was built on nine training folds using the CV scheme, and predictions were evaluated on the remaining held-out fold using the ROC (receiver operator characteristic) metric, obtaining a performance profile based on all the tuning parameters tested. After identifying the optimum model among the candidates based on their performance, this one was then re-built using the whole training data set (without fractions of the training data being held-out). To handle possibly unbalance between positive and negative classes, which could bias the model towards the positive class, a stratified version of the CV scheme was adopted. To that end, instances containing the majority (negative) class were randomly removed to ensure an approximate equal presence of both classes [9]. The *caret* package from the R software was used to build classifiers (*train* function), and the *down-sampling* argument in the *preProcess* function was used to implement the stratified CV.

Table 2. Candidate features used to build classification models for products.

Abbreviation	Type	Role	Value
Change in seller	Categorical	Response	1: The seller winning the buy-box has changed (positive class) 0: The seller winning the buy-box remains (negative class)
dPrLowestPr	Numeric	Predictor	Difference between the current price and lowest price
dHighestPrP	Numeric	Predictor	Difference between the highest price and current price
dPrRM32pr	Numeric	Predictor	Difference between current price and 32-prices rolling mean
dPrRM16pr	Numeric	Predictor	Difference between current price and 16-prices rolling mean
dPrRM8pr	Numeric	Predictor	Difference between current price and 8-prices rolling mean
dPrRM4pr	Numeric	Predictor	Difference between current price and 4-prices rolling mean
rPrLowestPr	Numeric	Predictor	Ratio between the current price and the lowest price
rPrHighestPr	Numeric	Predictor	Ratio between the current price and the highest price
rPrRM32pr	Numeric	Predictor	Ratio between the current price and 32-prices rolling mean
rPrRM16pr	Numeric	Predictor	Ratio between the current price and 16-prices rolling mean
rPrRM8pr	Numeric	Predictor	Ratio between the current price and 8-prices rolling mean
rPrRM4pr	Numeric	Predictor	Ratio between the current price and 4-prices rolling mean
rPr	Numeric	Predictor	Ratio between the current and previous price
Ops	Numeric	Predictor	Number of assessment the product has received by customers
ProdRating	Numeric	Predictor	0 to 5. Rating of the product received by customers

(continued)

Table 2. (*continued*)

Abbreviation	Type	Role	Value
Day	Numeric	Predictor	1 to 31
Wday	Categorical	Predictor	1: The product is displayed on a working day; 0: otherwise
AmChoice	Categorical	Predictor	1: The product is Amazon's choice; 0: otherwise
Bestseller	Categorical	Predictor	1: The product is a bestseller; 0: otherwise
Fulfilled	Categorical	Predictor	1: The product is fulfilled by Amazon; 0: otherwise
Stock	Categorical	Predictor	1: The product is in stock; 0: otherwise

Evaluation. To measure the classification accuracy, a 2×2 confusion matrix was set to summarize the number of instances which class label is predicted correctly or incorrectly. This classification accuracy was estimated for every predictive model built on each longitudinal dataset from products, and for every classifier. Considering that no one criteria is sufficient to assess the performance of a classifier [10], the accuracy, balanced accuracy and the kappa statistic (Cohen's kappa) [11] were used in this work.

The first metric, accuracy, measures the proportion of examples correctly classified. Balanced accuracy is estimated as the average value of sensitivity and specificity, and it provides an estimation on the average accuracy obtained on either class [12]. The third one, the kappa statistic takes into account the accuracy that would be generated simply by chance. The form of the statistic is $k = (O-E)/(1-E)$, where O is the observed accuracy and E is the expected accuracy based on the marginal totals of the confusion matrix. The statistic can take on values between -1 and 1: a value of 0 means there is no agreement between the observed and predicted classes, while a value of 1 indicates perfect concordance of the model prediction and the observed classes [7].

Relative Importance of Predictors. Once every predictive model was built on each longitudinal datasets from products, using the three different classifiers, their accuracy was evaluated on test sets and the relative importance of the predictors in the models estimated. On each predictor, a ROC curve analysis was conducted and a series of cut-offs applied to the predictor data to predict the class. ROC analysis is a useful metric since allows for estimating the optimal model independently from the class distribution. The area under to ROC curve was used as the measure of variable importance. Relative importance of the variables was estimated using the *varImp* function from the *caret* package.

The selection of the more important variables for sellers to win the buy-box after building a predictive model for each of 461 products, and for each classification model, was accomplished in a two-step process. Arbitrarily, the five more relevant variables (1-highest to 5-lowest) from classification models were estimated for every product. Then, considering all the products, the frequency distribution of the variables with highest relevance obtained. Secondly, from this frequency distribution, a tabulation scheme aggregated the range of highest frequencies containing the four more decisive variables for winning the buy-box. Thus, the most relevant features after considering all products were obtained.

Relevant Feature Analysis and Clustering of Sellers. Database was filtered by seller and their sold products obtained. Each seller was characterized by a single vector containing the average value of the relevant variables obtained from each product in its portfolio. Less representative sellers were removed and just those selling more than four products studied, obtaining a total of 525 sellers to be analyzed. From this characterization two analyses were conducted. The first one was a *bi-plot* study of relevant variables to understand their linear relation, using the *factoextra* library [13] in *R*, and secondly, a *k-means* cluster analysis of sellers. Intuitively, the latter analysis tries to detect patterns in sellers that can be aware of these relevant variables for considering them in their selling strategic decisions. The optimal number of clusters for grouping of sellers was obtained using the *NbClust* package [14] from *R*. The function *kmeans* from base *R* was used to perform the k-mean analysis.

3   Results and Discussion

3.1   Importance of Features

Figure 4 shows the frequency of the five more important features estimated after building the 461 predictive models (*x*-axis: from the 1-highest to 5-lowest importance). In Table 3, from variables with highest importance, the four more frequent features from each model are indicated as well as their percentage of occurrence. Some of these

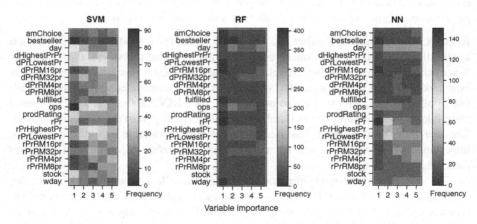

Fig. 4. Frequencies of variable importance in 461 predictive models using three different classifiers (support vector machine -SVM-, random forest -RF- and neural networks -NN-). In the *x*-axis, the relative importance of features is shown from left (1-highest) to right (5-lowest). By using a color code, each square indicated the number of times a variable is considered important in this ranking (1-highest to 5-lowest). (Color figure online)

variables (*Ops* and *Day*) are considered relevant in all classifiers and *rPr* in two of them (RF and NN). The predictive accuracy of each classifier was estimated after averaging the quality of the predictions accomplished in the 461 datasets (Table 4). As can be appreciated, RF provides the more accurate predictions in all the quality measures used.

According to the more accurate classifier (RF) the more decisive feature to be considered for gaining the buy-box is the ratio between the current price and the previous price of a product (*rPr*), followed by the number of assessment received by customers (*Ops*). According to [3], who used RF as only classifier using a different set of features, the most important one is the price difference to the lowest price (*dPrLowestPr*), followed by the price ratio to the lowest price (*rPrLowestPr*). Results of RF and NN are similar for the three more relevant features. Even SVM classifier provides the less accurate predictions, the variable importance estimations from this algorithm were also considered. The rest of features *Day*, *dPrLowestPr*, *rPrHigestPr* and *rPrRM32pr* seem to have a secondary, but worth to consider, role in this regard.

Table 3. Relevant features obtained from predictive models. Support vector machine (SVM), random forest (RF) and neural networks (NN). Relative frequency (%) is indicated in brackets.

Order of Importance	Classifiers		
	SVM	RF	NN
1	*Ops* (20%)	*rPr* (88%)	*rPr* (33%)
2	*Day* (9%)	*Ops* (4%)	*Ops* (28%)
3	*dPrLowestPr* (8%)	*Day* (3%)	*Day* (5%)
4	*Stock* (8%)	*rPrRM32pr* (1%)	*rPrHigestPr* (5%)

Complementarily to the estimation of the more relevant variables from predictive models, these variables were alternatively used to characterize sellers. Values of these variables in each product from seller's portfolio were averaged. Thus, it was possible to characterize each seller by a single vector defining its general behavior with respect the most relevant features to win the buy-box. Importantly, this approach allow for performing a bi-plot analysis of sellers to understand the linear relation among relevant variables. In Fig. 5, this relation is illustrated as well as the contribution of each of them to explain the variability of seller using two principal components (PCA-biplot). As expected, variables describing the relation of prices to the lowest (*dPrLowestPr*) and highest (*rPrHighestPr*) prices for products are negatively correlated, even quantifying a different measure (difference and ratio, respectively). Conversely, a high correlation is found between the variables studying the ratio between the price (*rPr*) and the 32-prices rolling mean (*rPrRM32pr*), indicating that this latter statistics describes effectively the trend of the prices for analyzed products. Remaining studied variables (*Stock*, *Day* and *Ops*) are not significantly useful to describe variability in sellers and do not show a remarkable association. All variables contributions explain around the 86% of variability for seller characterization.

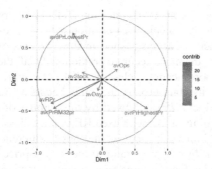

Fig. 5. Biplot analysis of the more relevant features. Color in arrows indicates contribution of each variable to explain the variability in seller characterization. Positive correlated variables point to the same side of the plot. (Color figure online)

Table 4. Quality measure results for predictive modeling. Support vector machine -SVM-, random forest -RF- and neural networks -NN-.

Classifiers			
Classifiers	Accuracy	Balanced accuracy	kappa
SVM	0.91	0.56	0.15
RF	0.94	0.76	0.52
NN	0.92	0.59	0.20

3.2 Importance of Features

A *k-means* analysis was carried out using the seller characterization from Sect. 3.1, considering six the optimum number of clusters. In the interest of space, graphical results are omitted. The value of the more relevant features (Table 3) from each cluster of sellers is indicated in Table 5, together with the size of each cluster.

Table 5. Value of analyzed features in cluster of sellers, including size of clusters (values in € when applicable).

Cluster	Size	Features						
		Ops	*Day*	*rPr*	*dPrLowestPr*	*rPrHighestPr*	*Stock*	*rPrRM32pr*
1	32	2027	15	−0.3	2.1	−4.2	0.8	−0.03
2	24	71	15	4.0	5.9	−19.6	0.9	0.8
3	103	220	15	0.06	0.9	−3.4	0.4	−0.02
4	1	202	19	24.6	0.4	−16.7	1.0	9.3
5	1	15	17	0.6	62.0	−23.1	0.9	−0.5
6	364	160	16	0.1	1.2	−4.3	0.9	0.05

First, third and sixth clusters are poorly delimited which centres are close to the axes origin. These three clusters hold most of analysed seller and as expected, they do not differ greatly in the value of the analyses features (Table 5). It is worth to note that Amazon seller is included in the sixth cluster, and also that 50% of sellers grouped in the second cluster are devoted to sell imitation jewellery items. Fourth and fifth clusters are composed by a single seller. Value of *Day* feature in clusters has approximately same value, indicating that most of the products are offered along the all days of the month. Short variations in these values are not conclusive enough to obtain an indication of product selling during specific days of the month and its analysis remains open for further investigation.

Seller in fourth cluster offered just six products competing by winning the buy-box, and none of its competitor was Amazon. The more relevant feature of this seller is the high value of the *rPr* feature and their products' permanent availability (stock presence). Surprisingly, this seller offers 6000 low-cost products through all product categories in Italy's Amazon webpage, enjoying a particular shop-window. After visiting many products displayed in this shop-window, it seems that those products are exclusively sold and fulfilled by this seller. Seller from fifth cluster is represented by an United State technological corporation presented in US's and all Europe's Amazon webpages, specialized in providing video and image processing chips for connected consumer camera applications. In the database, it was presenting just nine products competing for winning the buy-box. No other rival than Amazon was detected for selling products offered by this merchant.

4   Conclusions

This study aims to estimate the more relevant features of sellers to be eligible to occupy the buy-box, and to characterize sellers according to these features. Predictive models showed that the more relevant features are the ratio between consecutive prices in products (*rPr*) and the number of assessment received by customers for products (*Ops*). Cluster analysis of sellers considering these features showed a set of overlapped clusters which does not provide relevant information about these characteristics. However, this analysis revealed two clusters represented by singles sellers, together with another one, all of them with distinct characteristics.

Disclaimer. The views expressed are purely those of the authors and may not in any circumstances be regarded as stating an official position of the European Commission.

References

1. E-commerce News Europe (2018). https://ecommercenews.eu/the-most-visited-online-marketplaces-by-country/. Accessed 15 Feb 2019
2. Amazon: Buy box eligible status (2017). https://sellercentral-europe.amazon.com/forums/t/when-will-i-be-buy-box-eligible/157401. Accessed 20 Feb 2019

3. Chen et al.: An empirical analysis of algorithmic pricing on Amazon marketplace. In: WWW 2016 Proceedings of the 25th International Conference on World Wide Web, Montreal, Québec, Canada, 11–15 April 2016, pp. 1339–1349 (2016)
4. Vittinghoff, E., McCulloch, C.E.: Relaxing the rule of ten events per variable in logistic and cox regression. Am. J. Epidemiol. **165**(6), 710–718 (2007)
5. Austin, P.C., Steyerberg, E.W.: The number of subjects per variable rquired in linear regression analyses. J. Clin. Epidemiol. **68**(6), 627–636 (2015)
6. Kuhn, M.: Building predictive models in r using the caret package. J. Stat. Softw. **28**(5), 1–26 (2008)
7. Kuhn, M., Johnson, K.: Applied Predictive Modelling. Springer, New York (2013). https://doi.org/10.1007/978-1-4614-6849-3
8. R Development Core Team: R: A Language and Environment for Statistical Computing. R Foundation for Statistical Computing, Vienna, Austria (2018). http://www.R-project.org/. ISBN 3-900051-07-0
9. Galar, M., Fernández, A., Barrenechea, E., Bustince, H., Herrera, F.: A review of ensembles for the class imbalance problem: bagging-, boosting-, and hybrid-based approaches. IEEE Trans. Syst. Man Cybern. Part C (Appl. Rev.) **42**(4), 463–484 (2012)
10. Diettrich, T.G.: Approximate statistical tests for comparing supervised classification learning algorithms. Neural Comput. **7**(10), 1895–1924 (1998)
11. Carletta, J.: Assessing agreement on classification tasks: the kappa statistic. Comput. Linguist. **22**(2), 249–254 (1996)
12. Brodersen, K.H., et al.: The balanced accuracy and its posterior distribution. In: 2010 20th International Conference on Pattern Recognitio. IEEE Computer Society, Istanbul, Turkey (2010)
13. Kassambra, A., Mundt, F.: Factor extra: extract and Visualize the Results of Multivariate Data Analyses (2017). https://rpkgs.datanovia.com/factoextra/index.html
14. Charrad, M., Ghazzali, N., Boiteau, V., Niknafs, A.: NbClust: an R package for determining the relevant number of clusters in a data set. J. Stat. Softw. **61**(6), 1–32 (2014)

ISAMD Workshop

ISAMD 2019 Workshop Chairs' Message

We have a great pleasure to hand over to the readers the volume that contains papers selected for presentation at ISAMD 2019: First Workshop on Information Systems and Applications in Maritime Domain held during June 26–28, 2019, in Seville, Spain. The event was co-organized with the 22nd International Conference on Business Information Systems (BIS 2019).

The recent growth of the maritime sector is reflected by an increase of the global maritime traffic and of the activities exploiting the ocean environment and its resources. On the one hand the maritime sector contributes to the economic growth of societies, on the other hand it generates concerns at European and International level related to safety and security of maritime transportation, navigation, and exploitation.

Technological innovations led to the development of automated monitoring systems and maritime sensors networks, producing huge amounts of the maritime data, opening new avenues to science-driven maritime operations and policy making. Industry and academia willing to use the potential stemming from maritime data develop solutions, applications, and systems for maritime data sharing and advanced processing, fusion, and analysis, can develop added value products in support of the maritime operational and industrial communities.

The aim of the ISAMD 2019 workshop was to gather researchers as well as representatives of industry and maritime institutions to discuss research results and innovations in the maritime domain related to a widely understood information systems and applications. The workshop was a great opportunity to discuss novel data-driven solutions with applications for maritime security, safety and security of maritime navigation and transport, sustainable fisheries, and exploitation of ocean resources.

The workshop received nine articles. Each paper was evaluated by two or three independent reviewers of the Program Committee. The highest ranked four articles were accepted for presentation during the conference and for publication in the proceedings.

As a final point, the chairs would like to express their gratitude to all the participants and especially authors whose attendance and contribution allowed us to organize this event for the first, but for sure, not the last time. We believe that the workshop is all about community. Therefore we would like to thank all Program Committee members for their knowledge, sound judgment, and kind support during the review process. Without their hard work the organizers would not be able to make the selection of the best works.

Finally, we would like to direct our sincere appreciation to the organizers of the hosting conference (BIS 2019) for their effort and support.

Axel Hahn
Milena Stróżyna

Organization

Chairs

Axel Hahn | Carl von Ossietzky Universität Oldenburg, Germany

Milena Stróżyna | Poznań University of Economics and Business, Poland

Program Committee

Paolo Braca | Centre for Maritime Research and Experimentation, Italy

Dominik Filipiak | Poznań University of Economics and Business, Poland

Arne Lamm | University of Oldenburg, Germany

Po-Ruey Lei | ROC Naval Academy, Taiwan

Giuliana Pallotta | Lawrence Livermore National Laboratory, USA

Cyril Ray | Ecole Navale, France

Maria Riveiro | University of Skövde, Sweden

Matthias Steidel | Offis Institute for Information Technology, Germany

Krzysztof Węcel | Poznań University of Economics and Business, Poland

Spatial Query Processing on AIS Data Streams in Data Stream Management Systems

Tobias Brandt$^{(\boxtimes)}$ ⓘ and Marco Grawunder

Department of Computing Science, University of Oldenburg, Oldenburg, Germany
{tobias.leo.brandt,marco.grawunder}@uol.de

Abstract. Spatio-temporal data streams from moving objects have become ubiquitous in the recent years, not only, but also in the maritime domain. The Automatic Identification System (AIS) is an important technology in the maritime domain that creates huge amounts of streaming moving object data and enables new use cases. The data streams can improve the situation awareness, help Vessel Traffic Services (VTSs) to get an overview of certain situations and detect upcoming critical situations automatically. For these use cases, queries have to be processed on data streams with continuous results and little delay.

To reach this goal, Data Stream Management Systems (DSMSs) lay a foundation to process data streams, but lack the capabilities for spatio-temporal query processing. We tackle this research gap with techniques known from moving object databases and integrate those into the stream processing. We present a system that integrates the moving object algebra from moving object databases into the interval approach from data stream processing to run queries on AIS data. This new approach allows us to define very diverse spatio-temporal queries on AIS data streams, such as radius queries, k-nearest neighbors (kNN) queries as well as queries with moving polygons. Additionally, the approach allows us to use short-time prediction to detect situations before they occur, e. g., to avoid collisions. Our results show that the system is very flexible, offers a clear semantics and produces results on AIS streams with many vessels with low latency.

Keywords: Data Stream Management Systems · Maritime · Trajectories · Moving objects · Spatial-temporal systems · Data streaming · Stream management · Geographic information systems

1 Introduction

Today, moving objects such as vessels are commonly equipped with location tracking and communication capabilities to sense their location and share it

Supported by the Ministry of Science and Culture of Lower Saxony (Germany) with the graduate school *Safe Automation of Maritime Systems (SAMS)*.

ⓒ Springer Nature Switzerland AG 2019
W. Abramowicz and R. Corchuelo (Eds.): BIS 2019 Workshops, LNBIP 373, pp. 461–472, 2019.
https://doi.org/10.1007/978-3-030-36691-9_39

with others, e. g., using the Automatic Identification System (AIS). This development has allowed many new use cases beyond simple sharing of the raw location information. Vessel Traffic Services (VTSs) can better estimate risks in critical traffic [5], waypoint detection can help to get insights of maritime movement [17] and anomalies can be detected [17], for example, to find illegal activities [14,18].

All these use cases have in common that continuous spatio-temporal data streams from moving objects need to be processed. This can be done with custom implementations for each use case, which increases the development time and effort because common data stream challenges such as windows and out-of-order processing have to be re-implemented with each new application. Another approach is to use existing systems to implement the application on top. Moving object databases and Data Stream Management Systems (DSMSs) are system types than can assist in those cases.

Moving object databases mainly work on static data with one-time queries while DSMSs process data streams in various ways but typically lack the support for spatio-temporal data streams from moving objects. Due to these limitations, both are not ideal for the challenges posed by moving object data streams. Continuous queries need to consider both the temporal semantics from the data streams, i. e., the window semantics, and the temporal semantics of the spatio-temporal data itself. This is especially important if the moving objects send their locations unsynchronized, leaving gaps in-between the spatial information, as it is the case with AIS. Additionally, current systems have no support for queries that not only process the current situation, but also future or past situations while preserving the correct temporal semantics of the stream.

Our approach combines bitemporal data stream processing in a DSMS with the moving object algebra [10] from moving object databases [9,16] to solve this research gap. It allows to create very flexible spatio-temporal queries on continuous data streams. This is achieved with new temporal attributes that integrate seamlessly into the existing stream processing logic with a second time interval that flexibly defines for which points in time a spatial information such as a location is valid and needs to be predicted. Additionally, we introduce techniques for a spatio-temporal filter step to improve efficiency of the presented queries.

2   Background and Problem Description

This work aims to enable spatio-temporal query processing on moving object data streams. To lay a foundation, typical characteristics of data streams and data stream processing are described and the moving object algebra is introduced. Finally, example use cases in the maritime domain are outlined, which act as demonstration cases in the remainder of this paper.

2.1   Moving Object Data Streams

AIS streams are a good example for moving object data streams. The vessels send their location in irregular intervals every few seconds or minutes via radio signals.

The characteristics from data streams in general are typically outlined as follows [6,8,12]:

- **Active data sources** The sources actively push their data to the receiver(s).
- **Unbounded** The data stream can be assumed to be unbounded. The receiver does not know in advance if and when the stream will end and hence has to work with an infinite stream.
- **No control** The receiver has no control over the source.
- **Only once** The source sends its data only once.

For a comprehensive overview of moving object data streams, the reader may be referred to [4][1].

2.2   Windows and Time Intervals

To handle the unbounded nature of data streams, DSMSs offer concepts to work with this characteristic. Windows are a common approach for this purpose. They reduce the data stream to a certain amount of new stream elements. This can, for example, be the last hour or the last 100 elements. Windows have multifold tasks in stream processing. They allow to define temporal semantics on the stream to express the interest of the user in a certain time frame. For example, if a use case is only interested in the AIS messages in the last minutes, instead of all messages ever received, windows allow to express this requirement in a semantically clear manner. This also helps to deal with concept drifts, i. e., fundamental changes in the stream [6,11]. Additionally, windows limit the number of stream elements that need to be kept in memory and processed with non-incremental algorithms.

Time intervals are a way to implement windows in DSMSs [12]. With this approach, a time interval in the form [start, end) is attached to every stream element, e. g., [10,15). Operators in a stream processing graph, such as a join, an aggregation, etc., use the time intervals to decide which elements to keep and which to remove from their memory and which elements to use for a join, aggregation, or other respective operation.

2.3   The Moving Object Algebra

Moving object databases run queries on moving objects. A defining characteristic of moving objects is that they change over time. The moving object algebra, described by [10] and implemented in the moving object database SECONDO [9, 16], models this temporal behavior with temporal types and operations on these types. An attribute can be temporal. For example, for a vessel, the location

---

[1] The authors of this paper also authored this survey.

could be a temporal point that can change over time. In other words, a temporal attribute is a function over time which for every point in time returns a value of the according type, in this case a spatial point. A temporal point can be denoted as a *tpoint*[2].

Such a temporal point can be depicted as a trajectory with a timestamp at each point on this trajectory. When executing a query on a temporal attribute, the result is also temporal. For example, a query on a moving object, in contrast to a static situation, does not ask *if*, but *when* a point is within a certain region.

Existing functions over data types can be reused for temporal types. This is done with a process called *lifting* [10]. For example, the spatial *distance* function can be applied to any combination of temporal and non-temporal input values [1]:

$point \times point \rightarrow real$ [**distance**]

If at least one temporal input value is used, the result is also a temporal type, in this case a temporal real value [1]:

$tpoint \times point \rightarrow treal$ [**distance**]
$point \times tpoint \rightarrow treal$ [**distance**]
$tpoint \times tpoint \rightarrow treal$ [**distance**]

The result is a temporal type because the results can vary over time. For example, the distance between two temporal points can change over time.

2.4   Example Use Case 1: Nearby Vessels

Vessels which are or will be very close to each other can lead to risky situations. When tracking areas with a high density of vessels, automatically detecting such situations can be helpful. A query detecting such situations could use a radius query and filter for those pairs of vessels which are closer together than a certain threshold value. Another option would be to calculate the Closest Point of Approach (CPA) and search for CPAs where the distance is small.

The difficulty of this query is depicted in Fig. 1. Here, a radius query around vessel X is done at 12:00 o'clock. Nevertheless, the locations of the other vessels are not known at this point in time. Using the last known location would lead to a wrong result with vessel 1 not and vessel 2 being within the result set. The correct result, depicted with the dashed lines and points, is the other way around. This problem can be solved by using a prediction function for the locations of the vessels and predicting the locations to 12:00 o'clock. Having a prediction functionality build into the system, it can also be exploited to predict the movement even further into the future to have a picture of the situation a few minutes ahead of time.

Another use case with proximity between multiple vessels would be to find the closest vessels to a vessel, for example in case of an emergency. Here, a kNN could be applied on the same foundation as a radius query.

---

[2] Güting et al. [10] denote temporal types as moving types and hence a temporal point as *mpoint*. Nevertheless, to emphasize that the algebra is not only applicable to spatial objects, we use the notation from [7].

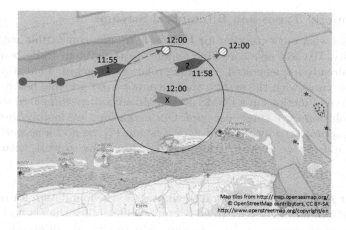

Fig. 1. Radius query with vessel x at the center at point in time 12:00 [3]

2.5   Example Use Case 2: Oil Spill

The previous use case works with multiple moving points. Nevertheless, other use cases may require other spatial objects. For example, in case of a moving oil spill, vessels that are about to enter this area need to be warned. Not only the vessels are moving, but also the region. It could even change its shape over time. Figure 2 depicts such a situation. The location of a vessel and a region (dashed circle) is predicted for the next ten minutes. Using the *in_interior* operation results in a temporal Boolean which tells when the vessel will be within the restricted area.

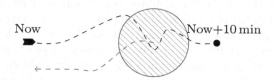

Fig. 2. A moving object and a moving area with prediction

3   Concept for Spatio-Temporal Streams

DSMSs are designed to lay a generic foundation so that they can be used for many different use cases. Our goal is it to also enable DSMSs to be applied on use cases with multiple moving objects as described in Sects. 2.4 and 2.5. To achieve this goal, we extend the interval approach for DSMSs by the moving object algebra using a bitemporal approach for the temporal metadata.

3.1   Temporal Types and Bitemporal Streams

A main goal with our extension for DSMSs is to stay compatible with existing functionality. We add new core functionality to the system while being able to reuse the already implemented streaming relational algebra. That way we allow to cover use cases with the system that have not been possible before.

The offered functions in a DSMS are a main advantage compared to a custom designed solution for a single use case. Our extensions are mainly threefold: (1) we add temporal attributes to the type system, (2) we add a second temporal metadata and (3) we allow existing and new functions to work with temporal attributes.

Temporal Attributes. Temporal attributes are the foundation for the moving object algebra and a key part to add temporal flexibility that is needed to run queries on spatio-temporal data streams with prediction. Internally, temporal attributes are functions that return, for a certain point in time, a value of their type. With our approach, a temporal attribute can be of every type that already exists in the system, for example, integers, spatial points or polygons.

Temporal attributes can be created by a map or aggregation operator. For example, the aggregation operator offers a function to use past movements of a vessel to create a linear or spline function of that movement. The resulting function is then used for the prediction of unknown or future locations of that vessel. Other options are possible as well, for example to use data from a navigation system to predict future locations more accurately.

Temporal Functions. DSMSs already offer many functions, for example arithmetic functions for select predicates, such as `temp_attr1 + attr2 > 42`. Following the lifting approach (cf. Sect. 2.3), the result of this function will be temporal if at least one of the involved attributes is a temporal attribute. This means that the function needs to consider the type of the input attributes. Instead of re-implementing all existing functions (such as the "+" function), the system detects if temporal attributes are involved in such an expression and then solves the expression for all points in time in a non-temporal fashion.

For this purpose, the temporal attributes, i. e., temporal functions, are solved for each point in time in a defined time interval. They result in values of their respective type. With these values, the expression is solved at each single point in time. The result again is a function from time to the respective type of the expression. That way, the system can automatically use temporal attributes in expressions without any work for the user to decide if a function needs to be temporal or not. Hence, expressions with temporal attributes can be defined as if no temporal attributes would be involved.

Additionally, the moving object algebra defines new functions that work directly on temporal attributes without the need to solve the temporal attributes for each point in time. The `atMin` function is an example. It takes a temporal real or integer value and returns the lowest value(s) in a certain time interval. It is a building block for a CPA query.

Bitemporal Streams. We refer to the previously mentioned time interval for which the temporal attributes are solved as the *prediction time interval*. It is an additional time interval in the metadata of a stream element next to the stream time interval for the window semantics. The prediction time interval defines if the stream element is predicted to the current point in time or to a future or even past time interval. The prediction time interval can be arbitrarily set in the query graph with a new operator called the "PredictionTime" operator.

Example Stream Element. The following table shows a single stream element with a temporal attribute (v), the stream time for the window semantics and the prediction time for the semantics of the moving object algebra. As can be seen, "v" is a function that for different points in time returns a different integer value (here written as "5→10", where "5" is the point in time and "10" is the value at this point in time).

v (tinteger)	stream time	prediction time
5→10, 6→10, 7→20, 8→40, 9→50	[0,2)	[5,10)

On this stream element, an expression can be applied. For example, "v + 5". The "+" operation does not know about temporal attributes, wherefore the system runs the expression five times, once for each point in the prediction time, and then combines the results to a new temporal integer:

v (tinteger)	stream time	prediction time
5→15, 6→15, 7→25, 8→45, 9→55	[0,2)	[5,10)

3.2   Spatio-Temporal Filter

Evaluating spatio-temporal queries on data streams can be computationally expensive. To increase the performance, we introduce three different spatio-temporal filtering techniques. These filter out elements in spatio-temporal queries, especially distance based queries, that are unlikely to be in the final result set of a query. They do this before the expensive spatio-temporal calculations take place and therefore reduce the costs of a query. The techniques are namely "approximate distance", "multi rectangle" and "single rectangle".

The basic idea of these techniques is to approximate the distance that the moving objects could have traveled between the time of the last known location and the predicted point in time. If the objects could reach the queried area, they are predicted. If not, the prediction is omitted. Hence, the filter is based on an estimation and could filter out elements which would have been part of the result. In consideration of the space, we omit a more detailed discussion about the filter approaches.

4   Experimental Evaluation

To evaluate the concept, we implemented it into an existing DSMS, which is build on top of the interval approach. We use the Odysseus DSMS[3] as the foundation, as it is very modular and with that easily extensible. The extensions are mainly wrappers around existing operators to handle temporal attributes and expressions internally. Additionally, we extended the operators with the bitemporal query semantics. In this evaluation we show both the feasibility to implement the use cases from Sects. 2.4 and 2.5 as well as the performance of the system.

4.1   Use Case 1: Nearby Vessels

In the first use case, vessels which are or will be very close to each other are aimed to be found. This can be realized with a radius query that filters for vessels that are within a certain radius to a center vessel. A generic query structure that can be used as a blueprint for such a query is depicted in Fig. 3. It is separated into multiple stages. In the preparation stage, the data is transformed into a common schema. For example, latitude and longitude values are combined to a spatial point object. In the temporalization stage, an aggregation function is used to create temporal attributes for the locations of the vessels, i. e., to create the prediction functions. The join stage is an important step to create all combinations of vessels that are necessary for the current use case. For example, if the radius query only has to be done for one element in the center (i. e., observing a specific set of vessels), this can be controlled in the join stage.

After this stage, a stream of combinations of all relevant vessels flows into the spatio-temporal stage. Here, the prediction time is set to the relevant time interval, for example the next ten minutes. Then, the spatial operation can be defined. In this case, it calculates the spatial distance between the vessels and selects only those where the distance is below a certain threshold.

The result of this query is a stream with stream elements of vessels that are close to each other. The result elements contain the information how far the vessels are from each other as well as when the respective distance will be reached. The whole query can be defined in a query language for data streams. Writing custom code is not necessary.

4.2   Use Case 2: Oil Spill

The second scenario can be realized in a very similar manner. Instead of one data source with the AIS data stream, two data sources are present: one for the AIS data and one for the current known polygon of the oil spill. These two streams again flow through the temporalization stage and the temporal attributes are joined together. In the spatio-temporal stage, instead of calculating the distance, the is_inside function is applied. The result is a stream that contains the information when a certain vessel is or will be within the moving oil spill.

---

[3] https://odysseus.informatik.uni-oldenburg.de/.

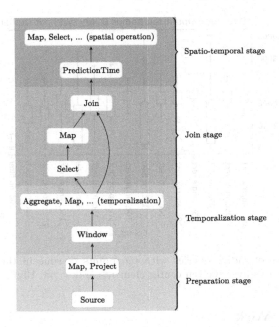

Fig. 3. Generic structure for a spatio-temporal query on moving object data streams with temporal functions

4.3 Performance Evaluation

To get insights on how many vessels can be observed at once, we did an experimental performance evaluation with real data from the US coast. We use the AIS messages from the US west coast in UTM-zone 10 and limited the dataset to messages from April 1st 2017, 10:00 to 12:00 o'clock. The dataset contains 88 132 AIS messages from 1171 vessels, which averages to 12 messages per second. Not all vessels are present in the area for the whole two hours. We did the performance evaluation on a 64 GiB system from which Odysseus was configured to use at maximum 50 GiB. The processor is an "Intel(R) Core(TM) i7-6700K CPU @ 4.00GHz". The data is read from the internal SSD. The system runs Java 8 on Ubuntu 18.04.

Figure 4 shows the data rate of the radius query for different numbers of observed vessels (i.e., the number of vessels for which the nearby vessels are continuously calculated) and different filtering techniques (cf. Sect. 3.2). As can be seen, the data rate can be above 3000 tuples per second in median for a query with 20 observed vessels (and roughly 1000 vessels in the area). Comparing this to the real-time data rate of the original data set of about 12 tuples per second, it can be seen that the system can handle scenarios with this amount of vessels. The latency values for this most demanding query with the single rectangle filter method is about 10 ms, wherefore this query can be considered as delivering near real-time results.

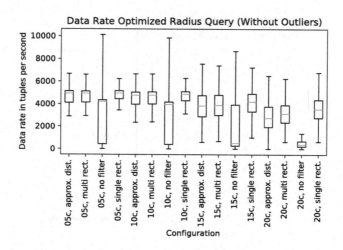

Fig. 4. Data rates of radius queries with ten points in time in the prediction time interval. 05c indicates five, 10c ten center elements and so on. Higher is better.

5   Related Work

Galić [6] presents two systems with a similar approach: OCEANUS and Moby-Dick. Both also use ideas from the moving object algebra for moving object stream processing, but lack the integration into the interval approach for a sophisticated window semantics. This leads to less possibilities to express streaming queries. Additionally, they do not include any filter approaches or queries including multiple moving objects.

Bakli et al. [2] used the moving object algebra to integrate it into Hadoop. While the motivation to process huge amounts of moving object data is similar, the target is different. Hadoop is designed for bulk processing, while we focus on near real-time results in stream processing.

Other works present solutions for smaller parts of moving object stream processing, but leave out the DSMS approach with reusable operators, query languages, window semantics, prediction time intervals, etc. Hence, in contrast, this work takes a more holistic approach to design a system for moving object queries with extension points for external algorithms instead of designing the specific algorithms but leaving out the system design. Mokbel et al. [15] present an algorithm for continuous radius and k-nearest neighbors queries on data streams. Lin et al. [13] also present an algorithm for moving object data streams and focus on the performance by estimating which parts of the stream may be part of future results. That way, elements that will not be part of future results can be discarded earlier, reducing the memory consumption.

6   Conclusion and Future Work

In this work we presented a system that can run continuous spatio-temporal queries in near real-time on moving object data streams from AIS data. To achieve this, we combine the moving object algebra with the interval approach for a flexible spatio-temporal semantics on the one hand and rich window semantics on the other. This allows the user to freely define a prediction time interval in which a query is evaluated. With this mechanism it is possible to calculate spatial expressions such as the distance between two vessels for future points in time. The underlying system reduces the effort for the user when developing such queries by allowing to define queries in a non-temporal way in a query language and automatically translating the queries into the temporal dimension.

In future work and applications of the system, the temporalization step can be improved. Currently, the functions to transform the history movement of a vessel to a prediction function, i. e., temporal point, are rather simple. For example, future prediction functions could consider typical waterways to improve prediction accuracy. To make the system more scalable to observe more vessels at once in more crowded areas, distribution strategies would be useful. Additionally, the development of more queries for the maritime domain would further show the capabilities as well as open issues of the system.

References

1. de Almeida, V.T., Güting, R.H., Behr, T.: Querying moving objects in secondo. In: 7th International Conference on Mobile Data Management (MDM 2006), vol. 6, p. 47. IEEE, May 2006. https://doi.org/10.1109/MDM.2006.133
2. Bakli, M.S., Sakr, M.A., Soliman, T.H.A.: A spatiotemporal algebra in Hadoop for moving objects. Geo-spatial Inf. Sci. **21**(2), 102–114 (2018). https://doi.org/10.1080/10095020.2017.1413798
3. Brandt, T., Grawunder, M.: Moving object stream processing with short-time prediction. In: Proceedings of the 8th ACM SIGSPATIAL Workshop on GeoStreaming, IWGS 2017, pp. 49–56. ACM, New York (2017). https://doi.org/10.1145/3148160.3148168
4. Brandt, T., Grawunder, M.: GeoStreams: a survey. ACM Comput. Surv. **51**(3), 44 (2018). https://doi.org/10.1145/3177848
5. Eide, M.S., Endresen, Ø., Brett, P.O., Ervik, J.L., Røang, K.: Intelligent ship traffic monitoring for oil spill prevention: risk based decision support building on AIS. Mar. Pollut. Bull. **54**(2), 145–148 (2007). https://doi.org/10.1016/j.marpolbul.2006.11.004, http://www.sciencedirect.com/science/article/pii/S0025326X06004735
6. Galić, Z.: Spatio-Temporal Data Streams. Springer, New York (2016). https://doi.org/10.1007/978-1-4939-6575-5
7. Galić, Z., Mešković, E., Križanović, K., Baranović, M.: OCEANUS: a spatiotemporal data stream system prototype. In: Proceedings of the 3rd ACM SIGSPATIAL International Workshop on GeoStreaming, IWGS 2012, pp. 109–115. ACM, New York (2012). https://doi.org/10.1145/2442968.2442982

8. Geisler, S.: Data stream management systems. In: Kolaitis, P.G., Lenzerini, M., Schweikardt, N. (eds.) Data Exchange, Integration, and Streams, Dagstuhl Follow-Ups, vol. 5, pp. 275–304. Schloss Dagstuhl-Leibniz-Zentrum fuer Informatik, Dagstuhl, Germany (2013). https://doi.org/10.4230/DFU.Vol5.10452.275, http://drops.dagstuhl.de/opus/volltexte/2013/4297

9. Guting, R.H., et al.: SECONDO: an extensible DBMS platform for research prototyping and teaching. In: 21st International Conference on Data Engineering (ICDE 2005), pp. 1115–1116, April 2005. https://doi.org/10.1109/ICDE.2005.129

10. Güting, R.H., et al.: A foundation for representing and querying moving objects. ACM Trans. Database Syst. **25**(1), 1–42 (2000). https://doi.org/10.1145/352958.352963

11. Hulten, G., Spencer, L., Domingos, P.: Mining time-changing data streams. In: Proceedings of the seventh ACM SIGKDD International Conference on Knowledge Discovery and Data Mining, KDD 2001, pp. 97–106. Association for Computing Machinery (2001). https://doi.org/10.1145/502512.502529

12. Krämer, J., Seeger, B.: Semantics and implementation of continuous sliding window queries over data streams. ACM Trans. Database Syst. **34**(1), 1–49 (2009). https://doi.org/10.1145/1508857.1508861

13. Lin, D., Cui, B., Yang, D.: Optimizing moving queries over moving object data streams. In: Kotagiri, R., Krishna, P.R., Mohania, M., Nantajeewarawat, E. (eds.) DASFAA 2007. LNCS, vol. 4443, pp. 563–575. Springer, Heidelberg (2007). https://doi.org/10.1007/978-3-540-71703-4_48

14. Mascaro, S., Nicholso, A.E., Korb, K.B.: Anomaly detection in vessel tracks using Bayesian networks. Int. J. Approximate Reasoning **55**(1), 84–98 (2014)

15. Mokbel, M.F., Aref, W.G.: SOLE: scalable on-line execution of continuous queries on spatio-temporal data streams. VLDB J. **17**(5), 971–995 (2008)

16. Nidzwetzki, J.K., Güting, R.H.: Distributed SECONDO: a highly available and scalable system for spatial data processing. In: Claramunt, C., Schneider, M., Wong, R.C.-W., Xiong, L., Loh, W.-K., Shahabi, C., Li, K.-J. (eds.) SSTD 2015. LNCS, vol. 9239, pp. 491–496. Springer, Cham (2015). https://doi.org/10.1007/978-3-319-22363-6_28

17. Pallotta, G., Vespe, M., Bryan, K.: Vessel pattern knowledge discovery from ais data: a framework for anomaly detection and route prediction. Entropy **15**(6), 2218–2245 (2013)

18. Patroumpas, K., Alevizos, E., Artikis, A., Vodas, M., Pelekis, N., Theodoridis, Y.: Online event recognition from moving vessel trajectories. GeoInformatica **21**(2), 389–427 (2017). https://doi.org/10.1007/s10707-016-0266-x

A Study of Vessel Trajectory Compression Based on Vector Data Compression Algorithms

Yuanyuan Ji®, Wenhai Xu^(✉)®, and Ansheng Deng®

Information Science Technology College, Dalian Maritime University,
Dalian 116026, China
yyjem@outlook.com, x_wenhai@163.com, asddmu@hotmail.com

Abstract. With the development of information technology and its vast applications in vessel traffic, such as the popular Automatic Identification System (AIS), a large quantity of vessel trajectory data has been recorded and stored. Vessel traffic has also entered the age of big data. However, the redundancy of data considerably reduces the availability of research and applications, and how to compress these data becomes a problem that needs to be solved. In this paper, several classical vector data compression algorithms are summarized, and the ideas of each algorithm and the steps to compress vessel trajectories are introduced. The vessel trajectory compression experiments based on the algorithms are performed. The results are analyzed, and the characteristics of each algorithm are summarized. The results and conclusions lay the foundation for the selection and improvement of the algorithms in vessel trajectory compression. Through the study of this paper, a systematic theoretical support for the compression of vessel trajectories is provided, which could guide practical applications.

Keywords: Vessel trajectory · Big data · Data compression algorithms · AIS

1 Introduction

Maritime transport plays a vital role in global supply chains. The Review of Maritime Transport published by United Nations Conference on Trade and Development (UNCTAD) in 2017 notes that over 80% of global trade by volume and more than 70% of its value being carried on board ships and handled by seaports worldwide, the importance of maritime transport for trade and development cannot be overemphasized. Ocean shipping will remain the most important mode of transport for international merchandise trade. However, maritime transport is facing many challenges to ensure a high level of efficiency, safety and

Supported by "the Fundamental Research Funds for the Central Universities" (No. 3132016021).

W. Abramowicz and R. Corchuelo (Eds.): BIS 2019 Workshops, LNBIP 373, pp. 473–484, 2019.
https://doi.org/10.1007/978-3-030-36691-9_40

environmental protection, which need academia to develop supporting models and methods of analysis [1].

Vessel trajectories are one of the main data sources for studying the characteristics of vessel traffic behaviors, which is an important basis for supporting the research and application of maritime transport. With the development of information technology and its vast applications in traffic, trajectory data becomes easy to be achieved and have been widely used in road, railway and air traffic researches and practical applications [5,15,19]. The researches and applications based on vessel trajectory data are less than the others, but with the popularity of Automatic Identification System (AIS), a large number of vessel trajectory data has been recorded and stored. Vessel traffic has also entered the age of big data [6,9,14]. Furthermore, increasingly numerous methods, theories and technologies of big data, knowledge mining and machine learning have been proposed. Therefore, how to take full use of the data to promote the development of the marine intelligent traffic system becomes one of the most important research topics [3,13,20–23,25]. Nonetheless, the AIS equipment of a vessel generally publishes a message within every 2 s to 6 min, which makes the trajectory data from the AIS notably large [2,8,17]. Because the AIS has a high frequency of information, the redundant problem of trajectory data from the AIS is highly serious. This problem makes it difficult to be used in research and actual applications. Therefore, the vessel trajectory data compression becomes particularly important [24]. There many methods to compress trajectory data, including clustering method, semantic trajectory compression method, context-aware method, piecewise linear segmentation method, directed acyclic graph method, offline direction-preserving trajectory simplification method, etc. [11,18]. It is noteworthy that as a type of vector data, vessel trajectory data can be compressed by the vector data compression algorithms. Generalized vector data compression should include the storage compression and re-sampling of the vector data [4,12]. The concept of storage compression reduces the amount of vector data by converting the data type or file type. The concept of resampling is to extract subset from set which is a collection of the points that compose the vector graphics. Subset should reflect the original data set within a certain accuracy as much as possible and should ensure that the points of subset are as little as possible. In this paper, the key study is of the re-sampling, which is the vector data compression in a narrow sense.

At present, several of the most widely used classic compression algorithms for vector data are the choosing interval points algorithm, limiting vertical distance algorithm, limiting angle algorithm, offset angle algorithm, Douglas Peucker algorithm and grating algorithm [7,10,16]. The research on vessel trajectory compression mainly focuses on the application and improvement of the Douglas Peucker algorithm, and some problems in the practical application of vessel trajectory data were effectively solved. However, many other vector data compression algorithms have not been applied to vessel trajectory compression. More testing and analysis of these algorithms in vessel trajectory compression are needed. Moreover, different algorithms have different characteristics, which may be highly effective in some specific data compression applications. Therefore, it is necessary to introduce the above vector data compression algorithms and to study the advantages and disadvantages of each algorithm in vessel trajectory compression through experiments. The remainder of this paper is organized as follows. Section 2 introduces the vessel trajectory data compression steps of the above five algorithms. Section 3 presents the data compression experiments in which the performances of the traditional algorithms are tested, and the results are analyzed and discussed. The study's conclusions are summarized in Sect. 4.

2   Compression Algorithms

Suppose a vessel's trajectory is composed by a set of points in chronological order, which can be represented by $A = P_1(x_1, y_1), P_1(x_2, y_2), ..., P_1(x_n, y_n)$, as shown in Fig. 1. P is a point on the trajectory, x is the abscissa and y is the ordinate. The subscript represents the number of the point ordered by time. n is the total number of points on the trajectory. The vessel sailed through each point in chronological order. Let subset B stand for the compression result of set A. The description of each algorithm is as follows.

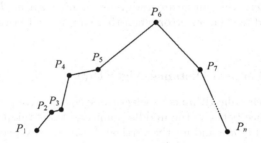

Fig. 1. Example of a vessel trajectory.

2.1   Choosing Interval Points Algorithm

The basic idea of this algorithm is to retain a point in interval k points or an inter-equal distance d on the trajectory. In addition, the first and last points should also to be retained. Let k stand for the number of interval points. The steps of trajectory data compression based on the choosing interval points algorithm are as follows.

(1) Calculate the number of intermediate points that need to be retain on the trajectory, $m = \lfloor (n-1)/k \rfloor$.
(2) Retain the points $P_{k+1}, P_{2k+1}, ..., P_{mk+1}$.
(3) Retain the first and last points P_1 and P_n.
(4) Take subset $B = P_1, P_{k+1}, ..., P_{mk+1}, P_n$.

Let $k = 2$ and $n = 8$. $\lfloor (n-1)/k \rfloor$ rounds $(n-1)/k$ to the nearest integers less than or equal to $(n-1)/k$. After the compression steps above, the result is shown in Fig. 2. The dashed line is the trajectory before compression, and the solid line is the compressed trajectory.

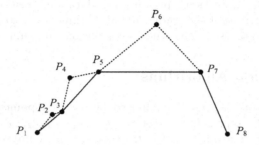

Fig. 2. Example of a vessel trajectory.

The choosing interval points algorithm is simple and easy to implement. This algorithm supports real-time compression processing. However, it is insensitive to the points where the curvature radius is small, such as P_6 in Fig. 2. This property may lead to a larger error when there are more twists and turns in the trajectory.

2.2 Limiting Vertical Distance Algorithm

The basic idea of this algorithm is to select three consecutive points and calculate the vertical distance between the middle point and the straight line between the other two points. Let d stand for the vertical distance. Next, compare d with the distance threshold D. If $d \geq D$, retain the middle point. Otherwise, if $d < D$, delete the middle point. After that step, select the second three consecutive points and continue the pattern until all of the points on the trajectory are processed.

The limiting vertical distance algorithm is simple and easy to implement. This algorithm supports the real-time compression processing of the vessel trajectory data and is sensitive to the distance that a point deviates from the vessel's previous course. However, occasionally, the extreme point of curvature may be deleted, thereby leading to compression error.

2.3 Limiting Angle Algorithm

This algorithm is similar to the limiting vertical distance algorithm. The basic idea is to select three consecutive points, such as P_1, P_2 and P_3. Next, calculate the degree of the angle $\angle P_2 P_1 P_3$. Next, compare it with a given threshold *theta*. If $\angle P_2 P_1 P_3 < theta$, delete the middle point P_2, otherwise retain P_2. The steps of trajectory data compression based on the limiting angle algorithm are similar to the limiting vertical distance algorithm above.

The limiting angle algorithm is simple and easy to implement. The algorithm supports the real-time compression processing of the vessel trajectory data, but it may delete the extreme point of curvature and result in compression error. It has high requirements for the curvature and point density of the trajectory, and it has not always been used in practical applications.

2.4 Offset Angle Algorithm

The offset angle algorithm is similar to the limiting vertical distance algorithm and the limiting angle algorithm. The basic idea of this algorithm is to select three consecutive points, such as P_1, P_2 and P_3. After that step, calculate the degree of the angle $\angle P_1 P_2 P_3$.

Next, compare it with a given threshold θ. If $\angle P_1 P_2 P_3 < \theta$, retain the middle point P_2, otherwise delete P_2. The steps of the trajectory data compression based on the offset angle algorithm are also similar to the limiting vertical distance algorithm above.

The offset angle algorithm is simple and easy to implement. This algorithm supports real-time compression processing of the vessel trajectory data, and it is sensitive to the course change of the vessel trajectory. However, when the point is dense or the course changes slowly, the algorithm may delete all the points on the curved segment and lead to compression error. To compensate for this defect, the course change is often highlighted by increasing the distance between the three selected points. Assuming that the middle point among the three points is P_j, the front and back points are P_{j-k} and $P_{j+k}, k \geq 1$. To a certain extent, the angle $P_{j-k} P_j P_{j+k}$ can reflect the course change from P_{j-k} to P_{j+k}. The value of k needs to be selected according to the data characteristics, related professional experience and application requirements.

2.5 Douglas Peucker Algorithm

The basic idea of the Douglas Peucker algorithm is to connect the first point P_1 and the last points P_n of the trajectory with a straight line, calculate the distance between the other points in the middle to this straight line, and discover the maximum distance d_{max} and the corresponding point P_i, then compare dmax with the maximum allowable error D_{error}. If $d_{max} < D_{error}$, delete all points between the first and last points. If $d_{max} \geq D_{error}$, retain the point P_i and divide the trajectory into two segments $P_1, P_2, ..., P_i$ and $P_i, P_{i+1}, ..., P_n$. Next, for each segment, repeat the above process until the end. The retained points and the first and last points constitute the compression result, subset B. Let the total number of track points be $n = 8$. The steps of trajectory data compression based on Douglas Peucker algorithm are as follows.

(1) Connect the points P_1 and P_8. Calculate the distances from $P_2, P_3, ..., P_7$ to the straight line $P_1 P_8$. The distance from P_6 to the straight line is the maximum, and it is denoted by dmax, as shown in Fig. 3(a).

(2) If $d_{max} < D_{error}$, delete the points $P_2, P_3, ..., P_7$. The remaining points, P_1 and P_8, are not satisfied by the conditions for repeating step (1), and thus go to step (3). The compressed result is $B = \{P_1, P_8\}$. The compressed trajectory is a straight line $P_1 P_8$, as shown in Fig. 3(b). If $d_{max} \geq D_{error}$, P_6 divides the trajectory into two segments, which are $P_1, P_2, ..., P_6$ and P_6, P_7, P_8. If each segment is a new trajectory, go to step (1), and process the two trajectories separately, as shown in Fig. 3(c).

(3) The points that have not been deleted through the above steps are the compressed results, which constitute the subset B. By adjusting the maximum allowable error D_{error}, let the number of points in subset B is 4, and then the result is shown in Fig. 3(d).

Compared with the above algorithms, this algorithm has better global characteristics, and it can retain the extreme point of curvature. After the compression, the spatial structural characteristics of the trajectory can be preserved well. However, the algorithm requires that the data of the entire trajectory must be obtained before the process, which means that it does not support real-time compression processing.

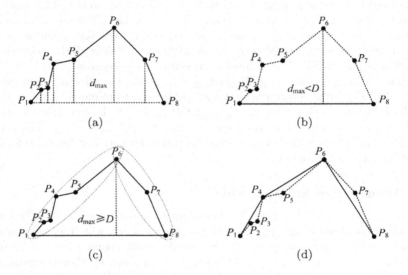

Fig. 3. Schematic diagram of the compression process based on the Douglas Peucker algorithm: (a) the d_{max} from P_6 to $P_1 P_8$; (b) the compression result P_1, P_8, if $d_{max} < D_{error}$; (c) the two new segments divided by P_6, if $d_{max} \geq D_{error}$; (d) the compression result when the number of points in subset B is 4.

2.6   Grating Algorithm

The basic idea of the grating algorithm is to define a fan-shaped region and judge whether the point on the trajectory is inside or outside the region. If it is inside, delete the related point. Otherwise, retain the related point. Let the caliber of the fan-shaped region be d. The steps of trajectory data compression based on grating algorithm are as follows.

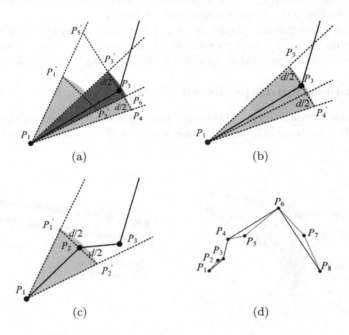

Fig. 4. Schematic diagram of the compression process based on the grating algorithm: (a) fan-shaped region $P_1'P_1P_2'$; (b) delete P_2 and the new fan-shaped region is $P_3'P_1P_4'$; (c) the overlapping area of $P_1'P_1P_2'$ and $P_3'P_1P_4'$; (d) compression result.

(1) Connect P_1 and P_2, and pass P_2 to make a straight-line perpendicular to P_1P_2. Take two points P_1' and P_2' on the line and let $P_2P_1' = P_2P_2' = d/2$. Then, $P_1'P_1P_2'$ constitutes a fan-shaped region, as shown in Fig. 4(c).

(2) Extend PP_1' and PP_2' to judge whether P_3 is inside the extended fan-shaped region or not. If P_3 is inside, delete P_2. Then, connect P_1 and P_3, and make a straight-line perpendicular to P_1P_3. Take two points P_3' and P_4' on the line and let $P_2P_1' = P_2P_2' = d/2$, as shown in Fig. 4(b).

(3) The line $P_3'P_4'$ intersects line P_1P_1' at point P_5' and intersects line P_1P_2' at point P_6'. If point P_3' or P_4' is located outside the extended region of the fan-shaped $P_1'P_1P_2'$, replace them with P_5' or P_6', respectively. As shown in Fig. 4(a), P_6' replaces P_4', the points P_3', P_1 and P_6' constitute a new fan-shaped region, which is the overlapping area of $P_1'P_1P_2'$ and $P_3'P_1P_4'$.

(4) Extend P_1P_3' and P_1P_6' to judge whether P_4 is inside the extended fan-shaped region or not. Repeat steps (1) to (3) until a new point is outside the newly constituted fan shape.

(5) If P_4 is outside the extended fan shape, P_3 should to be retained. Let P_3 be the new starting point (instead of P_1) and repeat steps (1)–(5) until the end of the trajectory. All the points that are retained (including the first and last points) constitute the compression result, subset B. The solid line, as shown in Fig. 4(d), is the compressed trajectory.

Although the grating algorithm is a little more complex than the above algorithm, it is also easy to implement. Besides, it is very sensitive to the curvature variation, and it supports real-time compression processing.

3   Compression Experiment

This section will introduce the compression experiments based on the compression algorithms above. The compression results will be compared and analyzed.

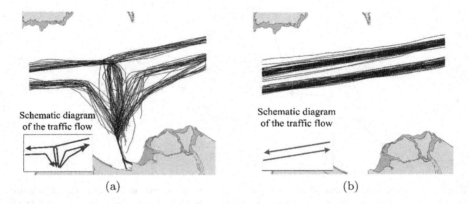

(a)   (b)

Fig. 5. Sample of vessel trajectories for the compression experiments: (a) the vessel trajectories of set C; (b) the vessel trajectories of set D.

3.1   Vessel Trajectory Data

In this paper, the trajectory data sample for experiments is from the AIS. The vessel trajectory data are mainly obtained from the position report messages of the AIS. The update frequency of this massage is related to the speed of the ship and the rate of turn (ROT). Therefore, the sample data should include the AIS messages when vessels have different speeds and ROTs. Taking the trajectories of vessels in the Qiongzhou Strait as an example, which contains AIS data of vessels with different sailing conditions.

The data of one hundred trajectories in the Qiongzhou Strait with obvious speed and ROT variations were taken as the sample for the experiments, as shown in Fig. 5(a), and is called set C. The data of another one hundred trajectories without obvious speed and ROT variations were also taken as a sample for the experiments, as shown in Fig. 5(b), and is known as set D. Set C includes 29429 points, and set D includes 26425 points.

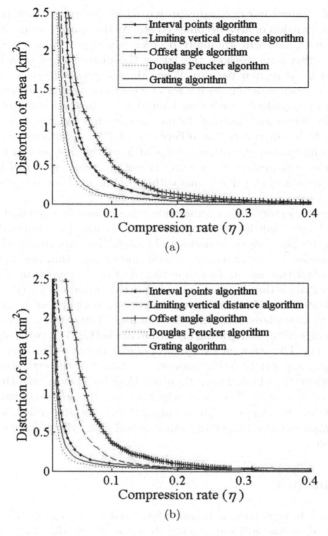

Fig. 6. Curves of the distortion of area with the compression rate: (a) Set C; (b) Set D.

3.2   Results and Discussion

The compression rate and compression error are the basic elements for evaluating a data compression algorithm. In this paper, the compression rate is defined as the ratio between the points' number of compressed trajectories and uncompressed trajectories. Suppose the number of trajectory points before compression is m and the number of compressed trajectory points is n. The compression rate is $\eta = n/m$.

The results shown in Fig. 6 indicate that when the compression rate becomes smaller, the distortion of area becomes larger. As the compression rate increases, the distortion of area will gradually decrease. In other words, the less points that are left after compression, the larger the distortion of area is, which is consistent with the regular pattern. When the compression rate is greater than 0.4, the distortion of area approaches zero for each compression algorithm. As the compression rate gradually decreases from 0.4, the distortion of area gradually increases. The extent and speed of the increase are different for each compression algorithm, which can reflect the differences of the algorithms' performances. Since each compression algorithm retains at least the first and last points, the compression rate is greater than zero. Therefore, this paper will analyze the compression results of the algorithms within the range of compression rate from 0.01 to 0.4.

The vessel trajectory data compression error caused by the offset angle algorithm is the largest, but it can be optimized by changing the interval parameter according to the data's characteristics and professional experience. The compression errors caused by the choosing interval points algorithm and limiting vertical distance algorithm are smaller than the offset angle algorithm. The choosing interval points algorithm is more suitable for the trajectories that are approximately straight lines. The limiting vertical distance algorithm is more suitable for the trajectories whose structures are complex. The performance of the Douglas Peucker algorithm and grating algorithm are better than other algorithms in the experiments. The error caused by the Douglas Peucker algorithm is minimal, but it does not support real-time processing. Although the error caused by the grating algorithm is a little larger than the Douglas Peucker algorithm, it support real-time processing. Therefore, when it needs to compress historical vessel trajectory data, the Douglas Peucker algorithm is recommended, and when it needs to compress vessel trajectory data in real time, the grating algorithm is recommended.

4   Conclusions

This paper introduces several classic vector data compression algorithms, as well as their ideas and implementation steps for vessel trajectory compression. Through the compression experiment, the performances of each algorithm are compared and analyzed. The result shows that the performance of the Douglas Peucker algorithm and grating algorithm are better than the other algorithms. The Douglas Peucker algorithm is suitable for historical data compression. The grating algorithm is suitable for real-time data compression. Furthermore, the advantages and disadvantages of each algorithm in compressing vessel trajectory data are also analyzed, which provides a basis for the selection and improvement of the algorithms in the future. The research described in this paper provides theoretical support for data compression in the application of vessel traffic research and practical applications based on AIS data.

Acknowledgments. This research was supported by "the Fundamental Research Funds for the Central Universities" (No. 3132016021). The authors thank the researchers who participated in the data processing and provided language assistance.

References

1. Bell, M.G., Meng, Q.: Special issue in transportation research part b-shipping, port and maritime logistics. Transp. Res. Part B: Methodol. **93**(PB), 697–699 (2016). https://doi.org/10.1016/j.trb.2016.09.003
2. Bole, A.G., Dineley, W.O., Wall, A.: Chapter 5 - automatic identification system (AIS). In: Radar and ARPA Manual, Oxford, 3rd edn, pp. 255–275 (2014). https://doi.org/10.1016/B978-0-08-097752-2.00005-2
3. Borkowski, P.: The ship movement trajectory prediction algorithm using navigational data fusion. Sensors **17**(6), 1432 (2017). https://doi.org/10.3390/s17061432
4. Chen, F., Ren, H.: Comparison of vector data compression algorithms in mobile GIS. In: 2010 3rd International Conference on Computer Science and Information Technology, vol. 1, pp. 613–617 (2010). https://doi.org/10.1109/ICCSIT.2010.5564118
5. Clements, J.C.: The optimal control of collision avoidance trajectories in air traffic management. Transp. Res. Part B: Methodol. **33**(4), 265–280 (1999). https://doi.org/10.1016/S0191-2615(98)00031-9
6. Dittmar, C.: Die nächste evolutionsstufe von AIS: big data. In: Gluchowski, P., Chamoni, P. (eds.) Analytische Informationssysteme, pp. 55–65. Springer, Heidelberg (2016). https://doi.org/10.1007/978-3-662-47763-2_4
7. Gudmundsson, J., Katajainen, J., Merrick, D., Ong, C., Wolle, T.: Compressing spatio-temporal trajectories. Comput. Geom. **42**(9), 825–841 (2009). https://doi.org/10.1016/j.comgeo.2009.02.002
8. Ifrim, C., Iuga, I., Pop, F., Wallace, M., Poulopoulos, V.: Data reduction techniques applied on automatic identification system data. In: International KEYSTONE Conference on Semantic Keyword-Based Search on Structured Data Sources, pp. 14–19 (2017). https://doi.org/10.1007/978-3-319-74497-12
9. Isenor, A.W., St-Hilaire, M.O., Webb, S., Mayrand, M.: MSARI: a database for large volume storage and utilisation of maritime data. J. Navig. **70**(2), 276–290 (2017). https://doi.org/10.1017/S0373463316000540
10. Ji, H., Wang, Y.: The research on the compression algorithms for vector data. In: 2010 International Conference on Multimedia Technology, pp. 1–4 (2010). https://doi.org/10.1109/ICMULT.2010.5631153
11. Lever, R., Hinze, A., Buchanan, G.: Compressing GPS data on mobile devices. In: Meersman, R., Tari, Z., Herrero, P. (eds.) OTM 2006. LNCS, vol. 4278, pp. 1944–1947. Springer, Heidelberg (2006). https://doi.org/10.1007/11915072_102
12. Li, Y., Zhong, E.: A new vector data compression approach for WebGIS. Geo-Spat. Inf. Sci. **14**(1), 48–53 (2011). https://doi.org/10.1007/s11806-011-0431-1
13. Mao, S., Tu, E., Zhang, G., Rachmawati, L., Rajabally, E., Huang, G.B.: An automatic identification system (AIS) database for maritime trajectory prediction and data mining. In: Proceedings of ELM-2016, pp. 241–257 (2018). https://doi.org/10.1007/978-3-319-57421-9_20
14. Moffitt, K.C., Vasarhelyi, M.A.: AIS in an age of big data. J. Inf. Syst. **27**(2), 1–19 (2013). https://doi.org/10.2308/isys-10372

15. Montanino, M., Punzo, V.: Trajectory data reconstruction and simulation-based validation against macroscopic traffic patterns. Transp. Res. Part B: Methodol. **80**, 82–106 (2015). https://doi.org/10.1016/j.trb.2015.06.010
16. Popa, I.S., Zeitouni, K., Oria, V., Kharrat, A.: Spatio-temporal compression of trajectories in road networks. GeoInformatica **19**(1), 117–145 (2015). https://doi.org/10.1007/s10707-014-0208-4
17. Tichavska, M., Cabrera, F., Tovar, B., Araña, V.: Use of the automatic identification system in academic research. In: Moreno-Díaz, R., Pichler, F., Quesada-Arencibia, A. (eds.) EUROCAST 2015. LNCS, vol. 9520, pp. 33–40. Springer, Cham (2015). https://doi.org/10.1007/978-3-319-27340-2_5
18. de Vries, G., van Someren, M.: Clustering vessel trajectories with alignment kernels under trajectory compression. In: Balcázar, J.L., Bonchi, F., Gionis, A., Sebag, M. (eds.) ECML PKDD 2010. LNCS (LNAI), vol. 6321, pp. 296–311. Springer, Heidelberg (2010). https://doi.org/10.1007/978-3-642-15880-3_25
19. Wang, P., Goverde, R.M.: Multi-train trajectory optimization for energy efficiency and delay recovery on single-track railway lines. Transp. Res. Part B: Methodol. **105**, 340–361 (2017). https://doi.org/10.1016/j.trb.2017.09.012
20. Wu, X., Mehta, A.L., Zaloom, V.A., Craig, B.N.: Analysis of waterway transportation in Southeast Texas waterway based on AIS data. Ocean Eng. **121**, 196–209 (2016). https://doi.org/10.1016/j.oceaneng.2016.05.012
21. Wu, X., Rahman, A., Zaloom, V.A.: Study of travel behavior of vessels in narrow waterways using AIS data-a case study in Sabine-Neches waterways. Ocean Eng. **147**, 399–413 (2018). https://doi.org/10.1016/j.oceaneng.2017.10.049
22. Zhang, L., Meng, Q., Fwa, T.F.: Big AIS data based spatial-temporal analyses of ship traffic in Singapore port waters. Transp. Res. Part E: Logist. Transp. Rev. (2017). https://doi.org/10.1016/j.tre.2017.07.011
23. Zhang, L., Meng, Q., Xiao, Z., Fu, X.: A novel ship trajectory reconstruction approach using AIS data. Ocean Eng. **159**, 165–174 (2018). https://doi.org/10.1016/j.oceaneng.2018.03.085
24. Zhang, S., Liu, Z., Cai, Y., Wu, Z., Shi, G.: AIS trajectories simplification and threshold determination. J. Navig. **69**(4), 729–744 (2016)
25. Zhang, S., Shi, G., Liu, Z., Zhao, Z., Wu, Z.: Data-driven based automatic maritime routing from massive AIS trajectories in the face of disparity. Ocean Eng. **155**, 240–250 (2018). https://doi.org/10.1016/j.oceaneng.2018.02.060

OCULUS Sea™ Forensics: An Anomaly Detection Toolbox for Maritime Surveillance

Stelios C. A. Thomopoulos[✉], Constantinos Rizogannis,
Konstantinos Georgios Thanos, Konstantinos Dimitros,
Konstantinos Panou, and Dimitris Zacharakis

Integrated Systems Laboratory, Institute of Informatics and Telecommunications,
National Center for Scientific Research "Demokritos", Patr. Gregoriou E & 27
Neapoleos str, 15341 Agia Paraskevi, Greece
{scat, crizogiannis, giorgos.thanos, k.dimitros, kpanou,
dzacharakis}@iit.demokritos.gr

Abstract. Maritime Surveillance command and control (C2) systems play a crucial role in ensuring the marine traffic safety and maritime border security. Through efficient integration of various sources (UAV, aircrafts, GIS data) and legacy systems (e.g. AIS, Radar, VMS) a more complete situational awareness picture of the activities at sea can be accomplished. This enhanced knowledge can be used to improve the detection capabilities related to vessel anomaly behavior and increase the efficiency, coordination, and quality of operational activities against existed maritime threats. In this paper, we present the Forensics toolbox of the OCULUS Sea maritime surveillance C2 platform which offers vessel anomaly behavior detection functionalities such as (i) Gap in Reporting, (ii) Speed Change, (iii) Fake MMSI, (iv) Risk Incident, and (v) Collision Notification. The performance effectiveness of the Forensics toolbox has been successfully tested under real world scenarios while its further enhancement is a work in progress.

Keywords: OCULUS Sea · Maritime surveillance · Border security · Forensics tool · Anomaly detection · Suspicious behavior · AIS

1 Introduction

Maritime Surveillance command and control (C2) systems play a crucial role in ensuring the navigation and marine traffic safety and maritime border security. Through efficient sharing of information among cross sector and/or cross border maritime authorities and integration of various sources (UAV, aircrafts, GIS data) and legacy systems (e.g. AIS, Radar, VMS) a more complete situational awareness picture of the activities at sea can be accomplished. This enhanced knowledge can be used to improve the detection capabilities related to vessel anomaly behavior and increase the efficiency, coordination, and quality of operational activities against threats related to environmental protection, illegal immigration, smuggling, trafficking of people or substances, piracy, search and rescue, fisheries, defense and border control and other. Moreover, the ships monitoring information is of special interest to many shipping companies for

W. Abramowicz and R. Corchuelo (Eds.): BIS 2019 Workshops, LNBIP 373, pp. 485–495, 2019.
https://doi.org/10.1007/978-3-030-36691-9_41

security, maritime logistics [2], and performance optimization purposes. For all the above mentioned reasons, systems and tools capable of storing and processing ships navigational information, in order to extract useful intelligence, are of great importance.

In this paper, we present the Forensics toolbox of the OCULUS Sea maritime surveillance C2 platform [3] which has been developed with the intent to offer event detection functionalities related to vessel anomaly behavior such as (i) Gap in Reporting, (ii) Speed Change, (iii) Fake MMSI, (iv) Risk Incident, and (v) Collision Notification. The aforementioned toolbox has been successfully tested in the context of the CY-CISE EU funded project[1] under real world scenarios and is a work under continuous improvement.

The structure of the paper is as follows. In Sect. 2, a brief presentation of the OCULUS Sea Maritime Surveillance C2 platform is given. In Sect. 3 the System Architecture and the User Interface (UI) of the Forensics tool are presented more thoroughly, while in Sect. 4 a description of the tool's Anomaly Detection capabilities along with real world detected cases are provided. Finally, the Sect. 5 concludes the paper.

2   The OCULUS Sea Maritime Surveillance C2 System

The OCULUS Sea C2 platform [3, 4] consists of National, Regional, and Local Control Centers (NCC/RCC/LCC's) which are governed in a centralized way. C2 Centers are located separately preserving their administrational and operational autonomy while share their Situational Pictures via a Message Oriented Middleware. At the NCC level there is a central governance mechanism that registers, authenticates and authorizes Regional and Local C2 centers into the OCULUS Sea network.

OCULUS Sea adopts a flexible expandable architecture which enables the system to easily add new C2 nodes while it is designed to be extensible, regarding the information sharing, notification, and communication level, in order to meet customer's requirements. Moreover, it facilitates the easy connection with other C2 systems using an interoperability framework and the ability to accommodate any future technology trends arising. Last, special emphasis has been given on interfacing integration with legacy sensors (Radar, AIS, other) and surveillance assets (e.g. patrol vessels, aircrafts) where an Ingestion server consists the integration point for sensor data available from external assets and other surveillance systems.

3   The OCULUS Sea Forensics Tool

3.1   System Architecture Overview

The system architecture encompasses a range of different languages and technologies depending on different needs. As shown in Fig. 1 the Database (MongoDB) is one of

---

[1] https://ec.europa.eu/easme/en/cypriot-information-sharing-environment-towards-integrated-national-maritime-surveillance-awareness.

the principal components of the architecture. It stores live vessel data along with historical tracks for vessels and information regarding all anomalies detected by the Anomaly detection backend system. The Database is being used by the Oculus Sea backend application, the Ingestion server and the Anomaly detection backend.

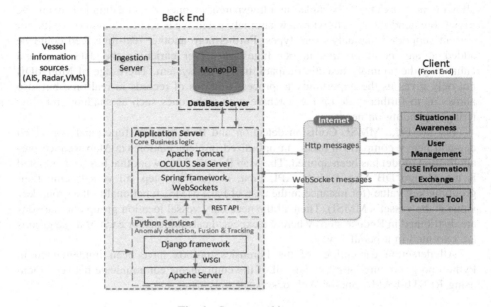

Fig. 1. System architecture.

The Oculus Sea backend acts as a middleware application being responsible for storing and retrieving data from the database and integrating with other applications such as the Front-end client and the Anomaly detection backend system. The application provides API's for clients to interact with the database in order to retrieve important information such as vessel information and tracks and Anomalies detected.

The Ingestion server is responsible for the collection of real time data, as it is emitted by the different feeds/sources, and its persistence in the database. With latency and effectiveness in mind, data ingestion is accomplished successfully and information from different sources (AIS, Radar, VMS) forms a complete view of the maritime domain.

The Anomaly detection backend system is monitoring vessel positions in near real time from the database and periodically communicates with the Oculus Sea server whenever a new anomaly is detected in order for the latter to store full information regarding that anomaly. The Django Python Web framework is adopted for the communication between the Anomaly detection backend and the Application server. This allows constant monitoring of the Maritime area and makes Forensics queries faster since we would only need to search the results of all anomalies generated during a period.

The system has been architected with extensibility in mind from the ground up, allowing new features to be added in a transparent manner. As an example it would be trivial to extend the system with new anomaly event types and to integrate it with our current supported anomaly event types. Furthermore another real-time feed could be added at any point in time in our Ingestion server enriching the data store and enhancing the anomaly detection capabilities of the system. The usage of MongoDB not only gives us the opportunity to process millions of records in real-time but also allows us to further scale up the database with techniques such as shading and clustering depending on needs.

For the Fake MMSI, Collision detection and Risk Incident functionalities which demand heavy comparison tasks, an optimized implementation via Map Reduce parallelization model has been applied. The Map Reduce framework that has been adopted is the Mongo DB Map Reduce API. First, in the Map step, all vessels emit their grouping key value (for instance in the case of Fake MMSI functionality the group key value is the vessel's MMSI). Then all the necessary vessel location group comparisons are distributed in Reduce steps where the expected calculations for each of these groups are executed in a parallel way.

All detection capabilities of the Forensics toolbox have been implemented in Python programming language and all of the components communicate between them using RESTful API's and/or Websockets securely using https.

3.2   Data Ingestion

OCULUS Sea integrates 3 types of vessel sources: VMS, AIS and RADAR. VMS messages contain information about fishing vessels. AIS may contain different types of vessels while RADAR reported vessels are targets sensed without identity information. Examples of VMS and AIS/RADAR information messages, received in the context of the CY-CISE EU funded project, are presented below prior to their corresponding integration to OCULUS Sea Server:

Sample VMS message:

```
https://service.oculus.eu/ingestion?application=NAF&method=send&message=//SR//
AD/DMS//TM/POS//IR/CYP000000XXX//TI/XXXX//DA/20180427//LT/%2B34%2
E899//LG/%2B033%2E640//SP/000//CO/103//NA/VESSELS_NAME//RC/Mini%2D
C%20Installed//FS/CYP//ER//
```

Sample AIS/RADAR message:

```
<?xml version="1.0" encoding="UTF-8"?>
<ns:MSG_IVEF
   xmlns:ns="http://www.iala-to-be-confirmed.org/XMLSchema/IVEF/0.2.4">
   <ns:Header      MsgRefId="0174eeb7-b9a0-44e5-9ecf-69d2c117ba07"      Ver-
sion="0.2.4"/>
   <ns:Body>
     <ns:ObjectDatas>
       <ns:ObjectData>
         <ns:TrackData             COG="0.000000"             SOG="0.000000"
Id="194345678083307253643"    Heading="90.000000"    Length="123.000000"
Width="21.000000"           SourceName="VTS"           UpdateTime="2018-09-
26T12:34:02.180Z" TrackStatus="2">
            <ns:Pos Lat="34.647345" Long="33.013123"/>
            <ns:NavStatus Value="5"/>
         </ns:TrackData>
         <ns:VesselData    Id="194345678083307253643"    SourceName="VTS"
SourceType="1" UpdateTime="2018-09-26T12:34:02.180Z">
            <ns:Identifier   Callsign="A1AA1"   IMO="1234567"   Name="*****"
MMSI="123456789"/>
         </ns:VesselData>
         <ns:VoyageData    Id="194345678083307253643"    Draught="2.700000"
DestName="RAVENNA"   ETA="2018-09-30T06:00:00.000Z"   SourceName="VTS"
SourceType="1" UpdateTime="2018-09-26T14:33:02.180Z"/>
         <ns:TaggedItem Key="VesselType" Value="Cargo ship"/>
         <ns:TaggedItem Key="AisFlag" Value="1"/>
         <ns:TaggedItem             Key="SourceTrackId"             Val-
ue="194345678083307253643"/>
       </ns:ObjectData>
     </ns:ObjectDatas>
   </ns:Body>
</ns:MSG_IVEF>
```

3.3   User Interface

OCULUS Sea Client. OCULUS Sea client is the main UI of the OCULUS Sea solution. Operator is offered a set of useful functionalities which enhance situational awareness and allow for quick inspection of suspicious maritime incidents. The main features of Oculus Sea client are:

- Situational awareness including:
  - Target identification from different sources (with search capabilities)
  - WMS layers support
  - Intra-authorities alerting capabilities
  - Fusion and tracking capabilities

- Information exchange through CISE [1] network (vessel, anomaly, action & document payloads)
- Multi-user environment with different access levels
- Forensic tool

OCULUS Sea Forensics Tool. OCULUS Sea[2] Forensics tool, depicted in Fig. 2, is the UI component of the OCULUS Sea client and is responsible for the retrieval and filtering of historical intelligence events which had already been logged in the system. Operator has the ability to create a geospatial query for a specific period of time while he can provide filters regarding the type of the events. More specifically, during the query preparation phase, date-picker controls are available where the user can pick a date and time of his preference for both the start and the end point in time (in order for a filter period to be created). Later on, user can right click multiple times on the map available in order for a filtering area bounding box to be created for the prepared request. Finally, user selects a specific type of events that are of his preference between (i) Gap in Reporting, (ii) Speed Change, (iii) Fake MMSI, (iv) Risk Incident, and (v) Collision Notification.

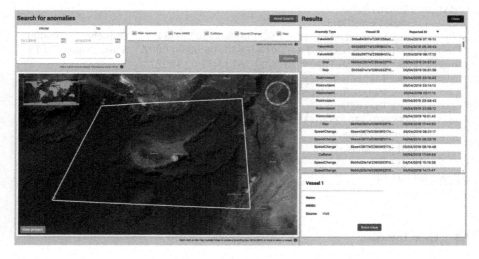

Fig. 2. The Forensics tool user interface

After the query has been submitted user awaits the system response. In case the provided criteria of the first phase are met, system returns the results and the interface

---

[2] Oculus Sea is using NASA WorldWind maps. NASA WorldWind maps support layers for enriching map content. Oculus Sea has integrated open source WMS layers with capability to integrate more in the future based on availability. Furthermore, Oculus Sea integrates Bing layers for more detailed satellite imagery. Bing imagery is available for non-commercial use only; otherwise, in coordination with Microsoft, it may be available for commercial applications too.

(table view on the right side of the UI) is updated. Operator can navigate to each separate result and provision intelligence results that the system has created at a specific timestamp in the past.

The Forensics tool is really useful for analysis of historical events in the maritime sector enabling professionals to gather resourceful insights about suspicious events and anomalies which are impossible to find using traditional means of maritime provisioning. It is designed to allow the operator to use it with ease and immediately understand most of its functionality without much training needed. It is implemented in order to be extensible and allow support of more types of events that may be of interest in the future.

4   Forensics Toolbox Anomaly Detection Capabilities

In this Section, a high level algorithmic description of the anomaly detection capabilities of the OCULUS Sea Forensics tool are presented along with real world detected events. To this end, a six months ships navigational information data originating from Radar, AIS, and VMS sources acquired during the CY-CISE project has been used. The whole system has been deployed on a 12 GB RAM Ubuntu Linux PC with an 8 core CPU running at 2.4 GHz.

4.1   Gap in Reporting

Gap in reporting functionality examines all vessels every T seconds in order to detect any time delay Δt in the transmission of the vessel's AIS message. The variables Δt, and T are modifiable. A Gap in reporting is not necessarily an index of a suspicious event since a vessel may sail in an area with no land AIS base stations or other ships nearby with an AIS transponder fitted on board or even because of attenuation of the transmitted signal. A Gap in Reporting incident is depicted in Fig. 3. As it is shown, the position and the course of the vessel during the gap period, between the two dots, are not known. Gap in reporting can be combined with other algorithms and/or with spatial information (e.g. geographic position of critical infrastructures, polygon of marine protected areas (MPAs), areas of suspicious meeting points) to detect other situations of interest.

4.2   Speed Change

Speed Change functionality detects any deviation of the current vessel's speed equal to or larger than p% of the mean vessel's speed. All vessels are examined every T seconds. Speed deviation percentage p, and variable T are modifiable. Figure 4 depicts a speed change event.

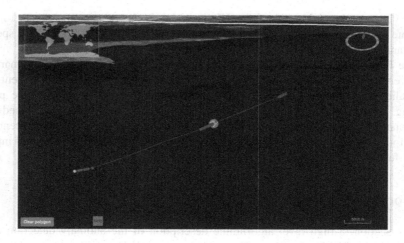

Fig. 3. Gap in reporting detected case.

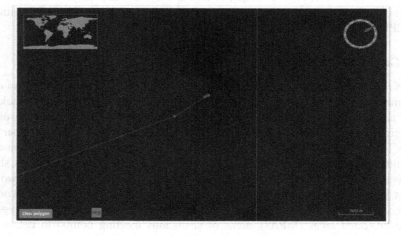

Fig. 4. Speed change detected case.

4.3 Fake MMSI

Fake MMSI functionality detects vessels which, within a time interval Δt, transmit the same MMSI code in their AIS messages. This function examines vessels every T seconds and generates alerts if vessels with a distance greater or equal to Δd emit the same MMSI. The variables Δt, T, and Δd are modifiable. A Fake MMSI detected event is depicted in Fig. 5. As one can see, the vessels which transmit the same MMSI are quite far from each other.

Fig. 5. Fake MMSI detected case.

4.4   Risk Incident

Risk Incident functionality detects, in real time, situations of suspicious vessel meetings that may correspond to illegal activities. This function examines all vessels every T seconds where variable T is modifiable. A Fuzzy Logic approach [4] is adopted where the time of the day, the region of the meeting place, the distance between the vessels, and the idle time of AIS transmitter are inputs to the Fuzzy Inference System (FIS). The algorithm provides the capability to define maritime areas of disparate risk classifications in order to prioritize high risk areas compared to low risk ones. Figure 6 depicts the trajectories of two vessels which sail very close to each other for a long period of time which may indicate a suspicious meeting event.

4.5   Collision Notification

Collision notification functionality [5] consists of a FIS system for the evaluation of collision risk between pairs of ships. Exploiting the AIS information available for every ship the Distance to the Closest Point of Approach (DCPA), the Time to the Closest Point of Approach (TCPA), and the Variation of Compass Degree (VCD) parameters [6, 7] are evaluated and used as inputs to the FIS system. Reduced computational complexity is achieved via the use of flow decision gateways which reject a large number of ships pairs at an early processing stage. This function examines all vessel pairs every T seconds, where T is modifiable. Figure 7 depicts a near ship-ship situation detected by the system for which collision notification has been generated.

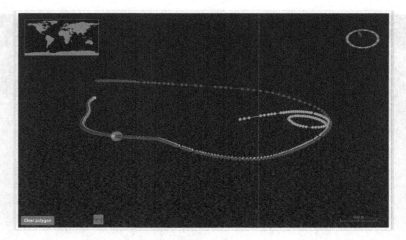

Fig. 6. Risk Incident detected case.

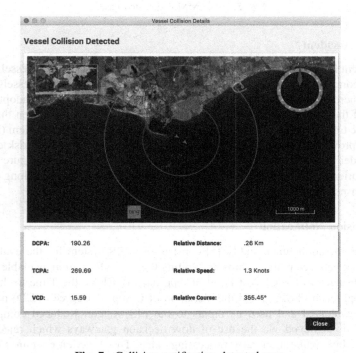

Fig. 7. Collision notification detected case.

5 Conclusion and Future Work

In this paper the OCULUS Sea Forensics toolbox for maritime surveillance is presented. Exploiting available sources of vessels' navigational information advanced intelligence is produced for the early detection of anomalies and suspicious incidents in the maritime domain. All functionalities of the proposed tool operate in real time or near real time examining all pairs of ships which transmit AIS messages at a selected area. The usage of the presented tool in real world scenarios has shown its effectiveness in detecting suspicious events and in generating automatic alerts at a reduced false alarm rate. The improvement of the proposed tool is a work in progress aiming to enhance the performance of the existed algorithms, add new anomaly detection capabilities which target more complex scenarios, and upgrade the available UI functionalities.

Acknowledgements. The work described in this paper is supported by the European research projects: (a) "CY-CISE: Cypriot information sharing environment towards an integrated national maritime surveillance awareness and enhancement of cross-sector and cross-border exchange of information," Grant Agreement No. EASME/EMFF/2015/1.2.1.5/003/SI2.739382, funded under programme EASME/EMFF/2015/1.2.1.5 – "ICT interoperability improvements in Member States to enhance information sharing for maritime surveillance" of the European Commission; (b) "TRESSPASS: Robust Risk Based Screening and Alert System for Passengers and luggage," Grant Agreement No. 787120, Call: H2020-SEC-2016-2017-2, and (c) "CIVILnEXt: Next generation of information systems to support EU external policies," Grant Agreement No. 786886, Call: H2020-SEC-2016-2017-2.

References

1. EUCISE 2020 project Homepage. http://www.eucise2020.eu/. Accessed 15 Apr 2019
2. Gudehus, T., Kotzab, H.: Maritime logistics. In: Gudehus, T., Kotzab, H. (eds.) Comprehensive Logistics, 2nd edn, pp. 823–842. Springer, Heidelberg (2012). https://doi.org/10.1007/978-3-642-24367-7_23
3. Kanellopoulos, S.A., et al.: OCULUS Sea™: integrated maritime surveillance platform. In: Proceedings of SPIE 9474, Signal Processing, Sensor/Information Fusion, and Target Recognition XXIV, vol. 94740N (2015)
4. Thomopoulos, S.C.A.: Maritime situational awareness with OCULUS Sea C2I and forensics tools for a Common Information Sharing Environment (CISE). In: Proceedings of SPIE 11018, Signal Processing, Sensor/Information Fusion, and Target Recognition XXVIII, Baltimore, Maryland, United States, 7 May 2019, vol. 110180C, SPIE Defense + Commercial Sensing (2019). https://doi.org/10.1117/12.2536966
5. Pedrycz, W., Gomide, F.: An Introduction to Fuzzy Sets: Analysis and Design. MIT Press, Cambridge (1998)
6. Rizogiannis, C., Thomopoulos, S.C.A.: A fuzzy inference system for ship-ship collision alert generation. In: Proceedings of SPIE 11018, Signal Processing, Sensor/Information Fusion, and Target Recognition XXVIII, Baltimore, Maryland, United States (2019)
7. Wang, X., Liu, Z., Cai, Y.: The ship maneuverability-based collision avoidance dynamic support system in close-quarters situation. Ocean Eng. **146**, 486–497 (2017)
8. Xu, Q.: Collision avoidance strategy optimization based on danger immune algorithm. Comput. Ind. Eng. **76**, 268–279 (2014)

Correcting the Destination Information in Automatic Identification System Messages

Matthias Steidel[1]([envelope]) [iD], Arne Lamm[2] [iD], Sebastian Feuerstack[1],
and Axel Hahn[2] [iD]

[1] OFFIS Institute for Information Technology Germany,
26121 Oldenburg, Germany
{matthias.steidel, sebastian.feuerstack}@offis.de
[2] Carl von Ossietzky University of Oldenburg, 26111 Oldenburg, Germany
{arne.lamm, axel.hahn}@uol.de

Abstract. The Automatic Identification System is a self-reporting system used by vessels and was introduced to enhance the operational picture on ship bridges. The Automatic Identification System destination port setting contains relevant information to anticipate a vessel's path. In future mixed traffic situations, autonomous vessels depend on correct destination port information specifically of human-operated ships to prevent dangerous encounter situations. In our Automatic Identification System data recordings of the last three months of 2018 a total of 4.988 unique vessels passing the German Bight with 13,216 different destinations were found. We found that at least 52.2% of all vessel destination settings are erroneous and a total of 1.3% (172) of the destination field settings were entirely conforming to the IMO UN/LOCODE recommendations. Our sample data indicates that no improvement in the percentage of correct destination settings has been made. Different to earlier studies, we report and quantify all eight error categories that we found and propose an algorithm that automatically adjusts the destination field settings. From those destination settings that two humans were independently of each other able to correct just by consulting a port and offshore dictionary (77,1%) the algorithm was able to correct 53,38% of the messages.

Keywords: Highly automated systems · AIS · String distance algorithms · E-Navigation · Natural Language Processing (NLP) · Collision avoidance

1 Introduction

The Automatic Identification System (AIS) is a well-established self-reporting system for vessels. It was introduced 2000 by the International Maritime Organization (IMO) as mandatory for all vessels with a gross tonnage above 300. Also vessels carrying more than 50 passengers or vessels with a length of more than 20 m are required to be equipped with an AIS transceiver. The International Convention for Safety of Life at Sea (SOLAS) recommend the use of AIS for collision avoidance [1]. Besides vessels also the Vessel Traffic Services (VTS) relies on AIS for surveillance of marine traffic. Typically AIS is

© Springer Nature Switzerland AG 2019
W. Abramowicz and R. Corchuelo (Eds.): BIS 2019 Workshops, LNBIP 373, pp. 496–507, 2019.
https://doi.org/10.1007/978-3-030-36691-9_42

used in combination with radar for generating a more precise operational picture as small vessels and obstacles are not required to broadcast AIS.

Three types of messages are broadcasted via AIS: Static messages contain general information about a vessel like its name, dimensions and its Maritime Mobile Service Identity (MMSI) - a nine-digit unique identifier. Voyage related messages provide information about the Estimated Time of Arrival (ETA), draught or the destination of the journey. Finally, dynamic messages contain information about a vessel's current position, speed and course. The broadcast frequency depends on the type of a message and on the vessel's speed and rate of turn [1].

Since AIS transceivers are typically connected to the on board sensors, information like positioning data gets automatically updated. Other data, like the destination field and the vessel's draught needs to be entered manually and is prone to human error. In encounter situations both provide relevant information about a vessel's planned route and its evasive maneuvering options [2].

While a human might be able to recognize erroneous entered destination port data also by considering several other information given by situational context in a potential encounter situation, a highly automated system in the end depends on algorithms that consider and value the sensed data based on error probabilities. Specifically in future mixed traffic situations wrong or inconsistent information might impact the overall safety.

This paper proposes an algorithm that aims to automatically adjust the destination field of a received AIS message to the IMO UN/LOCODE recommendations.

The paper is structured as follows: The upcoming section discusses related work on AIS data quality. Section 3 introduces the UN/LOCODE and error categories that can be found in the AIS destination field. In Sect. 4 the proposed algorithm is presented. Section 5 reports about the results of an evaluation based on AIS data that we recorded in the end of 2018 over a three month period for the German Bight. Section 6 discusses the results and suggests further improvements. Finally, Sects. 7 concludes the work.

2 Related Work

There is a long discussion about the reliability of AIS messaging. AIS is designed as a self-reporting system in which each reporting entity broadcasts messages. There are several aspects that impact reliability: The inefficiencies of the radio channel, which can cause transmitting incorrect or lost data [3, 4]. Defect sensors are also an often mentioned problem [5]. Furthermore, installation failures (intentionally or unintentionally) can result in erroneous AIS message data broadcasts [6, 7].

AIS information contributes to an operational picture. To avoid collisions the SOLAS recommended the use of AIS [5] but also pointed out explicitly that due to the reliability limitations of AIS, it should only be used in combination with radar-tracking applications to compensate radar signal clutter or target loss [1]. But AIS also offers some benefits for target identification and positioning. AIS complements radar information for vessels, which would be covered by radar shadows [8] and AIS positioning information is assumed to be more precise than the one gained by radar as AIS is directly connected to the GPS sensor [9]. In addition, the precision of the radar positions decreases with increasing distances [10].

AIS messages provide static, dynamic, and voyage related data. Static data such as: MMSI, IMO, call sign, name, vessel type, dimensions (location of the positioning system onboard) are usually entered during AIS transceiver installation and are thus less prone to operator errors [6]. Dynamic data is typically generated by systems i.e. bridge equipment [5, 8]. Studies have shown that from the dynamic AIS data the rate of turn (ROT) and the true heading (THDG) provide the highest amount of incomplete data [3].

As of today, voyage related data such as the Estimated Time of Arrival (ETA), draught, and destination information is set by operators manually before the start of a journey and therefore is prone to human errors.

The destination field supports predicting other vessels routes especially in areas of high traffic density, in port areas or at the entrance to inland waterways. [8] compared three studies regarding the reliability of the destination field. They reported that the use of numbers or country names instead of actual ports is the most common error. Also 'not available', 'not defined', 'null' or blank fields were often observed [8]. For this purpose, they analyzed 30,946 AIS transmissions. The errors mentioned above were detected for 49% of the AIS transmissions.

The study of [2] summarizes three studies that were carried out in 2004, 2005 and 2007. In each of these studies, they contacted all vessels passing the Strait of Dover via radio to learn about the discrepancy to the vessel's corresponding AIS broadcasts, including the destination field. In 2004, they contacted 806 vessels and detected an error rate of approximately 56% in the destination field. In the following year, 901 vessels were radioed, which revealed erroneous destination information for 38% of the contacted vessels. The last study in 2007 showed that the error rate is again decreased in comparison to the previous two studies: an error rate of around 18% were detected by contacting 940 vessels, yielding an average error rate of approximately 40.3%. Spelling errors, blank field, erroneous abbreviations and not updated destination information are the most common errors they observed. In addition to this, they observe a failure to use UN/LOCODE in the destination field. However, they are not providing specific numbers for each error category.

The information about the vessel's draught were the field with the second highest error rate [2].

The work of [7] presents an approach to estimate the trust of an AIS message. Two factors are relevant for this information: the reputation of the sender and the co-occurrence of multiple observations. In their approach they look in other sources like official ship registries in order to identify vessels that are trying to hide their real identity. They apply subjective logic with provenance information to calculate the probability of the correctness of an AIS message.

The work of [4] enhance the data availability of dynamic information, especially the positioning errors caused by electromagnetic interference, by using the piecewise cubic hermite interpolation and the cubix spline interpolation. The problem of dynamic AIS data is that they are often lost or mixed with inaccurate values.

Most work we are aware of focuses on identifying and estimating the reliability of the AIS message broadcasts. In contrast to these approaches, this contribution aims at correcting AIS destination port information and therefore proposes a constructive approach for the often discussed problem of erroneous AIS.

Prior studies that we summarized in this section reported spelling errors and ambiguities in the destination field as one of the major problems with the destination data. Unifying the destination field data, aligning it to the IMO recommendation, and correcting miss-spellings is the first step to improve the AIS destination data, which is currently still set manually by the crew.

3   UN/LOCODE and Error Categories

The work we are aware of that investigates the destination field does not provide a quantitative description of the found errors. In the following, we first give an overview about the IMO UN/LOCODE recommendations for the destination port, followed by a report of our findings for the most common error classes related to the works described in Sect. 2. This description includes an overview over the errors we found in our data.

3.1   IMO UN/LOCODE

The IMO recommended in 2004 the use of the UN/LOCODE in the destination field in order provide a consistent naming for ports [11]. The UN/LOCODE is a code for ports and locations. Each port is identified by an abbreviation for the country and is then followed by an abbreviation for the port. A country is identified by two letters, whereby a port is abbreviated with three letters. An example for this would be DE HAM, identifying the port of Hamburg in Germany. Table 1 shows the recommended format.

Table 1. IMO's recommendation on using the UN/LOCODE in order to fill the destination field in AIS messages.

Rule no.	Abbreviation	Meaning
R1	DE HAM>NL RTM	Hamburg to Rotterdam
R2	DE HAM>?? ???	Hamburg to unknown destination
R3	XX XXX>DE HAM	Unknown origin to Hamburg
R4	===Orrviken	If the destination does not have a UN/LOCODE, "===" should be entered, followed by the English name of the destination
R5	DE HAM> === US WC	If the destination is a general area, the known name or accepted abbreviation of the area should be used

See: [6]

3.2   Error Categories

The majority of the studies we found are focusing on the investigation of the reliability of the dynamic information transmitted (cf. Sect. 2). However, concrete numbers on the identified error categories in the destination field are not given by any author. Only a generalized statement about the error rate in the destination field is provided. Table 2 lists all error categories identified by prior work and is extended by further categories that we have found in our data.

Table 2. A summary of most common error categories found in related work and in our data.

	A in 2004	A in 2005	A in 2007	B in 2007	C in 2018
Category					
Total Vessel Destinations	806	901	940	30,946	13,216
IMO conform	?	?	?	?	178 (1.3%)
Wrong separator	?	?	?	?	448 (3.4%)
Non-IMO conform and no separator	?	?	?	?	12,590 (95.3%)
Total Erroneous Messages	~451 (56%)	~342 (38%)	~169 (18%)	~15,163 (49%)	6,901 (52.2%)
Empty	X	X	X	X	X (480; 3.6%)
Misspelling	X	X	X		X (4,355; 32.9%)
Abbreviation Error	X	X	X	X	X (2,684; 20.3%)
Not updated	X	X	X		
Number				X	X (0)
Country				X	X (0)
Not available				X	X (0)
Mischievous Input				X	
Not identifiable					X (232; 17.5%)
Invalid					X (3,397, 25.7%)

Key: A = [2], B = [8], C = This work

[2] provide error reports about AIS data for the year 2004, 2005 and 2007. In 2004, they revealed that around 56% of the considered AIS destination ports were erroneous. They observed a decreasing error rate in subsequent studies with 38% erroneous messages in 2005 and 18% erroneous messages in 2007. The most common errors that they have identified are marked with an "X" in Table 2. Based on their work it was not possible for us to identify a quantitative distribution over the error categories. In addition to this, the authors are not making a statement if the investigated destination fields were IMO compliant or not.

[8] investigated in total 30,946 AIS messages and found 49% with errors. The authors found several more errors compared to [2], but are also not providing numbers

for the found errors. A statement regarding the IMO compliance of the investigated destination fields is also missing.

In our work, we have analyzed three month of AIS data. The data was recorded by three stations that are located close to Brunsbüttel, in Cuxhaven, and in Wilhelmshaven. These stations are able to cover the southern German Bight [12].

In this period, the stations recorded a total of 4,489 unique vessels, which transmitted 13,216 destinations via AIS. We found just 1.3% of messages that were IMO conform. 3.4% are using an own defined separator such as "=>", "-", ">>", "->" and "<->". If a given string from a destination field contains one of these separators, it is assumed that the part of the string in front of the separator is the origin and the following part is the destination.

The remaining 95.3% are neither IMO compliant nor is a separator used. Furthermore, we have detected in 56% of our data errors. The found errors and their occurrence are depicted in Table 2. The most common error in our data are spelling mistakes (32.9%) followed by invalid data (25%). This includes the specification of the anchorage as the destination. 20.3% of all errors can be assigned to the use of incorrect abbreviations. This is followed by not identifiable data with 17.5% and unfilled destination fields with 3.7%. The errors described by [8] such as the use of numbers, the indication of a country, declaring "Not Available" as a destination or mischievous input could not be observed in our data.

In our dataset we have observed, that only 1.3% (172) of the destination field settings were conforming to the IMO UN/LOCODE recommendations. The studies of [2] indicate an improvement in the error rate, which cannot be confirmed with our data. We observed an error rate of 52.5%, which is in line with the results of [8]. Our study has been performed almost 11 years after the other studies we found and still no improvement in the error rate can be reported.

4   Algorithm for Correcting Destination Information

We have shown the most common error categories we found in our data and compared these findings with the findings from literature. In the following, we want to provide an approach for automatic error detection and correction of the destination field in AIS messages. Here, the challenge is to identify wrong used abbreviations and spelling errors, since these are the major problems in the destination field. The research field of Natural Language Processing (NLP) provides methods for the detection and correction of spelling errors. Two well established methods from this field have been selected in order to solve this problem. The idea is that a combined use of the Damerau-Levenshtein and Jaro-Winkler distance enables the identification and correction of wrong entries. This work adopts and extends the principles of [13].

The remaining of this section describes the applied text processing algorithms, the Damerau-Levenshtein distance and the Jaro-Winkler distance. The section concludes with the description of our approach, namely the Destination Field Corrector (DeFCorr).

Damerau-Levenshtein and Jaro-Winkler
The Damerau-Levenshtein distance is an extension of the Levenshtein distance, which is an algorithm in order to assess the edit distance between two given words. For this purpose, the algorithm calculates the amount of operations that have to be carried out in order to match both words. Here, three basic operations are available: insertion, substitution and deletion. Each operation is assigned a weight. At the end, the required operations are summed up, which identifies a distance between these two words [14, 15] stated that the transposition of a single letter is another common error. Thus, the Damerau-Levenshtein distance combines the operations described by [14, 15].

In contrast to the approach of Damerau-Levensthein, the Jaro-Winkler distance is not a distance in the mathematical sense but a similarity measure. The Jaro-Winkler distance is based on the Jaro Similarity, which evaluates the similarity between two words based on their length and matching letters [16–18]. The result is a similarity probability: the higher the result, the higher the similarity.

The use of string distance algorithms requires a dictionary containing the correct abbreviations and names for a port. Thus, such a dictionary must be created. For this specific problem here, a dictionary containing port names, the corresponding UN/LOCODEs and offshore platforms is needed.

Destination Field Corrector
As introduced above, DeFCorr is based on the combination of two well-known string distance algorithms, namely Damerau-Levenshtein and Jaro-Winkler distance (cf. Fig. 1).

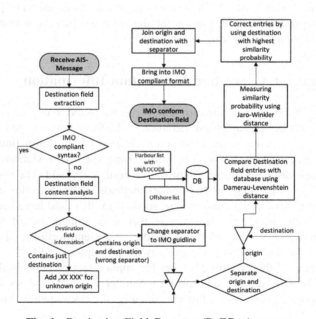

Fig. 1. Destination Field Corrector (DeFCorr) process

The first step is the pre-processing of the considered destination field. Here, it is checked whether only a destination has been entered or whether the port of departure has also been specified. The latter is the case if a separator defined by the IMO (cf. Table 1) has been identified. As described above, a custom separator is also frequently used. The separators described in Sect. 3.2 are also considered.

Following this, DeFCorr applies the Damerau-Levenshtein distance. As described above, this algorithm basically compares a given string with all strings in a given dictionary. For this purpose, a dictionary containing the correct UN/LOCODE and names for a port is required. For DeFCorr, such a dictionary was created based on data from United Nations website. Since offshore platforms are also valid destinations in AIS, a second dictionary containing offshore platforms was created with data from the website of the Federal Maritime and Hydrographic Agency of Germany. As a result of Damerau-Levenshtein, the three entries with the smallest edit distance are returned.

Afterwards, the Jaro-Winkler distance is used to decide which of the three entries most likely matches the given destination. For this purpose, the given destination is compared with each of the three entries and the similarity probability is given. At the end, the port or offshore platform with the highest probability is selected as the destination.

In order to meet IMO's recommendation, the result is converted into an UN/LOCODE, as described in Sect. 3. Offshore platforms are considered by applying rule 4.

5 Evaluation

In order to check the working principle of DeFCorr, we carried out a study that consists of three steps. First, a ground truth was created. This was done by manually correcting the historic AIS destination fields. Second, we have automatically corrected the destination fields by applying DeFCorr. Finally, we compared the manual corrected entries with the automatic corrected entries.

5.1 Manual Data Correction

The aim of our evaluation is to evaluate the algorithm performance against human error correction capabilities. For this purpose, we need a set of data that has been corrected by humans.

For this purpose, two independent raters corrected the data manually using the same two dictionaries that DeFCorr is using: one contains ports and the corresponding UN/LOCODE and the other contains offshore platforms.

The raters were given the following procedure for correcting the field:

1. Find the appropriate harbor name or UN/LOCODE from the port dictionary based on the given destination from AIS.
2. If no appropriate entry can be found in 1, then look for an appropriate entry in the offshore platform dictionary.

3. Give the IMO compliant destination declaration based on the found entry.
4. If no appropriate entry was found in either dictionary, apply IMO's rule 4 (cf. Table 1).

After both raters finished the correction, their results were compared. This was in 22.9% of the times the case, which shows one important aspect to be kept in mind: a distinct identification of the declared destination field is not always possible. The reasons for this vary. Either a port with the same name exists several times (e.g. Hamburg in Germany and Hamburg in the United States) or spelling errors in the harbor name were identified differently. For the evaluation of DeFCorr, we have used only the 77.1% of the data that were corrected in the same way by the raters.

5.2   Results

We have compared the automated corrected results with the manually corrected entries. As depicted in Table 3, 53.38% of the automatic corrected results matched with the manually corrected results.

Table 3.   Evaluation results of DeFCorr

	Match	No match
All messages (10,052)	53.38%	46.62%
DeFCorr performance results according to error categories (cf. Sect. 3.2)		
Category		
IMO-Compliant	91.47%	8.53%
Own Separator	5.17%	94.83%
Non-IMO conform and no separator	44.38%	55.62%

6   Discussion

When looking at the correction results, it becomes apparent that our proposed approach corrects only about half of all entries in the same way as the human raters. After looking into the results, the following reason might be decisive for this. Potential context knowledge that raters have may help in finding the correct harbor. In order to explain this, the following example from the data can be considered: The original message contained "DEHAM" in the destination field. Both raters corrected this declaration into the IMO compliant "XX XXX>DE HAM", stating that the vessel departed from an unknown origin heading to the port of Hamburg, Germany. DeFCorr found two similar destinations with "DE HAM" for Hamburg, Germany and "DENHAM", a port in Australia. Both declarations have the same Levenshtein distance with 1, because the transformation from "DEHAM" to both "DE HAM" and "DENHAM" only requires one operation. Hence, the similarity probability is also the same. DeFCorr selected here "DENHAM" and corrected the destination field IMO compliant to "XX XXX>AU DNM". Since the raters are both Germans, they considered "DE HAM" as the most possible destination, since only a whitespace is missing. DeFCorr does not use any context knowledge, meaning the decision for the allegedly correct port is made based on the Levenshtein distance and the Jaro-Winkler similarity. A possibility for integrating context knowledge into DeFCorr is either to add knowledge about the considered area of the AIS messages or to consider the direction of travelling of the respective vessels. A subsequent check for plausibility could help in the decision for one or the other.

Another challenge in this context is the detection of wrong used abbreviations and the assignment to the correct abbreviations. An example for this can be found in the used AIS data. Several messages stated "NL ROT" as a destination. The unanimous interpretation of this message by the raters is that "NL RTM", Rotterdam in the Netherlands, is meant with "NL ROT". DeFCorr identified "NL ROT" to "NL BOT", since this is an existing UN/LOCODE and just one operation is necessary to transform "NL ROT" into "NL BOT". In order to tackle this problem, DeFCorr must be extended by a component that is capable of detecting wrong used abbreviations.

In the German Bight, there are numerous offshore platforms, which includes oil platforms as well as offshore wind farms. For the purpose of maintenance and during the installation of such platforms it is necessary to transport personal and material from shore to these platforms. The current IMO recommendation to use UN/LOCODE in the destination field provides no method for declaring an offshore platform as a destination. This is due to the fact, that offshore platforms do not have a UN/LOCODE assigned. During the evaluation and the inspection of the results and the original message content it became apparent, that offshore platforms are often given as a destination. However, to be able to give a destination in AIS, the mariners of these supply vessels give the full name or an abbreviation of the offshore platform they are travelling to. The problem here is, that different names or abbreviations are used for the same offshore platforms, which makes it difficult for automatic identification with DeFCorr.

7 Conclusion

In this paper, we investigated the destination field in historic AIS messages regarding the correct use of UN/LOCODE recommended by the IMO. The data set contained just 3.4% IMO compliant and errorless messages. Among the most common errors are too many or no whitespaces, spelling mistakes and the use of wrong abbreviation. These findings correspond with findings of literature review.

Another finding of this work is the inconsistent declaration and use of names of offshore platforms as destinations. Since offshore platforms do not have a UN/LOCODE assigned, rule 4 of IMO's guideline applies here. Nevertheless, this format was never used in the data for setting an offshore platform as destination.

Furthermore, we provided a first and simple approach for correcting erroneous destination fields in AIS with DeFCorr. For this purpose, two well-known algorithms from Natural Language Process, the Damerau-Levenshtein and Jaro-Winkler distance, have been applied. DeFCorr was able to correct 53.38% of the messages in the same way the human raters did. A look into the results suggests that context knowledge about the considered sea area and about the travelling direction of a vessel may improve DeFCorr's performance.

Acknowledgement. This work has been conducted in the context of the HANSA project, which is funded by the MarTERA partners German Federal Ministry of Economic Affairs and Energy (BMWi), Polish National Centre for Research and Development (NCBR) and Research Council of Norway (RCN) and is co-funded by European Union's Horizon 2020 research and innovation program under the framework of ERA-NET co-fund.

References

1. International Maritime Organization: International Convention for the Safety of Life at Sea (SOLAS) (1974)
2. Bailey, N., Ellis, N., Sampson, H.: Training and Technology Onboard Ship: How Seafarers Learned to Use the Shipboard Automatic Identification System (AIS). Lloyd's Register Educational Trust, Cardiff (2008)
3. Felski, A., Jaskólski, K.: Analysis of AIS availability. Eur. J. Navig. **10**, 39–43 (2012)
4. Zhang, D., Li, J., Wu, Q., Liu, X., Chu, X., He, W.: Enhance the AIS data availability by screening and interpolation. In: 2017 4th International Conference on Transportation Information and Safety (ICTIS), pp. 981–986. IEEE, Banff (2017)
5. Banyś, P., Noack, T., Gewies, S.: Assessment of AIS vessel position report under the aspect of data reliability. Ann. Navig. **19**, 5–16 (2012). https://doi.org/10.2478/v10367-012-0001-0
6. Harati-Mokhtari, A., Wall, A., Brooks, P., Wang, J.: Automatic Identification System (AIS): data reliability and human error implications. J. Navig. **60**, 373 (2007). https://doi.org/10.1017/S0373463307004298
7. Ceolin, D., van Hage, W.R., Schreiber, G., Fokkink, W.: Assessing trust for determining the reliability of information. In: van de Laar, P., Tretmans, J., Borth, M. (eds.) Situation Awareness with Systems of Systems, pp. 209–228. Springer, New York (2013). https://doi.org/10.1007/978-1-4614-6230-9_13
8. Harati-Mokhari, A., Wall, A., Brooks, P., Wang, J.: Automatic Identification System (AIS): a human factors approach. J. Navig. **60**(3), 373–389 (2007)
9. Chang, L., Xiaofei, S.: Study of data fusion of AIS and radar. In: 2009 International Conference of Soft Computing and Pattern Recognition, pp. 674–677. IEEE, Malacca (2009)
10. Xiao, F., Ligteringen, H., Van Gulijk, C., Ale, B.: Artificial force fields for multi-agent simulations of maritime traffic and risk estimation. In: PSAM 11: 11th International Probabilistic Safety Assessment and Management Conference & ESREL 2012: The Annual European Safety and Reliability Conference Scandic Marina Congress Center, Helsinki, Finland, 25–29 June 2012. Curran Associates (2012)
11. International Maritime Organization: Guidance on the Use of the UN/LOCODE in the Destination Field in AIS Messages (2004)
12. Brinkmann, M., Hahn, A.: Testbed architecture for maritime cyber physical systems. In: 2017 IEEE 15th International Conference on Industrial Informatics (INDIN), pp. 923–928. IEEE, Emden (2017)
13. Christina Maria Tsiroglou: Automatic Identification System (AIS) – Probleme und Ansätze sie zu lösen (2018)
14. Levenshtein, V.I.: Binary codes capable of correcting deletions, insertions and reversals. Sov. Phys. Dokl. **10**(8), 707–710 (1966). Doklady Akademii Nauk SSSR, vol. 163, no. 4, pp. 845–848 (1965)

15. Damerau, F.J.: A technique for computer detection and correction of spelling errors. Commun. ACM **7**, 171–176 (1964). https://doi.org/10.1145/363958.363994
16. Jaro, M.A.: Probabilistic linkage of large public health data files. Stat. Med. **14**, 491–498 (1995). https://doi.org/10.1002/sim.4780140510
17. Jaro, M.A.: Advances in record-linkage methodology as applied to matching the 1985 census of Tampa, Florida. J. Am. Stat. Assoc. **84**, 414–420 (1989). https://doi.org/10.1080/01621459.1989.10478785
18. Winkler, W.E.: String comparator metrics and enhanced decision rules in the Fellegi-Sunter model of record linkage. In: Proceedings of the Section on Survey Research Methods, pp. 354–359 (1990)

QOD Workshop

QOD 2019 Workshop Chairs' Message

The Second Workshop on Quality of Open Data (QOD 2019) organized in conjunction with the 22nd Business Information Systems (BIS 2019) conference took place in Seville, Spain. The specific focused on bringing together different communities working on quality of information in Wikipedia, DBpedia, Wikidata, and other open knowledge bases.

There were 13 papers submitted for the conference and the Program Committee decided to accept 5 papers (an acceptance rate of 38%). There were 23 members in the Program Committee, representing 23 institutions from 13 countries.

The first paper "Evaluating the Quantity of Incident-Related Information in an Open Cyber Security Dataset" studied quality of the dataset under consideration through the analysis of the number of cybersecurity-related artifacts in the dataset. The approach focused on identifying and extracting information relevant to fundamental questions regarding seven concepts: Incident, Who, What, Asset, Victim, Result, and Impact. The paper presented experimental results including quantity of information related to each concept.

The second paper "Technical Usability of Wikidata's Linked Data: Evaluation of Machine Interoperability and Data Interpretability" focused on evaluation of the usability of Wikidata as a data source for robots operating on the web of data according to specifications and practices of linked data. Two use cases for data crawling robots were used for evaluation. The first use case regarded general data consumption applications based on RDF, RDF-Schema, OWL, SKOS, and linked data. The second use case regarded applications that explored semantics relying on Schema.org and SKOS.

The third paper "A New Tool for Automated Quality Control of Environmental Time Series (AutoQC4Env) in Open Web Services" proposed a statistical framework that can help to complement traditional data quality assessment and provide environmental researchers with a tool based on current statistical knowledge. The tool uses novel features to configure the sequence of tests for environmental data as well as their statistical parameters. Afer an experiment is conducted it also assigns probabilities if obtained data points are valid.

The fourth paper "Semantic Data Integration and Quality Assurance of Thematic Maps in the German Federal Agency for Cartography and Geodesy" was concerned with a new concept of geospatial quality assurance for thematic maps relevant to the population. These maps were enriched with semantic web data along with open data sets of the Federal Agency of Cartography and Geodesy.

The last paper "Approach to Improving the Quality of Open Data in the Universe of Small Molecules" contributed to open data related to small molecules, such as metabolites, drugs, natural products, food additives, and environmental contaminants. The proposed approach for the data quality improvement involved computer implementation of system that utilizes the three-dimensional structure of a compound to generate reproducible compound identifiers and universally reproducible designators for all constituent atoms of each compound. These compound and atom identifiers enable reliable federation of information from a wide range of freely accessible databases. Current database contains entries for more than 90 million unique compounds.

Włodzimierz Lewoniewski
Anisa Rula
Krzysztof Węcel

Organization

Chairs

Włodzimierz Lewoniewski	Poznań University of Economics and Business, Poland
Anisa Rula	University of Milano-Bicocca, Italy
Krzysztof Węcel	Poznań University of Economics and Business, Poland

Program Committee

Maribel Acosta	Karlsruhe Institute of Technology, Germany
Riccardo Albertoni	CNR-IMATI, Italy
Denilson Barbosa	University of Alberta, Canada
Volha Bryl	Springer Nature, UK
Ioannis Chrysakis	Foundation for Research and Technology – Hellas (FORTH), Greece
Vittoria Cozza	University of Padua, Italy
Gianluca Demartini	The University of Queensland, Australia
Wassim Dergeuch	Derilinx, Ireland
Anastasia Dimou	Ghent University, Belgium
Suzanne Embury	The University of Manchester, UK
Ralf Härting	Hochschule Aalen, Germany
Antoine Isaac	Europeana and VU University Amsterdam, The Netherlands
Tomas Kliegr	University of Economics in Prague, Czech Republic
Dimitris Kontokostas	University of Leipzig, Germany
Jose Emilio Labra Gayo	Universidad de Oviedo, Spain
Maristella Matera	Politecnico di Milano, Italy
Finn Årup Nielsen	Technical University of Denmark, Denmark
Matteo Palmonari	University of Milano-Bicocca, Italy
Simon Razniewski	Max Planck Institute for Informatics, Germany
Mariano Rico	Universidad Politécnica de Madrid, Spain
Blerina Spahiu	Università degli Studi di Milano Bicocca, Italy
Morten Warncke-Wang	Wikimedia Foundation, USA
Amrapali Zaveri	Maastricht University, The Netherlands

A New Tool for Automated Quality Control of Environmental Time Series (AutoQC4Env) in Open Web Services

Najmeh Kaffashzadeh[✉], Felix Kleinert, and Martin G. Schultz

Jülich Supercomputing Centre, Forschungszentrum Jülich GmbH, Jülich, Germany
{n.kaffashzadeh,f.kleinert,m.schultz}@fz-juelich.de

Abstract. We report on the development of a new software tool (AutoQC4Env) for automated quality control (QC) of environmental time series data. Novel features of this tool include a flexible Python software architecture, which makes it easy for users to configure the sequence of tests as well as their statistical parameters, and a statistical concept to assign each value a probability of being a valid data point. There are many occasions when it is necessary to inspect the quality of environmental data sets, from first quality checks during real-time sampling and data transmission to assessing the quality and consistency of long-term monitoring data from measurement stations. Erroneous data can have a substantial impact on the statistical data analysis and, for example, lead to wrong estimates of trends. Existing QC workflows largely rely on individual investigator knowledge and have been constructed from practical considerations and with a least theoretical foundation. The statistical framework that is being developed in AutoQC4Env aims to complement traditional data quality assessments and provide environmental researchers with a tool that is easy to use but also based on current statistical knowledge.

Keywords: AutoQC4Env tool · Quality control · Environmental time series

1 Introduction

Environmental monitoring is an essential component in humanity's quest to protect earth and mitigate adversarial effects of climate change, water, and soil pollution, and other transformations that are directly or indirectly caused by human activities. Moreover, environmental monitoring drives the development of advanced information technology. This is due to the exponential growth of monitoring data, the open data attitude in major parts of the environmental science communities and of many governmental agencies. Also, a high degree of standardization has been achieved with respect to geo-data and metadata. Users of environmental data services need to be able to assess the fitness-for-purpose of a data set and they need to find information that allows them to use the

© Springer Nature Switzerland AG 2019
W. Abramowicz and R. Corchuelo (Eds.): BIS 2019 Workshops, LNBIP 373, pp. 513–518, 2019.
https://doi.org/10.1007/978-3-030-36691-9_43

data set correctly. While numerous research institutions have implemented open data services for environmental data and metadata, less has been achieved with respect to facilitating the assessment of the data quality.

Although various software for checking the quality of time series have been developed by several environmental agencies and research institutions in the past, most of these have a rather specific application focus and they are generally deeply embedded in specific data processing workflows and thus not fully transparent to the data users. Examples of relatively well documented QC procedures include the QA/QC of Real-Time Oceanographic Data (QARTOD) [2], Carbon in the Atlantic Ocean (CARINA) [3], National Ecological Observatory Network (NEON) [1,5], US EPA Air Quality System (AQS), and European Air Quality Database Airbase. A common element of these QC procedures is the use of data quality flags as classifiers of the measured data values. The level of detail of the flagging schemes varies greatly, and this makes it difficult to automatically process the quality information and support user decisions on which data shall be accepted for a given analysis purpose, in particular, if data from different sources should be merged [4]. To provide one example: US air quality data can be flagged as "not-to-be-used-for-attainment-purposes" in the event that wildfires pushed air pollutant concentrations above the regulatory values. Thus, for an official air quality reporting, those data must be excluded. However, if these data are used in the evaluation of numerical air quality models, the omission of such events leads to substantial bias.

Here, we introduce a tool (AutoQC4Env) with a flexible software framework that allows users to configure the QC tests according to their needs. Moreover, the tool introduces a novel concept to environmental time series analysis based on statistical measures of testing uncertainty. While the concept and software framework may also be useful in other domains, we focus on environmental time series in this study in order to keep the problem tractable.

This paper is structured as follows: the methodology is presented in Sect. 2; Sect. 3 describes the software framework and implementation of the concept; Sect. 4 shows a case study of the tool's application, and Sect. 5 contains a short summary.

2   Methodology

The task of automated QC tests is to detect *abnormal* values. Statistically, this implies either that an individual value lies outside the expected distribution for a given variable at a specific time and location, or that some properties of a group of values are inconsistent with expectations. Although such *errors* are labeled according to their visual appearance on a time series graph, e.g. "outlier", "constant values", and "data out of range", or the result of a single test is typically categorized to "pass" or "fail", various statistical tests allow estimation of the uncertainty of a test result, for example via a *p-value* or from the probability density function (PDF) of an extreme value distribution (Fig. 1). We estimate such uncertainty by using them as proxies to obtain a probability that a given value is "valid" depending on the test outcome. For example:

$$\text{if test } t \text{ is passed:} prob_t = 1 - min(p\text{-}value, 0.5) \tag{1}$$

$$\text{if test } t \text{ fails: } prob_t = 0 + min(p\text{-}value, 0.5) \tag{2}$$

Effectively, test results with low *p-value* (i.e. low uncertainty) provide relatively strong confidence that a value is either "valid" or "invalid" with respect to the test's properties. If the uncertainty of the test result is large, the probability of a value being "valid" will approach 0.5 to indicate indifference.

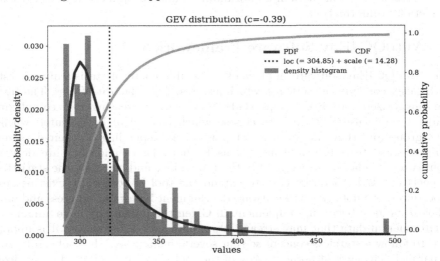

Fig. 1. Generalized extreme value (GEV) distribution and cumulative density function (CDF) derived from the 1000 largest ozone values measured after 1990 from the Tropospheric Ozone Assessment Report (TOAR) database [4]. The quantity $1 - CDF$ is used as a proxy for the validity of ozone measurements in a one-sided extreme value test. The c, loc, and scale show shape, location and scale parameters of the GEV distribution, respectively.

It is important to note that we do not use the *p-value* as a significance test, but only as a proxy. The overall likelihood of a value's validity is obtained by combining all the QC tests result. As the tests might not be independent, the final probability P approximates the conditional probability by using the minimum probability of all individual test result:

$$P = min(prob_t; t = 1 \ldots n), \tag{3}$$

where n is the number of QC tests that have been performed. If all tests are passed, the P will lie between 0.5 and 1. Conversely, if at least one test fails, the P will be between 0 and 0.5. Then the user can map the P into categorical flags. Thresholds can be defined according to the intended analysis, consequently balancing requirements for good quality data and sample size.

In closing this section, we emphasize that the statistical testing can only detect aberrations from expected data patterns and therefore does not constitute a judgment about the quality of a data value *per se*. Even though exceptional values often indicate some problem with the measurements or the data processing, they can also arise from exceptional measurement conditions, i.e. sampling of rare events. Therefore, a value with a low probability is not necessarily invalid, but may occasionally also point to an event of special significance. Detecting such events automatically will, if at all possible, require additional analyses with independent data or metadata. In future versions of AutoQC4Env we therefore plan to add consistency tests among multiple variables and multiple measurement locations as well as workflows to analyze numerical model results or metadata information.

3   AutoQC4Env Software Framework

The AutoQC4Env software implements a flexible chain of statistical QC tests with easily configurable settings, which are read from the *JSON* files. The tests are categorized into five groups (G0 – G4) with increasing test complexity (Table 1). The users are able to choose which tests shall be executed within each group and they can specify test parameters depending on their data set. All statistical tests are implemented as Python classes and they are derived from two base classes, which modify the probability and calculate the statistics, respectively. It is therefore easy to extend the tool or to modify existing test procedures. We note that the software development is work in progress and only a few tests have been fully implemented. Given the potentially huge amount of environmental data that may stream into a data processing center, it is important to follow a stateless concept so that several instances of the tool can be run in parallel. The current alpha version of the tool allows for a limited parallelization in that only full test suites can be run simultaneously. The software will be distributed via a git repository. The package includes automated documentation (Sphinx), unit-testing, and example applications. Functionality testing and the definition of new features are being conducted in the Digital Earth initiative of the German Helmholtz Association.

Table 1. Definition of test groups in the AutoQC4Env tool framework and implementation status of specific tests.

Group label	Scope of the group	Available QC tests
G0	Exclude the very gross errors for subsequent analysis (*sanity check*)	Range1 test outlier test
G1	Check a single value quality	Negative value test, range2 test
G2	Check the quality of a single value with adjacent data points	Spike test, step test, q test, constant value test
G3	Check consistency across multiple variables measured at the same site	Not yet implemented
G4	Check spatial consistency across nearby stations	Not yet implemented

4   Case Study Ground-Level Ozone Time Series

To demonstrate typical errors in ground-level ozone measurement time series and their *flagging* by the AutoQC4Env tool, we selected four time series of hourly ozone data from an arbitrarily data set of the TOAR database. Since these data had been already quality controlled (see [4]), we added some typical features of raw data sets for this demonstration. Figure 2 includes the probability from a run of the AutoQC4Env tool. The color shading clearly shows that the statistical tests capture several data artifacts and assign low probabilities to these values. Moreover, these figures highlight another feature of the AutoQC4Env tool: lower probabilities are not only assigned to the offending data values, but also to several neighbouring points. This reflects a common experience that certain data errors are usually indicative of a perturbation in a larger sub-sample of the data. Details about this will be provided in a subsequent paper.

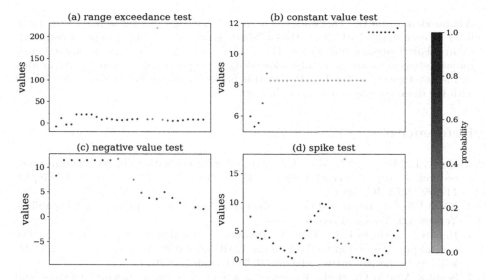

Fig. 2. Demonstration of typical environmental time series errors and their detection by the AutoQC4Env tool. The four panels show individual sub-samples of an arbitrarily selected ground-level ozone measurement series with added error features. (Color figure online)

5   Conclusion

The AutoQC4Env tool is still at an early development stage, but it has already attracted the attention of several researchers, because of its modern code design and its novel concept to estimate probabilities for the validity of measured data points. While existing QC tools have mostly been developed for specific data sets and applications, the AutoQC4Env provides a generic and self-consistent software framework, which can easily be adapted to specific user needs. While the tool may also work for time series data from other domains, we are currently concentrating on environmental measurement time series, which often show some commonalities, such as auto-correlation or the fact that a large fraction of the variability arises from more or less regular cycles, e.g. diurnal or seasonal. The AutoQC4Env combines a theoretical concept based on statistical test results with a flexible software toolkit that can easily be adapted to different workflows and user needs. By adapting the test sequences and parameters, the tool can be used during various stages of environmental data management: (i) initial checks in a real-time data transmission system, (ii) data review before ingestion into a database, and (iii) use case-specific data selection procedures, for example as part of open web services.

The present development status of the tool is a demonstrator version at alpha stage, where most of the statistical tests still need to be implemented and "calibrated" with respect to their uncertainty measures.

Acknowledgements. This work has been performed and funded as part of the IntelliAQ project under ERC-2017-ADG#787576 grant at the Jülich Super Computing Centre, Forschungszentrum Jülich. The TOAR community and various national environmental agencies are gratefully acknowledged for providing data and collaborating on the development of the TOAR database. Sabine Schröder and Lukas Leufen helped with the data analysis and software infrastructure.

References

1. Durre, I., Menne, M.J., Vose, R.S.: Strategies for evaluating quality assurance procedures. J. Appl. Meteorol. Climatol. **47**(6), 1785–1791 (2008). https://doi.org/10.1175/2007JAMC1706.1
2. IOOS-US: U.S. Integrated Ocean Observing System: a blueprint for full capability. Version 1.0. Technical report (2010)
3. Key, R.M., Schirnick, C., Velo, A., Tanhua, T., van Heuven, S., Olsen, A.: Quality control procedures and methods of the CARINA database. Earth. Syst. Sci. Data. **2**(1), 35–49 (2010). https://doi.org/10.5194/essd-2-35-2010
4. Schultz, Martin G., et.al.: Tropospheric Ozone Assessment Report: database and metrics data of global surface ozone observations. Elem. Sci. Anth. **5**, 58 (2017). https://doi.org/10.1525/elementa.244
5. Taylor, J.R., Loescher, H.L.: Automated quality control methods for sensor data: a novel observatory approach. Biogeosciences **10**(7), 4957–4971 (2013). https://doi.org/10.5194/bg-10-4957-2013

Approach to Improving the Quality of Open Data in the Universe of Small Molecules

John L. Markley[1]([✉]), Hesam Dashti[2], Jonathan R. Wedell[1],
William M. Westler[1], Eldon L. Ulrich[1], and Hamid R. Eghbalnia[1]

[1] University of Wisconsin-Madison, Madison, WI 53706, USA
jmarkley@wisc.edu
[2] Harvard Medical School, Medical School, Boston, MA 02215, USA

Abstract. We describe an approach to improving the quality and interoperability of open data related to small molecules, such as metabolites, drugs, natural products, food additives, and environmental contaminants. The approach involves computer implementation of an extended version of the IUPAC International Chemical Identifier (InChI) system that utilizes the three-dimensional structure of a compound to generate reproducible compound identifiers (standard InChI strings) and universally reproducible designators for all constituent atoms of each compound. These compound and atom identifiers enable reliable federation of information from a wide range of freely accessible databases. In addition, these designators provide a platform for the derivation and promulgation of information regarding the physical properties of these molecules. Examples of applications include, compound dereplication, derivation of force fields used in determination of three-dimensional structures and investigations of molecular interactions, and parameterization of NMR spin system matrices used in compound identification and quantification. We are developing a data definition language (DDL) and STAR-based data dictionary to support the storage and retrieval of these kinds of information in digital resources. The current database contains entries for more than 90 million unique compounds.

Keywords: Compound and atom identifiers · FAIR principles · Data dictionary · Compound dereplication · Nuclear magnetic resonance spectroscopy · Mass spectrometry · Force field description of small molecules

1 Introduction

Data quality is assessed by its completeness, consistency, validity, and accuracy. One domain in which data quality is of utmost importance is that involving natural and man-made chemicals. The universe of small molecules, which can be defined arbitrarily as compounds with molecular weight less than 1000, is enormous. Such compounds (metabolites, vitamins, drugs, toxins, environmental contaminants, food components, and other small molecules) underlie all life processes and can have positive or negative effects on them. The PubChem Compound database, which contains over 94 million entries, most of biological importance, represents only the tip of the iceberg, and other compounds known to be present remain to be catalogued. Additional open databases

© Springer Nature Switzerland AG 2019
W. Abramowicz and R. Corchuelo (Eds.): BIS 2019 Workshops, LNBIP 373, pp. 519–530, 2019.
https://doi.org/10.1007/978-3-030-36691-9_44

contain information about metabolites, drugs, natural products, and industrial chemicals. The naming of compounds in these databases is not unique: they may use the same name for different compounds or a given compound may be described by several different names. The descriptor with ultimate data quality for a compound is its complete three-dimensional (3D) structure (atomic, bonding, electronic, and stereochemical), which serves as a complete and valid description of the compound and provides a consistent method for distinguishing one compound from another (a process defined as "dereplication"). Two compounds are identical if their 3D structures are exactly congruent (neglecting exchangeable hydrogens). Note that, the data quality regarding compounds without a known 3D structure is low, because they inhabit a dark zone where they cannot be clearly distinguished from those with known 3D structures. The information on a compound may be partial (lower data quality); its atomic composition (formula) and even its covalent structure (how the atoms are joined) can be known, but without its 3D structure dereplication is not possible. Thus, the universe of small molecules consists of those with known 3D structures, those whose 3D structures need to be determined, and a vast number of unknown compounds. Compound data quality is of critical importance, as the inversion of a single chiral center (left-handed vs. right-handed) could turn a drug into a poison, or an incorrectly annotated atom in a particular position could mean the difference between an active or inactive metabolite.

Although accurate 3D structures provide optimal data quality, they are difficult to compare, catalog, and sort. What is required is a text string representation that can be sorted and compared while preserving the equivalent information content of the 3D structure of a compound with all of its atoms uniquely labeled. The representation must be bijective and provide for reproducible conversion from the 3D structure to the text string and from the text string to the structure. Algorithms have been developed to represent 3D structures of compounds by strings of characters. Of these approaches, the standard IUPAC International Compound Identifier (InChI) (https://iupac.org/) has proved to be the most applicable for database searches. In principle, an InChI string can be created from the 3D structural model of a compound and then used to recreate a congruent 3D model that reproduces the charge state and protonation state as well as the full stereochemistry of the molecule. In practice, we have found that InChI strings in databases do not consistently match the 3D models of the compounds. Moreover, although InChI provides a numbering system for all heavy atoms, it ignores hydrogen atoms and is incomplete for certain stereochemistry. These deficiencies have resulted in significant loss of quality in public data.

We have devised an algorithm and software to overcome problems regarding descriptors of (bio)chemical compounds. We describe here published and unpublished application of our approach to improve the data quality of small molecule databases as well as to solve data quality issues in the fields of structural biology and biomolecular nuclear magnetic resonance (NMR) spectroscopy. How data are defined is critical to data quality. Data without clear definitions are incomplete. We describe the versatile tag-value data definition system we have developed to make data at every step of analysis comprehensible. Finally, we discuss how our approach is already impacting the biomolecular field and how it likely can improve data quality in the fields as diverse as medicine, pharmaceuticals, food, and agriculture.

2 The ALATIS Algorithm and Software that Interconverts 3D Structures and InChI Strings

As described above, the critical problem is to derive a complete, consistent, and unique way to describe a compound as represented by its 3D structure in ways that can be sorted and compared. This requires that the compound itself and all of its constituent atoms have unique and reproducible names and that there is an algorithm for the bijective mapping between the descriptor and 3D structure. Ideally, the algorithm for carrying this out should be implemented in computer software to avoid human error, but it must also maintain a low time complexity order in order to mitigate very long computation times for molecules with a large number of atoms. Our approach to solving this problem is an algorithm called ALATIS (Atom Label Assignment Tool using InChI String) and an associated computer program that takes the 3D structure of a compound (in a variety of standard formats), generates a standard InChI string as the unique identifier for that compound, and assigns unique atom identifiers (numbers) to each atom in the molecule (Fig. 1) [1]. The software also can take this enhanced InChI string and generate a 3D model for the compound with all atoms reproducibly identified. Finally, because ALATIS uses computer software to generate unique identifiers and atom designators, their creation is not subject to human error and is fully reproducible anywhere in the world. The IUPAC International Chemical Identifier (InChI^{TM}), which is maintained by the InChI Trust, has acknowledged limitations. InChI currently does not support the representation of polymers, complex organometallics, generic representations of a group of structures (Markush structures), conformers, excited state and spin isomers, non-local stereochemistry/chirality, topological isomers, cluster molecules, polymorphs, unspecified isotopic enrichment, and reactions. InChI also is limited to compounds consisting of 1023 or fewer atoms.

InChI strings supported by ALATIS are highly versatile. They enable the modeling of compounds that interconvert between different conformations or configurations, such as glucose. They also can account for structural ambiguity, such as unknown configuration of chiral centers. As such, the tools are useful for studies aimed at determining complete 3D structures of compounds, and they also can be used to precisely define fragments in mass spectrometric analysis.

3 Application of ALATIS to Improving the Data Quality of Small Molecule Databases

In addition to ensuring high data quality, ALATIS is a useful tool for implementing, with regard to small molecule databases, the FAIR principles (findable, accessible, interoperable, and reproducible) [2]. Use of the enhanced InChI string as the identifier makes entries findable. The standardization of identifiers across databases makes the information accessible, and enables rigorous cross-references that make databases interoperable. We have used ALATIS to validate a number of databases containing 3D structural models and InChI designators for consistency between the two. We have found that all publicly available databases studied (HMDB, BMRB, RCSB PDB

Atom labeling and InChI string following ALATIS analysis of PubChem structure (below)

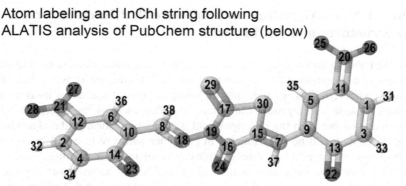

InChI=1S/C17H8N4O7S2/c22-13-3-1-11(20(25)26)5-9(13)7-15-16(24)19(17
(29)30-15)18-8-10-6-12(21(27)28)2-4-14(10)23/h1-8H/q-2

Structure and InChI from PubChem entry

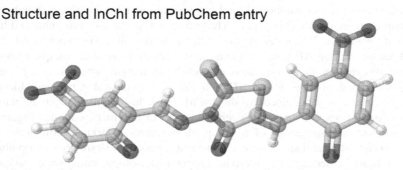

InChI=1S/C17H10N4O7S2/c22-13-3-1-11(20(25)26)5-9(13)7-15-16(24)19(17
(29)30-15)18-8-10-6-12(21(27)28)2-4-14(10)23/h1-8,22-23H/p-2/b15-7-,18-8?

Fig. 1. The 3D structure archived in PubChem entry CID 1551886 (below) has defined stereochemistry about the double bond between atoms C8 and N18 (see structure at top). However, the notation "18-8?" in the InChI string archived for this PubChem entry (bottom) denotes an ambiguous orientation (cis-/trans-configuration) around this double bond. This defect is corrected in the InChI string generated by ALATIS from the structure in the PubChem entry.

Ligand Expo, wwPDB Chem Comp, and PubChem Compound) contained files with an InChI string inconsistent with the corresponding 3D structure [1]. Errors presumably resulted from manual generation of the InChI string. We subsequently used ALATIS to analyze the 94,201,188 entries from the PubChem Compound database with 3D structures. (This database contains 2.5 million "dark" entries without 3D structures, which consequently could only be marked as incomplete but could not be analyzed.) In about 30% of the PubChem Compound entries, the InChI string failed to reproduce the 3D structure of the compound in that entry [3]. In nearly all of these cases, the inconsistency was in specifying the stereochemistry of the compound.

We have created a website called Gateway to the Universe of Small Molecules (http://gateway.nmrfam.wisc.edu/) that consolidates information on small molecules from the various websites that we have analyzed with ALATIS. The website can be searched by entering a compound name, InChI string, or structure. This returns a menu with the most probable matching entries. Each entry contains (a) a link to the corresponding ALATIS entry (with a 3D representation of the compound with the ALATIS atom nomenclature, and the corresponding standard InChI string, and with links to the identical compound in other databases with correspondence between atom naming in that database with ALATIS), (b) a link (if available) to the GISSMO entry for the compound (with spin system matrix), (c) a link to CAMP entries (with computational mapping of MS peaks to possible fragments of the compound, and (d) a link to BMOD entries (with force field parameters of the compound for use with different molecular modeling packages). By using ALATIS to federate these databases, we collected all names that have been associated with each unique identifier (standard InChI string) and have made these available for searching.

4   A Data Model and Data Dictionary Are Required to Ensure the Quality of Data

Data without a valid context are essentially useless. This context is provided by metadata through a data model and data dictionary (ontology). Because scientific data evolve with research and new findings require revisions to data content and their context, data models and data dictionaries need to be flexible and extensible and capable of supporting data integrity across versions of data. While ALATIS identifiers address the key element of findability for molecular data, additional information is required to define the data so as to make them accessible and ensure their quality and reproducibility. NMR-STAR is a data definition model that has been used to represent macromolecular and ligand data in the biomolecular NMR community for the past 20 years [4, 5]. It is a version of the STAR (Self-defining Text Archive and Retrieval) data model [6, 7] and dictionary definition language (DDL) [8] developed by N. Spadaccini and S.R. Hall. NMR-STAR, which makes use of "save frames", is fully compatible with mmCIF [9], which is an ASCII format and is used by the Protein Data Bank archive. NMR-STAR is a self-describing data model that is defined through a data definition language (DDL), and a dictionary. It is a highly flexible model that can be extended readily in a backward compatible way. Additionally, it provides an efficient model for data exchange by enabling robust transfer of sub-parts of the data (represented as save frames). NMR-STAR is useful for capturing workflows that operate on and transform data. As described below, we are utilizing NMR-STAR in our applications of ALATIS.

5   Applications of ALATIS-Based Methods to Biomolecular Nuclear Magnetic Resonance (NMR) Spectroscopy and NMR-Based Metabolomics and Ligand Screening for Drug Development

NMR spectra provide information on an atomic level about the structure, dynamics, and chemical properties of molecules. Because NMR signal intensities are proportional to concentration, NMR data can be used both to identify compounds in soluble mixtures and to determine their concentrations. NMR data of high quality include unique, complete, and accurate assignment of NMR spectral peaks to specific atoms in the 3D structure of a given compound. ALATIS is a boon for NMR in that it offers a universal atom nomenclature so that assignments made by one group are accurately available to others. NMR data are collected on NMR spectrometers, and different spectrometer models operate at different field strengths. Magnetic resonance imaging data, for example, are collected at a variety of low magnetic fields whereas chemical and biomolecular NMR data are collected at a variety of higher fields. This can impact data interpretation, because the pattern of peaks in an NMR spectrum of a given compound can differ greatly depending on the magnetic field strength of the spectrometer used to collect the data.

This problem has a theoretical solution, in that, if one solves for the quantum chemical spin system matrix of the compound, one can calculate the spectrum at any magnetic field. Although this is an old problem that has been addressed by computations, there has been no systematic approach to its solution. Because the computations need to keep track of individual nuclei and their interactions with other nuclei, ALATIS, by assigning atom names, facilitates this process. We have developed a software package called GISSMO (Guided Ideographic Spin System Model Optimization) that enables the efficient calculation and refinement of NMR spin system matrices (Fig. 2) [10]. GISSMO utilizes a graphical user interface (GUI) for guided optimization of spin system matrices against experimental 1D ^{1}H NMR spectra of small molecules. GISSMO provides a mechanism for the specification and exchange of NMR data in a robust way by parameterizing the description of the experimental data. Parameterization of experimental data is specialized work that entails expert modeling and detailed specification, but it is another key necessary step for advancing data quality. Associated NMR-STAR meta-data serve to define the calculated parameters and associates them with computer-readable information describing data collection, such as sample properties (concentration, pH, temperature, buffer), NMR instrument manufacturer, model, field-strength, type of probe, etc. The quality of the derived spin system is evaluated by calculating the RMSD between the experimental spectrum and the spectrum calculated from the spin system at the corresponding magnetic field.

The GISSMO website supports tools for simulating ^{1}H NMR spectra of mixtures of small molecules [11] and for automated analysis of ^{1}H NMR spectra of biological fluids or cell extracts to identify compounds present and determine their concentrations [11]. The GISSMO library currently represents more than 1100 compounds, including many key mammalian metabolites and drug-like molecular fragments used in ligand screening. The ^{1}H NMR spectrum of each compound is simulated at a variety of magnetic fields (40, 60, 80, 90, 100, 200, 300, 400, 500, 600, 700, 750, 800, 900, 950, 1000, 1100, and 1300 MHz). Every entry in the GISSMO library can be downloaded in NMR-STAR and NMReDATA [12] data format. Figure 2 shows the home page of the GISSMO website (http://gissmo.nmrfam.wisc.edu). Once the spin system matrix has been accurately modeled to represent an experimental NMR spectrum collected at a given magnet field strength, the matrix can be used to model spectra at any desired magnetic field strength (Fig. 3). This means that a spectral library of data collected at a single field strength (e.g., that corresponding to 600 MHz for protons) can be used to model data at another (e.g., 900 MHz for protons). As shown in Fig. 2, GISSMO offers

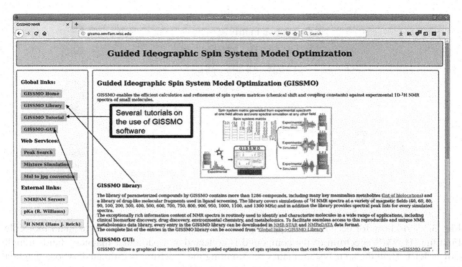

Fig. 2. Home page of the GISSMO website. The arrows point to the library of parameterized compounds, tutorials explaining the use of GISSMO software, and the GISSMO-GUI that provides tools for creating spin system matrices from a user-supplied ^{1}H NMR spectrum.

a menu of web services, including "Peak Search" and "Mixture Simulation". Figure 4 shows an example in which GISSMO data have been used to simulate the spectrum of the 33 most abundant metabolites in blood plasma.

We have used ALATIS/GISSMO to address issues of data quality in the field of metabolomics. Although, in principle, ^{1}H NMR spectra provide information about the identities and quantities of compounds present in biological fluids (plasma, cerebral spinal fluid, urine, and cell extracts), the reliable extraction of this information has been problematic. We have developed Bayes Explorer I, a tool that utilizes our database of GISSMO representations of NMR spectra in analyzing data from NMR spectra of mixtures of metabolites to yield a probabilistic list of compounds present in the mixture and the concentrations of these compounds with error estimates. This is an example in which the analysis of experimental data produces derived data (results) that themselves constitute source data for a curated public database. The Bayesian approach contributes to the quality of these public data because it provides highly enriched results that capture the uncertainty in the data as well as the assumptions about the data in the form of a probability distribution. This distribution, called the posterior distribution, often written as $P(M \mid D)$, is the conditional probability of the model M given the data D; it is derived by combining the data and the prior information to produce rigorous probabilistic results.

The quantity $P(M \mid D)$ is highly information-rich and can be readily used to calculate standard measures such as precision, recall, specificity, selectivity, and others. For example, when $P(M \mid D)$ is marginalized to the submodel M' – the submodel for the identification but not the quantification of each metabolite – then simulations using $P(M' \mid D)$ provide the true positive rate. The posterior can be used to calculate all essential measures of classification test accuracy as represented by the 2×2

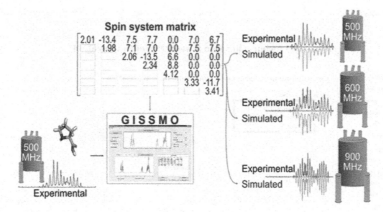

Fig. 3. Workflow for deriving and applying the NMR spin system matrix for a small molecule. First the ¹H NMR spectrum of the compound is collected at a particular magnetic field strength (lower left). Then the spin system matrix representing the spectrum is estimated, whose diagonal represents chemical shifts (ppm) of particular nuclei and whose off-diagonal elements represent spin-spin coupling (Hz) between pairs of nuclei (upper center). Tools on the GISSMO website are used to refine the spin system matrix so that it accurately predicts the experimental spectrum (lower center). The optimized spin system matrix can then be used to simulate ¹H NMR spectra at different magnetic field strengths (right). In the case shown, we have collected experimental spectra to verify the accuracy of the simulations.

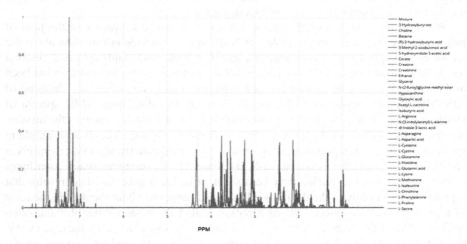

Fig. 4. Simulated spectrum of 33 metabolites found in blood plasma at their typical concentrations. The trace in magenta shows the simulated spectrum of all components, and the subspectra of individual components are shown in other colors. (Color figure online)

contingency table (true positive rate, true negative rate, false positive rate, and false negative rate) by simulating draws from the posterior distribution that is calculated in our Bayesian framework. Then, precision, for example, can be computed by dividing the true positive rate (distribution) by the sum of true positive and false positive rates (distribution). We note that because our "gold standard" for the results of these computations is often the human expert, additional computational procedures that control for verification bias must be undertaken; description of this complex set of procedures is beyond the scope of this report and will be published elsewhere.

By creating the representations that enable the preservation of posterior distributions along with the results, several aspects of data quality, including accuracy and precision, can be improved significantly. The beta version of this software tool has been released as a web server (Fig. 5). The quality of the automated analysis, which currently takes 2–4 h, now rivals that of an experienced spectroscopist working a full day with semi-automated tools.

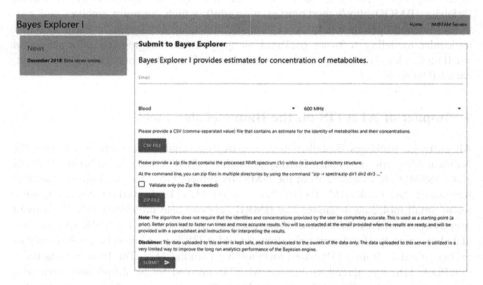

Fig. 5. Home page of the Bayes Explorer I web server (http://bayesxplorer.nmrfam.wisc.edu/).

6   Applications of ALATIS-Based Atom Nomenclature in Software for Calculating Force Fields, Molecular Structures, and Molecular Interactions

The physical and chemical properties and biological activities of small molecules are a manifestation of their configuration of atoms in 3D space. The "ALATIS identifiers" ensure that the 3D structural arrangements and the naming of subparts are captured in a unique and reproducible way. Many experimental and computational tools have been developed for determining and modeling important physical, chemical, and biological properties of small molecules. Because these tools utilize different naming conventions for atoms in molecules, nomenclature conversion steps need to be inserted when one tool is pipelined with another. The use of ALATIS identifiers eliminates such steps and ensures the interoperability of tools [13].

We have used ALATIS and associated NMR-STAR data format in the large-scale generation of force field parameters for small molecules by a software package called RUNER [14]. This software utilizes Open Babel to generate 3D structure files from input 2D structures and to add explicit hydrogen atoms to the structures when needed; then ALATIS and Antechamber are used to generate the force field parameters. ChemAxon Marvin is used to generate 2D images of structure files, which are displayed on entry pages.

Computationally derived data play a significant role in informing molecular modeling studies and are used routinely to enrich experimental data. At present, commonly accepted standards for the capture of maintenance of the derived data do not exist. As a result, publicly available data are often difficult to reproduce because much of the supporting data are "dark". We have developed the Biomolecular Modeling Database (BMOD http://bmod.nmrfam.wisc.edu/), which currently archives and provides force field parameters for more than 400,000 small molecules for use in different molecular modeling software packages along with other aggregated information on small molecules. This database utilizes a set of save frames/tags in NMR-STAR format, called BMOD-STAR

7   Impact of ALATIS on the Biomolecular Field

All software packages described here are freely available from the website of the National Magnetic Resonance Facility at Madison (NMRFAM). In addition, ALATIS and GISSMO are available from the NMRbox project [15]. The Biological Magnetic Resonance data Bank (BMRB) [16] has adopted ALATIS-derived atom nomenclature for its small-molecule database. The BMRB database also provides GISSMO-derived spin system matrices for most of these compounds as well as 1D NMR spectra simulated at a variety of different field strengths. ALATIS is proving to be a robust way of exchanging data from NMR-based metabolomics studies [17]. The Protein Data Bank (wwPDB) [18] has agreed to provide ALATIS-derived InChI strings and atom designators as part of its ligand database, and is utilizing this approach in remediating the annotation of carbohydrate ligands in this database. The NMReData initiative [12] has adopted ALATIS identifiers for its applications. The resources we have developed (GISSMO, RUNER, Bayes Explorer I), are already accessed by users worldwide. We are working to expand the GISSMO database of compounds, to enhance their quality by including effects on spin system matrices such as pH and the presence of metal ions. We also are implementing graphics processing units (GPUs) to accelerate the analysis of metabolomics data by Bayes Explorer I.

8   Summary and Future Prospects

ALATIS, GISSMO, and BMOD-STAR form the key axis in our efforts to create and maintain quality data on small molecules – data that can be checked for consistency on demand. Although we have developed these components in response to challenges in fields of metabolomics, ligand screening, ligand docking, mass spectrometry, and

NMR spectroscopy, we believe that the conceptual framework and the ideas can help stimulate parallel advances in support of data quality related to small molecules in other communities.

The curated federated database we have created on the basis of 3D structures can be expanded to include less stringent links to databases that contain entries on small molecules but do not include their 3D structure. Relevant databases include PubMed (NLM), Web of Science (Thompson Reuters), various university collections, and databases on toxicology, drugs, food additives, agricultural chemicals, and organic chemistry reactions. Links from the compound identifier used in these databases to the fully curated database can be made through artificial intelligence (AI) methods that provide the most likely link on the basis of information about compounds known by that identifier. Recommendations can be made to journals, database curators, drug manufacturers, and chemical companies to associate compound identifiers with standard or expanded InChI. Adherence to this practice will make the scientific literature much more accessible to computer searches that aggregate information and create knowledge.

Acknowledgments. This work was funded in part by NIH Grants P41GM103399 in support of the National Magnetic Resonance Facility at Madison (NMRFAM), R01GM 109046 in support of the Biological Magnetic Resonance data Bank (BMRB), and P41GM111135 in support of the NMRbox project.

References

1. Dashti, H., Westler, W.M., Markley, J.L., Eghbalnia, H.R.: Unique identifiers for small molecules enable rigorous labeling of their atoms. Sci. Data **4**, 170073 (2017)
2. Wilkinson, M.D., et al.: The FAIR guiding principles for scientific data management and stewardship. Sci. Data **3**, 160018 (2016)
3. Dashti, H., Wedell, J.R., Westler, W.M., Markley, J.L., Eghbalnia, H.R.: Automated evaluation of consistency within the PubChem compound database. Sci. Data **6**, 190023 (2019)
4. Ulrich, E.L., Argentar, D., Klimowicz, A., Markley, J.L.: STAR/CIF macromolecular NMR data dictionaries and data file formats. Acta Crystallogr. A **52**(a1), C577–C577 (1996)
5. Ulrich, E.L., et al.: NMR-STAR: comprehensive ontology for representing, archiving and exchanging data from nuclear magnetic resonance spectroscopic experiments. J. Biomol. NMR **73**, 5–9 (2019)
6. Hall, S.R., Spadaccini, N.: The STAR file: detailed specifications. J. Chem. Inf. Comput. Sci. **34**, 505–508 (1994)
7. Hall, S.R., Cook, A.P.F.: STAR dictionary definition language: initial specification. J. Chem. Inf. Comput. Sci. **35**, 819–825 (1995)
8. Spadaccini, N., Hall, S.R.: Extensions to the STAR file syntax. J. Chem. Inf. Model. **52**, 1901–1906 (2012)
9. Bourne, P.E., Berman, H.M., McMahon, B., Watenpaugh, K.D., Westbrook, J.D., Fitzgerald, P.M.D.: The macromolecular crystallographic information file (mmCIF). Meth. Enzymol. **277**, 571–590 (1997)

10. Dashti, H., Westler, W.M., Tonelli, M., Wedell, J.R., Markley, J.L., Eghbalnia, H.R.: Spin system modeling of nuclear magnetic resonance spectra for applications in metabolomics and small molecule screening. Anal. Chem. **89**, 12201–12208 (2017)
11. Dashti, H., et al.: Applications of parametrized NMR spin systems of small molecules. Anal. Chem. **90**, 10646–10649 (2018)
12. Pupier, M., et al.: NMReDATA, a standard to report the NMR assignment and parameters of organic compounds. Magn. Reson. Chem. **56**, 703–715 (2018)
13. Cornilescu, G., et al.: Progressive stereo locking (PSL): a residual dipolar coupling based force field method for determining the relative configuration of natural products and other small molecules. ACS Chem. Biol. **12**, 2157–2163 (2017)
14. Dashti, H., et al.: Robust nomenclature and software for enhanced reproducibility in molecular modeling of small molecules. *bioRxiv*, 429530 (2018)
15. Maciejewski, M.W., et al.: NMRbox: a resource for biomolecular NMR computation. Biophys. J. **112**, 1529–1534 (2017)
16. Ulrich, E.L., et al.: BioMagResBank. Nucleic Acids Res. **36**, 402–408 (2008)
17. Le Guennec, A., Tayyari, F., Edison, A.S.: Alternatives to nuclear overhauser enhancement spectroscopy presat and carr-purcell-meiboom-gill presat for NMR-based metabolomics. Anal. Chem. **89**, 8582–8588 (2017)
18. Burley, S.K., Berman, H.M., Kleywegt, G.J., Markley, J.L., Nakamura, H., Velankar, S.: Protein data bank (PDB): the single global macromolecular structure archive. Meth. Mol. Biol. **1607**, 627–641 (2017)

Evaluating the Quantity
of Incident-Related Information
in an Open Cyber Security Dataset

Benjamin Aziz$^{(\boxtimes)}$, John Arthur Lee, and Gulsum Akkuzu

School of Computing, University of Portsmouth, Portsmouth PO1 3HE, UK
{benjamin.aziz,gulsum.akkuzu}@port.ac.uk, John.Lee1@myport.ac.uk

Abstract. Data-driven security has become essential in many organisations in their attempt to tackle Cyber security incidents. However, whilst the dominant approach to data-driven security remains through the mining of private and internal data, there is an increasing trend towards more open data through the sharing of Cyber security information and experience over public and community platforms. However, some questions remain over the quality and quantity of such open data. In this paper, we present the results of a recent case study that considers how feasible it is to answer a common question in Cyber security incident investigations, namely that *"in an incident, who did what to which asset or victim, and with what result and impact"*, for one such open Cyber security database.

Keywords: Cyber security incidents · Open datasets · Quantity of information

1 Introduction

When designing a security system, data and information are imperative to creating the best solution. Most organisations will collect and analyse data from their own systems and use these and the experience, as well as the knowledge of the personnel involved, to design a security strategy. Cyber security practitioners working in an increasingly competitive environment face the challenge of providing security that is focused in the areas that threaten their business the most to reduce crime and loss. Because most organisations have limited resources, especially the smaller ones, the solution needs to be cost effective without exposing the organisations to unwarranted liability or embarrassment. Data-driven security, therefore, can help expose hidden patterns of errant behaviour and offer credible countermeasures and effective controls at such a cost effective level.

This obviously has restrictions, and a broader and deeper knowledge of security threats can mean a more robust and effective security system. At the same time, organisations can benefit from the combined knowledge, experience and competences of a wider community in order to improve their understanding of the risks that they may be facing. Sharing threat information through a community database enables organisations to do just this. By exploiting this shared

© Springer Nature Switzerland AG 2019
W. Abramowicz and R. Corchuelo (Eds.): BIS 2019 Workshops, LNBIP 373, pp. 531–542, 2019.
https://doi.org/10.1007/978-3-030-36691-9_45

knowledge, organisations can make more informed decisions to improve their own defences, threat detection practises and mitigation strategies. By collecting and analysing Cyber threat information from multiple sources, an organisation can also enrich existing information and make it more actionable [8]. In recent times, there has emerged a wealth of open data sources to assist Cyber security strategists in understanding systems and threats against them. Notable examples include SecRepo [11], VERIS/VCDB [18,19], CERT's Vulnerability Notes Database at Carnegie Mellon University [5], CAIDA [4], UNSW-NB15 [13] and the open datasets from the Los Alamos National Laboratory (LANL) [10]. As a result, data-driven security has emerged as a paradigm that uses such data sources effectively to manage the ever-changing risk landscape organisations operate in.

Nonetheless, a very important question in any data-driven technique is the quality of the dataset under consideration. This question is particularly critical in the context of Cyber security data, as was demonstrated recently for example in [9]. We aim in this paper to study this question through the analysis of the quantity of data in an example Cyber security dataset collected by Verizon [18]. Our approach focuses on identifying and extracting information from such dataset relevant to a fundamental question in Cyber incidents analysis, namely: *"in an incident, who did what to which asset or victim, and with what result and impact"*. Our findings show that while organisations are generally happy to report data for the majority of the elements of this question, they are particularly reluctant to report data related to the impact of Cyber incidents.

The rest of the paper is organised as follows. In Sect. 2, we discuss related work in literature where the problem of the quality of security data in open datasets has been tackled. In Sect. 3, we give an overview of the dataset used in our case study, namely the VERIS schema and dataset [18,19]. In Sect. 4, we describe the methodology used in extracting the sub-schema relevant to our research question highlighted above. In Sect. 5, we outline this scheme, and in Sect. 6, we present the results of our quantity of data analysis. Finally, in Sect. 7, we conclude the paper and outline directions for future research.

2   Related Work

Open Cyber security datasets, such as the ones we mentioned in the Introduction, are becoming increasingly popular, and as highlighted in [14], there is growing trend in encouraging the generation of such datasets. For example, [6] proposed ID2T, a DIY dataset creation toolkit for Cyber security incident detection. Another example of a data-driven security management approach was described in [3], who proposed a method for integrating security system data with systems engineering principles, in an attempt to increase the effectiveness of security systems being designed and implemented and to balance risk, effectiveness and cost. The method also proposes that human intelligence should not be ignored as a compliment to technological intelligence.

Whilst a few studies have been conducted to investigate the quality of data in more general datasets (e.g. for Wikidata and DBpedia as in [17] and more general, for any linked open data as in [20]), there is still no significant research effort done to understand the quantity of Cyber security data available. Perhaps the most interesting such research so far has been the work of [16], who proposed semiotic levels as a theoretical basis for the definition of data quality in the context of information systems security. For example, the relationship between data and information is an interpretation-related quality, which would affect security operations (e.g. confidentiality, integrity and availability controls), whereas that between information and knowledge is a usefulness-related quality, which in turn would affect decision-making processes (e.g. when enforcing security policies.) On the other hand, the authors in [7,15] proposed an approach that improves the sharing of Cyber security information through understanding the requirements and constraints underlying the collaborative system.

The work presented in this paper is based on current research effort by the authors, who in [1] demonstrated how open datasets can be effectively used to extract useful information for predicting features of future incidents. Similarly, in [2], the authors demonstrated how open data can be used to evaluate and reason about XACML [12] security policies based on risk probabilities, which offer a quantitative approach to security. However, none of the above works attempted to provide some understanding of the quality or quantity of data in Cyber security-related datasets or platforms.

3   VERIS: A Schema for Cyber Security Incidents

The Vocabulary for Event Recording and Incident Sharing (VERIS) [18] is a dataset and schema defining a set of metadata and metrics for describing Cyber security incidents. It is currently considered a leading provider of open quality information in the IT security domain and provides a framework that organisations can use to collect and share information on security incidents in a responsible and anonymous manner, with the aim of constructing a ground on which researchers and experts in the IT security industry can cooperate to learn from their knowledge and experiences. The VERIS schema itself consists of five general categories, containing descriptions of security incidents:

- *Incident Tracking*: this category contains general information about the incidents, for example, the source identity, summary of the incident and whether the incident is related to other incidents.
- *Victim demographies*: this category contains information related to the organisation being affected by the incident, for example, its country of operation, number of employees, revenue and industry type.
- *Incident description*: this category contains information related to the question of "who did what to what (or whom) with what result". It is based on the so-called A4 threat model developed by Verizon and contains descriptions related to the Actors, Assets, Actions and Attributes (A4) of an incident.
- *Discovery and response*: this category contains information related to the incident's timeline, its discovery method, root causes and corrective actions.
- *Impact assessment*: this last category contains information on loss categorisation and estimation and impact rating.

The significance of the VERIS dataset lies in the fact that it is a *community-based* dataset. This means that its data are collected from a wide range of industries and varied over different types and sizes of organisations, therefore providing a rich ground for organisations to learn about the various risks and threats that could exist on a global level. This renders the dataset more widely applicable than datasets that are generated in the context of single organisations. The VERIS dataset, known as VCDB [19], had at the time the work reported in this paper was carried out 7834 recorded incidents between 2010 and 2017, with its schema metadata described by some 2398 elements. Both the VERIS framework as well as the VCDB dataset are initiatives by the Verizon RISK team.

4   Data Extraction Methodology

Before evaluating the quantity of information available in VERIS to answer our research question, we can summarise our methodology used in extracting the relevant data by the diagram shown in Fig. 1.

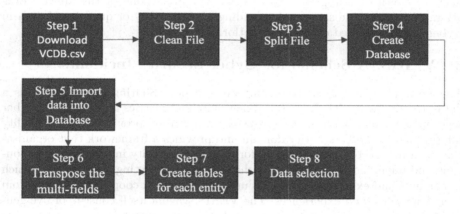

Fig. 1. Our data extraction methodology

This methodology comprises the following eight steps:

1. Download the dataset file, in this case "VCDB.csv". We used the version as of 15 March 2018, which contained 7834 records and 2398 fields, covering years 2010 to 2017.
2. Clean the file, as the file contained many non-standard characters, which had to be removed so that they would not interfere with the loading process. This was done manually in a basic text editor using find and replace.
3. Split the file, since there were 2398 fields in the file, these needed to be split into multiple files in order to make it possible for the data analysis server to process them. This step was performed using a VB.NET script. We used the Microsoft SQLServer Integration Services to perform this step.

4. Create a database, where we used the SQL Server database management studio system to create a database named VCDB, in order to receive the data from the newly created files.
5. Import data into the databse, where each file was imported into separate tables in the new VCDB database, each table having the name of the file from which the data came.
6. Transpose multiple fields, as many of the fields in the dataset are binary data that can be transposed into a single data field. For example, when asking if the ACTOR is of External, Internal or Partner type, the dataset uses 3 fields namely [actor#External], [actor#Internal] or [actor#Partner], each with a binary (i.e. True/False) value. One can instead optimise this into a single field with the three values (Internal, External or Partner).
7. Create tables for each entity, where we focused on the entities selected for the sub-schema. Each table contained also descriptions of the different records.
8. Data selection, which is the final step leading to our extracted sub-schema (described in the next section).

5   The Extracted Sub-schema

In order to answer the question *"in an incident, who did what to which asset or victim, and with what result and impact"*, we next need to identify the relevant part of the VERIS schema that contains enough information to answer the question. This information can be summarised in terms of the following four categories:

1. Incidents information, which captures some general information related to an incident, such as the various identifiers, date the incident occurred on, levels of confidence and so on.
2. A4 information, which represents information related to the A4 model (i.e. Actors, Actions, Assets and Attributes.)
3. Victims information, which is information related to the victims of the incident, the industry, organisation, revenue and country of the victim.
4. Impact information, which is essential information describing the impact of the incident, e.g. loss type, rating and overall amount.

More specifically, the sub-scheme of VERIS corresponding to these categorites of information is shown in Fig. 2. Furthermore, Table 1 defines how the mapping between our research statement concepts and the seven VERIS types captured in the sub-schema is done, indicating at the same time possible values for some of the sub-types of information in each type.

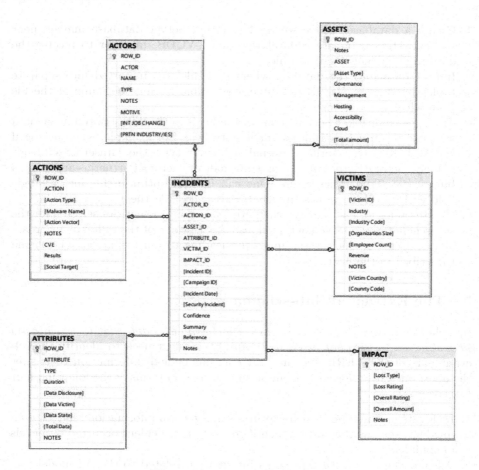

Fig. 2. The extracted sub-schema

Table 1. Mapping between research statement concepts and VERIS types

Statement concept	VERIS type	Possible values
Incident	INCIDENTS	Confirmed, Suspect False positive, Near miss
Who	ACTORS	External, Internal, Partner
What	ACTIONS	Hacking, Malware, Misuse Physical, Error, Social Environmental
Asset	ASSETS	Server, Network, User device Media, People, Kiosk/Public Terminal
Victim	VICTIMS	Demographic information
Result	ATTRIBUTES	Confidentiality/Possession
		Integrity/Authentication
		Availability/Utility
Impact	IMPACT	Impact assessment information

6   Quantity of Data Analysis

After identifying the relevant categories of information as outlined above in the extracted sub-schema, we next carried out an analysis to measure the amount of information for each element of this sub-schema. After filtering the original dataset of incorrectly inputted records, we ended up with 7210 records. For each of the seven elements of the extracted sub-schema, we measured the percentage of cases that had populated that element over the total number of cases. The results are shown in Tables 2, 3, 4, 5, 6, 7 and 8 for the extracted schema.

The first four tables, Tables 2, 3, 4 and 5, represent the quantity of information available in the A4 (i.e. Actors, Actions, Assets and Attributes) category. We found here that there was an abundance of data; Actors at 97%, Actions at 100%, Assets at 90% and Attributes at 97%. All percentages out of the 7210 records. Therefore, we were able to answer the sub-question *"who did what to which asset and with what result"* for about 90% of the incidents reported correctly.

In terms of the lack of data, we found that for the Actor category, the least populated data items were those related to their identity (10%), sources and capabilities of the actor (38%) and whether they had an internal job change (2%). For the Actions category, we found that the least populated data items were those related to the malware names (2.5%), CVEs exploited by the action (1%), results (3.6%) and social target (2.5%). For the Assets category, we found that the least populated data items were those related to the management and hosting of assets (0%), the accessibility of the assets (0.14%), whether the asset is a Cloud service (0.24%) and what the total amount of the assets was (3.3%). Finally, for the Attributes category, the least populated data item was the duration of the effect of loss or exposure (3%).

Table 2. Quantity of ACTORS information

Column name	Data type	Description	Percentage populated
ROW − ID	float	Unique Row ID	100.00%
ACTOR	varchar	Internal, External or Partner	97.00%
NAME	nvarchar	Name or ID of Actor	19.00%
TYPE	varchar	Defines resources and capabilities of capabilities of ACTOR	38.00%
NOTES	nvarchar	Extra information	10.00%
MOTIVE	varchar	Helps to understand intensions	50.00%
INT JOB CHANGE	varchar	Had the employee recently changed job?	2.00%
PRTN INDUSTRY/ IES	varchar	Type of industry of partner US Census NIACS codes	3.50%

Table 3. Quantity of ACTIONS information

Column name	Data type	Description	Percentage populated
ROW − ID	float	Unique Row ID	100.00%
ACTION	varchar	Primary Threat Action	100.00%
TYPE	varchar	What varieties or functions or methods of Primary action were involved	71.00%
Malware name	nvarchar	Common name or strain of the Malware	2.50%
Action vector	varchar	What were the vectors or paths of infection or attack	60.00%
NOTES	nvarchar	Enter any additional details deemed noteworthy	8.60%
CVE	nvarchar	Any CVEs exploited by this Action (1)	1.00%
Results	varchar	Exfiltrate, Exfiltrate or elevate	3.60%
Social target	varchar	Who was the target of these social tactics	2.50%

Table 4. Quantity of ASSETS information

Column name	Data type	Description	Percentage populated
ROW − ID	float	Unique Row ID	100.00%
ASSET	varchar	Asset Category	90.00%
TYPE	varchar	Specific type of asset	93.00%
Notes	nvarchar	Enter any additional details deemed noteworthy	2.20%
Governance	varchar	Who owns/governs the asset	10.00%
Management	varchar	Who manages the asset	0.00%
Hosting	varchar	Where (physically) is the asset hosted	0.00%
Accessibility	varchar	How accessible is the asset	0.14%
Cloud	varchar	If a cloud service what type is it	0.24%
Total amount	nvarchar	Total amount of assets of type affected	3.30%

Table 5. Quantity of ATTRIBUTES information

Column name	Data type	Description	Percentage populated
ROW − ID	float	Unique Row ID	100.00%
ATTRIBUTE	varchar	Confidentiality, Integrity and Availability (CIA)	97.00%
TYPE	nvarchar	What was the nature of integrity/authenticity loss	89.00%
Duration	varchar	Duration of effect of loss or exposure	3.00%
Data disclosure	varchar	Was non-public data disclosed	89.00%
Data victim	varchar	Who was the victim within the organisation	62.70%
Data state	nvarchar	State of data when disclosed	47.00%
Total data	nvarchar	Number of records affected	56.00%
Notes	nvarchar	Enter any additional details deemed noteworthy	10.60%

Table 6. Quantity of VICTIM information

Column name	Data type	Description	Percentage populated
ROW − ID	float	Unique Row ID	100.00%
VICTIM ID	nvarchar	Identifier or name of victim	96.00%
Industry	nvarchar	Industry	100.00%
Industry code	float	Industry (NAICS code)	100.00%
Organization size	varchar	Large or small	67.50%
Employee count	varchar	Number of employees	60.00%
Revenue	nvarchar	Annual revenue of the victim	7.00%
Total data	nvarchar	Number of records affected	56.00%
Notes	nvarchar	Enter any additional details deemed noteworthy	0.80%
Victim country	varchar	Country of operation	98.00%
Country code	varchar	ISO3166-1 two digit country code	98.00%

Table 7. Quantity of IMPACT information

Column name	Data type	Description	Percentage populated
ROW − ID	float	Unique Row ID	100.00%
Loss type	varchar	Specific category of loss	0.00%
Loss rating	varchar	Qualitative rating of impact	0.00%
Overall rating	varchar	Qualitative rating of overall impact	0.35%
Overall amount	decimal	Most likely estimated money amount	0.83%
Notes	nvarchar	Enter any additional details deemed noteworthy	1.66%

Table 6 shows the quantity of information in the VICTIM category. We found that this category of information was well-populated generally, with information supplied for at least 56% of cases, except for information related to the annual revenue of victims (7%), which can be sometimes sensitive information particularly for the case of privately-owned companies. We noticed that the least populated set of data were those belonging to the IMPACT category, shown in Table 7. Most of the fields had fewer than 1% reported data. Finally, for the category of INCIDENTS information, shown in Table 8, the most notable aspect was the hesitance of organisations to report their levels of confidence in the supplied data. Only 8.5% of cases reported any level of confidence.

Table 8. Quantity of INCIDENTS information

Column name	Data type	Description	Percentage populated
$ROW - ID$	float	Unique Row ID	100.00%
$ACTOR - ID$	float	ACTOR Row ID	100.00%
$ACTION - ID$	float	ACTION Row ID	100.00%
$ASSET - ID$	float	ASSET Row ID	100.00%
$ATTRIBUTE - ID$	float	ATTRIBUTE Row ID	100.00%
$VICTIM - ID$	float	$VICTIM - Row - ID$	100.00%
$IMPACT - ID$	float	IMPACT Row ID	100.00%
$Incident - ID$	nvarchar	To uniquely identify incidents for storage and tracking over time	100.00%
Incident date	date	Date the incident occurred	97.00%
Security incident	varchar	Was this a confirmed security incident? Confirmed, suspect, false positive or near miss	99.80%
Confidence	varchar	How certain are you that the information you provided about this incident is accurate? High, Medium, Low or None	8.50%
Summary	nvarchar	Brief summary of the incident	93.40%
Reference	nvarchar	URL or internal ticketing system ID	94.00%
Notes	nvarchar	Enter any additional details deemed noteworthy	5.30%

7 Conclusion

Since data-driven security management effectively helps organisations to understand their situations in terms of Cyber security, extracting knowledge from Cyber security datasets has been a crucial point in recent years towards this understanding. In this paper, we have given a representation of understanding if and to what extent useful free community Cyber security datasets can be to organisations when developing a Cyber security plan. We also showed the possibility of answering the fundamental question, *"in an incident, who did what to which asset or victim, and with what result and impact"*, with a subset of the VCDB dataset. A quantitative analysis was given, which measured the amount of information for each element of the extracted sub-scheme corresponding to the above question.

As a result, one can roughly illustrate quantity of information present in the various parts of the question, as follows:

93%	97%	100%	90%	56%	97%	0.35%

"in an incident, who did what to which asset or victim, and with what result and impact"

The significance of these results lies in the wider context of risk analysis. Risk is often defined as the product of the probability of a bad event happening and the impact of that event. Whilst the amount of information available in answering the majority of the above question helps calculate the probability part of risk, we find that we are quite poorly informed about the impact part.

For future research, we plan to apply more statistical calculations to the VERIS dataset, in particular to measure not just the quantity of information but also its quality. In fact, one important step is to develop open source tools that would automate such evaluations. We also plan to perform similar analyses for other open datasets, such as [4,5,11,13], and also importantly, for proprietary (non-open) data that would be more company-specific.

We consider this kind of research as initial experiments towards a more formal framework for evaluating quantity and quality of open data, where we would define a methodology for performing such evaluations.

References

1. Akkuzu, G., Aziz, B., et al.: Feature analysis on the containment time for cyber security incidents. In: 2018 International Conference on Wavelet Analysis and Pattern Recognition (ICWAPR), pp. 262–269. IEEE (2018)
2. Aziz, B.: Towards open data-driven evaluation of access control policies. Comput. Stan. Interfaces **56**, 13–26 (2018)
3. Cano, L.A.: A modern approach to security: Using systems engineering and data-driven decision-making. In: 2016 IEEE International Carnahan Conference on Security Technology (ICCST), pp. 1–5, October 2016
4. Center for Applied Internet Data Analysis: CAIDA Data. http://www.caida.org/data/overview/. Accessed 14 Aug 2017
5. CERT Coordination Center: CERT Vulnerability Notes Database. http://www.kb.cert.org/vuls. Accessed 14 Aug 2017
6. Cordero, C.G., Vasilomanolakis, E., Milanov, N., Koch, C., Hausheer, D., Mühlhäuser, M.: Id2t: a diy dataset creation toolkit for intrusion detection systems. In: 2015 IEEE Conference on Communications and Network Security (CNS), pp. 739–740. IEEE (2015)
7. Dandurand, L., Serrano, O.S.: Towards improved cyber security information sharing. In: 2013 5th International Conference on Cyber Conflict (CYCON 2013), pp. 1–16, June 2013
8. Johnson, C.S., Badger, M.L., Waltermire, D.A., Snyder, J., Skorupka, C.: Guide to Cyber Threat Information Sharing. Technical Report 800–150, NIST (2016)
9. Liang, G., Weller, S.R., Zhao, J., Luo, F., Dong, Z.Y.: The 2015 Ukraine blackout: implications for false data injection attacks. IEEE Trans. Power Syst. **32**(4), 3317–3318 (2017)
10. Los Alamos National Laboratory: Cyber Security Science Open Data Sets. http://csr.lanl.gov/data/. Accessed 14 Aug 2017
11. Sconzo, M.: SecRepo.com - Samples of Security Related Data. http://www.secrepo.com. Accessed 14 Aug 2017
12. Moses, T.: eXtensible Access Control Markup Language (XACML) Version 2.0. OASIS Standard (2005)

13. Moustafa, N., Slay, J.: Unsw-nb15: a comprehensive data set for network intrusion detection systems (unsw-nb15 network data set). In: 2015 Military Communications and Information Systems Conference (MilCIS), pp. 1–6, November 2015
14. Sangster, B., et al.: Toward instrumenting network warfare competitions to generate labeled datasets. In: CSET (2009)
15. Serrano, O., Dandurand, L., Brown, S.: On the design of a cyber security data sharing system. In: Proceedings of the 2014 ACM Workshop on Information Sharing & #38; Collaborative Security, pp. 61–69, WISCS 2014. ACM, New York (2014)
16. Tejay, G., Dhillon, G., Chin, A.G.: Data quality dimensions for information systems security: a theoretical exposition (Invited Paper). In: Dowland, P., Furnell, S., Thuraisingham, B., Wang, X.S. (eds.) Security Management, Integrity, and Internal Control in Information Systems. IICIS 2004. IFIP International Federation for Information Processing, vol. 193. Springer, Boston (2005). https://doi.org/10.1007/0-387-31167-X_2
17. Thakkar, H., Endris, K.M., Gimenez-Garcia, J.M., Debattista, J., Lange, C., Auer, S.: Are linked datasets fit for open-domain question answering? a quality assessment. In: Proceedings of the 6th International Conference on Web Intelligence, Mining and Semantics, p. 19. ACM (2016)
18. VERIZON: The Vocabulary for Event Recording and Incident Sharing (VERIS). http://veriscommunity.net/. Accessed 21 Nov 2016
19. VERIZON: VERIS Community Database. http://vcdb.org/. Accessed 21 Nov 2016
20. Zaveri, A., Rula, A., Maurino, A., Pietrobon, R., Lehmann, J., Auer, S.: Quality assessment for linked data: a survey. Seman. Web 7(1), 63–93 (2016)

Semantic Data Integration and Quality Assurance of Thematic Maps in the German Federal Agency for Cartography and Geodesy

Timo Homburg[1][✉], Sebastian Steppan[1], and Falk Würriehausen[2]

[1] Mainz University of Applied Sciences,
Lucy-Hillebrand-Straße 2, 55128 Mainz, Germany
{timo.homburg,sebastian.steppan}@hs-mainz.de
[2] Bundesamt für Kartographie und Geodäsie,
Richard-Strauss-Allee 11, 60598 Frankfurt am Main, Germany

Abstract. In this paper we present a new concept of geospatial quality assurance that is currently planned to be implemented in the German Federal Agency of Cartography and Geodesy. Linked open data is being enriched with Semantic Web data in order to create thematic maps relevant to the population. We evaluate the quality of such enriched maps using a standardized process and look at the possible impacts of enriching Semantic Web data with open data sets of the Federal Agency of Cartography and Geodesy.

Keywords: Data quality · GIS · Semantic technologies · Reasoning · OpenStreetMap · Official authority data

1 Introduction

The German Federal Agency for Cartography and Geodesy (BKG)[1] has the duty to collect certain geographic data of the federal states of Germany and to publish them as open data in various contexts. The collection of geodata can be done without a thematic context (e.g. building footprints without additional information) or within a thematic context possibly involving third-party datasources (e.g. data of the bureau for statistics) which are currently manually integrated using traditional RDBMS databases like PostGIS [28]. While BKG did not contribute to linked open data (LOD) in the past, the possibility to create LOD out of the existing datasets in order to provide datasets for other public agencies like the German National Library[2] relying heavily on a LOD infrastructure is becoming increasingly relevant. Linked Open Data also provides the possibility to enrich existing open data datasets (e.g. maps) with thematic content in a very easy fashion, as ontologies provide the opportunity to query sometimes

---

[1] https://www.bkg.bund.de/DE/Home/home.html.
[2] http://www.dnb.de/DE/Standardisierung/GND/gnd_node.html.

© Springer Nature Switzerland AG 2019
W. Abramowicz and R. Corchuelo (Eds.): BIS 2019 Workshops, LNBIP 373, pp. 543–555, 2019.
https://doi.org/10.1007/978-3-030-36691-9_46

georeferenced and more importantly thematically categorized data. However, as LOD repositories can very often be edited by anyone, a concept of quality assurance for such kinds of data is needed when being used in an official context. Our publication is therefore aimed at presenting a quality assurance concept for authority geospatial data which has been enriched with Semantic Web data in order to provide a user with a confidence score of data annotations. In order to achieve this we firstly discuss the State Of The Art in geospatial data quality in Sect. 2, elaborate on how thematic maps are created in BKG, explain our quality assurance approach in Sect. 3 and discuss a prototypical implementation of this approach in Sect. 4. Section 4.2.1 explains how our approach is used in a first real-world usecase concerning school data and how this can benefit end users of geographical authority data in Germany today. In Sect. 5 we summarize our results, elaborate on how to extend the approach to other usecases and by including other data quality concepts and discuss the potential success of a reversed process. Would it improve the quality of open data if BKG data was to be integrated in LOD and in what ways?

2   State Of The Art

In this section we revisit the State Of The Art in geospatial data quality, its measurement and the concept and intention of thematic maps.

2.1   Thematic Maps

[30] defines a thematic map as "a map that focuses on a specific theme or subject area". In that regard thematic maps highlight spatial patterns which may be used for comparison purposes or statistics and provide specific information about certain aspects of particular locations. This definition contrasts with the definition of general reference maps in which a variety of phenomena e.g. political map, points of interest or geological features might be highlighted all at once. Using the OpenStreetMap database [27] it is possible to create general reference maps like the default maplayer Mapnik visible on the main page of OpenStreetMap in which many points of interests and features are highlighted. Examples for thematic maps using OpenStreetMap content can be found in the various subcommunities of OSM like OpenSeaMap[3] or OpenRailwayMap[4]. Naturally, thematic maps are more sensitive to the provision or lack of certain data attributes, as in contrast to general reference maps, they have a particular focus which needs to be conveyed accurately to the respective user of the map.

2.2   Geospatial Data Provision

Even though geospatial data can be provided using Semantic Web technologies using for example triple stores for data distribution as shown on the example

---

[3] http://openseamap.org/.
[4] https://www.openrailwaymap.org.

of LinkedGeoData [2] or at least as coordinate annotations in [31], the most common way of geospatial data provision is using files (SHP [10], GML [7], KML [23], GeoJSON [5]), geospatial databases [28] or customized web services like WFS [17] which provide access to a single customized relational dataset. For a major provider of geospatial data like BKG it is therefore important to give access to data in at best all aforementioned forms. This involves uplift and downlift processes of geospatial data for data conversion and interpretation the kinds of which have been discussed in [25].

2.3   Semantic Uplift/Downlift

Semantic Uplift describes a process in which a relational dataset is converted to RDF [19] or OWL [21] in order to profit from possible interlinkings and data enrichment. This can be achieved by providing ontologies for certain dataformats as shown in the SemanticGIS project[5] and can be imported on-the-fly using a simple RDF-Converter such as GMLImporter[6]. Other methods include the customized creation of schema mappings such as R2RML [20] or fully automated approaches which mainly work on limited knowledge domains [25]. Downlift processes create a relational view on a subset of the knowledge graph present in the semantic datastore and export this relational view in the formats which are needed by the user (e.g. GML) while potentially validating the output with given schema validation processes. In the context of this publication, a downlift can also become the data basis of a thematic map, which is accessed in a typical export format like for example GeoJSON.

2.4   Geospatial Data Quality

The ISO8000 [16] standard definition describes data quality as "Quality is the degree to which a set of inherent characteristics fulfils requirements". Categories of geospatial data quality are commonly defined as Lineage [32], Positional Accuracy [9], Attribute Accuracy [11], Logical Consistency [18], Geometry and Attribute Completeness [12], Temporal Accuracy [6] and Semantic Accuracy [29]. As pointed out in [14] it is possible to extend this data quality definition if thematic attributes are needed to be evaluated by creating requirement profiles. As the aim of this publication is to present a new data quality concept to be used in BKG, both thematic attributes and the traditional ways of data evaluation are of importance. Currently, if geospatial data quality is evaluated in BKG, mainly said traditional means of geospatial data quality are evaluated pointing out only issues of the geometrical part of the dataset.

2.5   Equivalent Geometry Matching

In order to compare data quality in a certain way in a semantic context, firstly a data integration of non-semantic and semantic data sources needs to

---

[5] https://github.com/i3mainz/SemGISOntologies.

[6] https://github.com/i3mainz/GMLImporter.

be approached. Many approaches for interlinking and matching of relational to RDF data have been proposed in the literature. Commonly, a dataset is combined with Semantic Web data using appropriate vocabularies and is then to be matched using an appropriate algorithm or an appropriate manually created schema mapping sometimes formalized in language specifications such as R2RML [20].

Sometimes, mappings may already be provided by the respective communities, as can be shown on the example of Wikidata and OpenStreetMap which interlink equivalent properties using the equivalence relation wdt:P1282 (osm tag or key) and can be queried using an appropriate query language such as (Geo)SPARQL [3,24]. The given mapping provides the basis to match equivalent objects in a semantic web context and the basis for matching equivalent descriptions when an object pair has been matched.

3   Modelling

In this section we outline the construction of a semantic integrational system which includes and can integrate open data as well as linked data and how an automated data quality assurance and integration concept can help us to ensure the applicability of said datasources for thematic maps.

3.1   Semantic Integrational System

A semantic integrational system builds the foundation to store, quality assure and use semantically enriched datasets. Figure 1 shows the common components of a semantic integrational system. On the left, data sources in various formats are integrated into the triple store using one of the approaches explained in Sect. 2.5. If appropriate vocabularies have been used interlinks to other knowledge bases allow the enrichment of integrated data. The triple store then provides the basis for downlift methods e.g. exports of customized datasets, of views such as thematic maps, or as a service provider for other IT applications and service providers. In the integrational process, the following ontologies support the system in various aspects. The GeoSPARQL ontology [3] helps to model geometrical features in a unified way, the provenance ontology [22] gives help to cover the updating and data modification cycle, as BKG data is updated in regular intervals and the daQ vocabulary [8] as well as the QUDT ontology [13] provide the basis to cover data quality metrics and measurements.

3.2   A Quality Assurance Concept for Thematic Maps

Our quality assurance system for thematic maps combines general means of data quality measurements with thematic map attributes. [26] suggests the creation of thematic clusters on top of relational geospatial data for the purpose of selecting criteria for a successful automated semantic interpretation and integration. Such thematic clusters would highlight data columns with most semantic significance

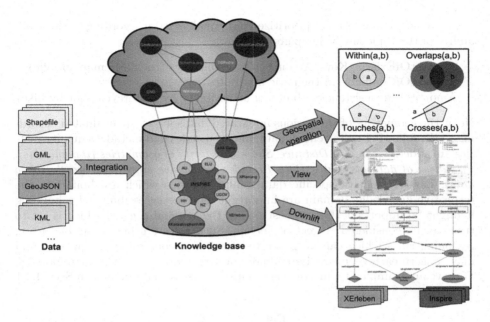

Fig. 1. Architecture Overview building up on the model of a semantic GIS system briefly shown in [15] highlighting integration, data storage and examplary downlift to INSPIRE [4] and XErleben [1]

and would be prioritized on import as well as subsequently when evaluated using quality assurance methods. Naturally, thematic clusters are also possible views for an upcoming thematic map implementation and could force an individual quality analysis as proposed in [14].

From Thematic Clusters to Quality Assurance. Having defined thematic clusters, i.e. relevant attributes for the proper creation and visualization of the thematic map, we follow [14] definition of requirement profiles to model requirements of the attributes describing the respective thematic cluster. We give an example of a map of the accessibility of a building given a set of keys (Listing 1.1) that signify accessibility in the sense of the presence of facilities to accommodate the respective means of transport.

Listing 1.1. Accessibility example

```
1   bicycle, car, bus, email, website, motorcycle
```

We define positive and negative outcomes in terms of quality of values for the respective keys as shown in Listing 1.2.

Listing 1.2. Positive and negative attribute descriptions. Here accurate representations receive 1 and inaccurate receive a 0 rating

```
{"bicycle":{"yes":1,"no":1,"unknown":0,"restricted":0.5}}
```

Next, we define a per-object prioritized data quality score according to the availability of the topic key/value pairs as follows:

– AmountOfExistingKeys/AmountOfAvailableKeys (thematic map specific)
– AmountOfConflicts (in thematic attributes)
– AmountOfInconsistencies (building accessibility by motorcycle, not by bike)

Next, the geometries of the various integrated datasources are evaluated according to the following more general data quality metrics and metadata quality metrics are added: *Geometry Distance, Shape Similarity of geometries (if applicable), Freshness of datasets* and a *Data Provider confidence score (trustworthy/open data)*. Lastly, thematic-specific data quality metrics which are bound to the respective knowledge domain are important. For the accessibility of a building it might be important that at least one of the attributes given which is set to true can be considered correct or certain. Such rules are best described using reasoning rules which can be generated from user constraint descriptions and may concern each geometry individually or targeted at the entire map globally. We give an example of a metric combination to assess data quality in Sect. 4.2.1

Fig. 2. Ontology ecosystem

Data Quality Representation
Data quality parameters are represented using an ontological structure in the knowledge base as shown in Fig. 2. Besides the integrated data the ecosystem includes data quality metrics and their units, data quality measurements from the aforementioned metrics, provenance information as well as evaluation logic parts which include reasoning rules, usecase descriptions (the topic of the map), the metrics to apply and the thematic attributes to apply the metrics on. Given the knowledge base and the data quality metric rules, the knowledge base can reason about the usefulness of data contents in every thematic map context included.

4   Implementation and Showcase

This section describes the proposed implementation of our approach and outlines the used architecture.

4.1   Data Integration

We integrate data according to [25] by matching a BKG dataset using a predefined mapping to attributes in usually Wikidata (Listing 1.3) This gives us the ability to predefine equivalent attributes.

Listing 1.3. Example schema manually created mapping. Name depicts the column name of the relational data set; prop the property type to convert to e.g. AnnotationProperty; propiri the URI of the property and the range of the property to be created

```
<column name="schulname" prop="annotation" propiri="http://www.w3.org
   /2000/01/rdf–schema#label" range="http://www.w3.org/2001/XMLSchema
   #string"/>
```

Geometry Matching
Equivalent geometrical representations in other ontologies are either matched via properties like the OSM wikidata tag[7] or via a positional and attribute matching approach described in [25]. This leaves us with a set of interlinked equivalent representations of the same geometry with an arbitrary amount of equivalent or conflicting attributes as shown in Fig. 3.

Conflicting and Complementing Attributes
Conflicting attributes will be considered by the quality metric calculation described in the previous section if they fall into any of the thematic clusters which are necessary to display the thematic map. As they add uncertainty to the quality of the overall map, they contribute to the overall quality score of the map. Complementing attributes will be identified during the semantic integrational process and can serve as the basis for potential thematic views of a map.

---

[7] https://taginfo.openstreetmap.org/keys/wikidata.

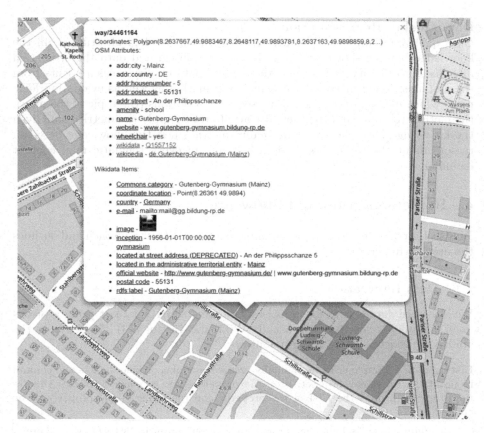

Fig. 3. Conflicting and matching attributes on the example of OpenStreetMap and Wikidata. Green colored items indicate a match, yellow colored items a value conflict, red and dark blue colored items an interlink and light blue items non-linked and therefore possibly complementing data (Color figure online)

4.2 Applications

In this section applications of the integrational and data quality assurance concept are presented on the example of school integration. We present three thematic maps of schools which can be automatically generated using our semantic integration system. Using the aforementioned quality assurance methods we show for one of the maps how the quality assurance will lead to either hints at uncertain map data or at the exclusion of problematic datasets from the map.

4.2.1 Integration of Schools

In Germany, the regulation of schools and the collection of school data is the task of the several German states. BKG recently received the task of creating a thematic map to incorporate schools and school related information. The first task is therefore to integrate school datasets of 16 German states which may be present. Table 1 presents an example of a school data file which contents commonly vary across the 16 states.

Table 1. School integration data excerpt, columns translated to English

Schoolname	Schooltype	Students	Address	Responsible entity
Karl Liebknecht Schule	Primary school	481	Gluckstraße 8	Potsdam

In Wikidata we commonly find annotations about historic information (*P571 inception, P1435 heritage category*) and accessibility information (Accessibility: *P856 official website, P17 image*) which can be potential sources for thematic maps. In OpenStreetMap we find the following attributes *name, start_date, website, address data, school type* and more detailed accessibility information such as *foot, bicycle, website, wheelchair, motorcycle, motorcar*.

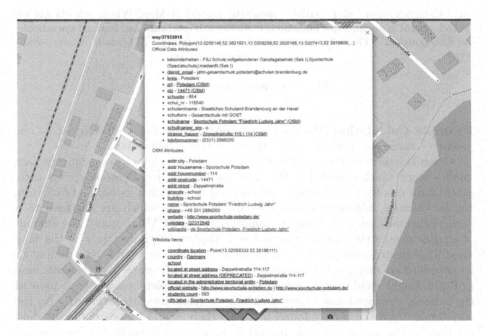

Fig. 4. School Interlinkage Screen: Official data (first part) is set into context with data from OSM (second part) and data from Wikidata (third part)

A customized map[8] also displayed in Fig. 4 shows the interlinkage between OpenStreetMap and Wikidata concerning schools.

---

[8] https://i3mainz.github.io/semgistestbench/school.html.

Thematic Map Creation: From the data given above thematic maps can be created on-the-fly as downlift export using the semantic integrational system. We show three examples in Figs. 5a, b and 6. The first map is based on BKG data only, the second and third map are only possible using data integration from either OpenStreetMap or Wikidata.

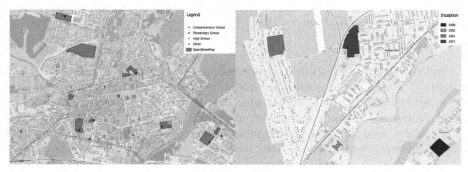

(a) Categorization Map (BKG data): Which school types and specializations can be distinguished? (Thematic cluster: schul-typ)   (b) Historical Map: Which schools are of historic importance and how old are schools within Germany? (Thematic cluster: wikidata:inception)

Fig. 5. Thematic map examples

Example Calculation: We show an example data quality metric set of one geometry using our method for the thematic accessibility map.

Given the data quality metrics in Table 2, we calculate a per-geometry data quality score which is added to the ontological structure. Reasoning rules categorize data quality metric results into several classes such as *bkg:CanBeShown*, *bkg:DoNotShow*, *bkg:ShowWithQualityIssueStatement* which are assigned to a defined thematic context. Using an appropriate GeoSPARQL query, the amount of eligible geometries can be assessed and displayed appropriately in the map view. This ensures only geometrical features which follow a predefined data quality standard are displayed or assigned with a confidence score. The thematic map in Fig. 6, might yield us with a low topic cluster completeness score, as some of the schools displayed have no wheelchair accessibility data attached. As the wheelchair attribute is only found in OSM, there would be no conflicting data attributes. The distance of the respective geometries is negligible (see Fig. 5a) and the freshness of the OSM data set is more recent than the governmental data. In our model this could result in the map being displayed (bkg:CanBeShown) on a geometrical feature level. However, users could be notified that the coverage of the map is of limited use to assess the accessibility of school buildings.

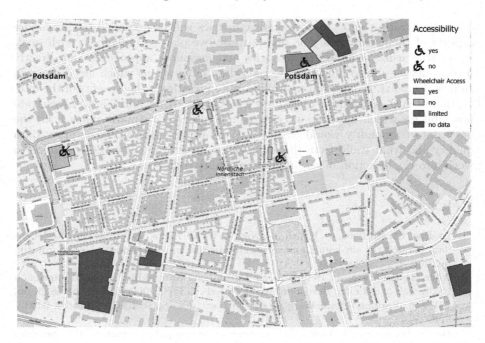

Fig. 6. School Accessibility Map (OSM): How accessible is the school by various means? (Thematic cluster: osm:wheelchair)

Table 2. Data Quality Metrics for the accessibility map calculated per geometry and aggregated for the whole map view. Priorities range from 1 to 4, whereas 1 is the most important criteria and 4 is the least important criteria. Exclusion criteria may signal that a geometry is not usable in the respective context.

Metric	Category	Description	Priority	Exclusion criteria
Topic cluster completeness	Dataset	Topic attribute available?	1	Yes
Topic cluster uncertainty	Dataset	Conflicting attributes	1	No
Distance	Geometry	Distance of geometries	4	No
Freshness	Metadata	Freshness of datasets	3	Yes

5   Conclusions and Future Work

In this publication we have described the concept of thematic map creation at the Federal Agency for Cartography and Geodesy of Germany and how thematic maps can be validated using a quality assurance concept based on a combination of thematic data quality metrics and standardized geographic data quality metrics on both an individual geometry level and aggregated on a map level. We have shown that data quality evaluation can be separated into geometrical data quality metrics, thematic cluster quality metrics and context dependent data quality metrics which can be aggregated from one geometry to a whole map view in order to get a general notion of the quality of geospatial data. In our future work, the set of data quality metrics will be extended to cover more aspects of thematic maps. For this purpose, we plan to implement such quality metrics using semantic technologies and reasoning approaches and directly use quality results to hide or show only data integrations which are deemed of sufficient quality. In addition we would like to investigate the benefits of the integration of BKG data in to open knowledge bases. We would like to investigate how and for which application cases/commonly used thematic maps from the open data community would an integration of BKG data would improve data quality and what could from the angle of a data provider like BKG be done to work into the direction of serving better quality data sets.

References

1. Andrae, C., Hinrichs, J., Kruth, F., Nienstedt, K., Pieke, B., Zolper, A.: Xerlebendatenmodell für ein kommunales freizeitkataster. In: Angewandte Geoinformatik, pp. 206–215 (2011)
2. Auer, S., Lehmann, J., Hellmann, S.: LinkedGeoData: adding a spatial dimension to the web of data. In: Bernstein, A., et al. (eds.) ISWC 2009. LNCS, vol. 5823, pp. 731–746. Springer, Heidelberg (2009). https://doi.org/10.1007/978-3-642-04930-9_46
3. Battle, R., Kolas, D.: GeoSPARQL: enabling a geospatial semantic web. Semant. Web J. **3**(4), 355–370 (2011)
4. Benner, J., Häfele, K.H., Geiger, A.: Transnational planning support by the European geodata infrastructure INSPIRE. In: Schrenk, M., Popovich, V., Zeile, P., Elisei, P. (eds.) Proceedings of REAL CORP, pp. 1009–1017 (2013)
5. Butler, H., Daly, M., Doyle, A., Gillies, S., Schaub, T., Schmidt, C.: The GeoJSON format specification. Rapport technique 67 (2008)
6. Chaudhuri, G., Clarke, K.C.: Temporal accuracy in urban growth forecasting: a study using the SLEUTH model. Trans. GIS **18**(2), 302–320 (2014)
7. Cox, S., et al.: OpenGIS® geography markup language (GML) implementation specification, version (2002)
8. Debattista, J., Lange, C., Auer, S.: DAQ, an ontology for dataset quality information. In: LDOW (2014)
9. Drummond, J.: Positional accuracy. In: Elements of Spatial Data Quality, pp. 31–58 (1995)
10. ESRI E.: Shapefile technical description. An ESRI White Paper (1998)
11. Goodchild, M.F.: Attribute accuracy. In: Elements of Spatial Data Quality, pp. 59–79 (1995)
12. Hecht, R., Kunze, C., Hahmann, S.: Measuring completeness of building footprints in OpenStreetMap over space and time. ISPRS Int. J. Geo-Inf. **2**(4), 1066–1091 (2013)
13. Hodgson, R., Keller, P., Hodges, J., Spivak, J.: QUDT-quantities, units, dimensions and data types ontologies, USA (2014)
14. Homburg, T., Boochs, F.: Situation-dependent data quality analysis for geospatial data using semantic technologies. In: Abramowicz, W., Paschke, A. (eds.) BIS 2018. LNBIP, vol. 339, pp. 566–578. Springer, Cham (2019). https://doi.org/10.1007/978-3-030-04849-5_49

15. Homburg, T., Prudhomme, C., Boochs, F.: Semantic geographic information system: integration and management of heterogeneous geodata. In: Fachaustausch Geoinformation 2018, November 2018

16. Data quality - Part 8: Information and data quality: concepts and measuring. Standard, International Organization for Standardization, Geneva, CH, November 2015

17. Jones, J., Kuhn, W., Keßler, C., Scheider, S.: Making the web of data available via web feature services. In: Huerta, J., Schade, S., Granell, C. (eds.) Connecting a Digital Europe Through Location and Place. LNGC, pp. 341–361. Springer, Cham (2014). https://doi.org/10.1007/978-3-319-03611-3_20

18. Kainz, W.: Logical consistency. In: Elements of Spatial Data Quality, pp. 109–137 (1995)

19. Klyne, G., Carroll, J.J.: Resource description framework (RDF): Concepts and abstract syntax (2006)

20. Kyzirakos, K., Vlachopoulos, I., Savva, D., Manegold, S., Koubarakis, M.: GeoTriples: a tool for publishing geospatial data as RDF graphs using R2RML mappings. In: TC/SSN@ ISWC, pp. 33–44 (2014)

21. McGuinness, D.L., Van Harmelen, F., et al.: OWL web ontology language overview. W3C Recommendation, vol. 10, no. 10, p. 2004 (2004)

22. Missier, P., Belhajjame, K., Cheney, J.: The W3C PROV family of specifications for modelling provenance metadata. In: Proceedings of the 16th International Conference on Extending Database Technology, pp. 773–776. ACM (2013)

23. Nolan, D., Lang, D.T.: Keyhole markup language. In: Nolan, D., Lang, D.T. (eds.) XML and Web Technologies for Data Sciences with R, pp. 581–618. Springer, New York (2014). https://doi.org/10.1007/978-1-4614-7900-0_17

24. Prud, E., Seaborne, A., et al.: SPARQL query language for RDF (2006)

25. Prudhomme, C., Homburg, T., Jean-Jacques, P., Boochs, F., Roxin, A., Cruz, C.: Automatic integration of spatial data into the semantic web. In: WebIST (2017)

26. Prudhomme, C., Homburg, T., Ponciano, J.J., Boochs, F., Cruz, C., Roxin, A.M.: Interpretation and automatic integration of geospatial data into the semantic web. Computing **2019**, 1–27 (2019)

27. Ramm, F., Topf, J., Chilton, S.: OpenStreetMap: Using and Enhancing the Free Map of the World. UIT Cambridge, Cambridge (2011)

28. Ramsey, P., et al.: PostGIS Manual. Refractions Research Inc., Victoria (2005)

29. Salgé, F.: Semantic accuracy. In: Elements of Spatial Data Quality, pp. 139–151 (1995)

30. Thrower, N.J.: Maps and Civilization: Cartography in Culture and Society. University of Chicago Press, Chicago (2008)

31. Vrandečić, D., Krötzsch, M.: Wikidata: a free collaborative knowledgebase. Commun. ACM **57**(10), 78–85 (2014)

32. Yue, P., He, L.: Geospatial data provenance in cyberinfrastructure. In: 2009 17th International Conference on Geoinformatics, pp. 1–4. IEEE (2009)

Technical Usability of Wikidata's Linked Data

Evaluation of Machine Interoperability and Data Interpretability

Nuno Freire[1]([⊠]) (iD) and Antoine Isaac[2,3] (iD)

[1] INESC-ID, Lisbon, Portugal
nuno.freire@tecnico.ulisboa.pt
[2] Europeana Foundation, The Hague, The Netherlands
antoine.isaac@europeana.eu
[3] Vrije Universiteit Amsterdam, Amsterdam, The Netherlands

Abstract. Wikidata is an outstanding data source with potential application in many scenarios. Wikidata provides its data openly in RDF. Our study aims to evaluate the usability of Wikidata as a data source for robots operating on the web of data, according to specifications and practices of linked data, the Semantic Web and ontology reasoning. We evaluated from the perspective of two use cases of data crawling robots, which are guided by our general motivation to acquire richer data for Europeana, a data aggregator from the Cultural Heritage domain. The first use case regards general data consumption applications based on RDF, RDF-Schema, OWL, SKOS and linked data. The second case regards applications that explore semantics relying on Schema.org and SKOS. We conclude that a human operator must assist linked data applications to interpret Wikidata's RDF because of the choices that were taken at Wikidata in the definition of its expression in RDF. The semantics of the RDF output from Wikidata is "locked-in" by the usage of Wikidata's own ontology, resulting in the need for human intervention. Wikidata is only a few steps away from high quality machine interpretation, however. It contains extensive alignment data to RDF, RDFS, OWL, SKOS and Schema.org, but a machine interpretation of those alignments can only be done if some essential Wikidata alignment properties are known.

Keywords: RDF · RDFS · OWL · Schema.org · Semantic Web

1 Introduction

Wikidata is an outstanding data source with potential application in many scenarios. Wikidata provides its data openly in RDF. Our study aims to perform an evaluation of the usability of Wikidata as a data source for robots operating on the web of data, according to specifications and practices of linked data and the semantic web. We evaluated from the perspective of two use cases of data crawling robots. The first use case regards general data consumption applications (potentially with Big Data requirements) based on RDF, RDF-Schema, OWL and linked data. The second case

© Springer Nature Switzerland AG 2019
W. Abramowicz and R. Corchuelo (Eds.): BIS 2019 Workshops, LNBIP 373, pp. 556–567, 2019.
https://doi.org/10.1007/978-3-030-36691-9_47

regards cross-domain applications that explore semantics relying on general-purpose, shared vocabularies like SKOS and Schema.org.

These uses cases are motivated by our long-term goal of using linked data as a source for descriptions of cultural heritage resources by large aggregators of cultural heritage data, in particular for Europeana[1]. Europeana has the role of facilitating the usage of digitized cultural heritage resources from and about Europe [1]. Although many European cultural heritage institutions do not yet have a presence in Europeana, it already holds metadata from over 3,700 providers, mostly libraries, museums and archives. Some of our early exploratory research on Wikidata has shown that it can be a rich source for data on cultural heritage and for digital representations of the cultural heritage objects (images, sounds, etc.). Wikidata uses an elaborate and complex data model, which supports good-quality data but may also require knowledge about the data model for its effective use. If a high demand of human resources is required, it may represent an obstacle for cultural heritage data aggregators that are already operating with limited resources, and searching for more efficient ways to perform their data aggregation needs and remain sustainable.

In our study, we tested the hypotheses that Wikidata can be used efficiently, and with leading to quality-data, by machine-based methods operating with the data technologies and practices of the Semantic Web and linked data.

We follow, in Sect. 2, by describing related work on data aggregation based on linked data in cultural heritage. Section 3 presents the linked data crawling use cases that guide us in the design of the study of Wikidata, in light of our hypothesis. The setup and workflow of the study are presented in Sect. 4. Section 5 describes our linked data crawling software's architecture, and its relevant functionality for this particular study. Section 6 presents the results and our analysis. Section 7 concludes by summarizing the conclusions of the study and presenting future work.

2 Related Work

Linked data has a large diversity of research topics related to our work. Scalability is one of the most addressed topics, with many facets such as indexing, federated querying, and aggregation. The reuse of published linked data by third parties has revealed data quality to be a challenge as well, at the level of semantics and at the level of syntax [2–4]. Significant work has been done to facilitate the reuse of linked data by aggregation and data cleaning [5, 6]. Reasoning on linked data is also an active research topic, and a comprehensive analysis and description of techniques has been published [7].

Regarding cultural heritage, although the use of linked data has been the focus of much research, most of published literature addresses mainly the aspect of the publication of linked data [8–10] and do not fully address how the aggregation approach of cultural heritage can be based on the existing published cultural heritage linked data.

---

[1] https://europeana.eu.

The most similar work to ours is that of the Dutch Digital Heritage Network[2] (NDE) and the Research and Education Space project[3] (RES). NDE is a Dutch national level program aiming to increase the social value of the collections maintained by the libraries, archives and museums in the Netherlands. NDE is still an ongoing project, and its initial proposals are based on specific APIs to enable data providers to centrally register the linked data URIs of their resources [11]. The current proposal of NDE, by being based in its own defined API, does not yet provide a solution purely based on linked data.

The Research and Education Space project finished in 2017, and has successfully aggregated a considerable number of linked data resources from cultural heritage sources. The resulting aggregated dataset can be accessed online[4], but an evaluation of its aggregation procedures and results was not published.

Generic technical solutions have been proposed by others for enabling aggregation of linked data (for example [12]). However, a standards-based approach has not yet been put into practice within cultural heritage.

The work presented in this paper is done in the context of the research activities, being carried out within the Europeana Network[5], for improving the network's efficiency and sustainability. Linked data has been identified in our past work as one of the technical solutions with application potential [13]. The work described in this paper is the continuation of a series of experiments addressing several Internet technologies for this purpose [14], particularly on the evaluation of Schema.org for cultural heritage [15] and linked data case studies [16].

3   Use Cases

Our study aims to evaluate the usability of Wikidata as a data source for robots operating on the web of data, according to specifications and practices of linked data and the semantic web. In particular, we evaluate the possibilities for machine ontology-based reasoning on the RDF output of Wikidata, for RDF-crawling processes by robots and for using its data in other general data applications.

Our study addresses two use cases, which are illustrated in Fig. 1. The use cases represent different applications that a data consumer may use for processing data at different levels of semantic detail.

- Semantic Web general application – this type of application processes data solely based on the bottom and middle layers of the Semantic Web Stack [17]. These applications use general technologies, especially "meta-languages" such as RDF, RDF-Schema, OWL and linked data for crawling linked data. These applications

---

[2] https://github.com/netwerk-digitaal-erfgoed/.

[3] https://bbcarchdev.github.io/res/.

[4] https://bbcarchdev.github.io/res/collections.

[5] The Europeana Network is a community of 1,700 experts with the shared mission to expand and improve access to Europe's digital cultural heritage, in the organization they work for and/or by contributing to shape Europeana's services.

require the use of properties that enable the crawling of linked data and the ontologies in use.

- Cross-domain semantic application – in addition to the functionality of Semantic Web general applications, this type of application processes data with additional requirements on the semantics of the data. They rely on general purpose, widely shared ontologies like the Schema.org vocabulary and SKOS (Simple Knowledge Organization System). These applications provide functionality that can be applied across different domains. They must either obtain the data that already use the ontologies they can consume (like Schema.org), or to find ontology alignments between these ontologies and the classes and properties used in the data. They thus require the ontologies used in the data source to be crawlable and to contain ontology alignments expressed in SKOS or OWL.

As mentioned in the introduction, these use cases are motivated by a third one, domain-specific semantic application, with data aggregation for Europeana being our core focus. This type of applications, while processing data like cross-domain applications, make further use of the semantics of the data. They indeed provide functionality for more specific purposes of a domain that requires a more detailed interpretation of the semantics of the data. They require the ability to convert the data to their domain-specific data model. Europeana uses the Europeana Data Model (EDM), which is its technological solution for data exchange with data providers. EDM is defined collaboratively withal the sectors represented in Europeana. Typically, they rely on ontology alignments defined by domain experts, whose work is enabled, or even only possible (regarding the amount of efforts these actors can afford), if widely used ontologies are used in the data.

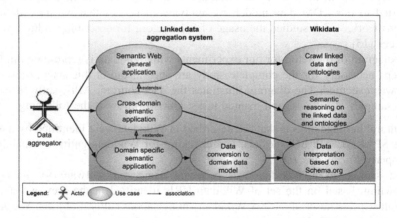

Fig. 1. Use cases of linked data consumption addressed in this study.

In this article, we present the results of our evaluation of the first two use cases. This work is the first milestone of our longer-term research interest to evaluate the use case of domain-specific applications. Note, however, that we include descriptions of the tasks involved in the third case at several points of this article, since it provides the complete context of our study.

4 Experimental Setup

To assess the usability of Wikidata as a data source for our use cases, we have developed and applied software that includes components for linked data crawling, reasoning on RDF data and ontologies, data processing and data analysis. This software represents an extra iteration over previous work done for earlier experiments with linked data crawling [16]. As data sources for our study, we used the Wikidata Ontology through its linked data publication. As we aim at eventually studying the usability of Wikidata for the Europeana case, we focus on Wikidata resources that correspond to the Europeana dataset of cultural heritage resources.

The general overview of the study is as follows:

- Cultural heritage objects that are described in both Europeana and Wikidata were identified. The corresponding subsets were harvested for supporting our study.
- The Wikidata sample was converted to Schema.org. The conversion was based on the ontology alignments to Schema.org that exist in the RDF of Wikidata properties and classes. Wikidata classes were also converted, when present as 'object' in RDF triples. The RDF data regarding Wikidata's classes contains alignments to equivalent Schema.org classes. When an alignment with Schema.org was not found, an equivalence was searched in a more generic property/class by crawling up the hierarchy of Wikidata's classes and properties.

In future work, the data from Wikidata, after conversion to Schema.org, will be converted to our EDM data model, by applying mappings that we have defined in previous work, which studied the usage of Schema.org for describing cultural heritage resources [15].

A diagram of the setup for our experiments with Wikidata is represented in Fig. 2. All steps necessary for the complete study are shown, but at this stage, only part of setup was executed. The diagram illustrates the data sources, APIs, software components, samples, dataflows, and manual tasks. Our workflow is the following:

- Cultural heritage objects that are described in Wikidata were identified by querying the SPARQL API of Wikidata, and checking for Wikidata entities containing the property *Europeana ID*[6].
- The sample from Wikidata was collected using our software for linked data crawling, based on the set of Wikidata URIs identified in the previous step. The result was a dataset of 11.798 Wikidata entities about cultural objects. We actually identified 77.103 Wikidata entities containing the *Europeana ID*, however, during the course of our study, we identified that the values were invalid or obsolete in 65.305 of the cases, and we removed those entities from the subset of Wikidata we used.

---

[6] https://www.wikidata.org/wiki/Property:P727.

- The values of the *Europeana ID* property were converted to their corresponding URIs at Europeana's linked data, by a simple process of prefixing the property value (a uniform URI structure is used by Europeana).
- The corresponding subset of Europeana was collected, also by our linked data crawler, based on the set of Europeana URIs. In future work, the Europeana subset will used for performing an evaluation of the data quality obtained from Wikidata.
- The Wikidata sample was further processed by conversion to Schema.org using our RDF converter software. At this stage of the workflow, we made our evaluation of the use cases for Semantic Web and cross-domain applications, and prepared reports about the RDF data, and about difficulties found during the crawling of Wikidata and the automatic interpretation of its RDF data.

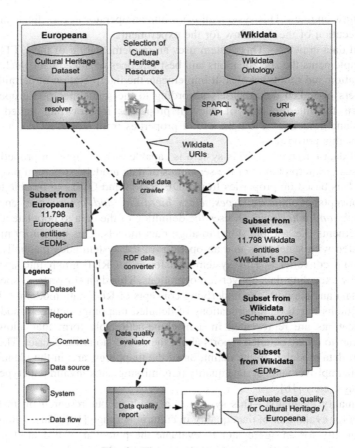

Fig. 2. The experimental setup

The remaining tasks of the workflow will be part of our future work. The Schema. org sample will then be converted to EDM, using the same software for conversion of RDF data. At this point, we will have two comparable subsets from both sources:

Wikidata's subset represented in EDM RDF; and Europeana's subset, directly obtained in EDM RDF. To measure the level of quality of the data, we will apply another software component, which implements a metric for measuring the completeness of the data in EDM. The software generates a report that will support our final evaluation of the cultural heritage use case.

5   Architecture of the System for Linked Data Aggregation

The architecture of the system supporting the execution of our experiment is illustrated in Fig. 3. The whole system is composed of 5 subsystems, supported by data repositories and resources that support its functions. The subsystems are the following:

- Workflow engine – This system allows a human operator to coordinate and monitor the execution of the workflow for the experiment.
- Linked data crawler – This system uses an implementation of the HTTP protocol, and implements the specifications and best practices of linked data, such as content negotiation and robots.txt files. It implements the interpretation of definitions of the members of linked data datasets according to the guidelines of Europeana[7], thus supports the interpretation of relevant properties for crawling linked data. The Europeana guidelines allow the use of properties from VoID, DCAT and Schema. org, for this purpose.
- Linked data interpreter – This system is capable of reasoning on properties for the purposes of interpretation of the semantics of data models' structural properties and URIs. It is based on properties from RDF, RDFS and OWL, to be able to interpret the concepts of *equality*, *types*, *class hierarchy and inheritance*, and *property hierarchy and inheritance*. It uses the definition of the data to populate a repository of statements (i.e. a triple store) to align data models. This repository may also be populated with statements that an operator of the system adds manually.
- RDF data converter – This system transforms an RDF graph into another RDF graph by executing data conversion operations. This data converter is specialized in RDF data and supports the underlying concepts of RDF data modeling. It converts RDF graphs based on specifications of detailed mappings between models. These specifications are represented in a machine-actionable form that allow the data converter to create detailed reports about the conversion of a dataset. These reports support data modelers in the definition of the mappings, and in the identification of possible improvements of data quality (e.g. missing data, invalid data types, missing mappings, etc.) [16].
- Data quality evaluator –This system is a result of our research on mathematical metrics for evaluation of data quality in cultural heritage [18]. This system provides functionality for an aggregator to evaluate the potential of a dataset for its own purposes. It is currently being implemented and will be applied in this experiment. The system functions based on plugins that implement particular metrics or

---

[7] https://github.com/nfreire/Open-Data-Acquisition-Framework/blob/master/opaf-documentation/ SpecifyingLodDatasetForEuropeana.md.

validations, and generates informative reports for the aggregator. In this study with Wikidata and Europeana, we will implement plugins for validation of EDM, and metrics of data completeness, whose definition has been in discussion within the Europeana Data Quality Committee[8].

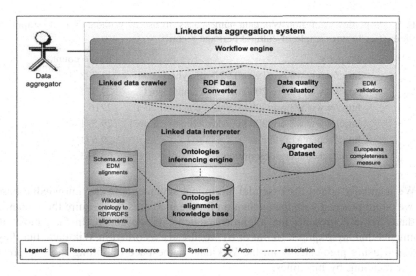

Fig. 3. High level system architecture of the linked data aggregation system

6   Results

In this section, we present the results of the study. It is important to note that the results of our study were gathered and checked for the last time on 12 of April 2019.

We observed that Wikidata's RDF presents some difficulties for cross-domain applications to aggregate and use the data. The difficulties are due to Wikidata's RDF using a very limited number of general data processing properties. Most of the properties in use, are labels, that are mostly useful for human users.

Wikidata has chosen to use properties from its own ontology instead of equivalent RDF, RDF-Schema, OWL or SKOS properties. Without some human intervention to support the application in interpreting Wikidata's properties, it would be impossible to use the data for any of our use cases. The count of occurrences of properties, in the collected dataset, of other namespaces than Wikidata's, are listed in Table 1. The main limiting aspect that blocks an advanced process in the interpretation of the data is the use of *rdf:type*. It is used just to state that the RDF resource is an Item from the Wikibase ontology (http://wikiba.se/ontology#Item), and for further types, the property *wdt:P31* is used. An advanced application that is able to search in all used properties'

---

[8] https://pro.europeana.eu/project/data-quality-committee.

RDF resources, could bypass this limitation and interpret the data, but not in the case of Wikidata. This impossibility comes from the fact that Wikidata's RDF resources' URIs are not resolvable in all cases. In the case of property wdt:*P31*, it is stated in the data as http://www.wikidata.org/prop/direct/P31, which is not resolvable. The resolvable corresponding URI is http://www.wikidata.org/entity/P31.

Table 1. Properties, from non-Wikidata namespaces, in use in Wikidata's RDF output, of the 11.798 entities in our sample of cultural heritage records.

Property	Usage count
http://www.w3.org/1999/02/22-rdf-syntax-ns#type	11.798
http://www.w3.org/2000/01/rdf-schema#label	29.571
http://www.w3.org/2004/02/skos/core#altLabel	2716
http://www.w3.org/2004/02/skos/core#prefLabel	29.571
http://schema.org/name	29.571
http://schema.org/description	64.563

We manually added the essential alignment statements in our knowledge base, so that we could proceed with the evaluation for the use cases that require the semantics of the data. Table 2 presents the alignment statements we added. In fact, most of the alignments that are required (6 out of 8) are already recorded in Wikidata, but they are expressed using predicates from the Wikidata namespace inhibiting the interpretation of their meaning by machines.

Table 2. Ontology alignments that were necessary for interpretation of semantics in Wikidata.

Aligned property	Wikidata property	Alignment existing in Wikidata (as wdt:P1628 or wdt:P1709)
rdf:type	wdt:P31(instance of)	*rdf:type*
rdf:Property	wdt:Q18616576 (instance of)	–
rdfs:Class	wdt:Q32753077 (instance of)	–
owl:sameAs	wdt:P2888 (exact match)	*skos:exactMatch*
owl:equivalentClass	wdt:P1709 (equivalent class)	*owl:equivalentClass*
owl:equivalentProperty	wdt:P1628 (equivalent property)	*owl:equivalentProperty*
rdfs:subClassOf	wdt:P279 (subclass of)	*rdfs:subClassOf*
rdfs:subPropertyOf	wdt:P1647 (subproperty of)	*rdfs:subPropertyOf*

For readability purposes, in this text we abbreviate namespaces as follows: *rdf* for http://www. w3.org/1999/02/22-rdf-syntax-ns; *rdfs* for http://www.w3.org/2000/01/rdf-schema; *owl* for http://www.w3.org/2002/07/owl; *skos* for http://www.w3.org/2004/02/skos/core; *schema* for http://schema.org/; *wikibase* for http://wikiba.se/ontology; *wd* for http://www.wikidata.org/entity/; *wdt* for http://www.wikidata.org/prop/direct/.

To evaluate the possibility of acquiring Schema.org semantics from Wikidata, we have used the equivalence relations that are stated in the RDF of the classes and properties' in Wikidata. When a resource does not state an equivalence with Schema.

org, our linked data interpreter navigates the ontology's class/property hierarchy searching for an equivalence. If one is found the interpreter assumes it by inheritance.

To perform this evaluation for cross-domain applications, we faced the same difficulty with Wikidata's RDF – the URI's of properties are not resolvable. It was only possible for us to continue the study by manually adapting the code of the linked data interpreter to convert the URI's to the ones that Wikidata is able to resolve.

An additional difficulty we have found, regards the interpretation of Wikidata's class and property hierarchy. It results from Wikidata using its own properties to state the class and property hierarchy. As in the first use case, we had to manually inject the essential alignment statements, which enable the interpretation of Wikidata's class and property structures (the alignments are listed in Table 2). Obtaining the equivalences between the classes and properties from Wikidata with Schema.org, faced the same difficulty – a Wikidata property is used to state the equivalences.

Table 3 presents statistics about the ontology alignments to Schema.org we found in Wikidata, considering only the classes and properties present in our subset. The listing of the individual alignments found may be consulted online[9]. In general, we found alignments for around 50% of the data elements in the sample. which, in our opinion, is a good indicative that many applications would be able to make use of the structured data. Particularly regarding classes, we found 102 distinct ones in use in the sample, 57% of which had alignments to Schema.org – 49% are direct alignments and 7,9% are alignments inherited from super classes. Regarding properties, we found 266 distinct ones in use in the sample, 44% of which had alignments to Schema.org – only direct alignments were found for properties.

Table 3. Statistics of the ontology alignments to Schema.org found in Wikidata, for the classes and properties in use in Wikidata's cultural heritage subset used in this study.

Type of data elements	Number of distinct data elements in Wikidata sample	Existing alignments	Existing alignments by inheritance	Total alignments
Classes	102	50 (49%)	7 (7,9%)	57 (55,9%)
Properties	266	44 (16,5%)	0 (0%)	44 (16,5%)

7   Conclusion and Future Work

Currently, a human operator must assist linked data applications to interpret Wikidata's RDF, thus it requires training on the data model behind Wikidata and its expression in RDF.

Our assessment is that Wikidata is only a few steps away from high quality machine interpretation, since there exists, in Wikidata, enough alignment data to RDF,

---

[9] https://github.com/nfreire/data-aggregation-lab/blob/master/data-aggregation-casestudies/documentation/wikidata/SchemaOrg-ontology-alignments-listing.md.

RDFS, OWL, SKOS and Schema.org. Unfortunately, the semantics of the RDF output of Wikidata is *locked-in* the usage of predicates from Wikidata's own ontology, making them uninterpretable for data crawlers based on of properties for general data processing that the Semantic Web relies on.

The second difficulty is the use of namespaces that are not resolvable for Wikidata's properties. The reasons for this use of namespaces are documented [19], and justified as a way to represent characteristics of the predicates or objects of the triples. This practice is not standard, however, and other standard options are available that could be applied to address the reasons behind it.

We will continue our evaluation of Wikidata in our future work, by evaluating the use case where detailed semantics is required, using the specific domain of the cultural heritage network of Europeana, as we briefly described throughout this article. In later work, we expect to perform similar studies as this one, but on linked data published by data providers from the Europeana network.

Acknowledgements. This work was partly supported by Portuguese national funds through Fundação para a Ciência e a Tecnologia (FCT) with reference UID/CEC/50021/2019, and by the European Commission under contract number 30-CE-0885387/00-80.e.

References

1. Niggermann, E., Cousins, J., Sanderhoff, M.: Europeana Business Plan 2018 'Democratizing culture'. Europeana Foundation (2018). https://pro.europeana.eu/files/Europeana_Professional/Publications/Europeana_Business_Plan_2018.pdf
2. Rietveld, L.: Publishing and Consuming Linked Data: Optimizing for the Unknown. Studies on the Semantic Web, vol. 21. IOS Press, Amsterdam (2016)
3. Radulovic, F., Mihindukulasooriya, N., García-Castro, R., Gomez-Pérez, A.: A comprehensive quality model for linked data. In: Semantic Web, vol. 9, no. 1/2018. IOS Press (2018)
4. Beek, W., Rietveld, L., Ilievski, F., Schlobach, S.: LOD lab: scalable linked data processing. In: Pan, J., et al. (eds.) Reasoning Web 2016. LNCS, vol. 9885, pp. 124–155. Springer, Cham (2017). https://doi.org/10.1007/978-3-319-49493-7_4
5. Beek, W., Rietveld, L., Schlobach, S., van Harmelen, F.: LOD Laundromat: why the Semantic Web needs centralization (even if we don't like it). In: IEEE Internet Computing, vol. 20, no. 2. IEEE (2016)
6. Fernández, J.D., Beek, W., Martínez-Prieto, M.A., Arias, M.: LOD-a-lot. In: d'Amato, C., et al. (eds.) ISWC 2017. LNCS, vol. 10588, pp. 75–83. Springer, Cham (2017). https://doi.org/10.1007/978-3-319-68204-4_7
7. Hogan, A.: Reasoning Techniques for the Web of Data. Studies on the Semantic Web, vol. 19. IOS Press, Amsterdam (2014)
8. Simou, N., Chortaras, A., Stamou, G., Kollias, S.: Enriching and publishing cultural heritage as linked open data. In: Ioannides, M., Magnenat-Thalmann, N., Papagiannakis, G. (eds.) Mixed Reality and Gamification for Cultural Heritage, pp. 201–223. Springer, Cham (2017). https://doi.org/10.1007/978-3-319-49607-8_7
9. Hyvönen, E.: Publishing and using cultural heritage linked data on the semantic web. In: Ding, Y., Groth, P. (eds.) Synthesis Lectures on the Semantic Web: Theory and Technology (2012). https://doi.org/10.2200/s00452ed1v01y201210wbe003

10. Jones, E., Seikel, M. (eds.): Linked Data for Cultural Heritage. Facet Publishing, London (2016)
11. Meijer, E., Valk, S.: A distributed network of heritage information. White paper (2017). https://github.com/netwerk-digitaal-erfgoed/general-documentation/blob/master/Whitepaper %20A%20distributed%20network%20of%20heritage%20information.md
12. Rietveld, L., Verborgh, R., Beek, W., Vander Sande, M., Schlobach, S.: Linked data-as-a-service: the semantic web redeployed. In: Gandon, F., Sabou, M., Sack, H., d'Amato, C., Cudré-Mauroux, P., Zimmermann, A. (eds.) ESWC 2015. LNCS, vol. 9088, pp. 471–487. Springer, Cham (2015). https://doi.org/10.1007/978-3-319-18818-8_29
13. Freire, N., Manguinhas, H., Isaac, A., Robson, G., Howard, J.B.: Web technologies: a survey of their applicability to metadata aggregation in cultural heritage. In: Chan, L., Loizides, F. (eds.) Expanding Perspectives on Open Science: Communities. Cultures and Diversity in Concepts and Practices. IOS Press, Amsterdam (2018). Inf. Serv. Use J. **37**(4)
14. Freire, N., Robson, G., Howard, J.B., Manguinhas, H., Isaac, A.: Metadata aggregation: assessing the application of IIIF and sitemaps within cultural heritage. In: Kamps, J., Tsakonas, G., Manolopoulos, Y., Iliadis, L., Karydis, I. (eds.) TPDL 2017. LNCS, vol. 10450, pp. 220–232. Springer, Cham (2017). https://doi.org/10.1007/978-3-319-67008-9_18
15. Freire, N., Charles, V., Isaac, A.: Evaluation of Schema.org for aggregation of cultural heritage metadata. In: Gangemi, A., et al. (eds.) ESWC 2018. LNCS, vol. 10843, pp. 225–239. Springer, Cham (2018). https://doi.org/10.1007/978-3-319-93417-4_15
16. Freire, N., Meijers, E., Voorburg, R., Cornelissen, R., Isaac, A., de Valk, S.: Aggregation of linked data: a case study in the cultural heritage domain. In: 2018 IEEE International Conference on Big Data (Big Data). IEEE (2018)
17. Curé, O., Blin, G. (eds.): RDF Database Systems, pp. 41–80. Morgan Kaufmann (2015). Chapter Three - RDF and the Semantic Web Stack. https://doi.org/10.1016/b978-0-12-799957-9.00003-1
18. Király, P., Stiller, J., Charles, V., Bailer, W., Freire, N.: Evaluating data quality in Europeana: metrics for multilinguality. In: Garoufallou, E., Sartori, F., Siatri, R., Zervas, M. (eds.) MTSR 2018. CCIS, vol. 846, pp. 199–211. Springer, Cham (2019). https://doi.org/10.1007/978-3-030-14401-2_19
19. Erxleben, F., Günther, M., Krötzsch, M., Mendez, J., Vrandečić, D.: Introducing Wikidata to the linked data web. In: Mika, P., et al. (eds.) ISWC 2014. LNCS, vol. 8796, pp. 50–65. Springer, Cham (2014). https://doi.org/10.1007/978-3-319-11964-9_4

SciBOWater Workshop

SciBOWater 2019 Workshop Chairs' Message

Currently, the processes in water resources management are undergoing major transformations during its transition from the sectoral approaches of the past (e.g., water use for only irrigation, hydropower, or navigation) to contemporary ones that are integrative and comprehensive approaching watersheds as a complex system with interrelated processes surrounding the water cycle. This transformation comes at a time when acute problems are rising in water resources by direct (land use change) or indirect (climate change) human interventions in the natural systems within which we live. Among the most obvious example of extreme events related to water are floods, droughts, excessive pollutant in streams, and an increasing demand of fresh water to sustain economic and social needs. Water is also close related with ecology topics, being affected directly or indirectly by pollutants, being also a strong pollution transportation medium. The new management approaches require processing of a huge amount of information with different levels of accessibility and availability and in various formats (from digital to hardcopy formats). Given the relevance of the data for practice, often the data acquisition needs to be acquired, transmitted, and accessed in real time. Not all the required data is critical nor of equal quality, therefore screening and conditioning has to also be conducted in real time. Equally important is to have access to historical data (raw, statistics, and post-processed) for calibration and validation of the models. With regard to the accessibility of stakeholders to information, there are as well different situations. There are situations when information is to be accessed only by designated stakeholders, but there is a huge amount of information that is, and should be handled, as public information. Thus, the workshop addressed relevant aspects of business information systems focusing on the theme of the conference "Data Science for Business Information Systems," reflected in water management problems. A special interest was given to water-ecology nexus.

Mariana Mocanu
Adrian Paschke
Naouel Karam

Organization

Chairs

Mariana Mocanu	University Politehnica of Bucharest, Romania
Adrian Paschke	Fraunhofer FOKUS Institute in Berlin, Germany
Naouel Karam	Freie Universität Berlin, Germany

Program Committee

Valentin Cristea	University Politehnica of Bucharest, Romania
Anca Ioniță	University Politehnica of Bucharest, Romania
Cătălin Negru	University Politehnica of Bucharest, Romania
Antonio Candelieri	University of Milano-Bicocca, Italy
Ito Wasito	Epoka University, Albania
Lucia Văcariu	Technical University of Cluj-Napoca, Romania
Anca Hangan	Technical University of Cluj-Napoca, Romania
Ajin R. S.	Hazard Analyst, Idukki District Emergency Operations Centre (DEOC), India

Telemetry System for Smart Agriculture

C. M. Balaceanu[1(✉)], I. Marcu[2], and G. Suciu[1]

[1] Beia Consult International, 16 Peroni Road, Bucharest, Romania
{cristina.balaceanu,george}@beia.ro
[2] University Polytechnic of Bucharest, Splaiul Independentei no. 313,
Bucharest, Romania
ioana.marcu@upb.ro

Abstract. The use of telemetry systems in SMART agriculture is an innovative approach which consists in the implementation of an information system able to provide data on irrigation parameters throughout a year, also taking into consideration other meteorological parameters. The need for a telemetry system for irrigation is emphasized by the market's interest in having access to fully automated monitoring and automation solutions for energy efficient and cost-effective agricultural crops. This paper aims to present a telemetry system for monitoring crops with an improved architecture from the point of view of very low energy consumption, low management costs, scalability, forecasting functions, and diagnosis. IoT devices are needed in the agriculture sector to monitor plant growth. This paper also brings to attention an analysis performed with an embedded implemented system. Measured data (collected using ADCON station) include air temperatures; relative humidity and soil temperature. These data are visualized and accessed on the IoT platform using an Internet connection. The ADCON station transmits data from the crop area where it is installed.

Measurements are performed considering energy efficiency criteria and the technologies available on the market. Enlargement facilities lead to an important technical impact and a high potential for marketing.

Keywords: Agriculture · Irrigation · IoT · Telemetry system · Meteorological parameters

1 Introduction

Climate changes contribute to different issues that occurred in the agriculture domain. To address them, the agricultural sector needs to adapt to the new technologies for data monitoring and transmission [1].

The history of agriculture began thousands of years ago when humans started to redirect nature's regular flow of the food web towards the benefit of human civilization. Since its beginning agriculture has suffered many changes in order to achieve improved productivity and increased quality. Significant improvements became obvious when machines and new tools such as milling machines, irrigation systems, harvest machines, farmland clearing machines, etc. were introduced in the primitive agriculture, where these activities were performed mainly by humans and animals. Still, agriculture

W. Abramowicz and R. Corchuelo (Eds.): BIS 2019 Workshops, LNBIP 373, pp. 573–584, 2019.
https://doi.org/10.1007/978-3-030-36691-9_48

has been affected by weather disasters (such as storms or extreme temperatures) and by biological disasters (such as pests and plant diseases) [2–4].

Smart Agriculture is a modern concept in which information and communication technologies are used to manage all activities and processes related to the agriculture field. Internet of Things (IoT) has the capability to influence many areas worldwide such as advanced industries, smart cities and novel technologies in connected vehicles [5]. However, IoT could have an even more significant impact on the agriculture domain. The presented solution for IoT-based smart agriculture consists in a system built to monitor the crop field using sensors (temperature sensor, the temperature of leaves and flower buds, level of oxygen in the soil, global shortwave radiation, UV global radiation, etc.) and to improve the irrigation system. One of the impacts that the system has is to enhance productivity while keeping the costs to a minimum [6, 7].

Water management and irrigation programming became the main subjects in numerous studies lately, taking into consideration their increased significance in precision agriculture. Irrigation quality is an indicator of performance, the influence which can be perceived both directly and indirectly. The need for crop irrigation differs depending on the area climate; therefore energy efficiency and economic use of water resources are strongly interconnected with the type of plantation and soil [8].

Protecting natural water resources through rational and effective use of water is one of the main challenges faced by the specialists. This way, concrete and sustainable measures are needed. Irrigated agriculture accounts for 20% of the total cultivated land with different irrigation solutions currently available, such as drip irrigation, irrigation surface leakage and sprinkler irrigation.

This paper proposes efficient energy system architecture for irrigation management and a demonstrative experimental part where motivation of soil irrigation is outlined. In order to establish an optimal configuration of the system, the monitored parameters having a significant influence on crop productivity (temperature and humidity) are explained as well as their use. Further the main control methods used in irrigation management are illustrated. Next an integrated automation and telemetry solution for water management in precision agriculture is detailed, by considering the criteria of energy and economic efficiency, as well as the leading driving technologies presented. Using this telemetry system different crop can be monitored.

The paper is structured as follows: Sect. 2 presents related work for smart agriculture, Sect. 3 introduces the main parameters monitored in irrigation, Sect. 4 presents the architecture for system irrigation, Sect. 5 the experimental data and finally, Sect. 6 concludes the paper.

2   Related Work

Agriculture plays a vital role in the lives and well-being of people throughout the world; it is also a process of producing food and a source of food for both the population and domestic animals. Over time, the climate has undergone changes that people had to adapt to and implicitly adjust the solutions used to ensure food or water quality, both irrigated and used daily [9]. In the field of agriculture, crops need to be watered whenever necessary and only with the amount of water required by the soil at that specific time of irrigation.

Water is eternally a needy part of everyone's survival. Due to environmental condition, water management and conservation will play a requisite role for human survivals. Lately, there were tremendous needs for consumer-based humanitarian projects that could be immediately improved using the Internet of Things (IoT) [10–14]. This introduces an IoT-based water monitoring scheme that measures the water level in real-time. The ideals are based on the water level which can be an essential parameter when it comes to the flood particularly in disaster regions. A water level sensor is employed to recognize the water level and depending on the fixed setting, and if the water level strikes the parameter, the alert will be feed in real- time to a social network like Twitter [15]. A cloud server was set up and configured as the data container. The ultrasonic sensor could be compensated by a specific water level sensor so that the system can function more accurately and provide greater accuracy of water level detection [15]. This system is set to maintain soil humidity levels and embrace the different watering needs.

To focus the consequence of using Wireless Sensors Network (WSN) in irrigation, comparison research between the automated drip irrigation system and non-automated drip irrigation was performed [16]. A similar method was implemented where the primary purpose was to administer water use productivity by monitoring soil moisture level [17, 18]. In [19], there is illustrated a process designed to achieve smart agriculture by applying automation and IoT technologies like ZigBee models, camera and actuators to manage smart irrigation on actual real-time field data. In [20], an automated irrigation system was developed using the wireless moisture sensor network and IoT technology. Based on temperature, humidity and moisture sensors, an automated irrigation system was implemented in order to supply water to the plant at scheduled intervals.

IoT technology is having disruptive impacts on an extensive range of industries including public transport, agriculture, environmental science, and robotics. In many of these fields, IoT is becoming a key enabler of innovation and success and corporations are willing to invest in such new technologies.

3   Parameters Monitored in Irrigation

Measurement accuracy is essential in agriculture. Monitored parameters on a plantation depend on the soil nature and region climate. Some of them are detailed as follows:

- *Temperature and humidity of the air*: Crops can be regarded as functions mainly reliant on temperature when irrigation is carried out suitable [21]. Temperature has a significant influence on seed germination because in biochemical processes germination phases include hydration and enzyme activation. Plant development process is dependent on temperature: high or low temperatures strongly influence the agricultural season. Considering that predictions for the coming years show increasing values of this parameter, the amount of water required for irrigation will increase according to the requirements of evaporation. A numerical method has shown that a 2°C increase in temperature leads to a rise of water demand of cultures by 19% [22].

Each plantation requires a specific temperature; otherwise, the seeds will not bloom and remain into the ground been therefore exposed to the attacks of some pests, diseases, or loss of germination. Optimal temperature does not generally correspond to vegetative growth, but it differs from one crop to another.

Absolute Humidity can be defined as the partial pressure of water vapour in wet air, usually expressed in millimetres mercury column. The partial pressure of water vapour in wet air and quantity of vapours contained in one m^3 of wet air, expressed in grams, are numerically equal [23].

Relative Humidity provides information on the water vapour in the air, parameter strongly interdepend to the temperature. On the other hand, dew point temperature explains the relationship between relative humidity and temperature because, with an increase in relative humidity, a decrease in temperature occurs, and if the temperature falls below a certain limit, the air reaches the point where it will contain the largest amount of water vapour [24].

- *Temperature and humidity of soil*: The soil is an essential resource in irrigation management, as it is a carbon storage tank. Soil humidity is identified as a critical parameter in precision farming. It has been demonstrated that monitoring of soil temperature and humidity are critical processes for precision agriculture. In some regions, irrigated farmers when soil moisture exceeds certain limit (50%) [25].

The frequency of irrigation depends on the equipment used for drip irrigation or the characteristics of deep wells. The primary objective of irrigation consists in optimizing plant water requirements; it can be achieved through active monitoring of soil moisture. It is considered that soil moisture should be measured by sensors that do not have moving parts and do not require calibration [26].

Soil temperature is greatly influenced by solar and humidity radiation. Usually, the soil temperature is higher than the air temperature, and the propagation of the heat in the soil is a slow process [27].

- *Evapotranspiration*: Evapotranspiration is one of the basic components of the hydrologic cycle. It influences the water balance from the moment it reaches the ground through precipitation until the residual water reaches the ocean. The consumptive use includes transpiration by vegetation, evaporation of water from the soil and from the water surfaces, and the small amount of water from harvests. These parameters continue to be very important in planning and managing water resources and irrigation. The term evapotranspiration (ET) has become more common than the term consumptive use. The difference between the term evapotranspiration and consumptive use is that the latter also refers to the amount of water found in plant tissue.

ET is required both in planning and operating water resource projects and necessary in problems regarding water supply, both surface and underground, water management, and in the economics of multipurpose water projects for irrigation, power, water transportation, flood control, municipal and industrial water uses, and wastewater reuse systems [28].

Evapotranspiration is an essential parameter for plant development and health, based on parameters weather. Water lost through evapotranspiration can be saved by proper irrigation that reduces evapotranspiration by 5–15% [29]. Evapotranspiration is closely related to meteorological parameters.

4 Architecture of the Irrigation System for Smart Agriculture

The proposed telemetry and automation system were designed to closely monitor the key parameters for agriculture. It brings to attention an automation system developed for irrigation control and reduced energy consumption [30].

The architecture of the ADCON telemetry station is presented in Fig. 1.

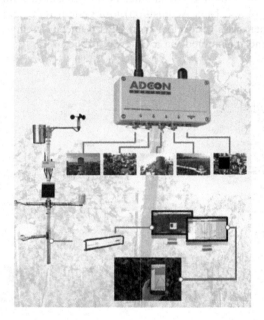

Fig. 1. Architecture of the ADCON telemetry

All data collected from the stations can be accessed, visualized and downloaded as table or graph. Every 10 min the acquisition platform (addVANTAGE Pro) receives data collected from stations (through sensors) related to temperature, soil air humidity. The sensors integrated at ADCON station level are supplied for a short period of time and their recorded data are read by the RTU (Remote Terminal Unit) every 5 min. Every 10 min, RTU performs average of data within the measurement range. Every hour, the RTU transmits the four average values computed for each parameter to Data Presentation Server through the gateway.

For the assessment of the quality of soil and crops in different area, IoT devices were deployed. Data flow architecture (Fig. 1) includes an acquisition platform (addVANTAGE Pro) composed of modular acquisition nodes addSWITCH A724 device, which acts as IoT-Gateway. The data acquisition modules connect via 4G/WiFi to the Internet or another (private) network and send data to it. The IoT gateway stored the data in a MySQL database that ensures local persistence of data. Data are transmitted to Cloud through a software component that serializes data to an MQTT broker. Next, the Adapter component (a software application developed in Python programming language), is basically an MQTT client that subscribes to several topics and stores the data received from the sensor in the database. Data visualization is then realized with an open platform for analytics and monitoring (Grafana).

The telemetry process for the proposed system (Fig. 2) is performed with an ADCON station that will measure field parameters (soil and air humidity and air temperature). All these monitored parameters are transmitted through the SCADA (Supervisory Control and Data Acquisition) to a system RTU and a communications server. These elements are connected to an OPC (Object Linking and Embedding for Process Control) and transmitted via a Gateway to the users.

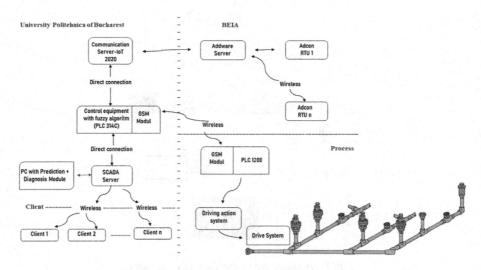

Fig. 2. Architecture of proposed irrigation system

The functions of SCADA system (adjustment, prediction, diagnosis) will be performed on a computer that has two-way connection means with the SCADA server and PLC (Programmable Logic Controller). It can support more customers depending on the number of users/beneficiaries of the telemetry and automation system. In order to ensure increased system efficiency, the drive equipment (pumps, valves) have low power consumption. With SCADA and PLC, parameters such as soil moisture, temperature, or health status of the crop are controlled remotely. These controllers inform whether it is necessary to take irrigation or fertilization measures.

The performance of the ADCON telemetry system consists in:

Datalogger Performance

- Very robust
- Extremely compact
- Extremely low power consumption
- High resolution (16 bit)
- Lots of memory (>2 000 000 value)
- Lots of inputs

Communication Options

- Only UHF/radio networks, short-range and long-range
- Only mobile data (2G/3G/4G/LTE)

ADCON telemetry station has a self-monitoring battery, a larger memory and wireless communication via Bluetooth.

In order to emphasize the significance of ADCON telemetry station, a comparison was performed of the two monitoring stations (Libelium and ADCON). Figure 3 presents a comparison of monitoring stations ADCON and Libelium.

Station	Parameter	Measurement unit	Min. value	Max. value	Board com	Data Query method
Libelium Smart Agriculture	Temperature	°C	-40	125	HTTP	MySQL
	Relative humidity	% RH	0	100		
	Atmospheric Pressure	kPa	15	115		
	Leaf Wetness Sensor	V	1	3.3		
	Soil Moisture	cb	0	200		
	Soil Temperature	°C	-50	300		
	Solar Radiation	nm	410	655		
	Ultraviolet Radiation	nm	250	400		
	Wind and speed direction	Km/h	0	240		
	Precipitation	mm of rain	-	-		
ADCON	Temperature	°C	-40	80	GPRS/ GSM	REST API (addUPI)
	Relative Humidity	% RH	0	100		
	Pressure	mbar	600	1500		
	Wind speed & Wind direction	m/s	0,4	65,56		
	Solar Radiation	w/m²	0	2000		
	Precipitations	mm/h	0	100		
	Leaf Wetness	V	0	10		
	Soil Moisture	%	0	100		
	Temperature Sensor for Soil, Water and Snow	°C	-20	60		
	Solar radiation	nm	310	2800		
	Ultraviolet radiation	nm	400	1100		

Fig. 3. Comparison of two monitoring stations

Taking into consideration the specifications of the two stations and the fact that ADCON station offers disease model, frost warming and degree days, for intelligent agriculture in our case, ADCON represents the best solution for this monitoring and forecasting implemented system.

5   Experimental Data

The agricultural decision-making system is a software program that collects multiple input data from crop sensors, data that helps farmers to make decisions related to issues that may occur at crops level (irrigation or diseases). Complex agricultural operations involve making daily decisions about chemical spraying, measures against frost and appropriate harvest period. This system should include a monitoring station equipped with crop sensors and an addVANTAGE Pro software for visualization of all collected data. The software program is designed to process data from sensors and to suggest actions beneficial to crops according to their status. These suggestions may be used as recommendations for treatment, frost alarms, or disease installs, all of which allow the user to act before affecting crops.

In Smart Agriculture, parameters such as temperature and humidity of air and soil humidity vary from one area to another, and these measurements lead to the need for a very flexible irrigation system easily adapted to all weather conditions. In order to have a good irrigation system, it is useful to have a communication network sensor to meet any requirements. Wireless sensors are essential for precision farming, being a solution for developing countries.

ADCON system telemetry measured the humidity of soil, air and temperature useful for the crop development in agriculture for a period of almost 55 h at the beginning of March 2019. The monitoring of parameters specific to agriculture was carried out in an area cultivated with tomatoes in a residential area in Bucharest. Following the measurements, a series of information on temperature, and humidity are stored in a database. Figures 4, 5 and 6 illustrate the variation of these parameters in the observed time interval.

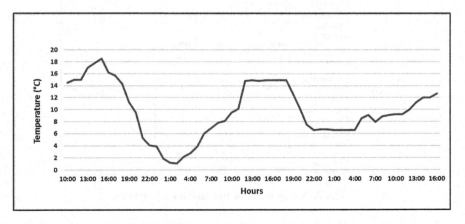

Fig. 4. Variation of air temperature

From Fig. 4 it can be noticed that the transition from winter season to spring season is correctly registered by ADCON telemetry system. As expected, an increase in temperature values is noticeable in the afternoon, starting at 11 o'clock, then the temperature drops in the evening. This parameter is an indicator that helps the farmers to choose the right period for tomato cultivation.

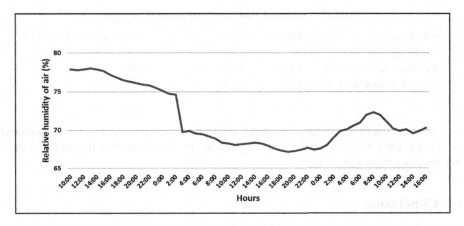

Fig. 5. Variation of relative humidity of air

Correlating data in Figs. 4 and 5 it can be observed a good connection between the variation of air relative humidity and temperature.

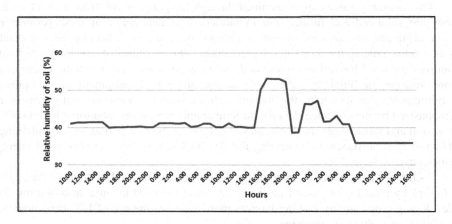

Fig. 6. Variation of relative humidity of soil

According to the technical data from the ADCON telemetry station, the relative humidity of soil varies between 40% and almost 60%, which means that the ground needs irrigation, although it is not yet very dry (values noticeable in Fig. 6). When soil humidity falls below 30%, crops need water. For an efficient and rapid development of tomatoes in the observed area an efficient telemetry system is necessary and the use of ADCON telemetry station can help farmers within this zone.

Table 1 presents a statistical analysis of the parameters measured during the monitored period.

Table 1. Statistical analysis of measured parameters

Parameters	Mean value	Standard deviation	Confidence level (95.0%)
Air temperature	9.8	4.57	1.23
Relative humidity of air	71.6	3.69	0.99
Relative humidity of soil	41.2	4.36	1.18

From the analysis of statistical data, it can be observed that for each monitored parameter, the confidence level (95%) is given by the probability that the studied values are included within this range.

6 Conclusion

ADCON platform used for parameters monitoring in smart agriculture prove its efficiency in various uses cases, including irrigation of soil. This paper aims to illustrate that such a platform is necessary for Romanian farmers in agricultural field and it is efficient in monitoring the humidity of soil and temperature of air (required parameters for plant growth).

The measured values are transmitted through the gateway A850 for ADCON, and they are validated and further sent to farmers. The emergence of these parameters monitoring and transmission systems highlights the need for collecting the soil-plant-soil actions crucial for agricultural production. The moisture of the monitored soil outlines the need for soil irrigation, and the measurement of solar radiation, temperature, relative air humidity offers information on crop development in an optimal environment. For example, the transition from winter season to spring season is emphasized by the collected data for air temperature parameter monitored by ADCON platform and farmers can use the values to determine the best period for crop planting. The use of solar panels for powering the ADCON station leads to very good energy efficiency.

As future plans, ADCON monitoring technology can be used to improve the health of crops by reducing the use of pesticides, creating the most favourable conditions for developing crops and by making farmers more aware of the use of IoT technology so useful in agriculture of precision.

Acknowledgment. The work presented in this paper has been funded by the SmartAgro project subsidiary contract no. 8592/08.05.2018, from the NETIO project ID: P_40_270, MySmis Code: 105976.

References

1. Nelson, M.C., et al.: Climate challenges, vulnerabilities, and food security. Proc. Natl. Acad. Sci. U.S.A. **113**(2), 298–303 (2016). https://doi.org/10.1073/pnas.1506494113
2. Rossati, A.: Global warming and its health impact. Int. J. Occup. Environ. Med. **8**(1), 7–20 (2017). https://doi.org/10.15171/ijoem.2017.963
3. Klomp, J., Hoogezand, B.: Natural disasters and agricultural protection: a panel data analysis. World Dev. **104**, 404–417 (2018)
4. Shelia, V., et al.: A multi-scale and multi-model gridded framework for forecasting crop production, risk analysis, and climate change impact studies. Environ. Model Softw. **115**, 144–154 (2019). https://doi.org/10.1016/j.envsoft.2019.02.006
5. Suciu, G., Bezdedeanu, L., Vasilescu, A., Suciu, V.: Unified intelligent water management using cyberinfrastructures based on cloud computing and IoT. In: 21st International Conference on Control Systems and Computer Science (CSCS), pp. 606–611, Romania (2017). https://doi.org/10.1109/cscs.2017.92
6. Kamienski, C., et al.: Smart water management platform: IoT-based precision irrigation for agriculture. Sensors **19**(2), 276 (2019)
7. Kapoor, A., Bhat, S.I., Shidnal, S., Mehra, A.: Implementation of IoT (Internet of Things) and image processing in smart agriculture. In: 1st IEEE International Conference on Computational Systems and Information Technology for Sustainable Solutions (CSITSS), WOS: 000390719100005, India, pp. 21–26 (2016)
8. Jianbang, L., Shuxue, Z., Aihua, L., Ye, Y.: Application of Internet of Things in weather modification service in Anhui Province. Meteorol. Sci. Technol. **42**, 1143–1146 (2014)
9. India set to become water scarce by 2025: report, Mumbai. http://www.thehindu.com/. Accessed 9 Apr 2019
10. Roopaei, M., Rad, P., Choo, K.-K.R.: Cloud of things in smart agriculture: intelligent irrigation monitoring by thermal imaging. IEEE Cloud Comput. **4**(1), 10–15 (2017)
11. Chaudhry, S., Garg, S.: Smart irrigation techniques for water resource management. In: Smart Farming Technologies for Sustainable Agricultural Development. Advances in Environmental Engineering and Green Technologies, WOS: 000461277400011, pp. 196–219 (2019)
12. Prathibha, S.R., Hongal, A., Jyothi, M.P.: IoT based monitoring system in smart agriculture. In: 1st IEEE International Conference on Recent Advances in Electronics and Communication Technology (ICRAECT), pp. 81–84, India (2017)
13. Rajalakshmi, P., Mahalakshmi, S.D.: IoT based crop-field monitoring and irrigation automation. In: 10th International Conference on Intelligent Systems and Control (ISCO), India, WOS: 000387435600028 (2016)
14. Pernapati, K.: IoT based low cost smart irrigation system. In: International Conference on Inventive Communication and Computational Technologies (ICICCT), WOS: 000456251700265, pp. 1312–1315, India (2018)
15. Difallah, W., Benahmed, K., Draoui, B., Bounaama, F.: Linear optimization model for efficient use of irrigation water. Int. J. Agron. 1–8 (2017). Article number: 5353648 https://doi.org/10.1155/2017/5353648
16. Gangadharan, A., et al.: Solar powered smart irrigation system. Int. J. Comput. Sci. Inf. Technol. Secur. 102–106 (2016)
17. Patil, S., Rudresh, S.M., Kallendrachari, K.M., Kiran, K., Vani, H.V.: Solar powered irrigation system with automatic control of pump and SMS alert. Int. J. Eng. Technol. Manag. Res. **3**(1), 90–94 (2015)

18. Nikesh, G., Kawitkar, R.S.: Smart agriculture using IoT and WSN based modern technologies. Int. J. Innov. Res. Comput. Commun. Eng. **4**(6), 12070–12076 (2016)
19. Ibrahim, M., Rawidean, M., Kassim, M., Harun, A.N.: IoT in precision agriculture applications using wireless moisture sensor network. In: IEEE Conference on Open Systems, WOS: 000411226100005, pp. 24–29, Langkawi, Malaysia (2016)
20. Rasul, G., Chaudhry, Q.Z., Mahmood, A., Hyder, K.W.: Effect of temperature rise on crop growth and productivity. Pak. J. Meteorol. **8**(15), 53–62 (2011)
21. Bellingham, K.: The role of soil moisture on our climate. http://www.soilsensor.com/climatech. Accessed 10 Apr 2019
22. Mareels, I., Weyer, E., Ooi, S.K., Cantoni, M., Li, Y., Nair, G.: Systems engineering for irrigation systems: success and challenges. Annu. Rev. Control **29**(2), 191–204 (2005). https://doi.org/10.1016/j.arcontrol.2005.08.001
23. Ahmad, L., Habib Kanth, R., Parvaze, S., Sheraz Mahdi, S.: Measurement of humidity. Experimental Agrometeorology: A Practical Manual, pp. 23–27. Springer, Cham (2017). https://doi.org/10.1007/978-3-319-69185-5_4
24. Sawant, S., Durbha, S.S., Adinarayana, J.: Interoperable agro-meteorological observation and analysis platform for precision agriculture: a case study in citrus crop water requirement estimation. Comput. Electron. Agric. **138**, 175–187 (2017). https://doi.org/10.1016/j.compag.2017.04.019
25. Davis, S.L., Dukes, M.D.: Landscape irrigation with evapotranspiration controllers in a humid climate. Trans. ASABE **55**(2), 571–580 (2012)
26. Prichard, T.: Vineyard irrigation systems. Raisin Production Manual University of California Agricultural and Natural Resources Publication, vol. 3393, pp. 57–63, Oakland (2000)
27. Jensen, M.E., Allen, R.G.: Evaporation, evapotranspiration and irrigation water requirements. ASCE Manuals and Reports on Engineering, no. 70 (2016)
28. Nabil, M.: Interaction of advanced scientific irrigation management with I-Scada system for efficient and sustainable production of fiber on 10,360 hectares. Resource Magazine, pp. 203–212 (2010)
29. OTT Hydromet. http://m.ott.com/index.php?id=93&L=2. Accessed 10 Apr 2019
30. Addvantage Pro. https://www.ADCON.com/products/software-285/ADCON-addvantage-6x-1485/. Accessed 12 Apr 2019

Increasing Collaboration and Participation Through Serious Gaming for Improving the Quality of Service in Urban Water Infrastructure

Alexandru Predescu[✉] and Mariana Mocanu[✉]

Department of Computer Science, University POLITEHNICA of Bucharest,
Bucharest, Romania
{alexandru.predescu,mariana.mocanu}@cs.pub.ro

Abstract. The transition towards sustainable developments is represented by the current industry trend. From the society perspective, raising awareness about water related problems is of particular interest. While there is an abundance of information available for the general public, a more interactive approach encourages participation in different aspects of government within a Smart City environment. Mobile crowdsensing has emerged as one of the most prominent paradigms for urban sensing, complementing the smart infrastructure. Serious gaming provides the spark in this interaction between the digital citizen and Artificial Intelligence. We consider the pervasive nature of serious gaming as a challenge that requires fusion between tech and non-tech industries. The proposed serious gaming platform combines crowdsensing with augmented reality for increasing active involvement of citizens in smart government. The core application was designed with a focus on rich user experience and game design elements while the game design is defined in the context of urban water infrastructure management and decision support.

Keywords: Serious gaming · Gamification · Crowdsensing ·
Augmented reality · Smart government · Urban water · Decision
support

1 Introduction

Sustainable developments require an extensive evaluation of impact factors across the industries and the society as a whole. The concept of Smart City is an example where multiple industries have to be orchestrated for reaching a level of sustainability in the context of the expansion of urban centers and the environmental impact.

In the domain of smart infrastructure, there are different approaches for sustainable developments and maintenance. A swift detection and solution of problems within a metropolitan infrastructure is required for improving the efficiency

© Springer Nature Switzerland AG 2019
W. Abramowicz and R. Corchuelo (Eds.): BIS 2019 Workshops, LNBIP 373, pp. 585–596, 2019.
https://doi.org/10.1007/978-3-030-36691-9_49

of operation and maintenance. However, it is often a trade-off between the time constraints and the accuracy requirements such as the case of leak detection.

A classification of leak detection methods includes:

– Hardware-based solutions
  For accurate detection of leaks, there are many hardware solutions such as using acoustic sensors, gas detectors, negative pressure detectors and infrared thermal sensors, as presented in many literature works such as [1,2]. These methods provide increased accuracy at the expense of time and cost requirements.
– Model-based solutions
  Using a hydraulic model and simulation is described in many literature works such as [3–7]. Modeling can be either based on physical laws of mass transfer or identified using experimental methods. The sensor placement can be evaluated in terms of sensitivity to leaks while the accuracy is influenced by the sensors (type, precision) that are installed within the network.
– AI-based solutions
  Machine Learning represents an alternative to the more traditional models and is currently used in many domains. In the context of water distribution systems, the applications include demand forecast, anomaly detection and priority evaluation as described in [8–11].
– Crowdsensing
  More than the electronic sensors, nowadays smartphones allow for transforming human observations into electronic data. This method can provide instant feedback on the current state of the infrastructure in a Smart City.

Data is essential for enabling intelligence in a Smart City infrastructure. IoT (Internet of Things) sensor networks are being installed to measure a broad range of parameters and provide large amounts of data for decision support systems. Digital sensors have become embedded in many consumer products of which mobile devices provide an entire ecosystem that can be used for mobile crowdsensing [12]. More than the electronic sensors, smartphones allow for transforming human observations into electronic data by connecting the people to the digital world. This way, the digital citizen can play an active role in the society and provide instant feedback to the authorities.

There are many challenges associated to the Utopian Society where everyone benefits from the synergy between people and digital devices, such as privacy and the associated derivatives with regards to cybersecurity. The collection of personally identifying information (PII) was not until recently covered by legal instruments such as the GDPR (General Data Protection Regulation).

Mechanisms of compliance to privacy obligations include avoidance (not collecting the PII in the first place), cryptography, anonymity and pseudonyms (protecting the real identity of users in a crowdsensing application, separate the location from the data), data obfuscation (adding randomness to the data) and access control mechanisms [13].

Crowdsensing emerged as a broad topic that encompasses the involvement of citizens in solving large scale problems. There are many applications that include collaborative navigation (Waze), ride sharing (Uber), food delivery (Uber Eats, Glovo), travel (Airbnb). A common trend is represented by a decentralization of services, in the sense that the individual can be both provider and consumer.

The collaborative aspect represents the main difference between electronic government and smart governance concepts. Social media, the Internet, open data and mobile technologies are some of the key enablers of a more citizen-centric approach in the context of Society 2.0.

Perspectives include:

- Smart Cities instrumented with data from IoT and citizens
- Cloud services that provide integrated decision support systems (DSS)
- Interactive participation through AI and gaming.

The transition towards an interactive participation in different aspects of government is already facilitated by the mobile gaming industry. The familiarity of the general public with Augmented Reality applications, and mobile games such as Pokémon GO, even though in the early stages, provides a bridge to a wide range of use cases in the real world.

Crowdsensing applications may prove to be essential for disaster management, where on-site observations can be the primary source of data. Many of the privacy issues regarding crowdsensing applications already exist as individual security risks associated to the enabling technologies.

From a large scale architectural perspective, enabling innovation through interoperability and system integration represents a real challenge because most technicians used to work with individual systems. In [14], Waze is given as an example for increasing collaboration and participation, that allows the individual to report a traffic situation, and many more use cases can be found for this class of geo-referencing applications. Data mining in this context, represents the background for a second stage of intelligence in the form of citizen-centric/crowdsourced/citizen-powered DSS.

Expanding on the user-centric approach, the concept of gamification has been applied in domains such as transport (Waze using social gamification e.g. "moods" or avatars that are unlocked through active participation and helping fellow Wazers through incident reporting), sports (e.g. Strava, Runtastic implemented social features to generate mutual support and competition and motivate users through peer pressure), social networks and applications (e.g. Foursquare using badges to motivate people to visit special places on a regular basis, LinkedIn acknowledging users with "strong profiles"), software development (e.g. Stack Overflow increasing community involvement in software development through rewards derived from reputation score), e-commerce (e.g. Amazon.com rewarding customers with points for good quality reviews), e-learning (e.g. Duolingo using interactive games and notifications to motivate the users learning a new language).

In [15], the scope of gamification is classified into three categories:

- background: academic/non-academic
- scope: complete/specific
- approach: wide spectrum of environments/specific business context.

In contrast to the more pragmatic tasks that are part of daily life, playing games is usually done voluntarily and often provides opportunities for social interaction in the digital world (e.g. multiplayer games) as well as real life (e.g. sports, social games).

Video games have been introduced since the beginning of the computer era and were, until recently, focused on the virtual reality more than the social and physical components. In this sense, mixed reality games represent the bridge between the two worlds.

Location-based games, augmented reality, persistent games and alternate reality games are expanding the traditional limits of games and are also known as "pervasive games".

The mixed reality continuum is described as the blend between the real environment (AR - Augmented Reality) and the virtual environment (VR - Virtual Reality).

The pervasive aspect of mixed reality games refers to the increased mobility (e.g. mobile games) and utilization of Pervasive Computing technologies (i.e. the integration of computers into our surroundings) [16].

In [17], gamification is defined as the "use of game design elements in non-game contexts". The concept of "serious games" even dates back several millennia [18,19].

Over the past few decades, video games have arguably become a cultural medium along with literature, movies or television with the added advantage of active participation. From this perspective, active learning is a powerful alternative to the more traditional forms, considering the fast-paced world of today that implies a "short" attention span as a direct consequence. Moreover, with the abundance of information, the cognitive functions have adapted to filter out unwanted details and while this is related to natural evolution, it makes it more difficult to present relevant information in a way that sparks the interest of general population.

For education, RPG games bring meaningful learning opportunities accounting for higher knowledge retention rate as well as the acquisition of general skills as described in [20].

Serious games are a particular form of pervasive games, where the use of game elements is directed towards a complete solution while the main goal extends outside the game itself. Flight simulators and virtual training games can be considered serious games with a virtual reality approach and some gamification elements.

2   Related Work

Recent developments in domains such as Machine Learning (ML), Augmented Reality (AR) and mobile technologies (e.g. smartphones, 5G) provide the ground for designing the Smart Cities of tomorrow. The key element that has to be addressed in the present context is sustainability (economic, environmental, social), while providing an increasing standard of living.

In the context of smart utility networks, modern solutions have to be developed to sustain the growth of urban areas, while improving the quality of service in aging infrastructure. The demand model and forecast in the scope of priority evaluation is a topic of unsupervised learning, combined with GIS (Geographic Information Systems) and SCADA systems (Supervised Control And Data Acquisition) [21,22].

A data-driven approach for water demand forecasting and anomaly detection, with results for the water distribution network in Milan is presented in [23] and [24]. Short-term demand forecasting is presented as a key component for encouraging water savings. Time series clustering is used to extract patterns from the data representing typical consumption behaviors, while the demand forecasting model is trained through SVM regression.

Industry 4.0 is changing the society as well (i.e. Society 2.0), and technological advancements have to be tuned to the needs and requirements of the modern citizen. While connecting things is possible with IoT, connecting people and involvement in the community is a challenge that extends beyond the scope of digital connectivity. The concept of serious gaming brings together the two pieces of the puzzle (the real world and the digital world) while enhancing the connection between the individual (digital citizen) and the public sector (smart government). In this context, gamification provides the means to motivate citizens' contribution while extending the concept of community and increasing social cohesion in a Smart City environment.

There are ongoing research projects on this topic as stated in [25], involving the public sector with regards to the economic sustainability (banking, e-government, infrastructure, job creation), environmental sustainability (water, energy, waste management) and social sustainability (health, education, food safety, leisure). The work presents a concept application of gamification in designing a virtual city, providing feedback for the authorities, badges, leaderboards, mini-games for solving potential problems and tax discounts from the authorities.

Raising consumer awareness and stimulating behavior change in the use of natural resources and providing actionable recommendations in the context of the consumer and the community of reference is a topic of particular interest. In [26] are presented some design guidelines for resource consumption awareness applications, the prototype of the application (featuring virtual points, badges, leaderboards) and a strategy to combine pragmatic use cases and gamification according to the target user profile.

Gamification in the context of water utilities is the scope of several research projects and SaaS products such as WaterSmart (personalized WaterScore, comparison with similar households, water-saving recommendations), WATER-NOMICS (integration of personalized feedback on water consumption, data from sensors and fault detection systems into decision support systems for water saving), WISDOM (water consumption data, awareness campaigns, customized feedback and rewards), SmartH2O (European project with results in data acquisition from smart meters, raising awareness through consumer portals, water analytics, user modeling and demand forecasting, engagement and behavior change through recommendations, goals, achievements, and rewards).

In terms of energy-saving and pro-environmental behavior, there is a great deal of inconsistency derived from both the user mentality and the legislation. In [27], the potential of serious games and gamification is examined. A computer-based search based on some inclusion criteria was performed on several databases to provide an overview on this subject, resulting in just about 10 relevant studies from three target areas: environmental education (EnerCities, Trashwar), consumption awareness (Power Advisor, Energy Chickens) and energy efficiency behaviors (Power Explorer, Power Agent) as well as comprehensive interventions (EcoIsland, Energy Battle, Social Power). The results of the studies point towards a short-term improvement in users' behavior, while the long-term effect is either observed to a lesser degree or not evaluated.

In this area, Augmented Reality and game concepts can be combined with "Waze-like" applications to create a universal platform for serious gaming in everyday life. With regards to the lack of data available at the moment, such platform has to be enabled with Machine Learning support to provide deeper insights on the effect of each component on the overall user behavior. The integration with sensors in the context of IoT is another possible scenario for improving the quality of data. Therefore, the potential of applied gaming is mostly untapped, and we consider a solution of convergence between practical and creative work towards developing entertainment-grade applications with a real-life purpose. In this sense, the concept of Industry 4.0 can extend across the tech and non-tech industries.

3   Proposed Solution

We consider that the ICT systems can be integrated into serious gaming platforms that bring together all aspects of smart government. We focus on broadening the scope of emerging technologies represented by interactive maps and AR as part of a collaborative platform for active participation in a Smart City.

We designed a mobile application with a serious gaming component that aims to bridge the gap between the general public and the authorities while providing entertainment-grade experience for the user. The involvement of the general public is encouraged through the use of gamification as well as real-life rewards. We present the game design and user interaction in Figs. 1 and 2.

The mobile application is based on Google Maps and Geolocation and the main view is similar to collaborative navigation applications e.g. Waze with the addition of AR technologies. There are two modes designed for the following use cases:

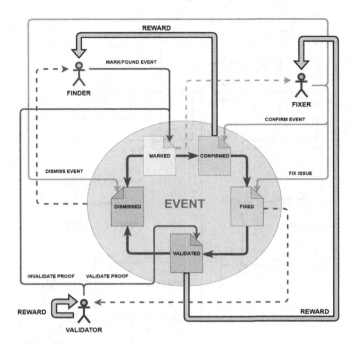

Fig. 1. SG design

Finder - the mode for the general user represented by the digital citizen that is involved in the community. The user opens the map showing infrastructure layers and is able to switch to an AR mode that overlays the information on the camera. In the event that an anomaly is identified, the user can report the event using the AR view. The location of the event is then registered on the map with absolute coordinates.

Fixer - the mode for experts or general users that are either qualified or just able to solve the specific events as reported by finders. The user opens the map showing nearby events and selects a target. The application switches into navigation mode and shows directions to the event.

The first task is to confirm or dismiss the event using the AR view. When the event is confirmed, the reward is issued to the Finder, otherwise the event can be dismissed/reported as a false positive and no reward is issued. The reward system can be further reinforced by negative rewards in the case of false positives, so that potential spam is reduced.

The second task is to fix the issue (in real life) and to upload a proof for validation. When the proof is validated by another expert (e.g. peer review), the fixer is given a reward.

Validator - the mode for verified experts that are qualified for evaluating the specific events and issues as confirmed by the fixers. The main task of the Validator is to evaluate the proof submitted by the fixers, with the advantage

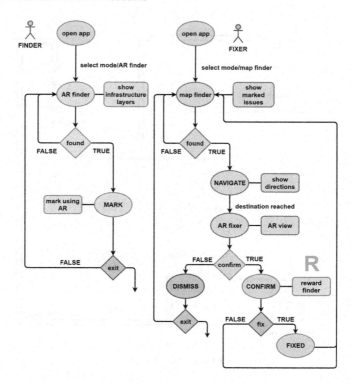

Fig. 2. SG interaction

that the field work is outsourced. The reward system in this case is based on reputation (e.g. similar to Stack Overflow). When the proof is validated, the reward is given to the Fixer.

While the first two use cases (i.e. Finder, Fixer) target the increased collaboration and participation in solving infrastructure problems in Smart Cities, the third use case ensures proof validation. This behavior is similar to some extent to the Blockchain technology. The interaction between the participants and with the real world is validated by trusted entities represented in this case by the verified experts.

4   Results

We developed the application with the core function of a treasure hunting platform that can be extended for multiple use cases in the context of serious gaming for the industry. The Geo-AR is designed to interact with the virtual components that are associated to real life treasures. The treasures, we consider a generic term for interest points that may be placed by the users.

The challenges that we encountered were related to the synchronization between the map geographical coordinates and the AR coordinate system. The

Fig. 3. Map view

accuracy of the AR relies to a great extent to the mobile sensors and geolocation, and this is an area of possible improvements in the future.

The gamification features include badges, leaderboards, player level and rewards. The UI includes fluid design elements and rich visual features such as photos, map themes and custom markers. We started from a broader scope of the application, including other game design elements such as inventory (special items, collectibles), random treasures, skill trees and game statistics.

The core platform includes stories and challenges that can be used for raising awareness about water related problems. This can bring interactive learning opportunities, combining the knowledge with the dynamic nature of the game.

Another aspect is that application encourages outdoor activities, providing rewards for finding treasures (generic term, e.g. water infrastructure problems) in the real world. With the increased participation, the user level and score increases, and real-life rewards can be unlocked. These can include discounts offered by the service providers for finding and solving problems.

In Fig. 2 is presented the flow diagram for the user interaction with the platform from the perspective of Finder and Fixer. The Finder mode is focused on AR clues, while the map view can be used as a guide for showing infrastructure layers. When the user finds a problem regarding the infrastructure, an event can be placed on the map, guided by the AR view.

The Fixer mode is focused on map navigation, showing nearby events as marked by finders. In Fig. 3 is shown the map view that reveals nearby events. Each event is represented by geographic coordinates, event code and specific icon. In the context of urban water, we considered the following events: flooding, water supply (e.g. leaks, service interruptions), pollution and hazards (other conditions).

The Fixer can investigate the issue and a reward is given to the Finder upon confirmation. When the issue is solved, the Fixer must submit a proof that will be evaluated by certified experts in the field.

5   Conclusion

Serious gaming is a topic of interest in the context of Smart Cities. While IoT and AI provide the backbone of a smart infrastructure, the human interaction provides the feedback and should set the standard for the digital world.

The driving force in the context of Society 2.0 is represented by the enhanced connectivity and collaboration. The increased participation in smart government through serious gaming provides valuable insights into the current state of the infrastructure. Moreover, the decision support is augmented by crowdsensing. This method can be used to validate the results of traditional sensor monitoring and reinforce the active participation of the digital citizens in solving large scale problems.

The serious game design that we propose in this work allows for a reliable, trust-based validation of crowdsensing data. The task of the maintenance teams are delegated to the general public, reducing the cost and improving the coverage. The issues and solutions can be validated remotely by verified experts, allowing for a collaboration between the citizens and the authorities.

The core application was designed with a focus on rich user experience and entertainment features. The game engine allows the extension towards serious gaming applications such as the case of urban water infrastructure. The visual design is key to the success of serious gaming for the general public that is accustomed to entertainment-grade applications. We focused on the gamification and visual elements to create an extensive platform that can be tailored for real world scenarios.

The user level, score and rewards provide a method to interact with the authorities (e.g. service providers), exchanging virtual points for discounts and real-life rewards. The multiple roles (e.g. Finder, Fixer, Validator) define the context of a real life RPG for water infrastructure management that can be extended for multiple scenarios as part of a smart government platform, encouraging collaboration and participation while improving the quality of service and solving large scale problems.

The validation of the proposed solution requires a progressive introduction of the general concept to the citizens, so that they are already accustomed to this form of digital interaction. This can be accomplished in the form of an entertainment oriented application such as the core application that we developed.

Acknowledgement. The core application was developed with LEPLACE GLOBAL - a tech startup in the industry of augmented reality games.

References

1. Turner, N.C.: Hardware and software techniques for pipeline integrity and leak detection monitoring. Society of Petroleum Engineers (1991)
2. Geiger, G.: Principles of Leak Detection. KROHNE Oil & Gas, Breda (2012)
3. Predescu, A., Mocanu, M., Lupu, C.: Modeling the effects of leaks on measured parameters in a water distribution system. In: 2017 21st International Conference on Control Systems and Computer Science (CSCS), pp. 585–590, May 2017
4. Predescu, A., Mocanu, M., Lupu, C.: Real time implementation of IoT structure for pumping stations in a water distribution system. In: 2017 21st International Conference on System Theory, Control and Computing (ICSTCC), pp. 529–534, October 2017
5. Lupu, C., Chirita, D., Iftimie, S., Miclaus, R.: Consideration on leak/fault detection system in mass transfer networks. Energy Proc. **112**, 58–66 (2017)
6. Isermann, R.: Process fault detection based on modeling and estimation methods—a survey. Automatica **20**(4), 384–404 (1984)
7. Oven, S.: Leak detection in pipelines by the use of state and parameter estimation. Master thesis, Norwegian University of Science and Technology, Department of Engineering Cybernetics, Technical report, January 2014
8. Predescu, A., Negru, C., Mocanu, M., Lupu, C.: Real-time clustering for priority evaluation in a water distribution system. In: AQTR 2018 (2018)
9. Predescu, A., Mocanu, M., Lupu, C.: A modern approach for leak detection in water distribution systems. In: 2018 22nd International Conference on System Theory, Control and Computing (ICSTCC), pp. 486–491 (2018)
10. Candelieri, A., Soldi, D., Conti, D., Archetti, F.: Analytical leakages localization in water distribution networks through spectral clustering and support vector machines. The icewater approach. Proc. Eng. **89**, 1080–1088 (2014). 16th Water Distribution System Analysis Conference, WDSA 2014. http://www.sciencedirect.com/science/article/pii/S1877705814023431
11. Candelieri, A., Soldi, D., Archetti, F.: Cost-effective sensors placement and leak localization - the Neptun pilot of the ICeWater project. J. Water Supply: Res. Technol.-AQUA **64**(5), 567–582 (2015). https://doi.org/10.2166/aqua.2015.037
12. Ganti, R., Ye, F., Lei, H.: Mobile crowd sensing: current state and future challenges. IEEE Commun. Mag. **49**, 32–39 (2011)
13. Gaire, R., et al.: Crowdsensing and privacy in smart city applications, Chap. 5. In: Rawat, D.B., Ghafoor, K.Z. (eds.) Smart Cities Cybersecurity and Privacy, pp. 57–73. Elsevier (2019). http://www.sciencedirect.com/science/article/pii/B9780128150320000056
14. Pereira, G.V., Cunha, M.A., Lampoltshammer, T.J., Parycek, P., Testa, M.G.: Increasing collaboration and participation in smart city governance: a cross-case analysis of smart city initiatives. IT Dev. **23**, 526–553 (2017)
15. Yen, B.T., Mulley, C., Burke, M.: Gamification in transport interventions: another way to improve travel behavioural change. Cities **85**, 140–149 (2019). http://www.sciencedirect.com/science/article/pii/S0264275118300039
16. Hinske, S., Lampe, M., Magerkurth, C., Röcker, C.: Classifying pervasive games: on pervasive computing and mixed reality. Concepts Technol. Pervasive Games-Reader Pervasive Gaming Res. **1**(20), 1–20 (2007)
17. Deterding, S., Dixon, D., Khaled, R., Nacke, L.: From game design elements to gamefulness: defining gamification, vol. 11, pp. 9–15, September 2011

18. Abt, C.C.: Serious Games. New York: Viking, 1970, 176 pp., $5.95, l.c. 79-83234. Am. Behav. Sci. **14**(1), 129 (1970). https://doi.org/10.1177/000276427001400113
19. Halter, E.: From Sun Tzu to Xbox: War and Video Games. Thunder's Mouth Press, New York (2006)
20. Randi, M., Carvalho, H.: Learning through role-playing games: an approach for active learning and teaching. Revista Brasileira de Educação Médica **37**, 80–88 (2013)
21. Moglia, M., Burn, S., Meddings, S.: Decision support system for water pipeline renewal prioritisation. In: ITcon. Special issue Decision Support Systems for Infrastructure Management, vol. 11, pp. 237–256 (2006)
22. Predescu, A., Negru, C., Mocanu, M., Lupu, C., Candelieri, A.: A multiple-layer clustering method for real-time decision support in a water distribution system. In: Abramowicz, W., Paschke, A. (eds.) BIS 2018. LNBIP, vol. 339, pp. 485–497. Springer, Cham (2019). https://doi.org/10.1007/978-3-030-04849-5_42
23. Candelieri, A.: Clustering and support vector regression for water demand forecasting and anomaly detection. Water **9**, 224 (2017)
24. Candelieri, A., Soldi, D., Archetti, F.: Short-term forecasting of hourly water consumption by using automatic metering readers data. Proc. Eng. **119**, 844–853 (2015)
25. Zica, M.R., Ionica, A.C., Leba, M.: Gamification in the context of smart cities. In: IOP Conference Series: Materials Science and Engineering, vol. 294, p. 012045, January 2018. https://doi.org/10.1088/1757-899x/294/1/012045
26. Micheel, I., Novak, J., Fraternali, P., Baroffio, G., Castelletti, A., Rizzoli, A.-E.: Visualizing & gamifying water & energy consumption for behavior change, September 2015
27. Morganti, L., Pallavicini, F., Cadel, E., Candelieri, A., Archetti, F., Mantovani, F.: Gaming for earth: serious games and gamification to engage consumers in pro-environmental behaviours for energy efficiency. Energy Res. Soc. Sci. **29**, 95–102 (2017)

Information Technology for Ethical Use of Water

Panagiotis Christias[(✉)] and Mariana Mocanu[(✉)]

University Politehnica of Bucharest, 060042 Bucharest, Romania
panagiotis.christias@cti.pub.ro,
mariana.mocanu@cs.pub.ro

Abstract. In this article, ethical considerations dealing with the proper use and the quality of water are examined based on literature resources. Principles of ethics and challenges when managing water resources are discussed. Subsequently, proposals are made on how information technology can assist assessments and decisions related to water. Additional proposals in the context of water well use relate information systems and artificial intelligence with citizens' participation and machine learning to predict unexpected or disastrous events.

Keywords: Ethics · Water resources management · Information systems · Artificial intelligence

1 Introduction

Global demands for water increase rapidly. In combination with factors like the change in Earth's climate, pollution, and urban growing populations, the requirement for applying proper ethical frameworks and legislation towards sustainability and preservation is unquestionable. Water deficiency or inadequate sanitation in large parts of the world places added consideration [1]. Governments, organizations and individuals have to treat water reserves wisely aiming towards to sustainability and equal distribution. Information technology can assist those efforts in order to preserve ethical principles and alleviate effects due to misuse and the global environmental change.

2 Why Water Resources Management Has Become More Significant

Ethical matters on water resources involve quantity and quality [1]. Ethical matters concerning water resource management and water quality assurance is a major topic worldwide and the European Union nowadays [2–5]. The first point which requires the moral values and obligations on this topic is the optimal and well use of water [1]. The latter relates to drinking water and water used in agriculture or livestock facilities. Intensive agriculture, manufacturing methods and cities overpopulation put the global water resources availability to the test [1]. The main activities which exhaust available water resources are [9]:

W. Abramowicz and R. Corchuelo (Eds.): BIS 2019 Workshops, LNBIP 373, pp. 597–607, 2019.
https://doi.org/10.1007/978-3-030-36691-9_50

1. Agricultural Water Use
2. Industrial Water Use
3. Water for Energy Production

When it comes to quality of water the scientific challenges lie around the following areas [7]:

1. Quality in water
2. Prevent pollution
3. Treat water once polluted
4. Dispose wastewater safely
5. Restore and protect vulnerable ecosystems

3 Principles in Water Ethics

We have to aim for a social change towards water, aided by the technological advances and innovation. A major priority must be the ethical use of water to sustain and promote human and ecosystemic health [1]. Additional principles of water are based on values, such as democratic governance rights, active participation of individuals, transparency, accountability, and public-private collaboration and partnership. Implementing these ethical ideals and obligations in practice depends on a number of factors: Who are the decision makers? Is participation active and contributing in formulating options or is it passive and reactive to proposals that are already well-developed? What kind of information is open to the public? How do professionals interact with non-professionals? Is there respect for cultural diversity and traditional beliefs and practices? And finally, how is a balance determined between the needs of human development and the need to preserve our natural resources?

Ethics can form both the source and normative content of a particular decision by providing reason and justification. The sub-commission of COMEST argued that, rather than analyzing once more the ethical issues of water management, it should try to promote best ethical practices [9]. They identified some fundamental principles, as follows.

3.1 The Principle of Equal Respect for Human Dignity

This is a fundamental principle of public health ethics; the concept of human dignity is not at odds with respect for other creatures and for nature and thus is fundamental to environmental ethics as well [1]. This principle encapsulates the basic needs and the promotion of human health and well-being. It incorporates the underlying notion behind the framework of universal human rights.– [9]. There is no life without water and those to whom it is denied they are denied life.

3.2   The Principle of Equity and Proportionality

Equity and proportionate response are required in the face of limited resources to give priority to the least well off, those most immediately at risk, and those who are made vulnerable by past discrimination, exclusion, and powerlessness [1].

3.3   The Principle of Solidarity

The notion of solidarity and interdependence applies in a social context, among human individuals and groups, but it applies with equal importance and resonance in an ecological context, between human and biotic communities [9]. This interdependence poses challenges for water management resulting in the need for integrated water management approaches [9].

3.4   The Principle of the Common Good

This principle calls for the recognition of situations in which the pursuit of rational self-interest by each individual leads to outcomes that are irrational and harmful to the interests of all individuals involved [1]. Water and the technologies of its utilization often present "tragedy of the commons" type scenarios, for which a conceptualization of water as a common resource and sustainable water utilization as a common good provides the ethically appropriate response.

3.5   The Principle of Right Relationship or Responsible Stewardship

The principles of solidarity and the common good call for collective action in relationship to public health and water management. The principle of right relationship addresses the substantive content and effects of such collective action [1]. The responsible course of action is closely tied with the actual properties and circumstances of what is being responded to. For example, the unsustainable use of an aquifer or the biological degradation of a watershed and its dependent ecosystems are forms of environmental malpractice. They do not establish right relationships between the human beings who use and affect water with artificial construction and technology, on the one hand, and the specific biological, chemical, and physical realities of water, on the other.

3.6   The Principle of Inclusive and Deliberative Participation

Just as the principle of right relationship and responsible stewardship addresses a substantive ethical standard for the content of public health and water management policies, so the principle of participation addresses the values inherent in the process of policymaking and decision making [1]. Often the mechanisms and institutions of democratic governance are selective and rely on bargaining and interest maximization strategies by powerful, well-organized, and well-represented groups. This type of governance and decision making may not be well suited to the protection, conservation, and equitable distribution of common goods. More adequate governance mechanisms, from an ethical point of view, involve a deliberative and participatory process marked by transparency, universal access to information, inclusiveness, and individual and community empowerment so that all may take advantage of the open information and the participatory opportunities.

4 Problems with Water Resources Management

Ecologically informed and ethically responsible water management are essential for public health and are necessary to secure these resources for future generations of all life forms [9]. Responsible behavior requires us to admit that all water cannot be considered ours for human uses. This conclusion rests on creating the proper social and political motivation to produce ethical policy and practice.

What needs to be understood as ultimate takeaway for the developed countries is the motivations and resulting commitments which can lead to a system centered around ecological conservation and protection and the preservation of quality in water. For the success of those aims each individual must value not only their own comfort and convenience, but also the dynamics and necessities of nature [1].

Water resource management problems can be seen at every stage of the development, utilization and management of water resources [8]:

1. Pollution. The widespread use of chemicals in industry and agriculture has led to the dispersal of rare chemical elements, antibiotics, pesticides, herbicides and fertilizers on fields.
2. Physical Problems. Physical problems deal with poorly developed water supply and wastewater treatment facilities, and incomplete water metering/monitoring systems.
3. Water Pricing Problems. Low water prices are one of the leading factors contributing to excessive water use in agriculture. The methods of determining the water price should be sufficient to meet operation and maintenance costs. China makes a striking example: Water pricing is generally based on irrigated land area or only based on the electricity used. The water prices applied for industrial and domestic uses do not reflect the actual cost of water.
4. Organizational Problems. Most of the water conflicts are caused by organizational problems. "Integrated Water Resources Management" (IWRM) is not been fully implemented or produces poor results [9].

5 Methods and Ideas Towards Better and Ethical Water Resource Management

The application of ethical concepts is directly related to water resource management. It can support the decision making process, which is a very complex issue involving a range of scientific domains (hydrology, groundwater, precipitation and runoff, water quality), and requires simultaneous consideration from different areas of water use, both from the supply and demand side (an integrated approach to water resource management), and their integration with socio-economic aspects. On the other hand, different tools and methodologies that are designed to support the knowledge base and decision making in the water sector are often technical. Review of state of the art and the application of these methodologies suggest that knowledge supporting tools and methodologies are not restricted to technical problems as they are also challenged by procedural items associated with stakeholder participation, especially at the level of communication with water managers and decision makers [9]. In this complex environment with different variables, the role of ethics is to provide operational assistance and conceptualization of different perspectives while helping to keep a focus on the actions, the consequences, or the motives, which examine the concepts of rights and duties, or effects and outcomes. From this perspective, the precautionary principle or cost benefit analysis for example, are useful.

Some of the main problems when dealing with water are going to be reviewed and we will try to make suggestions how information technology can contribute to offer candidate solutions. Methodologies already applied will be mentioned as well as our proposals to specific issues. The aforementioned ethics principles will form the framework which will highlight the working point of those ideas. Another reality that has to be respected is that water is inevitably considered a trading product. Without violating the primal human rights principles, this can be treated as a balancing factor towards a more sensible use of water.

5.1   Sharing Information and Knowhow

Available knowledge can improve water conditions and clearly benefit society, but achieving this goal means overcoming obstacles represented by cultural issues, local environment and population income levels [8]. There has to be commitments and actions in order for information to become available regarding water health, safety and resource use issues. Access to information, technological developments, sharing water resources with communities belonging to underdeveloped countries and transfer of knowledge especially from developed countries to those in great aid is important. It is an ethical issue crossing the social spectrum.

5.2   Balancing Economic Welfare and Ethical Behavior

Public health, economic growth, legitimate use, and equality to water distribution push governments to build effective integrated water resources management (IWRM) [10]. Integrated water resources management promote utilitarian governance where the goal is to maximize economic and social welfare without compromising the environment. A values approach to water governance (usage of water for economic growth and public well-being) is valuable, because it may not resolve ethical dilemmas, but it improves our understanding of how and why ethical issues are central to the task of adapting technical and political issues to changing patterns of water governance. The Santa Fe river case in New Mexico USA is a great example on this [10]. After many generations exploitation of the river resources, the government built a damn aiming to increasing the water availability to depending infrastructures (city populations, agriculture). At the same time it introduced modern ethical dilemmas because it transferred ownership to the private sector. As a result, adjacent areas were deprived of the river flow throughout the year. Moreover, there were periods that the river's flow was completely stopped. After assessing the situation, a new policy allows releases of surplus water from the dam more slowly to extend the period of the river flow.

The ideal situation for a sustainable use of water would require that the full cost of water should just equal its full value. At this point, according to classic economic models, the social welfare should be maximized [11]. Privatization seems an attractive path, but there are plenty of matters to consider. The most critical is ensuring a safe water supply. The expansion of multinational firms dealing with water supply and sanitation came along with a number of unsuccessful water privatization cases. Examples of such cases are the withdrawals of Suez from concession contracts in Argentina and the Philippines and of SAUR from a water supply contract in Mozambique [11]. Ideological, financial and pragmatic factors support the reasoning behind expecting better services from private water companies. They usually take up the water supply services and the waste water disposal services [12].

It is presently recognized that the implementation of proper water charging schemes is necessary to ensure efficient water services. Recently there has been a tendency to adopt charging schemes for water that progressively assume a full cost recovery to provide sufficient incentives for water conservation [11].

6 Information Technology for a Favorable Future in Water

6.1 Information Systems for Assessment and Decision

Environmental water organizations (EWOs) are identifiable organizations that can be held accountable for specific tasks in implementing environmental water policies. EWOs operate in a nested governance arrangement, building partnerships across spatial scales, policy areas, and between the public and private sectors. They promote active environmental water management, which is needed when environmental water allocation mechanisms and policy settings require ongoing active decision making to achieve the maximum environmental benefits [6].

Taking into account the ethics principles, legal frameworks concerning well use and quality of water and the problems as described above, let's examine how information technology and artificial intelligence can be of value to ensure better operations in governance (management, decision making), but conserving at the same time ethical values during those processes. The European Union has declared the necessity and the principal role information systems must have in management and operations. All financing and auditing procedures need to be transparent. Systems of financial control need to be rigorous in order to avoid the mismanagement or misapplication of funds associated with largescale investments in major construction works. Management information systems need to be suitable for the organizational level at which the relevant data collection and analysis activities are conducted. Inputs and outcomes need to be monitored in such a way that they provide information of value to managers when they require it [12].

Especially in the modern days where privatization takes control away from governments, central information repositories which produce high quality statistical calculations and observe water resources availability and disposal can ensure the purity of data eliminating events of manipulation and alteration. Study of data can also monitor activities results from companies related to water services across different areas and validate if the criteria and specifications are met in compliance with the government agreements. To go even further, intelligent decision systems can co-assist governance management. There have been attempts to incorporate decision support systems for groundwater and river construction works [13, 14]. Parameters like geophysical characteristics, climatic, water use but also socio-economic data are taken into account [14]. Results, show that active participation of stakeholders improve the decision process [13, 14].

We propose the gradual accumulation of data by involving citizens to this procedure. Modern software can accept information coming from devices of users which will declare observations and events from city or suburban environments. These may involve a broken water network pipe or imminent flood after heavy rainfall. Participation is a form of ethical position on water. Observing but doing nothing is as bad as acting maliciously. Those data can assist decisions on funding new infrastructure or restoring damages in areas where problems persist. The social aspect and character of each region is reflected to data coming from individuals, thus weighting more the appropriate alternatives for choice by the governance operators.

6.2   Social Media and Intelligent Forecasting

Long term planning and management is of high value but machine learning methods can take advantage of social media messaging flow to capture and predict unexpected and sudden events which can have dramatic effects. A broken water or sewage pipe, or sudden raise of water level after heavy rain, are all events which can occur and escalate in short time periods and have tremendous effects. Possible outcomes include massive loss of clean water, pollution of water reserves, cultivation destruction and dangers on human life. Messages on Twitter can help predict and act on time to these kind of situations. The application of such a system can really perform inside a city or urban environment where we have plenty of end users connected to the Internet. Twitter works with short length messages. Phrases in this messages form topics and when this phrases become very frequent then the topic becomes trending. Trends among a group of keywords related to our focus can warn us about harmful events, so that we have more time to react. How can we predict popular topics of interest before they become trending? Classification methods can give answer to that [15]. Logistic regression, linear discriminant analysis, quadratic analysis and K-Nearest neighbors can work with historical data which are available on Twitter and learn to predict if a critical topic will become trending. The challenge is how much earlier can we achieve a trustworthy prediction? We have to weigh important types of error more than less significant type of errors. With confusion matrices we can trade-off different types of errors which lead to a Receiver Operating Characteristic (ROC) curve. A true positive rate would classify correctly bad situations and a false positive rate would classify an event as trending without eventually becoming popular. Then we have to fine tune misclassification in our predictions. This way we can find the best point ahead of time where we have a strong probability for correctly classifying a bad event as likely to happen soon, at the cost of making a wrong assumption.

6.3   Information Systems and Water Resources Management

The ideas discussed in this section are visually expressed in the following figure where we can view the operation and interconnection of information technology with key factors in water use (Fig. 1).

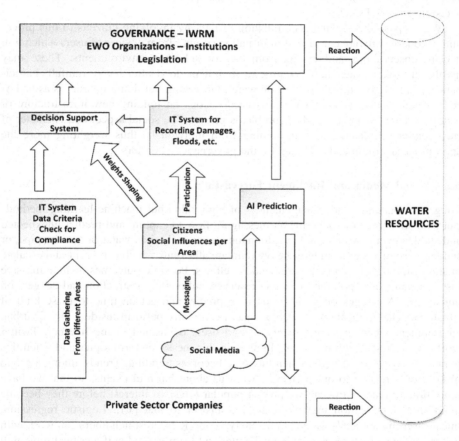

Fig. 1. Water management stakeholders and interconnected IT systems

7   Ethically Aligned Artificial Intelligence

The advent of artificial intelligence throws up ethical issues and considerations. Use of artificial intelligence should reflect the same ethical values which drive our efforts on ethical use of water. Should Artificial Intelligence be allowed to develop beyond the point where it surpasses, new intelligence? Furthermore, should Artificial Intelligence ethically be allowed not to be amenable to human will and instead take independent actions which could spell disastrous consequences for human society? [16]. Intelligent and autonomous technical systems are specifically designed to reduce human intervention in our day-to-day decisions. In doing so, these new fields are raising concerns about their impact on individuals and societies. Despite the positive impact, there are as well warnings, based on the potential harm on security of critical infrastructure, and the long-term effects on social well-being. As the use and impact of autonomous and intelligent systems (A/IS) become pervasive, we need to revisit the ethical framework from research and development phases to installing and using its products. Establishment of societal and policy guidelines is necessary in order for such systems to remain human-centric, serving humanity's values and ethical principles. These systems have to behave in a way that is beneficial to people beyond reaching functional goals and addressing technical problems. This will allow for an elevated level of trust between people and technology that is needed for its fruitful use in our daily lives. The ethical design, development, and implementation of these technologies should be guided by the following general principles which will actually benefit water resource management [17]:

- Accountability: Ensure that their designers and operators are responsible and accountable. Government and industry stakeholders should identify the types of decisions and operations that should never be delegated to such systems and adopt rules and standards that ensure effective human control over those decisions and how to allocate legal responsibility for harm caused by them.
- Transparency: Although self-improving algorithms can automate decision making with impact on citizens, legal requirements mandate transparency and accuracy. Legal representatives and courts must have reasonable access to all data and information generated and used by such systems. The logic and rules embedded in the system must be available and subject to testing. The systems should generate audit trails recording the facts. This way their reasoning and decisions can be explained in a transparent and comprehensive way.
- Embedding values into Autonomous Systems. If machines engage in human communities as autonomous agents, then those agents will be expected to follow the community's social and moral norms. Embedding norms in such systems requires a clear delineation of the community in which they are to be deployed. The first step is to identify the norms of the specific community in which the systems are to be deployed and, in particular, norms relevant to the kinds of tasks that they are designed to perform.
- Affective Computing. Affect is a core aspect of intelligence. Drives and emotions such as anger, fear, and joy are often the foundations of actions throughout our life. To ensure that intelligent technical systems will be used to help humanity to the greatest extent possible, artifacts should not cause harm either by amplifying or damping human emotional experience.

System developers should employ value-based design methodologies in order to create sustainable systems that can be evaluated in terms of both social costs and also advantages which may grow economic value for organizations.

8 Conclusions

Water in the 21st century is becoming what petroleum was in the 20th century. Demand growth due to population increase and requirements in agriculture and industry, combined with world climate changes in weather and temperature produce major considerations on our behavior and treatment of water. In this paper we discussed how ethical principles are bound to sustainable water management. After viewing the problems which affect quality and usable quantity of water globally, we examined how information technology can play major role to various steps of water management processes aligned with ethical values. Multiple stakeholders participate in the cycle of water distribution today. Governments, organizations, private sector companies and lastly citizens have their responsibility in the future of the planet's water resources. The assistance of information systems involve detailed and non-manipulated data, automated decision systems input. We proposed applications to enhance individuals' participation related to observations on unexpected and harmful water related events. Moreover machine learning is proposed to contribute to early prediction of such events giving authorities time advantage to act and conserve water or protect public health.

References

1. Jennings, B., Heltne, P., Kintzele, K.: Principles of water ethics. Minding Nat. **2**(2), 25–26 (2009)
2. European Commision. http://ec.europa.eu/environment/water/water-urbanwaste/index_en. html. Accessed 31 Mar 2019
3. European Commision. http://ec.europa.eu/environment/water/water-framework/index_en. html. Accessed 31 Mar 2019
4. European Commision. http://ec.europa.eu/environment/aarhus/index.htm. Accessed 31 Mar 2019
5. Horne, A.C., Angus Webb, J., Stewardson, M.J., Richter, B., Acreman, M.: Water for the Environment. From Policy and Science to Implementation and Management. Academic Press an Imprint of Elsevier, Cambridge (2017)
6. McNamara, P.: Water quality matters. In: Shroder, J.F., Ahmadzai, S.J. (eds.) Transboudary Water Resources in Afghanistan: Climate Change and Land-Use Implications, pp. 269–289. Elsevier, Amsterdam (2016)
7. Novo, F.G.: Morar drought: the ethics of water use. Water Policy **14**(S1), 65–72 (2012)
8. Regional Unit for Social and Human Sciences in Asia and the Pacific: Water Ethics and Water Resources Management. UNESCO Bangkok (2011)
9. Groenfeldt, D., Schmidt, J.J.: Ethics and water governance. Ecol. Soc. **18**(1) (2013). http://dx.doi.org/10.5751/ES-04629-180114
10. Veiga da Cunha, L.: Water: a human right or an economic resource? In: Ramon Llamas, M., Martinez-Cortina, L., Mukherji, A. (eds.) Water Ethics, Marcelino Botin Water Forum 2007, pp. 97–114. CRC Press, Boca Raton (2009)
11. Henriksen, H.J., Rasmusssen, P., Brandt, G., Bulow, D., Jensen, F.V.: Bayesian networks as a participatory modelling tool for groundwater protection. In: Castelletti, A., Soncini-Sessa, R. (eds.) Topics on System Analysis and Integrated Water Resource Management, pp. 49–72. Elsevier, Amsterdam (2007)

12. Georgakakos, A.P.: Decision support systems for integrated water resources management with an application to the Nile basin. In: Castelletti, A., Soncini-Sessa, R. (eds.) Topics on System Analysis and Integrated Water Resource Management, pp. 99–116. Elsevier, Amsterdam (2007)
13. European federation of national water services (EurEau). http://www.eureau.org/resources/news/1-the-governance-of-water-services-in-europe. Accessed 31 Mar 2019
14. United States Environmental Protection Agency. https://www.epa.gov/laws-regulations/summary-clean-water-act. Accessed 31 Mar 2019
15. James, G., Witten, D., Hastie, T., Tibshirani, R.: Classification. In: James, G., Witten, D., Hastie, T., Tibshirani, R. (eds.) An Introduction to Statistical Learning. STS, vol. 103, pp. 127–173. Springer, New York (2013). https://doi.org/10.1007/978-1-4614-7138-7_4
16. Stückelberger, C., Duggal, P.: Cyber Ethics 4.0 Serving Humanity with Values. Globethics. net, Geneva (2018)
17. The IEEE Global Initiative on Ethics of Autonomous and Intelligent Systems, Ethically aligned design: a vision for prioritizing human well-being with autonomous and intelligent systems, version 2 (2017). http://standards.ieee.org/develop/indconn/ec/ead_v2.pdf

Doctoral Consortium

Doctoral Consortium Chair's Message

The Doctoral Consortium was held in conjunction with the BIS 2019 conference, a well-respected event joining international researchers to discuss the wide range of the development, implementation, application, and improvement of business applications and systems. The goal of the Consortium was to allow doctoral students to present their research and obtain comments from the community. PhD Candidates also had a chance to hear about the work of their peers at other universities, and to interact with today's leading researchers from different universities and countries.

The Consortium was divided into two parts: plenary session and mentoring session. During the plenary session each student presented his or her work (research ideas, the current progress, future plans) and received constructive criticism and insights related to his or her paper. The mentoring session took place after the presentations. A dedicated Consortium Mentor was assigned to each student to provide individual feedback and advice on the paper, the focus of the work and further developments. PhD Candidates improved their papers based on the discussion and Mentors' advices.

All received submissions went through two rounds of review. Papers which qualified in the first round were presented at the Consortium, and the second round took place after the conference. The Program Committee consisted of 22 members from 15 countries. In total, we received 16 submissions from 5 countries. 7 papers were accepterd for publication, which amounts to an acceptance rate of 44%.

Accepted papers covered a wide range of topics, from theoretical studies to industry applications. All presented disseratation proposals followed the Design Science Research approach, but were on a different level of advancement, thus the discussion during the Consortium was not only limited to the research results and it's evaluation but also methodology, research problem, and artifacts specification, as well as analysis of prior research/theory.

June 2019

Elżbieta Lewańska
Jorge Marx Gómez

Organization

Chairs

Elżbieta Lewańska   Poznań University of Economics and Business, Poland

Jorge Marx Gómez   University of Oldenburg, German

Program Committee

João Barata	Universidade de Coimbra, Portugal
Jose Alejandro Cano	University of Medellin, Colombia
Tsung-nan Chou	Chaoyang University of Technology, Taiwan
Ioana Ciuciu	Babes-Bolyai University, Romania
Stéphanie Gauttier	University of Twente, The Netherlands
Ralf-Christian Härting	Aalen University, Germany
Inma Hernandez	University of Seville, Spain
Meena Jha	Central Queensland University, Australia
Patricia Jiménez Aguirre	University of Seville, Spain
Sesha Kethineni	Prairie View A&M University, USA
Włodzimierz Lewoniewski	Poznan University of Economics and Business, Poland
Xiufeng Liu	Technical University of Denmark, Denmark
Mariana Mocanu	University Politehnica of Bucharest, Romania
Marcin Pietranik	Wrocław University of Science and Technology, Poland
Panagiotis Sismanis	Sidenor Steel Industry, Greece
Piotr Stolarski	Poznań University of Economics and Business, Poland
Milena Stróżyna	Poznan University of Economics and Business, Poland
David Suda	University of Malta, Malta
Zinaida Taran	Delta State University, USA
Zuzana Tučkova	Tomas Bata University in Zlín, Czech Republic
Dustin van der Haar	University of Johannesburg, South Africa
Alfred Zimmermann	Reutlingen University, Germany

Towards a System for Data Transparency
to Support Data Subjects

Christian Janßen[(✉)]

Department Very Large Business Applications, University of Oldenburg,
Ammerländer Heerstr. 114-118, 26129 Oldenburg, Germany
christian.janssen@uni-oldenburg.de

Abstract. Data Transparency is one of the major challenges that comes
with the new European General Data Protection Regulation (GDPR).
In the age of Digital Transformation, more applications and processes
generate data that needs to be regulated under the requirements of
the GDPR. Concepts like Data Ownership or Data Sovereignty becomes
more popular and enable independent legal decisions for the data subject.
This research-in-progress aims to develop a data transparency system
that assists data subjects and companies. Therefore, a research roadmap
which includes research questions and the design have been developed.
First results, regard to research question one are mentioned. A structured
text analysis of the GDPR identifies articles and recitations in the categories Data Transparency and self-control (Data Ownership and Data
Sovereignty). In combination, a literature review of 1392 papers shows
possible solutions.

Keywords: GDPR · Data ownership · Data transparency · Data
sovereignty · Data science

1 Introduction

The Digital Transformation not only permeates the business world, but also
has fundamental implications for the whole society. This leads to interactions
between different actors. Individuals and communities have different expectations on state institutions and companies. In turn, institutions can exert regulatory influences in order to change the scope of action of all of those parties.
Companies and scientific institutions take up these regulatory guidelines and
create new insights through the development and advancement of digital technologies [3].

Within the growing amount of data in the age of the Digital Transformation through new applications, processes and technologies especially in companies, legal frameworks (e.g. General Data Protection Regulation (GDPR))
becomes more important. After the adoption in April 2016 and the ratification
by May 25th, 2018, the goal of the GDPR is to accelerate the economic and social

© Springer Nature Switzerland AG 2019
W. Abramowicz and R. Corchuelo (Eds.): BIS 2019 Workshops, LNBIP 373, pp. 613–624, 2019.
https://doi.org/10.1007/978-3-030-36691-9_51

progress of the EU society [26]. Also, the GDPR stipulates obligations of protection with respect to the processing and sharing of personal data between various entities. These entities could be the following: A data subject could be an individual, who's personal data are regulated by the GDPR [1]. A data controller could be a person or legal entity that controls both purpose and means of personal data processing. In combination, a data processor processes personal data on behalf of the data controller [1]. Specific obligations relate to obtaining consent from data subjects, the provision of transparency with respect to personal data processing and sharing, and ensuring compliance with usage restrictions [12]. Because of this, topics such as Data Transparency, Data Ownership and Data Sovereignty becomes popular again. Data Transparency ensures, that all privacy related data processing include the legal, technical, organizational and procedural settings can be understood and reproduced at any time. The information's has to be available before, during and after processing [18]. On the technical side, Data Lineage and Data Provenance solutions are promising implementations to reach Data Transparency. On the legal side, Data Sharing Agreements could be support legal rights by formulating clear rules. Data Ownership is defined as the legal right and complete control over a single piece or set of data elements [27]. In Combination, Data Sovereignty can be seen as an ethical and fundamental right-based informational self-determination. The data subject are able to make independent and autonomous decisions about their data [2,32].

Inside this paper, first steps of the realization of a transparency system which combines the mentioned aspects of transparency, ownership and sovereignty are described in a research roadmap. The data transparency system could enable data subjects and data controllers to interact with each other in order to increase and visualize the transparency of data related streams. The rest of the paper is organized as follows: Sect. 2 gives the motivation behind a system for data transparency. Section 3 shows a research roadmap that combines research questions, goals and the design. Also, preliminary results with reference to the first research question will be presented. Finally, Sect. 4 concludes the paper.

2   Motivation

Data is rapidly becoming a universal currency of our economy, a digital good whose value does not diminish with use and whose benefits are realized only when it can flow [14]. As already mentioned, there is a continuous increase in database through new applications, processes, technologies and the advancing digital transformation of analogue areas. For example, the global data traffic will increase to 163 Zettabytes by 2025 [25]. The administrative workload for data controller and processor in the areas of transparency of data use and data protection will increase tremendous [19].

Usually the processing of data, including personal data, requires the consent of the data subject. According to the GDPR, Art. 4 No. 11, several conditions must be respected. For example, consents have to be given voluntarily and without pressure or influence on the data subject. In addition, the data subject must be clearly and comprehensibly informed as to why his data is required and what happens to this stored data. This is linked to an active consent to the use of data, which is always designed for one or more specific purposes [24]. In particular, these limitations creates more questions than answers. Despite more precise legal regulations, it is often unclear how the stored data is processed or used for further purposes, such as sharing with third parties [33].

The lack of monitoring for the data subject makes it difficult to ensure the specified purpose limitation. Regarding the GDPR Art. 7 No. 1 and 3, the compliance of these limitations are main tasks of companies which process the data [24]. Therefore, the data subject need the possibility to interact with these companies, if his opinion in the use of data changed. In addition, the legal situation of data ownership is permeated by insufficiencies. Data protectors complained that there are only a few possibilities to establish clear ownership rights. Apart from that, the GDPR can be seen as chance to enhance digital rights by entrenching Data Transparency. Through more precise legal rules in the processing and use of data and the combination of technological development in this research area, data subjects could be supported.

3   Research Roadmap and Preliminary Results

This section introduces a research roadmap (research questions, goal and design) for the development of a data transparency system. Also, first results concerning to Data Transparency and self-control (Data Ownership and Data Sovereignty) are mentioned.

3.1   Research Questions, Goals and Design

Basically, the implementation of a data transparency system is oriented to the Design Science Research approach, according to Pfeffers [23] and Hevner [11], and it includes the following key objectives:

1. A data subject is supported and encouraged to make independent decisions regard to his data-basis which he generates.
2. On the basis of data-related interaction processes between companies and data subject, the participating interaction partners are provided with transparent ways of collecting, processing, using and passing on data for the purpose of traceability.
3. Through the use of Data Sharing Agreements and a better interaction with the data subject, companies could simplify their Data Governance/Data Compliance Policies.

The approach of a data transparency system focuses on the development of a technical system to support Data Ownership and Data Sovereignty by creating Data Transparency. As a central element on the technical level, the integration of a monitoring of data streams for data subject is made possible by using e.g. Data

Lineage, Data Provenance components. These components could be integrated into a data warehouse environment and will be used for tracing the data-related interactions of the data subject. Another important element of the system is the visualization of the traced data and the possibility for self-responsible decisions and interactions within an application for data subject. The research questions (RQ1–RQ3) in Fig. 1 have been derived from the key objectives. According to Wilde and Hess [31], research methods out of the methodical spectrum of business informatics will be used.

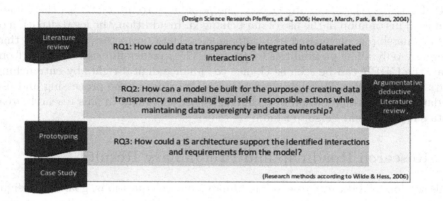

Fig. 1. Research questions and design

In the first research question (RQ1), requirements will be raised through a structured literature review and a text analysis of the GDPR. Therefore, legal frameworks and possible solutions (e.g. Data Lineage, Data Provenance) regard to Data Transparency, Data Ownership and Data Sovereignty will be analyzed. Also, questions in the motivation for using the system have to be considered. Within the second research question (RQ2) all aspects of RQ1 will be combined and used to develop a model of a transparency system. In addition, concepts of data sharing agreements have to be screened, set up and realized in the model. The research methods argumentative deductive analysis and literature review will be used. The major task of the third research question (RQ3) is to implement an IS architecture based on the developed model. Therefore, a software prototype will be set up and evaluated through case studies.

3.2   Preliminary Results

As already stated in the introduction, this research merges the areas of Data Transparency, Data Ownership and Data Sovereignty with legal components out of the GDPR to face the existing lack of transparency in use of data. Also, the connection between data subjects and companies should be enabled. With regard to RQ1, initial items have been conducted.

The first item is a text analysis of the GDPR with reference to Transparency and self-control. Following the approaches of Früh [9], Merten [17] and Krippendorff [13] the empirical method of a quantitative content analysis allows a systematic description of the given content and a formal characterization of messages. Therefore, Früh described four process steps. The conception phase characterizes the problem and focus the formation of hypothesis. The development phase forms different theoretical and empirically-driven categories. During the testing phase reliability and validation tests are performed. In the final application phase, data will be prepared, coded and analyzed. Through the help of MAXDictio, a tool for vocabulary analysis, dictionary creation and quantitative content analysis, result tables of different terms and categories have been developed. The following Fig. 2 gives an overview about the process of the used content analysis.

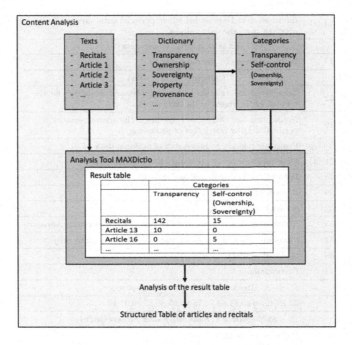

Fig. 2. Process content analysis

The starting point of the analysis are recitals and articles of the GDPR, which have been splitted up into different texts. This certain number of texts represent individual sections that are also called text units. In dictionary-based content analysis, they can also be used as analyzing units. Within the analysis, the associated dictionary consist different categories and words that are assigned to it. For the text analysis of the GDPR the categories Data Transparency and self-control (Data Ownership and Data Sovereignty) were created as well as connecting words (e.g. provenance, transparency, ownership, sovereignty, property). The quantitative content analysis allows the automatic counting of category frequencies in the texts on the basis of the dictionary [9]. Whenever a word contained in the dictionary is found in the text, the counter of the relevant category increases. After generating the result table, the stored findings were transformed into a structured table (Fig. 3) of articles and recitals regard to GDPR Data Transparency and self-control (Data Ownership and Data Sovereignty).

Article	Title
	Transparency
	Ex ante specific Transparency
13	Information to be provided where personal data are collected from the data subject
14	Information to be provided where personal data have not been obtained from the data subject
	Ex post specific Transparency
15	Rights of access by the data subject
	Transparency in general
12	Transparent information, communication and modalities for the exercise of the rights of the data subject
19	Notification and obligation regarding retification or erasure of personal data or restriction of processing
5 (1)a.	Principles relation to processing of personal data
21 (4)	Clear and separately presentation of informations
25	Data protection by design and default
30	Records of processing activities
32	Security of processing
33	Notification of a personal data breach to the supervisory authority
34	Communication of a personal data breach to the data subject
40	Codes of conduct
42	Certification
	Recitals with focus on Transparency
	32,29,42,58,60,61,63,74,78,84,85,86,87,90,91,100
	Self-control (Ownership and Sovereignty)
16	Right to rectification
17	Right to erasure
18	Right to restriction of processing
19	Notification and obligation regarding retification or erasure of personal data or restriction of processing
20	Right to portability
21	Right to object
22	Automated individual decision making and profiling

Fig. 3. Results content analysis

The second item is a qualitative literature review which makes it possible to review papers based on given context. Following the methodology by Webster and Watson [30], Cato [7] described four process steps for a qualitative literature review.

Database	Search String
1) Google Scholar 2) ORBIS 3) IEEE 4) ScienceDirect 5) Jstore 6) SpringerLink 7) ACM Digital Library 8) Web of Science	1) GDPR AND (Data Transparency OR Data Sovereignty OR Data Ownership) 2) GDPR AND (Model OR Framework OR Architecture) AND (Interoperability OR Data OR Consent OR Information OR Provenance OR Agreement)

Fig. 4. Database and search string

1. Definition of search strategy and parameter:
   The first process step defines the search process in order to record relevant publications. Also, different databases, where publications will be searched and the requirements should be defined. The following Fig. 4 shows, the research strategy and parameter that are used for this literature review.

   The search strings have been divided into two parts. All search terms are combined through the use of an or-operator for query-based search operation in the different databases. Also, specific limitations have been established. For example the search terms must be included in the abstract or key-words of the paper.
2. Identification and selection of relevant papers and forward and backward search:
   In the second process step, the literature research is executed with the defined search parameters. Based on the specific limitations, the titles and abstracts are screened in order to find the most relevant papers. The results of the findings, based on the search string are described in Fig. 5. Within the third process step, the forward and backward search are used to identify relevant papers in the bibliography of the already screened papers. In total, the literature research delivered 1392 papers of which 62 papers were relevant and selected for the related work path.
3. Analysis of relevant papers:
   Following the category-formation of the deductive qualitative content analysis by Mayring [16], the 62 relevant papers have been transferred into deductive categories. Therefore, the categories of the text analysis (Transparency, self-control (Ownership, Sovereignty)) have been reused and extended for the deductive category building. Figure 6 gives an overview about the different papers from 2013 to 2019 divided into the categories.

Database	Results	Selected papers
ORBIS	418	15
IEEE	47	2
ScienceDirect	113	10
Jstore	48	2
SpringerLink	625	24
ACM Digital Library	67	4
Web of Science	22	2
Forward and backward search	52	3
Total	**1392**	**62**

Fig. 5. Results structured literature review

After a closer look into the relevant papers, 49 Papers could be assigned to the mentioned categories. On the other side, 13 Papers shows a mixture and have not been added. With the adoption of the GDPR in April 2016, the numbers of papers are increasing continuously. More than 65% of the papers deals with the topic Data Transparency and 35% with the topic Data Ownership and Data Sovereignty. Researchers all over the world started to build different solutions on Data Transparency, Data Ownership and Data Sovereignty. According to Mayring [16] the inductive categories problem-based solutions and legal-based solutions have been formed. In total 13 problem-based solutions and 15 legal-based solutions have been resulted. Figure 7 gives an overview on specific problem and legal based solutions.

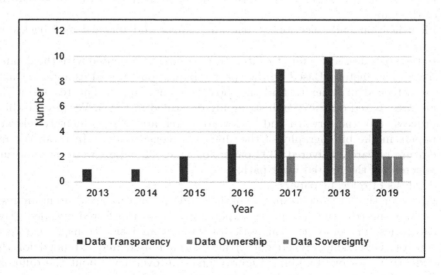

Fig. 6. Number of papers per year

Maguire et al. [14] shows, how a metadata-based architecture helps to balance the tensions between users and business. In combination, Tzolov [29] adopted a personal data model that allows a structured design process in line with the principles of privacy by design. For a better understanding of the interaction of different actors within the GDPR, Matulevicius [15] mapped the associated rights and responsibilities to each actor in order to reach GDPR compliance. Pandit et al. [20] described also a interoperability model that demonstrates how information flows between the actors. The research of Antignac et al. [6] indicates how some of the prescriptions of the privacy legislation and standards may be related to a technical design. Also, the extension of privacy language notations such as DFD, LPL, or ProvO in the GDPR context have been considered. The work of Alshammari et al. [5], Mougiakou et al. [18], Fatema et al. [8], Tom et al. [28], Agarwal et al. [4] and Pandit et al. [21, 22] can be used for this purpose. To demonstrate how transparency could be improved through a framework and data traceability controls, Gjermundrod et al. [10] introduced the privacyTracker.

Specific problem and legal based solutions	
Architecture	4
Data-Flow-Model	3
Meta-Model	3
Framework	3
Blockchain	3
LPL Model and Framework	2
System	2
Consent and Data Management Model	1
Flow-Chart	1
Data-Model	1
Design-Model	1
Data Interoperability Model	1
Graph Model	1
Data-Lifecycle-Model	1
Knowledge-based Model	1

Fig. 7. Legal and problem-based solutions

4   Conclusion

The emergence of data-driven economy has resulted in the need for a system, that empowers the data subject to make self-responsible decisions according to his database. One of the biggest barriers to reach this need, is the lack of transparency for data subjects in the use of data. Nowadays, the introduction of more stringent laws like the GDPR leads to the fact that data protection takes over as a cross-sectional task in companies. A data transparency system, which was briefly described in Sect. 3.1, should enable the connection between data subjects and companies for the purpose of enforcing Data Ownership and Data Sovereignty.

In this paper, a research roadmap for the development of a data transparency system have been proposed. Regarding to RQ1, initial items have been conducted. The results of the text analysis and the literature review will be used for the identification of requirements. Regarding to the findings of the literature review, none of the solutions can be used for the described problems and goals. As a next step, the information's of the findings needs to be combined through e.g. a Meta Model that shows all relations between entities, articles and possible solutions. With regard to RQ2 and RQ3 as future work, these information's will be used to set up a model of a data transparency system and an IS architecture.

References

1. Regulation (EU) 2016/679 of the European Parliament and of the Council - of 27 April 2016 - on the protection of natural persons with regard to the processing of personal data and on the free movement of such data, and repealing Directive 95/46/EC (General Data Protection Regulation), p. 88
2. Digitale Souveränität: Bürger, Unternehmen, Staat. iiT-Themenband. Springer Vieweg, Heidelberg (2017)
3. Abdolhassan, F.: Was treibt die Digitalisierung? Warum an der Cloud kein Weg vorbei führt. Springer Fachmedien (2016)
4. Agarwal, S., Steyskal, S., Antunovic, F., Kirrane, S.: Legislative compliance assessment: framework, model and GDPR instantiation. In: Medina, M., Mitrakas, A., Rannenberg, K., Schweighofer, E., Tsouroulas, N. (eds.) APF 2018. LNCS, vol. 11079, pp. 131–149. Springer, Cham (2018). https://doi.org/10.1007/978-3-030-02547-2_8
5. Alshammari, M., Simpson, A.: A UML profile for privacy-aware data lifecycle models. In: Katsikas, S.K., et al. (eds.) CyberICPS/SECPRE - 2017. LNCS, vol. 10683, pp. 189–209. Springer, Cham (2018). https://doi.org/10.1007/978-3-319-72817-9_13
6. Antignac, T., Scandariato, R., Schneider, G.: A privacy-aware conceptual model for handling personal data. In: Margaria, T., Steffen, B. (eds.) ISoLA 2016. LNCS, vol. 9952, pp. 942–957. Springer, Cham (2016). https://doi.org/10.1007/978-3-319-47166-2_65
7. Cato, P.: Einflüsse auf den Implementierungserfolg von Big Data Systemen. Verlag Dr. Kovac (2016)
8. Fatema, K., Hadziselimovic, E., Pandit, H., Debruyne, C., Lewis, D., O'Sullivan, D.: Compliance through informed consent: semantic based consent permission and data management model, p. 16 (2018)
9. Früh, W.: Inhaltsanalyse. Theorie und Praxis, vol. 7. Konstanz (2011)
10. Gjermundrød, H., Dionysiou, I., Costa, K.: privacyTracker: a privacy-by-design GDPR-compliant framework with verifiable data traceability controls. In: Casteleyn, S., Dolog, P., Pautasso, C. (eds.) ICWE 2016. LNCS, vol. 9881, pp. 3–15. Springer, Cham (2016). https://doi.org/10.1007/978-3-319-46963-8_1

11. Hevner, A., March, S., Park, J., Ram, S.: Design science in information systems research. MIS Q. **28**(1), 75–105 (2004)
12. Kirrane, S., et al.: A scalable consent, transparency and compliance architecture. In: Gangemi, A., et al. (eds.) ESWC 2018. LNCS, vol. 11155, pp. 131–136. Springer, Cham (2018). https://doi.org/10.1007/978-3-319-98192-5_25
13. Krippendorff, K.: Reliability in content analysis: some common misconceptions and recommendations. Hum. Commun. Res. **30**(3), 411–433 (2004)
14. Maguire, S., Friedberg, J., Nguyen, M.H.C., Haynes, P.: A metadata-based architecture for user-centered data accountability. Electron. Markets **25**(2), 155–160 (2015)
15. Matulevicius, R.: Privacy enhanced secure tropos: a privacy modeling language for GDPR compliance, p. 74 (2018)
16. Mayring, P.: Qualitative content analysis: theoretical foundation, basic procedures and software solution (2014)
17. Merten, K.: Inhaltsanalyse. Einführung in Theorie, Methode und Praxis. Opladen (1983)
18. Mougiakou, E., Virvou, M.: Based on GDPR privacy in UML: case of e-learning program. In: 2017 8th International Conference on Information, Intelligence, Systems and Applications (IISA), Larnaca, August 2017, pp. 1–8. IEEE (2017)
19. Otto, B., Österle, H.: Corporate Data Quality - Voraussetzung erfolgreicher Geschäftsmodelle. Springer Gabler, Berlin (2016)
20. Pandit, H.J., O'Sullivan, D., Lewis, D.: GDPR data interoperability model, p. 14 (2018)
21. Pandit, H.J., O'Sullivan, D., Lewis, D.: Towards knowledge-based systems for GDPR compliance, p. 8 (2018)
22. Pandit, H.J., O'Sullivan, D., Lewis, D.: Extracting provenance metadata from privacy policies. In: Belhajjame, K., Gehani, A., Alper, P. (eds.) IPAW 2018. LNCS, vol. 11017, pp. 262–265. Springer, Cham (2018). https://doi.org/10.1007/978-3-319-98379-0_32
23. Pfeffers, K., Gengler, T., Ross, C., Hui, W., Virtanen, V., Bragge, J.: The design science research process: a model for producing and presenting information systems. In: Proceedings of DESRIST, Claremont (2006)
24. Plath, K.U., Becker, T., Von Braunmühl, A., Frey, A.M., Grages, J.M.: BDSG/DSGVO: Kommentar zum BDSG und zur DSGVO sowie den Datenschutzbestimmungen von TMG und TKG. Otto Schmidt Verlag, Köln (2018)
25. Reinsel, D., Gantz, J., Rydning, J.: Data Age 2025: The Evolution of Data to Life Critical. Don't Focus on Big Data; Focus on the Data That's Big. IDC White Paper (2017)
26. Romansky, R., Kirilov, K.: Model investigation and realization of web-based application about GDPR. In: 2018 IX National Conference with International Participation (ELECTRONICA), Sofia, Bulgaria, May 2018, pp. 1–4. IEEE (2018)
27. Tapsell, J., Akram, R.N., Markantonakis, K.: Consumer Centric Data Control, Tracking and Transparency - A Position Paper, May 2018
28. Tom, J., Sing, E., Matulevičius, R.: Conceptual representation of the GDPR: model and application directions. In: Zdravkovic, J., Grabis, J., Nurcan, S., Stirna, J. (eds.) BIR 2018. LNBIP, vol. 330, pp. 18–28. Springer, Cham (2018). https://doi.org/10.1007/978-3-319-99951-7_2
29. Tzolov, T.: Data model in the context of the general data protection regulation. Int. J. Inf. Technol. Secur. **9**, 10 (2017)
30. Webster, J., Watson, R.: Analyzing the past to prepare for the future: writing a literature review. MIS Q. **36**, 13–23 (2002)

31. Wilde, T., Hess, T.: Methodenspektrum der Wirtschaftsinformatik: Überblick und Portfoliobildung, p. 20
32. Wittpahl, V.: Digitale Souveränität: Bürger, Unternehmen, Staat. iiT-Themenband. Springer Vieweg, Heidelberg (2017)
33. Woger, H.C.: Data Ownership - Keine Eigentumsrechte an Daten (2018). https://www.cmshs-bloggt.de/tmc/data-ownership-dateneigentum/

Towards a Record Linkage Layer to Support Big Data Integration

Felix Kruse[✉] [iD]

Department Very Large Business Applications,
University of Oldenburg, Oldenburg 26129, Germany
`felix.kruse@uni-oldenburg.de`

Abstract. Record linkage is a crucial step in big data integration (BDI). It is also one of its major challenges with the increasing number of structured data sources that need to be linked and do not share common attributes. Our research-in-progress aims to develop a record linkage layer that assists data scientist in integrating a variety of data sources. A structured literature review of 68 papers reveals (1) key data sets, (2) available classification algorithms (match or no match), and (3) similarity measures to consider in BDI projects. The results highlight the foundational requirements for the development of the record linkage layer such as processing unstructured attributes. As BDI emerges as a priority for industry, our work proposes a record linkage layer that provide similarity measures and integration algorithms while assisting its selection. A record linkage layer can contribute to big data adoption in industry settings and improve quality of big data integration processes to effectively support business decision-making.

Keywords: Big data integration · External data sources · Record linkage · Entity matching · Data science

1 Introduction and Motivation

Big Data is a phenomenon that describes the volume and variety of available data sources. The digitization of everyday life experiences is responsible for its continuous growth and makes data a crucial resource (cf. [13, pp. 55–56]; [2, pp. 1–2]; [12, pp. 4–5]). The global volume of data duplicates every twelve months and is estimated to grow to 44 zettabytes by 2020 (cf. [6]). However, Big Data definition can only be complete with other important dimensions of the 5V model that stands for Volume, Velocity, Variety, Value and Veracity. (cf. [2, p. 1]; [12, pp. 4–6]; [7, p. 1245]). The 5Vs describe the enormous challenges that companies need to address before using the available internal and external data sources for data product development (cf. [12, pp. 65–66]; [23, pp. 1–3]; see Fig. 1).

Big Data provides data sources from various domains. Moreover, the number of data sources per domain has grown rapidly, as the databases have often been created for a specific task (cf. [7, p. 1245]; [1, p. 1]; [28]). These internal

© Springer Nature Switzerland AG 2019
W. Abramowicz and R. Corchuelo (Eds.): BIS 2019 Workshops, LNBIP 373, pp. 625–636, 2019.
https://doi.org/10.1007/978-3-030-36691-9_52

and external data sources may contain different, complementary, or additional information, which together can provide more complete information (cf. [27, p. 3]; [24, p. 1]). This potential of Big Data should be used for data analyses in the analytics layer to develop useful data products for decision-making.

Various data sources must be integrated before the information base is ready for data analysis (cf. [5]; [28, p. 1]). Therefore, the aim of Big Data Integration (BDI) is the integration of different data sources (cf. [7, p. 1245]; [28]; [14, pp. 101–102]). BDI differs from traditional data integration by the 5Vs as influencing factors (see Fig. 1): (1) Volume - the number of data sources for a domain, (2) Velocity - the high dynamic data sources due to new or changing data, (3) Variety - the structural and semantic heterogeneity of the data sources and (4) Veracity and value - the different data quality in terms of completeness, accuracy and timeliness (cf. [7, p. 1245]). The core tasks of the BDI process are schema matching, record linkage (data matching, entity resolution) and data fusion (see Fig. 1) (cf. [7,10]). As these tasks are complex and in many cases not yet automated, a high level of research and development is invested in these various BDI tasks (cf. [12, pp. 51–52]). The reasons for this are, for example, data quality in terms of completeness, accuracy and timeliness, the different possibilities of the data source structure and the degree of structural and semantic heterogeneity of the data, which often happen due to the development of the data source for a specific purpose. As these general problems increase with the number of data sources to be integrated, most data integration methods are currently based on a few data sources (cf. [2,7,28]; [15, pp. 1–2]).

The most important BDI task is record linkage (RL) (cf. [2,8]; [15, pp. 1–2]; [5]). *Dong and Rekatsinas* define RL as an "unavoidable and arguably the most important problem in integrating data from different sources" ([8, p. 1646]). The goal of RL is to identify datasets that belong to the same entity of the real world. In this way, the BDI process merges the data about the entity (e.g. person, product or company) into an integrated database (see Fig. 1). The RL problem has existed since the beginning of relational databases and has been brought back into focus by the Big Data phenomenon (cf. [8]; ([9, p. 1454]); [15, p. 2])). The manual solution for record linkage is rarely an option because often several thousand entities from different data sources have to be linked in each data science project (cf. [8, p. 1646]).

The remainder of this paper is presented as follows. Section 2 defines the problem for our study and the related work. Subsequently, the research questions and the research methodology are introduced. A structured literature review of 68 papers was conducted to address the two initial research questions of a wider research project[1] with the purpose to improve BDI in data science development lifecycle. The presentation of the results follows and the paper closes with the main conclusions, limitations and future work opportunities.

---

[1] wwww.projekt-trace.de.

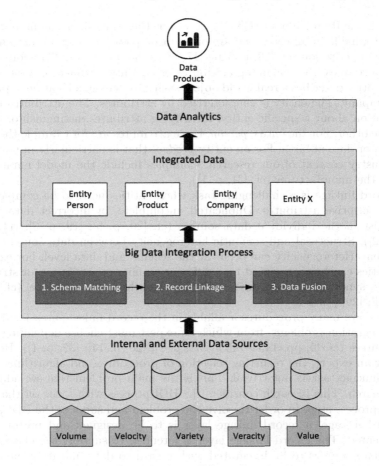

Fig. 1. Data flow in a data science project

2   Related Work and Problem Definition

Record linkage has been researched for about 70 years. To connect data sources, rule-based methods were used first, followed by unsupervised and supervised learning methods such as decision trees, logistic regression, or the support vector machine, and finally deep learning methods (cf. [8, p. 1646]; [20, pp. 97–105]; [21]; [26, pp. 19–20]; [9, p. 1454]). To compare character strings there exist various similarity measures. For example Levenshtein, Jaro-Winkler, Jaccard, or Tf-idf (cf. [19, p. 4]). These methods overcome simple character variations, or term changes, between different character strings (cf. [19, p. 4]).

RL procedures are needed when data sources cannot be linked via a unique identification number, which is often the case with external data sources in the context of Big Data. There are some efforts for globally standardized identification numbers, such as products with the Universal Product Code (UPC) or the

Global Trade Item Number (GTIN). However, these identification numbers may not be available in all cases and are often incomplete, so they are not sufficient as a linking criterion (cf. [22, p. 546]; [17, p. 1]; [30, pp. 1–2]). Therefore, to link the data sources, the remaining attributes of the entities must be used.

An entity describes a real world object such as a person, a location, a product, or a company. The entity is characterized by attributes. The attributes provide information about a specific entity. Identifying attributes distinguish one entity from the other. For the entity *person*, these attributes are for example the name, address, or date of birth. For an entity *product* that is particularly important to the industry context of our research, examples include the model number, the size, or the manufacturer (cf. [31, p. 1]).

Record linkage is a challenging task when entities need to be compared via their descriptive attributes. Duplicated, incomplete, or incorrect data records may exist in the individual data sources (cf. [20, p. 5]; [19, p. 3]; [11, p. 3]; [18, p. 2]). Structural and semantic heterogeneity between data sources is also a problem. Heterogeneity can occur at the schema and data level. For example, the entities can be represented by a different number of attributes, or structural conflicts, synonyms, or homonyms can exist at schema or data level (cf. [3, pp. 123–124]; [29, pp. 4–5]).

There are many procedures available in the record linkage area for different data integration problems, from which an expert must choose depending on the data sources (cf. [9, pp. 1454–1455]; [33, p. 1]; [20, p. 14]; [32, p. 1]). However, even for an expert, the recurring selection of procedures and algorithms for the record linkage task is not trivial. This is the main problem that we address in this research. This research considers the BDI process with focus on the record linkage process step. In order to solve the problem and support the BDI process in record linkage, a record linkage layer is to be designed and prototypically implemented. The record linkage layer is intended to support the classification of the data sources to be integrated with regard to data and data integration problems. On the basis of the classified data and data integration problems, the record linkage layer will support the selection of the methods and algorithms to be used. The next section details the research questions that were formulated to address the RL problem.

3   Research Questions and Methodology

In order to optimize the frequently recurring process steps of the selection of record linkage methods and algorithms to be used, a record linkage layer should be conceptualized. To do this the data integration problems should be classified and a recommendation for linkage methods and algorithms should be given on the basis of the classified problems. The following research questions are defined for this work:

Research Question 1 (RQ1): Which requirements exist for data sources in order to be integrated and how can these be classified?

Data sources should be analyzed with regard to their data integration problems to answer RQ1. The field experiment will be used as a research method. The results out of the experiments will be classified and provide the requirements for the record linkage layer.

Research Question 2 (RQ2): Which linkage methods exist to assign different data sets to a real world object?

A qualitative literature analysis will be carried out to answer RQ2 (cf. [16,25]). This should provide an overview of research in the field of linkage of data sources. This overview should provide possible solutions for the linkage algorithms to be used and integrate different data sources.

Research Question 3 (RQ3): How can a record linkage layer be conceptualized that supports data integration?

The record linkage layer is designed with the requirements determined from the field experiments (RQ1), the requirements from the literature review (RQ2) and the methods and algorithms potentially to be used from the literature review (RQ2). For this purpose, the argumentative deductive research method is applied. In addition, the concept will be evaluated through expert workshops.

Research Question 4 (RQ4): How must a record linkage layer be implemented to support data integration?

To answer RQ4, the concept for the record linkage layer is implemented. The research method case study will be used for this purpose (cf. [34]). Within these case studies, data integration cases will be defined. The case studies will be elaborated and evaluated in expert workshops. The evaluation is carried out in the research project TRACE (See Footnote 1). The project is a cooperation between Volkswagen AG and the University of Oldenburg.

4   Preliminary Results

In this section the first research results on RQ1 and RQ2 are presented and discussed. The qualitative literature review is an empirical method, which allows evaluating papers under consideration of the context (cf. [16,25]). A specific research goal is the basis of a literature review (cf. [25]). The research objective of this literature review is to provide an overview of the data, approaches, and algorithms used in record linkage. *Jane Webster and Richard T. Watson (2002)* and *Cato (2016)* describe a four-step process for a qualitative literature review. The four process steps are *definition of search strategy and parameters*, *identification and selection of relevant papers*, *forward and backward search*, and *analysis of relevant papers* (cf. [4,16]).

The selected search terms for this literature review are: *entity disambiguation*, *entity resolution*, *entity reconciliation*, *duplicate detection*, *deduplication*, *record linkage, object identification, reference matching, co-reference detection, non-identical duplicates, redundancy elimination, object matching, duplication detection, similarity join.* All search terms have been combined with an or-operator for the database query. We chose the databases IEEE[2], ScienceDirect[3] and ACM Digital Library[4] to search for relevant papers. Title, abstract, or keywords of identified papers must contain the search terms. The literature review provided 68 relevant publications on record linkage methods to integrate data sets related to the same real world object. The evaluation dimensions (1) dataset used, (2) similarity measure used and (3) algorithms and approaches used to decide match or no match are presented and discussed in relation to the record linkage layer.

Table 1. Dataset used in record linkage paper

Dataset	Real world object	Ground truth data
DBLP-ACM	Person	Yes
DBLP	Person	No
DBLP-Scholar	Person	Yes
Restaurant	Company	No
CORA	Person	No
FEBRL	Person	Yes
Abt-Buy	Product	Yes
Census	Person	No
Amazon-Google	Product	Yes

Table 1 lists the data sets most frequently used in publications[5,6,7,8]. For each dataset, the real world object for which information is available in the dataset is listed. The Ground truth data column also indicates whether labelled data (match/no match) exists. It is noticeable that record linkage research is limited to a few frequently used data sets. These include the bibliographic data sets *DBLP*, *ACM* and *Scholar*. Most data sets describe the entity person. Two often used data sets contain data on the entity product and have been provided

---

[2] https://ieeexplore.ieee.org/Xplore/home.jsp.

[3] https://www.sciencedirect.com/.

[4] https://dl.acm.org/dl.cfm.

[5] DBLP-ACM, DBLP-Scholar, Abt-Buy, Amazon-Google found here https://dbs.uni-leipzig.de/research/projects/object_matching/benchmark_datasets_for_entity_resolution.

[6] DBLP found here https://dblp.org/.

[7] Restaurant, Census, Cora found here https://hpi.de/naumann/projects/repeatability/datasets/.

[8] FEBRL found here https://recordlinkage.readthedocs.io/en/latest/ref-datasets.html.

by Köpcke et al. (cf. [21]). A data set with data on restaurants is also possible to find in the literature. This dataset represents the entity *company*. Traditionally, structured data sources are integrated with record linkage. Due to the Big Data phenomenon, unstructured attributes exist even in structured data sources. This occurs primarily in the data sets that contain data on products. There are often short product descriptions that are unstructured. To structure these product descriptions and thus make them usable for record linkage, Köpcke et al. first researched them in 2010 (cf. [21]). A first requirement for the record linkage layer is derived from this that the unstructured attributes should be made usable in structured data sources (variety in structured datasets).

Since a record linkage layer is to be designed and developed for practical use, further publicly accessible data sources were searched in addition to the provided research data sets. In order to be able to establish the link to the data sets from the papers (see Table 1), data sources with information on the entities product, company and person were sought. In Table 2 an extract of these data sources is described[9].

Table 2. Identified datasources

Dataset	Real world object	Ground truth data
Crunchbase	Person, Company	No
Standard and Poors 500	Company	No
GLEIF	Company	No
UPC Database	Product	No

Table 3 lists the most commonly used algorithms for classifying records into match and no match. In addition to its name, the algorithms are divided into the categories rule-based, supervised, unsupervised and deep learning. The *labeled data* column indicates whether the algorithm requires labeled data or not. For the record linkage layer, this is a requirement that the algorithm places on the data. Either algorithms are used that do not require labeled data or the effort is made to label data. This fact explains that rule-based approaches are still widespread and are being still researched.

Before an algorithm can make the classification into match and no match, the similarity of the records must be calculated. This is done using similarity measures. Table 4 lists the similarity measures used in the papers of the literature review. In addition, the category of similarity measures is listed. The category can be edit-based, token-based, hybrid, phonetic, domain-dependent or semantic. The categories are important because the procedures in the categories overcome different problems when comparing strings (cf. [19]):

---

[9] Crunchbase https://data.crunchbase.com/docs/; Standard and Poors 500 https://datahub.io/core/s-and-p-500-companies-financials; GLEIF https://www.gleif.org/en/lei-data/gleif-concatenated-file/; UPC Database https://www.upcitemdb.com/.

Table 3. Algorithms used in record linkage papers

Algorithm	Category	Labeled data
Rule-based	Rule-based	No
Support Vector Machine	Supervised	Yes
Decision Tree	Supervised	Yes
Neural Network	Deep Learning	Yes
Clustering	Unsupervised	No
Graph-based	Rule-based	No
Latent Dirichlet Allocation	Unsupervised	No
Logistic Regression	Supervised	Yes
Naive Bayes	Supervised	Yes

Edit-based: Similarity measures such as *Levenshtein, Jaro, Jaro-Winkler* or *Smith-Waterman* belong to the category edit-based. These methods can correct character variations. They are not able to overcome acronyms or abbreviations. For example, "Very Large Business Applications" and "VLBA" refer to the same department at University of Oldenburg.

Token-based: *Jaccard, Cosine distance* and the *Longest Common Sub-String Similarity* belong to the token-based similarity measures. Compared to the edit-based similarity measures, these terms can overcome term permutations, but no character variations.

Hybrid: The similarity measures *Monge-Elkan* and *Soft tf-idf* belong to the hybrid processes. These can overcome term permutations and character variations.

Phonetic: The similarity measures *Soundex* and *Metaphone* stand for phonetic procedures. These methods compare words and phrases according to their sound. They can be used to overcome spelling mistakes caused by human communication failures during input.

Domain-dependent: In addition to strings, numerical values or timestamps can also be compared. Procedures that calculate the similarity between these attributes fall into the domain-dependent category. An example is the *Euclidean distance*, which is used to calculate the distance between vectors.

Semantic: The methods mentioned so far cannot identify the similarity between the terms "Very Large Business Applications" and "VLBA". Although both terms refer to the same department at the University of Oldenburg. This requires semantic measures of similarity. Such semantic similarity measures are embeddings like *Word2Vec, GloVe* or *FastText*. For example, these can be used to overcome synonyms or abbreviations.

The results from the literature review on the use of similarity measures provide further requirements for the record linkage layer. The overview (see Table 4) shows which similarity measures should be provided. In addition, the record

Table 4. Similarity measures for record linkage papers

Similarity measure	Category
Levenshtein	Edit-based
Jaro Winkler	Edit-based
Jaccard	Token-based
Soundex	Phonetic
Cosine distance	Token-based
Jaro	Edit-based
Smith-Waterman	Edit-based
NYSIIS	Phonetic
Euclidean distance	Domain-dependent
Metaphone	Phonetic
Longest Common Sub-String Similarity	Token-based
Embedding (Word2Vec, GloVe, FastText)	Semantic
Monge-Elkan	Hybrid
Soft tf-idf	Hybrid

linkage layer should support the selection of the similarity measure, since a appropriate one must be selected for each attribute pair.

Summarizing, the following foundational requirements can be derived from the literature review:

- Provide similarity measures
- Support in selection of similarity measures
- Provide matching algorithms
- Support selection of matching algorithms
- Development and evaluation on different real-world datasets

5   Conclusion and Outlook

This paper describes a research project to create a record linkage layer for the development of new data products in the industry. The preliminary findings of the two initial research questions are presented, aiming to improve big data integration, namely, (1) the requirements and classification of possible data sources, and (2) the linkage methods available. The diffusion of Big Data in industry settings requires new tools to assist the integration of data sources and the adequate selection of algorithms. Our work is a first step in that direction, with the conceptualization of a record linkage layer.

This research in progress has limitations that must be stated. The first is a natural limitation of the databases and keywords used for our literature review. As the research evolves, other searches can be included to extend the results.

Secondly, we report the two findings of the initial questions of our research project, although already including an extensive selection of 68 papers, it needs to be improved during the field intervention.

In the Preliminary Results section, the first results on research questions one and two were presented. The data sources, similarity measures and algorithms identified in the papers of the literature review have been listed. The results show the existing variety of similarity measures and algorithms from which the data scientist has to choose.

This led us to the implication to support the data scientist in this selection process. For this purpose the first requirements for the record linkage layer were derived from these results. The record linkage layer should be able to handle unstructured attributes in structured data sources. The record linkage layer shall provide algorithms to integrate labeled and non-labeled data sources. Furthermore, a decision support for the selection of similarity measures should be available in the record linkage layer.

Future work will continue the requirements analysis to get further and more precise requirements. For this purpose, record linkage field experiments will be performed with the previously identified data sources. Another implication from the preliminary results is to search further industrial relevant data sources because the selection process of appropriate algorithms depends on the data used. The data sources could be classified for example by their content, represented real-world object(s) or descriptive statistics of the attributes to generate quantitative characteristics. These quantitative characteristics could be used as decision criteria for the selection process of algorithms to link the data sources. Subsequently, a concept will be developed using the argumentative deductive method to answer research question three. Industry case studies will be used to implement the concept to answer research question four. Within the case studies expert workshops will be conducted and data sources will be integrated with the record linkage layer.

References

1. Blanco, R., Enriquez, J.G., Dominguez-Mayo, F.J., Escalona, M.J., Tuya, J.: Early integration testing for entity reconciliation in the context of heterogeneous data sources. IEEE Trans. Reliab., 1–19 (2018). https://doi.org/10.1109/TR.2018.2809866
2. Blazquez, D., Domenech, J.: Big data sources and methods for social and economic analyses. Technol. Forecast. Soc. Change **130**, 99–113 (2018). https://doi.org/10.1016/j.techfore.2017.07.027
3. Bleiholder, J., Schmid, J.: Datenintegration und Deduplizierung. In: Hildebrand, K., Gebauer, M., Hinrichs, H., Mielke, M. (eds.) Daten- und Informationsqualität, vol. 1, pp. 123–142. Vieweg+Teubner, Wiesbaden (2011). https://doi.org/10.1007/978-3-8348-9953-8_7
4. Cato, P.: Einflüsse auf den Implementierungserfolg von Big Data Systemen. Dissertation, Verlag Dr. Kovač (2016)

5. Christen, P., Winkler, W.E.: Record linkage. In: Sammut, C., Webb, G.I. (eds.) Encyclopedia of Machine Learning and Data Mining, vol. 19, pp. 1–10. Springer, Boston (2016). https://doi.org/10.1007/978-1-4899-7502-7_712-1
6. Deloitte: Mission Zukunft: So treffen Sie die besten Entscheidungen für morgen! Unsere Experten zeigen, wie die Digitalisierung Entscheidungsprozesse in Ihrem Unternehmen nachhaltig verbessern kann (2018). https://www2.deloitte.com/de/de/pages/trends/zukunft-der-entscheidungsfindung.html
7. Dong, X.L., Srivastava, D.: Big data integration. In: 2013 IEEE 29th International Conference on Data Engineering (ICDE), pp. 1245–1248. IEEE (2013). https://doi.org/10.1109/ICDE.2013.6544914
8. Dong, X.L., Rekatsinas, T.: Data integration and machine learning. In: Das, G., Jermaine, C., Bernstein, P. (eds.) Proceedings of the 2018 International Conference on Management of Data - SIGMOD 2018, pp. 1645–1650. ACM Press, New York (2018). https://doi.org/10.1145/3183713.3197387
9. Ebraheem, M., Thirumuruganathan, S., Joty, S., Ouzzani, M., Tang, N.: Distributed representations of tuples for entity resolution. Proc. VLDB Endow. 11(11), 1454–1467 (2018). https://doi.org/10.14778/3236187.3236198
10. El-Ghafar, R.M.A., Gheith, M.H., El-Bastawissy, A.H., Nasr, E.S.: Record linkage approaches in big data: a state of art study. In: 2017 13th International Computer Engineering Conference (ICENCO), pp. 224–230. IEEE (27122017–28122017). https://doi.org/10.1109/ICENCO.2017.8289792
11. Enríquez, J.G., Domínguez Mayo, F.J., Escalona Cuaresma, M.J., Garcia-Garcia, J., Lee, V., Goto, M.: Entity identity reconciliation based big data federation - a MDE approach (2015)
12. Fasel, D., Meier, A. (eds.): Big Data: Grundlagen, Systeme und Nutzungspotenziale. Edition HMD. Springer, Wiesbaden (2016). https://doi.org/10.1007/978-3-658-11589-0
13. Gluchowski, P., Chamoni, P. (eds.): Analytische Informationssysteme. Springer, Heidelberg (2016). https://doi.org/10.1007/978-3-662-47763-2
14. Golshan, B., Halevy, A., Mihaila, G., Tan, W.C.: Data integration: after the teenage years. In: van den Bussche, J., Geerts, F., Sallinger, E. (eds.) Proceedings of the 36th ACM SIGMOD-SIGACT-SIGAI Symposium on Principles of Database Systems - PODS 2017, pp. 101–106. ACM Press, New York (2017). https://doi.org/10.1145/3034786.3056124
15. González Enríquez, J.: A model-driven engineering approach for the uniquely identity reconciliation of heterogeneous data sources. Dissertation, Universidad de Sevilla, Sevilla (2017)
16. Webster, J., Watson, R.T.: Analyzing the past to prepare for the future: writing a literature review. MIS Q. 26(2), 13–23 (2002). http://www.jstor.org/stable/4132319
17. Jupin, J., Shi, J.Y.: Identity tracking in big data: preliminary research using in-memory data graph models for record linkage and probabilistic signature hashing for approximate string matching in big health and human services databases. In: Chin, A., Zhan, J., Ding, W., Wu, J., Xu, W., Wang, F. (eds.) Proceedings of the 2014 International Conference on Big Data Science and Computing - BigDataScience 2014, pp. 1–8. ACM Press, New York (2014). https://doi.org/10.1145/2640087.2644170
18. Kong, C., Gao, M., Xu, C., Qian, W., Zhou, A.: Entity matching across multiple heterogeneous data sources. In: Navathe, S.B., Wu, W., Shekhar, S., Du, X., Wang, X.S., Xiong, H. (eds.) DASFAA 2016, Part I. LNCS, vol. 9642, pp. 133–146. Springer, Cham (2016). https://doi.org/10.1007/978-3-319-32025-0_9

636   F. Kruse

19. Kooli, N., Allesiardo, R., Pigneul, E.: Deep learning based approach for entity resolution in databases. In: Nguyen, N.T., Hoang, D.H., Hong, T.-P., Pham, H., Trawiński, B. (eds.) ACIIDS 2018, Part II. LNCS (LNAI), vol. 10752, pp. 3–12. Springer, Cham (2018). https://doi.org/10.1007/978-3-319-75420-8_1
20. Köpcke, H.: Object Matching on real-world problems. Dissertation, Universität Leipzig, Leipzig (2014)
21. Köpcke, H., Thor, A., Rahm, E.: Evaluation of entity resolution approaches on real-world match problems. Proc. VLDB Endow. **3**(1–2), 484–493 (2010). https://doi.org/10.14778/1920841.1920904
22. Köpcke, H., Thor, A., Thomas, S., Rahm, E.: Tailoring entity resolution for matching product offers. In: Rundensteiner, E., Markl, V., Manolescu, I., Amer-Yahia, S., Naumann, F., Ari, I. (eds.) Proceedings of the 15th International Conference on Extending Database Technology - EDBT 2012, p. 545. ACM Press, New York (2012). https://doi.org/10.1145/2247596.2247662
23. Kruse, F., Dmitriyev, V., Marx Gómez, J.: Building a connection between decision maker and data-driven decision process. Arch. Data Sci. Ser. A (Online First) **4**(1), 16 (2018). https://doi.org/10.5445/KSP/1000085951/03
24. Lin, Y., Wang, H., Li, J., Gao, H.: Data source selection for information integration in big data era (2016)
25. Mayring, P.: Qualitative content analysis: theoretical foundation, basic procedures and software solution (2014)
26. Mudgal, S., et al.: Deep learning for entity matching. In: Das, G., Jermaine, C., Bernstein, P. (eds.) Proceedings of the 2018 International Conference on Management of Data - SIGMOD 2018, pp. 19–34. ACM Press, New York (2018). https://doi.org/10.1145/3183713.3196926
27. Pershina, M.: Graph-Based Approaches to Resolve Entity Ambiguity. Dissertation, New York University, New York (2016)
28. Rahm, E.: The case for holistic data integration. In: Pokorný, J., Ivanović, M., Thalheim, B., Šaloun, P. (eds.) ADBIS 2016. LNCS, vol. 9809, pp. 11–27. Springer, Cham (2016). https://doi.org/10.1007/978-3-319-44039-2_2
29. Rahm, E., Hai Do, H.: Data cleaning: problems and current approaches. IEEE Data Eng. Bull. **23**, 3–13 (2000)
30. Schild, C.J., Schultz, S.: Linking deutsche bundesbank company data using machine-learning-based classification. In: Proceedings of the Second International Workshop on Data Science for Macro-Modeling (DSMM 2016), pp. 1–3. The Association for Computing Machinery, New York (2016). https://doi.org/10.1145/2951894.2951896
31. Talburt, J.R.: Entity Resolution and Information Quality. Elsevier (2011). https://doi.org/10.1016/C2009-0-63396-1
32. Peng, T., Li, L., Kennedy, J.: A comparison of techniques for name matching. GSTF Int. J. Comput. **2**(1) (2018)
33. Rekatsinas, T.I., Dong, X., Getoor, L., Srivastava, D.: Finding quality in quantity: the challenge of discovering valuable sources for integration. In: CIDR (2015)
34. Yin, R.K.: Case Study Research and Applications: Design and Methods, 6th edn. SAGE, Los Angeles (2018)

Incremental Modeling of Supply Chain to Improve Performance Measures

Szczepan Górtowski[1,2] and Elżbieta Lewańska[1(✉)]

[1] Department of Information Systems,
Faculty of Informatics and Electronic Economy, Poznań University of Economics,
al. Niepodległości 10, 61-875 Poznań, Poland
{szczepan.gortowski,elzbieta.lewanska}@ue.poznan.pl
[2] Żabka Polska, Plac Andersa 7, 61-894 Poznań, Poland

Abstract. Supply chain modeling is one of the key tools to improve its performance measures. This research follows the principles of Design Science Research (DSR). The paper presents the concept of incremental modeling, which helps quick adaptation of the suply chain model. This method uses Data Science methods and Big Data. Evaluation of the method will be conducted on the franchise network. Hence, new performance measures classification that contains measures specific to the needs of the franchise network, has been developed. In particular measures that allow assessing the level of cooperation around conflicting goals of franchise network participants are included. The results will improve the cooperation of entities within franchise networks.

Keywords: Supply chain · Performance measures · Supply chain design · Supply chain modeling · Big data · Data Science · Franchising · Retail

1 Introduction

Aitken defined supply chain as a network of connected and interdependent organizations [1]. They are cooperate to control, manage and improve the flow of materials and information between members of the chain. Efficient and integrated supply chain allows achieving a competitive advantage. One method of improving supply chain performance is modeling a supply chain and run a model-based analysis. In this context, the supply chain model is a simplified, abstract representation of a real-world supply chain. The model features, e.g., ability to represent the real-world system and to find an optimal network configuration and user-friendliness, are the essential characteristics for designing it. Using a supply chain model allows the faster, easier and more accurate answering to questions related to the supply chain which would not be possible otherwise [6,8]. As reported by Chopra and Meindl supply chain modeling includes many decisions related to the designation of network participants (warehouses, production facilities, points of sale, etc.) their number and location. Additionally it

© Springer Nature Switzerland AG 2019
W. Abramowicz and R. Corchuelo (Eds.): BIS 2019 Workshops, LNBIP 373, pp. 637–648, 2019.
https://doi.org/10.1007/978-3-030-36691-9_53

supports allocating resources to activities, assigning tasks to resources, decision on outsourcing part of the processes, selection of business partners, organization of the distribution network, choice of means of transport and type of information system [4]. The problem appearing in the literature is the assessment of supply chain performance. Many papers give for granted, without discussion, a specific goal (e.g., company net sales) or a set of goals for optimization. As noted by Calleja et al., for the whole supply chain, goal identification is complicated because of many partners and their partial goals [2]. They assume that the participants should include them in their measurement systems to improve the entire chain performance. Moreover, an example of an extensive and integrated supply chain with many participants and conflicting goals is franchise networks. The problem of the contradictory goals for such a network was previously discussed in [9].

This paper is structured as follows: In the next section, supply chain modeling approaches as well as performance measurement systems from literature will be discussed. Thereupon the methodology and research goals are presented. In Sects. 4 and 5, the research results regarding incremental modeling method and performance measures are described. The paper ends with a final conclusions.

2   Related Works

The approaches to modeling highlighted in the literature are simulation, analytical and hybrid approach [14]. Each of these approaches has specific drawbacks. Crespo and Marquez noticed that simulations do not generate a closed set of solutions. Also, some processes are difficult to describe and configure in the computer systems [6]. On the other hand, mathematical formulas used to describe the analytical models could be often intricate. It makes it challenging to apply them in everyday business conditions. Also, the lack of data in many papers from the company's environment is the main limitation when creating such models.

Review of the Big Data in logistics conducted by Wang et al. [20] showed that this is an essential trend in business analytics. They categorized and reviewed Supply Chain Analytics (SCA) literature depending on the application area as well as on descriptive, predictive, and prescriptive analyses. There is a shortage of papers related to descriptive and predictive analyses. Besides, as part of Supply Chain Analytics, the authors distinguished seven application areas: strategic sourcing, supply chain network design, product design and development, demand planning, procurement production, inventory, logistics. Implementation of SCA throughout the organization and supply chains to create comprehensive business analytics will bring benefits at the organizational level [20]. Big Data analytics allows to extract value from massive amounts of data and offers a new possibility to gain competitive advantage. According to Waller et al. [19], the combination of logistics and Big Data analytics could provide many opportunities for research. Business interest in new technologies, including those related to the collection and analysis of data is also significant.

One impediment in the supply chain's integration is the perception gap. It means that the business partners have different expectations and goals towards key performance criteria. It has presented the perception gap impact between suppliers and buyers in the literature, e.g., by Lu et al. [15]. Completion of this gap is significant for the full cooperation of members of the supply chain and its integration. Fulfillment of the perception gap between franchisor and franchisees is a strategic issue for some networks.

Performance measures are managerial tools adopted to assess the functioning of the supply chain. Supply chain measures help to manage the supply chain and provide the support required for performance improvement. Mishra's review suggests that both financial and non-financial measures, as well as Performance Management Systems, are necessary for the decision-making process [17]. Maestrini used the SCPMS (Supply chain performance measurement system) division in the review according to Internal SCPMS, Supplier PMS, Customer PMS, Multi-tier SCPMS, and Many-to-many SCPMS [16]. The study identified many papers in the first three components and only five in the SCPMS Multi-tier, of which only Mondragon et al. paper concerned practical implementation [5]. In the franchise network, used performance measures must match not only the strategic goals of the franchisor but must also correspond to the goals and values of the franchisees. In addition, many authors point to the link between maturity levels and supply chain performance [7,18]. Estampe et al. mention examples of maturity level classifications in supply chains. They note that when measuring the supply chain performance, one should take the level at which the supply chain is. As the chain matures, inter-relational processes develop and participants' goals should coincide, and thus, they should perceive the supply chain performance measures identically.

The Analytical Process Hierarchy (AHP) method supports performance measures systems creation. Jakhar and Barua [12] propose examples of applications for determining performance measures. They used the AHP method in combination with the BSc (Balanced Scorecard) proposed by Norton and Kaplan [13]. Studies show that both tools are complementary. BSc provides a way of processing business processes into perspectives, e.g., financial, customer, innovation. The method supports decomposing targets into tactical and operational levels. Cano et al. implemented this tool in exemplary company [3]. Besides, the AHP method allows the weighting of these goals.

3   Research Goal and Methodology

This research follows the principles of Design Science Research (DSR) guidelines by Hevner et al. in [11].

The DSR framework distinguishes the environment, knowledge base and scientific project. The environment defines business needs that shall be met by the results of the conducted research. The relevance cycle that connects the business environment with the scientific project, provides the requirements for designed artifacts and the test environment. The knowledge base consists of the assumption of previous research results, theories, methods and methods of conducting

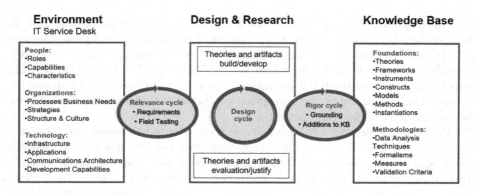

Fig. 1. Design science research cycles proposed by Hevner et al. [10,11]

the evaluation. The rigor cycle allows supplementing the knowledge base on the effect of scientific research. The focal point of the research design is the design cycle consisting of the phases of defining artifacts and their validation (Fig. 1).

The research goal is to develop a supply chain model that uses Data Science methods to improve supply chain performance measures. To achieve the main research goal, several specific objectives have been formulated:

- Presentation of the mechanisms of the supply chain used in the proposed solution. Justification of the importance of modeling the supply chain, improving its efficiency with the usage of Data Science.
- Selection of tools and techniques described in the literature in supply chain model building, Data Mining and Data-Driven Systems.
- Identification of the goals of franchisees and franchisor, important in the supply chain modeling. Collection of necessary data.
- Choosing performance measures, which will be used to assess the model. Determining how measures interact with each other and how they translate into achieving the goals of an entities.
- Building the supply chain model using Data Science methods.

Literature analysis has been conducted to analyse state of the art of research. Interviews with business experts were also used in the study.

4   Method of Supply Chain Incremental Modeling

According to the DSR, the environment provides requirements for the developed artifacts. They result from the business environment, technology availability, company strategy, etc. Environment for the research has specified the following major requirements for the supply chain modeling method:

- Because of the speed of changes both in the business environment and the business model, the primary requirement for the supply chain model is the possibility of its reconfiguration and adaptation to new conditions.

- Use the entire potential of data collected in the enterprise, both internally (from own systems) and from external sources.
- It should provide not only the value of the modeled target function but also extend the knowledge about functioning of the supply chain.

Bearing in mind the above requirements, the use of known modeling methods poses difficulties that can be addressed with emerging data science techniques. Successes in implementing Data Science methods in solving supply chain problems are the premise for developing a modeling method that will meet the needs. Figure 2 shows the general outline of this concept.

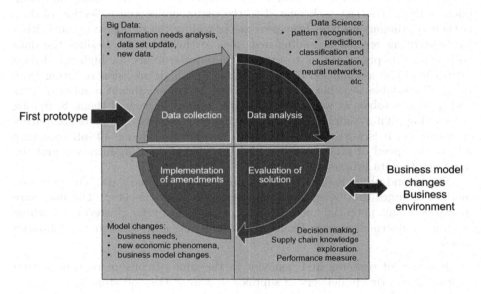

Fig. 2. Incremental modeling cycle [1]

The input to the developed method is the initial prototype of the retail supply chain. Initial model presented on Fig. 2 was created based on the interviews with business practitioners. It is necessary to designate the participants from the supply chain and identify the main processes occurring between them. Also creating a prototype requires setting a target for the whole supply chain in the form of performance measures. These measures are the primary determinant of the network performance assessment. After goal formulation, the method assumes the determination of the participants of this supply chain and their influence on the result of the whole chain. One way of presenting the model of the supply chain is in the graphical form, where processes are depicted as edges and participants as nodes. The next stage is to connect data sources with each of the nodes and edges. The main processes, participants and data sources determination is necessary to start the design cycle.

The cycle consists of four phases. In the phase related to data collection, Big Data technologies are used because of the large volume of data collected in the supply chains. This phase relates to information needs identification after the implementation of amendments stage. Satisfying information needs concerns the completeness, quantity and the quality of the data. With low data quality, it is necessary to increase it or find other data sources. Using data of uncertain quality is a frequent cause of incorrect results in subsequent phases. Potential sources of data may be the internal systems of the considered network, both transactional and analytical. It is worth to mention that data acquisition from other participants in the supply chain allows broadening analyses and performance measures calculation. Moreover, enterprises might download data from open sources. The last task related to the maintenance and collection of data is their continuous update. Processes are providing the database update either by overwriting records or adding new ones to the database. Besides the data collection, this phase goal is to provide the infrastructure for high-speed data processing. The assumption of the method is its high precision resulting from using all available, sensible data sources. It is both a significant number of facts and measures tables as well as the available volume in each of them. Searching data and applying complex Data Science methods requires adequate computing performance. It is worth noting here that not only the change of infrastructure affects the speed of processing but also the way of data organization and the approach to data processing.

The second phase is the analysis of previously prepared data. The proposed method assumes the use of Data Science methods in this step. The literature describes many potential methods, e.g., cluster analysis, clustering, machine learning, pattern discovery. Examples of their use may concern the following areas:

- Discovery of patterns and behavior in the time of consumers, orders from franchisees, timely delivery of supplies to warehouses and stores.
- Searching for the impact of factors on performance measures, e.g., what events affect the sales growth of a specific product group.
- Clustering within groups of goods, suppliers, stores, etc.
- Finding association rules, e.g., selling products.
- Predictive modeling both as a forecast of values, but also a simulation of results with a particular decision variant.

The diversity of data and methods of analysis allows to predict different phenomena and describe many processes using one supply chain model. Comprehensive analyses reduce the feeling of uncertainty and give a better picture of the situation. Therefore, the goal of the model is to provide enhanced insight into the behavior of the real-world supply chain. Thanks to this, managers can use it to support the decision-making process. Because the recipients of products from this phase are business decision makers, the analysis presentation need to be in a convenient form for them.

Having collected analyses, business practitioners will test them. At this stage, there is the practical use of the results of analyses to support both the current business and the formulation of the strategy. The results that get a positive assessment will be included in the knowledge base about the supply chain, allowing logistics managers to make better decisions. Negatively verified conclusions from analyses form a set of amendments aimed at improving the model.

In the last phase, the modeling team determines new needs for the model. The changing in business force the model change according to the company needs. The business environment is also changing, which has a significant impact on performance measures. Based on the requirements and expectations as well as amendments from the previous stage formed a list of model changes. This phase completes the supply chain model building cycle.

During the preparation of the model, managers should take into account human resources factors. First and foremost, people with varying degrees of technical and business knowledge are involved in building the model. Transmission of information between successive steps requires the involvement of the modeling process coordinator or people who understand various layers of analysis: technical, analytical, and business.

5   Performance Measures

The performance measures will be used to assess the functioning of the supply chain. Figure 3 shows the method of their composition. Results of defining performance measures are documents in the form of a list of indicators, their classification, and weights for groups and indicators. Performance measures are the basis for the assessment of the supply chain.

The proposed scheme presents the next stages of determining performance measures for the franchise network. Based on the process analysis, the method assumes creating a list of potential indicators, that describe critical aspects of the company's operation. An introduction to such a study may be the development of a model in the form of a list of participants and processes or graphic presentations as nodes and edges between them (1). The appointment of such a list of processes facilitates further stages of determining indicators. With such a collection and a review of the literature, one can formulate indicators, both financial and non-financial, serving the description of individual processes. Current trends show a gradual increase in the share of non-financial measures used in enterprises.

The selection of categories of indicators used in the measurement and assessment of supply chain performance measures depends on many factors, including industry, organizational structure, etc. In connection with the adoption as a test environment of a network of stores based on franchising, measures choice must take into account the needs of both franchisees and the franchisor. The sub-goals of the franchisees and the franchisor may be conflict, which is why it is reasonable to set a unique set of indicators describing these sub-goals. It allows to achieve a balance between meeting the goals of the franchisees and franchisor.

Hence in the franchising supply chain, it is suggested to use a separate classification of indicators. It is proposed to divide the indicators into five categories:

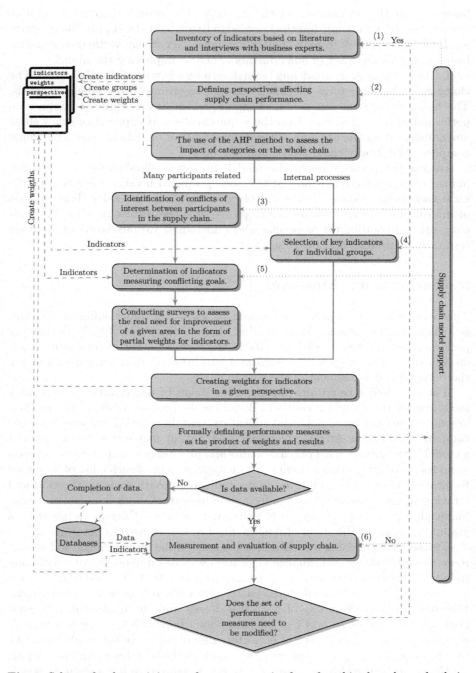

Fig. 3. Scheme for determining performance metrics for a franchise-based supply chain

- Transport, which includes both deliveries to the network and distribution between successive nodes of the supply chain. Indicators are distinguished because of the cargo type, e.g., freezer truck, or vehicle size.
- Internal processes excellence are including basic processes like inbound, storage, picking and outbound as well as all supporting processes like handling returns.
- Assets management, which contains indicators describing the level of inventory and its classification.
- Human resources and environment are related to employment and training.
- Supply chain cooperation, which defines the quality of collaboration within the franchise network.

This classification is related to the organizational division used in the enterprises implementing for functions or supply chain nodes or edges (2). Modeling team selected measures, which are strategic for executing key processes from among the operational indicators to evaluate the performance of the entire supply chain. The leading four categories are universal and can be adapted by companies not only based on a franchise. Particularly important for the franchise network are the supply chain cooperation measures.

Each of the groups could represent a different value for the analyzed company. Depending on the stage in which the business is more critical there may be indicators related to development (dynamics of the increase in the number of branches), process perfection (distribution level) or financial (investment profitability). Therefore, the AHP method assessed for choosing each of the previous groups. Business experts will consider whether a given group is more remarkable for the company's goals. The resulting ranking is then normalized, setting the weights for individual groups. Depending on the type of indicator, its optimal values are determined.

The analysis of the selection of indicators to further determine the efficiency of the supply chain is two-linear. Internal processes measures choosing based on interviews with business experts. The ones that describe these processes, which are the value for the company at a time, are selected. The advantage of setting indicators after their prior grouping is the possibility of conducting consultations among strict professionals in a given process. As before, the chain model itself is helpful here, which provides information on the relationship between operations and compliance with the company's objectives (3). Analysis of areas that go beyond the enterprise is much more complicated. Here, it is recommended to identify passive targets between the links. Research shows that processes in which there is a conflict of goals are the most crucial for franchise network. A chain model helps to identify such processes (3,4). In particular, using advanced data analysis methods and the model itself can help in the selection of relevant indicators for the network.

The qualitative indicators include opinions and assessments based on surveys and interviews. They can be directed to franchisees to assess the quality of cooperation with a franchisor. They are also a source of searching for places to improve collaboration with participants. Interviews and market surveys conducted among clients allow assessing how the network concept is implemented at the points of sale by franchisees and how it fits in with the client's requirements.

Quantitative indicators, however, contain those that result from previously identified conflicting goals. Some of them are the result of the strategy set by the franchisor that describes the level of implementation of this strategy by the participants. The second part is indicators whose keeping the target level is to prevent dissatisfaction among franchisees.

Some problems occur when taking into account the indicators calculated between many participants. Improvement of the indicator for one participant may be contrary to the goals of the other participants. An example of a franchise network may be the density of the sales network which causes a total increase in sales for the entire network, but the addition of a new point of sales may cause a drop in sales in the nearby outlet. Exceeding a specific value is disadvantageous for some parties, despite having a positive impact on other participants.

Within each of the perspectives, the weights for indicators containing them are determined similarly as before using the AHP method. In contrast to the previous stage, business experts are people closely associated with an area or process. The combination of these indicators builds the result for the whole perspective. In some cases, it is necessary to build combined performance measures using multiple performance measures. Complex indicators created in this way could be used as a target function for analytical models or be a way to evaluate a course in simulation models.

At this stage, it is need to consider the possibilities of providing data for the calculation of measures. Good data quality necessary for calculations is required. It is worth mentioning that data from many entities may need a strong standardization and adaptation of metadata. The data collection is a task considered in another part of the incremental method of building the supply chain. Only the fulfillment of data requirements allows moving to the next step.

Following the approaches presented in the literature review, the model of the supply chain may make up the basis for the construction of a decision-making support system. In this place, there is a significant interaction between the supply chain model and current results. Predetermined performance measures could be a compass for many decisions and a reference point for the predictive efficiency of the model.

With each change of the model and the next step in the rebuilding cycle, it needs checking whether the determined performance measures are in line with the company's goals. Performance measures in their assumptions should reflect the strategic needs of the company, so changes in the business should dictate their change.

6   Conclusions

The study is in initial stage. Limitation of this study is an economy sector restricted to franchising retail chains. The proposed solutions could not be applicable for other suppy chains.

The presented concept of incremental modeling of the supply chain responds to adapt to the changes in the business environment quickly to the model. The four main steps involved in this model are listed. Indicators have been proposed to assess performance based on the franchise supply chain. It was also underlined the necessity to set a group of indicators that describe conflicting goals of the supply chain's participants. A method for selecting such indicators based on conflicting goals between members of the network has been proposed.

The model can be extended by assigning the necessary human resources along with their competencies needed to build the model. It is also worth taking into account the flow of information between the members of the modeling team. Further work will consider what can be fully automated. The research will take into account what degree of self-driving may reach such a model. Also, in the case of indicators, it is worth considering research on the mutual impact of indicators on each other, aggregation method and the sensitivity of indicators.

In the next step, a prototype of entering the incremental cycle of supply chain construction will be built. Besides, the method of chain assessment at various management levels from the designated indicators and their target level will be determined.

References

1. Aitken, J.: Supply chain integration within the context of a supplier association: case studies of four supplier associations (1998)
2. Calleja, G., et al.: Methodological approaches to supply chain design (2018). https://doi.org/10.1080/00207543.2017.1412526
3. Cano, J.A., Vergara, J., Puerta, F.: Design and implementation of a balanced scorecard in a Colombian company. Espacios (2017)
4. Chopra, S., Meindl, P.: Supply chain management. strategy, planning and operation. In: Das Summa Summarum des Management. Pearson Education (2016). https://doi.org/10.1007/978-3-8349-9320-5_22
5. Coronado Mondragon, A.E., Lalwani, C., Coronado Mondragon, C.E.: Measures for auditing performance and integration in closed-loop supply chains. Supp. Chain Manag.: Int. J. **16**(1), 43–56 (2011). ISSN 1359-8549
6. Crespo Márquez, A.: Dynamic Modelling for Supply Chain Management. Springer, London (2010). https://doi.org/10.1007/978-1-84882-681-6
7. Estampe, D., et al.: A framework for analysing supply chain performance evaluation models. Int. J. Prod. Econ. **142**(2), 247–258 (2013). https://doi.org/10.1016/j.ijpe.2010.11.024
8. Goetschalckx, M.: Supply Chain Engineering: International Series in Operations Research & Management Science. Springer, New York (2011). https://doi.org/10.1007/978-1-4419-6151-8. arXiv:1011.1669v3. ISBN 9781441964717
9. Górtowski, S.: Supply Chain Modelling Using Data Science, vol. 339. Springer (2019). https://doi.org/10.1007/978-3-030-04849-5_54. ISBN 9783030048488
10. Hevner, A., Chartterjee, S.: Design Research in Information Systems : Theory and Practice. Springer, New York (2010). https://doi.org/10.1007/978-1-4419-6108-2. ISBN 9781441956521
11. Hevner, A., et al.: Design science in information systems research. MIS Q. **28**(1), 75–105 (2004). https://doi.org/10.2307/25148625. ISSN 02767783

12. Jakhar, S.K., Barua, M.K.: An integrated model of supply chain performance evaluation and decision-making using structural equation modelling and fuzzy AHP. Prod. Plann. Control (2014). https://doi.org/10.1080/09537287.2013.782616. ISSN 02767783

13. Kaplan, R.S., Norton, D.P.: Using the balanced scorecard as a strategic management system (2007)

14. Kleijnen, J.P.C.: Supply chain simulation tools and techniques: a survey. Other publications TiSEM, Tilburg University, School of Economics and Management (2005). https://doi.org/10.1504/ijspm.2005.007116. https://econpapers.repec.org/RePEc:tiu:tiutis:d0050225-57bd-4114-ab15-7be56d155eee

15. Lu, D., Ertek, G., Betts, A.: Modelling the supply chain perception gaps. Int. J. Adv. Manuf. Technol. **71**(1–4), 731–751 (2014). https://doi.org/10.1007/s00170-013-5504-x. ISSN 02683768

16. Maestrini, V.: Supply chain performance measurement systems a systematic review and research agenda. Int. J. Prod. Econ. **183**, 299–315 (2017). ISSN 09255273

17. Mishra, D., et al.: Supply chain performance measures and metrics: a bibliometric study. Benchmarking (2018). https://doi.org/10.1108/BIJ-08-2017-0224. ISSN 14635771

18. Trkman, P., et al.: Process approach to supply chain integration. Supp. Chain Manag. (2007). https://doi.org/10.1108/13598540710737307. ISSN 13598546

19. Waller, M.A., Fawcett, S.E.: Data science, predictive analytics, and big data: a revolution that will transform supply chain design and management. J. Bus. Logistics (2013). https://doi.org/10.1111/jbl.12010. ISSN 21581592

20. Wang, G., et al.: Big data analytics in logistics and supply chain management: certain investigations for research and applications. Int. J. Prod. Econ. **176**, 98–110 (2016). https://doi.org/10.1108/BIJ-10-2012-0068. https://doi.org/10.1016/j.ijpe.2016.03.014. ISSN 09255273

Use of Data Science for Promotion Optimization in Convenience Chain

Sławomir Mazurowski[1,2](✉) and Elżbieta Lewańska[1]

[1] Department of Information Systems, Faculty of Informatics and Electronic Economy, Poznań University of Economics and Business, al. Niepodległości 10, 61-875 Poznań, Poland
slawomir.mazurowski@ue.poznan.pl
[2] Żabka Polska, Plac Andersa 7, 61-894 Poznań, Poland

Abstract. This paper describes research being conducted in field of promotion planning and optimization for a chain of convenience stores. The motivation for choosing this subject is an important role of promotions in retail market and availability of large amount of data that can be used to improve profitability of promotions. In addition, most of existing studies analyzed promotions in super- and hypermarkets which have a different sales characteristic than a convenience chain. Since transaction amount is typically small (in comparison to transactions in bigger stores), we want to check whether findings from previous studies can be confirmed in our testing environment. In this paper, we show how both internal and external data can be used in order to improve accuracy of forecasts and obtain more reliable performance metrics. The thesis and research goals are presented along with key results of literature review.

Keywords: Promotion planning · Promotion optimization · Retail · Convenience store · Data-driven decision making

1 Introduction

Promotion is an important component of the retail companies' strategy. As the competition has recently become very fierce, many retailers look for competitive edge in promotion. A rapid growth of promotions has been noticed in most of Western countries [1]. There are many types of activities which are classified by researchers as a promotion. The most popular classification contains sales promotion, advertising, sales force, public relations and direct marketing [2,3]. From the perspective of retail company, sales promotion is probably the most important element on the list. It can be defined as "an action-focused marketing event whose purpose is to have a direct impact on the behavior of the firm's customer" [4].

Although promotions are so prevalent (e.g. almost 20% of total revenue in German grocery market is generated by promotions [1]), there is an evidence that only a half of all promotions is profitable for a retailer [5]. These facts show

W. Abramowicz and R. Corchuelo (Eds.): BIS 2019 Workshops, LNBIP 373, pp. 649–660, 2019.
https://doi.org/10.1007/978-3-030-36691-9_54

that implementing efficient promotion strategy is not trivial, but can lead to significant improvement in financial performance of a company. On the other hand, it is important to emphasize that immediate sales boost is not the only goal of promotions. Amongst other goals there are: a customer base growth, an opportunity to sell out seasonal products, an incentive for customers to start buying higher-margin more expensive products and creating a positive price image amongst customers [1,6,7]. Promotions are also intrinsic component of Hi-Lo pricing strategy, in which standard prices are high, but discounts are frequent and deep (as opposed to EDLP - everyday low prices) [8,9].

Nowadays there are very good prospects for building an effective model of promotional sales, which accounts for all major drivers of sales. Companies store a large amount of data in their data warehouses and operational databases, e.g. retailers can keep track of transactions, inventories, orders and deliveries at every store on daily basis. In addition, there are many open datasets (weather forecasts, social events, public holidays, points of interest, etc.[1]) that can be incorporated into such a model. It is also possible to obtain domain specific data from companies which monitor market trends and promotional activities[2].

The role of information in creation of competitive advantage was emphasized multiple times in literature [10]. The abundance of data that can be used for promotion optimization (and has never been used in full scale[3]) together with maturity and high availability of tools suitable for big data processing is one of the reasons to undertake the research in field of promotions. Another one is a high importance of promotional activities for company's revenue and an enormous number of unprofitable promotions reported by the researchers.

This study aims to build an efficient framework for promotion planning, optimization and evaluation. In order to achieve this goal, an innovative approach is proposed, which uses daily sales data and takes into account competitors' actions, weather and cross-item dependencies. It should lead to more accurate sales forecasts and allow to measure performance of promotion in a more reliable way. In addition, final solution should be able to handle new products. The study is focused on convenience stores because all the sales data come from them, but most of the outcomes should be applicable to any kind of market.

2   Related Work

This section contains detailed description of searching protocol along with results of the literature review. The entire process follows guidelines for Systematic Literature Review (SLR) proposed by Kitchenham et al. [11] and consists of 3 stages:

---

[1] e.g. OpenWeatherMap, Facebook, OpenStreetMap.

[2] An example of such company is FOCUS Marketing Research, https://www.focusmr.com (last accessed on 21 April 2019).

[3] Researchers have a limited access to retailers' internal data.

- Defining the research questions,
- Searching relevant documents in digital libraries,
- Study selection and quality/usefulness assessment.

Research questions are driven by actual business problems and have been formulated as follows:

- What methods are suitable for sales forecasting in a retail company in the presence of promotions?
- How to measure performance of promotional offer? How to account for shifts in demand caused by promotions in terms of time (acceleration/deceleration) and products (cannibalization)?
- Is it possible to obtain reliable predictions of sales for new products available only for a promotional period?
- How to determine the best mix of parameters for promotional offer in terms of time, products, prices and marketing support? How to optimize performance of promotion?

2.1   Searching Process

Several digital libraries and research databases have been used during the searching process, the list includes ScienceDirect, Springer, ResearchGate, Google Scholar, Jstor and multi search engine which is able to query against multiple database at once has been also in use. To answer research question stated before, a set of queries has been formulated using following patterns:

- promotion + models—retail—optimization—planning—effectiveness
- sales forecasting + retail—new products—promotion
- retail + price elasticity—demand models

The results have been limited to the domains of marketing and operational research because the number of initially obtained documents was very large (over 150 000 in some cases) and these areas seemed to be the most appropriate for the task at hand after inspection of first batches of documents. During first run only the papers from the period of 2015–2018 were reviewed, but application of forward and backward search (using references from initial set) led to extending the knowledge base with important studies and research papers from previous years. Eventually, the list of potentially useful documents includes 282 items.

2.2   Literature Review

The problem of promotion has been tackled many times in marketing literature, both store-level and household-level scanner data have been in use. The area that has seen the most interest is promotional sales decomposition - taking into account category growth, substitutions and temporal effects researchers have identified 24 scenarios of promotional sales increase during the promotional period [12].

The part of research body which has its roots in analyzing household data defines probability of a household buying a certain amount of the specific brand as a product of three probabilities: category incidence ($P(I_t^h = 1)$), brand choice ($P(C_t^h = b \mid I_t^h = 1)$) and quantity ($P(Q_{bt}^h = q_{bt}^h \mid I_t^h = 1, C_t^h = b)$) [12]. There are specific formulas for all the components of general equation. In the defined model probability of category incidence depends on maximal utility from buying a product from a category, average consumption rate and inventory prior to the shopping trip as it is shown in Eq. 1 [13].

$$P(I_t^h = 1) = \frac{1}{1 + e^{-(\gamma_0 + \gamma_1 CV_t^h + \gamma_2 I_{t-1}^h + \gamma_3 \overline{C}^h) + \gamma_5 INV_t^h)}} \tag{1}$$

where CV_t^h is the expected maximum utility from buying a brand in the category, I_{t-1}^h is an indicator of category incidence in previous period [14], $\overline{C}^h$ is the average daily consumption of the household h, INV_t^h is the current inventory of the household h [12].

In order to estimate brand choice probabilities model uses information about promotional characteristics of a brand (price, feature, display) and preferences of a household (operationalized as market share of brand and indicator for last purchase). All these variables form a "deterministic component" (V_{bt}^h), which measures the utility of a brand for a household at a given time (see Eq. 2).

$$\begin{aligned} V_{bt}^h &= u_b + \beta X_{bt}^h \\ &= u_b + \beta_1 price_{bt} + \beta_2 feat_{bt} + \beta_3 disp_{bt} + \beta_4 loy_b^h + \beta_5 last_{bt}^h \end{aligned} \tag{2}$$

where u_b is brand specific intercept, $price_{bt}$ is price of brand b in time t, $feat_{bt}$ is a feature indicator for brand b, $disp_{bt}$ is a display indicator for brand b, loy_b^h is an intrinsic preference of household h for brand b - calculated as the market share during initialization period, $last_{bt}^h$ is a state dependence parameter - operationalized as a dummy which is 1, if brand b was bought during the previous shopping trip, and 0 otherwise.

Eventually, brand probability, conditional on purchasing the category, is computed by multinomial logit model [15], which takes deterministic components as its input (see Eq. 3)

$$P(C_t^h = b \mid I_t^h = 1) = \frac{\exp(V_{bt}^h)}{\sum_{b'=1}^{B} \exp(V_{b't}^h)} \tag{3}$$

Probability of household buying a specific number of pieces, conditional on category incidence and brand choice, is estimated using Poisson model, which takes purchase rate of household h for brand b at time t (λ_{bt}^h) as its input and is truncated at 0. Equation 4 shows the exact formula [12].

$$P(Q_{bt}^h = q_{bt}^h \mid I_t^h = 1, C_t^h = b) = \frac{\exp(-\lambda_{bt}^h)(\lambda_{bt}^h)^{q_{bt}^h}}{[1 - \exp(-\lambda_{bt}^h)]q_{bt}^h!} \tag{4}$$

From the perspective of a retailer the most useful is store-level data because of its representativeness and easy availability, on the other hand household data can help understand customers' decisions better [16,17]. As far as setting optimal prices is concerned, use of store-level data should suffice [17]. The most well-established model built on store-level data is Scan*Pro, which uses price indexes (ratio of promotional and standard price) as well as promotional status (feature, display, feature and display) to estimate brand sales [12]. The model accounts for own- and cross-brand effects with regard to prices and promotions. Equation 5 describes the formula of the model:

$$S_{bst} = \lambda_{bs}\mu_{bt} \prod_{b'=1}^{B} \left(PI_{b'st}^{\beta_{b'b}} \times \gamma_{1b'b}^{feat_{b'st}} \times \gamma_{2b'b}^{disp_{b'st}} \times \gamma_{3b'b}^{feat\&disp_{b'st}} \right) e^{u_{bst}} \qquad (5)$$

where

S_{bt}	unit sales of brand b in store s in week t
λ_{bs}	brand-store specific intercept
μ_{bt}	brand-week specific intercept
PI_{bst}	price index
$feat_{bst}$	dummy for feature only advertising of brand b in store s in week t
$disp_{bst}$	dummy for display only of brand b in store s in week t
$feat\&disp_{bst}$	dummy for simultaneous use of feature and display
u_{bst}	disturbance term

The Scan*Pro model estimates sales of a brand directly, but this approach can lead to counter-intuitive signs of parameters in equation because of high dimensionality of data. Researchers have developed multiple strategies to overcome this issue. A one possible solution is to apply principal components analysis before fitting the model [18], the other one computes cross-effects between products based on measure of similarity of those products [19]. Finally, a market share model that estimates category sales and brand shares separately can be applied [20]. This approach imposes a structure on the own- and cross-effects, which makes obtaining the wrong signs much less likely.

As researchers have proven, own-brand effects can be decomposed into brand switching, cross-period and category expansion effects [16]. The idea behind this concept is based on the assumption that total category sales (TCS) throughout periods from $t - S'$ to $t + S'$ is equal to sales of the target brand in period t (OBS) plus total category sales in timespan of $t - S'$ to $t + S'$ excluding period t (PPCS) plus sales of competitive brands in period t (CBS). This method allows for decomposition of own-brand effect (β^{ob}) into sum of cross-brand switching (β^{cb}), acceleration and deceleration effects (β^{cp}), and pure category expansion (β^{ce}). Equations 6 and 7 describe these effects formally.

$$TCS = OBS + CBS + PPCS \qquad (6)$$

$$\beta^{ob} = \beta^{cb} + \beta^{cp} + \beta^{ce} \qquad (7)$$

It has been noticed in many studies that approach relying on use of ordinary time series might be a good solution for base sales forecasting, but doesn't perform well during promotional periods [21,22]. The method often used in practice assumes applying adjustments to base sales for the promotional periods, which are calculated based on past promotions and consulted with experts [22]. However, it has been also proven that in general statistical models perform better than relying on experts' opinions [23].

Multiple studies have demonstrated more sophisticated methods for promotional sales forecasting, which also include dimensionality reduction, feature selection and allow for inter-category dependencies [22,24,25]. Huang et al. [22] propose an autoregressive distributed lag model (ADL), which uses information about products' unit sales, price and promotion status (single indicator for all types). The model accounts for main calendar events in the U.S.A. and its specification includes prices of selected competitive product, which allows for substitution effects within category. However, feeding the model with all interaction between products can lead to overfitting or make computation infeasible because of a large number of parameters. For this reason, a mechanism for feature identification, selection and refining should be applied [26].

Over the last few years solutions that use multi-stage model fitting to manage complexity have been also presented [24,25]. The own-effects are obtained during the initial phase and the remaining ones are used in order to compute intra- and inter-category effects. In this case, final forecast is equal to the sum of partial forecasts from all the stages. In terms of the cross-price effects several scenarios are possible:

- using data about all product from a category,
- keeping information about the n best selling products only,
- performing a principal component analysis (PCA) and using LASSO to select the most important ones.

Other presented solutions assume use of regularization, promotion intensity indexes within a category or computing a top-down market-share model [25].

In summary, defining an efficient framework for automatic discovery of all significant dependencies in the presence of a large number of products and highly correlated data still seems to be area that needs more attention. Furthermore, vast majority of presented solutions use aggregated weekly data, whereas use of more granular data can lead to better estimation of some parameters in model equation, e.g. weather, holidays and social events. However, such a complex approach requires use of Big Data solutions.

Sales forecasting for new products is the area that has received relatively little research attention and existing studies examine opportunities mostly from the perspective of a manufacturer. This is justified by the fact that every algorithm requires some amount of historical data, which isn't available for products that have been just launched or are about to be launched, in order to built the model. Nonetheless, the case with the new products in retail (and convenience stores

especially) is a bit different as some products are introduced into assortment
only for promotional period ("in-out" products). In most scenarios they are
new variations of the well-established product, e.g. new flavor of soft drink or
chocolate bar. For such items Ma et al. [25] suggest using reference product
approach, i.e. finding a product similar in terms of flavor, size, etc. Baardman
et al. [27] extend this method with "cluster-while-estimate" approach, in which
model creates cluster based on similarity between products (both mature and
new ones) and generates predictions simultaneously. Kahn [28] on the other hand
insists on creating range predictions instead of point ones, but the author gives
recommendations for manufacturers and not retailers.

In recent years, a couple of complex solutions for forecasting and promotion
optimization have been published [29–31]. In either case, the demand model is
the most important component of the tool and the objective is to maximize total
sales or profit modifying the depth of the promotional discount and the time of
promotion. The presented models can account for business restrictions, but also
have some limitations, e.g. they are applicable for a small number of products [30]
or optimize profit at the level of single product not taking into account substitution effects [31]. Nonetheless, they are good solutions for the specific scenarios
and all authors have reported substantial improvement in analyzed companies'
profits. Table 1 briefly summarizes the key components of demand models found
in literature and proposed in this study. Subsequent sections describe this solution in more detail.

Table 1. Comparison of demand models used for promotion optimization

Paper, year	Product level	Time unit	Cross-product dependencies	Additional data
Divakar, 2005 [30]	Pack size	Week, month	No	Temperature, calendar events, season
Natter, 2007 [29]	SKU	Week	Yes	Reference prices
Ma, 2016 [24]; Ma, 2017 [25]	SKU	Week	Yes	Calendar events, cross-period variables
Cohen, 2017 [31]	Brand	Week	No	–
This study	SKU, brand, category	Day	Yes	Weather (temperature, insolation, etc.), competitors' actions, calendar events

Ma et al. [25] have presented the most sophisticated method for optimization
of promotional activities. Their approach relies on a genetic algorithm, which is
used to find the best combination of price (discount depth), marketing support
and the number of products in promotion. According to the authors, this solution
has fully met the business requirements of retailers as the first and the only one
so far. Their framework includes restrictions regarding the number of days with
lowered price and marketing support for every product.

3   Concept of the Thesis

The research assumes three preliminary steps to be performed. First, all factors which may affect sales must be identified and measured (e.g. price elasticities, impact of different types of marketing support, weather, etc.). Second, inter-action between items at multiple levels of product hierarchy[4] have to be dis-covered and quantified. Last, usefulness and applicability of all these elements must be assessed in order to find the most profitable combination of promotional attributes. Hence, the thesis is formulated as follows: *It is possible to improve promotions performance using appropriate analytical techniques.*

The detailed objectives are:

- to identify inter- and intra-category effects of promotions efficiently,
- to measure profitability at the level of entire promotional offer in given week (instead of measuring it for a single product),
- to prepare forecasting framework accounting for all major factors.

3.1   Performance Measures

There are 3 types of metrics associated with promotion performance that can be found in literature: sales, profit and traffic [32]. Furthermore, sales can be operationalized as total sales or sales per transaction and profit as total profit or profit margin. It is dependent on company's strategy, which one is the most important at the moment and this can change over time, but it is essential to note that there are some trade-offs between them, e.g. it is hard to keep both total sales and profit margin high.

In practice, computing profit margin in retail company is not a trivial task because of the complex nature of business contracts with suppliers, which can contain turnover threshold and marketing budgets, so the effective purchase price isn't known before end of the year. In addition, terms of contracts, including pur-chase prices, are company's secrets, which implies that they can't be published. Keeping in mind these two considerations, the research is focused on measur-ing performance in terms of total sales and store traffic with total profit highly simplified.

As far as sales forecasting is concerned, the most commonly used metrics are root mean squared error (RMSE), mean absolute error (MAE) and mean absolute percentage error (MAPE) [22,23,25,33]. This research implements the same scheme and RMSE has been chosen for the default forecasting error met-ric. That makes sure that result from this study will be comparable with the outcomes presented by other authors.

3.2   Units of Promotion

There are many possible levels of aggregations, at which promotions can be analyzed, but there are some trade-offs associated with each of them as well. A

---

[4] Retailers group products into hierarchical structure to manage them more easily.

brand is the unit, which is most commonly used in literature and this makes sense because typically all products within a brand have a very similar characteristic (in terms of price, volume and awareness), but for practical reasons there is also a strong need to provide exact forecasts for each product separately. This is necessary to ensure that more popular products are available for the entire promotional period, so the stock keeping unit (SKU) might be a natural choice for the default unit of promotion. The problem is that this approach does not take into account cannibalization between products, which means that efficiency measures at this level might not be reliable.

This research assumes use of multiple different units of promotion - each one for specific task. In order to measure efficiency of the promotional offer in the specific week, the promotions must be seen as a whole, since a mix of products with the best promotional lifts not necessarily results in the best overall performance. A promotional leaflet is a good tool for this task because it groups all activities in given week and sets a timeframe for implementing them. Furthermore, the sales of non-promoted products has to be also taken into account, to ensure that performance measures aren't affected by cannibalization and cross-category effects are included. In summary, this research will look for a balance between forecasts computed for single products and efficiency measures calculated at the level of product categories and promotional leaflet.

4   Methodology

The research will be conducted in accordance with Design Research Science guidelines formulated by Hevner et al. [34], which means that entire process is meant to have 3 cycles. The Relevance Cycle is the starting point for any research, which connects the research with the domain and the next two stages are called the Rigor and the Design Cycles. First one links ongoing research with existing knowledge base, while during the other one artifacts are iteratively constructed and evaluated [35].

A part of work from Relevance and Rigor Cycles has been already done as a set of actual business problem associated with promotions has been identified and mapped onto research questions. Furthermore, extensive literature review has been carried out as well and this paper contains a small excerpt from it. However, the process is iterative by nature, so there may be a need to repeat some stages or extend the literature review with papers, which are more recent or cover different methods.

Testing environment for the artifacts is composed of a large chain of convenience stores - it is possible to use raw data at the transaction level and aggregate it according to the needs. Although the access to the data is not limited, there are some restrictions on use of data in publications and only ex-post analysis can be assumed, so some analytical techniques, e.g. A/B testing [36] have to be excluded from the methodology. An important thing to mention is that the characteristic of those stores is completely different from super- and hypermarkets, which are often used as data providers for research in field of promotion. Typical store in chain is small - its floor area ranges from 30 to 80 square meters and has little storing capacity, so the number of products in assortment is relatively small compared to supermarkets. This limitation is in part the reason why "in-out" products are so frequent in the chain.

With respect to solution maturity and application domain maturity criteria, the research can be assigned to the "innovation" quadrant [35] because the problem itself has been tackled multiple times, but still there is a need for more efficient and complete solutions. The rapid development of Big Data tools and high availability of context datasets have both created a research opportunity in field of promotions.

The chain of interest consists of over 5000 stores and generates over 2 Mill. transactions a day. Other available datasets are also rather big (size of relevant tables spans from few thousands to over 60B records) and processing them requires use of Big Data and Data Science techniques - to join data from multiple sources, apply several analytical algorithms (e.g. mixed models, frequent itemset mining, dimensionality reduction), combine results and evaluate them efficiently. The whole process must be fully automated to meet business requirements.

5   Conclusion and Further Work

Promotions are a frequent topic in marketing literature and solutions to many basic problems in this field seem to exist. However, there still exists an area for further research as all existing studies appear to have some limitations and may be improved. Even the most sophisticated and complete solutions might not be directly applicable for a chain of convenience stores because they were designed with different business model in mind. In future the most promising models will be evaluated on internal data and treated as a benchmark.

Almost all models presented here are built on aggregated weekly data. This can be justified by the fact that most promotions last for a period, which is a multiple of a single week, but this doesn't have to be the case. Use of daily data could improve overall forecast accuracy and allow for more flexibility in evaluation of promotions, which don't follow this pattern. Furthermore, parameters in equation such as holidays and weather obtained in that way may be more accurate.

In future work a framework for forecasting and measuring the performance of promotion in presence of cross-effects will be presented. A working hypothesis is that inter-category dependencies may be difficult to operationalized at the product level, so a hierarchical approach might be needed. Hi-Lo pricing strategy may encourage customers to buy only the promoted items, so client who is interested in purchasing beer and salty snacks would buy the discounted ones. As a result, promotion of beer can induce additional sales of salty snacks, but this effect is independent of the specific products.

Ultimate goal of this research is to create a solution, which accounts for competitors' actions, weather and cross-item dependencies in order to improve performance of promotions. It should extend existing tools with better forecast for new products (mostly "in-outs") and use more detailed information about competitors' actions. Current state of technology allows to include in models detailed data about sales in specific store and its competitive environment. Other areas for further research are use of weather data at the store level and testing usefulness of weather forecast for short-term sales predictions.

References

1. Fassnacht, M., Koenigsfeld, J.: Spektrum sales promotion management in retailing: tasks, benchmarks, and future. Mark. Rev. St. Gallen **32**(3), 67–77 (2015)
2. Rajagopal: Promotion strategies. In: Sustainable Growth in Global Markets, pp. 280–306. Palgrave Macmillan, UK (2016)
3. Kotler, P., Keller, K.L., Brady, M., Goodman, M., Hansen, T.: Marketing Management. Prentice Hall, Upper Saddle River (2012)
4. Blattberg, R.C., Neslin, S.A.: Sales Promotion: Concepts, Methods, and Strategies. Prentice Hall, Upper Saddle River (1990)
5. Ailawadi, K.L., Harlam, B.A., César, J., Trounce, D.: Practice prize report—quantifying and improving promotion effectiveness at CVS. Mark. Sci. **26**(4), 566–575 (2007)
6. Ailawadi, K.L., Harlam, B., Cesar, J., Trounce, D.: Promotion profitability for a retailer: the role of promotion, brand, category, and store characteristics. J. Mark. Res. **43**(4), 518–535 (2006)
7. Blattberg, R.C., Briesch, R.A.: Sales Promotions. In: The Oxford Handbook of Pricing Management. Oxford University Press, Oxford (2012)
8. Ailawadi, K.L., Beauchamp, J.P., Donthu, N., Gauri, D.K., Shankar, V.: Communication and promotion decisions in retailing: a review and directions for future research. J. Retail. **85**(1), 42–55 (2009)
9. Shankar, V., Bolton, R.N.: An empirical analysis of determinants of retailer pricing strategy. Mark. Sci. **23**(1), 28–49 (2004)
10. Kubina, M., Varmus, M., Kubinova, I.: Use of big data for competitive advantage of company. Proc. Econ. Financ. **26**(15), 561–565 (2015)
11. Kitchenham, B., et al.: Systematic literature reviews in software engineering-a tertiary study. Inf. Softw. Technol. **52**(8), 792–805 (2010)
12. van Heerde, H.J., Neslin, S.A.: Sales promotion models. In: Handbook of Marketing Decision Models, vol. 254. Springer International Publishing (2017)
13. Bucklin, R.E., Gupta, S., Siddarth, S.: Determining segmentation in sales response across consumer purchase behaviors. J. Mark. Res. **35**(2), 189–197 (1998)
14. Ailawadi, K.L., Neslin, S.A.: The effect of promotion on consumption: buying more and it consuming faster. J. Mark. **35**(3), 390–398 (1998)
15. Guadagni, P.M., Little, J.D.C.: A logit model of brand choice calibrated on scanner data. Mark. Sci. **2**(3), 203–238 (1983)
16. van Heerde, H.J., Leeflang, P.S., Wittink, D.R.: Decomposing the sales promotion bump with store data. Mark. Sci. **23**(3), 317–334 (2004)
17. Song, I., Chintagunta, P.K.: Measuring cross-category price effects with aggregate store data. Manage. Sci. **52**(10), 1594–1609 (2006)
18. Kamakura, W.A., Kang, W.: Chain-wide and store-level analysis for cross-category management. J. Retail. **83**(2), 159–170 (2007)
19. Rooderkerk, R.P., van Heerde, H.J., Bijmolt, T.H.A.: Optimizing retail assortments. Mark. Sci. **32**(5), 699–715 (2013)

20. Breugelmans, E., Campo, K.: Effectiveness of in-store displays in a virtual store environment. J. Retail. **87**(1), 75–89 (2011)
21. Ali, Ö.G., Sayin, S., van Woensel, T., Fransoo, J.: SKU demand forecasting in the presence of promotions. Exp. Syst. Appl. **36**(10), 12340–12348 (2009)
22. Huang, T., Fildes, R., Soopramanien, D.: The value of competitive information in forecasting FMCG retail product sales and the variable selection problem. Eur. J. Oper. Res. **237**(2), 738–748 (2014)
23. Trapero, J.R., Kourentzes, N., Fildes, R.: On the identification of sales forecasting models in the presence of promotions. J. Oper. Res. Soc. **66**(2), 299–307 (2015)
24. Ma, S., Fildes, R., Huang, T.: Demand forecasting with high dimensional data: the case of SKU retail sales forecasting with intra- and inter-category promotional information. Eur. J. Oper. Res. **249**(1), 245–257 (2016)
25. Ma, S., Fildes, R.: A retail store SKU promotions optimization model for category multi-period profit maximization. Eur. J. Oper. Res. **260**(2), 680–692 (2017)
26. Castle, J.L., Doornik, J.A., Hendry, D.F.: Model selection when there are multiple breaks. J. Econom. **169**(2), 239–246 (2012)
27. Baardman, L., Levin, I., Perakis, G., Singhvi, D.: Leveraging Comparables for New Product Sales Forecasting, pp. 1–36. Ssrn (2017)
28. Kahn, K.B.: Solving the problems of new product forecasting. Bus. Horiz. **57**(5), 607–615 (2014)
29. Natter, M., Reutterer, T., Mild, A., Taudes, A.: Practice prize report— an assortmentwide decision-support system for dynamic pricing and promotion planning in DIY retailing. Mark. Sci. **26**(4), 576–583 (2007)
30. Divakar, S., Ratchford, B.T., Shankar, V.: Practice prize article—CHAN4CAST : a multichannel, multiregion sales forecasting model and decision support system for consumer packaged goods. Mark. Sci. **24**(3), 334–350 (2005)
31. Cohen, M.C., Leung, N.H.Z., Panchamgam, K., Perakis, G., Smith, A.: The impact of linear optimization on promotion planning. Oper. Res. **65**(2), 446–468 (2017)
32. Gauri, D.K., Ratchford, B.T., Pancras, J., Talukdar, D.: An empirical analysis of the impact of promotional discounts on store performance. J. Retail. **93**(3), 283–303 (2017)
33. Ramos, P., Santos, N., Rebelo, R.: Performance of state space and ARIMA models for consumer retail sales forecasting. Robot. Comput.-Integr. Manuf. **34**, 151–163 (2015)
34. Hevner, A.R., March, S.T., Park, J., Ram, S.: Essay in information design science systems. Manag. Inf. Syst. **28**(1), 75–105 (2004)
35. Hevner, A.R., Chatterjee, S.: Design Research in Information Systems. Springer, Boston (2010)
36. Siroker, D., Koomen, P.: A/B Testing: The Most Powerful Way to Turn Clicks Into Customers, 1st edn. Wiley Publishing, Hoboken (2013)

Towards a Cross-Company Data and Model Platform for SMEs

René Kessler[(⊠)]

Department Very Large Business Applications, University of Oldenburg,
26129 Oldenburg, Germany
rene.kessler@uol.de

Abstract. The global volume of data is increasing. As a result, companies are increasingly concerned with using the available data and generating added value from it. The development of data products is necessary to obtain information from data and to integrate it into decision making processes. One possibility is the application of artificial intelligence. However, large companies such as Google or Facebook benefit most from this technology. SMEs in particular are falling by the wayside and are confronted with many challenges. The cross-company platform presented in this article represents an approach to enable even smaller companies to access artificial intelligence and to support data management in machine learning projects.

Keywords: Artificial intelligence · Data science · Data management · Co-innovation · SMEs

1 Introduction

The global data volume has risen statically in recent years. IDC assumed that the current global data volume of 33 ZB will grow even faster than before and will reach a value of 175 ZB in 2025 [25]. At the same time, according this study, the use of public or shared cloud platforms is also increasing and more data is being stored in such platforms [25]. This trend is also having an impact on business and science, which can be seen from the increased relevance of the search term "big data"[1].

The existence of large amounts of data alone does not represent any added value for companies. Therefore, the aim must be to store and process the data volumes using suitable methods and to integrate them into the decision-making processes of companies. Decisions in companies are often made based on anecdotal evidence (feelings, intuition or experiences), which has to be distinguished from empirical evidence (quantifiable, measurable information or events)

PhD supervisor Prof. Dr. Jorge Marx Gómez, University of Oldenburg, Department Very Large Business Application, the PhD thesis will be written in the research cooperation POINT (project members: University of Oldenburg and abat AG).

[1] https://trends.google.com/trends/explore?date=all&q=Big%20Data.

© Springer Nature Switzerland AG 2019
W. Abramowicz and R. Corchuelo (Eds.): BIS 2019 Workshops, LNBIP 373, pp. 661–671, 2019.
https://doi.org/10.1007/978-3-030-36691-9_55

[2,3,15]. However, Data-driven decisions are more objective and of higher quality [3,5,6,20]. As a result, these can have positive effects on a company, such as the optimisation of lead times or the higher quality of produced goods [24].

In order to extract information from data and integrate it into decision making, the development of Data Products is necessary [12]. One possibility is the application of artificial intelligence, which has gained new momentum through the currently available hardware and databases, improved algorithms and the establishment of standards and frameworks [21]. The potential of the technology is expected to be cross-industry and cross-domain [4]. The high expectations of Artificial Intelligence (AI) can also be measured by indicators. The investments made in technology rose from 4.5 billion US dollars in 2013 to 39.2 billion US dollars in 2017, and the trend continues to rise [16]. In 2018 there was a total of 4925 AI-focused companies worldwide. 3039 of this companies are located in the United States or China [16], which means that many experts and people are trained in AI work in these countries (and India) [16]. It is alarming that IT-giants such as Microsoft, IBM, Google or Samsung, mainly drive the developments in the field of AI. This can be seen on acquired startups, but also in the number of published papers and patents [16]. Small and medium-sized companies currently benefit less from the current attention about artificial intelligence and thus from the advantages such as the development of new business models or the reduction of costs. This is a particular problem because SMEs are given special importance in Europe. The European Commission describes SMEs as the backbone of the European economy, since 99% of all European companies fall into this category and SMEs are responsible for 85% of the jobs created in the last 5 years. Furthermore, more than two thirds of all EU employees are hired by SMEs [11]. The central challenge for many companies is therefore how to keep up with the high speed of transformation in order to maintain their competitive position in the future or even improve their own positioning through the use of new technology [7].

According to the organizational theory of Hannan and Freeman (1977), small and medium enterprises have the prerequisites to adapt innovations. This states that the larger the organizations, the more sluggish and rigid companies become [14]. The more agile a company can act, the shorter the time periods required for change processes. However, SMEs play a special role here. Often the responsible decision-makers see no potential at all or there is a lack of IT competence [32]. In addition, digitisation projects in SMEs are often characterised by excessive complexity, legal uncertainties, financial expenditure, a lack of infrastructure and standards and simply excessive demands within the organisation [9,19,26]. With regard to the application of artificial intelligence, it is also argued that although IT know-how is available in SMEs, subject-specific data science knowledge is just as lacking as the necessary database [8].

2   Problem Statement

Based on the considerations above, it can be concluded that the use of AI can open up a wide range of opportunities for enterprises. At the same time SMEs have difficulties in implementing this technology adaption [8]. To bring about innovations independently, experience is often lacking, and to replace this experience with external services, the necessary monetary budget is lacking [17]. In the near past, innovation networks have proved their worth for the development of new knowledge and it has been shown that cross-company and cross-industry networks, in particular, can offer great advantages. The most common types of innovation networks are federal innovation networks and anarchic/clan innovation networks [31]. In order to achieve the objective, it is always necessary for the participating companies to provide input into the network in terms of content. Nevertheless, it is important for participating companies to maintain control over their own resources and possible results. Since the skills and knowledge of different actors are brought together through a cooperation in such a network, objectives and rights to results are in most cases regulated by contracts [31]. However, in order to apply the existing concepts of co-innovation in the context of AI and thus enable access to technology, there is a lack of suitable technical infrastructures which are indispensable for the management of data sets and the development of data products.

In both, European politics and national politics (Germany), the application of AI in SMEs is strongly discussed. This technology has a disruptive effect, which can concern all areas of life and work [7,10]. Politicians therefore demand access to AI for companies of all sizes [10].

In order to solve the problem of missing data, more and more cross-company data platforms are currently being proposed. Such data platforms should enable companies to share data sets with other companies, establish cooperations and create digital ecosystems [8]. Data is often a sensitive topic in companies. However, in times of a sharing economy the sharing of goods is more and more in vogue, as a monopolistic ownership of a good loses more of its value [23]. Therefore, data sharing is conceivable in the future, provided a suitable infrastructure is in place. Existing solutions from large vendors already address the problem of missing internal data and knowledge and offer AI-as-a-Service APIs that allow AI models to be developed in a short time without domain knowledge [13,18,22,27]. The problem, of course, is that each standard solution must be adapted to the individual needs of the company using it. It is also questionable whether the use of an interface alone can lead to an added value, since knowledge is still necessary to identify the right deployment scenarios in companies [8]. Even if the use of AI-as-a-Service would eliminate the need for knowledge to train a model, there are still problems regarding the missing database and at the same time the design of the deployment as well as the maintenance and optimization is unclear.

Existing approaches, such as the *Industrial Data Space* from the Fraunhofer Institute, are already adressing the problem described. The focus, however, is exclusively on the data, although possibilities for operationalization are being taking into account, but only as a boundary condition. Through close cooperation with an industry 4.0 initiative, it can also be assumed that it's problems, in particular, will flow into the architecture. A broad applicability is not shown.

From the consortium of the project, it becomes clear that especially large companies, such as Volkswagen, Thyssenkrupp, Siemens or Bosch are involved in the project. The project does not specialize in SMEs [23].

3   Research Goals and Methodology

Within the scope of this work, a cross-company data and model platform is to be designed and implemented. The main research objective is to provide SMEs with access to artificial intelligence. Several research questions can be derived from the problem described above and are shown in Fig. 1 together with the methods to be used. Sub-research questions 1.1 (RQ 1.1 "Which factors influence the success of AI implementations in SMEs") and 1.2 (RQ 1.2 "How can co-innovation concepts support SMEs in adapting AI?") will be dealt with in parallel. Independent literature studies will be prepared on both research questions, reflecting the state of the art. As soon as the first results from these studies are available, a mixed methods approach will be conducted to interview experts from practice on the topics dealt with. When selecting the experts, their field of activity and professional position play a particularly important role, i.e. that various IT decision-makers from SMEs represent the target group. The combination of qualitative and quantitative survey methods, which is an elementary component of mixed method approaches, is intended to ensure that, on the one hand, more experts are interviewed and thus more information can be collected and, on the other hand, that the evaluation of the surveys remains within a feasible timeframe.

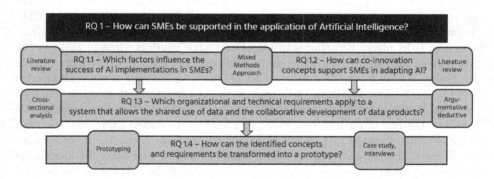

Fig. 1. Research methodology

From the results of the literature studies and the expert interviews, requirements are to be derived by cross sectional analysis and argumentative deductive in order to answer sub-research question 1.3 (RQ 1.3 "Which organizational and technical requirements apply to a system that allows the shared use of data and the collaborative development of data products"). On the basis of this requirements analysis, the next step will be to begin with the conception and implementation of the platform to be developed, which will lead to the sub-research question 1.4 (RQ 1.4 "How can the identified concepts and requirements be transformed into a prototype?"). The prototype will first be designed and conceptualized with the help of an iterative prototyping, in order to then implement this design in an iterative procedure as well. The first step is to create a technical basis in the form of a modular, extensible architecture, which can then be extended by the implementation of functional modules (business logic).

For quality assurance of the results, the developed prototype will be evaluated with the help of to be designed case studies and plausibility interviews/workshops. Again, experts from practical experience will be used to identify the practical suitability and possible problems of the prototype. In addition, an attempt will also be made to present interim results to experts during the development phase.

4 Cornerstones of the Platform

In the following first requirements and implications are explained and the cornerstones of the platform to be developed are presented. The concept of the platform is aligned to this.

4.1 Data Sharing as Support for the Applicability of AI in SMEs

A holistic approach consisting of a cross-company data and a model platform, makes a particular sense because it has proven itself in practice to rely on multi-layer model architectures [29]. Instead of training a completely separate and new model for each use case, a state-of-the-art model (e.g. in ImageNet image recognition) based on public data can be used as a base model. In the next step, this model can be re-trained with industry- or domain-specific data to improve the quality and accuracy of the results. In the last step, the technique of transfer learning can be used in order to archieve satisfying results by training with own, company- and application-specific data. As a result, models that consume comparatively less own data and are based on shared data sets, can be created and trained. The models are thus becoming more and more application-specific, which also limits the potential users. The computing effort can also be minimized, since the training time is reduced by the shared use.

In summary, it can be assumed that the shared use of data and the multi-layer architecture of ML models can reduce the need for own available data and the necessary computing power. This factor can support the applicability of AI in SMEs.

4.2 Life Cycle of an ML-Application

The lifecycle of machine learning applications can be described by different phases (see Fig. 2). The lifecycle phases are basically the cornerstones of the data and model platform, as it should be able to support the entire lifecycle.

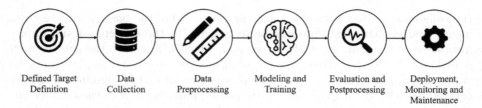

Fig. 2. Phases of a ML-Application (Own representation)

Target Definition. According to Kruse et al. (2018), the development and training of a machine learning model can be regarded as the development of a data product. Each data product serves to support a specific and defined decision. Accordingly, it is necessary to clearly define the purpose of an ML model before developing it. Questions that need to be answered are among others:

- Which decision(s) should be supported?
- What data is available?
- What quality of results is necessary to be able to use the model in the decision making processes?
- How should the finalized model be put into operation?

Data Collection. Although it is clear that data provides the basis for every machine learning model, even in companies it is not always clear what data is available. Therefore, when acquiring data, it must always be checked which internal and external data pools can be used to train a specific machine learning model. According to Agrawal et al. (2019), this phase is aggravated by the fact that the structure and type of data storage within the company is often very different. Machine Learning projects usually involve different experts. Machine learning specialists work together with developers, data engineers and data scientists. Each group of people may have different preferences in the way they work, which means that each team may maintain its own data silos and do so differently. This leads to a lack of transparency and an additional challenge in data exploration [1]. Within the work presented here, a concept is to be developed which makes it possible to maintain ML-relevant data silos uniformly and transparently. At the same time, it should also be shown how it is possible to share different data sets between different companies or organisations.

Data Preprocessing. During preprocessing, the data used (e.g. an annotated data set) is transformed into the form expected by the model. Typical, frequently occurring tasks are cleaning, transformation or scaling. As with data annotation, it therefore makes sense if preprocessing is performed only once and is also saved as the result or extension of a data set. This should also be considered in the data model of the platform to be developed.

Methods of supervised learning require not only data, but also annotations of the data. Only the annotation (e.g. labeling) of data entries makes it possible to use them for a classification algorithm, for instance. Annotation, however, requires a lot of time if this has to be done manually. It is therefore particularly negative for companies if data annotation tasks are performed several times, for example if a data set is used in different departments of a company.

Depending on the application, the same annotations can be helpful, but it is also conceivable that a data set has completely different annotations for the same data entries. This can be particularly the case if a data set is to be prepared for different usage scenarios. Within the framework of the platform to be implemented, a data format must therefore be developed that allows the annotation of data sets, is able to maintain and, if necessary, summarize different annotations, and at the same time offers the possibility of capturing the purpose of an annotation. Possibilities of tracing the annotation and, if necessary, versioning the data sets are also conceivable. It should also be noted that data sets and thus data maintenance are rarely completed. If new data is added, data maintenance must also be carried out again, whereby it must be observed and traceable which status of the data was used for training a model, since this can have far-reaching consequences for the performance of a model.

Modeling and Training. Once the data has been prepared, ML projects can begin to set up and train models. Models are no longer programmed from scratch, in the most cases the choice falls on various available ML frameworks. Frameworks such as Tensorflow[2], keras[3] or scikit-learn[4] are often open source and provide building blocks. By combining these building blocks, complex ML models can be built with simple means and relatively little programming effort. Frameworks and initiatives such as OPAL[5] are to be integrated into the Data and Model Platform in order to support the development workflow of ML teams. However, there is an almost unmanageable number of available frameworks. The integration of all frameworks into the platform is not possible due to the effort involved, which is why a selection must be made in the further conception of the platform (for example, based on the distribution of the respective framework). The training of models is very computationally intensive [28], which is why sharing models can save costs. But at least the data reference from the data platform to the training location should be made possible via an interface.

In order to increase the reproducibility of algorithms and model trainings, it is also necessary to establish back references between models and training data. The reproducibility of a model can only be guaranteed if the training data used and the model parameters are known. For the goal of sharing data and models between departments of a company and between companies, it is therefore necessary to create a possibility to share models and their descriptions in addition to the data sets. This would be possible, for example, in a model repository.

---

[2] https://www.tensorflow.org/.
[3] https://keras.io/.
[4] https://scikit-learn.org/stable/.
[5] https://www.opalproject.org/.

Evaluation and Postprocessing. Although various best practices have established themselves in the field of machine learning (e.g. the use of convolutional neural networks in image processing), the parameterization and configuration of these best practices is nevertheless characterized by an experimental procedure and "trial and error". The danger is that this usually iterative procedure is not sufficiently documented. The solution, which might be of interest for other applications, is lost and only the model with the best performance remains. If another ML team wants to solve a similar problem, it may make similar mistakes and make similar attempts as a previous team. If the entire solution path (including model parameterization and configuration as well as evaluation key figures such as Accuracy) is documented, the effort in this experimental phase of ML projects can possibly be massively reduced.

In addition to managing models that are ready for operation, the platform should therefore at least document such models, including their configuration, parameterization and data used, in order to trace how the solution came about at a later point in time.

Deployment, Monitoring and Maintenance. In addition to managing models that are ready for operation, the platform should therefore at least document such models, including their configuration, parameterization and data used, in order to be able to trace how the solution came about at a later point in time.

However, the model must also be monitored during operation. The training of a model always takes place in a defined context. The annotation of a data set can have a different meaning depending on the environment in which it is used, for example the attribute "fast" can have a different meaning to a speed measured in km/h, depending on which means of transport the speed refers to. If this is possibly not directly visible context changes, this can lead to changes in the model concept. This phenomenon is called Concept Drift in the literature [30].

As well as conventional software, ML applications must therefore also be consistently monitored so that they can be used in the long term. The Data and Model Platform should support the user by monitoring the models to ensure that different types of Concept Drifts, such as Rapid Drifts, Gradual Drifts, Reoccuring Drifts or Incremental Drifts [33], can be identified in order to take appropriate measures for improvement. The monitoring and modification of the operated ML applications and models is, however, only possible if the initial situation of the model creation is known. This point in particular should be addressed by the increased transparency (parameterization, configuration and data basis of the models) within the platform.

5   Conclusion and Further Steps

In this article the problem is identified and described that it is particularly difficult for SMEs to adapt the "AI" technology and implement their own application cases. It was derived from the existing literature and studies that these challenges can be attributed to the lack of data and know-how. The great effort behind the development of AI models also has an aggravating effect. Therefore, this paper presents the idea of a platform that enables SMEs to share data and models across companies and to adapt these models to their own needs by using transfer learning (see Sect. 4.1). The design and degree of support of this platform for the phases in the ML lifecycle (see Sect. 4.2) should be designed and implemented through the defined procedure and research questions (see Sect. 3).

In further research, the literature studies proposed will be started and the state of the art will be presented in full. Based on the extracted knowledge, the mixed-methods approach for interviewing experts will be derived and practical requirements will be determined. After combining the requirements from the literature with those from practice, the conception of the platform will begin.

The implementation of the concept should show that the requirements are met and that SMEs can be supported in the application of AI by the prototype. Experts will be consulted to assess the suitability of the system.

A continuous publication of relevant results during the research project is planned. At least one publication should be placed in a journal or at a conference for each listed research question.

References

1. Agrawal, P., et al.: Data platform for machine learning. In: Proceedings of the 2019 International Conference on Management of Data - SIGMOD 2019. ACM Press (2019). https://doi.org/10.1145/3299869.3314050
2. Anderson, C.: Creating a Data-Driven Organization. O'Reilly Media Inc., Sebastopol (2015)
3. BARC - Business Application Research Center: Data-Driven Decision-Making: 14 Recommendations on how to benefit (2017)
4. Batra, G., Queirolo, A., Santhanam, N.: Artificial Intelligence: the time to act is now, January 2018. https://www.mckinsey.com/industries/advanced-electronics/our-insights/artificial-intelligence-the-time-to-act-is-now
5. Beisswenger, A.: Anatomie strategischer Entscheidungen. Springer Fachmedien Wiesbaden, Wiesbaden (2016). https://doi.org/10.1007/978-3-658-12435-9
6. Brynjolfsson, E., McElheran, K.: Data in action: data-driven decision making in U.S. manufacturing. SSRN Electr. J. (2016). https://doi.org/10.2139/ssrn.2722502
7. Bundesministerium für Wirtschaft und Energie: Digitale Souveränität und Künstliche Intelligenz - Voraussetzungen, Verwantwortlichkeiten und Handlungsempfehlungen. Digital Gipfel Nürnberg 2018 (2018). https://www.de.digital/DIGITAL/Redaktion/DE/Digital-Gipfel/Download/2018/p2-digitale-souveraenitaet-und-kuenstliche-intelligenz.pdf?__blob=publicationFile&v=5
8. Bundesministerium für Wirtschaft und Energie: Künstliche Intelligenz. Website (2019). https://www.mittelstand-digital.de/MD/Redaktion/DE/Dossiers/A-Z/kuenstliche-intelligenz.html. abgerufen am 01 Apr 2019
9. Deloitte: Mission Zukunft: So treffen Sie die besten Entscheidungen für morgen! (2018). https://www2.deloitte.com/de/de/pages/trends/zukunft-der-entscheidungsfindung.html

10. European Commission: Artificial Intelligence for Europe. Communication from the Commission to the European Parliament, the European Council, the Council, the European Economic and Social Committee and the Committee of the Regions, April 2018. https://ec.europa.eu/digital-single-market/en/news/communication-artificial-intelligence-europe. abgerufen am 03 Apr 2019

11. European Commission: Entrepreneurship and Small and medium-sized enterprises (SMEs) (2019). http://ec.europa.eu/growth/smes_en

12. Felix Kruse, V.D., Gómez, J.M.: Building a connection between decision maker and data-driven decision process. Archives of Data Science, Series A (Online First) 4(1), 1–16 (2018). https://doi.org/10.5445/KSP/1000085951/03

13. Google: Google Cloud AutoML (2019). https://cloud.google.com/automl/

14. Hannan, M.T., Freeman, J.: The population ecology of organizations. Am. J. Sociol. 82(5), 929–964 (1977). https://doi.org/10.1086/226424

15. Hoeken, H., Hustinx, L.: When is statistical evidence superior to anecdotal evidence in supporting probability claims? The role of argument type. Hum. Commun. Res. 35(4), 491–510 (2009). https://doi.org/10.1111/j.1468-2958.2009.01360.x

16. Holst, A.: Artificial Intelligence (AI). Statista Study, December 2018

17. Hund, A., Wagner, H.T.: Innovation networks and digital innovation: how organizations use innovation networks in a digitized environment. In: Ludwig, T., Pipel, V. (eds.) WI2019 - Tagungsband, vol. 14, pp. 77–81 (2019)

18. IBM: IBM Watson: Products and services (2019). https://www.ibm.com/watson/products-services/

19. Leyh, C., Bley, K.: Digitalisierung: Chance oder Risiko für den deutschen Mittelstand? – Eine Studie ausgewählter Unternehmen. HMD Praxis der Wirtschaftsinformatik 53(1), 29–41 (2016). https://doi.org/10.1365/s40702-015-0197-2

20. Mcelheran, K., Brynjolfsson, E.: The rise of data-driven decision-making is real but uneven. IEEE Eng. Manag. Rev. 45(4), 103–105 (2017). https://doi.org/10.1109/emr.2017.8233302

21. McKinsey & Company: Ask the AI experts: Whats driving todays progress in AI? Interview, Jul 2017. https://www.mckinsey.com/business-functions/mckinsey-analytics/our-insights/ask-the-ai-experts-whats-driving-todays-progress-in-ai

22. Microsoft Azure: Azure Machine Learning Services (2019). https://azure.microsoft.com/de-de/services/machine-learning-service/

23. Otto, B., et al.: Industrial Data Space - Digitale Souveränität über Daten. White Paper (2016). https://www.fraunhofer.de/de/forschung/fraunhofer-initiativen/industrial-data-space.html, abgerufen am 03.04.2019

24. Pfliegl, R., Seibt, C.: Die digitale transformation findet statt! e & i Elektrotechnik und Informationstechnik 134(7), 334–339 (2017). https://doi.org/10.1007/s00502-017-0530-2

25. Reinsel, D., Gantz, J., Rydning, J.: The Digitization of the World: From Edge to Core. White Paper, November 2018. https://www.seagate.com/files/www-content/our-story/trends/files/idc-seagate-dataage-whitepaper.pdf. abgerufen am 14 Apr 2019

26. Saam, M., Viete, S., Schiel, S.: Digitalisierung im Mittelstand: Status Quo, aktuelle Entwicklungen und Herausforderungen. ZEW - Leibniz Centre for European Economic Research (2016). https://EconPapers.repec.org/RePEc:zbw:zewexp:145963

27. SAP: SAP Leonardo: Machine Learning (2019). https://www.sap.com/germany/products/leonardo/machine-learning.html

28. Shi, S., Wang, Q., Xu, P., Chu, X.: Benchmarking state-of-the-art deep learning software tools (2016)

29. Suzor, T.: IBMs data privacy policy for an AI-powered world, July 2018. https://www.ibm.com/blogs/watson/2018/07/ibms-data-privacy-policy-for-an-ai-powered-world/
30. Widmer, G., Kubat, M.: Learning in the presence of concept drift and hidden contexts. Mach. Learn. **23**(1), 69–101 (1996). https://doi.org/10.1007/bf00116900
31. Xu, T., Bernardy, A., Bertling, M., Burggräf, P., Stich, V., Dannapfel, M.: Development of a matching platform for the requirement-oriented selection of cyber physical systems for SMEs. In: Ludwig, T., Pipel, V. (eds.) WI2019 - Tagungsband, vol. 14, pp. 661–675 (2019)
32. Zimmermann, V.: Digitalisierung der Wirtschaft: breite Basis, vielfältige Hemmnisse, June 2017. https://www.kfw.de/PDF/Download-Center/Konzernthemen/Research/PDF-Dokumente-Unternehmensbefragung/Unternehmensbefragung-2017-%E2%80%93-Digitalisierung.pdf
33. Zliobaite, I.: Learning under concept drift: an overview. CoRR abs/1010.4784 (2010). http://arxiv.org/abs/1010.4784

Touchscreen Behavioural Biometrics Authentication in Self-contained Mobile Applications Design

Piotr Kałużny[(✉)]

Poznań University of Economics and Business,
Al. Niepodległości 10, 61-875 Poznań, Poland
piotr.kaluzny@ue.poznan.pl

Abstract. The article presents the research connected with developing a mobile touchscreen behavioural biometrics solution that may be applicable for authentication and improving transaction security of financial services. The article aims to present the research approach and a literature review that identified research gaps and performed a critical analysis of previous results. The goal is to suggest possible improvements over the existing methods in the literature. The motivation, methodology and main problem statements of the aforementioned research are presented, focusing on the characteristics of behavioural biometrics methods. The main contribution of the article consists of the literature review focused on the characteristics of the approaches used, differences in results caused by the evaluation criteria of the research processes and their comparability. Based on it insights are derived which can be used to build touchscreen based authentication method and validate the results.

Keywords: Behavioural biometrics · Authentication · Touchscreen biometrics · Interaction patterns · Mobile · Application security · Continuous authentication

1 Introduction

Mobile phones have became a widely used medium for customers. This growing tendency to use mobile phones also influences the financial sector change to a "mobile-centric" model [1] where all services are accessed by a mobile. Providing a high usability and safe services for their customers in this environment is important for the stakeholders [2]. Current point-of-access based authentication methods (PIN, password) are not sufficient for the users' needs - they require interaction, cannot provide constant authentication and are vulnerable to spoofing and fraud [2,3]. Current methods do not meet the usability criteria, stacking up multiple passwords in user's memory leads to frustration when forgetting them, password reuse and using weak patterns [4]. Developing new methods which may improve the authentication process is an important task from the service providers perspective. From a legal standpoint preventing frauds in financial

© Springer Nature Switzerland AG 2019
W. Abramowicz and R. Corchuelo (Eds.): BIS 2019 Workshops, LNBIP 373, pp. 672–685, 2019.
https://doi.org/10.1007/978-3-030-36691-9_56

services and protecting users from new types of malware also requires that financial institutions create additional mechanisms to minimize those threats and use multi-factor authentication [5]. Both of those issues may be solved by the use of behavioural biometrics, which can provide authentication with an increased usability of the process, while also enriching fraud detection systems [6] and reducing insider threat [7].

2 Research Methodology and Paper Structure

The goal of the PhD research is to create an authentication system which can be contained within the service provider's application, that can provide more usable authentication method and enrich fraud detection systems. The article presents the current state of research connected with fulfilling the goal presented. The methodology of the research itself follows the principles of Design Science and the special guidelines for Information Systems research [8,9]. The applied methodology consists of five phases:

- Awareness of Problem - presented in the introduction, focusing on new challenges in user authentication and fraud detection on mobile platforms.
- Suggestion - where a potential solution in terms of behavioural biometrics authentication system is be presented. This phase will be the main focus of this paper, presenting the characteristics and reasoning behind utilizing those methods for solving the problem mentioned.
- Development - in this phase, based on the findings from the literature review and own contribution a method will be designed, which will try to solve the problem presented. Outcomes of the literature review presenting all the possible advantages, disadvantages and research gaps to be studied for the development of the method will influence the development phase.
- Evaluation phase and Conclusion phase - where the results of the study and the artefacts designed will be evaluated based on the criteria that were used. In the last phase the discussion of the results importance will be present.

Based on this methodology the effects of the research can create multiple artefacts, in this case: models, methods, new design and developments models - focusing on a model of requirements for the method, the authentication method itself as an artefact and design of the authentication processes in which this method will be validated. The methodology includes a iterative approach, in which the method designed will be improved by new suggestions after the evaluation phase finishes. The main research hypothesis, which also defines the evaluation criteria, is as follows: *utilizing continuous touch patterns verification along with sequences of actions in a combined classifier can increase the accuracy and enable authentication in the application with error rates comparable to mobile face recognition methods.* The research is guided by the following research questions:

- **RQ1:** What are the requirements for the authentication method that can be used in financial applications from the perspectives of customers, providers (banks and financial institutions) and third parties and how behavioural biometrics fits into those requirements and needs?

- **RQ2:** What are the possible sensors and methods to be utilized for behavioural authentication on mobile devices that can be used for the mobile financial applications Use Case?
- **RQ3:** Can complementary methods be chosen based on defined characteristics and combined to provide a model which can satisfy the requirements?
- **RQ4:** How to benchmark and evaluate behavioural authentication method results in tasks and scenarios which may present the advantages and drawbacks of proposed method in real application scenarios and how to validate them?

Touchscreen biometrics are the chosen family of methods this article focuses on, as they have been proven by previous SOTA [3] to be the most promising in providing an authentication compliant with the model of requirements stated in RQ1, which is also described in Sect. 3 of this article. The work in this paper is connected with the RQ2 in terms of defining the characteristics, methods and approaches used for authentication and RQ3 in terms of defining the characteristics used by different approaches in the literature. It also briefly touches the RQ4 by describing approaches used for method evaluation in the literature and the datasets which may be used for this purpose. The outcomes of this article will lead to the development of the authentication method.

The paper is structured in as follows: the broader description of the problem, focused on the drawbacks of current authentication systems and characteristics of behavioural biometrics will be described in Sect. 3 along with the reasoning behind using touchscreen behavioural biometrics. The main contribution of the article consists of the literature review in Sect. 4, which differs from similar articles by focusing on the evaluation criteria and the the comparability of the results achieved in different studies. As the influence of the evaluation method and reasoning behind achieving vastly different results [10] are not explained by the literature. It explains different characteristics, features and methods that can be used for the authentication method creation. Further on other factors which may influence the results achieved: datasets and design of the experiment will be briefly discussed. The conclusions presented in Sect. 5 provide recommendations for building and evaluating a touchscreen authentication method.

3   Characteristics of Behavioural Biometrics

Physical biometric authentication (e.g. fingerprint) had became a standard login procedure for mobile banking already and is considered secure and acceptable [1,2]. Unfortunately, physical biometrics methods work as point-of-access mechanism, requiring user interaction to authenticate. Studies have shown that users see problems with this approach [2,4]. The new EU Payment Services Directive (PSD 2, Directive (EU) 2015/2366) [5] requires Strong Customer Authentication to strengthen transaction security. All banks across the European Union must add at least two-factor authentication by delivering a combination of at least two independent elements out of three categorized as: knowledge, possession or inherence factor. Also for assessing real-time transaction risk the directive allows using effective risk-based approaches which ensure the safety of the payment service user's funds and personal data. Current authorization being "all or nothing" access also make insider threat an increasingly important issue [11], as it is hard to differentiate between the rightful owner of the phone and their children or close relatives. Another problem is the lack of unified authentication method. With the number of possible combinations of phone models and built-in sensors (e.g. camera or fingerprint sensor) they may offer vastly different level of security. Solving those issues can lead to the improvement of the current authentication process or the development of a new process altogether.

Biometrics, being an inherence authentication factor, incorporate unique or at least sufficiently distinguishable traits which can be quantified and assigned to an individual for identification and confirmation of identity (authentication) [12]. Besides the "traditional" traits such as: fingerprint or palm print, iris and retina and face characteristics - a new family of methods using user behaviour as a pattern emerged recently. Some behavioural biometrics methods like behavioural profiling [13], can provide accuracy metrics in line with face or voice biometrics already utilized in smart phone authentication systems, providing below 1% EER (Equal Error Rate) and allowing for continuous authentication. Their characteristics may provide additional benefits, but the trade-off's in terms of privacy risk, convenience of use and security provided should be considered. The overall use of **behavioural biometrics methods** comes with potential advantages and drawbacks. The quick summary, partially based on previous work, is presented in Table 1. Even though the methods error rates may as low as for physical biometrics, they are inline with widely used mobile facial recognition [14]. Unfortunately, face recognition being a physical biometrics method does not solve the problems mentioned above as it is also a point-of-entry method which requires interaction. Behavioural biometrics on the other hand may offer new scenarios which can make the authentication process more usable or secure depending on the scenario of use, which may improve current services even if they don't offer performance similar to fingerprints or secure passwords. This brings up a potential of using behavioural biometrics systems as a factor in multi-factor authentication system that can work regardless of the physical biometrics sensors installed on it. It is also important to note that behavioural biometrics can be used for preventing the use of stolen or synthetic identities in applying for credit and preventing account takeovers once a user is logged into a session. The recognition of above mentioned situations, insider threat and malware protection is connected with new **Proof of Presence** type of authentication [15]. Continuous Proof of Presence (CPoP) is a crucial requirement for applications that deal with high risk. For example in a mobile banking app, if an unauthorized user accesses the phone while the intended user is still authenticated or by gaining user credentials, and begins interacting with the sensitive application. Above mentioned examples state that behavioural biometrics can be used in scenarios which benefit both security and usability of the solution provided.

One of such methods assumes utilizing user touchscreen dynamics to use as a pattern of user behaviour. This type of biometric can continuously (or at least with a high frequency) authenticate users, based on the way they interact with the touchscreen of a smartphone [7]. To fulfil this goal, right features for authentication need to be chosen from a wide family of sensors and statistics possible to be derived from user behaviour. Utilizing touchscreen provides less threat to privacy than keystroke analysis (which often effectively requires application to work as keylogger) and behavioural profiling (which, based upon examples in the literature requires access to user private data [13]). As an additional benefit it gives the possibility of extracting patterns specific for a given application environment. The methods results achieved (accuracy and error metrics) vary greatly in the literature [10], which clearly points to the need for thorough analysis of the methods, datasets and evaluation scenarios used by the authors, which will be described in Sect. 4.

Table 1. Advantages and drawbacks of using behavioural biometrics. Sources: [3,7,10, 11,15–17] and [14] as a reference for mobile face biometrics performance.

Topic	Advantages	Drawbacks
Usability	Continuous authentication and Continuous Proof of Presence scenario applicability. May lower the number of times user is asked for strong credentials	Requires additional algorithms implemented in mobile application
Security	Pattern theft is less dangerous as it can have features which are device or application specific in creating a pattern (in case of e.g. touchscreen). Can provide different levels of authentication. The pattern is inherent, not a knowledge factor	Achieved error rates of even 1% EER are less secure than the fingerprint scanner authentication. Learning user pattern takes time. The pattern may be subject to anomalies in behaviour, which requires different use case scenarios than just point-of-entry authentication
Technical complexity	Patterns are hard to spoof due to the use of multi-factor classifiers	May increase battery usage of the application. Requires use of sophisticated algorithms and infrastructure
Fraud detection	Can identify and differentiate user from an impostor with user credentials or malware simulating user behaviour. Can provide risk assessment and enrich fraud detection systems with behavioural information	May face high False Positives ratio when detecting an impostor. Some methods may use behaviour data that might be privacy threatening

4   Touchscreen Behavioural Biometrics

The touchscreen behavioural biometrics was a topic not widely discussed in the literature until recently, mostly due to the recent popularity of smartphones equipped with touchscreens. One of the first approaches is based on work of Saevanee in 2009, which enriched keystroke behavioural characteristics with touch pressure information to achieve about 1% EER on a small sample of users [18]. Later in the literature specific touch events actions, such as swipes and taps were identified as user distinguishing features [19] achieving about 3% EER. One of most widely known experiments was carried out by Frank et al. in 2013 [17] in the "Touchalytics" project, where "trigger actions" were defined. Those correspond to be frequent touch events for any usage and primitive, i.e. they should be part of all more complex navigational gestures. Over 30 features were extracted for every swipe/stroke identified as the above mentioned action for the purpose user authentication. The authors also presented different scenarios of use and validation for this type of authentication. Later work also included additional data sources - accelerometer readings [7]. Different classifiers were compared on multiple datasets by Serwadda et al. [20]. The outcome of this comparison and other reviews in the literature proves that the accuracy of the methods varies highly. Despite the fact that authors utilized the same aspect of user behaviour (e.g. touchscreen interaction patterns), they obtained different results of reported EER, which can be seen in Table 2. This points to the importance of discussing the reasons for this varying method performance observed. The gestures used, length of the learning process, time required for classification and the results evaluation methodology were also not discussed in the literature, but are very important for the use of those classifiers in a real world scenario.

Table 2. Comparison of the most widely discussed approaches for touch dynamics authentication methods best results. Source: [10]

Study	# of users	Classifiers	Feature dimension	Performance (%)
Frank et al. [17]	41	SVM, kNN	27	EER: 0.00–4.00
Zhang et al. [21]	50	Sparsity-based classifiers	27	EER: 0.77
Li et al. [7]	75	SVM	10	EER 3.00
Feng et al. [22]	40	Random Forest, J48 Tree, Bayes Net	53	FAR 7.50, FRR 8.00
Serwadda et al. [20]	138	10 different classifiers	28	EER:10.50
Zhao et al. [23]	78	L_1 distance	100 x 150 image	EER: 6.33–15.40

4.1   Characteristics of Events and Gestures

To better understand the differences in the approaches, the basic source of data must be described first. The major mobile platforms - Android OS, iOS provide a variety of APIs for the extraction of touchscreen events, including some low level information about pressure and position of user fingers [24]. Since the methods

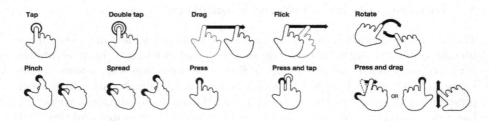

Fig. 1. Different gestures which can be captured on mobile applications. Source: [26]

depend on those APIs, approaches in the literature need to be evaluated considering different data used in their creation. Both Android and iOS prohibit access of touch data across different applications, i.e., each application can only read touch data produced by interacting with the application itself [17]. This reasonable limitation creates the need for application self contained authentication. For the **events** themselves, the device can (with limited frequency) monitor: x and y coordinate of the event, pressure and size registered[1]. While some approaches in the literature utilize this information "as is", they are strongly connected with the stability of the interface elements the user is tapping (e.g. if a confirm button is in the middle of an application screen all users would tap it, meaning the position variables are not so important). On the other hand Frank et al. [17] introduced the approach to characterise "trigger actions", which correspond to be frequent for any usage and primitive. They should be part of all more complex navigational gestures using vertical (scrolling) and horizontal (flicking or swiping) strokes. Those **actions, also often called gestures** in the literature, can be as simple as clicking (tapping) the screen or include multi-touch events which require more than one finger - like zooming in. The simple division of those gestures is shown in Fig. 1. During typical phone usage, drags/flicks (called strokes) and taps occur frequently as users browse pages to read text, or switch between two screens (e.g. while viewing images) [20] but some of the actions are more rare, which means they may be less useful for building the classifier. For characterization and measuring the uniqueness of both user overall profile gestures that are longer than one measurement and single measurement ones (e.g. tap) are often classified separately [25]. Events consisting of a few measurements only (e.g. <4 [20]) are often filtered out to increase the classifier reliability. The characteristics of each gesture may include:

– **Position** - initial and end coordinates, sometimes translated to relative screen position to compensate for screen resolution differences [17].

---

[1] developer.android.com/reference/android/view/MotionEvent, developer.apple.com/
documentation/uikit/uitouch.

- **Distance** - includes features characterizing the distance between consecutive measurements of the gesture compared to the start and end-point straight line distance.
- **Time** - how long the gesture took and how many measurements were taken.
- **Area/pressure/velocity characteristics** - often descriptive statistics such as mean, average, quartiles are calculated. What is important to note, is that characteristics of N beginning and ending of gesture are used, as they characterize the gestures well [17, 21].
- **Direction** - swipe and point curvature [27] of the gesture. Either expressed by an arctan value or mean direction for all of the pairs of measurements included in the gesture. The direction itself can be descriptive: horizontal/vertical or one of 8 directions in compass-like manner [19], or represented by an angle.
- **Finger orientation** and its changes - some approaches also use touch minors and majors [15] to characterize the specific size of user finger.
- **Phone orientation** - the gestures characteristics different dependent on the phone orientation, which makes the classifier trained on vertical mode unusable for user utilizing horizontal view.
- **MultiTouch events** - some approaches utilize number of fingers [15] observed during the interaction, mostly in a descriptive manner. Limited number of publications [27] include other gestures like zooming in and out.
- **Accelerometer, gyroscope data** - additionally characterizing the way the phone is held and it's position during the interaction may increase the classifier accuracy and decrease errors.

4.2   Comparison of Approaches in the Literature

The literature review was carried out, re-examining the approaches mentioned in the previous literature review studies [10, 20, 28] and including new examples that appeared after 2016. Characteristics of the methodologically sound approaches with low error rates are shown in Table 3. What is worth to note is that some of the studies have collected varying number of samples for different users. For example, in Li et al. [7] 75 users are listed, but only for 28 of them touchscreen data was used to build patterns and the rest were treated as impostors for testing the classifier. There are also approaches that differ in methods applied from the ones in Table 3. Zhao et al. [23] used a statistics based density estimator using Graphic Touch Gesture Features (GTGF) to represent the captured touch traces as an image. For 30 users, their approach achieved 2.62% EER by combining six gestures [23] using 6 sessions and 20 traces for learning including multitouch gestures such as zooming (pinch and spread).

Table 3. Characteristics and results of the touchscreen based mobile authentication approaches in the literature. Source: own work, partially based on [28] literature review.

	Position	Distance	Time	Area	Pressure	Speed	Acceleration	Direction	Finger orientation	Phone orientation	Multitouch events	Accelerometer	Gyroscope	Users	Training sessions per user	Phones	Dataset available	EER
Saevanee 2009 [18]	-	-	-	✓	-	✓	-	-	-	-	-	-	-	10	30	1	-	1% EER for session
Damopoulos et al. 2012 [29]	✓	-	✓	-	-	-	-	-	-	-	-	-	-	18	1 (24h)	18	-	0.205% EER for 24h session
Frank et al. 2013 [17]	✓	✓	✓	✓	✓	✓	✓	✓	✓	✓	-	-	-	41	7	4	✓	2-4% EER for 11 gestures
Li et al. 2013 [7]	✓	✓	✓	✓	✓	✓	✓	✓	-	✓	-	✓	✓	28	600 gestures	2	-	3% EER for 14/20 gestures
Serwadda et al. 2013 [20]	✓	✓	✓	-	-	-	-	-	-	✓	-	✓	✓	138	80 gestures	1	✓	10% EER for 10 gestures
Zhang et al. 2015 [21]	✓	✓	✓	✓	-	✓	✓	✓	-	✓	-	-	-	50	3	9	✓	1% EER for 70 gestures
Meng et al. 2018 [19]	✓	-	✓	-	-	✓	-	✓	-	-	✓	-	-	20	6	1	-	3% EER for 10 min session
Jain et al. 2015 [27]	✓	✓	✓	✓	-	-	-	✓	✓	-	✓	✓	✓	104	3 samples for 7 gestures	1	-	0.31% EER for session
Sameet et al. 2019 [15]	✓	✓	✓	✓	✓	✓	-	-	✓	✓	-	-	-	15	7	1	-	3% EER for session

4.3   Datasets Available

To compare the results achieved by different authors and to create a reliable method of authentication a study on multiple users is needed. It may also showcase the general nature of features across multiple environments and their ability to distinguish between users regardless of the task itself. The literature provides a list of accessible datasets with vastly different sizes and outcomes achieved by the researchers. The datasets that are available, to the best of the authors knowledge, have been presented in Table 4. The touchalytics dataset was provided by Frank et al. [17], BTAS 2013 dataset was created by Serwadda [20] and UMDAA02 touch dataset was provided by [21]. What is interesting to note, some of the very low EER papers have not published their datasets, and papers trying to provide evaluation on multiple datasets [20] have high error rates. Additionally, there are interesting datasets which were not obtained at the moment of conducting this research, like Syed Dataset [30][2] and the TouchMetric dataset [15], which seems to be unavailable by any openly known way. Additionally, there are some behavioural profiling datasets which could have captured natural touchscreen patterns with the device, such as the SherLock dataset [31][3].

---

[2] http://www.zasyed.com/jss18dataset.html.
[3] http://bigdata.ise.bgu.ac.il/sherlock/#/download#source_code.

Table 4. Analysis of the datasets in the literature Source: own work

Name	Event types	Aggregation	Position (x,y)	Pressure	Area	Direction	Additional sensors	Users/events	Sessions for user	Devices
Touchalytics [17]	Scrolling and strokes	–	Yes	Yes	Yes	Yes (possible to be calculated)	–	41 users 21k	7 (2 after a week)	4
Bioident [32]	Strokes	On stroke level	For start and end stroke	Yes	Yes	Yes	–	71 users 14k	4	8
H-Mog [33]	Scrolling, strokes, tapping, multitouch zoom events	–	Yes	Yes	Yes	Yes (possible to be calculated)	Keystroke, accelerometer, gyroscope and magnetometer	100 users >1.5 billion	24 (3 tasks)	10
UMDAA-02 Touch subset [34]	Scrolling and strokes	–	Yes	Yes	No	Yes (possible to be calculated)	–	48 users >1 billion	varying (avg. about 200)	9
BrainRun dataset [35]	Tapping and strokes	–	Yes	No	No	Yes (possible to be calculated)	Accelerometer, gyroscope, magnetometer	2218 users >3 billion gestures	varying (avg. about 50)	2418 (90% is Android)

5   Conclusions and Recommendations

Summarizing the results, focusing on information in Tables 3 and 4, a few conclusions can be drawn from comparing the approaches in the literature by the criteria of used features and evaluation procedure. Two most important parts of the research process may influence the result:

- **Length of the learning process and classification**, the amount of data collected about user behaviour, which may influence the robustness of the classifier results over large samples of users and allows to asses the performance correctly.
- **Repeatability and stability of actions used for learning the classifier**. Meaning how "controlled" was the scenario in which the behaviour was collected and reliant on the design of the application used for the experiment.

The features mentioned in the Table 3 may be calculated for the whole session [19], day [29], or for individual gestures (most often taps and swipes). The differences in those approaches may influence the true performance of the classifier that was observed, as the task to identify user after a day-long session, 10 min long session or 10 gestures differs significantly. This was not brought up in other literature reviews but greatly influences the classification result and is shown in EER column in Table 3. The question how test data is collected is important. It may include multiple session asking user to perform the same experiment (inter-session) or e.g. test data collected e.g. a week later to confirm the pattern stability (which [17] referred to as inter-week authentication scenario). When considering both the approaches and the datasets available, the task itself represented in the data-collecting application may influence the performance of the classifier. The application used for collecting the touch patterns may be collected:

- accompanying singular task in the application like writing user password [18].
- in a set of tasks, where user needs to apply gestures like swiping, scrolling [17, 21] to complete the process. The approaches in the literature (and especially the ones providing the datasets) should be thoroughly analysed with regards to the application design and general applicability of the results based on the tasks defined by the authors.
- in an uncontrolled environment [36], where the user behaviour is observed and basic user patterns like scrolling and tapping buttons in the application are used.

For testing the application in a more real world scenario, the stability of the pattern over time should be discussed. Some tasks in application design may require user to make gestures which are not often done, which may lower the classification error, but would require such action present in the application. For the results to be useful in the real authentication scenario - the tasks need to be prepared in a way that it would be possible to include them in a real application (like banking or payment app). Different tasks may also be useful in different scenarios of use, e.g.: enriching the current authentication in cases of high risk [3], inter-session authentication [17] where we apply Continuous Proof of Presence approach or continuous authentication, where we observe user behaviour and authenticate after some time period of observation, be it 10 actions, 10 s or full session length. This choice should influence the discussion of the results achieved and especially the validation scenario in which the classifier performance is evaluated.

Secondly, comparison of the results with the existing approaches should consider all of the above mentioned characteristics, for which the widely available datasets may be a good benchmark of performance. If additional features are used (such as accelerometer data or pressure measurements), which are not available in all of the datasets, additional description of results would be required. The feature importance of specific gestures should be considered and can influence the UI design of the applications utilizing this type of authentication. The overall gestures uniqueness should be tested on multiple datasets, as it would answer if the application design is determining the features, or are they inherently different between users regardless of the scenario.

Finally, based on the outcome of this study, a few areas of future research can be identified. As for now the main goal of the future work is twofold. First task is comparing the approaches among different datasets to research how the training time and validation scenario influences the classifier reliability. Second task is studying the design and UI elements of mobile banking and payment applications to design a mobile application which will include gestures which may be used for classifying a user being an addition to its normal functions.

References

1. Deloitte Center for Financial Services: 2018 banking outlook. https://www2.deloitte.com/content/dam/Deloitte/global/Documents/Financial-Services/gx-fsi-dcfs-2018-banking-outlook.pdf (2018). Accessed 10 Oct 2019
2. Visa USA: Visa biometrics payments study. https://usa.visa.com/visa-everywhere/security/how-fingerprint-authentication-works.html (2017). Accessed 10 Oct 2019
3. Kałużny, P.: Behavioral biometrics in mobile banking and payment applications. In: Abramowicz, W., Paschke, A. (eds.) Business Information Systems Workshops, vol. 339, pp. 646–658. Springer, Cham (2019). https://doi.org/10.1007/978-3-030-04849-5_55
4. Lawless Research: Beyond the password: the future of account security (2016). https://www.telesign.com/wp-content/uploads/2016/06/Telesign-Report-Beyond-the-Password-June-2016-1.pdf. Accessed 10 Oct 2019
5. Supplementing Directive (EU) 2015/2366 of the European Parliament and of the Council of the European Union, O.J. (2018)
6. Awad, A.: Collective framework for fraud detection using behavioral biometrics. In: Traoré, I., Awad, A., Woungang, I. (eds.) Information Security Practices, pp. 29–37. Springer, Cham (2017). https://doi.org/10.1007/978-3-319-48947-6_3
7. Li, L., Zhao, X., Xue, G.: Unobservable re-authentication for smartphones. In: NDSS, vol. 56, pp. 57–59 (2013)

8. Hevner, A.R., March, S.T., Park, J., Ram, S.: Design science in information systems research. MIS Q. **28**(1), 75–105 (2004)
9. Vaishnavi, V., Kuechler, W.: Design research in information systems (2004)
10. Patel, V.M., Chellappa, R., Chandra, D., Barbello, B.: Continuous user authentication on mobile devices: recent progress and remaining challenges. IEEE Signal Process. Mag. **33**(4), 49–61 (2016)
11. Hayashi, E., Riva, O., Strauss, K., Brush, A., Schechter, S.: Goldilocks and the two mobile devices: going beyond all-or-nothing access to a device's applications. In: Proceedings of the Eighth Symposium on Usable Privacy and Security, vol. 2, ACM (2012)
12. Saeed, K.: Biometrics principles and important concerns. In: Biometrics and Kansei Engineering, pp. 3–20. Springer (2012). https://doi.org/10.1007/978-1-4614-5608-7_1
13. Fridman, L., Weber, S., Greenstadt, R., Kam, M.: Active authentication on mobile devices via stylometry, application usage, web browsing, and GPS location. IEEE Syst. J. **11**(2), 513–521 (2016)
14. Rattani, A., Derakhshani, R.: A survey of mobile face biometrics. Comput. Electr. Eng. **72**, 39–52 (2018)
15. Samet, S., Ishraque, M.T., Ghadamyari, M., Kakadiya, K., Mistry, Y., Nakkabi, Y.: TouchMetric: a machine learning based continuous authentication feature testing mobile application. Int. J. Inf. Technol. 1–7 (2019)
16. Bo, C., Zhang, L., Li, X.Y., Huang, Q., Wang, Y.: SilentSense: silent user identification via touch and movement behavioral biometrics. In: Proceedings of the 19th Annual International Conference on Mobile Computing and Networking, pp. 187–190. ACM (2013)
17. Frank, M., Biedert, R., Ma, E., Martinovic, I., Song, D.: Touchalytics: on the applicability of touchscreen input as a behavioral biometric for continuous authentication. IEEE Trans. Inf. Forensics Secur. **8**(1), 136–148 (2013)
18. Saevanee, H., Bhattarakosol, P.: Authenticating user using keystroke dynamics and finger pressure. In: 2009 6th IEEE Consumer Communications and Networking Conference, pp. 1–2. IEEE (2009)
19. Meng, Y., Wong, D.S., Schlegel, R., Kwok, L.: Touch gestures based biometric authentication scheme for touchscreen mobile phones. In: Kutyłowski, M., Yung, M. (eds.) Inscrypt 2012. LNCS, vol. 7763, pp. 331–350. Springer, Heidelberg (2013). https://doi.org/10.1007/978-3-642-38519-3_21
20. Serwadda, A., Phoha, V.V., Wang, Z.: Which verifiers work?: a benchmark evaluation of touch-based authentication algorithms. In: 2013 IEEE Sixth International Conference on Biometrics: Theory, Applications and Systems (BTAS), pp. 1–8. IEEE (2013)
21. Zhang, H., Patel, V.M., Fathy, M., Chellappa, R.: Touch gesture-based active user authentication using dictionaries. In: 2015 IEEE Winter Conference on Applications of Computer Vision, pp. 207–214. IEEE (2015)
22. Feng, T., et al.: Continuous mobile authentication using touchscreen gestures. In: 2012 IEEE Conference on Technologies for Homeland Security (HST), pp. 451–456. IEEE (2012)
23. Zhao, X., Feng, T., Shi, W.: Continuous mobile authentication using a novel graphic touch gesture feature. In: 2013 IEEE Sixth International Conference on Biometrics: Theory, Applications and Systems (BTAS), pp. 1–6. IEEE (2013)
24. Masood, R., Zhao, B.Z.H., Asghar, H.J., Kaafar, M.A.: Touch and you're trapp(ck)ed: quantifying the uniqueness of touch gestures for tracking. Proc. Priv. Enhancing Technol. **2018**(2), 122–142 (2018)

25. Voris, J.: Measuring How we play: authenticating users with touchscreen gameplay. In: Murao, K., Ohmura, R., Inoue, S., Gotoh, Y. (eds.) MobiCASE 2018. LNICST, vol. 240, pp. 144–164. Springer, Cham (2018). https://doi.org/10.1007/978-3-319-90740-6_9
26. Examples of android gestures (2017). www.en.profit.me. https://en.proft.me/media/android/android_gestures.jpg. Accessed 10 Oct 2019
27. Jain, A., Kanhangad, V.: Exploring orientation and accelerometer sensor data for personal authentication in smartphones using touchscreen gestures. Pattern Recogn. Lett. **68**, 351–360 (2015)
28. Abdulhak, S.A., Abdulaziz, A.A.: A systematic review of features identification and extraction for behavioral biometrie authentication in touchscreen mobile devices. In: 2018 20th International Conference on Advanced Communication Technology (ICACT), pp. 68–73. IEEE (2018)
29. Damopoulos, D., Kambourakis, G., Gritzalis, S.: From keyloggers to touchloggers: take the rough with the smooth. Comput. Secur. **32**, 102–114 (2013)
30. Syed, Z., Helmick, J., Banerjee, S., Cukic, B.: Touch gesture-based authentication on mobile devices: the effects of user posture, device size, configuration, and inter-session variability. J. Syst. Softw. **149**, 158–173 (2019)
31. Mirsky, Y., Shabtai, A., Rokach, L., Shapira, B., Elovici, Y.: Sherlock vs Moriarty: a smartphone dataset for cybersecurity research. In: Proceedings of the 2016 ACM Workshop on Artificial Intelligence and Security, pp. 1–12. ACM (2016)
32. Antal, M., Szabó, L.Z., Bokor, Z.: Identity information revealed from mobile touch gestures. Stud. Univ. Babes-Bolyai, Inf. **59** (2014)
33. Sitová, Z., et al.: HMOG: new behavioral biometric features for continuous authentication of smartphone users. IEEE Trans. Inf. Forensics Secur. **11**(5), 877–892 (2016)
34. Mahbub, U., Sarkar, S., Patel, V.M., Chellappa, R.: Active user authentication for smartphones: a challenge data set and benchmark results. In: 2016 IEEE 8th International Conference on Biometrics Theory, Applications and Systems (BTAS), pp. 1–8. IEEE (2016)
35. Papamichail, M.D., Chatzidimitriou, K.C., Karanikiotis, T., Oikonomou, N.C.I., Symeonidis, A.L., Saripalle, S.K.: BrainRun: a behavioral biometrics dataset towards continuous implicit authentication. Data **4**(2), 60 (2019)
36. Feng, T., Yang, J., Yan, Z., Tapia, E.M., Shi, W.: Tips: context-aware implicit user identification using touch screen in uncontrolled environments. In: Proceedings of the 15th Workshop on Mobile Computing Systems and Applications, vol. 9. ACM (2014)

Data-Based User's Personality
in Personalizing Smart Services

Izabella Krzeminska[1,2]([envelope]) [ORCID]

[1] Poznan University of Economics and Business,
al. Niepodległosci 10, 61-875 Poznan, Poland
[2] R&D Labs, Orange Polska, Obrzezna 7, Warszawa, Poland
Izabella.Krzeminska@orange.com

Abstract. Currently, a lot of attention and commitment are paid to improving customer experience with services. More and more proposed solutions are data-based, human-centred services. The purpose of this article is to present the assumptions and evidence in order to create a method that will allow for customization of the service functionalities (e.g. a smart home service with a virtual personal assistant) to the nature of the user (personality in the Big 5 model). The article will present the results of the preliminary research concerning users' differentiation of needs, the definition of research problems and the idea for a research scheme. The aim of the research is creating a model that classifies users based on their personality indicated from mobile phone data. What distinguishes the proposed solution from others, is that many types of different data are used (call logs, photos, applications, data from telephone usage history, etc.), which can be beneficial for assessment accuracy. Additionally, the proposed method allows for adapting the service to the user needs from the beginning of usage, without the necessity of collecting data about user activity.

Keywords: User profiling · Service personalizing · Data based services · Detecting personality based on digital data · Smart services · Sensitive services · Human-centred services

1 Introduction and Motivation

A continuous digital transformation has been taking place for several years. The habits and ways of carrying out tasks, as well as the general functioning of people in the world are gradually enriched by an increasing number of helpful digital tools. For digital advanced services (e.g. sensitive or smart home) it's crucial to reduce the barriers related to anxiety over artificial intelligence, such as virtual robots or assistants. On the other hand, good determinants of diversifying user needs are always sought. Profiling based on demographic characteristics (such as gender, age, place of residence, education, economic status) seems to be insufficient as needs' predictor. In the context of the ongoing digital transformation, traces of the digital activity of users are increasingly being used to collect information about the client, as well as for profiling or classifying [1,2].

© Springer Nature Switzerland AG 2019
W. Abramowicz and R. Corchuelo (Eds.): BIS 2019 Workshops, LNBIP 373, pp. 686–696, 2019.
https://doi.org/10.1007/978-3-030-36691-9_57

The risk of service rejection and discontinuation of usage seems to be more important in the case of new, interactive and technologically advanced services based on artificial intelligence (intelligent services). This is due to individual differences and general concerns connected with new technologies. In addition, personalization seems to be beneficial before the service acquires data for profiling from activity history of user. An example to illustrate this problem can be the Amazon Alexa product, developed to encourage shopping by Amazon. In the report published in August 2018, we can find the claim "Of the people who did buy something using Alexa voice shopping, about 90% didn't try it again" [3]. Rejecting a service after one use completely excludes analytics based on usage history. Moreover, analyzing the smart speaker usage report (see Fig. 1), it seems that users limit the use of the service to basic functionalities known from their own experience. As we can also see, the list of used functionalities is the same for super users and average users. Based on experience, it's difficult for a user to find unknown functionalities available in the service, such as advanced shopping options. In this article [3], we can read that the representative of Amazon, who believes that the fact that so few people buy things through Alexa is a big challenge for the company, emphasizes also that the product will be able to be developed when the distinguishing features of individual customers are found. Also, recommendations based on analyzing behaviours in similar groups described by socio-demographic variables, or those based on segmentation will not allow for mapping any unused functionalities of the service. All these practices can be applied only if the services are actually used and are useless in the situation of leaving, discouragement or boredom of the user. One of the possible solutions is to have a basic usage profile already at the time of the service installation and to personalise the service from the first use according to the needs associated with the profile. The research program presented in the article has been developed simultaneously with the project of creating the service itself. Thanks to that the service, including the possibility of managing the

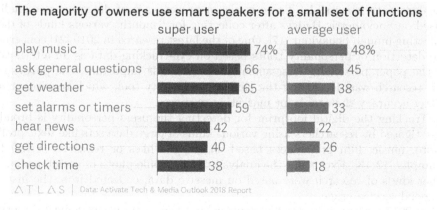

Fig. 1. The most popular question to smart speaker in group of super users (min. 3 times a day) and average service users. Source: [4].

functionalities of the service, is constantly adjusted to the results of the research on the classification of users. Taking the experience and effects of the work of other researchers, as well as the motivations resulting from the business need, presented above into account, the research program was created. In the article is proposed generic research framework for the detection of personality traits, which includes: (i) preparing the tool for data collection and creating a dedicated personality tool; (ii) a data processing stage for creating personality models and detecting the data required for personality detection; (iii) validation of usefulness of data-based automatically detected personality as a classifier of a service' user's needs.

2   Related Work

Personality has no singe definition shared by all psychologists. In general, personality is a set of traits or characteristics, which are organised, relatively stable and which influence the cognition and behaviour of individuals [5]. Within the existing personality theories one of the most influential and numerously validated ones is the Big 5 model. The model has been developed mainly by Costa and McCrae since 1978 and in the 90s it was confirmed in a large number of empirical studies [6–9]. There also are number of studies showing strong relationship between personality and behaviour, life satisfaction and achievements and preferences e.g. [10,11].

In the past 10 years, many researchers and many companies have attempted to determine the user's personality based on different kinds of digital data. Most of the attempts concerned data from social media (Facebook, Twitter) [12–14] or other personal data like call logs [15] or mobile applications [16]. There is also evidence that this kind of data-based personality diagnosis is accurate [17,18]. Concerning methods used, models of indicating data-driven users' personality are mainly based on text analysis (e.g. tweets or FB posts) using statistical regression or simply r-Pearson correlation [13,19].

In 2013 [13] researchers proved that predicting personality based on telephone call logs data is possible. There is also a proven case of detecting personality based on Sociometric Badges after collecting for 6 months various kinds of data reflecting human behaviour [17]. One of the latest research in 2019 [21] concerned the detection of personality traits based on eye-tracking data as an alternative to the paper personality assessment tools. What is important, the purpose of this research was developing the clinical personality tool, which requires much better accuracy than tools for marketing purposes.

Tracking the digital footprint for detecting the users personality is broadly investigated by researchers using various kinds of large data sets like text, profile photo, music, film preferences based on the FB likes or relations (SNA) for example: [12,13]. Except for the analysis of the profile photo in social media, all other kinds of research were based on massive data, collected from the history of social service usage.

In 2017 authors in paper [20] confirm that the use of psychological targeting allows to influence the behaviour of the social media users by adapting the message to the psychological needs of recipients defined by personality (Big 5). But at the beginning of using a new type of AI services, such as a virtual/voice assistant, data from the history of usage will not be available. In the context of even better regulations on the protection of users' privacy, we are slowly moving to a situation in which services will be limited to the use of own data, and data information systems will become more and more hermetic. Therefore, we are looking for methods that will allow services to detect user's personality based on even small amounts of data available at the time of service installation, e.g. from a mobile phone. In this paradigm, the assumption refers to determining the personality of each user of the smart home service, so the model should be based on the data available in each phone. Therefore, we have excluded such types of data which do not apply to everyone (e.g. social media or other specific services or applications).

3 Setting and Methods

3.1 Personality as a Classification of the Need

For this research, the "Big Five" model is used to describe the personality of an individual. Big 5 model basically claims that there are five dimensional factors of personality.

- **Openness to experience** which describe tolerance for the new and the unknown.
- **Extraversion** describes tolerance for big quantity of stimulus.
- **Neuroticism** describes intolerance to stress.
- **Agreeableness** is about concentration on others' needs and willingness for co-operation.
- **Conscientiousness** is about intolerance to chaos and disorder.

The description of the factors as dimensional is very important. This means that these are not "yes or no" factors but all individuals are described by each factor to some extent. In other words, the dimensions describe the variability among people. So you can be a little bit or a lot more (or less) extraverted than average, but it wouldn't be accurate to say that you have no extraversion.

Survey conducted in 2018 (own research[1]), delivered clear evidence that personality dimensions are good enough for discriminating users needs and expectations (see Table 1). Moreover respondents confirm that the services based on

---

[1] The research was carried out in the first half of 2018, on 60 users of mobile phones, residents of Warsaw. In order to emphasize the diversity between people resulting from their personality, the study was conducted on a very homogeneous group in terms of demographics (the aim was to reduce confounding factors). The age has been limited to 20–29 years, separate groups for both sexes, technologically advanced group, using many functionalities of mobile devices. The study was a multi-stage: filling of the personality questionnaire (Big 5), monthly observation of behaviors in social profiles and in the use of telephone, in-depth structured interviews aimed at getting as much information as possible about behavior patterns. The results of these studies were used for creating behavioral metrics for each of Big 5 dimensions.

Table 1. Different attitudes and expectations connected with virtual assistant (VA) dependable on personality dimensions (Big 5) (source: own research)

Personality dimension	High level	Low level
Extraversion	Rejection of VA, but if adapted to the user expectations (no advertisements) can be considered	Reject based on privacy (need for high protection), VA in role of invisible friend
Openness for experience	The repeatability based on usage history is irritating but the idea of smart proactive VA searching all they need is attractive, they would be first to try it, their interest is changing and evolving	They expect to do something easier and faster - but still only when they need it (they initiate the action) - their interests is rather stable
Conscientiousness	The only group which like personalization, VA for them can be useful tool for controlling themselves, keep schedule and order	They are aware of their own problems so they want the functionalities that helps them avoid errors due to lack of systematic or discretionary decision-making etc.
Neuroticism	They appreciate the convenience of this solution (it limits forgetting, helps), but skeptical about data transfer and risk of "manipulation"	If they will have enough time for adaptation they can go with it (the value for them is an effectiveness in real life)
Agreeableness	They are afraid but if it became popular (recommended by friends) they will accept it	Their main motivation is a pragmatic needs (usefulness in everyday life)

artificial intelligence are currently not adapted to them and this is the primary reason for their rejection or dissatisfaction with available services. The short summary in tabular data set shows (Table 1) how diverse the attitudes and expectations of mobile phone users towards virtual assistants are. Differences concern mainly the function of a virtual assistant and are a simple derivative of diversity of needs. At the same time, it can be seen that attitudes polarize with respect to personality dimensions. For example, people who are open to experience expect non-standard content, have a high level of cognitive needs, and high need to explore (curiosity). In turn, people with low openness expect only a sense of comfort in a world that is well known to them (they like only what they know, they are afraid of unknown). For another dimension, individuals with a high level of conscientiousness use mainly the functionalities that help in the implementation of the need for control, which mainly manifests itself in the control of time and in scrupulous planning. On the other hand people with a low level of conscientiousness, who accept life in chaos and disorder, need only very basic control functionalities and will never be interested in using advanced calendar or notebook functions.

Due to the specificity of research and linking it with electronic services, the decision of creating dedicated Big 5 tool was taken. Diagnostic tools for personality measurement are available on the market in the form of licensed commercial questionnaires (e.g. NEO Personality Inventory Revised) and NEO-FFI (NEO Five-Factor Inventory), created by Costa and McCrae (1992) [22, 23]. These tools are used primary for individual diagnosis and they are under protection. Psychological diagnostic tools cannot be disseminated, because it weakens their diagnostic power, nor be modified. The procedure of using them is very strict and can be conducted only by authorized psychologists. Another reason was the need for integration of Big 5 tool with electronic applications. The whole psychometric Big 5 tool creation procedure was processed from the beginning. In this way creation of a dedicated tool became possible and easy. Due to business needs, personality dimensions (Extraversion, Agreeableness, Conscientiousness, Neuroticism (Emotional Stability) and Openness to experience, will be treated independently - as if we were creating 5 separate tools. The issue of orthogonality of factors will also be examined due to theoretical foundations and due to the problem of interference between factors in the situation of building a model based on data.

3.2   Objectives of the Research and Thesis

Having in mind the presented motivation for the research, the following research questions were defined:

- RQ1. How to create method for determining the user's personality based on the available data (from mobile phone)?
- RQ2. How to evaluate the reliability of the method of personality detecting?
- RQ3. How to evaluate the utility of developed method in real service/data?

The main goal of the dissertation is to propose effective and accurate methods of assessing the user's needs defined by the dimensions of his personality (e.g. BIG 5) based on the data available from the moment of service installation without the delay connected with collecting user's data log. The specific objectives of the work are:

- Develop the method for determining user's personality based on the limited amount of data
- Develop reliability indicators for the method of personality determination based on the available amount of user data without having to collect usage history
- Develop the method for verifying a pre-designated personality based on dynamic data when using the service
- Assess the applied needs classifier by experiment based on laboratory measurement or measurement on a test group

– Assess reliability and accuracy of personality measurement (Big 5) based on user data in comparison to declarative data (personality questionnaire tool)

Hence the thesis was formulated as follows: **Automatic personality assessment (Big 5), based on user data of any interactive service, e.g. a virtual assistant, can be used as a classifier of user's needs for the way of interaction and the set of service functionalities, which will significantly speed up profiling of the service and will increase satisfaction with using it.**

4   Research Scheme

The overall methodology chosen for conducting required research is Design Science [24]. The main paradigm of Design Science Research, proposed by Hevner, is answering research questions by creating innovative artifacts, and in this way enhancing existing knowledge and science base by new knowledge [25]. In design science paradigm the main goal is to build and evaluate an artifact. To verify the defined thesis and to accomplish the research objectives, the following research scheme is designed (see Fig. 2):

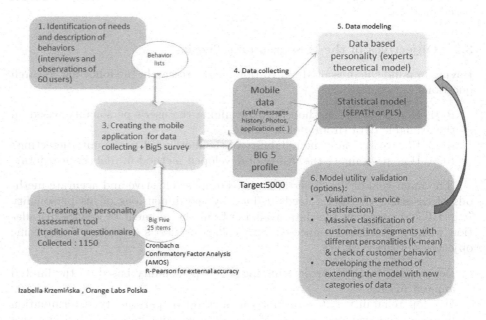

Fig. 2. Research scheme & methods

1. **Preliminary qualitative tests** carried out to identify needs and collect descriptions of discriminating behaviour.

2. **Creating the personality assessment tool**, which can be used for this specific research (low number of questions (25) and tool tested and created for online or mobile app usage). Standard psychometric procedures are applied.
3. **Developing the mobile application** dedicated for collecting data from mobile phone and Big 5 assessment. So far the data from the following user activities (sources) have been collected and analyzed on a mobile phone of a user:
   - Telco data – call logs statistics, text messages logs statistics etc. (collected from mobile phone logs)
   - Application data – applications on mobile phone, phone parameters, etc.
   - Photos – photos in user photo albums, etc.
   - Phone settings and statistics e.g. battery consumption, kind of security level, etc.
4. **Main research fieldwork** - data collecting required for creating the model - planned 5000 participants. This is the current point of the research.
5. **Creating the personality model** based on the mobile phone data, available at the moment of service installation (single drop without additional collecting of the activity logs). There is an idea to create at least 2 different models. The first will be theoretical model coherent with psychological Big 5 theory. The second will be pure statistical model based on SEPATH or PLS. From psychological point of view, it will be a very interesting and unique possibility of comparing these two differently created models.
6. **Validation stage** e.g. in interactive service which allows experimental manipulation based on personality adapted service. Or in laboratory simulation way comparing satisfaction metrics or checking the purchasing behaviour after a massive classification of the whole data base of mobile customers.

This is the plan of work stages. The presented user-oriented research program has been developed simultaneously with the project of creating the service itself. Thanks to that the service, including the possibility of managing the functionalities of the service, is constantly adjusted to the results of research on the classification of users. The research is now on stage 4 - collecting data for creating models. Stages 1, 2 and 3 have already been finished. The mobile application for data collection with implementing 25 questions tool for Big 5 assessment is ready.

The future works concern stages 5 and 6. The validation stage (6) is now rather a list of proposals and is not completely defined. The final shape will highly depend on the phase of maturity of the created parallel service, as well as on the availability of data on service platform. Stage 5 and stage 6 will run cyclically until satisfactory results are achieved. It will also be repeated if the data-set is expanded or the assumptions changed.

The planned comparison of the result based on behavioral metrics and personality test results can bring to very interesting conclusions. It can be said, that personality questionnaires reflect the image of how we see ourselves and not necessarily real behavior. If this image is biased (for various reasons, e.g. high need for social approval or cognitive defense mechanisms) the diagnosis will not be accurate. Moreover, the answers in the personality questionnaires are sometimes based on subjective perspective, e.g. the assessment of the amount of time spent with friends and social gathering may not be adequate to the real place in the distribution for the population. So if we create a model of predicting the personality questionnaire results (declarative), we will repeat this error. Therefore, in the research scheme, we included the creation of a personality profile based on theory and actual reference to the results of the whole representation of population. So potentially it will be possible to verify the declared behavior with the actual ones. Of course another issue is the interpretation of this possible gap.

5   Conclusion and Discussion

The preliminary research suggests that personality, as a predictor of user's needs, can significantly facilitate profiling of services. The results, based on the observation of behaviors related to the use of a mobile phone and experience with services based on AI algorithms, confirm the theory of personality in the Big 5 approach. It seems that extending the range of diagnostic tools measuring users' natural needs is an obvious step in the development of intelligent and sensitive services. The most important advantage of the proposed solution is not being limited to one type of data and basing the model on the data available at the time installing the service. This perfectly complements the currently used profiling methods (based on data from user activity registers). Fitting the service to the user's needs from the moment of installing the service can be crucial in prevention against rejection of innovative, technologically advanced and unknown services, such as a virtual assistant in a smart/sensitive home.

An additional contribution to the current state of knowledge is that the target solution will function on different types of data (call history, texts, photos). As a result, the solution will be more versatile and easier to implement in other applications. The planned research aims to provide evidence of the effectiveness of using the user's personality determined from digital data and significantly increase the satisfaction of using these services. The validation phase still needs to be refined and it will be a big challenge to find reliable measures to assess both user satisfaction and the accuracy of the profile of personality detected. Moreover comparing the effectiveness of differently created model (theoretical and statistical) can be interesting evidence for further psychological research.

The research carried out in this scheme will probably make a significant contribution to the discussion on the reliability of personality diagnostics based on questionnaires, in which information on behavior is declarative. This has significant consequences for the subsequent stages of work and for assessment of reliability and accuracy of profile detecting methods.

The potential of a solution that can be developed towards a faster psychological diagnosis is also important. Using a similar research program, tools for diagnose other features such as addiction to the phone, neuroses, depression and burnout can be created. In turn, the method of implementing knowledge about the user's personality in the service is relatively easy to implement in other types of activities such as creating applications and interfaces. It can be the first step for the development of automatically adaptable service interfaces. It is worth emphasizing that the presented solution is not an alternative to profiling solutions based on logs of activity. If the presented type of profiling proves to be effective, it can be used as a basis. In the future, IT systems should be designed in the way that will allow for validation of the initial model based on activity data. In the case of significant lack of coherence between initial profile and user choices, they will be able to update it.

References

1. Kosinski, M., Stillwell, D., Graepel, T.: Private traits and attributes are predictable from digital records of human behavior. Proc. Natl. Acad. Sci. (PNAS) **110**(15), 5802–5805 (2013)
2. Bachrach, Y., Kosinski, M., Graepel, T., Kohli, P., Stillwell, D.: Personality and patterns of Facebook usage. In: Proceedings of the 4th Annual ACM Web Science Conference, pp. 24–32. ACM (2012)
3. Anand, P.: The Reality Behind Voice Shopping Hype. https://www.theinformation.com/articles/the-reality-behind-voice-shopping-hype?. Accessed 15 Apr 2018
4. Activate-tech-media-outlook-2018. https://www.slideshare.net/ActivateInc/activate-tech-media-outlook-2018. Accessed 15 Apr 2019
5. Strelau, J.: Psychologia Temperamentu: Wydawnictwo Naukowe PWN (2019)
6. Costa Jr., P.T., Mc Crae, R.R.: Four ways Five Factors are basic. Personality Individ. Differ. **12**(13), 653–665 (1992)
7. McCrae, R.R., Costa Jr., P.T.: Toward a new generation of personality theories: theoretical context for the Five-Factor Model. In: Wiggins, J.S. (ed.) The Five-Factor Model of Personality: Theoretical Perspective, pp. 51–87. Guilford, New York (1996)
8. De Raad, B.: Structural models of personality. In: Corr, W.P.J., Methews, G. (eds.) The Cambridge Handbook of Personality Psychology, pp. 127–147. Cambridge University Press, New York (2009)
9. Goldberg, L.R.: The development of markers for the Big-Five factor Structure. J. Pers. Soc. Psychol., 99–110 (2016)
10. Barrick, M., Mount, M.: The Big Five Personality, dimensions and job performance: a meta-analysis. Pers. Psychol. **44**(1), 1–26 (1991)
11. Judge, T., Higgins, C., Thoresen, C., Barrick, M.: The Big Five Personality traits, general metal ability and career success across the life span. Pers. Psychol. **52**(3), 621–625 (1999)
12. Liu, L., Preotiuc-Pietro, D., et al.: Analyzing Personality Through Social Media Profile Picture Choice. Association for the Advancement of Artificial Intelligence (2016)
13. Kern, M.L., et al.: The online social self an open vocabulary approach to personality. University of Pennsylvania, University of Cambridge (2013)
14. Quercia, D., Kosinski, M., Stillwell, D., Crowcroft, J.: Our Twitter profiles, our selves: predicting personality with Twitter. In: IEEE SocialCom (2011)
15. de Montjoye, Y.-E., Quoidbach, J., Robic, F., Pentland, A.: Predicting Personality Using Novel Mobile Phone-Based Metrics. MIT, Harvard University, Ecole Normale Supérieure de Lyon (2013)

16. Xu, R., Frey, R.M., Fleisch, E., Ilic, A.: Understanding the impact of personality traits on mobile app adoption – insights from a large-scale field study. ETH Zurich (2016)

17. Kalimeri, K., Lepri, B., et al.: Going beyond traits: multimodal classification of personality states in the wild. MIT, ACM, 13 December 2013. ISBN 978-1-4503-2129-7

18. Back, M.D., et al.: Facebook profiles reflect actual personality not self-idealization. Psychol. Sci. 21(3), 372–374 (2010). https://doi.org/10.1177/0956797609360756

19. Goldbeck, J., et al.: Predicting personality from Twitter. In: IEEE International Conference on Privacy, Security, Risk, and Trust (2011)

20. Matz, S., Kosinski, M., Nave, G., Stillwell, D.: Psychological targeting as an effective approach to digital mass persuasion. Proc. Natl. Acad. Sci. 114 (2017). 201710966. https://doi.org/10.1073/pnas.1710966114

21. Berkovsky, Sh., et al.: Detecting personality traits using eye-tracking data. In: CHI Conference (2019). https://doi.org/10.1145/3290605.3300451

22. Costa, P.T., McCrae, R.R.: Revised NEO Personality Inventory (NEO-PI-R) and NEO Five-Factor Inventory (NEO-FFI) professional manual. Psychological Assessment Resources, Odessa, FL (1992)

23. Zawadzki, B., Strelau, J., Szczepaniak, P., Sliwinska, M.: Inwentarz Osobowości NEO-FFI Costy i McCrae. Adaptacja polska. Proffesional Manual. Warsaw, PTP (1998)

24. Hevner, A., March, S., Park, J., Ram, S.: Design science in information systems research. MIS Q. 28(1), 75–105 (2004)

25. Hevner, A., Chatterjee, S.: Design Research in Information Systems: Theory and Practice. Springer, Heidelberg (2010). https://doi.org/10.1007/978-1-4419-5653-8

Author Index